Casting Might-Have-Beens

*A Film by Film Directory
of Actors Considered for Roles
Given to Others*

Eila Mell

McFarland & Company, Inc., Publishers
Jefferson, North Carolina, and London

LIBRARY OF CONGRESS CATALOGUING-IN-PUBLICATION DATA

Mell, Eila, 1968–
Casting might-have-beens : a film by film directory of actors considered for roles given to others / Eila Mell.
p.   cm.
Includes bibliographical references and index.

ISBN-13: 978-0-7864-2017-9
(softcover : 50# alkaline paper) ∞

1. Motion pictures — Casting — United States.
2. Motion pictures — United States — Catalogs.
I. Title.
PN1995.9.C34M45   2005   791.4302'8'0973 — dc22   2004022515

British Library cataloguing data are available

©2005 Eila Mell. All rights reserved

No part of this book may be reproduced or transmitted in any form or by any means, electronic or mechanical, including photocopying or recording, or by any information storage and retrieval system, without permission in writing from the publisher.

On the cover: *background* ©2004 Thinkstock;
clockwise from top: Jessica Biel, Maria Conchita Alonso, Kelly McGillis, Aidan Quinn, Brandon Lee

Manufactured in the United States of America

*McFarland & Company, Inc., Publishers
Box 611, Jefferson, North Carolina 28640
www.mcfarlandpub.com*

For Jack and Erin

CONTENTS

Preface
1

The Films and Roles
3

Notes
263

Index
311

Preface

Screenwriter William Goldman has said that actors become stars by accident. Would Al Pacino be the star he is today had Robert Redford accepted the role of Michael Corleone in *The Godfather*? Then there's Humphrey Bogart, who practically owes his career to George Raft. Bogart made the following films Raft rejected: *Dead End, It All Came True, The Maltese Falcon, High Sierra, All Through the Night*, and *Casablanca*. Bogart is a legend; if not for Raft we might not even remember him.

Then there are the future stars who are turned down for roles. Imagine Tom Hanks rejecting Uma Thurman, saying that acting with her was like acting in a high school play. It's true! This was before *Pulp Fiction* made her an A-list actress and got her an Oscar nomination. Thurman auditioned to play opposite Hanks in *The Bonfire of the Vanities*. Although director Brian De Palma was interested in her, Hanks had casting approval, and Melanie Griffith (hot from *Working Girl*) was cast instead.

Casting Might-Have-Beens is full of such stories. The information was obtained through extensive research (see Notes section) and interviews.

The book is arranged alphabetically by film title (giving date). The actor who played the role is first listed along with the character's name. Immediately following, in parentheses, are the actors considered for the role, followed by one or more paragraphs telling the story behind the casting decision. Copious source notes accompany the entries, beginning on page 263; they are indicated by superscript numbers, which start over with each new letter of the alphabet.

An index of all actors, whether cast or considered, concludes the work.

In the book *Live from New York*, Lisa Kudrow gives some insight to the actor's point of view: "There've been a couple of things that I didn't get or got fired from, where friends who had a little more experience said, 'It's always a blessing when a door closes because another door's going to open.'"

Casting Might-Have-Beens gives you the chance to picture, for example, Danny Thomas as the Godfather, Michael Jackson as Edward Scissorhands, or Marilyn Monroe as Cleopatra. Imagine how different your favorite films might have been!

THE FILMS AND ROLES

About Last Night (1986)
Rob Lowe as Danny (Dan Aykroyd)
James Belushi as Bernie (John Belushi)

Paramount Pictures asked *Saturday Night Live* co-stars John Belushi and Dan Aykroyd to star in *About Last Night*. The movie was based on David Mamet's play, *Sexual Perversity in Chicago*. Belushi's younger brother, Jim Belushi, starred in the play. When John Belushi asked his brother how he would feel if he took the role in the film, Jim said that it would kill him. John Belushi turned the part down.[1] The movie was made a few years later with Jim who had, by that time, made a name for himself on the same show that made his late brother (John died of a drug overdose in 1982) famous—*Saturday Night Live*.

Above Suspicion (1943)
Fred MacMurray as Richard Myles (Clark Gable)

Clark Gable turned down Fred MacMurray's role in *Above Suspicion*.[2]

Abraham Lincoln (1930)
Kay Hammond as Mary Todd Lincoln (Una Merkel)

Una Merkel was originally cast as Mary Todd Lincoln. Director D.W. Griffith later changed his mind. He gave the part of Mary Todd Lincoln to Kay Hammond, while Merkel was switched over to the part of Ann Rutledge.[3]

Absence of Malice (1982)
Paul Newman as Michael Gallagher (Al Pacino)
Sally Field as Megan Carter (Diane Keaton)

Director Sydney Pollack originally wanted Al Pacino to star as libeled businessman Michael Gallagher in *Absence of Malice*. The two had previously worked together when Pacino starred in Pollack's 1977 film, *Bobby Deerfield*. Pacino agreed to take on the part of Gallagher. Soon after, Pacino dropped out unexpectedly. Pollack replaced him with Paul Newman.[4]

Diane Keaton was offered the part of Megan Carter. Keaton turned it down. Sally Field was cast in her place.[5]

Absolute Power (1997)
Ed Harris as Seth Frank (Clint Eastwood)

Clint Eastwood was initially sent the script of *Absolute Power* with the thought of him playing the role of detective Seth Frank. Eastwood read the script written by William Goldman. He liked it, but had a problem with the part of Seth. Eastwood felt that this role was something he had done many times before. Instead, Eastwood wanted to play thief Luther Whitney. In Goldman's screenplay Luther dies halfway through the film. If Eastwood were to star he would have to be in the film all the way through. Goldman altered the script to suit Eastwood and the actor signed on for the part. The role of Seth Frank was given to Ed Harris.[6]

The Accidental Tourist (1988)
William Hurt as Macon Leary (Kevin Costner)
Geena Davis as Muriel Pritchett (Ellen Barkin, Colleen Camp, Kate Capshaw, Laura Dern, Melanie Griffith, Amy Madigan, Mary Steenburgen, Victoria Tennant, Jo Beth Williams)

All of the above actresses auditioned for the part of Muriel Pritchett. Ellen Barkin had a particularly difficult time at the audition. She has said that during her reading she was just

Una Merkel switched roles in *Abraham Lincoln*.

waiting for it to be over, and was disappointed because she felt she was letting down William Hurt and director Lawrence Kasdan.[7] She told *Entertainment Weekly* that her audition was "terrible," and that she thought the part was very difficult to audition for.[8]

Kevin Costner was offered the starring role of Macon. He didn't want it, and it went instead to William Hurt.[9]

The Accused (1988)

Jodie Foster as Sarah Tobias (Rosanna Arquette, Kelly McGillis, Demi Moore, Meg Ryan, Meg Tilly)

Director Jonathan Kaplan wanted Kelly McGillis to star in *The Accused* as rape victim Sarah Tobias. McGillis refused the role. Some years earlier McGillis had been raped, and she felt that taking the part would be very painful. Kaplan still wanted McGillis in the film, and gave her the other starring role of lawyer Kathryn Murphy. Jodie Foster, whose career was in a slump at the time, desperately wanted the part of Sarah. The former child star of the 1970s, who received an Oscar nomination for her performance in 1976's *Taxi Driver*, was coming off a string of forgettable films in the 1980s. According to the actress, if she did not land the part in *The Ac-*

Jodie Foster has Kelly McGillis (above) to thank for her Academy Award for *The Accused*.

cused she was going to quit acting entirely and go to graduate school. Foster was at a disadvantage, because the executives at Paramount refused to even let her audition. Foster went to New York to meet with producer Stanley Jaffe. Jaffe was not sure that Foster was pretty enough to star in his film. After meeting with Foster Jaffe agreed to let her audition. Foster read the next day and wowed Jonathan Kaplan. The studio still had reservations about hiring her and continued to see other actresses. Demi Moore, Rosanna Arquette, Meg Tilly and Meg Ryan all auditioned. Co-star Kelly McGillis stepped in. McGillis was a big star and Paramount needed her. McGillis said that she would quit if Foster was not given the part. A week before shooting was set to begin Foster was cast.[10] *The Accused* earned her a second Oscar nomination — and this time she won the award. Foster's career has been going strong ever since: She went on to win a second Academy Award for 1991's *The Silence of the Lambs*, and also began directing films.

Kelly McGillis has made few films of note

since the 1980s and seems to have faded from the Hollywood scene. In 1988, she married Fred Tillman. In addition to raising two daughters, McGillis opened a restaurant called Kelly's in Key West, Florida. In 1999, she reemerged with a supporting role in the film *At First Sight*. McGillis' return was especially notable, because the film's star was Val Kilmer, who played a supporting role in *Top Gun*, McGillis' biggest hit.

Ace Ventura: Pet Detective (1994)

Jim Carrey as Ace Ventura (Whoopi Goldberg, Rick Moranis, Judd Nelson, Alan Rickman)
Courteney Cox as Melissa Robinson (Lauren Holly)

Rick Moranis was the first choice to play the title role in *Ace Ventura: Pet Detective*. Moranis turned it down, and Judd Nelson and Alan Rickman were both considered. At one point the producers contemplated changing the role to a female and casting Whoopi Goldberg.[11] Eventually Jim Carrey caught their attention. At the time Carrey was on the sketch comedy show *In Living Color*. Carrey had many memorable characters including the audience favorite Fire Marshall Bill. Carrey won the role and the film made him a big star.

In 1986 Lauren Holly joined the cast of the soap opera *All My Children*. One of her fans was an unknown Jim Carrey. Holly screen tested to play Melissa Robinson opposite Carrey's Ace Ventura. Her audition was impressive, and Holly was offered the role. Holly couldn't know that the film was going to be the blockbuster it turned out to be, and said no. She later admitted that she made the wrong decision. A few months later Holly was once again offered the chance to star opposite Carrey — this time in the film *Dumb & Dumber*. Holly took the part this time, which turned out to be a good decision. *Dumb & Dumber* was a runaway hit at the box office. Additionally, Holly and Carrey fell in love during the filming. The two married in 1996, but were divorced less than a year later.

Across 110th Street (1972)

Yaphet Kotto as Lt. Pope (Sidney Poitier)
Paul Benjamin as Jim Harris (Harry Belafonte)
Antonio Fargas as Henry J. Jackson (Sammy Davis, Jr.)

Not only did Anthony Quinn star in *Across 110th Street* as corrupt cop Captain Matteli, but he was also the co-executive producer. Quinn wanted to cast big stars for the other roles and hired Sidney Poitier, Harry Belafonte, and Sammy Davis, Jr. Shooting was on location in Harlem. The community objected to Quinn's choice of actors. They felt that these actors were from Hollywood, and were not familiar with the city streets. They wondered how they could accurately portray life in their community. Quinn knew that without the support of the community filming would be extremely difficult. He decided to take their and advice and recast the roles with Yaphet Kotto, Paul Benjamin, and Antonio Fargas.[12]

Act One (1963)

George Hamilton as Moss Hart (Warren Beatty)

Act One was the life story of playwright Moss Hart. The producers thought Warren Beatty would be a good choice to play Hart. Beatty wasn't interested in taking the part, and turned down the offer. The role went instead to George Hamilton.[13]

The Actress (1953)

Jean Simmons as Ruth Gordon (Debbie Reynolds)
Teresa Wright as Annie Jones (Maureen Stapleton)

Debbie Reynolds was MGM and director George Cukor's choice to play Ruth Gordon in her autobiographical film, *The Actress*.[14] After some time Cukor began to have his doubts about the actress. He thought that although she had some of the right qualities for the part, she was lacking in other areas. He especially didn't like that she wasn't familiar with Shakespeare. He didn't think her test was all that good, and gave the part to Jean Simmons instead.[15]

Maureen Stapleton was offered the role of Annie Jones. She wasn't interested and turned the part down. She was replaced by Teresa Wright.[16]

The Addams Family (1991)

Anjelica Huston as Morticia Addams (Cher)

Cher turned down the part of Morticia Addams in *The Addams Family*.[17] Anjelica Huston played it instead. *The Addams Family* was a big hit. So much so, that a sequel was made two years later called *Addams Family Values*.

The Adventures of Baron Munchausen (1989)

John Neville as Baron Munchausen (Sean Connery)
Robin Williams as King of the Moon (Sean Connery)

Sean Connery was considered for the role of the Baron. It was later decided that he would instead play the King of the Moon. Because of changes in the script Connery was no longer interested in playing the role and dropped out.[18]

The Adventures of Marco Polo (1938)

Gary Cooper as Marco Polo (Douglas Fairbanks)
Sigrid Gurie as Princess Kukachin (Merle Oberon)

It was Douglas Fairbanks' idea to make a film about Marco Polo. He planned it as a vehicle for himself to star in. Eventually, he decided against playing Marco Polo, and instead was going to produce the film.[19] Ultimately, Fairbanks dropped out of the film entirely. The role was taken by Gary Cooper when the film was later produced by Samuel Goldwyn and directed by Archie Mayo.

Merle Oberon was a consideration to play Princess Kukachin. At the time Oberon was working in England for Alexander Korda. Goldwyn decided to give the part to Sigrid Gurie instead.[20]

The Adventures of Pluto Nash (2002)

Rosario Dawson as Dina Lake (Halle Berry)

Halle Berry dropped out of *The Adventures of Pluto Nash* because the film's schedule would interfere with her wedding to Eric Benet. Rosario Dawson was brought in as a replacement.[21]

The Adventures of Robin Hood (1938)

Olivia De Havilland as Maid Marian (Anita Louise)

Anita Louise was the first choice for the role of Maid Marian. But audiences really liked Errol Flynn paired up with Olivia De Havilland.[22] The two had previously co-starred in *A Dream Come True* (1935), *The Irish in Us* (1935), and *A Midsummer Night's Dream* (1935). The producers wanted to cast the actress the audience wanted to see, and Louise was out.

Anita Louise almost got to play Maid Marian in *The Adventures of Robin Hood*.

Affectionately Yours (1941)

Merle Oberon as Sue Mayberry (Bette Davis, Olivia De Havilland)

Bette Davis was the original choice for the part of Sue Mayberry in *Affectionately Yours*.[23] Davis didn't make the film, and Olivia De Havilland was made an offer. She decided against making the film. The role was eventually played by Merle Oberon.[24]

The African Queen (1951)

Humphrey Bogart as Charlie Allnut (Charles Laughton)
Katharine Hepburn as Rose Sayer (Bette Davis, Deborah Kerr, Elsa Lanchester)

Columbia Pictures was the first studio to own the rights to *The African Queen*. It was, at that time, a project for the husband and wife team of Charles Laughton and Elsa Lanchester.[25] In 1939 the studio sold the rights to Warner Bros. Deborah Kerr was interested in the part of Rose. She went to MGM's Dore Schary to inquire about the film rights. Schary told her Warner Bros. already had them.[26] Warner Bros. planned to make the film with Bette Davis.[27] Bette Davis ultimately didn't work out, and Warners sold it to 20th Century–Fox. John Huston was assigned to direct. Huston cast Katharine Hepburn and Humphrey Bogart in the lead roles.

Agnes Browne (1999)

Anjelica Huston as Agnes Browne (Rosie O'Donnell)

Anjelica Huston set out to turn writer Brendan O'Carroll's book, *The Mammy*, into a film. She contacted Rosie O'Donnell about playing the lead role of an Irish mother. O'Donnell seriously considered the offer, but ultimately decided she would rather spend the summer with her family. Huston decided along with directing the movie, she would also become its star. The name of the film was changed to *Agnes Browne*.

Air Force One (1997)

Harrison Ford as James Marshall (Kevin Costner)

Producer Armyan Bernstein asked Kevin Costner to play President James Marshall in *Air Force One*. Costner was interested, but he had just finished shooting *Waterworld*. He was also in the process of getting divorced from his wife of about sixteen years, Cindy Silva. The actor requested a year off, and then he would make the film. Bernstein also made an offer to Harrison Ford. Like Costner, Ford would make the movie but needed a year off. Ford wanted to make the film *Six Days, Seven Nights* for Disney. Bernstein made a deal with Disney which resulted in *Air Force One* shooting before *Six Days, Seven Nights*. Costner was out, and Ford played the president.[28]

Airplane! (1980)

Kareem Abdul-Jabbar as Roger Murdock (Pete Rose)

The role of Roger Murdock was written for Cincinnati Reds star Pete Rose. However, the film was scheduled to shoot in the summer. Being a professional baseball player, Rose was unavailable during the summertime. The role went to another sports star—the NBA's Kareem Abdul-Jabbar.

The Alamo (2004)

Dennis Quaid as Sam Houston (Russell Crowe)
Patrick Wilson as William Barrett Travis (Ethan Hawke)

Ron Howard was originally going to direct *The Alamo*. His *A Beautiful Mind* star Russell Crowe was set to star as General Sam Houston. Howard's producing partner, Brian Grazer was going to act as producer. The team asked for so much money that Disney was unable to make a deal. John Lee Hancock signed on to replace Howard as director. Like Howard, Hancock cast the star from his latest hit, *The Rookie*, in the lead role (Dennis Quaid). Ethan Hawke had been considered for the part of William Barrett Travis, but Hancock gave the part to Broadway star Patrick Wilson instead.[29]

An Alan Smithee Film: Burn Hollywood Burn (1997)

Ryan O'Neal as James Edmunds (Mickey Rourke)
Eric Idle as Alan Smithee (Mick Jagger, Michael York)
Richard Jeni as Jerry Glover (David Paymer)
Jackie Chan as Himself (Bruce Willis)
Whoopi Goldberg as Herself (Arnold Schwarzenegger)

Mick Jagger, Michael York, David Paymer and Mickey Rourke were all considered for roles in *An Alan Smithee Film: Burn Hollywood Burn*.[30]

Bruce Willis was asked to play himself in the film. Willis said no and was replaced by Jackie Chan.[31]

Writer Joe Eszterhas tried to get Arnold Schwarzenegger to play himself. He wrote the actor a letter, but Schwarzenegger never responded. Whoopi Goldberg heard about the film and expressed interest. Eszterhas publicly said that Goldberg would replace Schwarzenegger. He added that she would be much better than he would have.[32]

Alfie (1966)

Michael Caine as Alfie Elkins (James Booth, Laurence Harvey, Anthony Newley, Terence Stamp)

Alfie began in 1964 as a Broadway play. Although the show was not a success, a film version was being planned. Director Lewis Gilbert wanted the actor who created the role on stage—Terence Stamp—to star. He offered Stamp the role. Stamp had no interest in taking the part. His experience with *Alfie* had not been good, and he wanted to end his association with the character. At this time Stamp was staying with a friend of his, another actor by the name of Michael Caine. Caine spent hours trying to convince his friend to take the part. Stamp would not budge. Gilbert offered the part to Anthony Newley, Laurence Harvey, and James Booth. All three actors rejected the role. Finally, Gilbert made an offer to Stamp's friend Michael Caine. Caine jumped at the opportunity.[33] The film went on to be a hit, and made Michael Caine a star. He received his first Academy Award nomination for his performance, but lost out to Paul Scofield, who won for the film *A Man for All Seasons*.

Algiers (1938)

Hedy Lamarr as Gaby [aka Gabrielle] (Dolores del Rio, Sylvia Sidney)
Sigrid Gurie as Ines (Sylvia Sidney)

Producer Walter Wanger wanted either Dolores del Rio or Sylvia Sidney for the role of Gaby, eventually played by Hedy Lamarr.[34] Sidney was also considered for the role of Ines, but Sidney felt that she had played that type of character many times before, and it went to Sigrid Gurie instead.[35]

Alice Doesn't Live Here Anymore (1975)

Ellen Burstyn as Alice Hyatt (Barbra Streisand)

Barbra Streisand was offered the starring role of Alice. At the age of 33, Streisand felt the part was too old for her, and said no.[36] The 43 year old Ellen Burstyn said yes, and won an Academy Award for the role.

Alice in Wonderland (1933)

Charlotte Henry as Alice (Ida Lupino)

Paramount Pictures saw Ida Lupino in a film called *Money for Speed*, and thought that she might be right for the title role of Alice. They later decided that she did not come off innocent enough and cast Charlotte Henry instead.[37]

Alice's Restaurant (1969)

Patricia Quinn as Alice Brock (Alice Brock)

Alice Brock, the real-life Alice of *Alice's Restaurant*, turned down the chance to play herself in the movie. Brock, who was not a professional actress, felt that there was no reason for her to recreate for film what she had already done in real life. Pat Quinn was cast in her place.[38]

Alien (1979)

Sigourney Weaver as Ripley (Jill Clayburgh)
John Hurt as Kane (Brad Davis)

Jill Clayburgh had the chance to star in *Alien*. She turned it down. Sigourney Weaver was cast instead. *Alien* was Weaver's breakthrough film.[39]

Brad Davis rejected the part of Kane, eventually played by John Hurt.[40]

All About Eve (1950)

Bette Davis as Margo Channing (Ingrid Bergman, Claudette Colbert, Joan Crawford, Marlene Dietrich, Joan Fontaine, Greer Garson, Paulette Goddard, Susan Hayward, Katharine Hepburn, Hedy Lamarr, Gertrude Lawrence, Ginger Rogers, Rosalind Russell, Norma Shearer, Barbara Stanwyck, Gloria Swanson)
Anne Baxter as Eve Harrington (June Allyson, Ann Blyth, Jeanne Crain, Olivia De Havilland, Mona Freeman, Donna Reed, Elizabeth Taylor)
George Sanders as Addison De Witt (Jose Ferrer, Charles Laughton, Adolphe Menjou, Vincent Price, Claude Rains, Basil Rathbone, Clifton Webb)
Celeste Holm as Karen Richards (Barbara Bel Geddes, Shirley Booth, Arlene Dahl, Joan Fontaine, Patricia Neal, Nancy Reagan, Alexis Smith, Ann Sothern, Margaret Sullavan, Jessica Tandy, Ruth Warrick)
Gary Merrill as Bill Sampson (Montgomery Clift, Robert Cummings, Glenn Ford, John Garfield, William Holden, Edmond O'Brien, Ronald Reagan, Zachary Scott, Robert Young)
Hugh Marlowe as Lloyd Richards (William Lundigan)
Gregory Ratoff as Max Fabian (Fred Clark, George Jessel, Zero Mostel, Walter Slezak, Everett Sloane)
Barbara Bates as Phoebe (Zsa Zsa Gabor)
Marilyn Monroe as Claudia Caswell (Lois Andrews, Karin Booth, Barbara Britton, Leslie Brooks, Myrna Dell, Zsa Zsa Gabor, Angela Greene, Adele Jergens, Pat Knight, Angela Lansbury, Joi Lansing, Ellie Marshall, Marian Marshall, Mari-

lyn Maxwell, Marie McDonald, Mary Meade, Cleo Moore, Dolores Moran, Joyce Reynolds, Marjorie Reynolds, Gale Robbins, Rowena Rollins, Randy Stuart, Virginia Toland, Arleen Whelan)

Many of the choices above are actors that were put on a list of possibilities by the 20th Century–Fox casting director to be presented to the director of *All About Eve*, Joseph L. Mankiewicz. Not all the actors were auditioned. Many were eliminated by Mankiewicz immediately. Nancy Reagan (then known as Nancy Davis) never even knew she was considered for the film![41] Others tested, and were later eliminated.

Darryl F. Zanuck originally considered Claudette Colbert, Barbara Stanwyck, and Marlene Dietrich for the role of Margo Channing.[42] He finally decided on Colbert, who eagerly signed on for the film. Before filming was set to begin Colbert had an accident. She suffered a ruptured disc and was put in traction.[43]

Zanuck expressed interest in Marlene Dietrich. Mankiewicz thought she was wrong for the part. Zanuck relented.[44] He suggested Susan Hayward. Again Mankiewicz disagreed with Zanuck. He thought that Hayward was too young to play the aging star. The actress Mankiewicz liked was stage star Gertrude Lawrence. She was sent a copy of the script. She was very enthusiastic after reading it. However she insisted on making two changes. She wanted all of Margo's drinking scenes taken out. The second request was regarding the party scene. Lawrence said that instead of the piano player playing Liebestraum, he would play Jerome Kern and Oscar Hammerstein II's Bill, which was to be sung by Lawrence. After all this, Lawrence ended up turning the part down.[45] Ingrid Bergman was briefly considered,[46] but Zanuck knew who he wanted — Bette Davis.

Jeanne Crain was the original choice for Eve Harrington. When she became pregnant, Anne Baxter inherited the role.[47]

Zanuck's first choice for Addison De Witt was Jose Ferrer. Ferrer was unavailable for the film and George Sanders was cast instead.[48]

Zanuck's first choice for the role of Margo Channing's boyfriend Bill Sampson was John Garfield.[49] Garfield lost the role to Gary Merrill, who married co-star Bette Davis shortly after making the film.

William Lundigan was mentioned early on for the part of Lloyd Richards.[50]

The 20th Century–Fox casting director made a long list of possible Claudia Caswells, as depicted above. One contender was Zsa Zsa Gabor. Gabor's husband, George Sanders, was cast as Addison DeWitt. Gabor was eager to join the cast. The part she wanted was Phoebe.[51] Joseph L. Mankiewicz preferred Barbara Bates, but did consider Gabor for Miss Caswell. Mankiewicz ultimately passed her over in favor of a still relatively unknown Marilyn Monroe.

All Night Long (1981)
Barbra Streisand as Cheryl Gibbons
   (Loni Anderson, Lisa Eichhorn)

All Night Long went into production with Lisa Eichhorn in the role of Cheryl Gibbons, even though Universal Studios had suggested Loni Anderson.[52] Early on director Jean-Claude Tramont felt there were problems with Eichhorn's characterization. He went on to say it was not a matter of her acting ability. He just felt that this part was too much of a reach for her. Eichhorn claimed that Tramont said that she wasn't funny. It didn't help Eichhorn's chances of staying in the film that Barbra Streisand expressed an interest in the part. Tramont, who was married to Streisand's agent, felt that she had the right natural quality he was looking for and replaced Eichhorn with her. Eichhorn said that she was shocked to have been fired.[53]

Lisa Eichhorn's role in *All Night Long* was coveted by Barbra Streisand.

All Quiet on the Western Front (1930)

Beryl Mercer as Mrs. Baumer (ZaSu Pitts)

All Quiet on the Western Front was originally shot with ZaSu Pitts in the role of Mrs. Baumer. Because of her reputation as a comedienne, preview audiences laughed during her scenes despite her serious portrayal. Based on this reaction, the studio believed that audiences would not accept her in this dramatic role. They played it safe and reshot her scenes with Beryl Mercer.[54]

ZaSu Pitts was so funny she actually lost a job (*All Quiet on the Western Front*).

All That Jazz (1979)

Roy Scheider as Joe Gideon (Alan Alda, Alan Bates, Warren Beatty, Robert Blake, Richard Dreyfuss, Bob Fosse, Elliott Gould, Gene Hackman, Jack Lemmon, Paul Newman, Jack Nicholson, George Segal, Jon Voight)

Leland Palmer as Audrey Paris (Shirley MacLaine)

All That Jazz was loosely based on the life of Broadway choreographer/director Bob Fosse. In the film, there is a Fosse-like character named Joe Gideon. Richard Dreyfuss was originally cast as Joe Gideon. Although Dreyfuss was not a dancer, the film's director (Guess who? Bob Fosse himself!) assured him that he would make it work for him. Fosse even decided to have Dreyfuss play the choreographer without the actor ever having to dance at all. Still, Richard Dreyfuss was uncomfortable with the role and with Bob Fosse himself. Dreyfuss accompanied Fosse to the dance rehearsals. Fosse confided to the actor that he was not getting the performances he wanted out of the dancers. Dreyfuss suggested ways to work with the dancers, and Fosse accused Dreyfuss of saying that Fosse was not a competent director. Dreyfuss was stunned at this comment. Fosse persisted until Dreyfuss finally said that, yes, he didn't think Fosse knew what he was doing. Dreyfuss quit the production, stating that the problem was an inability to work together. Years later Dreyfuss admits that he had made a mistake passing up the opportunity to work with Fosse.[55]

After Dreyfuss left, many actors were considered for the role including Robert Blake, Jack Nicholson, Elliott Gould, and George Segal. Sidney Lumet suggested Alan Alda and Gene Hackman. Producer Daniel Melnick contacted Paul Newman. But Newman was uncomfortable playing a dancer, and never bothered to read the script. Alan Bates was considered as was Jack Lemmon, but Bates was thought to be too "British" and Lemmon was too old for the role. Jon Voight was being wooed for the part. Fosse watched a copy of Voight's film, *Coming Home*, and decided that the actor was wrong for the part. Warren Beatty was interested as long as Joe Gideon didn't die at the end. Even Bob Fosse wanted the part. He wanted to test for Daniel Melnick who refused. Melnick stated that Fosse (who had a history of heart problems) would not survive the shoot, and he didn't want that on his head. Fosse realized that he had no chance to get the part, and concentrated on finding a suitable actor. Agent Sam Cohn recommended Roy Scheider. A meeting was scheduled with Fosse and writer/producer Robert Alan Aurthur. They liked Scheider immediately. Melnick flew into New York to discuss the matter. He decided that Scheider wasn't right for the part. Melnick didn't think the actor was appealing enough. Fosse told Melnick that he would spend a week working with Scheider. At the end of that week Fosse met with Melnick. Fosse said that he wasn't positive that Scheider would be believable playing a dancer, but that he saw something in the actor, and urged Melnick to give him the part. Melnick trusted Fosse, and finally agreed to cast Scheider.[56]

Bob Fosse briefly considered Shirley MacLaine for the role of Audrey Paris, which was loosely based on Gwen Verdon, Fosse's ex-wife.[57]

All the King's Men (1949)

Broderick Crawford as Willie Stark (Spencer Tracy)

The head of Columbia, Harry Cohn, wanted Spencer Tracy for the starring role of Willie Stark. Writer/director Robert Rossen disagreed with Cohn's choice. Rossen thought that audiences might like Tracy too much. He gave the part to Broderick Crawford instead. Crawford's performance was critically praised. He won the Academy Award for Best Actor for his performance in the film.[58]

All the Pretty Horses (2000)

Matt Damon as John Grady Cole (Leonardo DiCaprio, Nick Stahl)

For his first post–*Titanic* movie, Leonardo DiCaprio considered playing the lead role of John Grady Cole in *All the Pretty Horses*. It was reported at the time that DiCaprio was dragging his feet in committing to the film. The producers decided to not wait around for his decision and ultimately cast Matt Damon instead.[59] Damon was in great demand after the success of *Good Will Hunting*. Lesser-known actor Nick Stahl also read for the part of John Grady Cole. Stahl told *Movieline* magazine that losing this part to Damon hurt him very much.[60]

All Through the Night (1942)

Humphrey Bogart as Gloves Donahue (George Raft)

George Raft was offered the starring role of Gloves Donahue in *All Through the Night*. Raft, who has a long history of turning parts down, was uninterested. He let this role go to Humphrey Bogart.[61] Many of Bogart's most memorable roles had previously been rejected by Raft including Rick Blaine in *Casablanca*, Sam Spade in *The Maltese Falcon*, Baby Face Martin in *Dead End*, Roy Earle in *High Sierra*, and Chips Maguire in *It All Came True*.

Almost Famous (2000)

Billy Crudup as Russell Hammond (Roy Dupuis)
Kate Hudson as Penny Lane (Sarah Polley)
Zooey Deschanel as Anita Miller (Kate Hudson)

Roy Dupuis was asked to audition for the role of Russell Hammond. Dupuis didn't think the film was important, and turned down the audition.[62] Director Cameron Crowe cast Billy Crudup instead.

Cameron Crowe wanted Sarah Polley to play Band-Aid Penny Lane. Polley declined his offer. Kate Hudson was cast as teenage writer Will Miller's sister Anita. When she learned that the role of Penny Lane was free she went to Crowe

Nick Stahl wanted the part of John Grady Cole in *All the Pretty Horses*.

Cameron Crowe wanted Sarah Polley as Penny Lane in *Almost Famous*.

and asked for an audition. Crowe thought her audition was great and gave her the part.[63] *Almost Famous* was Hudson's big break. She quickly became an A-list star with her pick of parts. Hudson was nominated for an Oscar for her performance in *Almost Famous*, but lost out to Marcia Gay Harden (for *Pollock*).

The Alphabet Murders (1966)

Tony Randall as Hercule Poirot (Zero Mostel)

It was Zero Mostel's idea to make a film in which he would play Agatha Christie's famed detective, Hercule Poirot. Mostel was so serious about playing the part, that he left his starring role of Pseudolus in the Broadway production of *A Funny Thing Happened on the Way to the Forum* in order to make the film. A script called *The ABC Murders* was presented to the actor. Mostel was dissatisfied with the script and wanted to write his own version. MGM decided against this. They made the film (which was retitled *The Alphabet Murders*) with Tony Randall as Hercule Poirot.[64] Mostel filled the gap left in his schedule by creating the role of Tevye in *Fiddler on the Roof* on Broadway. Mostel never got to play Poirot, although Peter Ustinov, Albert Finney, and Dudley Jones all played the part in movies throughout the 1970s and 80s.

Always (1989)

Richard Dreyfuss as Pete Sandich (Paul Newman, Robert Redford)
Audrey Hepburn as Hap (Sean Connery)

Director Steven Spielberg wanted to cast both Robert Redford and Paul Newman in the two leading roles; one as Pete Sandich, the other as his best friend Ted Baker. Newman and Redford were an extremely popular onscreen team in the 1970s with the films *Butch Cassidy and the Sundance Kid* and *The Sting*. When Spielberg approached them about *Always* both men wanted to play Pete, and Spielberg was unable to work it out between them.

Sean Connery was the original choice for the role of angel Hap, but other film commitments made him unavailable. Steven Spielberg decided to change the character of Hap's gender from male to female in order to have superstar Audrey Hepburn play the role.[65]

Amadeus (1984)

F. Murray Abraham as Antonio Salieri (Walter Matthau)
Elizabeth Berridge as Constanze Mozart (Meg Tilly)

In 1994 F. Murray Abraham (who played Salieri in the film) said that director Milos Forman was interested in using the actors from the Broadway production for the film version. The catch was that he would only consider them for roles other than those they played on the stage. He would often tell the actors that he loved their performances in the play, and follow it up by asking what (different) part they were interested in playing in his movie. One example of this is actor Nicholas Kepros. Kepros originated the role of Joseph II, Emperor or Austria on Broadway. In the film however, he played the smaller role of Archbishop Collaredo.

Walter Matthau wanted to play Salieri very, very badly. Forman chose F. Murray Abraham instead.[66]

Meg Tilly was originally cast as Constanze, Mozart's wife. She was unable to go through with her commitment because she broke her ankle. Elizabeth Berridge was her replacement.[67]

American Beauty (1999)

Thora Birch as Jane Burnham (Leelee Sobieski)
Mena Suvari as Angela Hayes (Kirsten Dunst)

Leelee Sobieski auditioned for the role of Jane Burnham in *American Beauty*. The young actress told *Movieline* magazine that she felt that director Sam Mendes didn't like her for the role. Although it was a part she wanted to play very much, she also said that she didn't think she would have been a good match to work with Mena Suvari (the actress cast as Jane's friend Angela). Mendes cast Thora Birch instead.[68]

Popular actress Kirsten Dunst was offered the part of Angela Hayes. According to Dunst she read the script when she was 15 years old, and wasn't mature enough to fully understand it. She went on to say that she didn't want to kiss Kevin Spacey or lie naked in rose petals.[69]

American Gigolo (1980)

Richard Gere as Julian Kaye (Christopher Reeve, John Travolta)

American Gigolo began as a vehicle for John Travolta. The actor read the script and signed on, initially attracted by the glitziness of the character. Travolta went to Milan to meet with Giorgio Armani. The designer was hired to dress the character of Julian. Travolta began doing research for the film. Once again he read the script. At this point he had second thoughts. The film he once was enthusiastic about making now troubled him, partly because he was unclear of what the message of *American Gigolo* was. Another factor was that Travolta's mother had died very recently. Travolta decided he didn't want to be in the film after all. He called the president of Paramount Pictures, Michael Eisner, to ask to be released. Eisner agreed, but later asked Travolta to make it up to him by agreeing to star in *Urban Cowboy*.[70] Producer Jerry Bruckheimer had to come up with a replacement for Travolta. He was interested in Christopher Reeve. Reeve was made an offer of $1 million, but the actor said no. Reeve was put off by the fact that the character was a gigolo.[71] Finally, Bruckheimer found an actor who he thought was right: Richard Gere. *American Gigolo* was a big hit, and made Gere a major star.

American Graffiti (1973)

Charles Martin Smith as Terry Fields
 (Richard Dreyfuss)

Director George Lucas offered Richard Dreyfuss his choice of two roles in his film, *American Graffiti*: Curt Henderson or Terry "the Toad" Fields.[72] Dreyfuss passed on the role of the nerdy Terry the Toad and instead opted for the slightly cooler character Curt and spent most of the film looking for Suzanne Somers in her white T-Bird.

American Hot Wax (1978)

Fran Drescher as Sheryl Berkowitz
 (Marilu Henner)

Marilu Henner and Fran Drescher both went up for the role of Sheryl Berkowitz in *American Hot Wax*. Henner auditioned six times but ultimately lost out to Drescher.[73] Fran Drescher wouldn't get her big break for another 15 years, on her television series, *The Nanny*. Ironically, Marilu Henner's big break came only about a year after losing the role in *American Hot Wax*. In 1978 she was cast as Elaine Nardo in the TV series, *Taxi*, which ran for five years and has since become a television classic.

An American in Paris (1951)

Gene Kelly as Jerry Mulligan (Fred Astaire)
Georges Guetary as Henri Baurel
 (Maurice Chevalier, Yves Montand)

Fred Astaire was considered for the lead role, but another famous dancer, Gene Kelly also had his eye on the part. Since producer Arthur Freed wanted ballet dancing in the film Kelly was the logical choice.[74]

MGM wanted Maurice Chevalier to play the part of Henri Baurel in *An American in Paris*. Arthur Freed offered Chevalier a great deal of money. Chevalier said that he didn't like the script and turned down the offer.[75] Yves Montand was interested. He campaigned for the role, but was rejected by the studio. MGM thought Montand might be a communist, and instead gave the role to Georges Guetary.[76]

American Psycho (1999)

Christian Bale as Patrick Bateman
 (Leonardo DiCaprio)

American Psycho was originally planned by Lion's Gate Films as a small budget movie to be directed by Mary Harron. Harron wanted Christian Bale to play the part of Patrick Bateman. When Leonardo DiCaprio expressed some interest in starring, Harron's plans changed. Lion's Gate Films did not want a major star like DiCaprio to slip through their fingers and went over Harron's head to offer him the part. With DiCaprio in the lead the budget jumped from about $10-$15 million to about $40 million. Harron couldn't see him in the role, though, and decided to drop out as director. Finally, negotiations with DiCaprio fell through, with the official reason given as scheduling problems. Without him, the budget went back down and Harron returned as director. Meanwhile, Christian Bale had deliberately kept himself available and once again assumed the lead role.[77]

The Americanization of Emily (1964)

James Garner as Charles E. Madison
 (William Holden)
James Coburn as "Bus" Cummings
 (James Garner)

William Holden was the first choice to play Charles E. Madison in *The Americanization of Emily*. Holden wanted William Wyler to direct. Wyler was also the studio's first choice as director. However negotiations with Wyler and MGM were not smooth. Wyler asked for an extremely large sum of money to direct. In addition to that, he wanted $1250 a week for living expenses since they would be filming on location. Wyler also requested a car and a driver. He would travel to Europe at least twice for publicity; trips he expected to be reimbursed for. If his family were to visit him on location, he expected the studio to pay for their transportation. He wanted to be credited as a coproducer on the film. He wanted a lot of creative control in the editing. He also asked that his son be hired as his personal assistant. William Holden wanted approval of the director if Wyler were not the director. He made a list of acceptable directors which included David Lean, Howard Hawks, John Sturges, Blake Edwards, George Seaton, Joseph Mankiewicz, and Richard Quine. Ultimately, Wyler's demands proved too much, and he was out of the picture. None of the directors on Holden's list were available for the film. The studio hired Arthur Hiller. Holden did not like this choice and dropped out of the film. James Garner was cast in the supporting role of "Bus" Cummings. When Holden left, Hiller moved Garner into the starring role of Charles E. Madison. James Coburn replaced Garner as Cummings.[78]

America's Sweethearts (2001)

Catherine Zeta-Jones as Gwen Harrison (Julia Roberts)
John Cusack as Eddie Thomas (Billy Crystal)
Hank Azaria as Hector Gorgonzolas (Robert Downey, Jr.)

Billy Crystal wrote the script for *America's Sweethearts*. He envisioned himself playing the lead role of Eddie. A copy of the script was sent to Julia Roberts. She was told to consider the part of Gwen. Roberts read the script, but didn't want to play spoiled actress Gwen. She sent word back that she wanted the part of Gwen's sister Kiki. With Roberts set for Kiki, Crystal didn't quite mesh as her leading man. He was moved over to the role of publicist Lee Phillips. John Cusack was brought in to play Eddie, while Catherine Zeta-Jones was cast as Gwen.

Robert Downey, Jr., was originally set for the role of Hector. However, two weeks before shooting was set to begin Downey had a date in court. On November 25, 2000, Downey was arrested and charged with possession of cocaine and Valium as well as being under the influence of a controlled substance. If convicted, he would be unable to appear in the film. The producers wouldn't know until the last minute. Downey was let go, and Hank Azaria played Hector.[79]

Amistad (1997)

Matthew McConaughey as Roger S. Baldwin (Gabriel Byrne, John Cusack, Aidan Quinn)
Djimon Hounsou as Cinque (Denzel Washington)

Director Steven Spielberg's first choice for the role of lawyer Roger S. Baldwin was Matthew McConaughey. Spielberg offered the role, but also made a backup list in case the actor turned him down. The list included John Cusack, Gabriel Byrne, and Aidan Quinn. The list turned out to be unnecessary — McConaughey accepted the part.[80]

Denzel Washington had a meeting with Spielberg to discuss the part of Cinque. Washington didn't want to play a slave and turned Spielberg down. Djimon Hounsou was eventually cast.[81]

Analyze This (1999)

Donna-Marie Recco as Sheila (Amy Lynn Baxter)

Penthouse model Amy Lynn Baxter auditioned for the role of Sheila in *Analyze This*. As a guest on Howard Stern's radio show, Baxter told Stern about her audition with the star of the film, Robert De Niro. The part of Sheila is a small one; she appears in only one scene in the film, which is a sex scene. Baxter, who was new to acting, told Stern she had to audition by reading the sex scene with De Niro on top of her. Although Baxter said there was nothing inappropriate about the audition, Stern took the information and ran with it. Donna-Marie Recco, who ended up with the part, was also a relative newcomer at the time.

Anatomy of a Murder (1959)

Lee Remick as Laura Manion (Lana Turner)
Joseph N. Welch as Judge Weaver (Burl Ives, Spencer Tracy)

Lana Turner was originally set to play Laura Manion, but left the production due to problems between her and director Otto Preminger. It was reported that one of the problems was that Turner was unhappy with her costumes in the film. She wanted them to be more glamorous, but Preminger disagreed. Turner insisted that the reason was Preminger's temper.[82] Lee Remick was given the role instead, and it made her a star.

Burl Ives and Spencer Tracy were both offered the role of Judge Weaver, but turned it down.

The part went instead to real life lawyer Joseph N. Welch. Preminger said that since Welch was not an actor, he didn't ask him to walk and talk at the same time.[83] Welch is well known for his questioning of Senator Joseph McCarthy during the Army-McCarthy hearings. Said Welch to McCarthy, "Have you no sense of decency sir, at long last? Have you left no sense of decency?

Andy Hardy Comes Home (1958)
Polly Benedict (Ann Rutherford)

Ann Rutherford decided not to return to the Andy Hardy film series as Polly Benedict. The original idea was to have Polly married to Andy Hardy. Once Rutherford said no to the film the character of Jane was invented. Jane and Andy were married, and Polly was no longer necessary.[84]

Ann Rutherford did not want to marry Andy Hardy (*Andy Hardy Comes Home*).

Angel Eyes (2001)
James Caviezel as Catch Lambert (Aaron Eckhart)

Aaron Eckhart was originally cast as Catch Lambert in *Angel Eyes*. Shortly after, Eckhart had a change of heart and dropped out of the film.[85] James Caviezel eventually ended up with the part.

Angel Heart (1987)
Mickey Rourke as Harry Angel (Robert De Niro)

Robert De Niro was originally offered the lead role of Harry Angel. When director Alan Parker re-thought the idea, he decided he'd rather have De Niro in the role of Louis Cyphre. De Niro agreed to the switch, and Mickey Rourke joined the cast as Harry Angel.[86]

Angela's Ashes (1999)
Robert Carlyle as Malachy McCourt (Liam Neeson)

Liam Neeson was cast as Malachy McCourt in the film version of Frank McCourt's *Angela's Ashes*. However Neeson quit.[87] He was replaced with Robert Carlyle. Carlyle is best known for playing the lead role in the 1998 film, *The Full Monty*.

Robert Carlyle replaced Liam Neeson in *Angela's Ashes*.

Angels Over Broadway (1940)
Rita Hayworth as Nina Barone (Jean Arthur)

Jean Arthur was offered the role of Nina Barone in *Angels Over Broadway*. She turned it down, and it went to Rita Hayworth instead.[88]

Angie (1994)
Geena Davis as Angie Scacciapensieri (Madonna, Marisa Tomei)

Madonna was the original choice for the title role of Angie. She even worked with writer Todd Graff to develop the script. She lost the role, however, when executive producer Joe Roth would not postpone shooting to accommodate her schedule. An offer was made to Geena Davis, with Marisa Tomei waiting in the wings in case Davis turned it down.

Madonna, who co-starred with Davis in *A League of Their Own*, was furious. It seems her anger, however, was not directed towards Geena Davis, but rather towards Joe Roth's Caravan Pictures. In a letter to Roth, Madonna wrote: "I'm just grateful that I had the chance to inspire the writer to write the screenplay that is sure to make you happy fellas in Hollywood." In the end, it was Madonna who had the last laugh: *Angie* was a flop, both critically and at the box office.[89]

Animal House (1978)

John Belushi as John "Bluto" Blutarski (Meat Loaf)
Tim Matheson as Eric "Otter" Stratton (Chevy Chase, Mark Metcalf)
John Vernon as Dean Vernon Wormer (Jack Webb)
Verna Bloom as Marion Wormer (Kim Novak)
Peter Riegert as Donald "Boone" Schoenstein (Bill Murray, Harold Ramis)
Bruce McGill as Daniel Simpson "D-Day" Day (Dan Aykroyd)
James Widdoes as Robert Hoover (Brian Doyle-Murray)

Director John Landis wanted Chevy Chase for the role of Otter. According to screenwriter Harold Ramis, Chase felt that he was on the verge of a very big movie career and did not want to share the spotlight with his former *Saturday Night Live* co-star John Belushi. At the same time he was offered the leading role in another film, *Foul Play*. He decided to take the part in *Foul Play*, and turned Landis down, which indeed turned out to be a good career move for him. Another possibility for the part of Otter was Mark Metcalf. Director John Landis didn't think he was quite right for that part, but instead cast him as Doug Neidermeyer.

Both Bill Murray and his brother, Brian Doyle-Murray, were considered for roles in the film. Landis thought Brian Doyle-Murray would make a good Hoover, with Bill Murray as Donald "Boone" Schoenstein. They both turned down the parts. Harold Ramis (who co-wrote the film) auditioned for the part of Boone. Landis thought that Ramis looked too old to fit in with the rest of the cast and instead gave the role to Peter Riegert (who is two years younger than Ramis). This was particularly disappointing to Ramis because he wrote the part for himself to play. Dan Aykroyd was offered the part of D-Day. Aykroyd was more interested in spending his free time writing and said no. John Belushi was the first choice for the part of Bluto. However, Landis had a second choice waiting in the wings in case Belushi turned him down: Meat Loaf. For Dean and Mrs. Wormer, Landis was interested in Jack Webb and Kim Novak. He had a meeting with Webb. He has suggested that they did not hit it off with each other. He said that at their meeting Webb just sat there smoking and drinking Scotch. Eventually he decided to cast actors who were not so well-known, and gave the parts to John Vernon and Verna Bloom.[90]

The Animal Kingdom (1932)

Myrna Loy as Cecelia Henry Collier (Katharine Hepburn, Karen Morley)

Katharine Hepburn was interested in playing the role of Cecelia Henry Collier in *The Animal Kingdom*. Producer David O. Selznick had another actress in mind: Karen Morley.[91] When Morley did not pan out, Selznick turned not to Hepburn, but another actress entirely. He cast Myrna Loy, who is best known for her role as Nora Charles in The Thin Man film series.

Anna and the King of Siam (1946)

Irene Dunne as Anna Owens (Jean Arthur, Olivia De Havilland, Myrna Loy, Dorothy McGuire)
Rex Harrison as King Mongkut (Charles Boyer, William Powell)

Twentieth Century–Fox studio boss Darryl F. Zanuck wanted William Powell and Dorothy McGuire to star in *Anna and the King of Siam*. He contacted David O. Selznick to arrange a loan out for McGuire. Selznick made many demands, and Zanuck eventually decided it wasn't worth it. Jean Arthur informed Zanuck that if he were to give her the part, she would make it her top priority; even if she were already committed to another film. Arthur was given strong consideration. She was a major star, and would attract a large audience. Arthur eventually fell through. Olivia De Havilland campaigned for the role, but Zanuck kept searching. Myrna Loy was also interested, as well as Irene Dunne. Zanuck initially thought that Dunne, in her late forties, was too old for the part. He later changed his mind and cast her. Charles Boyer tried for the role of the king, but Zanuck had other ideas.[92] He gave the part to Rex Harrison.

Anna Karenina (1935)
Fredric March as Count Alexei Vronsky (Ronald Colman, Clark Gable)

Clark Gable was producer David O. Selznick's first choice to play Count Alexei Vronsky. Gable wasn't interested.[93] Ronald Colman was another consideration. Colman knew that the film belonged to costar Greta Garbo. Colman doubled his asking price, which took him out of the running.[94] Selznick contacted Fredric March. March, having had his fill of period pieces, did not want the part, but his studio ordered him to accept it.[95]

Anne of the Thousand Days (1969)
Genevieve Bujold as Anne Boleyn (Elizabeth Taylor)

Superstar Elizabeth Taylor wanted the part of Anne Boleyn. Taylor's then-husband Richard Burton was already cast in the film. But at 36 Taylor was too old for the part. Producer Hal B. Wallis instead decided to cast Genevieve Bujold, who is 10 years younger than Taylor.[96] Bujold was nominated for an Oscar for her performance, but lost out to Maggie Smith for *The Prime of Miss Jean Brodie*.

Annie (1982)
Albert Finney as Oliver Warbucks (Sean Connery)
Carol Burnett as Miss Hannigan (Bette Midler)

Sean Connery was offered, and strongly considered playing, the lead role of Oliver Warbucks. He took voice lessons in order to prepare for the role. Eventually he felt it was not the best idea for him, and he turned down the part.[97] Perhaps the singing was the reason for his decision. In 1998, Connery had a chance to sing when he was invited by record producer George Martin to record a track for the album *In My Life*. The album consisted of celebrities singing Beatles' songs. While the other celebrities on the album sang, Martin preferred to have Connery recite the lyrics to the song, "In My Life."

Executive producer Joe Layton talked to both Carol Burnett and Bette Midler about playing Miss Hannigan. Midler wasn't interested, while Burnett was very enthusiastic. Burnett was cast.[98]

Annie Get Your Gun (1950)
Betty Hutton as Annie Oakley (June Allyson, Judy Garland, Betty Garrett, Betty Grable, Ginger Rogers)
Louis Calhern as Buffalo Bill Cody (Frank Morgan)

Judy Garland was hired to star as cowgirl Annie Oakley in the film version of *Annie Get Your Gun*. Busby Berkeley was chosen to direct the film. However, Garland's erratic behavior started to cause problems for the famous director. Garland's apparent drug problem was getting in the way of shooting the film, and she was sent for shock treatments. When she returned to the set, Garland continued to have problems, including excessive lateness and absences. The actress was sick often and suffered from insomnia. She was unhappy with the performance she was giving, which caused her even more stress. Garland was also unhappy with Berkeley as director. Not only did she disagree with his interpretation of the material, but she also had problems with him personally. She disliked his treatment of her, and complained about it. It was decided by MGM that it would be best for everyone if Berkeley was replaced as director. Charles Walters stepped in to relieve Berkeley, but there were still problems. One day, Garland never showed up at the set. This was the last straw. She received a letter from the studio firing her from the picture. A replacement was needed. June Allyson was a possibility, as was Betty Grable and Betty Garrett. Grable's name was scratched off the list when her studio said no to a loan out.[99] Garrett had a good chance, until her agent made too many demands.[100] Ginger Rogers was interested in playing the part. She said she wanted it so much that she would have done it for a dollar.[101] Louis B. Mayer passed over Rogers; he thought the perfect choice was Betty Hutton.

Frank Morgan was cast as Buffalo Bill. Sadly, he died in his sleep. The part was recast with Louis Calhern.[102]

Annie Hall (1977)
Marshall McLuhan as Himself (Luis Bunuel, Federico Fellini)
Christine Jones as Dorrie (Sigourney Weaver)

Federico Fellini was Woody Allen's first choice to play himself in *Annie Hall*. Fellini said no and

Allen turned to Luis Bunuel. Bunuel also turned the film down. Allen gave the part to Marshall McLuhan.[103]

An unknown Sigourney Weaver was called in to audition for a role in *Annie Hall*. She met with the director and soon after was offered the role of Dorrie. This was the woman whom Allen's character dates after his breakup with Annie Hall. He tries to recreate the relationship he had with Annie with Dorrie, but it doesn't work out. Weaver told *Premiere* magazine that it had been a dream of hers to work with Woody Allen.[104] She saw this as a great opportunity. There was one problem. Weaver was opening a play called *Das Lusitania Songspiel* the following week, which conflicted with Allen's shooting schedule. The play was written by her best friend, playwright Christopher Durang. She would have had to drop out of the play in order to do the role in the film. The play meant too much to her and Durang for her to leave it, so Weaver reluctantly turned Allen down. She did appear in the film after all in a very small, nonspeaking role. There is a scene at the end of the film where Allen runs into Annie after not seeing her for a long time. They are both with dates. Weaver is Allen's date.

Annie Oakley (1935)

Barbara Stanwyck as Annie Oakley (Jean Arthur)

Barbara Stanwyck was cast in the title role of Annie Oakley only after it had been turned down by Jean Arthur.[105]

Another Woman (1988)

Gena Rowlands as Marion (Mia Farrow)
Mia Farrow as Hope (Dianne Wiest)

The role of Marion was originally to be played by Mia Farrow. Farrow became pregnant, and was unable to do the part. Dianne Wiest was set for the role of Hope, but decided that for personal reasons she would not be able to do the part. Writer/director Woody Allen made the character of Hope pregnant and switched Farrow over to that role. He now needed an older actress to play the now-vacant part of Marion and brought in Gena Rowlands as Farrow's replacement.[106]

Antwone Fisher (2002)

Derek Luke as Antwone Fisher (Cuba Gooding, Jr., Mekhi Phifer, Ja Rule, Will Smith)

Stars such as Will Smith, Cuba Gooding, Jr., Ja Rule and Mekhi Phifer all expressed interest in playing the title role of Antwone Fisher for first time director Denzel Washington. Washington didn't want a star. He gave the part to newcomer Derek Luke.[107]

Any Given Sunday (1999)

Dennis Quaid as Cap Rooney (David Duchovny)
Jamie Foxx as Willie Beaman #13 (Sean "P. Diddy" Combs)
Aaron Eckhart as Nick Crozier (Tony Goldwyn)
Matthew Modine as Dr. Allie Powers (David Duchovny)

David Duchovny, whom director Oliver Stone was pursuing for the supporting role of Dr. Allie Powers, was more interested in playing Cap Rooney, the aging quarterback. Stone didn't think the actor was right for the part, saying that Duchovny's neck was not thick enough to be believable as a quarterback, and cast Dennis Quaid instead.[108]

Sean "P. Diddy" Combs was originally cast as Willie Beaman. *Any Given Sunday* was to be the singer's film debut. According to Oliver Stone, there were delays which caused Combs to miss a concert in Japan. The missed performance cost Combs a lot of money.[109] Combs left the film and was replaced by Jamie Foxx. Scheduling conflicts were given as the official reason for his departure.[110]

Tony Goldwyn was originally cast as Nick Crozier. Goldwyn had to drop out, and Stone recast the role with Aaron Eckhart.[111]

The Apartment (1960)

Fred MacMurray as J.D. Sheldrake (Paul Douglas)

Paul Douglas was originally cast as Mr. Sheldrake in *The Apartment*. Douglas died of a heart attack just two weeks before shooting started.[112] Billy Wilder replaced him with Fred MacMurray, who had starred in Wilder's 1944 film, *Double Indemnity*. This was the second time Wilder cast MacMurray against type in the role of a bad guy. MacMurray is most often remembered as TV dad Steve Douglas in *My Three Sons*.

Apocalypse Now (1979)

Marlon Brando as Colonel Walter E. Kurtz (Steve McQueen, Jack Nicholson, Al Pacino, Robert Redford)

Paul Douglas (pictured) was replaced by Fred MacMurray in *The Apartment*.

Martin Sheen as Captain Benjamin L. Willard (John Aprea, James Caan, Keith Carradine, Clint Eastwood, Frederic Forrest, Tommy Lee Jones, Harvey Keitel, Michael Margotta, Tom Mason, Steve McQueen, Jack Nicholson, Nick Nolte, Al Pacino, Michael Parks, Robert Redford, Jack Thibeau, Robert Viharo, Alan Vint, Glenn Walken

There were many possibilities for role of Colonel Kurtz, which eventually went to Marlon Brando. Early suggestions included Steve McQueen, Robert Redford, Jack Nicholson, and Al Pacino. McQueen was the first one approached. At the time McQueen was married to actress Ali MacGraw. With their marriage failing, he did not want to leave his wife for the four months of location filming the movie required. McQueen's son Chad was also set to graduate from high school, and his father did not want to miss being there. There was still more going on in McQueen's personal life. He had just been diagnosed with cancer, and was actively trying to beat the disease. Instead of turning down the part, he asked for the large sum of $3 million, at which point director Francis Ford Coppola made an offer to Jack Nicholson. Nicholson had already turned down the role of Willard (played by Martin Sheen), and did not want to play this part either.[113] Next on the list was Al Pacino. Pacino didn't like the part and turned it down,[114] as did Clint Eastwood.[115] Finally, Marlon Brando agreed to do the role.

Steve McQueen was also on the top of the list for the role of Captain Willard, but for the aforementioned reasons, he wasn't interested.[116] Jack Nicholson was also offered the role, but turned it down. James Caan was offered $1.25 million to play the part. The actor instead wanted $2 million. Caan finally told director Francis Ford Coppola he couldn't do the movie because his wife was about to have a baby, and she didn't want to give birth in the Philippines. Al Pacino was made an offer, but the actor knew that working on this film would mean spending an excessive amount of time in the jungle, which he was not willing to do.[117] After considering many actors including Michael Margotta, Nick Nolte, John Aprea, Keith Carradine, Frederic Forrest, Alan Vint, Tommy Lee Jones, Tom Mason, Michael Parks, Glenn Walken, Jack Thibeau and Robert Viharo Coppola finally settled on Harvey Keitel.[118] Everything seemed fine until the end of the first week of shooting, when Coppola looked at all the film they had shot with him and decided that he needed to recast the role. However, according to Keitel's agent Harry Ufland, there was another reason for the firing — Marlon Brando. Supposedly, Brando wanted production on the film to shut down for the summer, and then resume shooting in September in order to accommodate his schedule. Keitel, who had another movie commitment, had a problem with this new arrangement. As a result, Keitel was fired and replaced with Martin Sheen.[119]

Apollo 13 (1995)

Ed Harris as Gene Kranz (John Travolta)

John Travolta was interested in the part of Gene Kranz.[120] Ed Harris was chosen instead. Harris was nominated for an Academy Award for his performance in the film. He lost the award to Kevin Spacey for the film *The Usual Suspects*.

The Apostle (1997)

Miranda Richardson as Toosie (Farrah Fawcett)

Farrah Fawcett was offered her choice of the two female leads by director/star Robert Duvall.

At first she chose the part of the radio station secretary, Toosie, but then changed her mind and asked for the part of the wife. Duvall allowed the switch. After Miranda Richardson was cast as the secretary, Fawcett changed her mind once again and said that she wanted that part back. Robert Duvall had had it. He said that either she played the wife or she was out of the movie.[121] Fawcett played the wife.

Apt Pupil (1998)

Ian McKellen as Arthur Denker (Richard Burton, James Mason, Nicol Williamson)
Brad Renfro as Todd Bowden (Rick Schroder)

In the early 1980s Richard Burton and James Mason were both offered the lead role of Arthur Denker, but both actors died before production began. In 1987 Nicol Williamson and Rick Schroeder were cast in the leads, but after 10 weeks of shooting the production company ran out of money and production was shut down. When they were finally ready to begin production again a year later, Schroder had aged too much for the role and the film shot with him was no longer usable. The movie was put on hold for about 10 years, when it was finally made by director Bryan Singer with Ian McKellen and Brad Renfro in the leads.[122]

Arabesque (1966)

Gregory Peck as David Pollock (Cary Grant)

Cary Grant was asked to star as David Pollock in *Arabesque*. Grant had recently been criticized for playing opposite the much younger Audrey Hepburn in *Charade*. He knew that it was likely that his co-star in *Arabesque* would be much younger than he was. Grant felt that it would be best for him to drop out of the film, and suggested a younger actor for the part — Gregory Peck. Peck was cast and his leading lady turned out to be Sophia Loren.[123] Incidentally, Grant was right. Sophia Loren is 30 years younger than Cary Grant.

Arizona (1940)

William Holden as Peter Muncie (Gary Cooper)

Gary Cooper was producer/director Wesley Ruggles first choice to star as Peter Muncie in *Arizona*. When Cooper turned the part down, Columbia chief Harry Cohn told Ruggles to cast William Holden. Ruggles was bothered by the fact that Holden was almost 20 years younger than his co-star Jean Arthur. Cohn wasn't concerned, and Holden got the part.[124]

Around the World in 80 Days (1956)

David Niven as Phileas Fogg (Cary Grant)
Cantinflas as Passepartout (Fernandel)
Shirley MacLaine as Princess Aouda (Donna Reed)
Tim McCoy as Colonel, U.S. Cavalry (Gregory Peck)

Cary Grant was the first choice to star in *Around the World in 80 Days* as Phileas Fogg. When he turned the part down, it went to David Niven.[125]

Director Mike Todd was interested in the French actor Fernandel for the part of Passepartout. Fernandel didn't think his English wasn't good enough. He opted for a cameo as a French coachman instead. The part of Passepartout went to Cantinflas.[126]

Donna Reed was offered the part of Princess Aouda. Reed had recently played Sacajawea in *The Far Horizons*. She didn't think that taking another ethnic part so soon after was a good idea, and turned the film down. Shirley MacLaine was cast instead.[127]

Mike Todd was unhappy with Gregory Peck, who was cast as the Colonel. He thought Peck

French actor Fernandel lacked confidence in his English (*Around the World in 80 Days*).

wasn't serious about the film and replaced him with the lesser-known Tim McCoy.[128]

The Arrangement (1969)
Kirk Douglas as Eddie Anderson (Marlon Brando)

Marlon Brando declined to appear in *The Arrangement* in order to work in the civil rights movement. Brando was deeply affected by the death of Martin Luther King, Jr. The actor announced on *The Joey Bishop Show,* that instead of making *The Arrangement*, he would go out and discover what it was like to be black in America.[129]

Arsenic and Old Lace (1944)
Cary Grant as Mortimer Brewster (Bob Hope)
Raymond Massey as Jonathan Brewster (Boris Karloff)

Cary Grant was cast in the role of Mortimer after Bob Hope turned it down. Cary Grant accepted, on the condition that the role be made bigger to suit a star of his magnitude.

According to the script, the character of Jonathan Brewster (played in the film by Raymond Massey) bears a striking to actor Boris Karloff. This is particularly interesting to note because guess who director/producer's first choice for the role was? Boris Karloff! He was unavailable at the time, so director Frank Capra hired Massey and had him made up to look like Karloff. Incidentally, Karloff played the role in the Broadway production.[130]

Arthur (1981)
Dudley Moore as Arthur Bach (John Travolta)
Liza Minnelli as Linda Marolla (Marilu Henner, Debra Winger)

John Travolta was an early possibility for the role of Arthur Bach, which was eventually played by Dudley Moore.[131]

Debra Winger turned down the role of Arthur's love interest, Linda Marolla.[132] Many other actresses were considered, and it finally came down to a choice between two for the role: Liza Minnelli and Marilu Henner. They were both very interested in playing the role, and the producers liked them both. They had to make a choice, and they picked Minnelli, the bigger star.[133]

As Good as It Gets (1997)
Helen Hunt as Carol Connelly (Melanie Griffith, Holly Hunter)

Director James L. Brooks originally wanted Holly Hunter to star alongside Jack Nicholson in *As Good as It Gets*.[134] Hunter, Brooks and Nicholson all previously worked together on *Broadcast News*. Hunter was unavailable and the role was up for grabs. Melanie Griffith desperately wanted the part, but she was pregnant. Brooks wouldn't delay production for her, and cast Helen Hunt instead.[135]

As Young as You Feel (1951)
Monty Woolley as John R. Hodges (Clifton Webb)

Clifton Webb was the original choice to play John R. Hodges. Webb's participation fell through, and the role was recast with Monty Woolley.[136]

The Asphalt Jungle (1950)
Marilyn Monroe as Angela Phinlay (Lola Albright)

Lola Albright was the first choice for the role of Angela Phinlay, but she turned it down. The producers found another actress who's career was just starting to take off: Marilyn Monroe.[137]

The Associate (1996)
Lainie Kazan as Cindy Mason (Cindy Adams)

Columnist Cindy Adams was asked to audition for the role of Cindy Mason, a gossip columnist who resembled Adams' real life persona. She read for the part, but ultimately was not chosen. The part went to actress Lainie Kazan instead.

Athena (1954)
Jane Powell as Athena Mulvain (Vera-Ellen, Esther Williams)

Director Chuck Walters, writer Leo Pogostin, and actress Esther Williams came up with the premise of *Athena* together. The three worked on the script for weeks which included Williams' trademark swimming sequences. Williams was about to give birth and so Walters and Pogostin were left to finish the script without her. When Williams was ready to go back to work, she made a lunch date with the men. Williams started talking about playing the title role at which point she noticed that her friends looked tense. She asked what the problem was. They informed her that *Athena* was already being shot, with Jane Powell in the lead and Dick Thorpe directing. The swimming scenes had been removed. Williams was furious and went to see studio head Dore Schary. Schary informed Williams that he was not going to do anything about the situation.[138] Incidentally, before Schary cast Powell as Athena, Vera-Ellen was a contender for the part.[139]

Auntie Mame (1958)

Coral Browne as Vera Charles (Vivian Vance)

Vivian Vance was very interested in playing the role of actress Vera Charles in *Auntie Mame*. However Vance had scheduling problems and was unable to commit to the film.[140] The role was played by Coral Browne instead.

The Avengers (1998)

Uma Thurman as Emma Peel (Elizabeth Hurley, Nicole Kidman, Gwyneth Paltrow)

Elizabeth Hurley met with director Jeremiah Chechik to discuss the possibility of her playing the role of Emma Peel.[141] Hurley wasn't quite what Chechik was looking for, and he continued to look at other actresses for the part. Gwyneth Paltrow was made an offer, which she turned down in order to be with her then-fiancé Brad Pitt.[142] At the time Pitt was doing the film *Meet Joe Black* in New York. Had Paltrow signed on to play Emma Peel the couple would have been apart for about four months. Paltrow chose to make the movie *Sliding Doors* instead.[143] Nicole Kidman also turned the part down.[144]

Awakenings (1990)

Robin Williams as Dr. Malcolm Sayer (Robert De Niro)
Ruth Nelson as Mrs. Lowe (Shelley Winters)

Robert De Niro was originally considered for the role of Dr. Malcolm Sayer in director Penny Marshall's *Awakenings*. De Niro chose to play patient Leonard Lowe instead, and Robin Williams was cast as the doctor.[145]

Robert De Niro wanted Shelley Winters to play his mother. However, the studio insisted that she read for the part first. Winters, having won two Academy Awards, felt that this was an insult to her. The story goes that when Winters met the casting director she put both of her Oscars on the desk and said, "Some people think I can act." Despite Ms. Winters' acting ability, Ruth Nelson ended up with the part.[146]

The Awful Truth (1937)

Cary Grant as Jerry Warriner (Ralph Bellamy)
Ralph Bellamy as Daniel Leeson (Cary Grant)

Initially Cary Grant was set to play the role of Daniel Leeson, with Ralph Bellamy cast as Jerry Warriner. Later Grant decided he would rather play the role of Warriner, which resulted in the two actors switching roles. Grant was still dissatisfied and asked to leave the film entirely. Director Leo McCarey agreed that Grant should be replaced. But studio head Harry Cohn said that Grant would stay on with the picture.[147] After all this upheaval, *The Awful Truth* went on to be a big hit.

The Babe Ruth Story (1948)

William Bendix as George Herman "Babe" Ruth (Jack Carson, Paul Douglas, Orson Welles)

Babe Ruth was a world famous icon of American pop culture for most of the 20th century. As such, several films were made depicting his story, beginning with Roy Del Ruth's biopic, *The Babe Ruth Story*. This film is widely held among baseball fans as one of the worst baseball movies ever made. While casting the larger-than-life Yankees' slugger, Del Ruth considered Orson Welles, Paul Douglas and Jack Carson.[1] Instead, the part went to a pre–*Life of Riley* William Bendix. Del Ruth's choice seemed to make sense: Not only was Bendix a former bat boy for both the New York Giants and the New York Yankees, he actually played professionally for a time, albeit in the minor leagues. Bendix was a successful actor; he was nominated for an Academy Award for his performance in 1942's *Wake Island*. He was, however, out of his element playing the charismatic Ruth. Bendix was best known for playing kindly, dimwitted characters, and the public did not accept his broad characterization of Babe Ruth. In addition to the miscasting of Bendix, the screenplay was implausible and notoriously bad.

Babes on Broadway (1941)

Virginia Weidler as Barbara Josephine "Jo" Conway (Shirley Temple)

Child star Shirley Temple was offered the role of Barbara Jo in *Babes On Broadway*. Temple's mother, Gertrude Temple turned it down. Gertrude's problem with *Babes on Broadway* was with its co-stars, Mickey Rooney and Judy Garland. Both young actors were extremely talented. Temple worried that her daughter would not stand out enough working with the two of them. Virginia Weidler was cast in her place.[2]

Baby Boom (1987)
Diane Keaton as J.C. Wiatt (Cher)

Cher was offered the starring role of J.C. Wiatt. She didn't think the part suited her, and said no.[4]

Baby Boy (2001)
Tyrese Gibson as Joseph "Jody" Summers (Tupac Shakur)

Writer/director/producer John Singleton originally planned to have Tupac Shakur in the starring role of Jody. Shakur was killed in Las Vegas in 1996, and Singleton's plans changed.[3] He decided to give the role to Tyrese Gibson. *Baby Boy* was Gibson's first film. He was formerly known to the public as a singer and a model.

Baby Doll (1956)
Carroll Baker as Baby Doll (Diane Cilento, Marilyn Monroe)

Superstar Marilyn Monroe desperately wanted to play the title role of Baby Doll. Director Elia Kazan instead offered the part to Diane Cilento. Cilento wasn't interested and turned it down.[5] Kazan finally filled the part with actress Carroll Baker. The movie was critically acclaimed with four Oscar nominations, including one for Baker. Although she didn't win, the film made her a star.

Baby, It's You (1983)
Vincent Spano as Albert "Sheik" Capadilupo (Maxwell Caulfield)

Writer/director John Sayles wanted Vincent Spano for the starring role of Albert "Sheik" Capadilupo. Studio executives were interested in Maxwell Caulfield. Caulfield had the lead in the upcoming *Grease 2*, which they thought was going to score well with audiences. Sayles insisted on Spano, who was ultimately approved by the studio.[6] *Grease 2* turned out to be a big flop.

Maxwell Caulfield was the studio's choice to star in *Baby, It's You*.

Bachelor Party (1984)
Tom Hanks as Rick Gassko (Paul Reiser)
Tawny Kitaen as Debbie Thompson (Kelly McGillis)

Paul Reiser and Kelly McGillis were originally cast as the couple about to be wed in *Bachelor Party*. A week into filming director Neal Israel realized he had made the wrong casting decision. He recast the roles with Tom Hanks and Tawny Kitaen.[7]

Back to the Future (1985)
Michael J. Fox as Marty McFly (C. Thomas Howell, Matthew Modine, Eric Stoltz)

Director Robert Zemeckis' first choice for the role of Marty McFly was Michael J. Fox. Fox was unavailable due to his commitment to the television series, *Family Ties*. Fox was unavailable because of the series.[8] The two final contenders for the part were C. Thomas Howell and Eric Stoltz. Eric Stoltz was hired.[9] Zemeckis and producer Steven Spielberg thought that Stoltz was playing the role as if it were a drama rather than a light comedy.[10] According to Stoltz, he just did not know how to do the part any other way.

Back to the Future Part II

Eric Stoltz was too serious for *Back to the Future*.

Halfway through the movie Spielberg and Zemeckis decided that Stoltz was too intense for their movie and fired him.[11] At this point, they contacted Matthew Modine, told him that Stoltz had been fired, and gave Modine 24 hours to decide if he would take over the part. Feeling uneasy about replacing Stoltz, he declined.[12] In the end it all worked out for Steven Spielberg and Robert Zemeckis. The delay caused by Stoltz's firing actually turned out to be a blessing in disguise for Spielberg and Zemeckis. Fox, who was on hiatus from *Family Ties*, was now available. The film went on to become a major hit which spawned two successful sequels.

Back to the Future Part II (1989)

Back to the Future Part III (1990)

Jeffrey Weissman as George McFly
(Crispin Glover)

Clashes over salary prevented Crispin Glover from reprising the role of George McFly in the *Back to the Future* sequels. Jeffrey Weissman was hired to replace Glover, who, since the film was released, had developed a reputation for erratic behavior. In an infamous appearance on NBC's *Late Night with David Letterman*, Glover wanted to arm wrestle with David Letterman. When Letterman declined, Glover stood up and tried to kick him in the head. Letterman stood up from his desk to leave, at which point Glover grabbed his jacket to keep him there. Letterman walked off the set and the show went to commercial. When they returned, Glover was gone. In a later appearance, Glover told Letterman that the person who tried to kick him was not him, but a Crispin Glover look-alike.

In the two *Back to the Future* sequels, Jeffrey Weissman was made up to resemble Crispin Glover as much as possible, so that the audience might not notice that a change had been made. Footage from Glover's performance in the original film was also used and edited in to make Weissman more believable as George McFly. Crispin Glover did not agree to allow the producers to use the film of him, and sued.[13] The Screen Actors Guild instituted new rules about the unauthorized use of an actor's work as a result of the case.

Bad Men of Missouri (1941)

Dennis Morgan as Cole Younger
(Humphrey Bogart)

Warner Bros. wanted Humphrey Bogart to star as Cole Younger in *Bad Men of Missouri*. Bogart refused to play the part, and was put on suspension from the studio.[14] Bogart was replaced by Dennis Morgan.

Bagdad (1949)

Maureen O'Hara as Princess Marjan
(Yvonne De Carlo)

When *Bagdad* started production, Yvonne De Carlo was cast in the role of Princess Marjan. De Carlo, who had been ill recently, had lost a great deal of weight, so much so that the producers decided to replace her with Maureen O'Hara.[15]

Bagdad Cafe (1988)

CCH Pounder as Brenda (Whoopi Goldberg)

Writer/director Percy Adlon's first choice for the role of Brenda was Whoopi Goldberg. He sent the script to her manager, but never heard back from anyone. Goldberg later said that she never received the script. The part of Brenda was played by CCH Pounder. However, when *Bagdad Cafe* was made into a television series, Goldberg jumped at the chance to play Brenda opposite Jean Stapleton as Jasmine.[16]

Ball of Fire (1941)

Barbara Stanwyck as Sugarpuss O'Shea (Jean Arthur, Lucille Ball, Betty Field, Carole Lombard, Ginger Rogers)

Sam Goldwyn's first choice for Sugarpuss O'Shea was Ginger Rogers. Rogers called it fluff and turned it down. She later said that she regretted her decision.[17] Jean Arthur was next on Goldwyn's list. Her studio, Columbia, would not loan her out. Carole Lombard did not like the script, and didn't want to do it.[18] Betty Field was another candidate. She was interested in the part and made a screen test.[19] Lucille Ball very much wanted to play the part. She thought it was the kind of role she could win an Oscar nomination for. She fought to win the role, and was eventually hired. At that point Barbara Stanwyck (who had originally turned down the offer to star) changed her mind. Lucille Ball was out and Barbara Stanwyck was in.[20] She was nominated for an Academy Award for her performance.

The Ballad of Cable Hogue (1970)

Jason Robards as Cable Hogue (Charlton Heston, James Stewart)
Stella Stevens as Hildy (Joanne Woodward)
David Warner as Joshua (Henry Fonda)

James Stewart was asked to play the title role of Cable Hogue. Stewart thought the part would be bad for his image and said no. Charlton Heston was approached. Heston thought it wasn't a great script, and passed on the film. Finally Jason Robards signed on for the part.

Director Sam Peckinpah met with Stella Stevens to tell her that she was the first choice to play Hildy. Stevens doubted that she was right for the part. Peckinpah reassured her that he was writing the role with her in mind. Stevens and the producers clashed over matters of money and billing. Executive producer Phil Feldman looked at Joanne Woodward as a possible replacement. Woodward asked for more money than they were willing to pay. Stevens got the part.

Henry Fonda was interested in playing Joshua.

Negotiations broke down, and the part went to David Warner instead.[21]

The Band Wagon (1953)

Jack Buchanan as Jeffrey Cordova (Clifton Webb)

Clifton Webb was the first choice to play the part of Jeffrey Cordova.[22] He turned it down, and Jack Buchanan was cast in his place.

Banjo on My Knee (1936)

Barbara Stanwyck as Pearl Holley (Janet Gaynor)

Janet Gaynor was originally scheduled to star in *Banjo on My Knee*. However Darryl F. Zanuck wasn't interested in Gaynor and he replaced her with Barbara Stanwyck.[23]

Barabbas (1962)

Anthony Quinn as Barabbas (Yul Brynner)
Silvana Mangano as Rachel (Jeanne Moreau)

Producer Dino De Laurentiis and director Richard Fleischer's first choice for the role of Barabbas was Yul Brynner. Brynner wasn't interested. He did, however, agree to meet with Fleischer. By the end of the meeting, Brynner had come around. He had agreed to play the part. De Laurentiis was thrilled they had gotten their first choice. A few days later Fleischer was called into De Laurentiis' office. De Laurentiis informed him that they would not be using Yul Brynner because he demanded too much money. Anthony Quinn was cast and the matter was settled. A few weeks later Fleischer received a letter from Brynner who was upset to have been let go from the film because Fleischer didn't like him. Fleischer could only assume that Brynner was told this lie because it was easier for Dino De Laurentiis to make it a personal issue than to pay him what he was asking.

Jeanne Moreau was brought to Rome to make a screen test. This was not to test her acting, but for hair, makeup, and costumes. The press was invited to cover her tests. This brought the production a great deal of publicity. It became front-page news that Moreau was to star in *Barabbas*. A week later De Laurentiis informed Richard Fleischer that he was not going to use Moreau, but instead his wife—actress Silvana Magnano—would play the part.[24]

Barbarella (1968)

Jane Fonda as Barbarella (Brigitte Bardot, Sophia Loren)

Producer Dino De Laurentiis offered Sophia Loren and Brigitte Bardot the title role of Barbarella. He was turned down by both actresses. He wrote to Jane Fonda to see if she might consider playing the part. She threw De Laurentiis' letter away. She mentioned the offer to her husband director Roger Vadim. Vadim took the letter out of the garbage. He wanted to make the film with Fonda as his leading lady. She wasn't enthusiastic about the idea, but he was eventually able to change her mind. Vadim was hired to direct the film. Jane Fonda starred as Barbarella.[25]

The Barefoot Contessa

Ava Gardner as Maria Vargas (Elizabeth Taylor)

Elizabeth Taylor lost out to Ava Gardner for the lead role in *The Barefoot Contessa*.[26]

Barefoot in the Park (1967)

Jane Fonda as Corie Bratter (Elizabeth Ashley, Natalie Wood)

Elizabeth Ashley created the role of Corie Bratter in *Barefoot in the Park* on Broadway. When casting began for the film version Ashley auditioned. However producers weren't satisfied with the Broadway star and kept looking for another actress.[27] They considered Natalie Wood for the part. Wood wasn't interested.[28] Meanwhile the actor who had originated the role of Paul on Broadway had, like Elizabeth Ashley, auditioned for the film. His name was Robert Redford and he fared much better than his former co-star. He won the role of Paul. With Redford cast as the male lead, director Gene Saks had to turn down Ashley. Since Redford was unknown, he needed a star in the female lead. Jane Fonda fit the bill, and she was given the part.

The Barkleys of Broadway (1949)

Ginger Rogers as Dinah Barkley (Judy Garland)

Judy Garland was the original actress cast in the role of Dinah Barkley in *The Barkleys of Broadway*. Garland started rehearsals and everything seemed fine. Soon after Garland started to not show up for work. Her doctor was contacted. He felt that the pressure of having to report to the set on a regular basis might result in a breakdown for the actress. It was decided that Ginger Rogers would replace Garland as Dinah Barkley.[29]

The Barretts of Wimpole Street (1934)

Norma Shearer as Elizabeth Barrett (Marion Davies)

MGM planned to star Norma Shearer as Elizabeth Barrett in *The Barretts of Wimpole Street*. Publishing magnate William Randolph Hearst had another idea. He thought that his girlfriend, Marion Davies, would be perfect for the part.[30] Apparently Hearst was the only one who thought so. Davies made a screen test in a black wig, to no avail.[31] She was told that she was too lively for Elizabeth Barrett, and to stick to comedy.[32]

Marion Davies was not considered enough of a serious actress to play literary figure Elizabeth Barrett (*The Barretts of Wimpole Street*).

The Barretts of Wimpole Street (1957)

Jennifer Jones as Elizabeth Barrett (Grace Kelly)

Grace Kelly was once considered for the part of Elizabeth Barrett, which eventually went to Jennifer Jones.[33]

Basic Instinct (1992)

Sharon Stone as Catherine Tramell (Isabelle Adjani, Ellen Barkin, Kim Basinger, Geena Davis, Melanie Griffith, Mariel Hemingway, Kelly Lynch, Kelly McGillis, Demi Moore, Lena Olin, Michelle Pfeiffer, Julia Roberts, Greta Scacchi, Emma Thompson, Debra Winger)
Jeanne Tripplehorn as Beth Garner (Linda Fiorentino)
Leilani Sarelle as Roxy (Jeanne Tripplehorn)

The role that made Sharon Stone a star was turned down by many other actresses. Lena Olin was the first to reject it.[34] Michael Douglas, the star of *Basic Instinct*, wanted Isabelle Adjani to be cast opposite him. Adjani was uncomfortable with the racy script and turned it down.[35] Geena Davis was approached, but the actress thought that the script would make women uneasy.[36] Julia Roberts,[37] Debra Winger,[38] Emma Thompson, Melanie Griffith,[39] Michelle Pfeiffer,[40] Kim Basinger[41] and Greta Schacchi[42] were all offered the part. Incredibly enough, Demi Moore wanted very much to play Catherine, but director Paul Verhoeven refused to even see her.[43] Kelly Lynch turned the part down, claiming it was too silly.[44] Ellen Barkin was offered the part, but thought the film was too graphic.[45] In the end it came down to a decision between three actresses: Mariel Hemingway, Kelly McGillis, and Sharon Stone.[46]

The role of Beth Garner was turned down by Linda Fiorentino.[47] Jeanne Tripplehorn was originally considered for the role of Catherine's lover Roxy. Director Paul Verhoeven said that she was wrong for the part. He was still interested in her, but for the larger role of Dr. Beth Garner. Leilani Sarelle was cast as Roxy.

The Basketball Diaries (1995)

Leonardo DiCaprio as Jim Carroll (Matt Dillon, Anthony Michael Hall, Rick Schroder, Eric Stoltz)

The role of Jim Carroll was sought after by many young actors including Matt Dillon, Rick Schroder, Anthony Michael Hall, and Eric Stoltz.[48]

Batman (1989)

Jack Nicholson as Jack Napier/The Joker (Robin Williams)
Michael Keaton as Bruce Wayne/Batman (Pierce Brosnan, Daniel Day-Lewis, Ralph Fiennes, Mel Gibson, Bill Murray, Tom Selleck, Charlie Sheen, Adam West)
Kim Basinger as Vicki Vale (Michelle Pfeiffer, Sharon Stone, Sela Ward, Sean Young)

Adam West, who rose to fame as Batman on television, felt disappointed and angry when director Tim Burton did not ask him to reprise the role for the movie.[49] Daniel Day-Lewis,[50] Mel Gibson,[51] Bill Murray,[52] Pierce Brosnan,[53] Charlie Sheen,[54] Ralph Fiennes,[55] and Tom Selleck[56] were all considered before Michael Keaton stepped into the part.

Sean Young was originally cast as photographer Vicki Vale until she broke a bone riding a horse. When they discussed who was going to replace her Burton brought up Michelle Pfeiffer. Keaton and Pfeiffer had just ended a romance, and Keaton thought it might be awkward to play opposite her so soon after (they did just that in the sequel: *Batman Returns*).[57] A pre–*Basic Instinct* Sharon Stone auditioned, but the mostly unknown actress was passed over.[58] Sela Ward auditioned for Tim Burton. According to the actress Burton loved her reading. He wanted her to fly to London to screen test. Producer Jon Peters requested that Ward audition for him as well. Ward refused. She felt that if Burton loved her, then she shouldn't have to impress the producer.[59] Her attitude wasn't appreciated, and Kim Basinger won the role instead.

Burton was interested in Robin Williams for the Joker. He tried to make a deal with him, but ran into trouble. Burton instead went with Jack Nicholson. Nicholson's performance stole the show.[60]

Batman & Robin (1997)

George Clooney as Bruce Wayne/Batman (Val Kilmer)
Uma Thurman as Pamela Eisley/Poison Ivy (Geena Davis, Julia Roberts)

Batman & Robin was the fourth installment in the series of Batman movies. The first two (*Batman* and *Batman Returns*) starred Michael Keaton as Bruce Wayne and his alter ego Batman. When Keaton declined to return for the third film, *Batman Forever*, Val Kilmer was given the part. When *Batman & Robin*, the fourth movie in the series, was being cast Kilmer was expected to participate. In fact, he was contractually bound to do so. At the same time Kilmer was offered *The Saint*. He was very interested in making that film. *The Saint* would require his presence until mid–July. He was scheduled to report for work as Batman on August 1. Paramount Pictures said that they would have to replace Kilmer. Kilmer threatened to quit *Batman & Robin*. Director Joel Schumacher had problems with Kilmer on the previous Batman film which led to a pushing match. Said Schumacher, "He was being irrational and ballistic with the first AD, the cameraman, the costume people. He was badly behaved, he was rude and inappropriate. I was forced to tell him this would not be tolerated for one more second. Then we had two weeks where he did not speak to me, but it was bliss." Warner Bros. let Kilmer out of his contract and replaced him with George Clooney.[61]

Reportedly Geena Davis expressed interest in playing Poison Ivy, but Schumacher said that the only actress he ever seriously considered was Uma Thurman.[62]

Batman Forever (1995)

Val Kilmer as Bruce Wayne/Batman (Ralph Fiennes, Michael Keaton, Liam Neeson, Keanu Reeves, Kurt Russell)
Chris O'Donnell as Dick Grayson/Robin (Leonardo DiCaprio, Mark Wahlberg)
Nicole Kidman as Dr. Chase Meridian (Sandra Bullock, Rene Russo, Robin Wright Penn)
Drew Barrymore as Sugar (Jenny McCarthy)

Michael Keaton decided to forego his $15 million paycheck and turn down *Batman Forever*. After Ralph Fiennes, Liam Neeson, Keanu Reeves, and Kurt Russell were all considered, Val Kilmer became the new Batman.[63]

Leonardo DiCaprio was asked to play the part of Robin, but declined. Mark Wahlberg was turned down for the part of Robin in favor of Chris O'Donnell.[64]

Rene Russo was originally set to costar as Dr. Chase Meridian. Director Joel Schumacher claims that she was replaced because of a scheduling conflict.[65] Sandra Bullock was considered but she was later told that she wasn't attractive enough for the role.[66] After Robin Wright Penn turned down the part Nicole Kidman was cast.[67]

Jenny McCarthy turned down Drew Barrymore's small role of Sugar because she didn't want to play a fluff.[68]

Batman Returns (1992)

Michelle Pfeiffer as Selena Kyle/Catwoman (Ellen Barkin, Annette Bening, Cher, Demi Moore, Sharon Stone, Sean Young)

Although superstar actresses like Cher[69] and Demi Moore[70] wanted the role of Catwoman director Tim Burton cast the well respected, but less famous, Annette Bening instead. Soon after getting the part Bening found out that she was pregnant by Warren Beatty. The actress decided the best thing to do was drop out of the film.[71] When Sean Young heard this she hatched a plan. Young was originally supposed to have been in Burton's first Batman movie. After her horse riding accident she was replaced with Kim Basinger. But now Young was better and she obviously still wanted to appear in a Batman movie. Wearing a Catwoman outfit she put together herself, Young snuck onto the Warner Bros. lot.[72] Burton was not amused by this and had her escorted off the set.[73] Young also showed up on a talk show being hosted by Joan Rivers wearing the same outfit to plead for the role. It didn't work. Burton refused to give Young the part. He was interested in Ellen Barkin, however. But the actress turned it down without even blinking.[74] Burton considered both Michelle Pfeiffer and Sharon Stone. Stone wanted the part, but Burton chose Pfeiffer.[75] The actress accepted the part and ended up stealing the movie.

Battle Circus (1953)

June Allyson as Ruth McGara (Shelley Winters)

Shelley Winters was originally set to play Lt. Ruth McGara in *Battle Circus*. Winters was pregnant however, and had to be replaced. The part went to June Allyson.[76]

Battle for the Planet of the Apes (1973)

Austin Stoker as MacDonald (Hari Rhodes)

Hari Rhodes played MacDonald in the 1972 film, *Conquest of the Planet of the Apes*. This film was the fifth in the *Planet of the Apes* series. The following year another ape film was being planned, entitled *Battle for the Planet of the Apes*. Rhodes was unavailable, and Austin Stoker took his place.[77]

The Beach (2000)

Leonardo DiCaprio as Richard (Ewan McGregor)

Ewan McGregor was the first choice for the role of Richard in *The Beach*. The character in the Alex Garland's novel is British, like McGregor. After the success of *Titanic*, director Danny Boyle became very interested in Leonardo DiCaprio. Actually, the director liked DiCaprio for the role before the phenomenal success of *Titanic*. But at that time he felt the rising star was too expensive for his budget and cast McGregor. But now DiCaprio was becoming a strong possibility. He liked the character and felt strongly about doing the film. McGregor was dropped in favor of the young star. Producer Andrew Macdonald has said that he and Boyle both thought that DiCaprio was the better choice for the part. McGregor said that their decision was based more on economics than anything else.[78]

Beaches (1988)

Barbara Hershey as Hillary Whitney Essex (Anne Archer)
Spalding Gray as Dr. Richard Milstein (David Lynch, Don Simpson)

Director Garry Marshall has said that Anne Archer came very close to landing the role of Hillary Whitney Essex in *Beaches*. Marshall also stated that David Lynch and producer Don Simpson (*Top Gun*) were considered for the part of Dr. Richard Milstein, played in the film by Spalding Gray.[79]

Beau Geste (1939)

Susan Hayward as Isobel Rivers (Frances Farmer)

Frances Farmer was originally chosen to play Isobel Rivers in *Beau Geste*. Farmer opted to do a play in New York and quit. Her replacement was Susan Hayward.[80]

A Beautiful Mind (2001)

Russell Crowe as John Forbes Nash, Jr. (Jim Carrey, Tom Cruise)

Initially Robert Redford was to direct *A Beautiful Mind*. Redford thought that Tom Cruise would be a great choice for the starring role. Redford ultimately decided against directing the film, opting instead to act in the film *Spy Game*. Soon after Ron Howard took over as director. Jim Carrey was also considered for the lead at one point, but Howard decided to go with Russell Crowe instead.[81]

Becket (1964)

Peter O'Toole as Henry II (Richard Burton)

Richard Burton was offered the chance to star in Becket as either Henry II or the title role of Becket. He went to Elizabeth Taylor for advice and she told him to play Becket.[82]

The Bedford Incident (1965)

Wally Cox as Seaman Merlin Queffle (Woody Allen)

Wally Cox was cast as Seaman Merlin Queffle in *The Bedford Incident* after the part was turned down by Woody Allen.[83]

Bedknobs and Broomsticks (1971)

Angela Lansbury as Eglantine Price (Julie Andrews)

Julie Andrews was the first choice for the starring role of Eglantine Price. Andrews had already had much success with the similar role of Mary Poppins, and turned it down.[84]

Before Night Falls (2000)

Javier Bardem as Reinaldo Arenas (Antonio Banderas, Benicio Del Toro)
Olivier Martinez as Lazaro Gomez Carriles (Javier Bardem)

Director Julian Schnabel wanted Benicio Del Toro to play Cuban poet and novelist Reinaldo Arenas. At the same time, Del Toro's friend, Christopher McQuarrie also wanted him for a film. Del Toro was in the 1995 film, *The Usual Suspects* written by McQuarrie. McQuarrie was making his directorial debut with the film *The Way of the Gun*, and wanted Del Toro for the starring role of Mr. Longbaugh. Del Toro chose McQuarrie's film and turned *Before Night Falls* down.[85] Antonio Banderas wanted to play Arenas, but was unable to.[86] Javier Bardem was already cast in the supporting role of Arenas' friend Lazaro Gomez Carriles. Schnabel bumped him up to the lead role, and cast Olivier Martinez as Carriles.[87] Bardem was nominated for an Academy Award for Best Actor for his performance. Coincidentally, Del Toro was nominated for a Best Supporting Actor award the same year for the film, *Traffic*. Del Toro won the Oscar, while

Bardem lost out to Russell Crowe (for *Gladiator*).

Being There (1979)
Melvyn Douglas as Benjamin Rand (Laurence Olivier)

Laurence Olivier was offered the role of Benjamin Rand in *Being There*. The actor turned it down because he was disgusted by Shirley MacLaine's masturbation scene. He referred to it as immoral.[88]

La Belle Meuniere (1948)
Tino Rossi as Franz Schubert (Fernandel)

Director Marcel Pagnol wanted Fernandel to play Franz Schubert. The actor was already committed to another film, *Emile l'African*, and had to turn down the offer. Tino Rossi was eventually cast.[89]

The Belle of New York (1952)
Vera-Ellen as Angela Bonfils (Judy Garland)

The score of *The Belle of New York* was written for Judy Garland. However, the project was put on hold for years. By that time Garland was no longer a possibility and Vera-Ellen was cast instead.[90]

Beloved (1998)
Danny Glover as Paul D Garner (Denzel Washington)

Denzel Washington was asked to play the role of Paul D in *Beloved*. Washington didn't like the character and turned it down. He went on to suggest another actor for the part: Danny Glover. Apparently it was a good suggestion. Glover was indeed cast in the role.[91]

Beneath the Planet of the Apes (1970)
James Franciscus as Brent (Burt Reynolds)
James Gregory as Ursus (Orson Welles)
David Watson as Cornelius (Roddy McDowall)

Burt Reynolds was the producers' first choice for the starring role of Brent in the sequel to the smash hit film, *Planet of the Apes*. Reynolds turned the part down, which was fine with director Ted Post. Post's first choice was James Franciscus. Franciscus' agent, Dick Clayton gave his client a copy of the script. Franciscus thought

Even though James Franciscus was the director's first choice for *Beneath the Planet of the Apes*, the producers wanted Burt Reynolds.

that the story was good enough, but the character of Brent was very weak. He expressed his concerns to producers Mort Abrahams and Arthur Jacobs. Franciscus also spoke with Charlton Heston the star of the original film. Heston had agreed to do a cameo in the sequel. Heston wasn't overly concerned, but did speak to Mort Abrahams on Franciscus' behalf. Abrahams agreed to make some changes in the script to appease Franciscus. The actor still wasn't satisfied and asked if he could make his own changes. Abrahams reluctantly agreed. Franciscus and writer John Ryan rewrote the entire script. Abrahams finally put his foot down and told Franciscus that they were going to use Abrahams revised script, although he did incorporate some of Franciscus' changes.

Orson Welles was pursued for the role of Ursus. Welles didn't want to wear the ape makeup and said no.

Roddy McDowall was scheduled to reprise the part of Cornelius. McDowall was more interested in directing the film, *Tam Lin*. Post allowed him to drop out of the film and replaced him with David Watson.[92]

Ben-Hur (1925)

Betty Bronson as Mary (Myrna Loy)

An unknown Myrna Loy made a screen test for the part of Mary in *Ben-Hur*. The studio decided they wanted a familiar name in the role and cast Betty Bronson instead. Loy was given a bit part as a consolation prize.[93]

Ben-Hur (1959)

Charlton Heston as Judah Ben-Hur (Marlon Brando, Cesare Danova, Kirk Douglas, Rock Hudson, Burt Lancaster)
Stephen Boyd as Messala (Charlton Heston)

The role of Ben-Hur was turned down by Marlon Brando,[94] Kirk Douglas[95] and Burt Lancaster. Lancaster felt that he couldn't play the part because he was an atheist, and besides he called the script a piece of crap.[96] Rock Hudson wanted to play the part, and MGM offered him $1 million. The only problem was that he was under contract at Universal Studios and they refused to loan him out. Hudson was very upset, and when he renegotiated his contract with Universal he included a clause allowing him to do at least one picture a year outside the studio.[97] Italian actor Cesare Danova was almost selected, but MGM worried that he didn't speak English well.[98] Director William Wyler concluded that the actor cast as Messala — Charlton Heston — would be better suited for the starring role of Ben-Hur.[99]

Benny and Joon (1993)

Mary Stuart Masterson as Juniper "Joon" Pearl (Laura Dern)
Aidan Quinn as Benny Pearl (Woody Harrelson)

Johnny Depp was cast as Sam, with Laura Dern as Joon. But Dern decided against doing the film and dropped out. Mary Stuart Masterson was cast in her place.

Woody Harrelson was originally cast to play Benny, but dropped out when he was offered *Indecent Proposal*. MGM was furious and sued Harrelson and Paramount. They later settled out of court.[100]

The Benny Goodman Story (1955)

Steve Allen as Benny Goodman (Tony Curtis)

Many actors auditioned for the title role in *The Benny Goodman Story*. The list of possible Benny Goodmans was narrowed down to two actors: Tony Curtis or Steve Allen. The real Benny Goodman had a say in which actor was chosen to play him. He felt that Allen had an advantage because he was also a musician. He also felt that Curtis was too good looking for the part, and Allen would be the best choice.[101]

Berkeley Square (1933)

Heather Angel as Helen Pettigrew (Loretta Young)

Loretta Young went after the part of Helen Pettigrew. She had a crush on the star of the film, Leslie Howard. She was very disappointed when she lost the part to Heather Angel. Young's disappointment didn't last long. *Berkeley Square* flopped.[102]

Best Foot Forward (1943)

Lucille Ball as Lucille (Lana Turner)

Lana Turner was initially cast in *Best Foot Forward*. When Turned learned she was pregnant she left the film and was replaced by Lucille Ball.[103]

Best in Show (2000)

Jennifer Coolidge as Sherri Ann Cabot (Catherine O'Hara)

Catherine O'Hara was initially considered for the role of Sherri Ann Cabot. O'Hara was moved over to the part of Cookie Guggelman Fleck. Jennifer Cabot was given the part of Sherri Ann.

The Best Little Whorehouse in Texas (1982)

Charles Durning as Governor (Mickey Rooney)

Director Colin Higgins thought that Mickey Rooney was the right choice to play the singing and dancing role of the governor of Texas. The star of the film, Burt Reynolds had another idea. He told Higgins that Mickey Rooney singing and dancing was just what people would expect. He went on to say that no one knew that Charles Durning could handle the part; Durning was a dance instructor. Higgins gave Durning the part. He was nominated for an Academy Award for his performance.[104]

The Best Things in Life Are Free (1956)

Sheree North as Kitty Kane (Mitzi Gaynor)

Twentieth Century–Fox was interested in having Mitzi Gaynor play Kitty Kane in *The Best Things in Life Are Free*. Gaynor didn't take the part; it was played by Sheree North instead.[105]

The Best Years of Our Lives (1946)

Harold Russell as Homer Parrish (Farley Granger)
Fredric March as Al Stephenson (Fred MacMurray)
Myrna Loy as Milly Stephenson (Olivia De Havilland)

At the age of 30, soldier Harold Russell lost both of his hands while he was training paratroopers at Camp McCall, NC. He was holding TNT, and it accidentally exploded. Unable to save his hands, doctors replaced them with hooks. Consequently, Russell was chosen to appear in the army training film *Diary of a Sergeant*. Around this time director William Wyler was preparing to make *The Best Years of Our Lives*, the story of three World War II veterans returning home. One of these soldiers was a character named Homer, who was originally intended to be a spastic. Wyler originally planned to cast Farley Granger in the role, but after seeing Russell's army film, Wyler changed his mind. He changed the part of Homer to an amputee and gave it to the newcomer, Russell.[106] Russell won two Oscars (Best Supporting Actor and a Special Award) for his performance. In 1993, Harold Russell auctioned off an Oscar to pay for an operation for his wife. The statuette sold for $125,000.

Fred MacMurray and Olivia de Havilland turned down the roles of Al and Milly because they felt the parts were not important enough.[107]

Betrayed (1988)

Debra Winger as Katie Phillips/Cathy Weaver (Melanie Griffith, Michelle Pfeiffer)
Tom Berenger as Gary Simmons (Kevin Costner)

Kevin Costner, Michelle Pfeiffer, and Melanie Griffith all turned down the chance to star in *Betrayed*.[108] Costner wasn't interested because he had another film on his plate, *Field of Dreams*.[109]

The Betsy (1978)

Robert Duvall as Loren Hardeman III (Steve McQueen)
Katharine Ross as Sally Hardeman (Ali MacGraw)

Robert Duvall and Katharine Ross were cast as Loren and Sally Hardeman after the roles were turned down by Steve McQueen and Ali MacGraw.[110]

Beverly Hills Cop (1984)

Eddie Murphy as Axel Foley (Mickey Rourke, Sylvester Stallone)

Sylvester Stallone and Mickey Rourke were both approached to star in *Beverly Hills Cop*. Stallone actually committed to the movie. He just had one problem with the script — he didn't like the way Foley spoke. He wanted to rewrite it to suit himself. When he came back with his version of the script, it was a totally different movie. He had eliminated much of the comedy and made it more of an action movie. The production team did not want to do this version and told Stallone that they were going to use the original script. Stallone dropped out of the project. His version of *Beverly Hills Cop* also became a movie: *Cobra*. Turns out the studio was right about Stallone's script. *Beverly Hills Cop* was a major hit grossing approximately $316 million, while *Cobra* only made about $49 million. Mickey Rourke had also committed to *Beverly Hills Cop*. He also dropped out because of the problematic script and decided to do *The Pope of Greenwich Village* instead.[111] The part was finally given to *Saturday Night Live* star Eddie Murphy. Murphy's humor changed the tone of *Beverly Hills Cop*. It was no longer only an action movie, it was also a comedy. That change gave the film a wider audience. Although Murphy had success with his first two films, *48 HRS.* and *Trading Places*, *Beverly Hills Cop* changed his career. The monumental success of the film enabled him to negotiate a $15 million film deal with Paramount Pictures. Murphy reprised the role of Axel Foley in two very successful sequels: *Beverly Hills Cop II* and *III*.

Beyond Borders (2002)

Clive Owen as Nick Ward (Kevin Costner, Ralph Fiennes)
Angelina Jolie as Sarah Jennings (Gwyneth Paltrow, Julia Roberts, Meg Ryan, Catherine Zeta-Jones)

Oliver Stone was originally supposed to write and direct *Beyond Borders*. Stone wanted Kevin Costner for the part of Nick Ward. He told the actor that the part was his as long as he said yes to the version of the script he already read. If he wanted changes made he could tell Stone, and Stone would see about it somewhere down the line. Costner wanted Stone to make changes before he signed a contract, exactly the opposite of what Stone wanted him to agree to. Catherine Zeta-Jones was hired to play opposite Costner. However, Jones learned that she was pregnant and dropped out of the film. Julia Roberts was a possible replacement. Roberts read the script. She eventually decided she would say yes, but by the time she did Stone and Costner were looking elsewhere. Gwyneth Paltrow was another possibility as well as Meg Ryan. Stone finally decided the right actress was Angelina Jolie. Very shortly before production was to start Costner said that he would be making another movie before starting work on *Beyond Borders*. Stone was annoyed by this and decided to offer the part to Ralph Fiennes. Stone eventually decided to quit the picture. He was replaced by Martin Campbell. Campbell kept Jolie as Sarah Jennings. The part of Nick Ward went to Clive Owen.[112]

The Bible (1966)
John Huston as Noah (Charlie Chaplin, Alec Guinness, Orson Welles)
Ava Gardner as Sarah (Maria Callas)

Charlie Chaplin refused the role of Noah because he didn't want to appear in a film that was not his own. Alec Guinness was also approached, but turned it down.[113] Orson Welles was unavailable.[114] Unable to cast the role, Director John Huston played the part himself.

Producer Dino De Laurentiis wanted opera star Maria Callas to play Sarah. John Huston didn't agree. He gave the part to Ava Gardner.[115]

Bicentennial Man (1999)
Robin Williams as Andrew (Tom Hanks)

At one point Tom Hanks considered starring in *Bicentennial Man* with Wolfgang Petersen as director.[116] Eventually Chris Columbus signed on as director and Robin Williams was cast in the lead role.

The Bicycle Thief (1948)
Lamberto Maggiorani as Antonio Ricci (Cary Grant)

An American company wanted to make the film on the condition that Cary Grant play Antonio Ricci. Director Vittorio De Sica rejected that idea, and cast Lamberto Maggiorani instead.[117]

Big (1988)
Tom Hanks as Josh Baskin (Warren Beatty, Albert Brooks, Kevin Costner, Robert De Niro, Clint Eastwood, Harrison Ford, Dennis Quaid)

Steven Spielberg considered directing *Big* with Harrison Ford as Josh. The director later decided against the project. Spielberg's sister, Anne Spielberg, had co-written the script and he thought his participation on the project might take the attention away from her.[118] Albert Brooks was made an offer, but said no. He didn't want to play a kid at the time.[119] Warren Beatty was asked. Beatty's asking price of $7.5 million was too high.[120] Penny Marshall was hired as director. Her first choice for the role was Tom Hanks. Hanks turned down the part. Marshall went down her list, which included Kevin Costner, and then Dennis Quaid, Clint Eastwood, and Robert De Niro. De Niro was made an offer and the actor accepted. He and Marshall spent months working on the character of 12-year-old Josh Baskin. De Niro even practiced skateboarding. Soon after 20th Century–Fox created a problem. They refused to pay De Niro the amount he had been promised. Marshall and producer James L. Brooks offered to give De Niro their own money to arrive at De Niro's price, but the actor refused to let them and quit the film. In the meantime, Tom Hanks knew that De Niro had been associated with the film. An actor like Robert De Niro gave respectability to the film, and Hanks was now very interested. An offer was made, and Hanks accepted.[121] *Big* turned Hanks' career around. The actor had become famous on the TV series *Bosom Buddies*. He went on to make movies, without any big successes. He was nominated for an Academy Award for his performance in *Big* and from that point his career skyrocketed. He went on to be nominated for an Oscar three more times, with two consecutive wins.

The Big Broadcast of 1938 (1938)
Bob Hope as Buzz Fielding (Jack Benny)

Jack Benny, the star of *The Big Broadcast of 1937*, was offered the chance to star in the 1938 version of the series. Benny was unavailable, and turned it down.[122] Paramount Pictures searched for a replacement. They had just signed an actor who was straight from Broadway. He had never made a film, but Paramount decided to give the role to Bob Hope anyway.

The Big Chill (1983)
Kevin Kline as Harold (Mickey Rourke)

Director Lawrence Kasdan offered Mickey Rourke the role of Harold in *The Big Chill*. At the same time Francis Ford Coppola had asked him to star in *Rumble Fish*. Rourke chose to work with Coppola and Kasdan gave the part of Harold to Kevin Kline.[123]

The Big Sky (1952)
Dewey Martin as Boone (Ken Tobey)

The final two candidates to play Boone in *The Big Sky* were Ken Tobey and Dewey Martin. Director Howard Hawks decided that Dewey Martin was the better choice.[124]

A Bill of Divorcement (1932)
Katharine Hepburn as Sydney Fairfield (Jill Esmond, Anita Louise)

Jill Esmond lost out to newcomer Katharine Hepburn for the role of Sydney in *A Bill of Divorcement*.

Laurence Olivier's then wife, Jill Esmond, fought very hard to win the role of Sydney Fairfield. Director George Cukor didn't agree that she was right for the part, and turned her down.[125] He also considered Anita Louise until he decided to cast Katharine Hepburn.[126]

Billy Budd (1962)
Terence Stamp as Billy Budd (Warren Beatty, Anthony Perkins, Dean Stockwell)

An unknown Terence Stamp won the title role of Billy Budd over Warren Beatty, Anthony Perkins and Dean Stockwell.[127]

Billy Liar (1963)
Julie Christie as Liz (Topsy Jane)

Director John Schlesinger was interested in having Julie Christie play the role of Liz in *Billy Liar*. He invited the actress to make a screen test. Schlesinger felt the test was poor and kept looking for an actress to play the part. He later decided to re-test Christie, with the same results. Schlesinger chose instead Topsy Jane. Jane had originated the role of Liz in the stage production and was now hired to recreate it in the film version. However the actress became ill midway through the filming. Another actress was needed in a hurry. Schlesinger reconsidered Julie Christie — the actress he rejected twice for the part. He now decided she would be the best choice and she was brought in to replace Topsy Jane.[128]

The Birdcage (1996)
Nathan Lane as Albert Goldman (Robin Williams)

When director Mike Nichols initially approached Robin Williams about starring in *The Birdcage*, he wanted the actor to play the role of Albert Goldman. The part of Albert is the type of flamboyant part Williams is famous for doing, but the actor had a different idea. Williams told Nichols he was interested in doing the film, but in the part of Armand instead. Nichols agreed and cast Broadway star Nathan Lane as Williams' co-star.[129]

The Birds (1963)
Rod Taylor as Mitch Brenner (Cary Grant)
Suzanne Pleshette as Annie Hayworth (Anne Bancroft)
Tippi Hedren as Melanie Daniels (Grace Kelly)

Director Alfred Hitchcock's first choices for

the lead roles in *The Birds* were Grace Kelly and Cary Grant. The former actress was now Princess of Monaco which made her unavailable. Hitchcock didn't want to pay Grant as much as he thought the actor would ask for. Rod Taylor and Tippi Hedren were cast instead.[130]

Hitchcock originally considered casting Anne Bancroft as Annie Hayworth. He later changed his mind, feeling he did not want a star in the role.[131] He instead chose the much lesser known Suzanne Pleshette instead.

Bitter Sweet (1933)

Anna Neagle as Sarah Linden (Jeanette MacDonald)

Jeanette MacDonald was mentioned for Anna Neagle's role in *Bitter Sweet*.[132]

The Black Bird (1975)

Stephane Audran as Anna Kemidov (Glenda Jackson)

Glenda Jackson and George Segal starred in the hit film *A Touch of Class*. After the success of the film Columbia wanted to reteam the actors in *The Black Bird*. Segal accepted the part of Sam Spade. Glenda Jackson was offered the part of Anna Kemidov. She didn't want to do it, and Stephane Audran filled in.[133]

Black Hand (1949)

Gene Kelly as Johnny Columbo (Robert Taylor)

The first choice for the starring role of Johnny Columbo was Robert Taylor. Taylor thought that his good looks were wrong for the part and turned it down.[134] Next on the list was Gene Kelly. Kelly had one problem with the part — the fact that Taylor had been offered it first. Kelly and Taylor were not friends. In fact Kelly resented the way Taylor testified in at a HUAC hearing in Washington. Kelly wasn't happy to find out that he was runner-up to Robert Taylor for a part.[135] However Kelly wanted the role enough that he was able to put his bad feelings aside and accept.

Black Knight (2001)

Martin Lawrence as Jamal Walker (Chris Tucker)

Director F. Gary Gray cast Chris Tucker in the starring role in his forthcoming film, *Black Knight*. The film is loosely based on Mark Twain's *A Connecticut Yankee in King Arthur's Court*. Tucker and Gray worked together previously on the 1995 film *Friday*. Tucker eventually dropped out of the project, as did Gray.[136] Gil Junger took over as director with Martin Lawrence in the lead role.

The Black Orchid (1959)

Sophia Loren as Rose Bianco (Anna Magnani)

Paramount Pictures acquired *The Black Orchid* for Anna Magnani to star in. Magnani's schedule was full and Carlo Ponti was brought on board. He gave the part to his wife, Sophia Loren.[137]

Black Rain (1989)

Kate Capshaw as Joyce (Marilu Henner, Cathy Moriarty)

Both Marilu Henner and Cathy Moriarty screen tested for the female lead in *Black Rain*. However Kate Capshaw was cast because director Ridley Scott wanted an actress who had recently been in a hit movie. This gave Capshaw, hot off the success of *Indiana Jones and the Temple of Doom*, the edge over Henner and Moriarty.[138]

Black Widow (1987)

Theresa Russell as Catherine Petersen (Cher)

Cher turned down the part of Catherine Peterson.[139]

Blade Runner (1982)

Harrison Ford as Rick Deckard (Dustin Hoffman, Tommy Lee Jones, Robert Mitchum, Christopher Walken)
Sean Young as Rachael (Barbara Hershey)

In 1975 writer Hampton Fancher was planning to make the film *Blade Runner*. He thought that Robert Mitchum was ideal for the starring role of Rick Deckard. Nothing much happened. A few years later he changed his mind and considered Christopher Walken and Tommy Lee Jones. However director Ridley Scott wanted Dustin Hoffman. Fancher disagreed with Scott's choice. Hoffman met with the writer and requested rewrites. Fancher agreed. Hoffman continued to be involved with the film for a couple of months, but then abruptly dropped out. Scott replaced him with Harrison Ford.

Barbara Hershey screen tested for Sean Young's role of Rachael.[140]

Blame It on Rio (1984)

Michelle Johnson as Jennifer Lyons (Suzy Amis)

Suzy Amis could have starred in *Blame It on Rio*, but chose not to because she did not want to do a topless scene.[141] Michelle Johnson was given the role instead.

Suzy Amis could have starred in *Blame It on Rio* if she had been willing to take her top off.

Blaze (1989)

Paul Newman as Earl Long (Gene Hackman)
Lolita Davidovich as Blaze Starr (Melanie Griffith, Michelle Pfeiffer)

Writer/director Ron Shelton sought Paul Newman for the starring role of Earl Long in *Blaze*. Newman, who was around 64 at the time, didn't like the idea of playing a 70-year-old character. Gene Hackman was approached. Hackman didn't have any problems with the part, and wanted to do it. Everything was all set until Paul Newman changed his mind. Shelton took Hackman out, and gave the part to Newman.

Melanie Griffith was Shelton's first choice to play the stripper Blaze. The problem was that after Newman's salary there was not enough money to pay Griffith. Griffith was also pregnant, which didn't help matters. Michelle Pfeiffer was interested, but Shelton thought that her body type was wrong to play the voluptuous stripper. The role ended up going to newcomer Lolita Davidovich, who would later become Ron Shelton's wife.[142]

Blazing Saddles (1973)

Cleavon Little as Sheriff Black Bart (James Earl Jones)
Gene Wilder as Waco Kid (Dan Dailey)

Andrew Bergman wrote a treatment for *Blazing Saddles* and sold it to Warner Bros. Alan Arkin was to direct and James Earl Jones was slated for the lead role. However, that deal fell apart and Mel Brooks was brought in to write and direct.[143] Dan Dailey was set to play the Waco Kid, but the actor changed his mind and dropped out of the film. He was replaced by Gene Wilder.[144]

Blessed Event (1932)

Lee Tracy as Alvin "Al" Roberts (James Cagney)

James Cagney was supposed to play the part of Al Roberts. On the first day of shooting Cagney was nowhere to be found. He ignored his commitment and was traveling to New York. Lee Tracy was Cagney's replacement.[145]

Blind Date (1987)

Kim Basinger as Nadia Gates (Madonna)
Bruce Willis as Walter Davis (Sean Penn)

Newlyweds Madonna and Sean Penn considered playing the leads in *Blind Date*. Madonna made a deal for the film. The actress' contract stipulated that she had approval of the director, co-star and script. She wanted James Foley to direct and Sean Penn to play opposite her. However the producers ignored hr contract and hired Blake Edwards to direct. Bruce Willis was hired to play Walter Davis. This angered her so much that she dropped out of the film, although she publicly said she was overworked.[146]

The Bliss of Mrs. Blossom (1968)

Shirley MacLaine as Harriet Blossom (Anouk Aimee)

It was announced that Anouk Aimee would star in *The Bliss of Mrs. Blossom*. Aimee's association with the film eventually fell through. Shirley MacLaine took the starring role of Harriet Blossom.[147]

Blithe Spirit (1945)
Kay Hammond as Elvira Condomine (Myrna Loy)

Noel Coward wanted Myrna Loy to star in the film version of his play *Blithe Spirit*. She wanted the part very much. The problem was with her studio, MGM. They refused to loan Loy out. She ended up losing the part to Kay Hammond. Shortly after Loy left MGM.[148]

Blood Alley (1955)
John Wayne as Tom Wilder (Humphrey Bogart, Robert Mitchum, Gregory Peck)

Robert Mitchum was originally cast as Captain Tom Wilder. He was fired shortly after filming began. A replacement was needed. Offers went out to Humphrey Bogart and Gregory Peck. Neither actor was willing to play the part. John Wayne was finally cast.[149]

Blood and Sand (1941)
Rita Hayworth as Dona Sol des Muire (Maria Montez)

Studio head Darryl F. Zanuck considered Maria Montez for the part of Dona Sol des Muire, but he didn't think much of her screen test.[150] Zanuck eventually chose Rita Hayworth instead.

Blood Simple (1984)
Frances McDormand as Abby (Holly Hunter)

Holly Hunter was offered the part of Abby. She was already booked for another job. She suggested her former roommate, Frances McDormand. McDormand auditioned and won the part.[151] She later married writer/director Joel Coen.

Bloodline (1979)
Audrey Hepburn as Elizabeth Roffe (Candice Bergen, Jacqueline Bisset, Diane Keaton)

Director Terence Young offered the part of Elizabeth Roffe to Diane Keaton, Candice Bergen, and Jacqueline Bisset. None of these actresses were interested. Young's search for a leading lady ended when Audrey Hepburn accepted the role.[152]

Blow Out (1981)
John Travolta as Jack (Harrison Ford, Richard Gere, Al Pacino)

Harrison Ford and Richard Gere were candidates for the lead role in *Blow Out*.[153] Al Pacino was another possible choice.[154] Director Brian De Palma instead chose an actor he had worked with previously — John Travolta. Five years earlier De Palma directed Travolta in the film *Carrie*.

Blowing Wild (1953)
Barbara Stanwyck as Marina Conway (Lauren Bacall)

Lauren Bacall was offered the chance to star in *Blowing Wild*. After she said no the part was given to Barbara Stanwyck.[155]

Blowup (1966)
David Hemmings as Thomas (Terence Stamp)

Director Michelangelo Antonioni gave the part of Thomas to Terence Stamp. Soon after he decided that Stamp was not going to work out and fired the actor.[156] He brought in David Hemmings as his replacement.

Blue (1968)
Terence Stamp as Blue (Robert Redford)

Robert Redford was originally cast as the title role in *Blue*. He dropped out a week before shooting was to begin, and Paramount Pictures sued him for breach of contract. The vacant part was taken by Terence Stamp.[157]

The Blue Angel (1930)
Marlene Dietrich as Lola Frohlich (Brigitte Helm, Trude Hesterberg, Lucie Mannheim)

Director Josef von Sternberg's first choice for the role of Lola was Brigitte Helm until he discovered Marlene Dietrich. The director had to convince everyone that Dietrich was a better choice than the other possible candidates including Lucie Mannheim and Helm.[158] Dietrich was also competing with Trude Hesterberg for the part.[159] In the end it turned out von Sternberg was right. *The Blue Angel* was a big success and made Dietrich a major star.

The Blue Lagoon (1980)
Brooke Shields as Emmeline (Jodie Foster, Diane Lane)

A 14-year-old Jodie Foster auditioned for the starring role of Emmeline in *The Blue Lagoon*. During her audition producer Dino De Laurentiis made a joke about Foster's body, which hurt the young actress. It was decided that Foster was not right for the role.[160] Diane Lane was offered the part, but turned it down.[161] Brooke Shields signed on and had one of the biggest hits of her career.

Blue Skies (1946)
Fred Astaire as Jed Potter (Paul Draper)

Fred Astaire replaced dancer Paul Draper as Jed Potter.[162]

Blue Velvet (1986)
Laura Dern as Sandy Williams (Helen Hunt)

Helen Hunt auditioned to play Sandy Williams, but director David Lynch cast Laura Dern instead.[163]

Blues Brothers 2000 (1998)
J. Evan Bonifant as Buster Blues (Macaulay Culkin)

When the movie was first being discussed Macaulay Culkin was a possibility to play the role of Buster. Years later when the film finally went into production, Culkin was much too old for the part, and J. Evan Bonifant was cast instead.

Blues in the Night (1941)
Richard Whorf as Jigger Pine (Humphrey Bogart, John Garfield, Anthony Quinn, George Raft)

Jack Warner's first choice for the starring role of Jigger Pine was George Raft. Raft was sent a copy of the script, but the actor was not interested. Next on the list was Humphrey Bogart. Like Raft, Bogart turned Warner down. Warner then turned his attention to John Garfield, who also said no. Anthony Quinn was sent a copy of the script. Quinn thought the script was terrible, but needed the work. He made some notes about how he thought the script could be improved and scheduled a meeting with Warner. At the meeting Warner asked Quinn what he thought of the script. Quinn started to answer by saying, "Well, Jack...." At this point Warner stopped him. He told Quinn that he didn't like the little Quinn had already said and told him to forget it. He escorted Quinn out, and that was that. Warner gave the part to Richard Whorf instead.[164]

Blume in Love (1973)
George Segal as Stephen Blume (Warren Beatty)
Susan Anspach as Nina Blume (Julie Christie)

Writer/director Paul Mazursky wanted Warren Beatty to play the title role in his film, *Blume in Love*. Beatty was interested, but only if his then-girlfriend Julie Christie was cast opposite him. Mazursky was not opposed to Christie as Nina Blume. He agreed that they would be great in the parts. A few months later he learned that Christie and Beatty were no longer available for the film. He replaced them with Susan Anspach and George Segal.[165]

Bob & Carol & Ted & Alice (1969)
Elliott Gould as Ted Henderson (Alan Alda, Richard Benjamin, James Caan)
Dyan Cannon as Alice Henderson (Paula Prentiss)

When Paul Mazursky set out to direct *Bob & Carol & Ted & Alice* he needed to cast two couples. For the sophisticated main couple Bob & Carol, Mazursky cast Robert Culp and Natalie Wood. He needed to find two more actors to play Ted & Alice. He tried out Elliott Gould, Alan Alda, James Caan, and Richard Benjamin for the role of Ted. Benjamin's real-life wife Paula Prentiss auditioned to play Alice as well as Dyan Cannon. Cannon and Gould made a screen test together. Once Mazursky saw their chemistry, he knew they were perfect together.[166]

Bobby Deerfield (1977)
Al Pacino as Bobby Deerfield (Paul Newman)

Paul Newman was offered the title role of Bobby Deerfield. He considered it, but ultimately decided it wasn't for him. After he turned it down Al Pacino was cast.[167]

Body Double (1984)
Melanie Griffith as Holly (Jamie Lee Curtis, Annette Haven)

Director Brian De Palma wanted to see porn star Annette Haven for the part of Holly. She rehearsed with the star of the film Craig Wasson.

According to Wasson, Haven was hardened by having to defend her chosen profession. He said that she had built up a shell around her. Wasson said this was to her detriment for acting. De Palma made an offer to Jamie Lee Curtis. Curtis had played similar characters before, and worried that another one might typecast her. She turned down the offer. He gave the part to Melanie Griffith.[168]

Body Heat (1981)

William Hurt as Ned Racine (Christopher Reeve)
Kathleen Turner as Matty Walker (Catherine Hicks)

Christopher Reeve was offered the role of lawyer Ned Racine in *Body Heat*. Reeve didn't think he was right for the part; he couldn't see himself playing the seedy lawyer. He said no, and the part went to his friend William Hurt.[169]

Catherine Hicks was offered the chance to star in *Body Heat*. She turned it down because of the overt sexuality in the film.

Body Heat was too sexy for Catherine Hicks.

The Bodyguard (1992)

Kevin Costner as Frank Farmer (Steve McQueen, Ryan O'Neal)
Whitney Houston as Rachael Marron (Diana Ross)

The history of the film *The Bodyguard* dates back to the 1970s. The producers were interested in having Diana Ross star in the film.[170] Steve McQueen and Ryan O'Neal were strong contenders for the part of the bodyguard, although McQueen never knew he was being considered.[171] According to O'Neal, Ross had problems with the language and sex scenes. The film was put on hold for about 15 years until Kevin Costner got a hold of the script, which was written by his old friend Lawrence Kasdan. Costner decided to make the film and gave pop star Whitney Houston a chance to make her acting debut in the role of Rachel Marron, with Costner as her bodyguard.[172] The film was a huge hit, and Houston received good reviews playing this character whose life seemed to be quite similar to Houston's own life. She went on to star in other successful films such as *Waiting to Exhale* and *The Preacher's Wife*.

The Bonfire of the Vanities (1990)

Tom Hanks as Sherman McCoy (Kevin Costner, Tom Cruise, Steve Martin, Christopher Reeve)
Bruce Willis as Peter Fallow (John Cleese, Jack Nicholson)
Melanie Griffith as Maria Ruskin (Lolita Davidovich, Lena Olin, Michelle Pfeiffer, Uma Thurman)
Morgan Freeman as Judge Leonard White (Alan Arkin, Walter Matthau, Judge Burton Bennett Roberts)

For the starring role of Sherman McCoy the studio was interested at one point in Tom Cruise and Steve Martin.[173] Kevin Costner was made an offer, which he refused.[174] Christopher Reeve auditioned. At his interview Reeve was told that, although he was perfect for the part, he was not going to be cast. Reeve knew that the reason was that outside of the Superman movies, his films hadn't done well at the box office.[175] Brian De Palma decided to go with the very popular Tom Hanks.

Michelle Pfeiffer was the first choice to play Maria Ruskin, Sherman's girlfriend, but she was not interested. Lolita Davidovich and Lena Olin both read for the part unsuccessfully. Melanie Griffith was the front runner. Brian De Palma, though, became extremely interested in Uma

Thurman. He brought her in to read with Hanks. De Palma and casting director Lynn Stalmaster were impressed with her. Hanks didn't say anything to the two men, but he did not think that Thurman was right for the part at all. It was written in his contract that he had casting approval, so his opinion was very important. He reluctantly made a screen test with Thurman. Afterwards he told the studio that he thought her acting was high school material and that he couldn't act with her. Eventually, De Palma changed his mind about her too. He felt that although she was a good actress, she did not have the comic timing that was necessary for the role. Front runner Griffith was cast after all.[176]

Bruce Willis was brought in as journalist Peter Fallow after both John Cleese and Jack Nicholson turned it down. Walter Matthau was the first choice to play Judge Myron Kovitsky. His asking price of $1 million took him out of the running. Real life judge Burton Bennett Roberts, a friend of Tom Wolfe (author of the novel), very much wanted to test for the role. After a while De Palma reluctantly agreed to see him, more out of obligation to Tom Wolfe. To their surprise, De Palma and Stalmaster were impressed with the judge. They considered casting him in the role until De Palma decided that the part was too important for a non-actor. They cast Alan Arkin, but then changed their minds. They wanted to go another way with the part. They changed the name from the Jewish Myron Kovitsky to Leonard White.[177] Morgan Freeman was offered the role. Freeman said that he had reservations about taking the part. First of all, he thought that Arkin was perfectly cast as the judge. Freeman also didn't like the fact that he was being offered the part was because of the filmmakers' political correctness. He realized that no matter what he decided, Alan Arkin wasn't going to get the part back. Freeman accepted the role, but said that he felt like a "suck-ass" for doing so.[178]

Bonnie and Clyde (1967)

Warren Beatty as Clyde Barrow (Bob Dylan)
Faye Dunaway as Bonnie Parker (Leslie Caron, Jane Fonda, Carol Lynley, Sue Lyon, Shirley MacLaine, Tuesday Weld, Natalie Wood)

French actress Leslie Caron was dating Warren Beatty when he decided to produce *Bonnie and Clyde*. She became interested in playing Bonnie. Beatty thought that the part called for an American actress. He turned Caron down. He made an offer to Natalie Wood. She refused the part because she did not want to be away from her therapist for the three months shooting would take.[179] Jane Fonda did not like the part either and said no.[180] Tuesday Weld turned it down; she was pregnant.[181] Carol Lynley was another possibility.[182] Sue Lyon and even Beatty's sister, Shirley MacLaine were considered before an unknown Faye Dunaway stepped into the part.[183]

Beatty briefly considered casting singer Bob Dylan as Clyde.[184] He changed his mind and played the part himself.

Boogie Nights (1997)

Mark Wahlberg as Eddie Adams/Dirk Diggler (Leonardo DiCaprio)
Burt Reynolds as Jack Horner (Warren Beatty)
Heather Graham as Rollergirl/Brandy (Gwyneth Paltrow)

Although Leonardo DiCaprio was considered for the starring role of Eddie Adams/Dirk Diggler, director Paul Thomas Anderson gave the part to Mark Wahlberg.[185]

Warren Beatty was asked to play Jack Horner. Beatty turned it down and Burt Reynolds was cast instead. *Boogie Nights* was Reynolds' first hit in almost twenty years. He was nominated for an Oscar for his performance, but lost out to Robin Williams (*Good Will Hunting*).[186]

Gwyneth Paltrow was asked to play Rollergirl. She worried that her grandfather would have been upset had she played the part. Paltrow said that it wasn't worth upsetting him and turned the part down. The role was played by Heather Graham.[187]

Bopha! (1993)

Danny Glover as Micah Mangena (Morgan Freeman)

Acclaimed actor Morgan Freeman was asked to star in *Bopha!* as Micah Mangena. Freeman was more interested in directing the film. He felt that Danny Glover was more connected to Africa, and therefore better suited to the part. Glover accepted the job. *Bopha!* was Freeman's directorial debut.[188]

The Border (1982)

Jack Nicholson as Charlie Smith (Robert Blake)

The Border was originally intended as a starring vehicle for Robert Blake. Blake, who was best known for his television series *Baretta*, was not a big movie star, and financing was difficult to obtain. Eventually Blake grew impatient and dropped out of the film. Jack Nicholson, a major movie star, was cast in his place. Money was suddenly available and shooting began shortly after.[189]

Born on the Fourth of July (1989)

Tom Cruise as Ron Kovic (Nicolas Cage, Al Pacino, Sean Penn, Charlie Sheen)

In the late '70s Al Pacino was the choice to play Vietnam vet Ron Kovic. There were problems with the financing of the film, and Pacino moved on.[190] Ten years later when Oliver Stone was casting the role he considered Sean Penn, Nicolas Cage, and Charlie Sheen.[191]

Born to Be Bad (1934)

Loretta Young as Letty Strong (Jean Harlow)

Jean Harlow was originally sought for the part of Letty Strong. When Harlow was unable to do the film, the part was assigned to Loretta Young. Young didn't want the part, but couldn't get out of the assignment.[192]

Born Yesterday (1950)

Judy Holliday as Billie Dawn (Lucille Ball, Alice Faye, Gloria Grahame, Jean Hagen, Barbara Hale, Rita Hayworth, Evelyn Keyes, Marie MacDonald, Barbara Stanwyck, Jan Sterling, Lana Turner, Cara Williams, Marie Wilson

Broderick Crawford as Harry Brock (Paul Douglas)

MGM originally considered making *Born Yesterday* with Lana Turner as Billie Dawn. A representative was sent to see the play. He reported that it was the worst show he had ever seen and that it should never be made into a movie.[193] That was the end of MGM and *Born Yesterday*. Enter Columbia Pictures. Paul Douglas, who originated the Harry Brock role on Broadway, did not wish to appear in the film and turned it down.[194] Harry Cohn refused to see the screen test of Judy Holliday, who had originated the role on Broadway. He demanded that the part called for a star. His first choice was Rita Hayworth.[195] Cohn was also willing to settle on Barbara Stanwyck or Lucille Ball;[196] possibly even Alice Faye.[197] Evelyn Keyes auditioned but failed to win the part.[198] Other actresses tested include: Jan Sterling, Jean Hagen, Cara Williams, Marie MacDonald and Barbara Hale. Marie Wilson and Gloria Grahame were turned down for the part. The writers—Garson Kanin and Ruth Gordon—were determined to have Holliday in the role. They joined forces with Katharine Hepburn, Spencer Tracy and George Cukor, who shared their opinion. Gordon and Kanin were working on a film—*Adam's Rib*—with the trio. They decided to write a part for Holliday to play, and this would be her screen test. Their plan worked. Holliday scored raves for *Adam's Rib* and Cohn finally cast her as Billie Dawn.[199]

Bound for Glory (1976)

David Carradine as Woody Guthrie (Robert De Niro)

David Carradine was cast as Woody Guthrie in *Bound for Glory* after his part was turned down by Robert De Niro.[200]

The Bounty (1984)

Mel Gibson as Fletcher Christian (Christopher Reeve)

Christopher Reeve was presented with the possibility of playing opposite Anthony Hopkins in *The Bounty*. Reeve was intrigued by the offer. Working with Hopkins appealed to him, as well as the location shoot in Tahiti. Reeve ultimately decided it wasn't right for him. He turned it down and made *The Bostonians* instead.[201]

The Bourne Identity (2002)

Matt Damon as Jason Bourne (Brad Pitt)

Brad Pitt considering playing the lead role in *The Bourne Identity*. He chose instead to star opposite Robert Redford in the film *Spy Game*.[202]

Boxing Helena (1993)

Sherilyn Fenn as Helena (Kim Basinger, Madonna)

Julian Sands as Dr. Nick Cavanaugh (Ed Harris)

The script of *Boxing Helena* was so shocking that many producers passed on the project. They feared the story of a surgeon who amputates the arms and legs of the girl he loves and keeps her in a box was too controversial to be made into a film. Finally writer/director Jennifer Lynch (daughter of director David Lynch) struck a deal with Main Line Films' Carl Mazzocone.

Madonna was originally set to star as Helena but pulled out of the production a month before shooting was to start. She claimed she was overwhelmed. Jennifer Lynch hired Kim Basinger as a replacement by the way of a verbal agreement. Basinger too, later changed her mind about starring, and also backed out of the project. Basinger claimed that she had problems with some of the sex scenes and with the script in general. Said Basinger: "Though well-constructed, it was probably the strangest piece I ever read. The idea of a woman with no arms and legs was very bizarre to me." Basinger also went on to say that she was advised that the part would be detrimental to her career.[203] Perhaps Basinger knew what she was talking about. Sherilyn Fenn, her replacement, has yet to have a hit film, while Basinger later won an Academy Award for 1997's *L.A. Confidential*. Lynch sued Kim Basinger, and won, which resulted in Basinger filing for bankruptcy. Basinger's bankruptcy forced her to sell off the town of Braselton, GA, which she purchased in 1989. However, the ruling against her was later overturned by an appeals court. This was not the only lawsuit involving an actor and *Boxing Helena*. Ed Harris, who was to play Dr. Nick Cavanaugh, had to drop out when the production was delayed. He sued Main Line Pictures for beach of contract. Although Harris quit, he had a pay or play cause in his contract which meant that he would be paid whether or not he made the movie. Producer Carl Mazzocone claimed that the lawsuit was unnecessary and that Harris would get the money he was entitled to.[204]

The Boy Who Could Fly (1986)

Lucy Deakins as Milly Michaelson (Martha Byrne)

Lucy Deakins was the first choice to play Milly Michaelson. Deakins was starring on the soap opera *As the World Turns* at the time. The show wouldn't release her for the film. Martha Byrne was brought in to audition. Coincidentally Byrne auditioned for *As the World Turns* but lost out to Deakins. While Byrne was meeting with the producer he was lamenting that Deakins was not there. Deakins decided to quit the soap in order to do the film. Although Byrne lost the movie, *As the World Turns* called her to replace Deakins on the show based on her audition about eight months before.[205]

Bram Stoker's Dracula (1992)

Gary Oldman as Prince Vlad Dracula (Armand Assante, Antonio Banderas, Gabriel Byrne, Daniel Day-Lewis, Andy Garcia, Jeremy Irons, Viggo Mortensen, Eric Roberts)

Keanu Reeves as Jonathan Harker (Johnny Depp)

Sadie Frost as Lucy Westenra (Juliette Lewis, Ione Skye)

Director Francis Ford Coppola was interested in having Daniel Day-Lewis star as Dracula. The actor was unavailable because he was already working on the film, *The Last of the Mohicans*. Also considered were Jeremy Irons and Eric Roberts. Andy Garcia was interested, but ultimately decided he wouldn't be comfortable playing the part. Coppola tested Gabriel Byrne, Antonio Banderas and Armand Assante.[206] Viggo Mortensen auditioned, but Coppola gave the part to Gary Oldman.[207]

Winona Ryder brought the film's script to Coppola's attention because she wanted to play Mina. Coppola gave Ryder the part.[208]

Johnny Depp was Coppola's first choice to play Jonathan Harker. Columbia didn't want Depp, and Coppola had to go with another actor. He chose Keanu Reeves.

Juliette Lewis and Ione Skye auditioned to play Lucy Westenra, but lost out to the lesser-known Sadie Frost.[209]

Brazil (1985)

Michael Palin as Jack Lint (Robert De Niro)

Jonathan Pryce as Sam Lowry (Tom Cruise, Rupert Everett)

Kim Greist as Jill Layton (Rosanna Arquette, Ellen Barkin, Rae Dawn Chong, Jamie Lee Curtis, Rebecca De Mornay, Madonna, Kelly McGillis, Joanna Pacula, Michelle Pfeiffer, Kathleen Turner)

Robert De Niro initially wanted to play the lead role of Jack Lint, but director Terry Gilliam already gave the part to Michael Palin. Gilliam persuaded De Niro to instead take the role of Tuttle.[210]

Gilliam considered both Rupert Everett and Tom Cruise for the part of Sam Lowry. Cruise didn't want to test, and Gilliam decided to move on. The part was eventually cast with Jonathan Pryce.[211]

Jamie Lee Curtis, Rebecca De Mornay, Rae

Dawn Chong, Ellen Barkin, Kelly McGillis, Rosanna Arquette, and Joanna Pacula were all tested for the part of Jill Layton.[212] Gilliam also considered Madonna,[213] Michelle Pfeiffer,[214] and Kathleen Turner[215] before giving the part to Kim Greist.

Breakfast at Tiffany's (1961)

Audrey Hepburn as Holly Golightly [aka Lulamae Barnes] (Marilyn Monroe)
George Peppard as Paul Varjak (Steve McQueen)

Writers Truman Capote and George Axelrod wanted the role of Holly Golightly to be played by Marilyn Monroe. Her studio — 20th Century-Fox — did not want her playing the role of a prostitute and refused to loan her out to make the film.[216]

Steve McQueen was offered the role of Paul Varjak. He was unable to sign on because he was already committed to the film, *Wanted: Dead or Alive*.[217]

Breaking the Waves (1996)

Emily Watson as Bess McNeill (Helena Bonham Carter)

Helena Bonham Carter turned down the role of Bess in *Breaking the Waves*. Carter objected to the film's explicit sexuality. Emily Watson was cast instead. Watson received an Oscar nomination for her performance in the film.[218]

Breezy (1973)

Kay Lenz as Edith Alice "Breezy" Breezerman (Jo Ann Harris, Sondra Locke)

Clint Eastwood was set to direct *Breezy*. Screenwriter Jo Heims told Sondra Locke that Jo Ann Harris was a strong contender for the title role, and that Harris and Eastwood had had an affair during the shooting of the film *The Beguiled*. Heims also went on to say that the voluptuous Harris was the wrong type for the part. She saw the character as a waif, which was Locke's type. Heims arranged an audition for Locke. Neither Locke nor Harris won the role. Eastwood gave the part to Kay Lenz instead. A few years later Locke and Eastwood began a relationship that lasted about thirteen years. He then told Locke that he made a big mistake in passing her over for Lenz.[219]

Brewster's Millions (1985)

Richard Pryor as Montgomery Brewster (John Ritter)

At one point, Peter Bogdanovich was planning to direct *Brewster's Millions* with John Ritter as star.[220] Eventually Walter Hill directed the film with Richard Pryor playing the role of Montgomery Brewster.

The Bride Goes Wild (1948)

June Allyson as Martha Terryton (Donna Reed)

Donna Reed was assigned the part of Martha Terryton in *The Bride Goes Wild*. Reed didn't want the part. The role was recast with June Allyson.[221]

The Bride of Frankenstein (1935)

Elsa Lanchester as Mary Wollstonecraft Shelley/The Monster's Bride (Louise Brooks, Brigitte Helm)
Ernest Thesiger as Dr. Pretorius (Claude Rains)

Director James Whale originally wanted Claude Rains for Dr. Pretorius. He didn't get him, and he gave the part to Ernest Thesiger.

Louise Brooks and Brigitte Helm's names were mentioned as possibilities for the title role.[222]

The Bridge on the River Kwai (1957)

Alec Guinness as Colonel Nicholson (Humphrey Bogart, Noel Coward, Laurence Olivier)
William Holden as Shears (Cary Grant)

Laurence Olivier was producer Sam Spiegel's first choice to play the part of Colonel Nicholson. Olivier turned it down in order to make *The Prince and the Showgirl*. Olivier said he would rather stay home and work with Marilyn Monroe than go off to Ceylon to make *The Bridge on the River Kwai*.[223] Noel Coward rejected the role because he didn't want to be on location for the amount of time required,[224] although he later said that his tuning the role down was a mistake.[225] Humphrey Bogart was also considered before they finally settled on Alec Guinness.[226]

Cary Grant had the chance to play the role of Shears, but he chose not to. Like Coward, Grant also came to regret his decision very much.[227] William Holden went on to play the part.

A Bridge Too Far (1977)
Robert Redford as Maj. Julian Cook (Steve McQueen)

Steve McQueen was offered the part of Major Julian Cook. He asked to be paid $3 million, which producer Joe Levine felt was too much. He gave the part to the more affordable Robert Redford instead.[228]

The Bridges of Madison County (1995)
Meryl Streep as Francesca Johnson (Cher, Glenn Close, Catherine Deneuve, Barbara Hershey, Anjelica Huston, Jessica Lange, Susan Lucci, Mary McDonnell, Isabella Rossellini, Susan Sarandon, Kathleen Turner)
Clint Eastwood as Robert Kincaid (Robert Redford)

In the early stages of production on *The Bridges of Madison County* Robert Redford was the front runner for the part of Robert Kincaid, although Clint Eastwood ended up with both the part and as director. Many, many actresses were very interested in playing the Italian housewife including Susan Sarandon, Cher, Mary McDonnell, Kathleen Turner, Glenn Close, Barbara Hershey and Anjelica Huston.[229] Jessica Lange was another possibility.[230] Isabella Rossellini and Catherine Deneuve were also mentioned.[231] Soap star Susan Lucci was interested enough to try to option it for herself to star. She was unable to because it had already been optioned by Steven Spielberg. Lucci wrote to Spielberg in order to win the role but never heard anything back from him.[232] Meryl Streep went on to play the role and earned an Oscar nomination for her performance.

Bridget Jones's Diary (2001)
Renee Zellweger as Bridget Jones (Cameron Diaz, Emily Watson, Rachel Weisz, Kate Winslet)

British actresses Kate Winslet, Emily Watson, and Rachel Weisz were considered for the very British starring role of Bridget Jones as well as American actress Cameron Diaz.[233] Many English fans of Helen Fielding's book were upset when the part went to Texas born Renee Zellweger. Fielding consoled them by saying that Scarlett O'Hara was played by an English woman.

Brief Moment (1933)
Carole Lombard as Abby Fane (Barbara Stanwyck)

Carole Lombard won the role of Abby Fane over Barbara Stanwyck.[234]

Bright Lights, Big City (1988)
Michael J. Fox as Jamie Conway (Tom Cruise)

Tom Cruise turned down the lead role in *Bright Lights, Big City* because he did not want to appear in a film that glorified the use of drugs.[235]

Bring Me the Head of Alfredo Garcia (1974)
Warren Oates as Bennie (James Coburn, Peter Falk)
Isela Vega as Elita (Aurora Clavel)
Gig Young as Quill (Mort Sahl)

Director Sam Peckinpah sought James Coburn to play the part of Bennie in *Bring Me the Head of Alfredo Garcia*. Coburn disliked it so much that he even questioned why Peckinpah would want to make the film. Peter Falk was up next. Falk was interested, but the schedule for his television series *Columbo* was in production at the same time. Peckinpah gave the part to Warren Oates.

Peckinpah considered giving his then girlfriend Aurora Clavel the part of Elita. He instead decided to go with Isela Vega.

Mort Sahl was cast as Quill. However Warren Oates got sick, and production was halted for about two weeks. Sahl had concerts booked. The two week delay was a major issue for him, and he was forced to leave the film. Gig Young was cast in his place.[236]

Bringing Up Baby (1938)
Katharine Hepburn as Susan Vance (Carole Lombard)
Cary Grant as David Huxley (Ronald Colman, Leslie Howard, Fredric March, Ray Milland, Robert Montgomery)

Carole Lombard was a possible choice for the part of Susan Vance. The role later went to Katharine Hepburn.[237]

Cary Grant, Leslie Howard, Fredric March, Ronald Colman, Ray Milland, and Robert Montgomery all turned down the role of paleontologist David Huxley. Director Howard

Hawks asked Cary Grant to reconsider. Grant wasn't sure he wanted to take on a role so different from his usual persona, but was persuaded when Hawks suggested he use Harold Lloyd as a model for the character.[238]

Broadcast News (1987)

Holly Hunter as Jane Craig (Kathleen Turner, Debra Winger)

Debra Winger was unable to play Jane Craig because she was pregnant.[239] Holly Hunter won the role after Kathleen Turner was considered.[240]

Broadway Danny Rose (1984)

Nick Apollo Forte as Lou Canova (Danny Aiello, Robert De Niro, Sylvester Stallone)

Robert De Niro and Sylvester Stallone both turned down the part of singer Lou Canova. Danny Aiello wanted the part but lost out to Nick Apollo Forte. Aiello was extremely disappointed to lose the part. Aiello got to work with director Woody Allen after all. Allen gave him a supporting part in his next film, *The Purple Rose of Cairo*.[241]

Broadway Melody of 1936 (1935)

Una Merkel as Kitty Corbett (Eleanor Powell)

An unknown Eleanor Powell was working on Broadway when she was spotted by MGM producer Sam Katz. He thought that Powell would be good for a role in MGM's upcoming film, *Broadway Melody of 1936*. He brought her to MGM. The other executives were not impressed. They told Katz that she was not feminine enough. The studio beauticians were assigned to make her over. She was assigned a small role in the film. She started shooting, and her talent shone through. Her small role of Kitty Corbett was reassigned to Una Merkel. They created the lead role of Irene Foster especially for Powell.[242] Sam Katz's hunch paid off. When *Broadway Melody of 1936* was released Powell became a star.

Broadway Nights (1927)

Lois Wilson as Fanny Franchette (Barbara Stanwyck)

An unknown Barbara Stanwyck screen tested for *Broadway Nights*. When it came time to cry in the scene, she couldn't. Director Joseph C. Boyle gave her an onion to help, but that didn't work.[243] Not surprisingly Stanwyck lost the lead in the film to Lois Wilson, but was cast in the film as a fan dancer.

Brokedown Palace (1999)

Kate Beckinsale as Darlene Davis (Jennifer Love Hewitt)

Jennifer Love Hewitt read for the part of Darlene with star of the film Claire Danes twice. Hewitt had scheduling problems and lost the role to Kate Beckinsale. Hewitt said that she was heartbroken to have to miss out on making the film.[244]

Broken Arrow (1996)

Samantha Mathis as Terry Carmichael (Jennifer Aniston, Helen Hunt)

Helen Hunt was offered the role of Terry Carmichael, but she chose to do *Twister* instead.[245] Jennifer Aniston was also considered before Samantha Mathis was cast.[246]

Broken Lance (1954)

Katy Jurado as Sra. Devereaux (Dolores del Rio)

Mexican actress Dolores del Rio was asked to star in *Broken Lance*. del Rio was without a visa, and thereby unable to appear in the film.[247]

The Broken Land (1962)

Jack Nicholson as Will Brocious (Burt Reynolds)

Jack Nicholson auditioned for the part of Will Brocious in *The Broken Land*. It came down to a choice between him and another actor whose name was Burt Reynolds. At the audition Nicholson was asked if he could ride a horse, to which he responded "yes."[248] Perhaps Reynolds' answer was different. Producer Leonard Schwartz decided that Nicholson was the better choice.

Bronco Billy (1980)

Sam Bottoms as Leonard James (Gordon Anderson)

Director Clint Eastwood suggested sometime actor Gordon Anderson for the part of Leonard James. Anderson was the husband of his then girlfriend Sondra Locke. Locke and Anderson had separated a year earlier and remained dear friends. Anderson wasn't interested in continu-

A Bronx Tale (1993)
Taral Hicks as Jane Williams (Naomi Campbell)

A Bronx Tale was Robert De Niro's directorial debut. Naomi Campbell, who he was dating at the time, wanted the part of Jane. The English model worked with De Niro's former voice coach Sam Chwat to transform her British accent to one from the Bronx. De Niro didn't think she was right for the part, and publicly announced that the decision against Campbell was professional, and had no bearing on their personal relationship. A week later they split up.[250]

The Browning Version (1951)
Jean Kent as Millie Crocker-Harris (Margaret Lockwood)

Margaret Lockwood was offered the part of Millie Crocker-Harris. When she turned it down it was played by Jean Kent.[251]

The Buccaneer (1938)
Fredric March as Jean Lafitte (Clark Gable, Anthony Quinn)

When producer Cecil B. DeMille started the casting process for his upcoming film, The Buccaneer, he thought of Anthony Quinn for the starring role of pirate Jean Lafitte. Quinn made a screen test for DeMille, which the producer showed to some of his friends and family. His daughter Katherine told DeMille that Quinn was too young, and encouraged her father to think about Clark Gable instead. DeMille agreed with his daughter and contacted Gable. He was unavailable, and DeMille cast Fredric March instead.[252] As a consolation prize DeMille cast Quinn in a supporting role as a lieutenant of Lafitte's. Quinn, not one to hold a grudge, married Katherine DeMille soon after.

Bull Durham (1988)
Kevin Costner as Crash Davis (Kurt Russell)
Susan Sarandon as Annie Savoy (Michelle Pfeiffer, Debra Winger)

Writer/director Ron Shelton wrote the part of Crash Davis with his friend Kurt Russell in mind. Russell actually played AA ball for the California Angels. Russell wasn't available when Shelton wanted to start filming, and Kevin Costner was cast instead.[253]

Debra Winger was asked to play Annie Savoy. She wasn't interested, and turned the part down.[254] Michelle Pfeiffer was another possibility to play Annie Savoy, along with Susan Sarandon. Sarandon was so determined to win the role that she spent her own money to fly to California to meet with Shelton and Kevin Costner. She successfully won over both men and was cast in the role.[255]

Burglar (1987)
Whoopi Goldberg as Bernice "Bernie" Rhodenbarr (Eddie Murphy, Bruce Willis)
Bobcat Goldthwait as Carl Hefler (Whoopi Goldberg)

Both Eddie Murphy and Bruce Willis were sought for the lead role in Burglar. Willis tentatively agreed to do the film, but eventually dropped out. Whoopi Goldberg, who was already cast in the film as the sidekick, had an idea. She contacted Warner Bros. and was able to persuade them to change the lead character to a woman! Her now vacant role of the dog groomer was changed to a male character. Her replacement in the role was comedian Bobcat Goldthwait.[256]

Bus Stop (1956)
Marilyn Monroe as Cherie (Dorothy Dandridge, Kim Stanley)
Don Murray as Beauregard "Beau" Decker (Rock Hudson)

Kim Stanley originated the role of Cherie on Broadway, and wanted to play it in the film version.[257] Dorothy Dandridge went after the part. Darryl F. Zanuck told her this was not possible; that if she were cast the film would have a racial theme that wasn't there previously. She ultimately lost the role to superstar Marilyn Monroe.[258]

Monroe wanted Rock Hudson to play opposite her. He didn't want to make the film, and Don Murray stepped into the part.[259]

Butch and Sundance: The Early Days (1979)
Tom Berenger as Young Butch Cassidy (Harrison Ford)

Harrison Ford turned the part of Young Butch Cassidy down to avoid being compared with Paul Newman, who had played the part originally.[260]

Butch Cassidy and the Sundance Kid (1969)

Paul Newman as Butch Cassidy [aka Robert Leroy Parker] (Jack Lemmon, Steve McQueen, Robert Redford)
Robert Redford as The Sundance Kid [aka Harry Longbaugh] (Warren Beatty, Marlon Brando, Paul Newman)
Katharine Ross as Etta Place (Jacqueline Bisset)

Screenwriter William Goldman had originally thought of Jack Lemmon as Butch Cassidy with Paul Newman playing the Sundance Kid.[261] It turned out that 20th Century–Fox wanted Steve McQueen instead. The teaming of McQueen as Butch and Marlon Brando as Sundance was explored. Brando said no,[262] and Warren Beatty's name was mentioned as a possibility.[263] Finally Paul Newman was signed to play the Sundance Kid. Steve McQueen was all set to play Butch Cassidy. But the deal was never finalized because of billing. Even though both actors wanted to star in the film, their agents could not agree on who was to receive top billing. It was suggested that since Paul Newman had been signed for the film first, he should receive top billing. Another argument was that McQueen was the bigger star, so he should receive top billing. It was even suggested that McQueen would be billed first on screen, and Newman would be billed first in the print ads. Or that McQueen's name would come first, but Newman's name would appear higher up. Or that their names would be crossed with each other, etc., etc, etc. In the end the deal was scrapped, and McQueen was out of the film.[264] Warren Beatty was considered for a while, but instead Robert Redford was chosen. Director George Roy Hill decided to switch the parts and had Newman play Butch with Redford as Sundance, which turned out to be a good idea.[265] The film was a major hit, and has since become a classic.

Jacqueline Bisset was mentioned as a possible choice for the role of Etta Place. There a question as to whether or not she could lose her English accent, and the American-born Katharine Ross won the role instead.[266]

Butterfield 8 (1960)

Eddie Fisher as Steve Carpenter (David Janssen)

David Janssen was originally set for the part of composer Steve Carpenter. The star of the film, Elizabeth Taylor, wanted the part for her husband, singer Eddie Fisher. Fisher wasn't overly enthusiastic about doing the film, but he did it for Taylor.[267]

Cabaret (1972)

Liza Minnelli as Sally Bowles (Shirley MacLaine, Barbra Streisand)
Michael York as Brian Roberts (John Rubinstein)

Barbra Streisand turned down the lead role of Sally Bowles.[1] Shirley MacLaine was also considered, but it went to Liza Minnelli instead.[2]

Michael York was the first choice for Brian, however there was a time when it was unclear as to whether he would be available for the movie. At that time John Rubinstein was brought in for a screen test.[3] In the end it was not necessary. York went on to star with Liza Minnelli. Minnelli won an Oscar for her portrayal of Sally.

Cactus Flower (1969)

Ingrid Bergman as Stephanie Dickinson (Lauren Bacall, Lucille Ball)

Cactus Flower began as a Broadway play which starred Lauren Bacall. When it came time for the film version Bacall was very much interested in bringing the character she created to the screen. A meeting was arranged with Mike Frankovich at Columbia Pictures. Frankovich told Bacall that although he wanted to cast her, Walter Matthau, the star of the film and director Gene Saks were not sure. Bacall was led to believe that the part was hers. When she found out that they had decided to go with Ingrid Bergman, Bacall was extremely upset. She felt unimportant in Hollywood, and couldn't understand why the producers would cast a woman who was ten years older than she was.[4]

Producers had also been interested in Lucille Ball, but the famous comedienne turned them down.[5]

Caesar and Cleopatra (1945)

Stewart Granger as Apollodorus (James Mason)

James Mason was pursued for *Caesar and Cleopatra*. Mason said no to the film. Stewart Granger was hired instead.[6]

Cairo (1942)

Ethel Waters as Cleona Jones (Lena Horne)

Lena Horne auditioned for the part of Cleona Jones. She lost out to Ethel Waters.[7]

California Split (1974)

Elliott Gould as Charlie Waters (Robert De Niro, Peter Falk)

Both Peter Falk and Robert De Niro tried for the part of Charlie Waters. They lost the part to Elliott Gould.[8]

Camelot (1967)

Richard Harris as King Arthur (Richard Burton)
Vanessa Redgrave as Guinevere (Julie Andrews)

Director Joshua Logan was not interested in casting Richard Burton and Julie Andrews in the roles they created on Broadway. He decided, instead, to go with Richard Harris and Vanessa Redgrave for the film version.[9]

Camille (1937)

Henry Daniell as Baron de Varville (John Barrymore)

John Barrymore was considered for Baron de Varville. Barrymore was in no shape to take any role at this time. His drinking was out of control and he checked himself into a clinic.[10] His brother Lionel took the part of Duval, while Henry Daniell played de Varville.

Cannery Row (1982)

Debra Winger as Suzy (Raquel Welch)

MGM claims that Raquel Welch was fired from *Cannery Row* because it took her three hours to put her makeup on, resulting in production being held up too long. Welch countered that the studio wanted to save money by replacing her with Debra Winger. Welch sued the studio.[11] Burt Reynolds testified on her behalf. The two worked together on the films *100 Rifles* and *Fuzz*. Reynolds claimed that Welch was always on time, well prepared, and acted in a professional manner.[12] The suit took over five years to settle, at which point the actress was awarded approximately $11 million.[13]

Cannonball Run (1981)

Sammy Davis, Jr., as Morris Fenderbaum (Tom Selleck)

Tom Selleck was forced to turn down *Cannonball Run* because it interfered with the schedule of his television series, *Magnum, P.I.*[14]

Can't Stop the Music (1980)

Ray Simpson as Police Officer (Victor Willis)

The band The Village People was the invention of Jacques Morali. Morali was living in New York in 1976. One night he went to the Greenwich Village bar The Anvil. While there he noticed a young man dressed in full Native American clothes. This was Felipe Rose. Rose gave Morali the idea of starting a band made up of men dressed as macho stereotypes. Rose was enlisted. The lead singer was Broadway actor Victor Willis. Willis dressed as a cop. Other members dressed as a GI, a construction worker, a biker, and a cowboy. The band was immensely popular with hits such as "Y.M.C.A." and "In the Navy." They were such a hit that Hollywood came calling. Morali teamed with Allan Carr and Henri Belolo to produce a movie starring the band called *Can't Stop the Music*. Less than a week before the film was to start shooting Willis decided he no longer wanted to be a Village person and quit the band. He was quickly replaced with Ray Simpson, the brother of Ashford & Simpson's Valerie Simpson. *Can't Stop the Music* was an enormous flop, from which the band never fully recovered.

Cape Fear (1991)

Juliette Lewis as Danielle Bowden (Reese Witherspoon)
Robert Mitchum as Lt. Elgart (George C. Scott)

Reese Witherspoon was asked to audition for the part of Danielle Bowden. To Witherspoon this was just another audition. On the plane she became friendly with a man sitting next to her. She mentioned her upcoming audition and that she was meeting with Martin Scorsese and Robert De Niro. The man raved about how talented they were. This made Witherspoon so nervous that she blew her audition.[15] Scorsese decided to cast Juliette Lewis. The young actress' performance was critically acclaimed, resulting in an Oscar nomination.

George C. Scott was given the part of Lt. Elgart. Scott quit and left behind a note. The note said that the little people had to be taken care of. Martin Scorsese was confused. Nick Nolte told him to check the minibar, which was almost empty.[16] He was replaced in the film by Robert Mitchum. Mitchum played Max Cady in the original *Cape Fear* (1962).

Captain Blood (1935)
Errol Flynn as Peter Blood (George Brent, Ronald Colman, Robert Donat, Clark Gable, Leslie Howard, Ian Hunter, Fredric March)
Olivia De Havilland as Arabella Bishop (Bette Davis, Anita Louise, Jean Muir)

Ian Hunter was considered for the role of Peter Blood.[17] Fredric March, Leslie Howard, Clark Gable, and Ronald Colman were all unavailable.[18] George Brent was tested, but not chosen.[19] Robert Donat was cast, but ultimately dropped out.[20]

For the female lead both Bette Davis[21] and Anita Louise[22] made screen tests. Jean Muir was a strong contender, but only if it were Donat opposite her.[23] Donat's leaving made it possible for Olivia de Havilland and Errol Flynn to assume the roles.

Captain Corelli's Mandolin (2001)
Penelope Cruz as Pelagia (Katie Holmes)

Katie Holmes was up for the part of Pelagia in *Captain Corelli's Mandolin*. She was disappointed when she lost the role to Penelope Cruz.[24]

Captain Horatio Hornblower (1951)
Gregory Peck as Capt. Horatio Hornblower (Errol Flynn)

Errol Flynn was the original choice for the role of Horatio Hornblower. It was eventually decided that Flynn was too old for the part, and he was replaced by Gregory Peck.[25]

The Captain's Paradise (1953)
Alec Guinness as Captain Henry St. James (Ray Milland, Michael Wilding)

Director Anthony Kimmins contacted Yvonne De Carlo about starring in his upcoming film, *The Captain's Paradise*. De Carlo told Kimmins she was interested, but on the condition that Alec Guinness was cast in the lead role of Captain Henry St. James. Kimmins told De Carlo that he thought Guinness would be hard to get, but that he thought that either Ray Milland or Michael Wilding would be fine. De Carlo asked Kimmins to just send Guinness the script. She thought that once he read it, he would become interested. She was right. Guinness accepted the role and starred alongside De Carlo.[26]

The Cardinal (1963)
Carol Lynley as Mona Fermoyle/Regina Fermoyle (Audrey Hepburn)

Audrey Hepburn was pregnant, and turned down the role that went to Carol Lynley in *The Cardinal*.[27]

Carnal Knowledge (1971)
Ann-Margret as Bobbie (Jane Fonda)

Although Jane Fonda would have loved to work with Mike Nichols, she just couldn't see herself in the role of a character described to have a forty-inch bustline. Instead, the bustier Ann-Margret assumed the role.[28]

Carousel (1956)
Gordon MacRae as Billy Bigelow (Frank Sinatra)

Frank Sinatra was originally cast opposite Shirley Jones in the film version of Rodgers & Hammerstein's *Carousel*. Sinatra quit after one day's work. He was unhappy with the fact that every scene in the film was going to be shot twice, one time the usual way and the other time in Cinemascope. Doing multiple takes was a pet peeve of Sinatra. He felt that if a shot was good, it was unnecessary to shoot it over and over again. In later years if Sinatra was asked to do more takes than he wanted he would say no and leave for the day, rather than quit. Director Henry King brought in Jones' former *Oklahoma!* co-star Gordon MacRae as a replacement.[29]

Carrie (1952)
Laurence Olivier as George Hurstwood (Humphrey Bogart, Charles Boyer, Ronald Colman, Fredric March, William Powell, Spencer Tracy, John Wayne)
Jennifer Jones as Sister Carrie Meeber (Ava Gardner, Elizabeth Taylor)

Laurence Olivier and Elizabeth Taylor were director William Wyler's first choices for the starring roles in *Carrie*. Olivier was very interested, but MGM refused to loan out Taylor. Paramount wanted Ava Gardner to play the part. David O. Selznick called Olivier on behalf of his wife, Jennifer Jones. Selznick wanted Jones to play Carrie. Olivier wasn't a sure thing and Selznick suggested other actors for the part of George Hurstwood including: Spencer Tracy,

Fredric March, William Powell, Humphrey Bogart, John Wayne, Charles Boyer and Ronald Colman. When Selznick found out that Jones had competition (Taylor and Gardner) he was incensed. He accused Wyler of double dealing. Wyler sent Selznick a letter apologizing to him. Two weeks later Jones signed for the film with Laurence Olivier cast opposite her.[30]

Carrie (1976)

Sissy Spacek as Carrie White (Carrie Fisher)
Nancy Allen as Chris Hargensen (Sissy Spacek)

Directors Brian De Palma and George Lucas were both casting films at the same time. De Palma was doing *Carrie*, while Lucas was making *Star Wars*. They decided to hold their auditions together. Carrie Fisher was up for the starring role of Carrie White. She instead got the part of Princess Leia in *Star Wars*. De Palma originally wanted Sissy Spacek to play bad girl Chris Hargensen. But Spacek wanted the lead. She came to read dressed down, as Carrie would dress. De Palma changed his mind and gave her the part.[31]

Casablanca (1942)

Humphey Bogart as Rick Blaine (James Cagney, George Raft, Ronald Reagan)
Ingrid Bergman as Ilsa Lund Laszlo (Hedy Lamarr, Michele Morgan, Ann Sheridan, Tamara Toumanova)
Paul Henreid as Victor Laszlo (Jean-Pierre Aumont, Joseph Cotten, Philip Dorn, Dean Jagger, Herbert Marshall, Ronald Reagan)
Dooley Wilson as Sam (Ella Fitzgerald, Lena Horne, Clarence Muse, Hazel Scott)
Conrad Veidt as Major Heinrich Strasser (Otto Preminger)

It's hard to believe Humphrey Bogart was not the first choice for Rick in *Casablanca*, but originally the producers wanted to hire James Cagney or George Raft. Raft felt that the part was not right for him.[32] Actually, Humphrey Bogart inherited many roles that Raft turned down including *High Sierra* and *The Maltese Falcon*. In a press release from the studio it was announced that Ronald Reagan would star along with Ann Sheridan as Lois. The character of Lois was to be a jet-setting American married to Victor Laszlo.

Eventually the writers changed Lois to the Scandinavian Ilsa, which was no longer appropriate for Sheridan. Hedy Lamarr might have been Ilsa, but MGM would not loan her out to Warner Bros.[33] Ballet dancer Tamara Toumanova was auditioned, but passed over.[34] Michele Morgan was tested, but instead Jack Warner hired Ingrid Bergman.[35]

Jean-Pierre Aumont was considered for the part of Victor Laszlo. Jack Warner didn't think he was a big enough star, and turned him down. Philip Dorn was made an offer, but Dorn chose to make the film *Random Harvest* instead.[36] Ronald Reagan's name was mentioned as a possible choice.[37] Other potential Victor Laszlos included: Joseph Cotton, Dean Jagger and Herbert Marshall. The actor Jack Warner was interested in was Paul Henreid. Henreid was used to playing lead roles, and didn't want to take this supporting role. He changed his mind when he was promised equal billing with Humphrey Bogart and Ingrid Bergman.[38]

Clarence Muse was the first choice for Sam, but then there was a time when Sam was to be played by a woman![39] Lena Horne, Ella Fitzgerald and Hazel Scott were all considerations.[40] However, if Sam was to be played by a woman, the character might have been viewed as a possible love interest for Rick. Sam was always intended to be a black character. A possible interracial romance was apparently not what Warner Bros. wanted. The part of Sam was given to Dooley Wilson.

Otto Preminger tested for the part of Major Strasser.[41]

The Case of the Howling Dog (1934)

Helen Trenholme as Della Street (Bette Davis)

Bette Davis was so set against playing the role of Della Street that she refused to show up on the set. She claimed that this film was not on a par with her recent film, *Of Human Bondage*. Subsequently, she was put on suspension from her studio for two weeks.[42]

Casino (1995)

Sharon Stone as Ginger McKenna (Kate Capshaw, Melanie Griffith, Nicole Kidman)

Melanie Griffith screen tested for the role of Ginger McKenna in director Martin Scorsese's *Casino*.[43] Scorsese also considered Nicole Kidman[44] and Kate Capshaw,[45] but instead chose Sharon Stone. Stone won raves for her performance, and was nominated for an Oscar.

Cass Timberlane (1947)
Lana Turner as Virginia Marshland (Esther Williams)

Esther Williams was a swimming champion whose movies always featured elaborate diving and swimming scenes. Williams was eager to do other types of films. She tried for the lead in the drama *Cass Timberlane*. Williams was turned down in favor of Lana Turner, who was considered a serious actress.[46]

The Cassandra Crossing (1976)
Richard Harris as Dr. Jonathan Chamberlain (Burt Lancaster)

Burt Lancaster was asked to star in *The Cassandra Crossing* as Dr. Jonathan Chamberlain. Lancaster wasn't interested. He did not want to work the amount of hours necessary for such a large part. He also felt that at 62 he was too old for the role. Lancaster agreed to take the smaller role of Mackenzie instead, and the lead went to Richard Harris.[47] Harris is 17 years younger than Lancaster.

Cat on a Hot Tin Roof (1958)
Paul Newman as Brick Pollitt (James Dean)
Elizabeth Taylor as Maggie Pollitt (Grace Kelly, Marilyn Monroe)

James Dean was the first choice to play Brick, but was killed in an automobile accident. For the role of Maggie, Grace Kelly was at the top of the list. She instead married Prince Rainier and retired from acting.[48] Marilyn Monroe sought the lead. Although writer Tennessee Williams thought she was perfect for the part, Monroe lost out to Elizabeth Taylor.[49]

Catch-22 (1970)
Martin Balsam as Colonel Cathcart (Charles Grodin)

When Charles Grodin first came in to read for director Mike Nichols one of the parts he auditioned for was Colonel Cathcart. Grodin did not get that part, but was still cast in the movie in the smaller role of Aarfy Aardvark.[50]

Catherine the Great (1934)
Douglas Fairbanks, Jr., as Czar Peter III (Joseph Schildkraut)

Joseph Schildkraut was selected to join the cast of *Catherine the Great* in the role of Czar Peter III. Elisabeth Bergner was already cast in the title role of Catherine. Both Schildkraut and Bergner were from Vienna, Austria, and had thick German accents. United Artists felt that two accents were too many for their film. They decided to keep Bergner, which meant that Schildkraut was now out of the picture. A replacement was needed, and producer Alexander Korda gave the part to Douglas Fairbanks, Jr.[51]

Joseph Schildkraut's German accent prevented him from appearing in *Catherine the Great*.

Cecil B. Demented (2000)
Stephen Dorff as Cecil B. Demented (Johnny Depp)

Director John Waters was interested in Johnny Depp for the title role of Cecil B. Demented.[52] Instead of Depp, Waters gave the part to Stephen Dorff.

Ceiling Zero (1936)
Stuart Erwin as Texas Clarke (G. Albert Smith)

Martha Tibbetts as Mary Miller Lee (Ann Dvorak)

G. Albert Smith played the part of Texas Clarke on Broadway. When the film version was being planned Smith made a test for the part. He lost out to Stuart Erwin.

Ann Dvorak was offered the part of Mary Miller Lee. Dvorak dismissed the role as too insignificant, and Martha Tibbetts was cast in her place.[53]

Celebrity (1998)

Kenneth Branagh as Lee Simon (Alec Baldwin)
Winona Ryder as Nola (Drew Barrymore, Kate Winslet)

Woody Allen claims that he wrote the role of Lee Simon with an actor like Alec Baldwin in mind. He thought Baldwin would have been perfect for the role, but other commitments prevented him from appearing in the film.[54]

Drew Barrymore was unable to appear in the film because of a commitment to star in the Cinderella story *Ever After*.[55] Kate Winslet was up for the part. Her audition consisted of Allen asking her a few questions and taking a Polaroid of her. The whole thing lasted about ninety seconds. Winslet wasn't optimistic about her chances of landing the role. She knew that both Kenneth Branagh and Judy Davis were already in the cast. Davis is Australian, while Branagh and Winslet are British. Winslet had a feeling that Allen did not want another actor doing an American accent. Allen's reasons for turning Winslet are unknown, but the actress lost the role to the American Winona Ryder.[56]

Chain Reaction (1996)

Rachel Weisz as Dr. Lily Sinclair (Mira Sorvino)

Twentieth Century–Fox executives were interested in Mira Sorvino for the female lead in their upcoming film, *Chain Reaction*. Sorvino was very hot at the moment. She had just won an Oscar for her breakthrough performance in Woody Allen's *Mighty Aphrodite*. Fox and Sorvino were unable to negotiate a deal, and British stage actress Rachel Weisz was cast instead.[57]

The Champ (1979)

Jon Voight as Billy Flynn (Ryan O'Neal)
Ricky Schroder as T.J. Flynn (Griffin O'Neal)

Griffin O'Neal made a screen test for *The Champ*.

Ryan O'Neal was set to play the lead role of the champ. He wanted his son Griffin to play the boy. Franco Zeffirelli granted him a screen test, which did not impress the director. He cast Ricky Schroder instead. Ryan O'Neal quit and was replaced by Jon Voight.[58]

Charade (1963)

Cary Grant as Peter Joshua/Alexander Dyle/ Adam Canfield/Brian Cruikshank (Warren Beatty)
Audrey Hepburn as Reggie Lampert Vass (Natalie Wood)

Director Stanley Donen's first choices for the leads in *Charade* were Cary Grant and Audrey Hepburn. Hepburn liked the script, and agreed to make the film as long as Grant accepted the male lead. Grant read the script, which he didn't like and decided to make another film, *Man's Favorite Sport?*, instead. After Grant's refusal, Donen knew he no longer had Hepburn. Donen went to the executives at Columbia and said he wanted to make the film with Warren Beatty and Natalie Wood in the leads. Columbia wouldn't give Donen enough money to make the film and he went to Universal Studios instead. At this point, Donen received a call from Cary Grant! It turns out that Grant didn't like the script for

Man's Favorite Sport?, and now wanted the role he had been offered in Charade. Grant met Donen the next morning, and by the end of the meeting Grant was set for the film. Audrey Hepburn, who only wanted to work with Cary Grant on this film, was still available, and she was given the part she was originally offered.[59]

Chariots of Fire (1981)

Nigel Davenport as Lord Birkenhead (Sean Connery)

Sean Connery turned down Nigel Davenport's role in *Chariots of Fire*.[60]

Charlie's Angels (2000)

Lucy Liu as Alex Munday (Halle Berry, Penelope Cruz, Lauryn Hill, Thandie Newton, Gwyneth Paltrow, Jada Pinkett Smith, Liv Tyler)

   [*Jill Munroe*— Farrah Fawcett; *Sabrina Duncan*— Kate Jackson; *Kelly Garrett*— Jaclyn Smith]

Since Drew Barrymore was producing the movie version of *Charlie's Angels*, she was the first actress cast in the film. The next Angel cast was Cameron Diaz. Gwyneth Paltrow was offered the role of the third Angel. Paltrow liked the idea, and wanted to sign on. Reportedly a problem arose when she was offered less than the $12 million Cameron Diaz was getting. Unable to work out the financial situation, Paltrow dropped out of the film. Liv Tyler, Jada Pinkett Smith, Penelope Cruz and Lauryn Hill were considered.[61] Halle Berry was another possible Alex Munday.[62] Thandie Newton came very close to landing the part, but *Ally McBeal* star Lucy Liu was chosen instead.[63]

Farrah Fawcett, Jaclyn Smith, and Kate Jackson, the original Charlie's Angels, were offered $100,000 each to make a cameo appearance in the film. The proposed scene would have them meeting the new Angels, and would have taken about three hours to shoot. Fawcett was interested, but wanted a say over the way her character was written. She wanted her character, Jill Munroe, to have fallen in love with Charlie. Jaclyn Smith had zero interest in the movie. For Smith, it was a character she had long since moved on from. Kate Jackson was more interested in playing a bad guy than reprising her role of Sabrina Duncan.[64]

Charly (1968)

Claire Bloom as Alice Kinnian (Anne Heywood)

Anne Heywood was originally cast as therapist Alice Kinnian in *Charly*. Heywood eventually dropped out over problems with the script. Claire Bloom was already cast in another film, *Shalako*. She quit in order to replace Heywood in *Charly*.[65]

Anne Heywood had concerns about the script for *Charly*.

The Chase (1966)

Marlon Brando as Sheriff Calder (Robert Redford)
Jane Fonda as Anna Reeves (Faye Dunaway)

Robert Redford was offered the part of Sheriff Calder. Redford wanted to make the film, only in another role. He chose to play the prison escapee Charlie "Bubber" Reeves. Marlon Brando was cast as Sheriff Calder.[66]

Faye Dunaway wanted the part of Anna. She was told she wasn't attractive enough. Jane Fonda got the part instead.[67]

Cheyenne Autumn (1964)

Edward G. Robinson as Carl Schurz (Spencer Tracy)

Poor health forced Spencer Tracy to drop out of *Cheyenne Autumn*.[68] Edward G. Robinson replaced him as Carl Schurz.

Chicago (2002)

Renee Zellweger as Roxie Hart (Cameron Diaz, Goldie Hawn, Gwyneth Paltrow, Charlize Theron)
Catherine Zeta-Jones as Velma Kelly (Nicole Kidman, Madonna)
Richard Gere as Billy Flynn (Rupert Everett, Hugh Jackman, Kevin Kline, Kevin Spacey, John Travolta)
Queen Latifah as Matron "Mama" Morton (Kathy Bates)
Lucy Liu as Kitty Baxter (Mandy Moore, Britney Spears)

Chicago originated as a hit Broadway show in 1975. Director Bob Fosse wanted to bring the musical to the big screen. It took him about ten years, at which point he had a concept for the film. However Fosse died in 1987. He never said publicly how he saw the film being made. Producer Marty Richards acquired the film rights, but without Fosse, Richards didn't see much of a future for the property. That is, until Miramax's Harvey Weinstein got involved. Weinstein and Richards made a deal for the film. Baz Luhrmann, Herbert Ross, Stanley Donen, Nicholas Hytner and Milos Forman were all possibilities for the directing job. None of these established directors would do it. Rob Marshall directed the television version of *Annie*. Weinstein's children had a copy of the video and played it often. Marshall came in to meet Weinstein and Meryl Poster (co president of Miramax). They liked Marshall's concept for the film and he was hired. Before Marshall came on board, Goldie Hawn and Madonna were the choices to play Roxie Hart and Velma Kelly. Hawn thought Nicholas Hytner was a good choice to direct. Hytner thought that Hawn was too old to play Roxie. Hytner wanted Charlize Theron in the part. Marty Richards didn't agree with his choice. Madonna eventually left the movie. Nicole Kidman was approached to replace her. She was enthusiastic about it, but at the same time she was offered the starring role in *Moulin Rouge*. Kidman took *Moulin Rouge* and was out of the running. Gwyneth Paltrow was considered, but Paltrow said no. Cameron Diaz worried that she wouldn't be able to tackle the singing and dancing. Renee Zellweger didn't want to do it, but agreed to meet Rob Marshall. Marshall obviously changed her mind. Zellweger accepted the part of Roxie. Her performance was critically acclaimed. She was nominated for an Oscar for her performance.

John Travolta, Kevin Kline, Kevin Spacey, Rupert Everett and Hugh Jackman were all considered for the part of lawyer Billy Flynn.

Kathy Bates starred as Miss Hannigan in Marshall's *Annie*. Marshall thought that Bates would be great as Mama Morton. Queen Latifah was another possibility. She auditioned, and won the role.[69]

Harvey Weinstein worried that the film wouldn't appeal to younger audiences. He thought that he might be able to bring in that audience with Britney Spears in the small part of Kitty Baxter. He wanted Spears to also make a video in relation to the film. Meryl Poster thought this was a bad idea. She saw Spears as too contemporary for the movie.[70] Mandy Moore auditioned, but was told she was too young.[71] Lucy Liu was cast instead.

Chicago was a major hit. The film was nominated for 13 Oscars, and won 6 including Best Picture and Best Supporting Actress (Catherine Zeta-Jones as Velma Kelly).

Chicken Every Sunday (1948)

Celeste Holm as Emily Hefferan (Jeanne Crain, Gene Tierney)

Twentieth Century–Fox assigned Gene Tierney the role of Emily Hefferan in their upcoming film, *Chicken Every Sunday*. Tierney refused to do the film and was put on suspension. Jeanne Crain was briefly considered, but the role eventually went to Celeste Holm.[72]

Chicken Run (2000)

Mel Gibson as Rocky (Will Smith, John Travolta)

Both John Travolta and Will Smith were mentioned for the role of Rocky, eventually played by Mel Gibson.[73]

A Child Is Waiting (1963)

Judy Garland as Jean Hansen (Ingrid Bergman)

Ingrid Bergman was originally cast as Jean Hansen. She dropped out of *A Child Is Waiting* and was replaced by Judy Garland.[74]

The Children's Hour (1961)

Fay Bainter as Mrs. Amelia Tilford (Merle Oberon)

Merle Oberon turned down the role of Mrs. Amelia Tilford in *The Children's Hour*.[75]

Child's Play (1972)
Robert Preston as Joseph Dobbs (Marlon Brando)

Marlon Brando was originally cast as Joseph Dobbs in *Child's Play*. He and producer David Merrick clashed. Brando was replaced by Robert Preston.[76]

The China Syndrome (1979)
Jane Fonda as Kimberly Wells (Richard Dreyfuss)

The role of reporter Kimberly Wells was originally written as a man to be played by Richard Dreyfuss.[77] When Dreyfuss changed his mind producer Jane Fonda took over and the character was rewritten.

Chinatown (1974)
Faye Dunaway as Evelyn Mulwray (Jane Fonda, Ali MacGraw, Cybill Shepherd)

Producer Robert Evans wanted Peter Bogdanovich to direct the upcoming film, *Chinatown*. Bogdanovich wanted his girlfriend, Cybill Shepherd, to play the female lead. Evans thought that at 23, Shepherd was too young for the role and turned her down.[78] Bogdanovich told Evans that he wouldn't direct the film without Shepherd. Evans hired Roman Polanski to direct. Jane Fonda was Polanski's first choice to play Evelyn Mulwray. She met with him and listened as he told her the plot of the movie. Polanski got the impression that Fonda would agree to do it, but she ended up turning it down a few days later.[79] Fonda thought that the part was not large enough.[80] Ali MacGraw was another possibility. She was married to the movie's producer, Robert Evans. When MacGraw left Evans for Steve McQueen that was the end of that.[81] Faye Dunaway was brought in and the film was a great success.

A Chorus Line (1985)
Michael Douglas as Zach (John Travolta)
Audrey Landers as Val (DeLee Lively)
Tony Fields as Al DeLuka (Eddie Mekka)
Nicole Fosse as Kristine Evelyn Erlich-DeLuka (DeLee Lively)

John Travolta was offered the chance to star as choreographer Zach in the film version of *A Chorus Line*. Travolta turned it down, saying that he was too big for the film. It was a film about people in the chorus, and Travolta felt that since he was a big star, his presence might offset the balance of the film. An offer was made to another big star, Michael Douglas, who obviously didn't agree with Travolta. Douglas agreed to the part, and turned out to not be too much of a distraction for anyone.[82]

Eddie Mekka (of *Laverne & Shirley*) and his wife DeLee Lively auditioned for the parts of husband and wife Al and Kristine. Lively played Val in the Broadway show. She asked if she could try for the part in the film. She was given a screen test. Director Richard Attenborough told Lively that she was great, but he had one more actress to see. As she was leaving she saw television star Audrey Landers there. Lively knew that she was going to lose the part to Landers, which is exactly what happened. Lively was asked to dub Landers' dancing. She wouldn't.[83]

The Chosen (1981)
Rod Steiger as Reb Saunders (Maximilian Schell)

Maximilian Schell was originally cast as orthodox rabbi Reb Saunders. Rod Steiger was also in the cast, but really wanted Schell's part. Schell allowed Steiger to take his role. Schell was cast as professor David Malter instead.[84]

A Christmas Story (1983)
Darren McGavin as Mr. Parker [aka The Old Man] (Paul Dooley, Jack Nicholson)

Paul Dooley was asked to play Mr. Parker. Dooley didn't participate in the film. The role went to Darren McGavin, even though Jack Nicholson had briefly been interested.[85]

Christopher Strong (1933)
Katharine Hepburn as Lady Cynthia Darrington (Ann Harding)

The role of Lady Cynthia Darrington was originally planned for Ann Harding. Harding fell through, and the part was played by Katharine Hepburn instead.[86]

The Cider House Rules (1999)
Michael Caine as Wilbur Larch (Paul Newman)
Paul Rudd as Wally Worthington (Colin Irving)

The Cider House Rules was a popular novel written by John Irving. When a film version was being planned, the author's son Colin Irving was set for the role of soldier Wally Worthington. However the film was delayed so long that Colin Irving lost the role of Wally to Paul Rudd. Instead director Lasse Hallstrom cast Irving as Major Winslow (the soldier who brings the news of Wally's paralysis).

Paul Newman was offered the part of Dr. Wilbur Larch. Newman was uneasy about the scenes which involved an incinerator, and Michael Caine was cast instead. Caine won an Oscar for his performance.[88]

The Cincinnati Kid (1965)

Edward G. Robinson as Lancey Howard (Spencer Tracy)

Tuesday Weld as Christian Rudd (Sharon Tate)

Spencer Tracy was set to star as Lancey Howard. Tracy quit at the last minute and was replaced by Edward G. Robinson.[89]

Sharon Tate screen-tested for the role of Christian. Although producer Martin Ransohoff and Steve McQueen both liked her reading very much, director Sam Peckinpah gave the part to Tuesday Weld instead.[90]

City for Conquest (1940)

Ann Sheridan as Peggy "Peg" Nash (Ginger Rogers, Sylvia Sidney)

Both Ginger Rogers and Sylvia Sidney turned down the chance to play Peggy in *City for Conquest*.[91]

City Heat (1984)

Burt Reynolds as Mike Murphy (John Travolta)

Clint Eastwood as Lieutenant Speer (Charles Durning)

Madeline Kahn as Caroline Howley (Kim Basinger, Marilu Henner, Sondra Locke)

Jane Alexander as Addie (Julie Andrews, Marilu Henner, Marsha Mason)

Writer Blake Edwards originally saw John Travolta and Marilu Henner as the stars of his upcoming film, *City Heat*. Travolta had no interest and passed on the project. Henner, however, was enticed by Edwards' script. Edwards told Henner to look at the role of socialite Caroline Howley. Henner considered the part but thought it was dull. She told Edwards the part she was interested in was the secretary, Addie. The director did not agree with her and told her to forget it. By this time he had another actress in mind for Addie—Marsha Mason.[92] Mason's interest wasn't peaked. Edwards wife, Julie Andrews, was considered, but Edwards gave the part to Jane Alexander instead.[93]

At this point the director was still short an actress to play Caroline Howley. He considered Kim Basinger as well as Sondra Locke. Locke was excited at the possibility of playing this part and told Edwards she would love to be in his film. Edwards casually mentioned to Locke that she should show the script to her then boyfriend Clint Eastwood, which she did. Soon after Edwards and Andrews had dinner with Locke and Eastwood.[94] Edwards had originally planned to use Charles Durning as Lieutenant Speer.[95] Now his mind was changed. He offered the role to Eastwood, who accepted. Burt Reynolds was brought in as his co-star. All was set until a few weeks later when Locke discovered that she was out of the film. Edwards had replaced her with Madeline Kahn. Locke was very upset. She felt that the director had used her in order to get Clint Eastwood to star in his film.[96]

City Lights (1931)

Virginia Cherrill as A Blind Girl (Georgia Hale)

Director Charlie Chaplin gave the key role of the blind girl to Virginia Cherrill. This was the

Virginia Cherrill was fired then rehired by Charlie Chaplin (*City Lights*).

20 year old's first movie. He later became aggravated by Cherrill's attitude on the set, as well as by her active night life. He fired her from the cast of *City Lights*. Chaplin considered replacing her with Georgia Hale, but the thought of refilming all the scenes he had already shot with Cherrill stopped him. He rehired her at a higher salary.[97]

City Streets (1931)
Sylvia Sidney as Nan Cooley (Clara Bow, Nancy Carroll)

The part of Nan was originally meant for Clara Bow. Bow fell through, as did another candidate, Nancy Carroll. The role was played by Sylvia Sidney.[98]

Class Action (1991)
Mary Elizabeth Mastrantonio as Maggie Ward (Julia Roberts)

Julia Roberts wanted the part of Maggie Ward in *Class Action*. She personally called Joe Roth, the head of 20th Century-Fox to inquire about it. Roth told her she was too young to play Maggie. The part went to Mary Elizabeth Mastrantonio.[99]

Classe Tous Risques (1960)
Jean-Paul Belmondo as Eric Stark (Dario Moreno)

The producers of *Classe Tous Risques* wanted Dario Moreno for the part of Eric Stark. Director Claude Sautet disagreed. His choice was Jean-Paul Belmondo. He was able to give Belmondo the part, but only after fighting with the studio.[100]

Claudia (1943)
Dorothy McGuire as Claudia Naughton (Jennifer Jones, Phyllis Thaxter)

At one point Selznick International Pictures owned the rights to *Claudia*. Phyllis Thaxter was tested, but deemed unsuitable.[101] Jennifer Jones screen tested as well. But writer Rose Franken didn't want Jones cast. She preferred Dorothy McGuire. Selznick eventually sold the rights to the film. Franken got her first choice when Dorothy McGuire was signed for the part.[102]

Claudine (1974)
Diahann Carroll as Claudine (Diana Sands)

Diana Sands chose Diahan Carroll to replace her in *Claudine*.

Diana Sands was originally cast as Claudine. Sands was suffering from cancer at the time. On the first day of filming she realized that she would not be able to go through with the picture; she was in too much pain. Sands asked that Diahann Carroll replace her as Claudine.[103]

Cleopatra (1963)
Elizabeth Taylor as Cleopatra (Brigitte Bardot, Joan Collins, Susan Hayward, Audrey Hepburn, Gina Lollobrigida, Marilyn Monroe, Joanne Woodward)
Richard Burton as Mark Antony (Stephen Boyd)
Rex Harrison as Julius Caesar (Peter Finch)

Cleopatra was first conceived in 1958 for Joan Collins to star.[104] Her costars were to be Peter Finch as Julius Caesar and Stephen Boyd as Mark Antony.[105] The project was put on hold, and Collins was out. A search was on for a new leading lady. Audrey Hepburn was considered.[106] Susan Hayward was another possible choice. The contenders were finally narrowed down to five: Marilyn Monroe, Elizabeth Taylor, Brigitte Bardot, Gina Lollobrigida and Joanne Woodward. Monroe was eliminated. The studio was afraid she wasn't up to the task, and audiences would laugh at her. Woodward and Bardot were also out of the running. It was between Gina Lollobrigida and Elizabeth Taylor. It was decided that Taylor would bring in a bigger audience. She won the part.[107] However, Taylor became ill with pneumonia and it was unclear as to whether or not she would be able to perform. At this point Collins received a call from her agent. She was informed that the producers thought that Taylor was dying, and that they needed Collins to replace her. Collins thought that this was terribly cold. She knew Elizabeth Taylor, and this felt like a betrayal. Her agent reminded her that Cleopatra was a star making role, and to think about it. Later that night Collins' agent called back to tell her that Taylor was recovering. Collins was relieved.[108]

Peter Finch and Stephen Boyd were chosen by director Rouben Mamoulian for Julius Caesar and Mark Antony. After Taylor's illness, Mamoulian was replaced by Joseph Mankiewicz who decided to replace Finch and Boyd with Rex Harrison and Richard Burton.[109]

Clerks (1994)

Jeff Anderson as Randal Graves (Kevin Smith)
Jason Mewes as Jay (Jeff Anderson)

Writer/director Kevin Smith wrote the part of Randal for himself. Smith was too busy to play such a big part. His high school friend Jeff Anderson auditioned for the part of Jay. Smith wrote the part for Jason Mewes, but he wasn't sure if Mewes wanted to be in the film or not. After Anderson's initial audition he and Smith read through the whole script together, at which point Smith decided to cast him as Randal. Smith gave himself the supporting role of Silent Bob. He was happy because he didn't have to memorize dialogue. Mewes accepted the part of Jay.[110]

The Clock (1945)

Robert Walker as Cpl. Joe Allen (Van Johnson)
Keenan Wynn as Luncheonette Drunk (Hume Cronyn)

Van Johnson was considered for the role of Joe Allen.[111]

Hume Cronyn was cast as the Luncheonette Drunk. MGM later decided they would rather have him in *The Valley of Decision*. Keenan Wynn replaced him. Cronyn was eventually removed from *The Valley of Decision* and replaced by Marshall Thompson.[112]

Clockers (1995)

Harvey Keitel as Rocco Klein (Robert De Niro)

Early on, Martin Scorsese planned to direct *Clockers*. His choice for the pivotal role of Rocco Klein was his longtime friend Robert De Niro. Scorsese eventually decided to produce the film, and left the directing task to Spike Lee. Scorsese and De Niro made the film *Casino* instead. Lee gave the part of Rocco Klein to Harvey Keitel.[113]

Close Encounters of the Third Kind (1977)

Richard Dreyfuss as Roy Neary (James Caan, Gene Hackman, Steve McQueen, Jack Nicholson, Al Pacino)
Teri Garr as Ronnie Neary (Amy Irving, Meryl Streep)
Francois Truffaut as Claude Lacombe (Yves Montand, Phillippe Noiret, Jean-Louis Trintignant, Lino Ventura)

The role of Roy Neary was turned down by some of Hollywood's biggest stars. Jack Nicholson didn't want to appear in a film in which the special effects played a larger role than him. He felt so strongly about this point that he would not even meet with Steven Spielberg to discuss it. Al Pacino was approached, but he wasn't interested.[114] Steve McQueen didn't want the part either.[115] Gene Hackman didn't want to be away on location for the many months filming required.[116] James Caan accepted the job but got himself out of it by asking for $1 million plus ten percent of the gross. Richard Dreyfuss wasn't asking for anything near that amount, and Spielberg cast him in the part.[117]

An unknown Meryl Streep auditioned for the part of Ronnie Neary, as did Amy Irving. Irving met with Spielberg (whom she would later marry), but the director thought that she looked too young for the part.[118] Spielberg gave the part to Teri Garr.

Spielberg's first choice to play Claude Lacombe was Lino Ventura. However, the actor didn't speak English. Philippe Noiret was considered, as well as Jean-Louis Trintignant and Yves Montand. Montand and Trintignant were both made offers, which they both rejected. Spielberg then offered the part to Francois Truffaut, who accepted.[119]

Cobra (1925)
Gertrude Olmstead as Mary Drake (Myrna Loy)

After high school graduation, Myrna Loy was hired to be in the chorus of *The Ten Commandments* at Grauman's Chinese Theatre. Photographer Henry Waxman took a picture of all the chorus girls. The photo came to the attention of Rudolph Valentino. Valentino was about to start work on the film *Cobra*. Loy's picture impressed Valentino. The actor pulled some strings and got Loy a screen test for the part of Mary Drake. Valentino's wife, Natacha Rambova, wanted to help the budding actress, and helped her with her makeup and wardrobe. Loy was so unhappy with the way she performed in her test that she went home and cried for hours. She was ashamed, and embarrassed to face Rambova. Loy was turned down for *Cobra*. Rambova was also about to start a film — *What Price Beauty?* Rambova (the star of the film) made sure that Loy was given the small role of a model.[120]

The Cobweb (1955)
John Kerr as Steven W. Holte (James Dean)

James Dean was sought to star in *The Cobweb*. Dean wanted the part, but MGM refused to loan him out. John Kerr took his place in *The Cobweb*.[121]

Cold Mountain (2003)
Jude Law as Inman Balis (Tom Cruise, Matt Damon, Daniel Day-Lewis, Tom Hanks, Brad Pitt)

The part of Inman Balis interested many actors including Tom Cruise, Brad Pitt, Daniel Day-Lewis, Tom Hanks and Matt Damon. Cruise was offered the part. According to producer Sydney Pollack, Miramax chief Harvey Weinstein refused to pay Cruise the amount he was asking for. However, both Cruise and Weinstein disagree with Pollack. Cruise said that he just didn't want to make the film at the time. He starred in *The Last Samurai* instead. Director Anthony Minghella gave the part to Jude Law. Law was nominated for an Oscar for his performance in Minghella's film, *The Talented Mr. Ripley*. Law was also nominated for his performance in *Cold Mountain*.[122]

The Color Purple (1985)
Oprah Winfrey as Sofia (Whoopi Goldberg)

Margaret Avery as Shug Avery (Lola Falana, Patti La Belle, Diana Ross, Tina Turner)

Whoopi Goldberg originally went after the role of Sofia. Director Steven Spielberg thought she was the wrong physical type for the part; he wanted a larger actress. Spielberg decided that Goldberg would be better cast as Celie. Producer Quincy Jones was instrumental in finding the actress for Sofia.[123] One day he turned on the television and saw talk show host Oprah Winfrey. He thought that Winfrey had the right quality to play Sofia. He arranged for the acting novice to audition. Spielberg loved Winfrey and gave her the role.

Spielberg offered Tina Turner the role of Shug Avery three times. She turned him down saying that the abuse storyline hit too close to home for her.[124] Diana Ross, Lola Falana and Patti La Belle were all considered, but instead Spielberg gave the part to Margaret Avery.[125] Goldberg, Winfrey, and Avery all received Academy Award nominations for their work in the film.

Come and Get It (1936)
Edward Arnold as Barney Glasgow (Spencer Tracy)
Frances Farmer as Lotta (Miriam Hopkins, Andrea Leeds)

Louis B. Mayer refused to loan Spencer Tracy out, and Edward Arnold was cast as Barney Glasgow instead. Miriam Hopkins was supposed to play Lotta until director Howard Hawks decided he didn't want her for the role. He preferred newcomer Andrea Leeds, but studio head Samuel Goldwyn though she might be too inexperienced to handle the lead in a film. She remained in the film, although in the smaller role of Evvie Glasgow.[126]

Come Back Little Sheba (1952)
Shirley Booth as Lola Delaney (Bette Davis)

Producer Hal Wallis asked Bette Davis to play the lead role of Lola Delaney. She had seen the show on Broadway and thought that no one could play the role as well as the star of the production, Shirley Booth. Wallis tried to convince her otherwise, to no avail. Booth reprised the role in the film. Davis later said that turning the film down was a big mistake.[127]

Come Back to the Five and Dime, Jimmy Dean, Jimmy Dean (1982)

Karen Black as Joanne (Cher)

Director Robert Altman originally wanted Cher to play Joanne. Cher preferred the part of Sissy, which Altman gave her. Karen Black played Joanne.[128]

The Comedians (1967)

Elizabeth Taylor as Martha Pineda (Sophia Loren)

Sophia Loren was supposed to star opposite Richard Burton in *The Comedians*. That is, until Burton's wife, Elizabeth Taylor, decided she wanted the part too. This same situation had come up four years earlier when Taylor replaced Loren opposite Burton in *The VIPs*. Like the last time, Taylor offered to do the part for about half the amount of money Loren was asking for. And just like last time Taylor's offer was accepted. Loren was out, and Taylor was given the role of Martha Pineda.[129]

Comet Over Broadway (1938)

Kay Francis as Eve Appleton (Bette Davis)

Bette Davis was offered the role of Eve Appleton. She read the script and decided that the film was exactly the kind of film she did not want to make. The part went instead to Kay Francis.[130]

Coming Home (1978)

Jon Voight as Luke Martin (Jack Nicholson, Al Pacino, Sylvester Stallone)
Bruce Dern as Captain Bob Hyde (Jon Voight)

Jack Nicholson, Al Pacino, and Sylvester Stallone all turned down the part of Luke Martin. Jon Voight had originally been cast in *Coming Home* as Jane Fonda's husband Captain Bob Hyde. When Voight was promoted to the starring role of Luke Martin Bruce Dern was brought in to play Hyde.[131]

Confessions of a Dangerous Mind (2002)

Sam Rockwell as Chuck Barris (Johnny Depp)

In 2001 Bryan Singer was signed to direct *Confessions of a Dangerous Mind*. He cast Johnny Depp in the starring role of Chuck Barris. However, there was a problem with the financing for the film, and everything was up in the air. A few months later George Clooney was set to direct. According to Clooney, he was still interested in Depp, but Depp's agent interfered. Depp's agency, United Talent Agency, claims that Depp's agent, Tracey Jacobs, never spoke to Clooney. Clooney cast Sam Rockwell as Chuck Barris.[132]

The Conqueror (1956)

John Wayne as Temujn, later Genghis Khan (Marlon Brando)

Marlon Brando was asked to star in *The Conqueror*, but his schedule was filled. John Wayne was cast in the role instead.[133]

The Constant Nymph (1943)

Joan Fontaine as Tessa Sanger (Olivia De Havilland, Merle Oberon)

Merle Oberon was the original choice to play Tessa. Oberon was ill, and unable to make the film. Joan Fontaine was considered. Production was delayed and Oberon fought to get her part back, to no avail. Fontaine's sister, Olivia De Havilland, also wanted the part. Director Edmund Goulding passed over De Havilland in favor of Fontaine.[134]

Continental Divide (1981)

John Belushi as Ernie Souchak (Robert De Niro, Richard Dreyfuss, Peter Falk, Elliott Gould, Dustin Hoffman, Al Pacino, George Segal, Barbra Streisand)
Blair Brown as Nell Porter (Julie Christie, Jill Clayburgh, Kate Jackson, Robert Redford)

Al Pacino, Elliott Gould and Peter Falk were all in and out of the project at one time or another. There was a chance that Jill Clayburgh and Robert De Niro would play the leads but that fell through. The same was true for Robert Redford and Barbra Streisand. However, in that pair, Streisand would have played the Souchak role, and Redford the Nell role. Julie Christie was considered for Nell, as well as Kate Jackson, while Dustin Hoffman, Richard Dreyfuss, and George Segal were possibilities for Ernie. Director Michael Apted finally went with John Belushi and Blair Brown.[135]

The Conversation (1974)
Gene Hackman as Harry Caul (Marlon Brando)
Frederic Forrest as Mark (Harrison Ford)

Marlon Brando was director Francis Ford Coppola's choice for the role of Harry Caul. He turned down the role and it went to Gene Hackman.[136]

Harrison Ford made a screen test for the part of Mark. Coppola chose Frederic Forrest instead, but liked Ford enough to give him the smaller role of Martin Stett.[137]

Conversation Piece (1974)
Silvana Mangano as Bianca Brumonti (Audrey Hepburn)

Audrey Hepburn turned down the role of Bianca.[138]

Convoy (1978)
Kris Kristofferson as Rubber Duck (Steve McQueen)

Steve McQueen was offered the male lead in *Convoy*. He turned it down and the project stalled for a few years, at which point Kris Kristofferson was cast. Incidentally, McQueen's wife Ali MacGraw was cast in the female lead. This caused some friction between the couple. McQueen had recently turned down *Sorcerer* in order to stay at home with his wife. Now MacGraw was in the same position, but she accepted the role in *Convoy*. The two were divorced soon after.[139]

A Cool Dry Place (1998)
Vince Vaughn as Russell Durrell (Chris O'Donnell)

Chris O'Donnell's wedding prevented him from taking the lead in *A Cool Dry Place*.[140]

The Corn Is Green (1945)
Joan Lorring as Bessie Watty (Angela Lansbury)

Angela Lansbury was turned down by the studio for the role of Bessie Watty in favor of Joan Lorring.[141]

The Cotton Club (1984)
Richard Gere as Dixie Dwyer (Al Pacino, Sylvester Stallone)
Gregory Hines as Sandman Williams (Richard Pryor)

Al Pacino was producer Robert Evans' first choice to play the lead role of Dixie Dwyer. Pacino didn't want to do it and told Evans no. Sylvester Stallone wanted to play the part, and Evans was interested. Stallone, however, took himself out of the running by asking to be paid twice the amount Evans was willing to pay. Ultimately, Richard Gere was cast as Dixie Dwyer.[142]

The part of Sandman Williams was originally intended for Richard Pryor. It was actually producer Robert Evans' 11-year-old son Joshua who persuaded his father not to cast Pryor. He explained that using Pryor, who was a major movie star at the time, would take away from the film. It would just be another Richard Pryor movie. His surprised father agreed as did the studio. Gregory Hines replaced Pryor.[143]

Counsellor at Law (1933)
John Barrymore as George Simon (Paul Muni, William Powell, Edward G. Robinson, Joseph Schildkraut)

Counsellor at Law was a successful Broadway play. Universal Studios decided to turn the play into a movie. Their first choice for the part of lawyer George Simon was the actor who played it on Broadway—Paul Muni. Muni didn't want to be typecast in Jewish roles and turned it down. Universal then considered John Barrymore, William Powell, Edward G. Robinson and Joseph Schildkraut. Barrymore was such a big star that Universal couldn't resist. He got the part.[144]

The Count of Monte Cristo (1934)
Robert Donat as Edmond Dantes (Fredric March)

The role of Edmond Dantes was originally written for Fredric March. When he was unavailable Robert Donat was cast.[145]

The Country Girl (1954)
Grace Kelly as Georgie Elgin (Greta Garbo, Jennifer Jones)

Jennifer Jones was originally cast in the lead. She became pregnant and the role had to be recast.[146] Greta Garbo was made an offer, which she refused. Grace Kelly was another possibility. The studio contacted MGM to see about a loan out. MGM wasn't interested. They had Kelly scheduled to make *Green Fire*. However, Kelly was very interested in playing Georgie Elgin. MGM eventually gave her permission to make *The Country Girl*. Kelly won an Academy Award for her performance in the film.[147]

The Courtship of Andy Hardy (1942)

Donna Reed as Melodie Nesbit (Ava Gardner)

Mickey Rooney tried unsuccessfully to get Ava Gardner, his wife, the part of Melodie Nesbit in *The Courtship of Andy Hardy*. Producer Carey Wilson thought Gardner was too inexperienced and the role went to Donna Reed instead.[148]

Cover Girl (1944)

Gene Kelly as Danny McGuire (Larry Parks)
Cornelia R. Von Hessert as Cover Girl: *Harper's Bazaar* (Lauren Bacall)

Larry Parks was considered for the lead role of Danny McGuire.[149] The role went to Gene Kelly instead.

Real life *Harper's Bazaar* cover girl, Lauren Bacall, was asked to appear in the film. At the same time Bacall was offered the chance to screen test for Howard Hawks. If Bacall passed the test Hawks would sign her to a contract. Bacall passed her test.[150] Shortly afterwards Hawks cast her in the female lead in *To Have and Have Not*. The film made her a star. Humphrey Bogart played opposite her. Bacall and Bogart were married a few months after the release of the film.

Crimes and Misdemeanors (1989)

Jerry Orbach as Jack Rosenthal (Martin Landau)

Martin Landau was originally cast as Jack Rosenthal. Director Woody Allen later changed his mind and decided that Landau would be better in the larger role of Judah Rosenthal (Jack's brother). He replaced Landau with Jerry Orbach.[151]

Crimes of Passion (1983)

John Laughlin as Bobby Grady (Tom Berenger)

Tom Berenger was offered the part of Bobby Grady in *Crimes of Passion*. He chose to do the film *Firstborn* instead.[152]

Crimes of the Heart (1986)

David Carpenter as Barnette Lloyd (Brad Davis)

Casting director Susan Bluestein Davis suggested her husband, actor Brad Davis, for the part of lawyer Barnette Lloyd. Davis auditioned, but didn't do very well. Director Bruce Beresford reassured Bluestein Davis that her husband was a good actor, but he was too sexy and dangerous to play Barnette.[153] The part went to newcomer David Carpenter.

Crimson Tide (1995)

Denzel Washington as Ron Hunter (Andy Garcia, Val Kilmer, Brad Pitt)
Gene Hackman as Captain Frank Ramsey (Warren Beatty, Al Pacino)

Producers Don Simpson and Jerry Bruckheimer wanted Warren Beatty to play the role of Captain Frank Ramsey. Beatty met with the pair repeatedly, but was reluctant to make a firm commitment. The producers could not wait any longer. Al Pacino was their next choice. Brad Pitt learned that Pacino was seriously considering the part. Pitt was eager to work with him, and looked into the co-starring role of Lieutenant Commander Hunter. Like Beatty, Pacino was taking too long to decide. Once he was eliminated Pitt dropped out of the running. The producers finally chose Gene Hackman as their star.[154] Val Kilmer and Andy Garcia were considered to play opposite Hackman, but Simpson and Bruckheimer chose Denzel Washington instead.[155]

Criss Cross (1949)

Yvonne De Carlo as Anna Dundee (Ava Gardner, Shelley Winters)

Yvonne De Carlo beat out contenders such as Ava Gardner and Shelley Winters to land the role of Anna in *Criss Cross*.[156]

Critical Condition (1987)

Richard Pryor as Eddie/Kevin (Eddie Murphy)

Eddie Murphy turned down Richard Pryor's role in *Critical Condition*.[157]

The Crow (1994)

Brandon Lee as Eric Draven (River Phoenix, Charlie Sexton, Christian Slater)

Christian Slater, River Phoenix and Charlie Sexton were all candidates to play Eric Draven.

Brandon Lee starred as Eric Draven in *The Crow*.

Brandon Lee was also considered. Executive producer Edward R. Pressman was so impressed with Lee that he thought that there could be a whole series of films with Lee as Eric Draven.

On March 31, 1993, Lee was scheduled to film a scene in which his character is shot. Michael Massee, the actor playing the character of Funboy, was supposed to fire a 44-caliber revolver from approximately 15 feet away. Lee was supposed to detonate a squib. A squib is an explosive charge that would safely replicate the bullet. Massee fired the gun and Lee collapsed. No one realized that anything was wrong until the end of the scene when Lee didn't get up. It soon became apparent that Lee was bleeding from his abdomen. Lee was rushed to a hospital and into surgery. The doctors were unable to save the 28-year-old Lee's life. It was theorized that the gun used in the scene was loaded improperly, and the dummy bullet became a lethal weapon.[158] Michael Massee was distraught at the thought that he fired the shot that killed Brandon Lee. The film was subsequently completed without Lee.

The Crow was a big hit. There was a sequel two years later, *The Crow: City of Angels*, with the Draven character replaced by a new character, Ashe Corven (played by Vincent Perez).

The Crow: City of Angels (1996)

Vincent Perez as Ashe Corven (Jon Bon Jovi)

Vincent Perez won the role of Ashe Corven over rock star Jon Bon Jovi.[159]

The Crucible (1996)

Winona Ryder as Abigail Williams (Jennifer Love Hewitt, Kate Winslet, Renee Zellweger)

Joan Allen as Elizabeth Proctor (Emma Thompson)

Joan Allen was cast as Elizabeth Proctor after Emma Thompson took herself out of the running.[160]

Kate Winslet was desperate to play her dream role of Abigail.[161] Jennifer Love Hewitt auditioned, but failed to make the cut.[162] Winona Ryder was director Nicholas Hytner's first choice with Renee Zellweger as a backup in case Ryder didn't work out.[163]

Cruising (1980)

Al Pacino as Steve Burns (Treat Williams)

Treat Williams was considered for the part of undercover cop Steve Burns. Al Pacino got hold of the script. Pacino liked the script very much and wanted the part. Director William Friedkin agreed to give him the part. The movie was originally supposed to be made by Warner Bros. They didn't want to pay Al Pacino's $2 million salary. The studio dropped the film. It was produced by Lorimar instead.[164]

The Cry Baby Killer (1958)

Jack Nicholson as Jimmy Walker (Tom Pittman)

Initially, the role of Jimmy Walker was earmarked for Hollywood newcomer Tom Pittman. Producer David Kramarsky was unable to settle on a contract with Pittman, and he lost the role. Kramarsky asked acting teacher Jeff Corey to recommend someone as a replacement. Corey suggested his student, Jack Nicholson. He auditioned for Kramarsky, and the producer liked what he saw. Nicholson was rewarded with the part, which was his first role in a motion picture.[165]

Cul-De-Sac (1966)

Donald Pleasence as George (Roman Polanski)
Francoise Dorleac as Teresa (Barbara Lass)

Writer/director Roman Polanski's *Cul-de-Sac* was a fictionalized account of his marriage to Barbara Lass. He wanted Lass to play the film version of herself with him playing his onscreen counterpart. Lass' husband didn't want her to make the film, and producer Michael Klinger didn't want Polanski acting and directing, so neither one was cast. Instead, Polanski gave the starring roles to Francoise Dorleac and Donald Pleasence.[166]

Cynara (1932)

Kay Francis as Clemency Warlock (Dorothy Hale)

Socialite Dorothy Hale was originally thought of for the role of Clemency Warlock. Those plans fell through and another actress was needed to fill in. Kay Francis was sought. Francis was supposed to have been shooting *42nd Street*, but had been replaced by Bebe Daniels. She was suddenly available, and won the lead in *Cynara*.[167]

Dakota Incident (1956)

Linda Darnell as Amy Clarke (Anne Baxter)

Anne Baxter was originally cast as Amy Clarke in *Dakota Incident*. She eventually decided against doing the film and dropped out. Linda Darnell was brought in to replace her.[1]

Damage (1992)

Juliette Binoche as Anna Barton (Isabelle Adjani, Jodie Foster)

Juliette Binoche beat out the more established Jodie Foster and Isabelle Adjani to win the lead role of Anna Barton in *Damage*.[2]

Damn Yankees (1958)

Ray Walston as Mr. Applegate (Cary Grant)

Cary Grant turned down the role of the devil.[3] Ray Walston was cast instead. Walston originated the role on Broadway. He won a Tony Award for his work on the show.

A Damsel in Distress (1937)

Joan Fontaine Lady Alyce Marshmorton (Ruby Keeler)

Ruby Keeler was considered for the part of Lady Alyce Marshmorton. The star of *A Damsel in Distress*, Fred Astaire, said that Keeler was unsatisfactory; that no one would believe that she was a member of English aristocracy.[4]

Dancing Lady (1933)

Joan Crawford as Janie "Duchess" Barlow (Jean Harlow)
Clark Gable as Patch Gallagher (Robert Montgomery)
Fred Astaire as Himself (Clifton Webb)

Clark Gable and Joan Crawford were the proposed stars of *Dancing Lady*. David O. Selznick thought he might like to replace Crawford with Jean Harlow. When Crawford got wind of this she went right to Selznick, who told her that the character was "a bit of a hooker." He went on to say that Harlow was a better fit. Crawford countered saying, "Listen, David, I could be a better hooker than Harlow any day of the year." The two shared a laugh over this exchange, and Selznick kept her in the role.

Shortly before filming was to begin Clark Gable fell ill with a dangerous infection. He had to have most of his teeth pulled and replaced with false ones. Shooting went on without Gable. He was finally well enough to work, but after only one day he was back in the hospital. The infection had spread to his gallbladder, which had to be removed. He would not be able to return to work for a month. Selznick thought about putting Robert Montgomery in Gable's part and moving forward with the film. Studio boss Louis B. Mayer refused. After filming as much as they could without Gable production was put on hold until he was healthy enough to return to the set.[5]

Clifton Webb was asked to appear in the film. Webb would do it, if he had star billing with Joan Crawford. MGM refused, and gave the part to Fred Astaire.[6]

Darby's Rangers (1958)

James Garner as William Orlando Darby (Charlton Heston, John Hudson, Robert Stack)
Edd Byrnes as Arnold Dittman (Dennis Hopper, Tab Hunter)

Agent Bill Shiffrin wanted the starring role of William Orlando Darby to go to his client John Hudson. He hired a helicopter to hover over Warner Bros. for 25 minutes. The helicopter had a banner which read: John Hudson for Darby!

The helicopter was extremely disruptive to the studio. Director William Wellman told Shiffrin that he would see Hudson, but that he must get the helicopter to come down. Robert Stack was another candidate, but the studio had another actor in mind. Charlton Heston was Warner Bros.' choice for the part of Darby. Heston wanted to make the film, and a contract was drawn up. Heston had a problem with the contract. He claimed that it was worded differently than what had been agreed to previously. Warner Bros. did not like what Heston said and decided to make the film without him. James Garner was hired for the part of William Orlando Darby.

Tab Hunter was offered the supporting role of Arnold Dittman. Hunter thought that the part wasn't big enough and said no. Dennis Hopper wanted the part, but studio head Jack Warner passed him over in favor of Edd Byrnes.[7]

Daredevil (2003)
Ben Affleck as Matt Murdock/Daredevil (Vin Diesel, Edward Norton, Guy Pearce)
Colin Farrell as Bullseye (Vin Diesel)

Writer/director Mark Steven Johnson thought that Ben Affleck might be right for the title role of superhero Daredevil. However Affleck wasn't going to be available when Johnson wanted to stat shooting. Affleck was scheduled to make *Gigli* at the time. Universal suggested Vin Diesel, but Johnson thought he was the wrong type. He thought that Diesel would be better as Bullseye. But Diesel was offered another film, and was no longer available. Johnson continued to search for a leading man. Other candidates were Edward Norton and Guy Pearce. Norton was very familiar with the character, but wasn't sure he wanted to don the Daredevil suit.[8] Filmmaker Kevin Smith arranged a meeting between Johnson and Affleck. Johnson offered Affleck the role of Bullseye, but later admitted that he really wanted him to play the lead. Affleck was a fan of the Daredevil comics. He arranged for the *Gigli* schedule to be changed so that he could do *Daredevil*.[9]

Dark City (1950)
Charlton Heston as Danny Haley (Burt Lancaster)

Producer Hal Wallis of Paramount Pictures wanted to cast Burt Lancaster as Danny Haley. However, Lancaster was offered a deal too good to pass up from another studio (20th Century–Fox), and Charlton Heston played the part instead.[10]

Dark Victory (1939)
Bette Davis as Judith Traherne (Kay Francis, Greta Garbo, Janet Gaynor, Katharine Hepburn, Merle Oberon, Barbara Stanwyck)
George Brent as Dr. Frederick Steele (Fredric March, Spencer Tracy)

Before *Dark Victory* came to Warner Bros., David O. Selznick owned the rights. He tried to persuade Greta Garbo to take the starring role of Judith Traherne with Fredric March[11] as her co-star, but the elusive actress wasn't interested. He also considered Katharine Hepburn, Janet Gaynor, and Merle Oberon. He was never quite happy with the script and sold it to Warner Bros. Their first choice for the role was Kay Francis. As a policy she refused to play death scenes, her reason for turning down *Dark Victory*. Barbara Stanwyck unsuccessfully tried to win the role.[12] Finally, Bette Davis was cast. She requested Spencer Tracy as her leading man, but he was not available.[13] George Brent was cast instead.

Darling (1965)
Dirk Bogarde as Robert Gold (Gregory Peck)
Julie Christie as Diana Scott (Shirley MacLaine)

The studio wanted Shirley MacLaine to play the lead role in *Darling*. Director John Schlesinger liked the virtually unknown Julie Christie. He successfully fought the studio to have her star as Diana Scott.[14] Schlesinger must have been right because Christie won the Academy Award for *Darling*. Gregory Peck turned down the male lead.[15]

Darling, How Could You (1951)
Joan Fontaine as Mrs. Alice Grey (Gloria Swanson)

Gloria Swanson was considered for the part of Alice Grey in *Darling, How Could You*. Paramount Pictures asked her to test for the part. Swanson found that disrespectful and the role was played by Joan Fontaine instead.[16]

David and Bathsheba (1951)
Gregory Peck as King David (Laurence Olivier)
Susan Hayward as Bathsheba (Anne Baxter, Vivien Leigh)

Anne Baxter was considered for the part of Bathsheba.[17] Screenwriter Philip Dunne was interested in Laurence Olivier as David, with Vivien Leigh as Bathsheba.[18] Anne Baxter wasn't considered as popular with audiences as Susan Hayward, and Baxter lost the part.[19] Gregory Peck was cast opposite Hayward as David.

David Copperfield (1935)

W.C. Fields as Micawber (Charles Laughton)
Freddie Bartholomew as David as Child (Jackie Cooper)

For the role of Micawber it had come down to two actors: Charles Laughton and W.C. Fields. David O. Selznick chose Laughton. After a few days of filming Laughton wanted out. He even told Selznick to replace him with Fields, which he did.

Studio head Louis B. Mayer wanted child star Jackie Cooper to play young David. Selznick and director George Cukor disagreed with Mayer. They looked at about 10,000 child actors and chose Freddie Bartholomew.[20]

The Day of the Locust (1975)

Karen Black as Faye Greener (Cybill Shepherd)

Cybill Shepherd tried for the role of Faye Greener in director John Schlesinger's *The Day of the Locust*. Schlesinger didn't think Shepherd was right for the part. He felt that Shepherd was too old for it. He turned her down, and cast Karen Black instead.[21] Black is eight years older than Shepherd.

The Day the Earth Stood Still (1951)

Michael Rennie as Klaatu (Claude Rains, Spencer Tracy)

Spencer Tracy was considered for the part of Klaatu.[22] Director Robert Wise liked Claude Rains for the part. Rains was involved with a play and was unavailable. Darryl F. Zanuck decided that he wanted an unknown actor in the part, feeling an unknown would make the film seem more realistic. Michael Rennie was tested, and won the role.[23]

Daylight (1996)

Sylvester Stallone as Kit Latura (Harrison Ford)

Harrison Ford was offered the starring role of Kit Latura. Ford said no, and the part went to Sylvester Stallone instead.[24]

Days of Heaven (1978)

Richard Gere as Bill (Dustin Hoffman, Al Pacino, John Travolta)
Brooke Adams as Abby (Genevieve Bujold)

Director Terrence Malick wanted Genevieve Bujold and John Travolta in the leads.[25] Travolta was forced to turn it down. Shooting would have interfered with his schedule for his television series, *Welcome Back Kotter*. Malick and Travolta met to discuss this news. Malick was very upset, and couldn't help but cry.[26] Dustin Hoffman and Al Pacino were both asked to star as Bill. Neither actor wanted the part.[27] The leads were eventually played by Richard Gere and Brooke Adams.

Dead End (1937)

Humphey Bogart as Baby Face Martin (James Cagney, George Raft)

James Cagney was the first choice for the role of Baby Face Martin but a legal battle with the studio disqualified him. The next choice was George Raft. But true to his reputation, he turned it down.[28] Once again Humphrey Bogart inherited a role rejected by Raft (*Casablanca, The Maltese Falcon, High Sierra*).

Dead Poets Society (1989)

Robin Williams as John Keating (Tom Hanks, Liam Neeson)

Tom Hanks turned down the starring role of teacher John Keating.[29] Jeff Kanew was hired as director. He thought Liam Neeson was the right choice to star.[30] Ultimately, Kanew was replaced by Peter Weir. Weir had his own ideas about who would make the perfect John Keating. He gave the part to Robin Williams, who was nominated for an Oscar for his performance.

The Dead Zone (1983)

Christopher Walken as Johnny Smith (Nicholas Campbell, Bill Murray)
Tom Skerritt as Sheriff Bannerman (Hal Holbrook)

When director David Cronenberg began production on *The Dead Zone*, he thought that Nicholas Campbell would be right for the starring role of Johnny Smith. Campbell and Cronenberg worked together previously on the film

Nicholas Campbell played a small role in *The Dead Zone*, but director David Cronenberg originally wanted him for the lead.

The Brood. Stephen King, the writer of the novel on which the movie was based, had other ideas. He went to Dino De Laurentiis and told him that he wanted Johnny Smith to be played by Bill Murray. Had Murray been available, *The Dead Zone* would have been a very different type of film for him. He was mainly known as a comic actor. However, Murray did not sign for the film, and De Laurentiis hired the Academy Award winning actor Christopher Walken to play Johnny. Meanwhile, David Cronenberg gave his friend Nicholas Campbell the featured role of the Castle Rock killer, Frank Dodd.

Cronenberg thought of Hal Holbrook for the part of Sheriff Bannerman. Producer Dino De Laurentiis had never heard of Holbrook and cast Tom Skerritt as Sheriff Bannerman instead.[31]

Death Becomes Her (1992)

Bruce Willis as Ernest Menville (Kevin Kline)

Robert Zemeckis cast Kevin Kline opposite Meryl Streep and Goldie Hawn in *Death Becomes Her*. However, when his contract was being negotiated, a problem arose. Kline's agent was asking for him to be paid the same amount as his female co-stars. Zemeckis refused to budge. The roles that Streep and Hawn were playing were the starring roles, while Kline's was a supporting part. Zemeckis also felt that the women were bigger stars than Kline, and he just didn't think he should have to pay him any more than he was offering. Kline, an Oscar winning actor himself, would not give in, and dropped out of the film. Zemeckis gave the part to Bruce Willis.[32]

Death on the Nile (1978)

Lois Chiles as Linnet Ridgeway (Cybill Shepherd)

Cybill Shepherd was offered the role of Linnet Ridgeway. Shepherd didn't want to play the part. She would have had to play a dead body for the bulk of the film. Shepherd turned it down, and Lois Chiles was cast instead.[33]

Death Wish (1974)

Charles Bronson as Paul Kersey (Burt Lancaster)

Director Michael Winner wanted Burt Lancaster for the starring role of Paul Kersey. The producers of the film disagreed and gave the part to the more popular Charles Bronson instead.[34]

The Decision of Christopher Blake (1948)

Alexis Smith as Mrs. Blake (Norma Shearer)

Studio head Jack Warner asked Norma Shearer to play Mrs. Blake. She declined because she didn't think it was an important enough film or part. Alexis Smith was cast as Mrs. Blake.[35]

Deep in My Heart (1954)

Jose Ferrer as Sigmund Romberg (Kurt Kasznar)

Kurt Kasznar was briefly considered for the lead role of Sigmund Romberg.[36]

The Delicate Delinquent (1957)

Darren McGavin as Mike Damon (Dean Martin)

The Delicate Delinquent was originally meant to be a Martin & Lewis vehicle. Then suddenly Dean Martin and Jerry Lewis split up as a team. Jerry Lewis got custody of the film, and Darren McGavin was cast in the role intended for Martin.[37]

Deliverance (1972)
Jon Voight as Ed Gentry (Henry Fonda)
Burt Reynolds as Lewis Medlock (Marlon Brando, Charlton Heston)

Charlton Heston turned down the starring role of Lewis Medlock in *Deliverance*. It was a role he would have liked to do, but at the same time he was also offered the role of Mark Antony in *Antony and Cleopatra*. He chose to play Mark Antony.[38] Marlon Brando was also a consideration with Henry Fonda playing opposite him.[39] In the end the part went to Burt Reynolds with Jon Voight cast as Ed Gentry. *Deliverance* was a breakthrough for Reynolds, who soon became Hollywood's top leading man.

Demolition Man (1994)
Sandra Bullock as Lenina Huxley (Lori Petty)

After three days of filming Lori Petty was replaced by Sandra Bullock. Petty claimed that she and Sylvester Stallone did not work well together.[40]

Lori Petty was dropped from the cast of *Demolition Man*.

Design for Living (1933)
Fredric March as Tom Chambers (Douglas Fairbanks, Jr.)

Douglas Fairbanks, Jr., was offered the role of Tom Chambers in *Design for Living*. Fairbanks was ill at the time which prevented him from making the film. The part was played by Fredric March instead.[41]

Designing Woman (1957)
Lauren Bacall as Marilla Hagen (Grace Kelly)
Gregory Peck as Mike Hagen (James Stewart)

First choice Grace Kelly turned down the lead because she was marrying Prince Rainier of Monaco. She later said that she was upset that she never got to play the part. Jimmy Stewart turned it down because he only wanted to do the film with Grace Kelly opposite him. He, too, claimed later that he was unhappy he was not in the movie.[42]

Desire Me (1947)
Richard Hart as Jean Renaud (Robert Montgomery)

MGM assigned the role of Jean Renaud to Robert Montgomery. He started shooting the film, but problems arose and he was replaced by Richard Hart.[43]

Desperately Seeking Susan (1985)
Rosanna Arquette as Roberta Glass (Cher, Goldie Hawn, Diane Keaton)
Madonna as Susan (Ellen Barkin, Rebecca De Mornay, Melanie Griffith, Jennifer Jason Leigh, Kelly McGillis)
Aidan Quinn as Dez (Bruce Willis)

Warner Bros. Pictures was the first studio to handle *Desperately Seeking Susan*. Executives wanted to make the film with an established star in the lead. They considered Cher, Goldie Hawn, and Diane Keaton. Producers of the film, Sarah Pillsbury and Midge Sanford, eventually left Warner Bros. and went to Orion Pictures. Director Susan Seidelman said that Orion agreed to do the film with Rosanna Arquette already cast in the lead role of housewife Roberta Glass.[44] Melanie Griffith, Ellen Barkin, Jennifer Jason Leigh and Kelly McGillis were all tested for the part of Susan.[45] Rebecca De Mornay auditioned, but lost out to Madonna.[46]

An unknown Bruce Willis went up for the male lead in *Desperately Seeking Susan*. In order to look the part, Willis cut his hair and got fake tattoos put on. He made a screen test, but lost the part to the more established actor, Aidan Quinn.[47]

Destry Rides Again (1939)
Marlene Dietrich as Frenchy (Paulette Goddard, Hedy Lamarr)

Producer Joe Pasternak wanted Marlene Dietrich for the part of Frenchy. Universal Pictures didn't want Dietrich. They claimed that she was box office poison. They suggested he cast either Hedy Lamarr or Paulette Goddard. Pasternak refused and gave the part to Dietrich.[48]

The Detective (1968)
Jacqueline Bisset as Norma MacIver (Mia Farrow)

Frank Sinatra was cast in the starring role of Detective Joe Leland in *The Detective*. He wanted his wife Mia Farrow to play the part of Norma MacIver. Sinatra wanted filming to begin in November. The start date wouldn't work for Farrow; she was busy at work in the starring role of Rosemary Woodhouse in *Rosemary's Baby*. She would not be done with that film in time to start shooting *The Detective* until January. Sinatra wanted Farrow to quit *Rosemary's Baby*, which was already in production. He threatened to divorce her if she didn't. Farrow told producer Robert Evans that she had no choice but to quit. Evans took Farrow into a screening room and showed her some of the film. He told Farrow that he thought she was so good in the film that she would be nominated for an Academy Award. Farrow decided to stay with the film. Sinatra served her with divorce papers on the set of *Rosemary's Baby*.[49] Although *Rosemary's Baby* was a smash hit Farrow was not nominated for an Academy Award.

Detective Story (1951)
Kirk Douglas as Detective James "Jim" McLeod (Charlton Heston, Alan Ladd)

Alan Ladd had a surprise one day while reading the *Hollywood Reporter*. There was a headline saying that Paramount had purchased the film rights for *Detective Story*, and that Ladd would be playing the starring role. He asked a studio executive if the headline was true. Ladd was told that a deal would be made in the next few days. The part of detective James "Jim" McLeod was a part that appealed to Ladd. Paramount's deal for the film was set the following week, although nothing was mentioned about Ladd's participation. Ladd was eventually passed over for the part.[50]

Charlton Heston made a screen-test. Heston found out that director William Wyler had rejected him in favor of the more established Kirk Douglas by listening to gossip columnist Louella Parsons' radio show. In his autobiography, *In the Arena*, a gracious Heston admits that Douglas was better in the part than he would have been.[51]

The Devil to Pay! (1930)
Loretta Young as Dorothy Hope (Constance Cummings)

After two weeks of shooting Constance Cummings was fired and replaced by Loretta Young.[52]

The Devils (1971)
Vanessa Redgrave as Sister Jeanne (Glenda Jackson)

Glenda Jackson turned down the role of Sister Jeanne. It went to Vanessa Redgrave instead.[53]

The Devil's Disciple (1959)
Kirk Douglas as Richard "Dick" Dudgeon (Montgomery Clift)

The part of Dick Dudgeon was originally meant for Montgomery Clift. Burt Lancaster was raising the money to get the film produced. He made a deal with Kirk Douglas' company, Byrna Production Company. Part of the deal was that Douglas play Dick Dudgeon.[54]

The Devil's Holiday (1930)
Nancy Carroll as Hallie Hobart (Jeanne Eagels)

Jeanne Eagels was set to play the starring role of Hallie Hobart in *The Devil's Holiday*. When Eagels died of a drug overdose she was replaced in the role by Nancy Carroll.[55]

The Devil's Own (1997)
Harrison Ford as Tom O'Meara (Sean Connery, Gene Hackman)

Both Sean Connery and Gene Hackman were considered for the part of Tom O'Meara, but were eventually deemed too old for the part. Brad Pitt was already signed for the film and suggested Harrison Ford to play opposite him.[56] Ford was offered the part, and he accepted. De-

Jeanne Eagels died of a drug overdose after being cast in *The Devil's Holiday*.

spite the two strong leading men, *The Devil's Own* was not a major hit.

Diamond Head (1962)

Charlton Heston as Richard "King" Howland (Clark Gable)

The role of Richard "King" Howland had originally been planned for Clark Gable. Gable died shortly after the project was green lighted. The role was then revamped for Charlton Heston to play.[57]

Diamonds Are Forever (1971)

Sean Connery as James Bond (John Gavin, Burt Reynolds)
Lana Wood as Plenty O'Toole (Jill St. John)

Burt Reynolds was mentioned as a possible James Bond. John Gavin was set for the part. He lost the role when Sean Connery was made a generous offer to reprise the role he created.[58]

Jill St. John was first brought in for the part of Plenty O'Toole. Director Guy Hamilton thought her acting was too good for that part. He gave her the leading role of Tiffany Case instead.[59]

The Diary of Anne Frank (1959)

Millie Perkins as Anne Frank (Audrey Hepburn)

Audrey Hepburn was the first choice to play Anne Frank. She turned it down, feeling she was not right for the role.[60]

Dick Tracy (1990)

Warren Beatty as Dick Tracy (Harrison Ford)
Madonna as Breathless Mahoney (Kim Basinger, Melanie Griffith, Michelle Pfeiffer, Sharon Stone, Kathleen Turner)
Glenne Headly as Tess Trueheart (Sean Young)

Harrison Ford was made an offer to play Dick Tracy, which he rejected.[61] Warren Beatty stepped in as both star and director. Michelle Pfeiffer, Kim Basinger, and Kathleen Turner were all too expensive to cast as Breathless Mahoney.[62] Sharon Stone auditioned, but was turned down.[63] Production designer Richard Sylbert suggested two actresses to Beatty: Melanie Griffith and Madonna. It was Madonna herself who first initiated contact with Warren Beatty. She wanted the part of Breathless Mahoney, and called up Beatty to discuss it.[64] After about a year he finally decided to give her the part. He must have liked her forwardness. The two became an item during the making of the film.

Sean Young was set to play Tess Trueheart. Young publicly accused Beatty of sexually harassing her. She was replaced by Glenne Headly.[65]

Die Hard (1988)

Bruce Willis as John McLean (Clint Eastwood, Richard Gere)

Richard Gere was the first choice to play the lead role of John McLean in *Die Hard*. Gere turned it down, saying he had no interest in the project. Producer Joel Silver wanted Gere so much that he added another million dollars to the actor's proposed salary in order to get him to sign on. Gere resisted and Silver turned to Clint Eastwood who also turned him down. Bruce Willis was suggested. At the time, Willis was best known for his starring role in the TV series, *Moonlighting*. Because of the series, Silver saw Willis as a comedian, and thought he wouldn't be right for the lead of an action movie. He did, however, agree to meet with Willis. The two hit it off, and Willis won an audition.[66] He was later given the role, and the film was a huge success. Willis' career was completely changed by the film. He went on to make two sequels to *Die Hard*, and is now known as one of the most successful action movie stars.

Dinner at Eight (1933)
Edmund Love as Wayne Talbot (Clark Gable)

Clark Gable was considered for the film *Dinner at Eight*. However the only role that Gable was right for was a supporting one. Louis B. Mayer thought that Gable (by then a big star) would be wasted in the part. Edmund Love was cast instead.[67]

Dirty Dancing (1987)
Miranda Garrison as Vivian Pressman (Kelly Bishop)

Kelly Bishop got the part of Jennifer Grey's mother by being in the right place at the right time. The actress originally cast in the role was complaining that she didn't feel well. Even after a doctor found nothing wrong with her she still persisted. By lunchtime she went home and needed to be replaced immediately. They were ready to do her scene that day. Kelly Bishop, originally cast in the smaller role of Vivian, arrived on the set for a wardrobe fitting. When the producers saw her they realized she could do it. She was upgraded to the mother role on the spot.[68]

The Dirty Dozen (1967)
Lee Marvin as John Reisman (John Wayne)
Telly Savalas as Archer Maggott (Jack Palance)

John Wayne turned down the starring role of Major John Reisman in order to direct and star in *The Green Berets*.[69]

Jack Palance rejected part of Archer Maggott. The role was eventually played by Telly Savalas.[70]

Dirty Harry (1971)
Clint Eastwood as Harry Callahan (Burt Lancaster, Walter Matthau, Steve McQueen, Robert Mitchum, Paul Newman, Frank Sinatra, John Wayne)

John Wayne was the first actor offered the role of Harry Callahan. After he turned it down, it was then offered to Frank Sinatra. Like Wayne, he rejected the role[71] as did Steve McQueen,[72] Walter Matthau,[73] Paul Newman[74] and Robert Mitchum. Mitchum called the film a piece of junk.[75] Burt Lancaster was considered, but the part went to Clint Eastwood.[76]

Dirty Rotten Scoundrels (1988)
Steve Martin as Freddy Benson (Tom Cruise)

In the very early stages of production, Tom Cruise was the leading contender for the role of Freddy Benson in *Dirty Rotten Scoundrels*, with Michael Caine playing opposite him. Financing for the film fell through, and the project was put on hold for a few years. When the film was finally ready to be made, Tom Cruise was a major star and very expensive. The part went instead to Steve Martin, with Michael Caine, who was still available, playing opposite him.[77]

Dirty Work (1998)
Adam Sandler as Satan (Howard Stern)

Before Adam Sandler was cast, Howard Stern was considered for the role of Satan.

Disclosure (1994)
Demi Moore as Meredith Johnson (Annette Bening)
Allan Rich as Ben Heller (Don Simpson)

Kelly Bishop was in the right place at the right time on the set of *Dirty Dancing*.

Annette Bening's pregnancy prevented her from playing the role of Meredith Johnson.[78]

Director Barry Levinson was very interested in casting producer Don Simpson as Moore's lawyer, but instead went with Allan Rich.[79]

Do the Right Thing (1989)

Danny Aiello as Sal (Robert De Niro, Joe Mantegna, Joe Pesci)
Giancarlo Esposito as Buggin' Out (Kadeem Hardison)
Bill Nunn as Radio Raheem (Laurence Fishburne)
John Turturro as Pino (Matt Dillon, James Russo)
Paul Benjamin as ML (Bill Cobb, James Earl Jones, Joe Seneca)
Samuel L. Jackson as Mister Senor Love Daddy (Bill Nunn)

Robert De Niro was writer/director Spike Lee's first choice to play Sal. However, De Niro felt that he had already played characters which were very similar to this one. For that reason he turned Lee down. Lee considered Joe Pesci and Joe Mantegna, but finally gave the part to Danny Aiello.

Kadeem Hardison was considered for Buggin' Out. Instead Lee gave the part to his *School Daze* co-star Giancarlo Esposito.

Spike Lee offered another *School Daze* alum a part in the film—Laurence Fishburne. He wanted Fishburne to play Radio Raheem. Fishburne wanted to play leading roles, and turned this supporting part down.

Matt Dillon was asked to play Sal's son Pino. In Lee's journal he said that Dillon was jerking him around, and he went on to consider James Russo. Lee eventually chose John Turturro instead.

Joe Seneca rejected the role of ML. Lee contemplated James Earl Jones and Bill Cobb before deciding to cast Paul Benjamin.

Lee thought of Bill Nunn when casting the part of Mister Senor Love Daddy. He instead gave Nunn the part of Radio Raheem, and cast Samuel L. Jackson instead.[80]

Do You Love Me (1946)

Maureen O'Hara as Katherine Hilliard (Betty Grable)

Betty Grable turned down *Kitten on the Keys* which was later renamed *Do You Love Me*.[81]

Dr. Jekyll and Mr. Hyde (1941)

Spencer Tracy as Dr. Henry Jekyll/Mr. Hyde (Robert Donat)
Ingrid Bergman as Ivy Peterson (Katharine Hepburn, Lana Turner)
Lana Turner as Beatrix Emery (Ingrid Bergman, Katharine Hepburn)

Robert Donat was an early consideration for the dual title role, but MGM eventually chose Spencer Tracy instead.

Spencer Tracy suggested to the studio that Katharine Hepburn should play both of the female leads, but they didn't go for it. Instead, they cast Lana Turner and Ingrid Bergman. Bergman was the ingénue and Turner was cast as the bad girl. Ingrid Bergman begged for them to switch roles, in order to play against type.[102]

Dr. No (1962)

Sean Connery as James Bond (Richard Burton, Peter Finch, Cary Grant, Trevor Howard, Richard Johnson, James Mason, Patrick McGoohan, Roger Moore, David Niven, Michael Redgrave, Bob Simmons, James Stewart)
Joseph Wiseman as Dr. No (Noel Coward)

Patrick McGoohan turned down the chance to play James Bond because he didn't like the way the character was written. After James Stewart, future Bond Roger Moore, Richard Burton, David Niven, Michael Redgrave, Peter Finch, Cary Grant, Trevor Howard, Richard Johnson, and Bob Simmons were all considered, Sean Connery assumed the role.[103]

Bond creator Ian Fleming wanted his friend Noel Coward to play the title role of Dr. No. Coward responded by saying "No! No! No!"[104] Joseph Wiseman was cast instead.

Dr. Seuss' The Cat in the Hat (2003)

Mike Myers as The Cat (Tim Allen)

Tim Allen was originally cast as the Cat. Allen dropped out to make *The Santa Clause 2*. Mike Myers was brought in as a replacement.[105]

Dr. Strangelove or: How I Learned to Stop Worrying and Love the Bomb (1964)

George C. Scott as General "Buck" Turgidson (Peter Sellers)
Slim Pickens as Major T.J. "King" Kong (Peter Sellers)

Peter Sellers was supposed to have played the role of Major Kong in *Dr. Strangelove*. He suffered a broken ankle and was unable to continue in the physically demanding role.[106] Director Stanley Kubrick hired Slim Pickens as a replacement. Sellers was also offered the part of General "Buck" Turgidson. He said no and George C. Scott was cast instead.[107]

Doctor Zhivago (1965)

Omar Sharif as Yuri Zhivago (Paul Newman, Peter O'Toole)
Julie Christie as Lara (Jane Fonda, Sophia Loren, Sarah Miles, Yvette Mimieux, Jeanne Moreau)
Geraldine Chaplin as Tonya (Audrey Hepburn)
Rod Steiger as Victor Komarovsky (Marlon Brando, James Mason)
Tom Courtenay as Pasha Antipova/Strelnikov (Omar Sharif)

MGM wanted Paul Newman to play the title role of Zhivago. Director David Lean disagreed with their choice. He couldn't see Newman as a dreamer. Lean also considered Peter O'Toole. Omar Sharif was originally set for the part of Strelnikov. When O'Toole fell through Lean moved Sharif over to the starring role. Tom Courtenay was cast as Strelnikov.

Carlo Ponti owned the rights to the film. He wanted his wife, Sophia Loren, to play Lara. Lean said that he didn't think that the 30-year-old Loren would be believable as a 17-year-old virgin. Loren was out of the running. Lean thought Jeanne Moreau might be right for the part. But screenwriter Robert Bolt didn't like this choice. Robert Weitman from MGM suggested Yvette Mimieux. Lean liked Jane Fonda. However he thought her American accent would be a problem. He considered dubbing her lines. Lean also mentioned Sarah Miles to Bolt. Bolt dismissed her as a north country slut. Lean told Bolt he was wrong, but Miles did not win the part. Lean saw the film *Billy Liar* starring Julie Christie. He was very interested in the actress. He asked director John Ford what he thought of her work. Ford was working with her at the time on the film *Young Cassidy*. Ford told Lean that Christie was the best young actress to ever work in films.

David Lean offered the role to Jane Fonda. She rejected it because she did not want to be apart from Roger Vadim, her then boyfriend. It would take about nine months of filming on location in Spain, and she worried that the relationship would not survive the separation. After a while she changed her mind and decided she wanted to be in the film. It was too late. Lean signed Julie Christie to play Lara. Fonda later admitted she was very unhappy to not have been a part of the film.

Lean wanted Audrey Hepburn to play Tonya, but Carlo Ponti wanted Geraldine Chaplin to be tested. Lean brought Chaplin in. He was so impressed with her audition that he nixed the idea of Hepburn and gave Chaplin the part.

Marlon Brando was the first choice to play Victor Komrovsky. Lean wrote to Brando, but Brando never answered. James Mason was next on the list. Mason wanted to do it, but was eventually replaced by Rod Steiger.[82]

Dodsworth (1936)

Mary Astor as Edith Cortwright (Dolores Costello, Rosalind Russell, Nan Sunderland)

Dodsworth was a Broadway play starring Nan Sunderland as Edith. When she learned that a film version was planned, Sunderland wanted the part. Producer Samuel Goldwyn didn't want Sunderland. He wanted either Rosalind Russell or Dolores Costello. Director William Wyler liked the idea of Costello but not Russell. He didn't think that Russell's personality was prominent enough for the part. Goldwyn eventually discarded both choices in favor of Mary Astor.[83]

Dogma (1999)

Linda Fiorentino as Bethany Sloane (Holly Hunter, Emma Thompson)

Both Emma Thompson and Holly Hunter were considered for the part of Bethany.[84] Director Kevin Smith eventually gave the part to Linda Fiorentino.

La Dolce Vita (1960)

Anouk Aimee as Maddalena (Gina Lollobrigida, Silvana Magnano)
Alain Cuny as Steiner (Henry Fonda)

74 Don Juan

Nan Sunderland starred in *Dodsworth* on Broadway.

Nepotism did not help Dolores Costello win a part in *Don Juan*.

Annibale Ninchi as Marcello's father (Maurice Chevalier)

Director Federico Fellini unsuccessfully pursued Henry Fonda,[85] Maurice Chevalier,[86] Silvana Magnano,[87] and Gina Lollobrigida for roles. Lollobrigida never even knew she had been offered the part! Her manager (and former husband) read the script, disliked it, and rejected it without ever telling her about it. The rejection caused Fellini to be quite upset with Lollobrigida for many years. When she found out about it, she was so embarrassed that she promised to appear as an extra in any of his movies. Fellini forgave her, and did not hold her to her offer.[88]

Don Juan (1926)

Mary Astor as Adriana della Varnese (Dolores Costello)

John Barrymore, the star of the film *Don Juan*, wanted his wife (Dolores Costello) cast in the role of Adriana della Varnese. Warner Bros. had other ideas, and gave the part to Mary Astor instead.[89]

Donnie Brasco (1997)

Johnny Depp as Joe Pistone (John Travolta)

John Travolta was considered for the part of Joe Pistone.[90]

Double Indemnity (1944)

Fred MacMurray as Walter Neff (Alan Ladd, George Raft)
Jean Heather as Lola Dietrichson (Yvonne De Carlo)

The first choice for Fred MacMurray's role of Walter Neff was Alan Ladd. He turned it down and director Billy Wilder then offered it to George Raft.[91] As Wilder explained the story to Raft, it became clear to him that Raft didn't get the movie's concept.[92]

Wilder screen tested Yvonne De Carlo for the part of Lola Dietrichson.[93] He decided to go with another actress instead — Jean Heather.

Double Jeopardy (1999)

Ashley Judd as Elizabeth Parsons (Jodie Foster, Michelle Pfeiffer, Meg Ryan)
Bruce Greenwood as Nick Parsons (Greg Kinnear)

Producer Leonard Goldberg wanted Ashley Judd to play the starring role of Elizabeth Parsons. Judd wanted the part, but the studio executives wanted a more popular actress. Goldberg gave the part to Jodie Foster. A few months before shooting was set to begin Foster quit. She was pregnant. Goldberg was still interested in Judd, but the studio made offers to Meg Ryan and Michelle Pfeiffer. Neither actress wanted the part and Goldberg went to bat for Ashley Judd. The studio agreed to cast her on the condition that a star was cast as the male lead. Goldberg gave the part of Travis Lehman to Oscar winner Tommy Lee Jones.[94]

Greg Kinnear was considered for the part of Nick Parsons, eventually played by Bruce Greenwood.[95]

A Double Life (1947)

Ronald Colman as Anthony John (Laurence Olivier)
Shelley Winters as Pat Kroll (Yvonne De Carlo, Lana Turner)

Laurence Olivier was offered the starring role in *A Double Life* but was unable to take the job.[96] The part went to Ronald Colman instead.

Yvonne De Carlo approached studio executive Nate Blumberg about the possibility of her taking on the role of waitress Pat Kroll. Blumberg told De Carlo that she was too big a star to take on this small role.[97] Lana Turner screen-tested for the part, but instead it was given to Shelley Winters, and it made her a star.[98]

Down and Out in Beverly Hills (1986)

Nick Nolte as Jerry Baskin (Warren Beatty, Richard Dreyfuss, Jack Nicholson)
Richard Dreyfuss as David "Dave" Whiteman (Paul Mazursky)

Director Paul Mazursky's first choice for the part of homeless man Jerry Baskin was Jack Nicholson. Nicholson told Mazursky that he was interested, but only if Mazursky played Dave Whiteman opposite him. Mazursky is primarily a director, but has plenty of acting experience. He told Nicholson that both starring and directing would be too much for him. Nicholson then told Mazursky that if he did it, he would not be available for about a year because he was committed to make *The Two Jakes*. Mazursky couldn't wait that long and decided to move on.

Mazursky arranged a meeting with Richard Dreyfuss. Dreyfuss said that he would be interested in playing either Jerry or Dave. He asked Mazursky who he saw him as. Mazursky cast him as Dave.

Mazursky discussed the part of Jerry with Warren Beatty. Beatty told Mazursky that he knew that his friend, Jack Nicholson, had already been offered the part. Beatty had a problem with being the second choice. He told Mazursky that he would call him with a decision. He never called. Mazursky decided to move on. He met with Nick Nolte. Nolte liked the part and agreed to star.[99]

Down Argentine Way (1940)

Betty Grable as Glenda Crawford (Alice Faye)
Leonid Kinskey as Tito Acuna (Cesar Romero)

The casting of *Down Argentine Way* was greatly impacted by health problems. Alice Faye was supposed to play Glenda Crawford. Soon before production was to begin she had to have an emergency appendectomy which would require about six weeks of recovery. The studio decided to replace her with Betty Grable. Surprisingly, Grable did not want the part. Grable humbly told studio chief Darryl F. Zanuck that Alice Faye was a major star, and that she would not be able to do the part as well as Faye would have. Grable sympathized with Faye, because Grable had previously lost a part in a film due to a bout with appendicitis. Zanuck confided to Grable that Faye did not really have appendicitis; her real illness was hemorrhoids. She required surgery, and the recovery time was longer than he could wait. Grable realized that there was no way Faye would keep the part, and so she signed on.

Cesar Romero was cast as Tito Acuna but fell ill. He was replaced with Leonid Kinskey.[100]

Down to You (2000)

Henry Winkler as Ray Connelly (Gene Wilder)

Miramax was interested in having Gene Wilder play chef Ray Connelly. However, Wilder did not sign on for the film.[101] Henry Winkler was given the part instead.

Dracula (1931)

Bela Lugosi as Count Dracula (Lon Chaney)
David Manners as Jonathan Harker (Lew Ayres)

Lon Chaney was set to play Dracula. When he died, Bela Lugosi was brought in to play the role he became famous for.

Lew Ayres was cast as Jonathan Harker. He left the film and was replaced by David Manners.[108]

Dragnet (1987)
Tom Hanks as Pep Streebek (John Candy)

The part of Pep Streebek was originally intended for John Candy. Candy eventually decided against doing the film, and he was replaced by Tom Hanks.[109]

Dragon: The Bruce Lee Story (1993)
Jason Scott Lee as Bruce Lee (Brandon Lee)

Brandon Lee was offered the chance to play his father in *Dragon: The Bruce Lee Story*. He wanted a career based on his own merit, and therefore turned the part down.[110]

Dragonheart (1996)
Dennis Quaid as Bowen (Harrison Ford, Mel Gibson, Patrick Swayze)

Director Rob Cohen's first choice for the starring role of dragon slayer Bowen was Patrick Swayze. The executives at Universal wanted as big a star as possible. They mentioned Harrison Ford and Mel Gibson.[111] After numerous rejections, Cohen thought of Dennis Quaid. Quaid was made an offer, which he accepted.

Dressed to Kill (1980)
Michael Caine as Robert Elliott (Sean Connery)
Angie Dickinson as Kate Miller (Liv Ullman)
Keith Gordon as Peter Miller (Cameron De Palma, Matt Dillon)
Dennis Franz as Detective Marino (Paul Mazursky)

Sean Connery was a contender for the part of Dr. Robert Elliott. The actor was already set for another film and was unable to play the part. Michael Caine was cast instead.

Director Brian De Palma asked Liv Ullman to play Kate Miller. Ullman found the film to be very violent and said no. De Palma thought that Angie Dickinson had the look he wanted and gave her the part.

Keith Gordon beat out Matt Dillon and Cameron De Palma (director Brian De Palma's nephew) for his role.

Paul Mazursky was unable to play Detective Marino because he was busy with a film of his own.[112]

Drive, He Said (1971)
Michael Margotta as Gabriel (Richard Dreyfuss, Jack Nicholson)

Jack Nicholson was hired to direct *Drive, He Said*. He considered playing the part of student radical Gabriel, but eventually decided against it. Richard Dreyfuss made a screen test for the role, which impressed executive producer Bert Schneider. He was ready to give Dreyfuss the part. Nicholson disagreed and cast Michael Margotta instead.[113]

The Driver (1978)
Ryan O'Neal as The Driver (Steve McQueen)

Steve McQueen was offered the part of the Driver. He thought it was too similar to parts he had played before and turned it down. He was replaced by Ryan O'Neal.[114]

Driving Miss Daisy (1989)
Jessica Tandy as Daisy Werthan (Shirley MacLaine)

Producers Richard D. Zanuck and Lili Fini Zanuck wanted Shirley MacLaine to play the title role of elderly Miss Daisy. MacLaine felt she was too young for the part and said no. Jessica Tandy was given the role. Tandy was 24 years older than MacLaine.[115]

Drugstore Cowboy (1989)
Matt Dillon as Bob Hughes (Jack Nicholson, Mickey Rourke, Charlie Sheen)
Kelly Lynch as Dianne (Jamie Lee Curtis, Patti D'Arbanville, Mare Winningham)
Heather Graham as Nadine (Traci Lords)
Max Perlich as David (Rodney Harvey)

Writer/director Gus Van Sant's dream choice for the starring role of Bob Hughes was Jack Nicholson. However, Nicholson was not the right choice for various reasons. Nicholson was 51 at the time, which was much older than the character was supposed to be. If he were even available, there was no way that Avenue Pictures Productions could afford to pay him the kind of salary he was accustomed to receiving. Mickey Rourke and Charlie Sheen were considered, but Van Sant decided Matt Dillon was the best choice.

To play Bob Hughes' wife Dianne, Van Sant

considered Jamie Lee Curtis, Patti D'Arbanville, and Mare Winningham. Like Nicholson, Curtis was too expensive for the film's budget. Gus Van Sant decided to cast former model Kelly Lynch.

Heather Graham beat out former porn star Traci Lords for the role of Nadine.

Kelly Lynch's agent Allan Mindel suggested his client, Rodney Harvey, for the part of David. Van Sant liked the actor and gave him the part. During preproduction Mindel called Van Sant to tell him that Harvey had a drug problem, which was now out of control, and that he was removing him from the film. Van Sant quickly replaced him with Max Perlich.[116] Sadly, Harvey never overcame his addiction. He was found dead of a drug overdose in April of 1998 at the age of 30.

The Duchess and the Dirtwater Fox (1976)

Goldie Hawn as Amanda Quaid (Glenda Jackson)

Initially, writer/director Mel Frank wanted Glenda Jackson for the part of Amanda Quaid. Jackson was made an offer, but turned it down. Goldie Hawn was cast instead.[117]

Duel in the Sun (1946)

Gregory Peck as Lewton "Lewt" McCanles (John Wayne)
Jennifer Jones as Pearl Chavez (Veronica Lake, Hedy Lamarr, Teresa Wright)

Niven Busch sold the film rights to his novel, *Duel in the Sun*, to RKO. Busch was set to produce with John Wayne as the star. For the part of Pearl he thought of Hedy Lamarr, Veronica Lake and his wife, Teresa Wright. Lamarr was pregnant and therefore unavailable. Lake would have to dye her trademark blonde hair black. Wright thought that the part was beyond her. Busch soon learned that David O. Selznick was willing to loan out Jennifer Jones. However, Selznick thought that Wayne was wrong for the movie. He also wanted to make changes in the script. Selznick eventually got his way. RKO sold the rights to Selznick's company, Vanguard Pictures. Selznick changed the script and replaced Wayne with Gregory Peck. Jennifer Jones was cast as Pearl.[118]

Duets (2000)

Scott Speedman as Billy Hannon (Brad Pitt)

In June of 1997 director Bruce Paltrow intended to star his daughter Gwyneth Paltrow and her fiancé Brad Pitt in his upcoming film, *Duets*. The pair met when they played a married couple in the 1995 film, *Seven*, and began dating soon after. The two were engaged by December of 1996. *Duets* was planned to start production on September 15, 1997.[119] However, within weeks of agreeing to make the film together, Paltrow and Pitt broke up. Paltrow said publicly that the reason for the split was because neither one felt that they could pursue their careers with enough time to devote to making a marriage work. With their romance over, Bruce Paltrow re-cast Pitt's role with *Felicity* star Scott Speedman.

Dumb and Dumber (1994)

Jeff Daniels as Harry Dunne (Rob Lowe)

Rob Lowe passed up the chance to work opposite Jim Carrey in *Dumb and Dumber*.[120]

Dune (1984)

Dean Stockwell as Wellington Yueh (John Hurt)

John Hurt was pursued to play Dr. Wellington Yueh. Hurt and director David Lynch worked together previously on *The Elephant Man*. Hurt was unavailable, and Dean Stockwell got the job.[121]

E.T. the Extra-Terrestrial (1982)

Dee Wallace as Mary (Shelley Long)

Director Steven Spielberg wanted Shelley Long to play the part of Mary in *E.T. the Extra-Terrestrial*. At the same time Long was offered another job, the part of Tala in *Caveman*. *E.T.* was one of the biggest hits of all time, and has become a modern classic. *Caveman* on the other hand, was a flop at the box office. Spielberg gave the part of Mary to Dee Wallace.[1]

East of Eden (1955)

James Dean as Cal Trask (Marlon Brando, Montgomery Clift, Paul Newman, Anthony Perkins)
Richard Davalos as Aron Trask (Paul Newman)

Anthony Perkins auditioned for the part of Cal Trask.[2] Director Elia Kazan's first choice for the role was Marlon Brando.[3] Montgomery Clift was also considered, as was Paul Newman. Once Clift turned the part down[4] Paul Newman made a screen test alongside James Dean. Dean won the role and Newman tested for the role of the older brother Aron as well, but lost out to Richard Davalos.[5]

East Side, West Side (1949)
Barbara Stanwyck as Jessie Brown (Ava Gardner, Greer Garson)

Greer Garson was MGM's first choice to star as Jessie Brown.[6] Ava Gardner was cast in the role, until it was decided that Barbara Stanwyck would replace her. At the time Stanwyck was the bigger star, and Gardner was reassigned to the smaller role. Gardner didn't mind. She felt the smaller role was the better of the two.[7]

Easter Parade (1948)
Fred Astaire as Don Hewes (Gene Kelly)
Ann Miller as Nadine Hale (Cyd Charisse)

Judy Garland was set to star in *Easter Parade*. She and Gene Kelly had recently had a big hit with their film *The Pirate*, so Kelly was given the part of Hewes. The week that shooting was to begin Kelly hosted a volleyball game in his backyard. Kelly was very serious about playing, so much so that the game became tense. Other players such as Farley Granger, Arthur Laurents, and Kelly's wife Betsy Blair broke out in laughter. Knowing that Kelly was getting upset, they tried to suppress their laughter. The knowledge that they shouldn't laugh made it even harder to stop until finally the game came to an abrupt end when Kelly was hit by a ball. He accused the others of playing badly on purpose. He was so enraged that he was screaming at his guests, even cursing at them. He marched off to his house and opened the kitchen door. He yelled at the group and pounded his foot down so hard that his ankle was broken. The hobbled Kelly was replaced by Fred Astaire.[8]

Cyd Charisse was set for the part of Nadine Hale. Ironically, she also hurt her leg (in a non-volleyball–related accident) and had to be replaced by Ann Miller.[9]

Easy Rider (1969)
Jack Nicholson as George Hanson (Bruce Dern, Rip Torn)

Bruce Dern was the original choice for the role of George Hanson. Dern asked for too much money, and Rip Torn was hired instead.[10] It is not exactly clear why Torn left the production. He and director/costar Dennis Hopper had a fight during dinner one night. Costar Peter Fonda said he remembered both of them fighting with butter knives.[11]

Ed (1996)
Matt LeBlanc as Jack "Coop" Cooper (Matthew Perry)

Friends costars Matthew Perry and Matt LeBlanc competed for the lead role in *Ed*, with LeBlanc eventually winning the part.[12]

Educating Rita (1983)
Julie Walters as Rita (Dolly Parton)

Director Lewis Gilbert chose Julie Walters over Columbia Pictures' choice of Dolly Parton for the starring role in *Educating Rita*.[13]

Edward Scissorhands (1990)
Johnny Depp as Edward Scissorhands (Tom Cruise)

Director Tim Burton met with Tom Cruise to discuss the part of Edward Scissorhands. Cruise had a lot of questions for the director. Burton didn't think that Cruise was exactly right for the part. He was glad that Cruise didn't do the film. Burton got the actor he really wanted all along—Johnny Depp.[14]

The Egyptian (1954)
Edmund Purdom as Sinhue (Marlon Brando)
Gene Tierney as Baketamon (Marilyn Monroe)

Marlon Brando was cast in the lead role and all was set. After one rehearsal, Brando left for New York. A letter from his psychiatrist arrived at 20th Century–Fox stating that Brando was too sick to appear in *The Egyptian*.[15] He was sued by the studio and ended up paying $75,000 for delaying production. Another part of his settlement was to appear in the movie *Desiree*.[16] Marilyn Monroe, on the other hand, wanted very much to be in *The Egyptian*. She even offered to make a screen test, but Darryl F. Zanuck cast Gene Tierney instead.[17]

The Eiger Sanction (1975)
Clint Eastwood as Jonathan Hemlock (Paul Newman)

Paul Newman was originally supposed to star in *The Eiger Sanction*. He thought the film was too violent and said no. Clint Eastwood replaced him.[18]

Eight Men Out (1988)
John Sayles as Ring Lardner (Sam Waterston)

Writer/director John Sayles initially thought of Sam Waterston as Ring Lardner. Sayles was going to play one of the baseball players. However, by the time Sayles was ready to go into production it was some years later. He was in his late thirties then; the right age to play Lardner himself.[19] Sam Waterston did not appear in the film.

El Cid (1961)
Herbert Lom as Ben Yussef (Orson Welles)

Orson Welles was offered the chance to play Ben Yussef in *El Cid*. Yussef's face is hidden until the last scene of the film. Welles wanted to do the part, but had the idea to do it as a voice-over, with another actor's face on the screen. Producer Samuel Bronston didn't like the idea at all, and gave the part to Herbert Lom instead.[87]

The Electric Horseman (1979)
Jane Fonda as Alice "Hallie" Martin (Diane Keaton)

Diane Keaton rejected the role of Hallie Martin.[20]

Elephant Walk (1954)
Elizabeth Taylor as Ruth Wiley (Olivia De Havilland, Katharine Hepburn, Vivien Leigh, Jean Simmons)
Peter Finch as John Wiley (Marlon Brando, Clark Gable, Laurence Olivier, Claude Rains, Ralph Richardson)

The role of Ruth Wiley was originally to be played by Vivien Leigh. For her leading man, Leigh's husband Laurence Olivier was pursued. He had just done *The Beggar's Opera* and wanted to take a break. Clark Gable, Marlon Brando, Claude Rains and Ralph Richardson were all unattainable. Leigh saw Peter Finch in a play and was impressed by his performance. She went to him and said that she wanted him as her leading man. Paramount agreed to give him the part.[21]

Leigh was unable to finish the film, and director William Dieterle needed an actress to replace her.[22] Elizabeth Taylor was cast after Katharine Hepburn, Olivia De Havilland and Jean Simmons all refused the part.[23]

Elizabeth (1998)
Cate Blanchett as Elizabeth (Nicole Kidman, Gwyneth Paltrow, Winona Ryder, Emily Watson)

Both Nicole Kidman and Emily Watson turned down the chance to play Queen Elizabeth.[24] Director Shekhur Kapur chose Cate Blanchett over better known actresses such as Gwyneth Paltrow and Winona Ryder.[25] Coincidentally, at that year's Oscar ceremony Blanchett competed with Emily Watson and Gwyneth Paltrow for best actress. The Oscar went to Paltrow.

Endless Love (1981)
Brooke Shields as Jade (Sharon Stone)
Martin Hewitt as David (Tom Cruise, Timothy Hutton)

An unknown Sharon Stone was the producers' choice for the role of Jade until major star Brooke Shields entered the picture. Tom Cruise auditioned for the male lead as did Timothy Hutton. Hutton was considered too ordinary looking.[26] Cruise lost the lead, but still got into the movie, in a much smaller role.

Enemies: A Love Story (1989)
Ron Silver as Herman Broder (Richard Dreyfuss)

Director Paul Mazursky was interested in Richard Dreyfuss for the starring role of bigamist Herman. Mazursky and Dreyfuss worked together twice before with the films *Down and Out in Beverly Hills* and *Moon Over Parador*. Dreyfuss agreed to take the part. He told Mazursky that he wanted to come to dailies. Mazursky has a strict policy that he does not allow actors to watch the dailies. Dreyfuss tried to convince him to change his mind, to no avail. The next day Richard Dreyfuss dropped out of the film. Less than a week later Mazursky saw the Broadway play *Speed the Plow* to see Ron Silver. He thought that Silver would be perfect for Herman. He cast Silver the next day.[27]

An Enemy of the People (1977)
Charles Durning as Peter Stockman (Nicol Williamson)

Nicol Williamson was originally cast as Peter Stockman. Director George Schaefer said that Williamson was a nightmare. He failed to show up for the first day of rehearsals, and Schaefer

Nicol Williamson was cast in *An Enemy of the People* but never showed up for work.

later found out he had had a fight with his girlfriend, gotten drunk, and had gone to Hawaii. Steve McQueen (the executive producer and star of the film) and Schaefer immediately replaced him with the very reliable Charles Durning.[28] Williamson has a history of outrageous behavior. In 1991 he starred on Broadway in *I Hate Hamlet*. During a performance Williamson got so carried away that he stabbed his co-star Evan Handler in the derriere with a sword. Handler walked off in the middle of the performance and quit the production. *I Hate Hamlet* closed shortly after.

Enemy of the State (1998)

Will Smith as Robert Clayton Dean (Tom Cruise)

Will Smith won the part of Robert Clayton Dean after it was turned down by Tom Cruise.[29]

Enigma (2001)

Kate Winslet as Hester Wallace (Natasha Little)

Natasha Little was originally cast as Hester Wallace in *Enigma*. The film was being produced by Lorne Michaels and Mick Jagger. The two soon learned that Kate Winslet was pregnant. She was going to be able to make one film before having her baby. They decided to grab the available Winslet, and let Little go. Little was paid in full however. She moved on, and was cast in the play *The Novice* in London.[30]

Eraser (1996)

James Caan as Robert Deguerin (Jonathan Pryce)

Jonathan Pryce was offered the part of Deguerin, but chose to play Juan Peron in *Evita* instead.[31]

Escapade (1935)

Luise Rainer as Leopoldine Dur (Myrna Loy)

Myrna Loy was originally cast in the role of Leopoldine Dur. However Loy wanted more money than MGM was willing to pay, and she dropped out of the film. She was replaced in the role by Luise Rainer.[32]

Escape from the Planet of the Apes (1971)

William Windom as The President (Henry Fonda)

Producer Arthur Jacobs wanted Henry Fonda to play the president. Director Don Taylor disagreed with his choice. He felt that Fonda was too big a star for the role. Taylor got the actor of his choice — William Windom.[33]

Even Cowgirls Get the Blues (1993)

Uma Thurman as Sissy Hankshaw (Shelley Duvall)
Lorraine Bracco as Delores Del Ruby (Lily Tomlin)
Angie Dickinson as Miss Adrian (Faye Dunaway)
John Hurt as The Countess (Willem Dafoe, Daniel Day-Lewis, Peter O'Toole)

In 1977 producer Robert Wunsch optioned the screen right to Tom Robbins' novel, *Even Cowgirls Get the Blues*. His option eventually expired, at which point Warner Bros. acquired it. They planned it as a vehicle for Shelley Duvall. Two years later that plan was also scrapped. The project sat on a shelf for years until Gus Van Sant expressed interest in directing.

Lily Tomlin discussed the possibility of playing cowgirl Delores Del Ruby. Van Sant eventually went with Lorraine Bracco instead. Faye Dunaway was up for Miss Adrian, but lost out to Angie Dickinson.

For the part of the transsexual countess, Van

Sant considered Peter O'Toole, Daniel Day-Lewis, and Willem Dafoe before finally deciding on John Hurt.[34]

Ever After (1998)

Dougray Scott as Prince Charming (Jude Law, Jonny Lee Miller)

Both Jude Law and Jonny Lee Miller rejected the chance to play Prince Charming. The part was played by Dougray Scott.[35]

Everybody's All-American (1988)

Dennis Quaid as Gavin Grey (Kevin Costner)

Kevin Costner rejected the part of college football star Gavin Grey in *Everybody's All-American*.[36]

Eve's Bayou (1997)

Debbi Morgan as Mozelle Batiste Delacroix (Angela Bassett, Alfre Woodard)

Angela Bassett and Alfre Woodard both turned down the role of Aunt Mozelle due to previous commitments.[37]

Evita (1996)

Madonna as Eva "Evita" Duarte de Peron (Ann-Margret, Sarah Brightman, Mariah Carey, Cher, Glenn Close, Jennifer Lopez, Patti LuPone, Bette Midler, Liza Minnelli, Olivia Newton-John, Marie Osmond, Michelle Pfeiffer, Meryl Streep, Barbra Streisand)
Antonio Banderas as Che (Mandy Patinkin)
Jonathan Pryce as Juan Peron (Julio Iglesias)

Very early on Barbra Streisand and Liza Minnelli were mentioned as possibilities for the role of Eva Peron. Other candidates included Cher, Bette Midler, Olivia Newton-John, Ann-Margret, Marie Osmond, and Patti LuPone.[38] LuPone had originated the role on Broadway. Former contender Barbra Streisand thought that *Evita* composer Andrew Lloyd Webber's ex-wife Sarah Brightman was the right choice.[39] Glenn Close was interested in the part as was Mariah Carey.[40] Oliver Stone was set to direct. He considered Michelle Pfeiffer as Eva Peron.[41] Stone met with Meryl Streep and decided that she was the right choice. He contemplated having Mandy Patinkin reprise the role of Che Guevara, the part he originated on Broadway.[42] Stone had Robert Stigwood set to produce and Paula Abdul was hired to choreograph the film. Then Streep dropped out. She said in the press that she was exhausted from making *Postcards from the Edge*, but Stone felt the real issue was money. At that point Stone was fed up and left the film.[43] Alan Parker replaced him as director. Jennifer Lopez auditioned, but eventually Madonna won the role.[44]

When Oliver Stone was going to direct he wanted Julio Iglesias to play Juan Peron.[45] After Stone dropped out Alan Parker cast Broadway star Jonathan Pryce in the role.

Executive Suite (1954)

William Holden as McDonald Walling (Henry Fonda)

Henry Fonda was producer John Houseman's first choice for the role William Holden went on to play. Fonda was not able to appear in the film because he was committed to a Broadway musical at the time.[46] Incidentally, the musical was cancelled prior to opening.

The Exorcist (1973)

Ellen Burstyn as Chris MacNeil (Anne Bancroft, Carol Burnett, Jane Fonda, Audrey Hepburn, Shirley MacLaine)
Linda Blair as Regan MacNeil (Anissa Jones, Dana Plato)
Jack MacGowran as Burke Dennings (J. Lee Thompson)
Jason Miller as Father Damien Karras (Marlon Brando, Stacy Keach, Jack Nicholson, Al Pacino, Roy Scheider)
Lee J. Cobb as William Kinderman (Studs Terkel)

Director William Friedkin's first choice for the part of Chris MacNeil was Carol Burnett. He soon reconsidered. Friedkin worried that audiences might expect her to be her usual funny self in the movie. Friedkin then mentioned Ellen Burstyn. Warner Bros. was opposed to his choice. They said they would okay Jane Fonda, Audrey Hepburn, Shirley MacLaine or Anne Bancroft. Fonda called the film, "Rip-off capitalist bullshit." Bancroft was pregnant and didn't sign for the film. Friedkin was eventually able to convince Warner Bros. to agree to casting Ellen Burstyn.[47]

J. Lee Thompson was the model for the part of Burke Dennings. Thompson was going to play the part in the film, but just before shooting was to start he changed his mind.[48]

Marlon Brando[49] and Al Pacino[50] were considered to play Father Karras. Stacy Keach was cast, but ended up not making the film. Jack Nicholson and Roy Scheider were both interested in playing the part, but William Friedkin wanted an unknown actor instead. He gave the part to Jason Miller. It was Miller's first film.[51]

Anissa Jones, best known as Buffy on *Family Affair*, auditioned for the role of Regan. Jones was actually relieved when the part went to Linda Blair and not her. It was Jones' mother who wanted to get the film. Jones wanted to retire from show business. When she lost the part she was able to just that. Dana Plato auditioned and impressed Friedkin. She was offered the role, but her mother Kay didn't think it would be good for her daughter and turned it down. The film was so popular that a few years later a sequel was made called *Exorcist II: The Heretic* in which Plato was cast in a small role. Unfortunately it flopped. In an eerie coincidence, both actresses died at a young age of a drug overdose.

William Friedkin cast Lee J. Cobb as William Kinderman. Friedkin thought that audiences would be comfortable with Cobb. He later said that this decision was a mistake. He wanted to give the part to writer Studs Terkel. Friedkin thought that Terkel would have been more genuine in the part.[52]

Eye of the Devil (1966)

Deborah Kerr as Catherine de Montfaucon (Kim Novak)

Kim Novak was originally cast as Catherine in *Eye of the Devil*. Filming was just about done when Novak had an accident and was unable to complete the film. Deborah Kerr replaced her.[53]

The Eyes of Laura Mars (1978)

Faye Dunaway as Laura Mars (Barbra Streisand)

Barbra Streisand turned down the role of Laura Mars because she didn't like scary movies.[54]

Eyes Wide Shut (1999)

Tom Cruise as Dr. William Harford (Alec Baldwin)
Nicole Kidman as Alice Harford (Kim Basinger)
Sydney Pollack as Victor Ziegler (Harvey Keitel)
Marie Richardson as Marion Nathanson (Jennifer Jason Leigh)

Stanley Kubrick liked the idea of having a real-life married couple play the married couple in *Eyes Wide Shut*. His first idea was Alec Baldwin and Kim Basinger. Instead, he cast Tom Cruise and Nicole Kidman.[55]

Harvey Keitel was originally cast in *Eyes Wide Shut*. Kubrick delayed production for weeks. Keitel grew tired of waiting, and left the production to do another film. He was replaced by Sydney Pollack.[56]

Jennifer Jason Leigh was the original choice to play Marion. The movie was actually filmed with her in the role. When director Stanley Kubrick wanted to do a reshoot Leigh was busy making the film *eXistenZ*. Kubrick needed her for about 2 to 4 weeks, which for Leigh was impossible. Leigh loved the experience of working with Kubrick and was disappointed to not be able to finish up the film. However, she was unable to hold up the shooting of *eXistenZ*, and Kubrick reshot her scenes with Marie Richardson.[57]

The Fabulous Baker Boys (1989)

Michelle Pfeiffer as Susie Diamond (Madonna)

Madonna was offered the part of Susie. She disliked the script and said no.[1] Michelle Pfeiffer was eventually cast. She was nominated for an Academy Award for her performance.

Fahrenheit 451 (1967)

Oskar Werner as Guy Montag (Warren Beatty)

Warren Beatty was interested in *Fahrenheit 451*, and spoke to director Francois Truffaut about it. He told him it was not possible since Oskar Werner was already cast in the role.[2]

Family Plot (1976)

Karen Black as Fran (Cybill Shepherd)
Barbara Harris as Blanche Tyler (Liza Minnelli)
William Devane as Arthur Adamson (Roy Thinnes)
Cathleen Nesbitt as Julia Rainbird (Lillian Gish)

Universal Pictures suggested Liza Minnelli for the part of Blanche Tyler to director Alfred Hitchcock. Hitchcock thought she was the wrong type, and gave the part to Barbara Harris instead.[3]

Cybill Shepherd tried fort he role of Fran. Director Alfred Hitchcock turned her down and cast Karen Black instead.[4]

Hitchcock gave the part of Arthur Adamson to Roy Thinnes. He was unhappy with Thinnes' performance and fired him a month into shooting. William Devane was his replacement.[5]

Lillian Gish asked Hitchcock for the part of Julia Rainbird. Hitchcock wanted Cathleen Nesbit instead. He was forced to turn Gish down.[6]

The Fan (1996)

Robert De Niro as Gil Renard (Wesley Snipes)
Wesley Snipes as Bobby Rayburn (Brad Pitt, Denzel Washington)

Brad Pitt was offered the part of the baseball star Bobby Rayburn. Pitt wanted instead to play the fan. Denzel Washington was offered the Rayburn role after that. He was not interested and turned it down.[7] Next, Wesley Snipes was approached. Like Pitt, he too wanted to play the fan instead. Director Tony Scott wanted him for the ball player.[8] Snipes signed on as Rayburn and Robert De Niro was cast as Gil Renard, the fan.

Fanny (1961)

Leslie Caron as Fanny (Jane Fonda, Audrey Hepburn)

When director Josh Logan set out to cast the title role of Fanny, he thought of an actress he had recently worked with — Jane Fonda. Fonda made her film debut in Logan's *Tall Story*. Fonda was up for the part of Fanny, but was not cast.[9] Audrey Hepburn could have had the role but turned it down.[10] Logan finally gave the part to Leslie Caron.

A Farewell to Arms (1932)

Helen Hayes as Catherine Barkley (Eleanor Boardman, Claudette Colbert)
Gary Cooper as Lt. Frederick Henry (Fredric March)

Helen Hayes replaced both Claudette Colbert and Eleanor Boardman as Catherine Barkley. Actually, *A Farewell to Arms* was written for Claudette Colbert to star in with Fredric March. That fell through and Gary Cooper and Helen Hayes stepped into the parts.[11]

A Farewell to Arms (1957)

Rock Hudson as Lieutenant Frederick Henry (Rod Steiger)

David O. Selznick wanted Rod Steiger to play the starring role of Lieutenant Frederick Henry in his version of *A Farewell to Arms*. Part of the deal was a long term contract with 20th Century–Fox, which turned off Steiger. He turned it down and Rock Hudson was cast instead.[12]

Fargo (1996)

Larry Brandenburg as Stan Grossman (William H. Macy)

William H. Macy had to campaign to win the role he was nominated for an Oscar for. When he first came to read, the Coen brothers had Macy in mind for the part of Stan Grossman, the accountant.[13]

The Farmer Takes a Wife (1935)

Henry Fonda as Dan Harrow (Gary Cooper, Joel McCrea)

Gary Cooper and Joel McCrea both rejected the role of Dan Harrow, leaving it free for Henry Fonda.[14] Fonda previously originated the role in the Broadway version.

The Farmer's Daughter (1947)

Loretta Young as Katrin Holstrom (Ingrid Bergman, Sonia Henie)

Ingrid Bergman was not interested in playing Katrin Holstrom in *The Farmer's Daughter*, and turned it down.[15] Sonia Henie was contemplated.[16] Loretta Young was finally cast and was rewarded with an Oscar for her performance.

Fast Times at Ridgemont High (1982)

Sean Penn as Jeff Spicoli (Anthony Edwards, Eric Stoltz)
Jennifer Jason Leigh as Stacy Hamilton (Ally Sheedy, Meg Tilly)
Judge Reinhold as Brad Hamilton (Nicolas Cage, Sean Penn)
Robert Romanus as Mike Damone (Scott Thomson)
Ray Walston as Mr. Hand (Fred Gwynne)
Stu Nahan as Himself (Johnny Carson, Tom Snyder)

Sean Penn, Anthony Edwards and Eric Stoltz all auditioned for the part of Jeff Spicoli. Director Amy Heckerling thought that Stoltz gave the best reading. But she knew that Sean Penn was a great actor. Penn said not to worry, that his performance would be what was needed. Penn got the part. Stoltz and Edwards were cast as his stoner buds.

Heckerling auditioned Jennifer Jason Leigh, Meg Tilly and Ally Sheedy for the part of Stacy. The teenage character gets pregnant in the film. Heckerling thought that Sheedy and Tilly seemed capable of handling the tough circumstances. Leigh was smaller than they were. Heckerling saw her as being more able to convey the difficulty of the situation.

Before Sean Penn was set for Spicoli, Heckerling asked him to read for Brad, Stacy's older brother. Penn refused. The only part he was interested in was Jeff Spicoli. A 17-year-old Nicolas Cage auditioned for Brad. Although Cage gave a very good audition Heckerling felt there were a couple of things going against him. First of all, Heckerling thought that Jennifer Jason Leigh had a sad quality. She saw the same thing in Cage. She thought that the two of them together might make the middle of the film too dark. Another obstacle was his age. Since he was 17, the number of hours he would be able to work was limited. Judge Reinhold also auditioned for the part. He had the light quality Heckerling was looking for. He was also older, which was another plus. Reinhold was cast as Brad. Cage made his film debut in the small role of Brad's bud. He was billed as Nicolas Coppola. The following year the film *Valley Girl* was released. Cage was the leading man. After Heckerling saw his performance in the film she thought she might have made a mistake not giving him the part of Brad.

Casting director Don Phillips knew he wanted Scott Thomson in the movie. According to Thomson, "I don't remember reading for Amy any particular part but she said, "Stick around. I want you to read the part of Damone." I went, "Damone? Well, sure. Okay." They were reading the role of Forest Whitaker's part. So I got to read with Forest and Forest is very intimidating and very big and I think out of that the character of Arnold was sort of born because he was sort of a factor to deal with. So I became this person who's sort of shrinking all the time, became the invisible man trying to fit in."

Fred Gwynne was sought to play Mr. Hand. Gwynne objected to the script and turned it down.

In Cameron Crowe's book, Spicoli had a fantasy about being on *The Tonight Show with Johnny Carson*. Carson was offered the chance to play himself, but said no. The next offer was made to Tom Snyder. Crowe spoke with Snyder the day he left *The Today Show*. Snyder was down, and declined the offer. Stu Nahan was cast instead. Crowe adapted the scene for the film to suit Nahan.

Fat City (1972)
Stacy Keach as Tully (Marlon Brando)
Jeff Bridges as Ernie (Paul Le Mat)

Director John Huston's first choice to play Tully was Marlon Brando. Brando couldn't decide whether or not he would do it. Meanwhile, Huston saw Stacy Keach's work and decided that he might be right. Brando didn't get back to him, and so Huston gave the part to Keach.[17]

Jeff Bridges won his role in *Fat City* because Paul Le Mat's manager wanted too much money for his client to star.[18]

Fatal Attraction (1987)
Glenn Close as Alex Forrest (Barbara Hershey, Sharon Stone, Debra Winger)

Debra Winger and Barbara Hershey turned down the role of Alex Forrest in *Fatal Attraction*.[19] An unknown Sharon Stone wanted the part, but was unable to get an audition.[20] Director Adrian Lyne gave the part to Glenn Close. The film was a smash hit. Close's performance was critically acclaimed. Close was nominated for an Oscar for playing the obsessed Alex Forrest.

Fatal Beauty (1987)
Whoopi Goldberg as Rita Rizzoli (Cher, Tina Turner)
Sam Elliott as Mike Marshak (Billy Dee Williams)

Cher was initially contacted for the starring role in *Fatal Beauty*. She considered taking the part, but eventually decided to turn it down. Whoopi Goldberg called MGM to ask to be considered. The studio bluntly told her they were looking for a more attractive actress. They had Tina Turner in mind. However, the director of the film, Tom Holland, liked the idea of having Goldberg play the lead. To Goldberg's surprise, the part she previously was unable to get was now offered to her.[21]

Father of the Bride (1950)

Spencer Tracy as Stanley T. Banks (Jack Benny)

Jack Benny very much wanted to play the father in *Father of the Bride*. The studio agreed to give him a screen test. Although Benny was a gifted comedian, they thought his screen test showed that his style of comedy was wrong for their film.[22] Spencer Tracy was cast instead.

Fearless Fagan (1952)

Janet Leigh as Abby Ames (Deborah Kerr)

When director Stanley Donen signed on to direct *Fearless Fagan*, he envisioned Deborah Kerr in the role of Abby Ames. Donen was unable to get Kerr, and the part was played by Janet Leigh instead.[23]

A Few Good Men (1992)

Demi Moore as Lieutenant Commander JoAnne "Jo" Galloway (Linda Hamilton, Penelope Ann Miller, Elizabeth Perkins, Michelle Pfeiffer, Nancy Travis, Julie Warner)

Kiefer Sutherland as Lieutenant Jonathan James "John" Kendrick (Kevin Bacon)

Michelle Pfeiffer was an early consideration to play opposite Tom Cruise in *A Few Good Men*. The producers decided against her, however, because they felt the audience would expect a romance between her and Tom Cruise's character. Linda Hamilton, Elizabeth Perkins, Julie Warner, Nancy Travis, and Penelope Ann Miller all read for the part.[24] But it was Demi Moore who ended up with the role of Joanne Galloway. Kevin Bacon initially wanted to play Kiefer Sutherland's role of Jonathan Kendrick, but director Rob Reiner felt it was a typical role for him.[25] He wanted to give a more challenging role, and cast him as Captain "Smiling" Jack Ross instead.

Fiddler on the Roof (1971)

Topol as Tevye (Zero Mostel)

Even though Zero Mostel originated the role of Tevye on Broadway, director Norman Jewison preferred Topol for the film version.[26]

Field of Dreams (1989)

Kevin Costner as Ray Kinsella (Tom Hanks)

Tom Hanks was offered the starring role of Ray Kinsella. Hanks said no, and the part went to Kevin Costner.[27]

55 Days at Peking (1963)

Ava Gardner as Baroness Natalie Ivanoff (Anne Bancroft, Jeanne Moreau)

Flora Robson as Dowager Empress Tzu-Hsi (Myrna Loy)

Anne Bancroft was very briefly considered for the part of Baroness Natalie Ivanoff.[28] Producer Samuel Bronston and Charlton Heston, the star of *55 Days at Peking*, disagreed on the question of who should get the part. Bronston liked Ava Gardner for the role of Baroness Natalie Ivanoff, while Heston thought Jeanne Moreau was the better choice. According to Heston, Moreau was a better actress than Gardner, plus she was more believable as a Russian. Since Heston had casting approval in his contract, this created a problem for Bronston. Finally Bronston acquiesced and gave Moreau the part. The next day Heston and Bronston met for lunch, where Bronston said that he deeply regretted his decision to go with Moreau. He begged Heston to change his mind. Heston's opinion of Gardner for the part hadn't changed and he told Bronston so. At this point Bronston broke out in tears. Heston tried to comfort him, but it was no use. He cried even harder until Heston agreed to let Ava Gardner play the part.[29]

Myrna Loy's name came up as a possible Dowager Empress Tzu-Hsi. It was decided that the American actress would not be able to convincingly play a Chinese woman. Loy found this amusing since in the early days of her career she played many exotic roles.[30]

Fight Club (1999)

Brad Pitt as Tyler Durden (Sean Penn)

Helena Bonham Carter as Marla Singer (Courtney Love)

For a short time Sean Penn was mentioned to play Tyler Durden. Courtney Love was a contender for the part of Marla Singer. Love couldn't fit the film into her busy schedule. Helena Bonham Carter was cast instead.[31]

Finian's Rainbow (1968)

Tommy Steele as Og (Donal Donnelly)

Director Francis Ford Coppola was interested in having Donal Donnelly play Og in *Finian's Rainbow*.[32] In the end Coppola decided Tommy Steele would be the better Og. But Coppola never forgot Donnelly. He later cast him as Archbishop Liam Francis Gilday in *The Godfather Part III*.

Although it took 22 years, Francis Ford Coppola eventually cast Donal Donnelly in one of his films (*Finian's Rainbow*).

Firestarter (1984)

Martin Sheen as Captain Hollister (Burt Lancaster)

Burt Lancaster was set to play the role of Captain Hollister in *Firestarter* for director John Carpenter. However production was halted before shooting ever began. Eventually producer Dino De Laurentiis decided to make the film. He hired Mark L. Lester to direct and gave Lancaster's part to Martin Sheen.[33]

The Firm (1993)

Tom Cruise as Mitch McDeere (Jason Patric)
Jeanne Tripplehorn as Abby McDeere (Julia Roberts, Robin Wright Penn)
Gene Hackman as Avery Tolar (Meryl Streep)
Holly Hunter as Tammy Hemphill (Park Overall)

Jason Patric was an early consideration for the role of lawyer Mitch McDeere. When Tom Cruise signed on to star, the rest of the cast fell into place. Director Sydney Pollack thought of changing the part of Avery Tolar into a female character. He thought of Meryl Streep for the role. But ultimately, it was decided that fans of the novel would have a problem with such a major change, and Gene Hackman was cast instead.[34]

Both Julia Roberts[35] and Robin Wright Penn[36] turned down the role of Tom Cruise's wife, leaving the door open for Jeanne Tripplehorn.

Although Holly Hunter was Oscar nominated for her performance as Tammy, she was not the first choice. It was Park Overall. Overall wanted very much to be in the film. The problem was that she was on a television series — *Empty Nest*. The producers of *Empty Nest* refused to give her the time off to make the film. She was extremely upset at missing the chance to play the role.[37]

First Blood (1982)

Sylvester Stallone as John Rambo (Powers Boothe, Brad Davis, Robert De Niro, Michael Douglas, Clint Eastwood, Steve McQueen, Paul Newman, Nick Nolte, Al Pacino, Steve Railsback, John Travolta)
Richard Crenna as Colonel Samuel Trautman (Kirk Douglas, Burt Lancaster, George C. Scott)
Brian Dennehy as Will Teasle (Charles Durning, Gene Hackman, Burt Lancaster, Lee Marvin, Robert Mitchum)

Many actors were considered for the Rambo role including: Robert De Niro, John Travolta, Paul Newman Michael Douglas, Steve McQueen, Clint Eastwood, Steve Railsback, Brad Davis, Nick Nolte, and Powers Boothe. Al Pacino was a possibility, but decided against it. At one point, it was possibly going to be a TV movie with David Soul as the star.

Burt Lancaster and George C. Scott were contenders fort he role of Colonel Samuel Trautman. Kirk Douglas had the part but dropped out. He was replaced by Richard Crenna.

Brian Dennehy won the part of Will Teasle after Burt Lancaster, Robert Mitchum, Gene Hackman, Lee Marvin and Charles Durning were all considered.[38]

First Monday in October (1981)

Walter Matthau as Dan Snow (Henry Fonda, William Holden)
Jill Clayburgh as Ruth Loomis (Ellen Burstyn)

William Holden fell in love with the script for *First Monday in October*. He wanted to play the lead role of Supreme Court Justice Dan Snow, a role that Henry Fonda had created on Broadway. Holden was so excited about the film that he met with Ellen Burstyn to discuss the script. Burstyn was originally scheduled for the part that Jill Clayburgh played. Fonda was sick at the time, but still wanted to do the film. When he learned of Fonda's illness, Holden sympathized and immediately took himself out of the running. Unfortunately for Fonda, the studio was not as compassionate as William Holden. They thought that more money was to be made with Walter Matthau, and Matthau was chosen.[39]

The First Wives Club (1996)
Elizabeth Berkley as Phoebe La Velle (Jenny McCarthy)

Jenny McCarthy rejected the part that went to Elizabeth Berkley. The character was a girl who was sleeping with a man to advance her acting career. McCarthy, a former *Playboy* centerfold, felt that that was not the image she wanted to project.[40]

The Fisher King (1991)
Jeff Bridges as Jack Lucas (Kevin Kline, Ron Silver)

Director Terry Gilliam signed Robin Williams to star in his upcoming film, *The Fisher King*. For the other male lead he considered Kevin Kline. He wanted to meet with the actor but they were unable to do so. He did interview Ron Silver, but eventually gave the part to Jeff Bridges instead.[41]

Fitzcarraldo (1982)
Klaus Kinski as Brian Sweeney Fitzgerald — "Fitzcarraldo" (Jason Robards)

Jason Robards was cast as Fitzcarraldo. Halfway through filming Robards was diagnosed with amoebic dysentery and was replaced with Klaus Kinski.[42]

5 Against the House (1955)
Kim Novak as Kay Greylek (Mary Costa)

The part of Kay Greylek was to have been played by Mary Costa. Costa did not end up in the film; the part was taken by Kim Novak.[43]

The Flamingo Kid (1984)
Matt Dillon as Jeffrey Willis (Matthew Broderick)

Matthew Broderick was director Garry Marshall's first choice to star in *The Flamingo Kid*. When the deal fell through Matt Dillon was cast instead.[44]

Flap (1970)
Anthony Quinn as Flapping Eagle (Richard Harris)

Richard Harris agreed to play the part of Flapping Eagle. He later changed his mind and dropped out of the movie. His replacement was Anthony Quinn.[45]

Flashdance (1983)
Jennifer Beals as Alex Owens (Demi Moore, Leslie Wing)
Michael Nouri as Nick Hurley (Gene Simmons)

The starring role of Alex Owens came down to three actresses: model Leslie Wing, Demi Moore (who at this point was known primarily as a soap opera actress), and Jennifer Beals. The decision was so difficult to make that a group of 50 men were brought in to see the audition tapes. They were asked which one of the three actresses they would most want to sleep with. Jennifer Beals ran away with it and was cast in the role.[46]

Rocker Gene Simmons considered playing Nick. Simmons said that he wasn't interested in making the disco movie and turned it down.[47]

Flatliners (1990)
Julia Roberts as Rachel Mannus (Nicole Kidman)

Director Joel Schumacher originally wanted Julia Roberts to star in *Flatliners*. Schumacher was under the impression that Tom Cruise was interested in having Roberts as his costar in *Days of Thunder*, so he discussed the part with Nicole Kidman. However Roberts still wanted to do *Flatliners*, so Schumacher got his first choice after all. Coincidentally, Nicole Kidman was cast opposite Tom Cruise in *Days of Thunder*.[48]

The Flintstones (1994)
John Goodman as Fred Flintstone (James Belushi)
Elizabeth Perkins as Wilma Flintstone (Geena Davis, Faith Ford, Catherine O'Hara)
Rick Moranis as Barney Rubble (Danny De Vito)

Rosie O'Donnell as Betty Rubble (Janine Turner, Tracey Ullman, Daphne Zuniga)
Halle Berry as Sharon Stone (Anna Nicole Smith, Sharon Stone)
Elizabeth Taylor as Pearl Slaghoople (Audrey Meadows, Elizabeth Montgomery)

Jim Belushi and Danny De Vito were possibilities to play Fred Flintstone and Barney Rubble. Several actresses were considered to play Wilma including Geena Davis, Catherine O'Hara, and Faith Ford. Tracey Ullman and Janine Turner were possible Bettys[49] along with Daphne Zuniga who auditioned for the role.

The role of sexy secretary Sharon Stone was offered to actress Sharon Stone.[50] She decided against doing it. Anna Nicole Smith was a candidate but failed to win the part.[51]

Elizabeth Taylor was signed for the role of Pearl Slaghoople after both Audrey Meadows and Elizabeth Montgomery were contemplated.[52]

Flying Down to Rio (1933)

Ginger Rogers as Honey Hale (Dorothy Jordan)

Dorothy Jordan was originally cast as Honey Hale. She wanted to marry producer Merian Cooper and quit. Her replacement was Ginger Rogers.[53]

Follow the Fleet (1936)

Harriet Hilliard as Connie Martin (Irene Dunne)

Irene Dunne was not available to take the role Harriet Hilliard played in *Follow the Fleet*.[54] Hilliard later married Ozzie Nelson and came to fame with the television series *Ozzie and Harriet*.

Fools Rush In (1997)

Salma Hayek as Isabel Fuentes (Jennifer Lopez)

Jennifer Lopez was given two movies to choose from—*Fools Rush In* or *Anaconda*. She felt the *Fools Rush In* script was not especially good and did *Anaconda* instead.[55]

Footloose (1984)

Kevin Bacon as Ren MacCormack (Tom Cruise)
Lori Singer as Ariel Moore (Valerie Bertinelli, Madonna)

Director Herbert Ross was interested in Kevin Bacon for the starring role of Ren MacCormack. He presented his casting choice to Paramount Pictures. Producer Dawn Steel was opposed to Bacon. She didn't think Bacon was attractive and doubted if she would ever approve of him for the part. Tom Cruise was brought in to audition. Dancing played a pivotal role in the film, and whoever was cast in the lead had to be able to dance. Cruise danced at his audition, but Ross was unimpressed. At this point Bacon was given a makeover. A screen test was made with the new and improved actor. Steel still didn't like him, but the other executives overruled her. Bacon was cast, and *Footloose* became a smash hit.[56]

Madonna[57] and Valerie Bertinelli auditioned for the role of Ariel but lost out to Lori Singer.

For Me and My Gal (1942)

Gene Kelly as Harry Palmer (Dan Dailey, George Murphy)
Judy Garland as Jo Hayden (Eleanor Powell)

Eleanor Powell and Dan Dailey were originally set to star in *For Me and My Gal*. One day at rehearsal, to their surprise, they learned they had been replaced.[58]

George Murphy was initially set to play Harry. Judy Garland went over the director's head to producer Arthur Freed. She asked Freed to hire Kelly to play Harry Palmer. Freed agreed, to the dismay of Busby Berkeley. George Murphy was relegated to the supporting role of Jimmy Metcalf. Both Berkley and Murphy were angry at the situation and let it show in their attitudes toward Kelly. Berkeley eventually warmed up, although Murphy never did.[59]

For Whom the Bell Tolls (1943)

Ingrid Bergman as Maria (Betty Field, Vera Zorina)

Even though Ingrid Bergman was many people's first choice (including writer Ernest Hemingway), Paramount cast former ballerina Vera Zorina as Maria. They were already paying a lot of money to Gary Cooper and figured that Zorina would not cost as much as Bergman[60] or other contenders such as Betty Field.[61] After a few days of shooting, it was decided that Zorina was unsuitable.[62] She was replaced with Bergman.

Vera Zorina was originally cast as Maria in *For Whom the Bell Tolls*.

Foreign Correspondent (1940)

Joel McCrea as Johnny Jones (Gary Cooper)
Laraine Day as Carol Fisher (Joan Fontaine)

Director Alfred Hitchcock wanted Gary Cooper to star as Johnny Jones. Cooper read the script and dismissed it as a thriller.[63] He later told Hitchcock that he regretted not taking the part.[64] Hitchcock ultimately gave the part to Joel McCrea.

Hitchcock considered Joan Fontaine for the part of Carol Fisher, but eventually chose Laraine Day instead.[65]

Forever Amber (1947)

Linda Darnell as Amber St. Clair (Peggy Cummins, Angela Lansbury, Vivien Leigh, Margaret Lockwood, Lana Turner)
George Sanders as King Charles II (Vincent Price)

The original list of possible Amber St. Clairs included Linda Darnell,[66] Margaret Lockwood,[67] Vivien Leigh[68] and Peggy Cummins.[69] Cummins was selected after both Leigh and Lockwood turned the part down.[70] Shortly after it was decided that Cummins was not working out, and she was fired. Linda Darnell was considered, but director Otto Preminger was also interested in Lana Turner. Darryl F. Zanuck said no to Turner.[71] Angela Lansbury was interested, but was turned down in favor of Linda Darnell.[72]

Forever Female (1953)

Patricia Crowley as Sally Carver (Audrey Hepburn)

Paramount Pictures was not able to sign their first choice, Audrey Hepburn, for the role of Sally Carver.[73]

Fort Apache: The Bronx (1981)

Paul Newman as John Murphy (Steve McQueen, Nick Nolte)
Ken Wahl as Corelli (John Travolta)

Paul Newman's role of John Murphy was turned down by both Steve McQueen and Nick Nolte.[74] Newman was interested in having John Travolta play his partner, Corelli. Travolta's agent asked for more money than the studio was willing to pay, and Ken Wahl was cast in his place.[75]

The Fortune (1975)

Stockard Channing as Fredrika Contessa "Freddie" Biggars/Sullivan (Cher, Bette Midler)

Cher wanted to be in *The Fortune*, but director Mike Nichols was not interested.[76] Another singing star, Bette Midler, was offered the female lead. Nichols offered Midler the same deal he was giving to the other stars of the film, Warren Beatty and Jack Nicholson. Both men were seasoned performers, while Midler was new to movies. Midler asked the veteran director what other films he'd directed. Nichols gave the part to Stockard Channing instead.[77]

Forty Carats (1973)

Liv Ullman as Ann Stanley (Audrey Hepburn)

William Wyler wanted to direct Audrey Hepburn in *Forty Carats*. Hepburn wanted to stay in Europe and turned Wyler down. When she declined the offer, Wyler dropped out of the project.[78]

40 Days and 40 Nights (2002)
Josh Hartnett as Matt (Ashton Kutcher)

Ashton Kutcher owed Miramax a film. The studio wanted him to appear in *40 Days and 40 Nights*. However, Kutcher had to make a screen test. The test wasn't especially good. Miramax replaced him with Josh Hartnett.[79]

Forty Guns (1957)
Barbara Stanwyck as Jessica Drummond (Marilyn Monroe)

Marilyn Monroe wanted to play Jessica Drummond in *Forty Guns*. Director Samuel Fuller turned her down in favor of Barbara Stanwyck, whom he said he envisioned in the part all along.[80]

48 Hrs. (1982)
Nick Nolte as Jack Cates (Burt Reynolds)
Eddie Murphy as Reggie Hammond (Bill Cosby, Gregory Hines, Richard Pryor)

Producer Larry Gordon wanted Burt Reynolds and Richard Pryor to star in *48 Hrs*. The actors were ready to do it, but then a problem arose. Richard Pryor wanted top billing. This caused the whole project to be put on hold. Gordon recast Reynolds' role of Jack Cates with Nick Nolte. Gregory Hines was asked to be his costar. Hines turned the film down, as did Bill Cosby. The part went to Eddie Murphy.[81]

49th Parallel (1941)
Glynis Johns as Anna (Elisabeth Bergner)

Elisabeth Bergner was cast in the role of Anna in *49th Parallel*. She went to Canada for location shots. She was next scheduled to go to England to shoot her scenes. She refused to go, and instead went to the United States. It was said that Bergner was afraid that Hitler was going to invade, and that she would be sent to a concentration camp. The part of Anna was recast with Glynis Johns.[82]

42nd Street (1933)
Bebe Daniels as Dorothy Brock (Kay Francis)
Ruby Keeler as Peggy Sawyer (Loretta Young)
Ginger Rogers as Ann "Anytime Annie" Lowell (Joan Blondell)

The film version of *42nd Street* was originally planned as a non-musical with Loretta Young

Did Hitler cost Elisabeth Bergner a job? (*49th Parallel*)

and Kay Francis in the leads.[83] Francis was shooting *Trouble in Paradise*. Shooting took longer than expected, and Francis was not going to be available for the start date for *42nd Street*. She hoped that Warner Bros. would wait for her, but instead they recast the role with Bebe Daniels.[84] Joan Blondell was the original choice for Anytime Annie, but her schedule forced her to pull out of the project.[85] Director Mervyn LeRoy persuaded his then girlfriend Ginger Rogers to take her place.

The Fountainhead (1949)
Gary Cooper as Howard Roark (Humphrey Bogart, James Cagney)
Patricia Neal as Dominique Francon (Greta Garbo, Ida Lupino, Barbara Stanwyck)

Gary Cooper was director King Vidor's third choice to play Howard Roark. His first two choices, which didn't work out, were Humphrey Bogart and James Cagney.

Greta Garbo was the first choice for the role of Dominique Francon. She had retired by that point and turned down the role.[86] Ida Lupino was also considered. Barbara Stanwyck wanted very much to play the part. She even claimed that she was the one to bring the project to

Four Rooms (1995)
Tim Roth as Ted the Bellhop (Steve Buscemi)
Marc Lawrence as Sam the Bellhop (Lawrence Tierney)

The starring role of Ted the Bellhop was written for Steve Buscemi to play. However, Buscemi turned the part down, feeling the bellhop character he played in *Barton Fink* was too similar to this one.

Lawrence Tierney was considered for Sam the Bellhop. Eventually it was decided that Marc Lawrence would be easier to work with and he was cast instead.[88]

Four Weddings and a Funeral (1994)
Andie MacDowell as Carrie (Sarah Jessica Parker)

Sarah Jessica Parker auditioned for the part of Carrie, but lost out to Andie MacDowell.[89]

Foxes (1980)
Scott Baio as Brad (Buddy Foster)

Buddy Foster lost the male lead in *Foxes* because his sister, Jodie Foster, was chosen to play the female lead. The two characters were romantically involved.[90]

Frances (1982)
Jessica Lange as Frances Farmer (Kim Basinger)

Kim Basinger auditioned for the role of Frances Farmer, but lost out to Jessica Lange.[91]

Francis (1950)
Donald O'Connor as Peter Stirling (Mickey Rooney)

Untied Artists was originally set to make *Francis* with Mickey Rooney in the starring role of Peter Stirling. They eventually dropped the project, which was picked up by Universal Studios. They put Donald O'Connor in the lead role and scored a major hit.[92]

Frankenstein (1931)
Colin Clive as Dr. Frankenstein (Leslie Howard)
Boris Karloff as The Monster (John Carradine, Bela Lugosi)
Mae Clarke as Elizabeth (Bette Davis)

Leslie Howard was the original choice to play Dr. Frankenstein. However, he really wasn't interested, and director James Whale preferred Colin Clive.

Bela Lugosi gave his rival Boris Karloff a break when he turned down the part of the monster. He really didn't like the script, and wasn't interested in sitting in a makeup chair for the amount of time necessary to become the monster. John Carradine also turned down the part.

Bette Davis was almost cast as Elizabeth, but the studio and Whale agreed that Mae Clarke would be better for the part.[93]

Frankie and Johnny (1991)
Al Pacino as Johnny (F. Murray Abraham, Elliott Gould, Jack Nicholson)
Michelle Pfeiffer as Frankie (Penny Marshall, Barbra Streisand)
Kate Nelligan as Cora (Emma Thompson)

Director Garry Marshall considered several pairings to play Frankie and Johnny. One possible duo was his sister Penny Marshall and Jack Nicholson in the roles. He also thought about Barbra Streisand starring with her ex-husband Elliott Gould. He finally cast Michelle Pfeiffer and Al Pacino. Many people objected to this casting. The characters were originally intended to be unattractive, and the actors he cast were anything but.

Emma Thompson auditioned for the role of Cora, but lost out to Kate Nelligan.[94]

Fraulein (1958)
Dana Wynter as Erika Angermann (May Britt)

May Britt screen tested for the part of Erika Angermann in *Fraulein*. She was passed over in favor of Dana Wynter.

Freaks (1932)
Olga Baclanova as Cleopatra (Jean Harlow)

Jean Harlow was scheduled to play the female lead in the film *Freaks*. When she found this out, she was very upset. She did not want to be a part of this controversial film, and begged to be released from it. She got her wish, and the part of Cleopatra was played by Olga Baclanova.[95]

A Free Soul (1931)

Clark Gable as Ace Wilfong (John Gilbert)

Clark Gable's role was originally intended for John Gilbert. However, producer Irving Thalberg had a hunch that the up and coming Gable might be right for this part. He sent the actor to meet screenwriter Adela Rogers St. Johns to make sure she approved of his casting. St. Johns liked Gable, and he won the part.[96]

The French Connection (1971)

Gene Hackman as Jimmy "Popeye" Doyle (Peter Boyle, Jimmy Breslin, Eddie Egan, Jackie Gleason, Steve McQueen, Robert Mitchum, Paul Newman, Rod Taylor)
Roy Scheider as Buddy "Cloudy" Russo (Sonny Grosso)

Many actors were considered for the role of Popeye Doyle. The character was based on Eddie Egan. Egan wanted to play the part with his real life partner Sonny Grosso playing the silver screen version of himself (Russo) opposite him. Egan even auditioned for it, but failed to win the part. The part of Doyle was rejected by Paul Newman[97] and Peter Boyle. Boyle wanted to play romantic leads at the time. Boyle later deeply regretted not taking the role.[98] Robert Mitchum,[99] Jackie Gleason,[100] Steve McQueen,[101] and Rod Taylor[102] were all possible choices. Director William Friedkin was very interested in casting a non-actor in the role. He felt that writer Jimmy Breslin would make the perfect Popeye Doyle. Breslin rehearsed the role and it became apparent there was a problem. Breslin wasn't an actor. He also couldn't drive a car which presented another problem.[103] He was replaced by Gene Hackman. Hackman went on to win an Oscar for his portrayal.

The French Lieutenant's Woman (1981)

Meryl Streep as Sarah and Anna (Vanessa Redgrave)

Writer John Fowles first wanted Vanessa Redgrave to star as Sarah and Anna. When the film went into production, Redgrave was out, and Meryl Streep was in.[104]

Friday the 13th: A New Beginning (1985)

Dick Wieand as Jason Voorhees (Ted White)

Ted White decided against reprising his role as Jason.[105] White played the part in 1984's Friday the 13th: The Final Chapter.

Friendly Persuasion (1956)

Gary Cooper as Jess Birdwell (Bing Crosby)
Dorothy McGuire as Eliza Birdwell (Jean Arthur, Ingrid Bergman, Katharine Hepburn, Vivien Leigh, Mary Martin, Maureen O'Hara, Eleanor Parker, Martha Scott, Teresa Wright, Jane Wyman)
Anthony Perkins as Josh Birdwell (James Dean)

Friendly Persuasion was planned ten years before production ever started. At that time, Frank Capra was set to direct, with Bing Crosby and Jean Arthur in the leads.[106] William Wyler eventually took over the directing job. He signed Gary Cooper for the part of Jess Birdwell. His first choice to play Eliza was Katharine Hepburn. She was not available. The same went for Vivien Leigh and Ingrid Bergman. Dorothy McGuire won the part after Jane Wyman, Maureen O'Hara, Mary Martin, Eleanor Parker, Teresa Wright and Martha Scott were all considered.[107]

Wyler wanted James Dean to play the part of Josh Birdwell. Dean's agent said that Dean would not play any supporting parts. Wyler cast Anthony Perkins instead.[108]

From Hell (2001)

Johnny Depp as Fred Abberline (Sean Connery, Daniel Day-Lewis, Anthony Hopkins, Jude Law, Brad Pitt)

Sean Connery, Brad Pitt, Jude Law, Daniel Day-Lewis and Anthony Hopkins were all considered for the starring role of Fred Abberline. Connery, Pitt and Law all met with directors Albert and Allen Hughes. Anthony Hopkins was supposed to meet with them, but he decided against it. The Hughes brothers got together with Johnny Depp. The meeting lasted for hours. They were impressed with Depp and gave him the part.[109]

From Here to Eternity (1953)

Burt Lancaster as Sgt. Milton Warden (Robert Mitchum, Edmond O'Brien)
Montgomery Clift as Robert E. Lee Prewitt (John Derek, Aldo Ray)
Deborah Kerr as Karen Holmes (Joan Crawford)
Frank Sinatra as Angelo Maggio (Eli Wallach)
Donna Reed as Alma [aka Lorene], Gloria Grahame, Julie Harris, Roberta Haynes, Shelley Winters)
Philip Ober as Dana "Dynamite" Holmes (Walter Matthau)

Columbia studio head Harry Cohn was interested in Robert Mitchum for the starring role of Sgt. Milton Warden.[110] He also envisioned Edmond O'Brien as Warden, along with Aldo Ray or John Derek as Prewitt.[111] None of these choices were obtained, and the parts went to Burt Lancaster and Montgomery Clift.

Joan Crawford was originally cast as Karen Holmes. However, she and director Fred Zinnemann clashed over her costumes. He felt the fashionable wardrobe she chose was inappropriate for the plain character she was hired to play. This disagreement led to Deborah Kerr replacing Crawford in the role.[112]

It came down to Frank Sinatra and Eli Wallach for the role of Maggio. It was decided that Wallach was the first choice. But, at this point, Wallach had also been offered the chance to star in Tennessee Williams' *Camino Real* on stage. The production was to be directed by Elia Kazan and was a very big deal. Wallach turned down *From Here to Eternity*.[113] Frank Sinatra was cast as Maggio. Sinatra went on to win an Oscar for his performance.

Director Fred Zinnemann was interested in Julie Harris for the part of Alma. Other contenders were Roberta Haynes and Gloria Grahame.[114] Shelley Winters was offered the part. She turned it down because she had just had a baby and didn't want to be away.[115] Donna Reed was finally chosen for the part.

Walter Matthau was asked to play Captain Holmes. Matthau thought that it wasn't a very good part and said no. Philip Ober later won the role.[116]

From Russia with Love (1963)

Daniela Bianchi as Tatiana Romanova (Elga Anderson, Pia Lindstrom)
Desmond Llewellyn as Boothroyd (Peter Burton)

German actress Elga Anderson was the first choice to play Tatiana Romanova. However there was a rumor about Anderson being promiscuous. Director Terence Young later realized this rumor was false. He was still unable to get her casting approved. Pia Lindstrom (the daughter of Ingrid Bergman) auditioned, but the part went to Daniela Bianchi.

Peter Burton played Boothroyd in *Dr. No*. He wasn't available to make *From Russia with Love*, and Desmond Llewellyn was cast in his place.[117]

The Front Page (1931)

Pat O'Brien as Hildy Johnson (James Cagney, Clark Gable)
Adolphe Menjou as Walter Burns (Louis Wolheim)

Director Lewis Milestone wanted either Clark Gable or James Cagney in the starring role of Hildy Johnson. Producer Howard Hughes was under the false impression that Pat O'Brien played the part in the stage version and insisted he repeat his performance in the film.

Louis Wolheim was originally cast as Walter Burns. When he died of a stroke, he was replaced by Adolphe Menjou.[118]

Frontier Gal (1945)

Yvonne De Carlo as Lorena Dumont (Maria Montez)

Maria Montez was offered the chance to star in *Frontier Gal* as Lorena Dumont. Montez had problems with the film. She was not happy with the studio's choice of possible leading men. Another sticking point was that Montez did not want to play opposite a child. She ended up turning the part down, at which point it was assigned to Yvonne De Carlo.[119]

The Fugitive (1993)

Harrison Ford as Richard Kimble (Alec Baldwin)

Producer Arnold Kopelson wanted Alec Baldwin to play the starring role of Richard Kimble. However Warner Bros. was not sure he was their man. Kopelson then passed the script along to Harrison Ford. Since Ford wanted to do the part Alec Baldwin was out of the running.[120]

Maria Montez turned down the lead in *Frontier Gal.*

The Funeral (1996)
Chris Penn as Chez (Vincent D'Onofrio)

Vincent D'Onofrio was director Abel Ferrara's choice to play Chez. When he proved unavailable Chris Penn was cast.[121]

Funny Face (1957)
Audrey Hepburn as Jo Stockton (Leslie Caron, Cyd Charisse, Carol Haney, Grace Kelly, Debbie Reynolds)

The role of Jo Stockton was originally set for Carol Haney. Haney was well known for her starring role of Babe in the Broadway hit *The Pajama Game*. MGM eventually decided that Haney wasn't a big enough star and she was out of the running.[122] Other actresses were considered including: Grace Kelly, Debbie Reynolds, Cyd Charisse, and Leslie Caron. Caron, Reynolds, and Charisse were not what the studio was looking for. Kelly might have played the part, but she was retiring from acting to become Princess of Monaco.[123] Screenwriter Leonard Gershe thought Audrey Hepburn might be right. Hepburn loved the script and signed on enthusiastically.[124]

Funny Girl (1968)
Barbra Streisand as Fanny Brice (Shirley MacLaine)
Omar Sharif as Nicky Arnstein (Marlon Brando, Sean Connery, Tony Curtis, James Garner, David Janssen, Gregory Peck, Frank Sinatra)

Even though Barbra Streisand had been a big success playing the role of Fanny Brice on Broadway, Columbia Pictures did not want her to recreate the role for the film version. Executives at Columbia Pictures said that she wasn't pretty enough, and that she was also too Jewish. Streisand had never been in a film before, and that too was a problem. They wanted a more established movie star — namely Shirley MacLaine. Producer Ray Stark would not hear of this. Stark had produced the show on Broadway, and was now working on the film version. He knew what Streisand brought to the role, and insisted that she be given the part. Columbia finally agreed.[125] Streisand won the Academy Award for her performance.

Early on it was reported that David Janssen would co-star with Streisand. This deal eventually fell through and the search was on for a replacement.[126] The question of billing prevented other stars from appearing in *Funny Girl*. Frank Sinatra was composer Jule Styne's favorite to play Nicky Arnstein. In order for the deal to go through, Sinatra would have to receive top billing. Barbra Streisand, who in all fairness was the star of the movie, didn't want to take second billing. Ray Stark was also concerned about Sinatra's age, and the $750,000 he was asking for, so the deal was scrapped.[127] Both Marlon Brando and Gregory Peck preferred to have top billing, and declined the part.[128] Sean Connery, Tony Curtis, and James Garner were all considered. Stark worried about their singing ability.[129] One day William Wyler was in Columbia's cafeteria, where he saw Omar Sharif. He brought Sharif in for a screen test with Streisand. There was an immediate chemistry between the two actors. Wyler quickly signed Sharif for the film.[130]

Funny Lady (1975)
James Caan as Billy Rose (Robert Blake, Robert De Niro, Richard Dreyfuss, Dustin Hoffman)

Robert Blake was the first to audition for the part of Billy Rose. Streisand read with Blake. She thought his reading was very good.[131] Dustin Hoffman,[132] Robert De Niro,[133] Richard Dreyfuss,[134] and James Caan also auditioned. It came down to a choice between Caan and Blake. James Caan was chosen because he had more sex appeal.[135]

The Fuzzy Pink Nightgown (1957)

Ralph Meeker as Mike Valla (Dean Martin)

Director Norman Taurog contacted Dean Martin about starring as Mike Valla in *The Fuzzy Pink Nightgown*. Martin was interested in taking the part. He was very disappointed when he learned that he lost the role to Broadway actor Ralph Meeker.[136]

Gable & Lombard (1976)

James Brolin as Clark Gable (Warren Beatty, Steve McQueen, Burt Reynolds)
Jill Clayburgh as Carole Lombard (Sally Kellerman, Ali MacGraw, Valerie Perrine)

Husband and wife Steve McQueen and Ali MacGraw were considered for the leads. McQueen thought better of it. He was later quoted as saying, "That was one less turkey in my life!"[1] Burt Reynolds and Warren Beatty were asked to play Gable. Reynolds wasn't interested. Beatty wanted to make too many changes in the script, including the names of the characters.[2]

Sally Kellerman and Valerie Perrine lost out to Jill Clayburgh for the role of Carole Lombard.[3]

The Gambler (1974)

James Caan as Axel Freed (Robert De Niro)

Robert De Niro was a strong contender for the starring role of Axel Freed. Director Karel Reisz didn't think he was the right choice for the part and cast James Caan instead.[4]

Gandhi (1982)

Ben Kingsley as Mahatma Gandhi (Dirk Bogarde, Tom Courtenay, Peter Finch, Albert Finney, Alec Guinness, Anthony Hopkins)

Director Richard Attenborough was all set to have Anthony Hopkins play the title role of Gandhi. Hopkins doubted his ability to play the part. He didn't want to lose the substantial amount of weight necessary for the part. He also thought the best idea was to cast an Indian actor in the role. He called up Attenborough to pull out of the film. Attenborough graciously let him off the hook.[5] Hopkins was not the only actor to say no to this role. Others include Albert Finney, Alec Guinness, Peter Finch, Tom Courtenay, and Dirk Bogarde.[6] Attenborough finally found Ben Kingsley. The role made him a star and earned him an Academy Award.

The Gang That Couldn't Shoot Straight (1971)

Robert De Niro as Mario Trantino (Al Pacino)

Al Pacino was signed to play Mario in *The Gang That Couldn't Shoot Straight*. Two days later producer Robert Evans called Pacino's agent to tell him his client had won the role of Michael Corleone in *The Godfather*. Evans tried to persuade the agent to pull him out of the film, but he said the studio wouldn't allow it. Evans called the studio and spoke to Jim Aubrey. Aubrey refused to let Pacino out of *The Gang That Couldn't Shoot Straight*. Evans then called a friend, Sidney Korshack, who also called Aubrey. Korshack went over Aubrey's head and was able to get Pacino released. Robert De Niro (who had also auditioned to play Michael Corleone) replaced Pacino.[7]

Gangs of New York (2002)

Daniel Day-Lewis as Bill Poole (Robert De Niro)

Robert De Niro contemplated taking the role of Bill the Butcher in director Martin Scorsese's *Gangs of New York*. De Niro ultimately said no to the project, reportedly because the film was scheduled for a long shoot in Italy.[8]

The Garden of Allah (1936)

Marlene Dietrich as Domini Enfilden (Greta Garbo, Merle Oberon)
Charles Boyer as Boris Androvsky (Brian Aherne, George Brent, Noel Coward, Robert Donat, Maurice Evans, Jean Gabin, John Gielgud, Fredric March, Ivor Novello, Laurence Olivier, Vincent Price, Basil Rathbone, Gilbert Roland, Robert Taylor)
Alan Marshal as De Trevignac (Ray Milland, David Niven, Cesar Romero)

Merle Oberon was considered to play the role of Domini Enfilden in *The Garden of Allah*. The film was costing more than originally anticipated, and David O. Selznick wanted an actress with more box office clout.⁹ An offer was made to Greta Garbo. Garbo said no, and it was presented to Oberon who was interested and signed on.¹⁰ David O. Selznick had other ideas. He thought that Marlene Dietrich was one of the best actresses around, and he wanted her to star in the film. Oberon did not go quietly. She sued for the salary she would have been paid—$25,000. Selznick gave her the money and got Dietrich in return.¹¹

Many actors were tested for the starring role of Boris Androvsky. Some of the candidates were Vincent Price, Laurence Olivier, Noel Coward, Robert Donat, John Gielgud, Robert Taylor, Fredric March, Brian Aherne, Maurice Evans, Gilbert Roland, Basil Rathbone, George Brent, Ivor Novello and Jean Gabin. David O. Selznick didn't find anyone he thought was as good for the part as Charles Boyer. David Niven, Ray Milland, and Cesar Romero all screen tested for the featured role of De Trevignac. Selznick instead chose Alan Marshal.¹²

Garden of the Moon (1938)
Margaret Lindsay as Toni Blake (Bette Davis)

Bette Davis turned down the role of Toni Blake.¹³

Gas Food Lodging (1992)
Ione Skye as Trudi (Christina Applegate)
Fairuza Balk as Shade (Drew Barrymore)
Robert Knepper as Dank (Hugh Grant)

Writer/director Allison Anders wrote the part of Trudi with Christina Applegate in mind. She was unable to sign Applegate, and Anders gave the part to Ione Skye instead.

Drew Barrymore was suggested for the part of Shade numerous times. Anders didn't think that Barrymore projected the innocent quality she was looking for in the character. Anders eventually cast Fairuza Balk.

Anders had a hard time casting the part of Dank. She wanted an unknown actor named Hugh Grant. The producers gave her a hard time over Grant because he was unknown. Anders was finally able to cast him, but then Grant dropped out at the last minute. Anders replaced him with Robert Knepper.¹⁴

Gaslight (1944)
Ingrid Bergman as Paula Alquist (Irene Dunne, Hedy Lamarr)

Gaslight was first purchased by Columbia for Irene Dunne to star in.¹⁵ They later sold it to MGM who wanted it for Hedy Lamarr. Lamarr, however, wasn't interested.¹⁶ Ultimately, the part went to Ingrid Bergman.

Gattaca (1997)
Jude Law as Jerome/Eugene Morrow (John Cusack, Johnny Depp, Sean Penn)

The role Jude Law played was first offered to Johnny Depp, Sean Penn, and John Cusack. Depp chose to direct the film *The Brave* instead, and Jude Law was cast.¹⁷

The Gauntlet (1977)
Clint Eastwood as Ben Shockley (Marlon Brando, Steve McQueen)
Sondra Locke as Gus Mally (Barbra Streisand)

The Gauntlet was written with Marlon Brando and Barbra Streisand in mind. Brando didn't want to do it, and the next actor considered was Steve McQueen. Streisand didn't want to work with McQueen, and she suggested Clint Eastwood instead. Eastwood loved the project and signed up for the lead. Streisand eventually decided to drop out of the film, and Eastwood, who was also now directing, replaced her with his girlfriend at the time, Sondra Locke.¹⁸

The Gay Sisters (1942)
Barbara Stanwyck as Fiona Gaylord (Bette Davis)

Bette Davis was offered the part of Fiona Gaylord in *The Gay Sisters*. Davis had no interest in the film and gladly gave the part to Barbara Stanwyck.¹⁹

The General's Daughter (1999)
Madeleine Stowe as Sara Sunhill (Laura Dern)

Laura Dern was reportedly offered $1 million to co-star with John Travolta. Instead she chose to make a film with Billy Bob Thornton, whom she was living with at the time. The film was called *Daddy and Them*, and reports stated that Dern worked for scale, making about $100,000 for the entire shoot. Shortly after, Thornton shocked everyone, including his still-girlfriend Laura Dern, by marrying Angelina Jolie, his co-star in the film *Pushing Tin*.²⁰

Gentleman's Agreement (1947)
Gregory Peck as Phil Green (Tyrone Power)

Tyrone Power turned down *Gentleman's Agreement* in order to star in *The Razor's Edge*.[21]

Gentlemen Prefer Blondes (1953)
Jane Russell as Dorothy Shaw (Betty Grable)
Marilyn Monroe as Lorelei Lee (Betty Grable, Judy Holliday, Betty Hutton)

Twentieth-Century–Fox, Columbia, and Paramount wanted to buy the rights to *Gentlemen Prefer Blondes* to star, respectively, Betty Grable, Judy Holliday, and Betty Hutton. Fox ended up with the property. It was suggested that Grable play the Jane Russell role, but studio chief Darryl F. Zanuck wouldn't hear of it.[22]

The George Raft Story (1961)
Ray Danton as George Raft (Robert Evans)

Actor-turned-producer Robert Evans turned down the role of George Raft.[23] The part was played by Ray Danton.

George White's Scandals (1934)
Alice Faye as Mona Vale (Lilian Harvey)

Lilian Harvey was originally set to play Mona Vale in *George White's Scandals*. She had a fight with George White and left the film. Alice Faye was already cast in a smaller part. Now that there was a vacancy, she was bumped up to the lead. This was her film debut, and she became a star.[24]

Geronimo: An American Legend (1993)
Jason Patric as Lt. Charles Gatewood (Alec Baldwin, Patrick Swayze)

Scheduling problems prevented both Alec Baldwin and Patrick Swayze from starring in *Geronimo*.[25]

The Getaway (1972)
Ali MacGraw as Carol McCoy (Dyan Cannon, Angie Dickinson, Farrah Fawcett, Mariette Hartley, Cybill Shepherd, Stella Stevens)
Al Lettieri as Rudy Butler (Jack Palance)

At one point Peter Bogdanovich was slated to direct *The Getaway*. He wanted his then-girlfriend, Cybill Shepherd, as the female lead. Steve McQueen objected to Shepherd.[26] Bogdanovich left the project and Sam Peckinpah came on board as director. Peckinpah's first choice for the part of Carol was Stella Stevens, with Angie Dickinson, Farrah Fawcett, Dyan Cannon, and Mariette Hartley as possible backup choices. Finally producer David Foster came up with the actress everyone agreed would be perfect—Ali MacGraw. At first MacGraw had no interest in the film, but after a meeting with Peckinpah and the star of the film, Steve McQueen, MacGraw was convinced.[27] She and Steve McQueen fell in love on the set, and MacGraw left her husband producer Robert Evans to marry him.

Peckinpah wanted Jack Palance to play Rudy Butler. Palance's asking price was around $100,000. Peckinpah only had $50,000 to offer. Peckinpah tried to get more money for Palance, even offering to pay the actor himself. Producer David Foster finally persuaded him to look for another actor. Producer Albert S. Ruddy suggested Al Lettieri for the part. Peckinpah liked the idea and gave Lettieri the part. Palance was under the impression that Peckinpah had agreed to give him the part. He sued the director for breach of contract. The case was eventually dismissed.[28]

Ghost (1990)
Patrick Swayze as Sam Wheat (Harrison Ford, Mel Gibson)
Demi Moore as Molly Jensen (Nicole Kidman, Meg Ryan)
Whoopi Goldberg as Oda May Brown (Nell Carter, Patti LaBelle, Tina Turner, Alfre Woodard)

Mel Gibson and Harrison Ford were considered to play Sam Wheat.[29]

The first choice for the role of Molly Jensen was Meg Ryan. Ryan planned to do the film, but just before shooting was to begin she dropped out.[30] Nicole Kidman was considered, but lost out to Demi Moore.[31]

Tina Turner, Patti LaBelle, Nell Carter, and Alfre Woodard were all considered for the role of Oda May, which won Whoopi Goldberg an Oscar.[32]

The Ghost and Mrs. Muir (1947)

Gene Tierney as Lucy Muir (Claudette Colbert, Olivia De Havilland, Katharine Hepburn, Norma Shearer)
Rex Harrison as Capt. Daniel Gregg (Spencer Tracy)
Robert Coote as Coombe (Richard Haydn)

Originally, Spencer Tracy and Katharine Hepburn were set for the leads in *The Ghost and Mrs. Muir*. Suddenly, Tracy changed his mind and dropped out of the film. Without Tracy involved Hepburn also quit. Rex Harrison replaced Tracy while several actresses were considered to play Mrs. Muir including Claudette Colbert and Olivia De Havilland.[33] Norma Shearer was offered the part, but she was retired and turned it down.[34] Eventually Darryl F. Zanuck chose Gene Tierney for the role.

Although Zanuck thought Richard Haydn was perfect for Coombe the part ended up going to Robert Coote instead.[35]

The Ghost & the Darkness (1996)

Val Kilmer as John Henry Patterson (Kevin Costner, Tom Cruise, Mel Gibson)
Michael Douglas as Remington (Sean Connery, Gerard Depardieu, Anthony Hopkins)

Paramount Pictures was interested in making *The Ghost & the Darkness*, on the condition that they could get either Tom Cruise, Mel Gibson, or Kevin Costner to star as John Henry Patterson. As it turned out, Kevin Costner was interested. Now even though Costner was on the list of acceptable male stars, the executives at Paramount were not satisfied. They wanted to wait for Tom Cruise, who was making *Days of Thunder* at the time. Six months later Tom Cruise turned down the part. The once interested but now very angry Kevin Costner also passed. The film was in danger of never getting made until Val Kilmer decided he wanted the part. At this time Kilmer had just become the new Batman, and was very hot. So once he came on board, the film was safe again. Now the search for a co-star was on. Sean Connery was the first to be offered the part of Remington. He turned it down in order to do another film, *The Rock*, which proved to be a big hit. Anthony Hopkins was another possibility. He was unavailable. Gerard Depardieu was the next name on the list, but was never made an offer. This is because Michael Douglas, who was working as a producer on the film, decided to play the part himself.[36]

Ghostbusters (1982)

Bill Murray as Doctor Peter Venkman (John Belushi, Eddie Murphy)
Harold Ramis as Doctor Egon Spengler (Jay Leno)

Ghostbusters was originally intended as a project for Dan Aykroyd and John Belushi to star. However, Belushi died before production began.[37] Eddie Murphy was offered the part of Peter Venkman, but he turned it down.[38] Bill Murray was eventually given the part.

Jay Leno auditioned for the role of Egon Spengler, but lost out to Harold Ramis.

Giant (1956)

James Dean as Jett Rink (Alan Ladd)
Rock Hudson as Bick Benedict (Gary Cooper, Clark Gable, William Holden, Alan Ladd)
Elizabeth Taylor as Leslie Benedict (Grace Kelly)

Director George Stevens was interested in having Alan Ladd star in *Giant*. After reading the book, Ladd was enthusiastic about making the film. He wanted to play the part of Bick Benedict. The problem was, George Stevens wanted Ladd for the part of Jett Rink. Ladd was not interested in playing Jett and said no. Stevens tried to persuade Ladd to take the part. He told him that Jett Rink was the better part. Ladd was torn; he wanted to work with George Stevens, but he also did not want to play a supporting part. He finally turned Stevens down.[39]

Both Clark Gable and Gary Cooper were interested in the role of Bick Benedict.[40] One actor who wanted the part very badly was William Holden. He had gotten together with Stevens a couple of times to discuss it. What he didn't know was that Stevens was also interested in Rock Hudson. Stevens thought that it would be easier to age Hudson for the role than it would be for him to make Holden appear younger. Ironically, Holden was born only seven years before Rock Hudson. When Holden found out that he lost the part to Hudson he was upset, but still made a point to congratulate Hudson personally.[41]

Grace Kelly turned down the part of Leslie Benedict.[42]

Gidget Goes Hawaiian (1961)
Deborah Walley as Gidget [aka Frances Lawrence] (Sandra Dee)

Sandra Dee scored a big hit in the title role of Gidget. The film was so successful that a sequel was planned called *Gidget Goes Hawaiian*. Dee's studio, Universal, was contacted about the new film. The studio had other plans for Dee. They refused to loan her out to Columbia Pictures. Instead they starred her as Tammy Tyree in *Tammy Tell Me True*. Deborah Walley became the new Gidget.[43]

Gigi (1958)
Leslie Caron as Gigi (Audrey Hepburn)
Louis Jourdan as Gaston Lachaille (Dirk Bogarde)
Hermione Gingold as Madame Alvarez (Jeanette MacDonald)
Isabel Jeans as Tante Alicia (Ina Claire, Yvonne Printemps)

Audrey Hepburn's big break came when she starred in *Gigi* on Broadway. Five years later it was being made into a movie. Now a major star, Hepburn was offered the chance to recreate the role for the screen. She declined, feeling she had grown in five years and might not be able to play the part in the same way.[44]

Dirk Bogarde wanted to play Gaston Lachaille, but was unable due to a studio contract with J. Arthur Rank.[45]

Jeanette MacDonald was considered for the part of Madame Alvarez, ultimately played by Hermione Gingold.[46]

Director Vincente Minnelli was turned down by Ina Claire[47] and Yvonne Printemps[48] for the part of Tante Alicia.

A Girl, a Guy, and a Gob (1941)
Lucille Ball as Dot Duncan (Maureen O'Hara)

Maureen O'Hara turned down the role of Dot Duncan. It was O'Hara who suggested Lucille Ball for the part.[49]

The Girl in the Red Velvet Swing (1955)
Joan Collins as Evelyn Nesbit (Marilyn Monroe, Terry Moore, Debra Paget

Marilyn Monroe was the first choice to play Evelyn Nesbit in *The Girl in the Red Velvet Swing*. She turned it down, and Terry Moore, Debra Paget, and Joan Collins were tested. The producers eventually chose Collins.[50]

Girl, Interrupted (1999)
Angelina Jolie as Lisa Rowe (Courtney Love)

Courtney Love and Angelina Jolie vied for the part of Lisa Rowe in *Girl, Interrupted*. Jolie won the part. Her performance was critically acclaimed. She was rewarded with an Academy Award for her work in the film.[51]

The Girl Next Door (1953)
June Haver as Jeannie Laird (Betty Grable)

Instead of reporting for work on *The Girl Next Door*, Betty Grable went on vacation with her family. She was replaced by June Haver.[52]

The Girl of the Golden West (1938)
Jeanette MacDonald as Mary Robbins (Joan Crawford)
Nelson Eddy as Ramerez/Lieutenant Johnson (Allan Jones)

Joan Crawford tried for the role of Mary Robbins in *The Girl of the Golden West*. Director Robert Z. Leonard preferred Jeanette MacDonald and gave her the part instead. MacDonald thought that Allan Jones would be perfect to play opposite her. Louis B. Mayer didn't agree with her. MacDonald and Eddy had worked in four films together already, and Mayer thought that audiences liked the MacDonald-Eddy pairing, and might not accept her with a new leading man. Meanwhile, Nelson Eddy had heard that Allan Jones was being talked about for the role. He told Mayer that he would not take it lightly if he lost the role to Jones. Mayer, who preferred Eddy from the beginning, did not want to upset his leading man. He gave the part to Nelson Eddy.[53]

Glengarry Glen Ross (1992)
Jack Lemmon as Shelley Levine (Robert De Niro)

In the very early planning stages Ulu Grosbard was mentioned to direct with Al Pacino and Robert De Niro starring in the screen version of

God Is My Co-Pilot (1945)

Dennis Morgan as Col. Robert L. Scott (Humphrey Bogart)

Humphrey Bogart turned down the role of Col. Robert L. Scott. Jack Warner was upset by his decision. He called Bogart ungrateful. Bogart responded by tearing up his studio contract. He said that the part of Robert L. Scott was mediocre. He went on to say that he did not have confidence in Michael Curtiz, the director. He also claimed that he needed the time to prevent a breakdown. The part was recast with Dennis Morgan. Bogart was put on suspension.[55] Incidentally, Curtiz was replaced by director Robert Florey.

David Mamet's hit play, *Glengarry Glen Ross*. The project was dropped for about five years. Al Pacino remained in the cast, but Grosbard was out as the director. In his place was James Foley, who cast Jack Lemmon in the co-starring role of Shelley Levine.[54]

The Godfather (1972)

Marlon Brando as Don Vito Corleone (Melvin Belli, Ernest Borgnine, Richard Conte, Vince Edwards, David Janssen, Burt Lancaster, John Marley, Laurence Olivier, Carlo Ponti, Anthony Quinn, George C. Scott, Rudy Vallee, Raf Vallone)

Al Pacino as Michael Corleone (Warren Beatty, Charles Bronson, James Caan, Alain Delon, Robert De Niro, Dustin Hoffman, Tony Lo Bianco, Jack Nicholson, Ryan O'Neal, Robert Redford, Martin Sheen, Rod Steiger, Dean Stockwell)

James Caan as Sonny Corleone (Carmine Caridi, Robert De Niro, Burt Reynolds, John Saxon)

Diane Keaton as Kay Adams (Anne Archer, Karen Black, Susan Blakely, Genevieve Bujold, Jill Clayburgh, Blythe Danner, Veronica Hamel, Ali MacGraw, Jennifer O'Neill, Michelle Phillips, Jennifer Salt, Cybill Shepherd, Trish Van Devere)

Robert Duvall as Tom Hagen (James Caan, Peter Donat, Martin Sheen, Rudy Vallee)

Al Martino as Johnny Fontane (Frankie Avalon, Vic Damone, Eddie Fisher, Buddy Greco, Frank Sinatra, Jr., Bobby Vinton)

Talia Shire as Connie Corleone Rizzi (Julie Gregg, Penny Marshall, Maria Tucci, Brenda Vaccaro, Kathleen Widdoes)

Gianni Russo as Carlo Rizzi (John Ryan)

Lenny Montana as Luca Brasi (Richard Castellano)

Morgana King as Mama Corleone (Anne Bancroft, Alida Valli)

John Martino as Paulie Gatto (Robert De Niro)

In 1968, producer Robert Evans acquired the rights to writer Mario Puzo's new script called *Mafia*. A little over a year later the script was turned into a novel and retitled *The Godfather*. The novel was a huge hit, and Evans was ready to start production on the film version. There was, however, a problem. Paramount Pictures didn't want the film made. They said that Sicilian mob movies weren't successful. Evans was undaunted and continued to look for a director to make the film. No one wanted the job including Elia Kazan, Arthur Penn, Costa-Gavras, and Richard Brooks. They all felt that it was wrong to show the Mafia in a glamorous light. Burt Lancaster had the same vision Evans did. He thought the picture would be a hit, and wanted very much to play the title role. An offer was made to buy the rights, which Paramount was interested in taking. Evans had to prove to the studio that this property was worth keeping. He told the studio that the reason mob movies hadn't fared well lately was because they were not made by Italians. *The Godfather* would be different, he promised them. The studio reluctantly decided not to sell to Lancaster, and Evans hired Italian-American director Francis Ford Coppola to direct the film.[56]

Coppola considered hundreds of actors for the starring role of Don Vito Corleone in *The Godfather* including David Janssen, Rudy Vallee, John Marley, and Vince Edwards.[57] Richard Conte was another Vito Corleone candidate. Coppola said that he videotaped every old Italian actor around, until he realized that he wanted a star for the role.[58] There were many stars that were interested. Ernest Borgnine[59] wanted the part, as well as the famous lawyer Melvin Belli.[60] Evans suggested having director Carlo Ponti play the role. Anthony Quinn was considered, along with Raf Vallone. Finally Coppola and casting director Fred Roos narrowed the choice down to three: Laurence Olivier, George C. Scott, and Marlon Brando. Coppola said that it became clear to him that the thing to do was to hire the best actor in the world for the part. Scott was eliminated and Brando and Olivier were pursued. Olivier was sick with cancer, which made him unavailable for the movie. There was one actor left: Brando. Brando told Mario Puzo that Paramount would not want to hire him, which turned out to be true. Many of his recent films had not done well, and the great actor had a reputation for being difficult on the set. The studio told Coppola that Brando would have to make a screen test for the part. This was clever on their part, because it was widely known that Brando never made tests. Coppola met with Brando and brought along a video camera. They discussed how he might play the character, and Coppola slyly suggested trying it out on tape. Brando, not knowing this was a test, agreed. The actor stuffed his cheeks with tissues and played the part. Coppola presented the tape to the studio. The executives loved the test, and Marlon Brando became the Godfather.[61]

For the role of Michael Corleone, producer Albert Ruddy wanted to cast Robert Redford. Although Redford was a superstar, nobody liked the idea of him as Michael. Ruddy told Mario Puzo that in order to have Redford in the film he would have to change the script. He said that the film would need to open with a love scene between Kay and Michael. Puzo was contractually obligated to write the scene. Robert Redford was made an offer, but to everyone's (except Ruddy's) delight, he turned it down. Rod Steiger was interested, but Puzo felt he was way too old for the part.[62] Dustin Hoffman[63] was considered, as well as Alain Delon,[64] Charles Bronson,[65] and Warren Beatty,[66] who turned it down. Robert Evans had just completed the film *Love Story*. He thought that Ryan O'Neal, the star of that film, would be a good match for Michael. O'Neal screen-tested, but the test did not turn out well.[67] Coppola tested many other actors including Jack Nicholson,[68] Robert De Niro, Martin Sheen,[69] Dean Stockwell,[70] Tony Lo Bianco,[71] James Caan,[72] and Al Pacino. Pacino was unknown at the time, but Coppola thought he was perfect. The studio disagreed at first but was eventually won over. The offered the part to Pacino. He took the role, even though it meant he had to drop out of the film *The Gang That Couldn't Shoot Straight*. His replacement in that film was another Michael Corleone contender — Robert De Niro.[73]

Burt Reynolds expressed interest in playing the supporting role of Sonny Corleone. Marlon Brando didn't think that Reynolds was right, and the studio agreed.[74] Actors such as Robert De Niro,[75] John Saxon,[76] James Caan, and Carmine Caridi were tested. Coppola decided to give the part to Caridi. But it was not meant to be. Robert Evans decided that if James Caan was not going to play Michael Corleone, Coppola would have to cast him as Sonny. Coppola reluctantly agreed, and Caridi lost the role he had already celebrated getting.[77]

Jill Clayburgh, Michelle Phillips, and Susan Blakely all screen tested for the role of Kay Adams. Coppola and Roos didn't think any of them were exactly what they were looking for and also considered Cybill Shepherd, Jennifer O'Neill, Karen Black, Anne Archer, Genevieve Bujold, Trish Van Devere, Blythe Danner, Jennifer Salt, and Veronica Hamel. Robert Evans' wife Ali MacGraw was also up for the part. Coppola's search for a leading lady ended when he decided to cast Diane Keaton as Kay.

Martin Sheen, James Caan, and Peter Donat were all considered for the role of Tom Hagen. Rudy Vallee's agent called Albert Ruddy to say that Vallee would be perfect as Tom. Vallee was then in his sixties, and the character was supposed to be thirty-five! Coppola kept looking, and finally found Robert Duvall.

Coppola wanted to cast a star for the part of singer Johnny Fontane. He considered real-life singers such as Eddie Fisher, Bobby, Vinton, Frankie Avalon, Buddy Greco, and Frank Sinatra, Jr. Rumor had it that Sinatra Jr. was persuaded by his father to turn down the part. Many have speculated that the part of Johnny Fontane was based on Frank Sinatra, who wanted to have nothing to do with the film. Coppola cast Vic Damone in the part, but Damone later dropped out. He said that the film was "not in the best interests of Italian-Americans," although he later said the real reason was that he was not being paid enough money. Coppola replaced him with singer Al Martino.

Penny Marshall, Brenda Vaccaro, Kathleen Widdoes, Maria Tucci, and Julie Gregg all tried for the part of Connie Corleone Rizzi. Coppola liked Gregg, and gave her the smaller role of Sonny's wife Sandra. He gave the role of Connie to his sister, actress Talia Shire.

Coppola signed John Ryan for the part of Connie's husband, Carlo. When he had to drop out, the part went to Gianni Russo.

Richard Castellano tried for the role of Luca Brasi. Coppola decided Castellano would make a better Clemenza, and gave the role of Luca Brasi to Lenny Montana.

Coppola wanted Anne Bancroft, Alida Valli, or Morgana King to play Mama Corleone. He gave the part to King. Although this was her first acting job, King was already famous as a singer.

Robert De Niro was cast in the role of Paulie Gatto until he got the chance to star in *The Gang That Couldn't Shoot Straight*. He dropped out, and was replaced by John Martino.[78]

The Godfather Part II (1974)

Robert De Niro as Young Vito Corleone (Marlon Brando)
Lee Strasberg as Hyman Roth (Elia Kazan)
James Gouranis as Anthony Corleone (Robby Benson)

[*Vito Corleone*— Marlon Brando; *Peter Clemenza*— Richard Castellano]

Francis Ford Coppola wanted Marlon Brando to return for the sequel *The Godfather Part II*. Since Brando's character, Don Vito Corleone, died in the first film, the only part he could play was the young version of Vito. Brando wanted no part of this film. He had a problem with the head of Paramount, Frank Yablans. Brando asked for a lot of money, which Paramount wouldn't pay. Coppola remembered an actor who had tested for the part of Michael Corleone in the first film, Robert De Niro. At the time, Coppola thought that De Niro resembled Brando. Coppola was interested, but Paramount didn't want him. Coppola insisted, and finally won. Makeup artist Dick Smith tried to use makeup to make De Niro look even more like Brando, but the idea was eventually scrapped. Like Brando, De Niro won an Academy Award for his portrayal of Vito Corleone.

Legendary director Elia Kazan was Coppola's first choice to play Hyman Roth. One hot summer day Coppola and Fred Roos traveled to Kazan's office to discuss the film. They opened the door and found a shirtless Kazan working. This image struck Coppola as being totally right for the character. Kazan was too busy to make the film and turned them down. The next choice was Lee Strasberg. Coppola and Roos were unsure of how to approach him. When Sally Kirkland learned of their problem, she decided to throw a party. On the guest list were Francis Ford Coppola, Fred Roos, and Lee Strasberg, who all attended. At the party the pair approached Strasberg and offered him the part.

Strasberg accepted the role, which now included a brand new scene in which Hyman Roth appears without his shirt on.

An eighteen-year-old Robby Benson was initially linked to the part of Anthony Corleone. Since the role called for a child, Benson was obviously the wrong choice. He was replaced by nine-year-old James Gouranis. Incidentally, Gouranis' brother Anthony Gouranis played Anthony Corleone in the first film.

Coppola wanted Marlon Brando to reprise his role of Vito Corleone in a flashback for the sequel. The problem was that Brando was feuding with Frank Yablans. Yablans had been so angered by Brando's refusal of his Oscar (for the first *Godfather* film) that he was openly hostile towards the actor. Brando demanded a high salary to appear in the film, and was unwilling to come down in price. Paramount finally decided that *The Godfather Part II* would proceed without Marlon Brando.

Richard Castellano wanted an exorbitant amount of money to reprise his role of Clemenza. In addition, Castellano also wanted to rewrite his dialogue and for his girlfriend to be cast in the film as well. Coppola eliminated his part in the film, and replaced the character with a new one—Frankie Pentangeli played by Michael V. Gazzo.[79]

The Godfather Part III (1990)

Andy Garcia as Vincent Mancini (Kevin Anderson, Alec Baldwin, Nicolas Cage, Robert De Niro, Matt Dillon, Val Kilmer, Charlie Sheen, Vincent Spano, Billy Zane)
Eli Wallach as Don Altobello (Frank Sinatra)
Joe Mantegna as Joey Zasa (Mickey Rourke, John Turturro)
Sofia Coppola as Mary Corleone (Trini Alvarado, Bridget Fonda, Madonna, Julia Roberts, Winona Ryder, Laura San Giacomo, Annabella Sciorra)
Bridget Fonda as Grace Hamilton (Diane Lane, Madonna, Virginia Madsen)
Donal Donnelly as Archbishop Liam Francis Gilday (Albert Finney, Vittorio Gassman, Marcello Mastroianni, Yves Montand, Phillippe Noiret, Gian Maria Volonte)
Franc D'Ambrosio as Anthony Corleone (John Travolta)

Raf Vallone as Cardinal Lamberto
  (Vittorio Gassman, Yves Montand, Michel Piccoli)
Vittorio Duse as Don Tommasino
  (Corrado Gaipa, Tom Hagen, Robert Duvall)

Robert De Niro went after the role of Vincent Mancini. Francis Ford Coppola thought that he was ineligible, having played young Vito Corleone in *The Godfather Part II*. De Niro argued that the two characters are related, thus explaining the physical resemblance. Coppola tested him, but eventually decided it would be better to go with a different actor. Many actors were tested including Alec Baldwin, Kevin Anderson, Matt Dillon, Charlie Sheen, Val Kilmer, Vincent Spano, and Billy Zane. Coppola even had his nephew Nicolas Cage audition, but in due time chose Andy Garcia instead.

Frank Sinatra was interested in the part of Don Altobello. The legendary singer ultimately decided that the shooting would take too long. Coppola cast Eli Wallach in his place.

The part of Joey Zasa came down to a decision between two actors—Mickey Rourke and Joe Mantegna. The deciding factor was that Mantegna was Italian. Coppola's back-up choice in case there was a problem with Mantegna was John Turturro.

The actress Coppola wanted for Mary was Julia Roberts. When she proved unavailable the part was up for grabs. Madonna was a strong contender. It was decided that at 31 she was too old to be convincing as the young Mary Corleone. Coppola looked at Annabella Sciorra, Laura San Giacomo, Trini Alvarado, Winona Ryder, and Bridget Fonda. Fonda was deemed too WASPy. Coppola decided that Winona Ryder was the best choice. Ryder had just finished working on *Welcome Home Roxy Carmichael* and *Mermaids*. She began work on *The Godfather Part III*. About a month later Ryder felt that she would be unable to complete the film. She couldn't get out of bed and was sent to a doctor who informed Coppola that the young actress was exhausted. Ryder was released from the film. Coppola again asked about Julia Roberts, who was still unattainable. He reconsidered both Annabella Sciorra and Laura San Giacomo, but then realized that the actress he was looking for was right under his nose. He gave the part to his daughter Sofia Coppola. The script was rewritten to make Mary (then 26) younger since Sofia was only 19 at the time. When the film came out Coppola was criticized for his nepotism. Sofia Coppola's performance was widely panned. Sofia Coppola didn't do much acting after the film. She did have success later on, though, as a director, most notably for the 2003 film *Lost in Translation*.

After Coppola rejected Madonna for the part of Mary Corleone he thought that maybe she would be right for journalist Grace Hamilton. Madonna wanted $500,000 for the part. Paramount balked at her salary request and told Coppola that she was too big a star for the part, that people would see Madonna and not the character. Other contenders were Diane Lane and Virginia Madsen, but Coppola chose Bridget Fonda instead.

Albert Finney, Phillippe Noiret, Yves Montand, Vittorio Gassman, Marcello Mastroianni, and Gian Maria Volonte were all considered for the part of Archbishop Liam Francis Gilday. Coppola decided to make the character Irish to accommodate an actor he had admired for years—Donal Donnelly. Over twenty years earlier Donnelly auditioned for Coppola when he was directing the film version of *Finian's Rainbow*. Although Coppola didn't think he was right for that film, he was impressed by his audition. When the role of the Archbishop came up Coppola remembered Donnelly and gave him the part.[80]

Paramount considered having John Travolta play Anthony Corleone.[81] However, once Coppola signed on to direct he hired newcomer Franc D'Ambrosio. Since Anthony is an opera singer Coppola went for a singer. D'Ambrosio was appearing on Broadway in *Sweeney Todd*. Coppola wanted him so much that he had Paramount buy out his contract.[82]

Yves Montand, Vittorio Gassman, and Michel Piccoli were all considered for the part of Cardinal Lamberto.

Corrado Gaipa died before shooting commenced. Coppola replaced him with Vittorio Duse.[83]

Robert Duvall was asked to return as lawyer Tom Hagen. Duvall asked for $5 million.[84] The studio wouldn't pay, and Duvall's character was written out of the film.

Godzilla (1998)

Matthew Broderick as Nick Tatopoulos
  (Bill Paxton)
Maria Pitillo as Audrey Timmonds
  (Helen Hunt, Sarah Jessica Parker)

Bill Paxton and Helen Hunt were a possible pair for the leads in *Godzilla*.[85] They previously starred in *Twister* together. Matthew Broderick's wife, Sarah Jessica Parker, tried for the role of Audrey but lost out to Maria Pitillo.[86]

Goin' South (1978)

Mary Steenburgen as Julia Tate (Jane Fonda, Jessica Lange)

Jane Fonda was sought for the part of Julia Tate. Jessica Lange auditioned for the part.[87] Director Jack Nicholson's search ended in an office building in New York City where he encountered Mary Steenburgen, who was not there to audition. Nicholson spotted her, and invited her in to read for the part. She was flown to Hollywood for a screen test and won the role.

Going My Way (1944)

Bing Crosby as Father Chuck O'Malley (James Cagney, Spencer Tracy)

Neither Spencer Tracy nor James Cagney were available to star in *Going My Way*, leaving the part free for Bing Crosby.[88] Crosby won the Best Actor Oscar for his performance.

The Gold Rush (1925)

Georgia Hale as Georgia (Lita Grey, Carole Lombard)

A 15-year-old Carole Lombard lost out to Lita Grey for the part of Georgia in *The Gold Rush*. However, Grey became pregnant (with director Charlie Chaplin's baby) and was replaced by Georgia Hale.[89]

Golden Boy (1939)

Barbara Stanwyck as Lorna Moon (Jean Arthur)

William Holden as Joe Bonaparte (John Garfield, Alan Ladd, Tyrone Power, Gene Raymond)

Initially Frank Capra planned to make *Golden Boy*. He imagined Jean Arthur as his leading lady. However Capra decided he would rather make *Mr. Smith Goes to Washington* and traded films with director Rouben Mamoulian. The new director gave the part of Lorna Moon to Barbara Stanwyck.[90]

Studio head Harry Cohn wanted John Garfield to play Joe Bonaparte. Garfield was the original star of *Golden Boy* when it premiered as a Broadway play. Garfield was under contract to Warner Bros. When Cohn contacted Jack Warner, Warner told him that he was not willing to lend out Garfield.[91] The next actor Cohn considered was Tyrone Power. He ran into the same problem with Power's studio, 20th Century–Fox.[92] Gene Raymond tried for the part, but was turned down.[93] It was at that point that Harry Cohn decided that the starring role in *Golden Boy* was to be played by a newcomer. An open audition was announced. Hundreds and hundreds of actors came to audition, including Alan Ladd.[94] Ladd was not a star at the time. He was instructed to show up at the audition looking Italian. He sent his wife Midge to buy mascara which she later applied to his blond hair. The day of the audition was very hot. During his reading the mascara began to run down his neck.[95] One actor who caught Harry Cohn's eye was an unknown William Holden. Cohn noticed that Holden had the look he wanted for the part. He gave Holden a screen test. After some deliberation Holden had the part. The role of Joe Bonaparte made William Holden a star.

Goldeneye (1995)

Pierce Brosnan as James Bond (Ralph Fiennes, Mel Gibson, Hugh Grant, Liam Neeson, Adrian Paul, Sharon Stone)

Mel Gibson was the first choice to be the new James Bond. Gibson wasn't interested and turned down the $15 million he was being offered. Next on the list was Liam Neeson, who

Lita Grey missed out on starring in *The Gold Rush*.

felt it wasn't enough of a serious role. Ralph Fiennes was a strong contender, but he and producer Cubby Broccoli saw the character in very different ways, which squashed the deal. Adrian Paul was considered, as was Hugh Grant.[96] There was even talk of having a female James Bond as the film's star and Sharon Stone's name was mentioned.[97] In the end the part went to Pierce Brosnan, who had been waiting for about eight years for another chance to play Bond. Brosnan was offered the Bond role in *The Living Daylights*, but was forced to turn it down because of his contract with the TV series *Remington Steele*.

Goldfinger (1964)

Austin Willis as Mr. Simmons (Cec Linder)
Cec Linder as Felix Leiter (Austin Willis)

Austin Willis was originally cast as Felix Leiter. He and co-star Cec Linder exchanged roles at the last minute, and Willis became Mr. Simmons with Linder now playing Leiter.[98]

Gone with the Wind (1939)

Clark Gable as Rhett Butler (Warner Baxter, Ronald Colman, Gary Cooper, Errol Flynn, Fredric March, Groucho Marx, Basil Rathbone)
Vivien Leigh as Scarlett O'Hara (Katharine Aldridge, Mary Anderson, Ardis Ankerson, Jean Arthur, Lucille Ball, Tallulah Bankhead, Diana Barrymore, Joan Bennett, Em Bowles Locker, Catherine Campbell, Claudette Colbert, Nancy Coleman, Joan Crawford, Doris Davenport, Bette Davis, Fleurette DeBussy, Frances Dee, Marie Dressler, Irene Dunne, Joan Fontaine, Diana Forrest, Susan Fox, Paulette Goddard, Jean Harlow, Susan Hayward, Katharine Hepburn, Miriam Hopkins, Linda Lee, Shirley Logan, Carole Lombard, Adele Longmire, Anita Louise, Marcella Martin, Dorothy Mathews, Austine McDonnel, Lynn Merrill, Louise Platt, Mary Ray, Terry Ray, Alicia Rhett, Norma Shearer, Ann Sheridan, Haila Stoddard, Margaret Sullavan, Lyn Swann, Margaret Tallichet, Lana Turner, Linda Watkins, Liz Whitney, Shelley Winters, Loretta Young)
Leslie Howard as Ashley Wilkes (Lew Ayres, Melvyn Douglas, Jeffrey Lynn, Ray Milland, Shepperd Strudwick)
Olivia De Havilland as Melanie Hamilton Wilkes (Ann Dvorak, Joan Fontaine, Janet Gaynor, Linda Gray, Julie Haydon, Dorothy Jordan, Priscilla Lane, Andrea Leeds, Maureen O'Sullivan, Anne Shirley)
Hattie McDaniel as Mammy (Louise Beavers, Lizzie McDuffie, Hattie Noel)
Oscar Polk as Pork (Eddie Anderson)
Barbara O'Neil as Ellen O'Hara (Lillian Gish, Cornelia Otis Skinner)
Harry Davenport as Dr. Meade (Lionel Barrymore)
Leona Roberts as Mrs. Meade (Janet Beecher)
Jane Darwell as Dolly Merriwether (Janet Beecher)
Laura Hope Crews as Pittypat Hamilton (Billie Burke)
Ona Munson as Belle Watling (Tallulah Bankhead, Joan Blondell, Gladys George, Mae West, Loretta Young)
Ann Rutherford as Careen O'Hara (Judy Garland)

Although producer David O. Selznick sent talent scouts across the country to find an unknown actress for the starring role of Scarlett O'Hara, he knew that this was more for publicity than anything else.[99] Selznick wanted Bette Davis to star as Scarlett with Errol Flynn as Rhett Butler. Davis wouldn't hear of it. She felt that Flynn was wrong for the role, which would make her look bad.[100] She also stated that Flynn didn't respect her as an actress. Davis said no to Scarlett, but played a similar role in the film *Jezebel* instead.

Selznick's brother, agent Myron Selznick, suggested his client, Paulette Goddard. Goddard was tested for the part. Selznick liked her so much that he called her back numerous times. Goddard was Jewish, which worried Selznick. He thought audiences might not accept her as Scarlett. Her tests were too good to ignore however.[101] He and George Cukor (then set to direct) decided to give her the part. A problem soon arose. At the time Goddard was living with Charlie Chaplin. The two stated that they were married, but were unable to produce a marriage certificate. This, along with the fact Chaplin was accused of being a communist, was enough to incite thousands of people to write letters of protest to Selznick-International. Not wanting the film boycotted, Selznick chose to look for another actress.[102] He considered Norma Shearer. To test the waters Selznick decided to leak the news of her as a possible Scarlett to Walter Winchell. The public reaction was not good. Shearer's fans wrote letter after letter saying that she was all wrong for the part, that she was too nice and ladylike to play the part. Shearer withdrew her name from consideration.[103]

George Cukor's dear friend Katharine Hepburn was another prospect. Selznick felt that she was the wrong type for the part. For one thing, she was from New England. Selznick also complained that Hepburn was not sexy enough. Hepburn was such a big star, though, that Selznick still considered her. He told Cukor to test her. Hepburn refused to audition.[104] She agreed that if it were the day shooting was to start and no suitable Scarlett had been found, she would step into the role.[105]

Alabama born Tallulah Bankhead went after the role. Her southern upbringing was a plus, but at 35 Bankhead seemed too old for the part.[106] David O. Selznick thought Bankhead would make a better Belle Watling. He wanted to offer her the part, but dropped the idea worrying that it would infuriate her.[107]

Ben Piazza, the head of casting at RKO, informed Lucille Ball that she would be auditioning to play Scarlett.[108] Ball thought she was completely wrong for it, and didn't even show up for her audition. David O. Selznick called RKO to make sure she would come in to see him.[109] Ball worked with Will Price on her southern accent. Price was hired by Selznick as an advisor on the film. The day of her audition, Ball drove to Selznick's office in an open convertible. A heavy rain started to fall as she was in the car. By the time she reached the studio, she was drenched. Selznick's assistant Marcella Rabwin felt for her. She gave her a fresh sweater to put on, as well as a glass of brandy. Selznick arrived to find Ball waiting in his office, sitting by the fire. Ball read three scenes, but failed to nab the part.[110]

Miriam Hopkins seemed to many the perfect choice. She was from Georgia, just like Scarlett. She had also played the title role of *Becky Sharpe*, a character very similar to Scarlett. David O. Selznick considered Hopkins. Unfortunately for Hopkins, after Selznick saw *Becky Sharpe* he was no longer interested in her for Scarlett.

Myron Selznick submitted Margaret Sullavan's name for consideration. David Selznick agreed to see her, but only as a courtesy.[111]

An 18-year-old Lana Turner was tested with Melvyn Douglas playing Ashley. Selznick knew she was too young for the part, and lacked the acting experience to pull it off.[112]

Selznick briefly considered Ann Sheridan, but eventually dropped her from the list of possibilities.[113]

Jean Arthur was tested on December 17, 1938.[114] Before Selznick was married to Irene Mayer, he had been in love with Arthur.[115]

A pairing of Clark Gable and Carole Lombard intrigued Selznick. He ultimately decided that Lombard's comic persona was wrong for Scarlett.[116]

An unknown named Edythe Marrener traveled to California for a screen test. Although Cukor was impressed with the young actress, he felt that she was not experienced enough to handle a role such as Scarlett. Unknown to Marrener she was never really a contender for the part. Cukor thought she was too young, and utterly inexperienced. She continued to make screen tests, but only as a reader in other actor's tests. Selznick thought she had potential, and put her under contract. Marrener later changed her name to Susan Hayward.[117]

Joan Crawford was briefly considered.[118]

An unknown Margaret Tallichet was tested, as was Joan Bennett and Doris Davenport, then known as Doris Jordan. Also considered were Anita Louise, Frances Dee, Marcella Martin, and Nancy Coleman.[119] Alicia Rhett auditioned, but didn't make the cut.[120] Rhett and Mary Anderson turned up at an audition for unknowns. Although they lost the role of Scarlett, Selznick found a place for them in the film. Rhett was cast as India Wilkes, and Anderson played Maybelle Merriwether.[121]

A teenage Shelley Winters learned where auditions for Scarlett were being held. Winters was a big fan of the book, and was confident that she was right for the part. She made herself up as her version of a southern belle and went to see Selznick. She was led into the office where she found not only Selznick, but George Cukor and talent scout Bill Grady. She announced in a southern accent that she should play Scarlett O'Hara. Selznick and Grady laughed at her, but George Cukor stopped them. Cukor asked her to sit down, and asked her about her future goals. He advised her to finish college, study acting, and work in the theater before trying to conquer Hollywood. Winters was impressed by his kindness, so much so that she wasn't too disappointed by losing the part.[122]

Other Scarlett contenders included Louise

Platt, Susan Fox, Diana Barrymore, Shirley Logan, Austine McDonnel, Mary Ray, Katharine Aldridge, Terry Ray, Fleurette DeBussy, Haila Stoddard, Lyn Swann, Em Bowes Locker, Linda Watkins, Linda Lee, Adele Longmire, Ardis Ankerson, Dorothy Mathews, Diana Forrest and Lynn Merrill.[123]

Time was drawing to a close and Selznick began to consider just about anyone else he hadn't already seen. He wanted to test Loretta Young. Young refused to audition, and Selznick dropped her from consideration.[124] Other possibilities were Jean Harlow, Irene Dunne, Claudette Colbert, and Marie Dressler.[125] Liz Whitney and Catherine Campbell were potential Scarletts,[126] as well as Joan Bennett.[127]

Vivien Leigh told her agent Harry Ham to put her up for Scarlett. Leigh was unaware that Selznick had already been thinking of her as a possibility. In fact, he was intent on having her play the part, but kept it a secret from the public. At the time Leigh was married to Herbert Leigh Holman, but was carrying on an affair with Laurence Olivier. Olivier was then married to Jill Esmond. Leigh and Olivier were in love and planned to divorce their respective spouses. Selznick urged them to wait until after he could publicly announce the casting of Scarlett. Selznick negotiated to buy out Leigh's contract with from Alexander Korda. At first Korda was not cooperative, which forced Selznick to keep testing other actresses. Finally, Korda relented. Selznick instructed his brother Myron to bring Leigh to the *Gone with the Wind* set the night the burning of Atlanta scene was being shot. While there, Selznick would supposedly "discover" Vivien Leigh. Leigh and Olivier arrived on the set as planned. However, Myron Selznick failed to show up. Selznick went along with the hoax as planned, and Myron finally showed up. The story of Leigh's supposed discovery was reported to the press and has become Hollywood legend.

Polls showed that the public wanted Clark Gable to play Rhett Butler. Gable was under contract to MGM at the time. Gable was wary of the part. He knew that the public had expectations of how the character should be, and he didn't want to be disappointing in the role. He wasn't interested, and Selznick was forced to look at other actors. Warner Bros. offered to loan out the package deal of Bette Davis and Errol Flynn. Davis didn't want to work with Flynn. Selznick thought that Flynn's acting was not up to the demands of Rhett Butler and eliminated him from consideration.

Selznick wanted to borrow Gary Cooper from Sam Goldwyn. Goldwyn refused to lend Cooper out, and Selznick continued his search.

Selznick was briefly interested in Ronald Colman. Colman told Selznick that he thought *Gone with the Wind* was tremendous, and that he would love to play Rhett Butler. Colman's English accent eventually turned the producer off, and Colman was out of the running.

Basil Rathbone was a contender, as well as Fredric March. However, March had been publicly accused of being a communist, which was the end of his possible involvement with the film.

Southerner Warner Baxter was considered. It was determined that Baxter lacked the sex appeal necessary for Rhett.

Author Margaret Mitchell stayed out of the making of *Gone with the Wind* for the most part. Her one casting suggestion was Groucho Marx as Rhett Butler.

Unable to find an appropriate Rhett Butler, Selznick went back to Clark Gable. Selznick's father-in-law, Louis B. Mayer, offered Gable a $100,000 bonus for taking the part. At the time Gable needed the money. He had fallen in love with Carole Lombard, and wanted to divorce his wife, Rhea Langham. Langham's lawyer asked for a hefty settlement of $265,000. Gable agreed to play Rhett. Once his divorce was finalized, he wasted no time and married Lombard.[128]

Melvyn Douglas was tested to play Ashley Wilkes. Selznick and Cukor thought his test was great, but that he was physically wrong for the part.[129] Irene Mayer Selznick suggested Ray Milland. Her husband, however, was bothered by Milland's Welsh accent. Jeffrey Lynn tested, but Selznick was unimpressed.[130] Also considered were Lew Ayres[131] and Shepperd Strudwick.[132] Selznick finally decided that the one actor he wanted was Leslie Howard. This was problematic, because Howard did not want the part. Howard saw Ashley as weak. Howard had played a long line of similar characters, and was ready for a change. Selznick made Howard an offer, which he refused. Selznick was determined to sign Howard. He knew that the actor wanted to also work behind the camera. He proposed to Howard that if he played Ashley, then Selznick would not only have him as the star of *Intermezzo*, but he would also hire him as the associate producer. Howard reluctantly accepted this offer. Howard had to shoot both *Gone with the Wind* and *Intermezzo* at the same time. Ironically, Howard was so busy acting in both films that he didn't have the time to do the one job he most enthusiastic about — produce *Intermezzo*.[133]

Janet Gaynor was an early contender for the role of Melanie.[134] Other possibilities included Priscilla Lane, Maureen O'Sullivan and Ann Dvorak.[135] Andrea Leeds was considered,[136] as well as Julie Haydon, Anne Shirley, Olivia De Havilland, Dorothy Jordan, Linda Gray and Scarlett contender Joan Fontaine.[137]

Olivia De Havilland went to Selznick's home to read for the part. De Havilland read for Melanie with Selznick reading Scarlett opposite her. He was so impressed with her audition that he decided to look no further. De Havilland was under contract to Warner Bros.[138] Jack Warner told Selznick that he would not loan her out for *Gone with the Wind*. De Havilland was determined to change his mind. She arranged to meet Warner's wife at the Brown Derby. De Havilland plead her case to Mrs. Warner, who proved sympathetic. She persuaded him to loan out the actress for the film. In exchange he borrowed Jimmy Stewart to star in *No Time for Comedy*.[139]

Louise Beavers was a possibility for Mammy.[140] FDR's White House cook, Lizzie McDuffie, auditioned for the part[141] as well as Hattie Noel. Noel came close to landing the part but lost out to Hattie McDaniel.[142] McDaniel won an Oscar for her performance in the film.

Eddie Anderson was a consideration to play Pork. He was later cast as Uncle Peter instead.[143]

Cornelia Otis Skinner was considered for the part of Ellen O'Hara,[144] as was Lillian Gish. Gish turned the part down, and Barbara O'Neil was cast instead.[145]

Lionel Barrymore was Selznick's first choice to play Dr. Meade. While the film was being planned, Barrymore suffered from crippling arthritis and was confined to a wheelchair.[146] Selznick eventually settled on Harry Davenport instead.

Selznick was interested in Janet Beecher for both roles of Mrs. Meade and Mrs. Merriwether. However Beecher was not cast in the film and the roles were played by Leona Roberts and Jane Darwell.[147]

Billie Burke coveted the role of Scarlett's aunt Pittypat Hamilton. Pittypat was written to be much heavier than Burke was. For her screen test she wore a great deal of padding. The test was unsuccessful (largely due to the padding) and the part was played by Laura Hope Crews.[148]

Scarlett contender Tallulah Bankhead was considered for madam Belle Watling, as well as Mae West, Loretta Young and Joan Blondell.[149] Gladys George was another possibility, but the part went to Ona Munson instead.[150]

Selznick wanted Judy Garland to test for the part of Scarlett's youngest sister, Careen O'Hara. Garland had been cast in the starring role of Dorothy in *The Wizard of Oz*, and the part of Careen was too small for her at this point in her career. Ann Rutherford was cast in her place.[151]

The Good Mother (1988)

Diane Keaton as Anna Dunlap (Debra Winger)

Debra Winger turned down the part of Anna Dunlap.[152]

The Good Son (1993)

Macaulay Culkin as Henry Evans (Jesse Bradford)

Jesse Bradford was hired by 20th Century–Fox for the starring role of Henry in *The Good Son*. Macaulay Culkin's father, Kit Culkin, wanted this part for his son. A couple of years prior, Macaulay starred in one of the studio's biggest hits ever—*Home Alone*. A sequel was being planned. Kit Culkin implied that his son would not appear in *Home Alone 2* if he were not given the part in *The Good Son*. Fox fired Bradford and gave the part to Culkin.[153]

Good Will Hunting (1997)

Minnie Driver as Skylar (Claire Danes, Kate Winslet)

Director Gus Van Sant wanted Kate Winslet to play Skylar. Winslet was wiped out from making *Titanic* and said no. The role went to Minnie Driver instead.[154] Driver was nominated for an Oscar for the film.

Goodbye, Columbus (1969)

Ali MacGraw as Brenda Patimkin (Lesley Ann Warren, Natalie Wood)

Lesley Ann Warren was cast as Brenda Patimkin in *Goodbye, Columbus*. Two months before production started Warren dropped out because she was pregnant.[155] Natalie Wood was made an offer but turned it down.[156] Ali MacGraw was eventually cast.

The Goodbye Girl (1977)

Richard Dreyfuss as Elliot Garfield (James Caan, Robert De Niro, Dustin Hoffman, Raul Julia, Tony Lo Bianco, Jack Nicholson)

Mike Nichols was signed to direct Neil Simon's script, originally titled *Gable Slept Here*. Simon's wife Marsha Mason was set for the female lead. Dustin Hoffman was the first choice for the part of actor Elliot Garfield. Hoffman took too long deciding whether or not he wanted the part. Another strike against Hoffman was that he was expensive. The lesser known Robert De Niro was cast instead. After two weeks De Niro was let go from the film. Neil Simon has stated that De Niro is an intense actor who doesn't play joy well. According to *Variety* the reason for his departure was artistic differences between him and director Mike Nichols.[157] De Niro called Mason and asked her to rehearse with him. He wanted to prove that he could do the part. He was fired anyway.[158] Production was shut down, at which point Jack Nicholson, James Caan, and Tony Lo Bianco were considered as possible replacements. Dustin Hoffman was interested in doing the film but was already committed to *Marathon Man*.[159] Nichols also considered Raul Julia, but he ultimately decided to leave the film.[160] Herbert Ross replaced him as director. Ultimately the part of Elliot Garfield went to Richard Dreyfuss who won an Oscar for his performance in the film and made Academy Award history. Dreyfuss is the youngest actor to win the Best Actor award.

Goodbye, Mr. Chips (1939)

Robert Donat as Charles Chipping (Charles Laughton)

Charles Laughton came close to playing the starring role of Charles Chipping.[161] The part was ultimately played by Robert Donat. *Goodbye, Mr. Chips* was one of Donat's most successful films. He won the Academy Award for Best Actor for his performance in the movie.

Goodbye, Mr. Chips (1969)

Peter O'Toole as Arthur Chipping (Richard Burton)
Petula Clark as Katherine Bridges (Audrey Hepburn)

Audrey Hepburn turned down the role of Katherine because she felt it was too soon after *My Fair Lady* to do another musical. Richard Burton was mentioned as a possible choice to play Chipping.[177]

Goodfellas (1990)

Lorraine Bracco as Karen Hill (Ellen Barkin)

Ellen Barkin tried unsuccessfully for the part of Karen Hill. She didn't mind though, because it went to her good friend Lorraine Bracco.[178]

Grace Quigley (1984)

Nick Nolte as Seymour Flint (Steve McQueen)

Katharine Hepburn met with Steve McQueen to try and persuade him to co-star with her in *Grace Quigley*. McQueen wasn't interested, and the script sat around for about ten years when it was filmed with Nick Nolte opposite Hepburn.[179]

The Graduate (1967)

Dustin Hoffman as Benjamin Braddock (Warren Beatty, Tony Bill, Chris Connelly, Harrison Ford, Charles Grodin, Robert Lipton, Jack Nicholson, Robert Redford)
Anne Bancroft as Mrs. Robinson (Doris Day, Ava Gardner, Jeanne Moreau, Patricia Neal)
Katharine Ross as Elaine Robinson (Candice Bergen, Cathy Carpenter, Sally Field, Jennifer Leak)
William Daniels as Mr. Braddock (Ronald Reagan)
Murray Hamilton as Mr. Robinson (Gene Hackman)

Dustin Hoffman was far from the first choice for the part of Benjamin Braddock. More conventional leading man types such as Warren Beatty and Robert Redford were considered. Beatty wasn't interested.[165] Redford made a screen test with Candice Bergen as Elaine.[166] Others who tested were Tony Bill, Chris Connelly, Robert Lipton, Charles Grodin and Dustin Hoffman. Jack Nicholson was also considered.[167] Columbia Studios acting teacher Walter Beakel thought that his student, Harrison Ford, was perfect for the role. Beakel was friends with director Mike Nichols and arranged an audition for Ford. Nichols allowed him to audition twice, but ultimately rejected Ford.[168] The actor Mike Nichols was interested in was Charles Grodin. Grodin had to work hard to even get an audition because at 32, he was about ten years older than the character. Grodin read for Nicholas and that same night received a call from the director. He was told that he was their number one choice, and that there was no second choice. Grodin was overjoyed. That is, until he found out how much money he would be paid. He was being offered $500 a week to play Benjamin Braddock. At the time Grodin had done several guest appearances on television. For these guest spots he was paid $1000 a week. He could not believe he was being offered half that to star in a movie. He felt that it was exploitation and was not fair. After a couple of weeks the offer was upped to $1000 a week, but Grodin was required to make a screen test. Grodin felt that the nature of the relationship between him and the production team had changed. During his test (with Katharine Ross) Grodin felt uncomfortable and became argumentative with Nichols. He finished the test and returned home feeling regret for the way he handled the whole situation. Soon after Nichols called him to offer him a part — not in *The Graduate*, but in his next film, *Catch-22*.[169] Mike Nichols finally gave the part of Benjamin to newcomer Dustin Hoffman. The film earned him an Oscar nomination and made him a star.

Doris Day was offered the part of Mrs. Robinson. What intrigued the production team about Day was her wholesome image.[170] Mrs. Robinson was anything but, and they found the contrast interesting. Day read the script and was horrified. She found the script offensive and turned down the part.[171] Many actresses were considered including Ava Gardner[172] and Jeanne Moreau. Nichols first thought that a European Mrs. Robinson would be interesting. He was later convinced otherwise, and Moreau was out of the running. Nichols offered the part to Patricia Neal. Neal wanted to play the part, but was unable to because she had had a stroke and was still recovering.[173] Nichols cast Anne Bancroft as the older woman, Mrs. Robinson. Bancroft is five years older than Hoffman.

Candice Bergen was the first actress Mike Nichols thought of to play Elaine Robinson.[174] But Katharine Ross seemed to be a better match with Dustin Hoffman. They felt Bergen was too beautiful for the part. Sally Field auditioned but Nichols felt she lacked movie experience. Another problem was that she had just finished with her television series, *Gidget*, and was too closely associated with that part.[175] Cathy Carpenter and Jennifer Leak screen tested, but Nichols gave the part to Katharine Ross instead.

Ronald Reagan was a possible Mr. Braddock, but Nichols decided to go with William Daniels.[176]

Dustin Hoffman had gotten his friend Gene Hackman a role in the film as Mr. Robinson. During rehearsals Hackman had trouble giving Nichols the performance he was looking for. He was fired and replaced by Murray Hamilton.[177]

Grand Hotel (1932)

John Barrymore as Baron Felix Von Geigern (Clark Gable, John Gilbert, Robert Montgomery)
Wallace Beery as Preysing (Jean Hersholt)
Lionel Barrymore as Otto Kringelein (Buster Keaton)

Clark Gable, John Gilbert and Robert Montgomery were considered for the role that ultimately went to John Barrymore in *Grand Hotel*. Jean Hersholt wanted to play the part of Preysing, but producer Irving Thalberg convinced him that he would be better as Senf.[178]

MGM considered changing the great comic actor Buster Keaton's image by giving him a dramatic role in a film. He was tested for the part of Otto Kringelein in *Grand Hotel*, but lost out to Lionel Barrymore.[179]

Grandview U.S.A. (1984)

Jamie Lee Curtis as Michelle "Mike" Cody (Cher)

Cher was signed for *Grandview U.S.A.* She later changer her mind about the film and dropped out. Jamie Lee Curtis replaced her.[180]

The Grapes of Wrath (1940)

Henry Fonda as Tom Joad (Don Ameche, Tyrone Power)
Jane Darwell as Ma Joad (Beulah Bondi)
Russell Simpson as Pa Joad (James Barton, Walter Brennan, Warren Hull)
O.Z. Whitehead as Al Joad (James Stewart)

For the starring role of Tom Joad, producer Darryl F. Zanuck envisioned either Don Ameche or Tyrone Power.[181]

Beulah Bondi lost the part of Ma to Jane Darwell. Bondi was unhappy to have this role slip away, and rightly so.[182] Darwell won an Oscar for her performance.

Zanuck looked at Walter Brennan, James Barton, and Warren Hull as possibilities for Russell Simpson's role of Pa Joad. He briefly considered having James Stewart play the small part of Al Joad.[183]

Grease (1978)

John Travolta as Danny Zuko (Elvis Presley, Henry Winkler)
Olivia Newton-John as Sandy Olson

(Ann-Margret, Susan Buckner, Susan Dey, Carrie Fisher, Marie Osmond)
Stockard Channing as Betty Rizzo (Lucie Arnaz, Annette Cardona)
Dinah Manoff as Marty Maraschino (Debralee Scott)
Frankie Avalon as Teen Angel (Fabian)
Lorenzo Lamas as Tom Chisum (Steven Ford)

Long before *Grease* actually went into production producer Allan Carr thought that the starring roles of Danny and Sandy should go to Elvis Presley and Ann-Margret.[184] Years later when Carr was ready to cast the parts he approached Henry Winkler to play Danny Zuko. At the time Winkler was starring on the television series *Happy Days*. He was a huge star. Winkler graciously turned Carr down. He said that the part of Danny Zuko was very much like Fonzie, his character on the show. He wanted to play different kinds of roles. John Travolta played Doody in *Grease* on stage. Carr decided Travolta was the best choice to play Danny Zuko in the film.[185]

For the role of Sandy, Susan Dey was the number one choice. Dey came to fame playing the teenage character Laurie on *The Partridge Family*. Dey's agent said that she was no longer playing teenage roles and turned the movie down.[186] Carrie Fisher was also considered.[187] Marie Osmond auditioned, and came close to getting the part.[188] Carr was very interested in both of them until he met Olivia Newton-John. Carr wanted her in the film, and Sandy Dumbrowski was now Sandy Olson, an Australian just like Newton-John. Newton-John wanted to make a screen test. If she didn't like what she saw in the test she would turn down the part. Susan Buckner was a possible choice if Newton-John passed on the part. To Carr's delight she liked what she saw and joined the cast. Buckner was given the supporting role of cheerleader Patty Simcox.[189]

Lucie Arnaz wanted to play Rizzo, but her mother (Lucille Ball) told her not to screen-test. This ended negotiations with Arnaz.[190] Annette Cardona was up for the role but lost out to Stockard Channing. Cardona's consolation prize was the role of Cha Cha.

The two final candidates for the part of Marty were Dinah Manoff and Debralee Scott. Manoff thought that she didn't stand a chance against Scott. Scott was starring on the series *Mary Hartman, Mary Hartman* at the time. Scott had also had a recurring role as Rosalie "Hotzie"

Debralee Scott came close to getting the part of Marty in *Grease*.

Totzie on the smash hit series *Welcome Back Kotter*. One of the stars of *Kotter* was John Travolta, who was already signed to star in *Grease*. Manoff was surprised to learn that she won the part of Marty.[191]

The Teen Angel character was originally intended to be an Elvis Presley–type singer. Carr said that Fabian was originally thought of for the role. However, Fabian was not made an offer. Instead, Frankie Avalon was invited to join the cast. He agreed, on the condition that they drop the Elvis Presley idea. Avalon wanted to play the part in his own style. Carr agreed.[192]

Steven Ford was originally cast as jock Tom Chisum. He dropped out and Allan Carr needed a replacement. Two weeks prior Carr ran into his friend Arlene Dahl at the Academy Awards. She was with her son, Lorenzo Lamas. Carr decided that Lamas was the right choice to replace Ford. Incidentally, Steven Ford is the son of former president Gerald Ford.[193]

Great Expectations (1934)

Jane Wyatt as Estella (Valerie Hobson)

Universal Studios wanted Valerie Hobson for the part of Estella in *Great Expectations*. They later changed their mind cast the role with Jane Wyatt.[194]

The Great Gatsby (1974)

Robert Redford as Jay Gatsby (Warren Beatty, Marlon Brando, Steve McQueen, Jack Nicholson)
Mia Farrow as Daisy Buchanan (Candice Bergen, Lois Chiles, Faye Dunaway, Ali

MacGraw, Katharine Ross, Cybill Shepherd, Natalie Wood)
Bruce Dern as Tom Buchanan (Jack Nicholson)

The Great Gatsby started out as a project that was being developed by producer Robert Evans to star his then-wife Ali MacGraw. MacGraw loved F. Scott Fitzgerald's novel and wanted very much to play Daisy Buchanan in a film version. Evans needed to find a co-star for her. He asked friends Warren Beatty and Jack Nicholson. Both actors shared the opinion that the part wasn't right for MacGraw, and turned down the offer,[195] although Nicholson later said that he regretted his decision.[196] Marlon Brando was approached but asked for more money than the studio was willing to pay.[197] Before a Gatsby was secured the project changed. MacGraw left Evans for Steve McQueen. Now Evans was determined to keep MacGraw out of the film. However it was brought to his attention that she and McQueen were interested in starring in the film together. It was also brought up that these two actors were extremely popular. Evans didn't change his mind and a search for a new Daisy began.[198] It was offered to Natalie Wood. She was told the part was hers, but only if she made a screen-test first. Wood was a very big star and saw this as a slight. She refused to test and relinquished the part.[199] Cybill Shepherd wanted the role. Shepherd was asked to test. Like Wood, Shepherd was offended by the request. She thought she was perfect for the part, and didn't understand why no one else realized it.[200] Several actresses auditioned until it finally came down to five: Faye Dunaway, Mia Farrow, Katharine Ross, Candice Bergen, and Lois Chiles. Chiles was dating Evans at the time. All the tests were reviewed and it was decided that Farrow had the best hold on the character. Chiles received the role of Daisy's friend Jordan Baker as a consolation prize. When she found this out, she was angry. She told Evans she had wanted to pay Daisy, not Jordan. Although she did go on to play the role of Jordan, her relationship with Evans was over.[201]

Jack Nicholson was a possible choice to play Jay Gatsby, but the role went to Robert Redford instead.[202]

Evans considered Jack Nicholson to play Tom Buchanan before settling on Bruce Dern.[203]

The Greatest Show on Earth (1952)

Betty Hutton as Holly (Hedy Lamarr)
Cornel Wilde as "The Great Sebastian" (Burt Lancaster)
Gloria Grahame as Angel (Lucille Ball, Paulette Goddard)

Director Cecil B. DeMille offered Hedy Lamarr the part of Holly in *The Greatest Show on Earth*. The two had worked together previously on the film *Samson and Delilah*. Lamarr said that working with DeMille was too much for her. She turned the part down and DeMille cast Betty Hutton instead.[204]

Former real-life circus performer Burt Lancaster was courted to play trapeze artist "The Great Sebastian." Lancaster was signed with Warner Bros., who didn't make the deal to loan him out to Paramount for the film.[205]

Director Cecil B. DeMille wanted to have Lucille Ball play Angel in *The Greatest Show on Earth*. Ball wanted the role and went to her Columbia boss Harry Cohn. He refused to loan her out and so she became unavailable.[206] Paulette Goddard campaigned heavily for the part,[207] but De Mille decided instead to cast Gloria Grahame.

The Greatest Story Ever Told (1965)

Dorothy McGuire as Mary (Audrey Hepburn)

Director George Stevens thought of Audrey Hepburn for the role of Mary, but instead gave the part to Dorothy McGuire.[208]

The Greeks Had a Word for Them (1932)

Joan Blondell as Schatze (Ina Claire, Jean Harlow, Carole Lombard)

Ina Claire was originally cast as Schatze. She was switched over to the role of Jean because studio head Samuel Goldwyn wanted more of a sexpot for the Schatze role. He considered Jean Harlow until he heard that she was difficult to work with. Carole Lombard was cast but eventually dropped out. The part finally went to Joan Blondell.[209]

Green Mansions (1959)

Audrey Hepburn as Rima (Pier Angeli)

Green Mansions went into production with Pier Angeli in the role of Rima. The project was soon dropped. A few years later it was resumed with Audrey Hepburn replacing Angeli.[210]

The Green Mile (1999)
Dabbs Greer as Old Paul Edgecomb (Tom Hanks)

The original plan was to have Tom Hanks play his character, Paul, as an old man. The problem was that the makeup on Hanks was not believable. Eighty-something Dabbs Greer was brought in and solved the problem.[211]

Greystoke: The Legend of Tarzan, Lord of the Apes (1984)
Christopher Lambert as John Clayton/Tarzan (Viggo Mortensen)

Viggo Mortensen auditioned for the starring role of Tarzan. He was flown to England, but still lost the part to Christopher Lambert.[212]

Groundhog Day (1993)
Andie MacDowell as Rita (Jeanne Tripplehorn)

Jeanne Tripplehorn lost the part of Rita in *Groundhog Day* to Andie MacDowell.[213]

The Group (1966)
Candice Bergen as Lakey Eastlake (Faye Dunaway)

Faye Dunaway lost out to Candice Bergen for the part of Lakey Eastlake in *The Group*. Dunaway said that she felt that Bergen was more beautiful than her.[229]

Gung Ho (1986)
Michael Keaton as Hunt Stevenson (Eddie Murphy, Bill Murray)

Executives at Paramount wanted either Eddie Murphy or Bill Murray to play Hunt Stevenson in *Gung Ho*. Neither actor signed for the film The part was played by Michael Keaton instead.[230]

Gunga Din (1939)
Cary Grant as Archibald Cutter (Robert Donat, Douglas Fairbanks, Jr., Roger Livesey, Jack Oakie
Victor McLaglen as Sgt. "Mac" MacChesney (Spencer Tracy)
Douglas Fairbanks, Jr., as Thomas "Tommy" Ballantine (Cary Grant, Robert Montgomery)

Director Howard Hawks was interested in either Robert Donat or Roger Livesey to play Sgt. Archibald Cutter. He also wanted to sign Spencer Tracy as Sgt. "Mac" MacChesney with Robert Montgomery as Sgt. Thomas "Tommy" Ballantine. None of these casting choices panned out and Hawks moved on to other actors.[216] Cary Grant was signed for the part of Ballantine. The studio hoped that they could sign Jack Oakie to play opposite Grant as Sergeant Cutter. Oakie had scheduling problems and was unable to do the film.[217] Douglas Fairbanks, Jr., was cast as Grant's co-star, although at this point it was unclear if Grant was still going to play Ballantine. He had also expressed interest in the role of Cutter. Fairbanks asked Grant what he intended to do. Grant told Fairbanks to pick whichever part he liked better, and that he would play the other one. He went on to say that what was important to him was that they were in the film together, not which part he played. Fairbanks suggested they decide on a coin toss. From that toss Grant won the role of Cutter, and Fairbanks was Ballantine.[218]

Guns at Batasi (1964)
Mia Farrow as Karen Eriksson (Britt Ekland)

Britt Ekland dropped out of *Guns at Batasi* to placate her jealous husband Peter Sellers.[219]

Guys and Dolls (1955)
Marlon Brando as Sky Masterson (Cary Grant, Gene Kelly, Burt Lancaster)
Frank Sinatra as Nathan Detroit (Bob Hope, Sam Levene)
Jean Simmons as Sarah Brown (Grace Kelly, Deborah Kerr, Jane Russell)
Vivian Blaine as Adelaide (Betty Grable, Marilyn Monroe)

The role of Sky Masterson was coveted by many big stars. Burt Lancaster and Cary Grant were among those who were considered.[220] Gene Kelly wanted it, but his studio, MGM, wouldn't allow him to be loaned to make the film.[221]

Frank Sinatra was offered the supporting role of Nathan Detroit, although director Joseph Mankiewicz's first choice was Sam Levene.[222] Levene had originated the role on Broadway. Bob Hope had also been considered.[223] It was studio boss Samuel Goldwyn who favored Sinatra as Nathan.

Grace Kelly and Deborah Kerr both turned down the part of Sarah Brown.[224] Jane Russell was considered, but the part was eventually taken by Jean Simmons.[225]

Marilyn Monroe wanted to play Adelaide, but was turned down.[226] Betty Grable had prior commitments which prevented her from signing on.[227] The role finally went to the actress who created the part in the Broadway production, Vivian Blaine.

Halloween (1978)

Donald Pleasence as Dr. Sam Loomis (Peter Cushing, Christopher Lee, Christopher Reeve)
Jamie Lee Curtis as Laurie Strode (Anne Lockhart)

Peter Cushing and Christopher Lee were offered the part of Dr. Loomis. Neither actor wanted to do it. Lee later said it was the biggest mistake he ever made.

Anne Lockhart (daughter of June) was asked to play Laurie Strode. She said no and the part went to Jamie Lee Curtis. *Halloween* was Curtis' debut film.

Hamlet (1948)

Jean Simmons as Ophelia (Vivien Leigh)

Vivien Leigh wanted very much to star as Ophelia in her husband Laurence Olivier's adaptation of *Hamlet*. But Olivier felt that she was too famous; that the audience would see Vivien Leigh and not Ophelia. He gave the part to Jean Simmons.[1]

Hamlet (2000)

Kyle MacLachlan as Claudius (Nick Nolte)

Kyle MacLachlan was cast as Claudius after the part was turned down by Nick Nolte. It makes sense that Nolte would receive the offer before MacLachlan. Nolte is undeniably a bigger star, and more important, a bigger movie star. MacLachlan is best known for his work on *Twin Peaks*, a television series. Nolte is also closer to the age of the character. But Nolte said no, and director Michael Almereyda gave the part to MacLachlan who, for the record is 19 years younger than Nick Nolte.[2]

The Hand (1981)

Michael Caine as Jon Lansdale (Dustin Hoffman, Jon Voight, Christopher Walken)

Writer/director Oliver Stone's first choice for the lead role of Jon Lansdale was Jon Voight. According to Stone Voight said no, and he was persuaded by Mike Medavoy to meet with Dustin Hoffman. The two had a breakfast meeting, but Stone was unable to sign him for the film. Next up was Christopher Walken, who also passed. Stone found his leading man eventually in Michael Caine.[3]

Hannah and Her Sisters (1986)

Barbara Hershey as Lee (Mia Farrow)
Dianne Wiest as Holly (Mia Farrow)
Michael Caine as Elliot (Woody Allen)
Max Von Sydow as Frederick (Woody Allen)

Writer/director Woody Allen gave Mia Farrow the choice of playing Hannah, Lee or Holly. She chose to play Hannah, a character based on herself. Allen considered playing Elliot or Frederick, but eventually decided to play Mickey Sachs.[4]

Hannibal (2001)

Julianne Moore as Clarice Starling (Gillian Anderson, Cate Blanchett, Jodie Foster, Angelina Jolie, Ashley Judd, Gwyneth Paltrow, Hilary Swank)

Jodie Foster won her second Academy Award for playing the part of Clarice Starling in *The Silence of the Lambs*. When the sequel was being planned, Foster declined to reprise the role. She was committed to direct the film *Flora Plum*. Foster also didn't agree with the way the character was written in the sequel. Producer Dino De Laurentiis publicly stated that Foster's agent asked for $20 million plus 15 percent of the gross.[5] De Laurentiis said the film didn't need Foster and looked for a replacement.[6] Possibilities included Cate Blanchett, Ashley Judd, Angelina Jolie, Hilary Swank and Julianne Moore.[7] Gwyneth Paltrow and Gillian Anderson were also mentioned. The competition was narrowed down to four actresses: Julianne Moore, Angelina Jolie, Hilary Swank and Cate Blanchett. Director Ridley Scott discussed the part with each of them. It was concluded that Swank was too young, and was eliminated.[8] Moore was the favorite. Scott asked costar Anthony Hopkins what he thought of this choice. Hopkins gave his approval, and Moore was awarded the part.[9]

Hanover Street (1979)

Harrison Ford as David Halloran (Kris Kristofferson)
Lesley-Anne Down as Margaret Sellinger (Genevieve Bujold)

Kris Kristofferson was scheduled to star as David Halloran with Genevieve Bujold playing Margaret Sellinger opposite him. Kristofferson and Bujold quit shortly before production was set to begin. Their replacements were Harrison Ford and Lesley-Anne Down.[10]

Hans Christian Andersen (1952)

Danny Kaye as Hans Christian Andersen (Gary Cooper)
Zizi Jeanmaire as Doro (Moira Shearer)

Gary Cooper was an early choice to play the lead in *Hans Christian Andersen*. He turned it down, and when production began, Danny Kaye was the star.

Moira Shearer was pregnant, so Zizi Jeanmaire won the ballerina role.[11]

The Happy Time (1952)

Kurt Kasznar as Uncle Louis (Zero Mostel)

Kurt Kasznar had played the part of Uncle Louis in the Broadway production of *The Happy Time*, and was a big success. When the time came to cast the part for the film version Kasznar was the first choice. He was offered the part, but asked for more money than the studio wanted to pay. The next choice was Zero Mostel. At this time Mostel was having trouble finding work, because he was believed to be a communist and had been blacklisted. When he received the offer, he was overjoyed and immediately accepted. Studio boss Harry Cohn heard about this casting and got involved. He refused to have Mostel appear in the film. He objected to his politics so much he paid Kasznar the large sum he had asked for.[12]

Hardcore (1979)

George C. Scott as Jake Van Dorn (Warren Beatty)

Warren Beatty refused the lead role in *Hardcore* because he didn't want to play a teenager's father. Beatty was in his early forties at the time.[13]

Harlem Nights (1989)

Jasmine Guy as Dominique La Rue (Michael Michele)

Michael Michele claims that she was fired from *Harlem Nights* because she was not interested in star Eddie Murphy romantically. Murphy denies these charges. Michele was replaced with Jasmine Guy.[14]

Harlow (1965)

Ginger Rogers as Mama Jean Bello (Judy Garland, Eleanor Parker)

Ginger Rogers was the third actress cast as Mama Jean Bello. Judy Garland was originally cast. She was subsequently replaced by Eleanor Parker, who was replaced by Rogers.[15]

Harold and Maude (1971)

Ruth Gordon as Maude (Peggy Ashcroft, Elisabeth Bergner, Gladys Cooper, Mildred Dunnock, Edith Evans, Edwige Feuillere, Mildred Natwick, Dorothy Stickney)
Bud Cort as Harold Chasen (Bob Balaban, John Rubinstein)

Paramount's Robert Evans was interested in Ruth Gordon for the starring role of Maude. Hal Ashby was selected to direct. Ashby questioned Evans' choice of Gordon. Gordon expressed her concern to Evans, who assured her she would play the part. Ashby arranged a meeting with Gordon. At the meeting Gordon asked him if he wanted her for the part. He told her that he still needed to meet with other actresses. Gordon was upset by this. She later heard that Ashby was meeting with many actresses including Peggy Ashcroft, Elisabeth Bergner, Mildred Natwick, Edwige Feuillere, Dorothy Stickney, Gladys Cooper, Mildred Dunnock and Edith Evans. Evans herself told Ashby that she was not right for the part. She also suggested that he hire Ruth Gordon. Gordon spoke with Robert Evans once again. Ashby called her in for another interview. At the end he thanked her for coming, but said nothing about whether or not she had the part. Gordon was not pleased. However, a week later Gordon got the official word that she had the part.

Writer Colin Higgins wrote the part of Harold Chasen with John Rubinstein in mind. Rubinstein still had to test. Ashby had five other actors who were to screen test including Bud Cort and Bob Balaban. Ashby narrowed it down to

The part of the suicidal Harold was written with John Rubinstein in mind (*Harold and Maude*).

just Cort and Rubinstein. Although Ashby thought that Rubinstein was a great actor he gave the part to Bud Cort instead.[16]

Harper (1966)

Paul Newman as Lew Harper (Frank Sinatra)

Frank Sinatra was the first choice for the role of Lew Harper. Sinatra turned it down, and it went to Paul Newman instead.[17]

Harry and Son (1984)

Paul Newman as Harry Keach (Gene Hackman)
Robby Benson as Howard Keach (Tom Cruise)

Gene Hackman was director Paul Newman's first choice to star in *Harry and Son*. The studio refused to take a chance on the film unless Newman agreed to star in it as well as direct.[18]

An unknown Tom Cruise auditioned to play Newman's son. Although his reading was good, Newman thought he was too young for the part.[19] The role went to the Robby Benson, who is six years older than Cruise. Newman and Cruise would have to wait two more years to work together in Martin Scorsese's *The Color of Money*.

Harry and Tonto (1974)

Art Carney as Harry Coombes (James Cagney, Cary Grant, Danny Kaye, Laurence Olivier, Frank Sinatra, James Stewart)

The starring role of Harry in *Harry and Tonto* was first offered to James Cagney. Cagney turned it down. Also approached were Laurence Olivier and Frank Sinatra, to no avail.[20] Olivier thought that an American should play the part.[21] Writer/director Paul Mazursky decided to approach Danny Kaye. Kaye was an attractive choice for more than one reason. First of all, Mazursky thought that Kaye would be great in the role. Second, the director was having trouble finding money for the film. The problem he encountered time and again was that the lead character was 70, and producers weren't sure if audiences would respond. Kaye was sent a copy of the script, which he approved of. A meeting was set up at Kaye's house to discuss the film. Kaye expressed concern to the director that, at age 60, he was too young to play Harry. Kaye was also concerned that the film wasn't funny enough. Mazursky knew that this wasn't going to work out. *Harry and Tonto* was never intended to be a comedy. Kaye's wife, Sylvia Fine Kaye, and Mazursky explained to him that while the film had humorous moments, it was not a laugh a minute comedy. The meeting eventually ended with Mazursky deciding to look elsewhere for a leading man.[22] James Stewart was interested, but Mazursky didn't think he was the right actor for the part. Cary Grant was pursued unsuccessfully. Mazursky gave Art Carney a copy of the script. Carney was a television personality, most famous for his role of Ed Norton on *The Honeymooners*. Carney wasn't sure if he was the right actor to play Harry, a character 18 years older than he was. Mazursky assured him that he would be fine. Carney thought about it and eventually decided to accept the part.[23] Carney won an Oscar for his portrayal of Harry.

Harry Potter and the Chamber of Secrets (2002)

Kenneth Branagh as Gilderoy Lockhart (Hugh Grant)

Hugh Grant was considered for the part of Gilderoy Lockhart. Director Chris Columbus eventually decided against Grant. He thought that Kenneth Branagh was the better choice.[24]

Harry Potter and the Sorceror's Stone (2001)

Alan Rickman as Professor Severus Snape (Tim Roth)

Tim Roth was offered the role of Professor Snape. Roth turned it down and took the part of Thade in the 2001 remake of *Planet of the Apes* instead.[25]

Hart's War (2002)

Colin Farrell as Thomas W. Hart (Edward Norton)

Edward Norton dropped out of *Hart's War* and was replaced by Colin Farrell. Norton decided he would rather make the film *Death to Smoochy* instead.[26] According to director Gregory Hoblit, Norton didn't want the other characters to be built up. Screenwriter Billy Ray claimed that Norton didn't like the choice of Bruce Willis for a costar. However Edward Norton's agent, Brian Swardstrom, said that their claims were ridiculous. He said his client never actually committed to the film.[27]

The Harvey Girls (1945)

Judy Garland as Susan Bradley (Lana Turner)
Angela Lansbury as Em (Lucille Ball, Ann Sothern)

Lana Turner was an early choice to star in *The Harvey Girls*. When Bernie Hyman, the original producer, died, Judy Garland was cast in the role.[28]

Although Lucille Ball and Ann Sothern were considered for the role of Em, the madam, the part ended up going to the unlikely choice of Angela Lansbury.[29]

Hatari! (1962)

Hardy Kruger as Kurt Muller (Patrick McGoohan)
Elsa Martinelli as Anna Maria "Dallas" D'Alessandro (Claudia Cardinale, Antonella Lualdi)
Red Buttons as Pockets (Theodore Bikel, Art Carney)
Michele Girardon as Brandy de la Court (Ingrid Thulin)

Patrick McGoohan was considered to play Kurt Muller in *Hatari!* Director Howard Hawks preferred Hardy Kruger instead.

Hawks thought that Claudia Cardinale might be right to play Anna Maria "Dallas" D'Alessandro. However, Cardinale lost the part because she didn't speak English well enough. Antonella Lualdi was another possibility, but Hawks cast Elsa Martinelli.

Art Carney met with Hawks to discuss the part of Pockets. Theodore Bikel was also a contender, but Hawks decided that Red Buttons was the right choice.

Ingrid Thulin auditioned for the part of Brandy de la Court. She lost the part to Michele Girardon.[30]

Hatter's Castle (1942)

Deborah Kerr as Mary Brodie (Margaret Lockwood)

Margaret Lockwood originally had the part of Mary Brodie in *Hatter's Castle*. Lockwood announced she was pregnant, and the part was recast with Deborah Kerr.[31]

Hawaii (1966)

Julie Andrews as Jerusha Bromley Hale (Audrey Hepburn)

Audrey Hepburn was offered the role of Jerusha Bromley Hale. Hepburn didn't commit, and the film was shelved for several years. It was finally made in 1966 with Julie Andrews in the part.[32]

He Got Game (1998)

Ray Allen as Jesus Shuttlesworth (Travis Best, Kobe Bryant, Rick Fox, Allen Iverson, Walter McCarty)

Real-life basketball players Kobe Bryant, Travis Best, Allen Iverson, Walter McCarty, and Rick Fox were all considered for the lead role, but lost out to fellow real-life basketball player Ray Allen.[33]

Head Over Heels (2001)

Monica Potter as Amanda Pierce (Claire Danes)

When Claire Danes left *Head Over Heels* Monica Potter was brought in as a replacement. Incidentally, Potter dropped out of *Mission to Mars* to make *Head Over Heels*.[34]

The Heart Is a Lonely Hunter (1968)

Sondra Locke as Mick Kelly (Mary Badham, Lorna Luft)
Chuck McCann as Spiro Antonapoulos (Jackie Vernon)

The Heart Is a Lonely Hunter began pre-production with Joseph Strick as the director. Strick was searching the country to find an unknown actress to play the part of 14-year-old Mick Kelly. A 20-year-old Sondra Locke went to the open call in Birmingham, Alabama, accompanied by her good friend and future husband Gordon Anderson. Anderson advised Locke to tell the casting director, Marion Dougherty, that she was only 17. At the audition Locke and Anderson noticed a young woman come in with an entourage. Anderson recognized her as Mary Badham, the young star of *To Kill a Mockingbird*. Badham was quickly brought in to audition, breezing past the many unknown hopefuls waiting and waiting. Locke's audition was successful — Dougherty asked her to come to New York City for a final audition. Locke and Anderson spent much of their time in Dougherty's office. One day an agent came in with a young girl of about 15. He explained that the girl was Lorna Luft, the daughter of Judy Garland, and that she would be perfect for the part of Mick Kelly. Without missing a beat, Anderson acted like he worked in the office and told Luft's agent that the part had already been cast. Soon after Joseph Strick offered the part to Sondra Locke.

Strick gave the part of the retarded deaf mute Spiro Antanapoulos to Jackie Vernon. Unfortunately for Vernon, Strick had differences with the studio about the direction of the film. Strick wanted to play up the implied homosexual relationship between Antonapoulos and the lead character John Singer. This was not a popular idea and Strick was replaced by Robert Ellis Miller. Miller let Vernon go and brought in Chuck McCann as a replacement.[35]

Heartbreakers (2001)

Jennifer Love Hewitt as Page Conners (Jennifer Aniston)

Jennifer Aniston was offered the part of con artist Page Conners.[36] Aniston said no, and Jennifer Love Hewitt was cast instead.

Heartburn (1986)

Jack Nicholson as Mark Louis Forman (Mandy Patinkin)

After a day of filming director Mike Nichols dropped Mandy Patinkin from *Heartburn*.[37] It was reported that the problem with Patinkin's performance was that he and co-star Meryl Streep had no chemistry.[38] Streep, being the bigger star, remained with the film, and Jack Nicholson was brought in to replace Patinkin.

Mandy Patinkin worked on *Heartburn* for one day.

Heaven Can Wait (1978)

Warren Beatty as Joe Pendleton/Leo Farnsworth/Tom Jarrett (Muhammed Ali)
Julie Christie as Betty Logan (Stephanie Zimbalist)
Dyan Cannon as Julia Farnsworth (Susan Lucci)
James Mason as Mr. Jordan (Cary Grant, Senator Eugene McCarthy)

Director Warren Beatty originally wanted Muhammed Ali to star in *Heaven Can Wait*. The film was a remake of *Here Comes Mr. Jordan*, and the lead character was a boxer. Due to previous commitments, Ali turned the part down.[39] Beatty decided to change the profession of the character to football player and take the part himself.

A 20-year-old Stephanie Zimbalist was considered for Betty Logan. Beatty (who is about 19 years older than she) thought he might look old next to her. He gave the part to Julie Christie instead.⁴⁰

Casting director Dianne Crittenden was interested in soap star Susan Lucci as a possible choice for the part of Julia Farnsworth. However, it would have been necessary for Lucci to go out to California for at least two months to even try for it. Lucci had a contract with *All My Children*, and also didn't want to leave her family for such a long period of time. The role went to Dyan Cannon.⁴¹

Beatty offered Cary Grant $1 million to co-star as Mr. Jordan. But Grant said the part wasn't good and turned it down.⁴² Beatty also considered Senator Eugene McCarthy before settling on James Mason.⁴³

Heaven Knows, Mr. Allison (1957)

Deborah Kerr as Sister Angela (Donna Reed)
Robert Mitchum as Marine Corporal Allison (Marlon Brando)

Donna Reed wanted the part of Sister Angela. Her husband Tony Owen tried to buy the rights to the film, to no avail. Reed lost the role to Deborah Kerr.⁴⁴

Marlon Brando felt the script for *Heaven Knows, Mr. Allison* was weak and turned down the part of Allison.⁴⁵

Heaven's Gate (1980)

Kris Kristofferson as James Averill (Clint Eastwood, Steve McQueen, Paul Newman, Robert Redford, John Wayne)
Christopher Walken as Nathan D. Champion (Jeff Bridges)
Isabelle Huppert as Ella Watson (Jane Fonda, Diane Keaton, Ali MacGraw, Raquel Welch)
John Hurt as William C. Irvine (Jack Lemmon)

Many actors were considered for the planned epic, *Heaven's Gate*. Robert Redford, Paul Newman, Steve McQueen, John Wayne, and Clint Eastwood were possibilities to star. The role ultimately went to Kris Kristofferson. Jeff Bridges was considered for the part of Nathan D. Champion. The part went, instead, to Christopher Walken. Walken had just won an Academy Award for *The Deer Hunter*, which helped him win the role over the more established Bridges. Isabelle Huppert was cast as the female lead in spite of the fact that much more well-known actresses including Jane Fonda, Ali MacGraw, Diane Keaton, and Raquel Welch had been considered. Jack Lemmon's name was brought up as a possibility to play William C. Irvine, but instead it went to John Hurt.⁴⁶

The Helen Morgan Story (1957)

Ann Blyth as Helen Morgan (Yvonne De Carlo)

Yvonne De Carlo was offered the starring role of Helen Morgan. At the same time, she was also offered a role in *Band of Angels*. De Carlo's mind was made up upon the discovery that the star of *Band of Angels* was Clark Gable. She promptly turned down *The Helen Morgan Story*.⁴⁷ Director Michael Curtiz chose Ann Blyth for the part.

Helldorado (1935)

Richard Arlen as Art Ryan (Spencer Tracy)

Spencer Tracy was originally set for the role of Art Ryan. Tracy changed his mind, and dropped out. He was replaced by Richard Arlen.⁴⁸

Hello, Dolly! (1969)

Barbra Streisand as Dolly Levi (Lucille Ball, Carol Channing, Doris Day, Shirley MacLaine, Elizabeth Taylor)
Michael Crawford as Cornelius Hackl (Hampton Fancher)
Marianne McAndrew as Irene Molloy (Tricia Noble)
Danny Lockin as Barnaby Tucker (James Dybas)
E.J. Peaker as Minnie Fay (Sandy Duncan)
Tommy Tune as Ambrose Kemper (Ron Rifkin)
Judy Knaiz as Gussie Granger (Peggy Murray, Joanne Worley)

Carol Channing was interested in recreating the role she created on Broadway in the film version of *Hello, Dolly!* At first the producers were enthusiastic about the idea, but then they saw a film that Channing was in, *Thoroughly Modern Millie*. They were dismayed by Channing's broad performance. The decision was quickly made that Channing's personality was not right for the screen.[49] Lucille Ball was considered,[50] along with Doris Day and Shirley MacLaine.[51] Elizabeth Taylor was a possibility. Producer Ernest Lehman mentioned it to her. Taylor was very interested, but Lehman later reconsidered.[52] The role was finally cast with Barbra Streisand. The very gracious Carol Channing sent Streisand flowers to congratulate her.

Hampton Fancher was tested for Cornelius. He lost the part to Michael Crawford.

Tricia Noble auditioned for the part of Irene Molloy but lost out to newcomer Marianne McAndrew.

Sandy Duncan screen tested for the part of Minnie Fay.

James Dybas made a test to play Barnaby. He lost the part to Danny Lockin. Lockin had played the part in several of the show's touring companies.

Ron Rifkin auditioned to play Ambrose, but lost out to dancer Tommy Tune.

Peggy Murray and Joanne Worley tested for the part of Gussie Granger.

Hell's Angels (1930)

Jean Harlow as Helen (Greta Nissen)

Greta Nissen had to be replaced in *Hell's Angels* because her Norwegian accent was not understandable, nor was it suitable for the character of a British woman. A search for a replacement dragged on for six months when the role was given to an actress with absolutely no film experience—Jean Harlow.[53]

Hemingway's Adventures of a Young Man (1962)

Richard Beymer as Nick Adams (Warren Beatty)

Warren Beatty turned down the role of Nick Adams.[54]

Henry V (1944)

Leslie Banks as Chorus (Robert Donat)
Renee Asherson as Katharine (Vivien Leigh)

Robert Donat turned down the Chorus role.[55] Director Laurence Olivier wanted his wife, Vivien Leigh, to play Katharine, but producer David O. Selznick (he held her contract) would not allow it.[56]

Heroes (1977)

Sally Field as Carol Bell (Beverly D'Angelo, Mary Beth Hurt, Andrea Marcovicci, Meryl Streep)

Meryl Streep, Beverly D'Angelo, Mary Beth Hurt, and Andrea Marcovicci were all up for the part of Carol. The role was won by Sally Field.[57]

High Noon (1952)

Gary Cooper as Will Kane (Marlon Brando, Montgomery Clift, Charlton Heston, Gregory Peck, John Wayne)

John Wayne was offered the starring role of Will Kane. Wayne hated the script: He felt it was un–American.[58] Marlon Brando, Montgomery Clift and Charlton Heston were all considered.[59] Gregory Peck was offered the part, but turned it down. He thought that the part was too similar to the part he played in *The Gunfighter*. Peck later regretted his decision.[60]

High Road to China (1983)

Tom Selleck as Patrick O'Malley (Roger Moore)

Roger Moore was originally set to star in *High Road to China*. When Moore left the production the role went to Tom Selleck.[61]

Greta Nissen's accent lost her a job in *Hell's Angels*).

High Sierra (1941)
Humphey Bogart as Roy Earle (James Cagney, John Garfield, Paul Muni, George Raft, Edward G. Robinson)

The part of Roy Earle was turned down by George Raft (who didn't want the character to die at the end),[62] Paul Muni (who didn't want the part because it had already been offered to George Raft),[63] James Cagney,[64] Edward G. Robinson,[65] and John Garfield.[66]

The Hi-Lo Country (1998)
Woody Harrelson as Big Boy Matson (Sean Penn)
Billy Crudup as Pete Calder (Jim Caviezel)

Director Stephen Frears considered Sean Penn for the role that eventually went to Woody Harrelson. Jim Caviezel auditioned for the role of Pete Calder. He says that losing that film was a serious blow for him.[67]

The Hired Hand (1971)
Verna Bloom as Hannah Collings (Lee Grant)

Peter Fonda directed and starred in *The Hired Hand*. When casting the film Fonda's sister, Jane Fonda, suggested Lee Grant for the part of Hannah Collings. Fonda liked Grant, but wasn't sure she was right for the part. Actress Sylvia Miles suggested Verna Bloom.[68] Fonda took her advice and gave Bloom the part.

His Girl Friday (1940)
Rosalind Russell as Hildy Johnson (Jean Arthur, Claudette Colbert, Irene Dunne, Katharine Hepburn, Carole Lombard, Ginger Rogers, Margaret Sullavan)

The role of Hildy Johnson was rejected by Jean Arthur, Ginger Rogers, Carole Lombard, Claudette Colbert, and Irene Dunne.[69] Other possibilities were Katharine Hepburn and Margaret Sullavan, but neither actress was interested. The part was finally played by Rosalind Russell.[70]

His Kind of Woman (1951)
Raymond Burr as Nick Ferraro (Robert J. Wilke)

Robert J. Wilke was originally cast as Nick Ferraro. When he left the cast he was replaced by Raymond Burr.[71]

Hit the Deck (1955)
Jane Powell as Susan Smith (Vera-Ellen)

Vera-Ellen came very close to landing the lead role of Susan Smith in *Hit the Deck*. The part went to Jane Powell instead.[72]

Hobson's Choice (1983)
John Mills as Willie Mossop (Robert Donat)

Robert Donat was originally set to star, but he became ill and was replaced by John Mills.[73]

Hocus Pocus (1993)
Kathy Najimy as Mary Sanderson (Rosie O'Donnell)

Rosie O'Donnell rejected the role of Mary Sanderson. O'Donnell is a mother, and felt uneasy about playing a witch who kills children.[74]

Hold 'Em Jail (1932)
Betty Grable as Barbara Jones (Dorothy Lee)

Dorothy Lee wanted too much money to star in *Hold 'Em Jail*. Instead of paying her, Betty Grable was brought in to replace her.[75]

A Hole in the Head (1959)
Frank Sinatra as Tony Manetta (James Cagney)

James Cagney's name was discussed as a possible Tony Manetta in *A Hole in the Head*.[76]

Holiday (1938)
Katharine Hepburn as Linda Seton (Irene Dunne)
Doris Nolan as Julia Seton (Rita Hayworth)

Columbia Pictures boss Harry Cohn wanted Irene Dunne to play the starring role of Linda Seton. Director George Cukor was able to persuade him that the best possible choice was Katharine Hepburn.[77]

Rita Hayworth auditioned for the part of Julia Seton but lost out to Doris Nolan.[78]

Honeymoon (1947)
Franchot Tone as David Flanner (Joseph Cotten)

Joseph Cotten was asked to play the part of American consul David Flanner. Cotten's co-star was to be 18-year-old Shirley Temple. Cotten turned the part down, saying that Temple was too young to play opposite him (Cotten is about 23 years her senior). Franchot Tone (older than Cotten by about three months) had no such problem and replaced Cotten.[79]

Honeymoon in Vegas (1992)

Nicolas Cage as Jack Singer (Billy Crystal)

Director Andrew Bergman thought Billy Crystal was a little too old for the lead in *Honeymoon in Vegas*. He cast Nicolas Cage who is 16 years Crystal's junior.[80]

The Honeymoon Machine (1961)

Steve McQueen as Lieutenant Fergie Howard (Cary Grant)

Cary Grant was the first choice to play Fergie Howard in *The Honeymoon Machine*. Grant wasn't interested and the part went to Steve McQueen instead.[81]

Hook (1991)

Bob Hoskins as Smee (Richard Dreyfuss)
Arthur Malet as Tootles (Richard Attenborough)
Maggie Smith as Wendy (Peggy Ashcroft)
Charlie Korsmo as Jack "Jackie" Banning (Joseph Mazzello)

Richard Dreyfuss wanted to be in *Hook*. He offered his services for the part of Smee, but director Steven Spielberg gave the part to Bob Hoskins instead.

Richard Attenborough was pursued for the part of Tootles. Attenborough was unavailable. He was directing *Chaplin* at the time. Arthur Malet was cast in his place.

Peggy Ashcroft was given the part of Wendy. Ashcroft had a bad back and had to drop out. Producer Frank Marshall asked costume designer Anthony Powell who he thought should replace her. Powell knew that Maggie Smith had played Peter Pan on stage in the early 1970s. He passed that along to Marshall. Marshall took the suggestion and gave Smith the part.

Joseph Mazzello auditioned to play Jack Banning. He lost the part to Charlie Korsmo. Spielberg later gave Mazzello a part in his next film, *Jurassic Park*.[82]

The Horse Whisperer (1998)

Kristin Scott Thomas as Annie MacLean (Emma Thompson)
Scarlett Johansson as Grace MacLean (Natalie Portman)

Emma Thompson considered playing Annie, but eventually turned it down.[83]

Natalie Portman was originally cast as Grace until the start of production was delayed. She had been offered the chance to star in *The Diary of Anne Frank* on Broadway and the new start date would have interfered.[84]

Hot Millions (1968)

Maggie Smith as Patty Terwilliger (Lynn Redgrave)

Lynn Redgrave was set for the part of Patty Terwilliger in *Hot Millions*. She became pregnant and had to drop out. Her replacement was Maggie Smith.[85]

Hot Saturday (1932)

Cary Grant as Romer Sheffield (Gary Cooper)

Gary Cooper was asked to play the lead role of Romer Sheffield. He said no, and it was played by Cary Grant instead.[86]

The Hotel New Hampshire (1984)

Jodie Foster as Frannie Berry (Diane Lane)

Diane Lane turned down the part of Frannie Berry. It was eventually played by Jodie Foster.[87]

The Hours (2002)

Jeff Daniels as Louis Waters (Zeljko Ivanek)
Julianne Moore as Older Laura Brown (Betsy Blair)

Zeljko Ivanek was cast as Louis Waters. Ivanek shot his scenes, but was let go afterwards. Producer Scott Rudin said that Ivanek was too young to play opposite Ed Harris; one wouldn't accept them as old friends. Ivanek was replaced by Jeff Daniels, who is two years older than Ivanek.

Director Stephen Daldry was concerned about aging Julianne Moore to play the older Laura Brown. He decided to cast an actress the right age and chose Betsy Blair. After he saw footage of Blair in the part, Daldry and all involved changed their minds. Even though it meant waiting about a year, they chose to reshoot the scenes with Julianne Moore.[88]

A House Divided (1931)

Helen Chandler as Ruth Evans (Bette Davis)

Bette Davis screen-tested for the role of Ruth Evans in *A House Divided*. In order to win the role Davis went to her audition in a low-cut dress, which was not typically her choice of dress. Director William Wyler was unimpressed, and even commented that showing off your chest was not the way to get a job. Davis lost the part to Helen Chandler.[89]

Houseboat (1958)

Sophia Loren as Cinzia Zaccardi (Betsy Drake)

Cary Grant originally intended to star in *Houseboat* with his then-wife Betsy Drake as his co-star. As they got closer to the start of production, Grant developed a crush on Sophia Loren, and she was cast opposite him instead. The character was changed to the glamorous Italian Cinzia Zaccardi to suit Loren.[90] Grant and Drake were divorced four years after the film was released.

How Green Was My Valley (1941)

Walter Pidgeon as Mr. Gruffyd (Brian Aherne, George Brent, Ray Milland, Laurence Olivier)
Maureen O'Hara as Angharad Morgan (Katharine Hepburn, Vivien Leigh, Ida Lupino, Merle Oberon, Gene Tierney)
Anna Lee as Bronwyn Morgan (Geraldine Fitzgerald, Greer Garson, Martha Scott, Gene Tierney)
Roddy McDowall as Huw Morgan (Tyrone Power)
Lionel Pape as Mr. C. Evans (Donald Crisp)

Producer Darryl F. Zanuck considered casting Ray Milland or George Brent as Mr. Gruffyd.[91] He also thought about Brian Aherne, but later decided against him. Zanuck thought that Laurence Olivier might be the right choice. Olivier was unavailable, and Zanuck cast Walter Pidgeon instead.[92]

Before Maureen O'Hara was signed for the part of Angharad, Katharine Hepburn, Vivien Leigh, Merle Oberon, and Ida Lupino were considered.[93] Zanuck contacted director John Ford to sing the praises of Gene Tierney. He told Ford that she was perfect for the part; she was young and sexy.[94]

Gene Tierney was also a contender for the role of Bronwen, but it was decided she was too young. Other candidates were Greer Garson and Geraldine Fitzgerald.[95] Martha Scott was considered, but the part went to Anna Lee instead.[96]

The character of Huw was originally intended to be played by two actors. One would play him as a young boy, and the other as an adult. The adult Huw was to have been played by Tyrone Power. It was later decided to have Huw only as a young boy and Power was out of the film.[97]

Donald Crisp was considered for the part of Evans.[98]

Betsy Drake was thrown over both on and off screen by Cary Grant (*Houseboat*).

How the Grinch Stole Christmas (2000)

Jim Carrey as The Grinch (Jack Nicholson)

Jack Nicholson's name was mentioned as a possible Grinch.[99]

How to Be Very, Very Popular (1955)

Sheree North as Curly Flagg (Marilyn Monroe)

Instead of reporting for work on *How to Be Very, Very Popular*, Marilyn Monroe took off for New York.[100] She was subsequently suspended and replaced by Sheree North.[101]

How to Lose a Guy in 10 Days (2003)

Kate Hudson as Andie Anderson (Gwyneth Paltrow)

Gwyneth Paltrow was originally set to star as Andie Anderson. She left in order to make the film *View from the Top*.[102] Kate Hudson replaced her.

How to Steal a Million (1966)

Eli Wallach as Davis Leland (George C. Scott)

George C. Scott was originally cast as Davis Leland in *How to Steal a Million*. On the first day of filming Scott was late to the set. He was replaced by Eli Wallach.[103]

The Hucksters (1947)

Clark Gable as Victor Albee Norman (Errol Flynn)

Clark Gable was offered the part of Victor Albee Norman in *The Hucksters*. Gable wasn't sure he liked the part, and took a long time deciding if he wanted to do it or not. He took so long, in fact, that MGM borrowed Errol Flynn from Warner Bros. to play the part. Gable then decided he would do it, and Flynn was out.[104]

Hudson Hawk (1991)

Andie MacDowell as Anna Baragli (Marushka Detmers)

Marushka Detmers was originally cast as Anna Baragli. She was suffering from back problems and wanted to be let go from the film. Andie MacDowell was brought in to replace her.[105]

The Hudsucker Proxy (1993)

Tim Robbins as Norville Barnes (Ethan Coen)
Jennifer Jason Leigh as Amy Archer (Jeanne Moreau, Winona Ryder)

According to producer Joel Silver, writer/directors Ethan and Joel Coen's first choices for the leads were Ethan Coen and Jeanne Moreau. Silver wanted a younger actress.[106] Coen did not play the part of Norville Barnes; it went to Tim Robbins instead. Winona Ryder lost the part of Amy to Jennifer Jason Leigh.[107]

The Hulk (2003)

Eric Bana as Bruce Banner (Billy Crudup)

Director Ang Lee wanted Billy Crudup to play Bruce Banner. When Crudup turned the part down Lee cast unknown actor Eric Bana.[108]

Human Desire (1954)

Glenn Ford as Jeff Warren (Marlon Brando, Montgomery Clift, Kirk Douglas, Burt Lancaster, Robert Mitchum)
Gloria Grahame as Vicki Buckley (Olivia De Havilland, Rita Hayworth, Barbara Stanwyck)

The female lead in *Human Desire* went through several actresses. First Barbara Stanwyck was supposed to play it. She turned it down, as did Rita Hayworth. An offer was made to Olivia De Havilland. De Havilland was interested but had to have a say in who her leading man was. She made a list which included Marlon Brando, Burt Lancaster, Kirk Douglas, Robert Mitchum, and Montgomery Clift. De Havilland didn't work out, and Gloria Grahame was cast with Glenn Ford playing opposite her.[109]

The Hunchback of Notre Dame (1956)

Anthony Quinn as Quasimodo (Marlon Brando)

Anthony Quinn was all set for the role of Quasimodo in the 1956 remake of *The Hunchback of Notre Dame*. Quinn stayed up nights worrying about how he was going to play this classic role. One morning he woke up to find that he had what looked like a terrible rash on his face. Quinn was convinced that his physical condition was caused by all his worrying. His face was in such bad shape that makeup would not conceal it. Shooting was postponed until Quinn was better. The producers sent him to many doctors hoping someone could figure out a way to help him. This went on for weeks until finally the producers could wait no longer. They asked Marlon Brando if he was available, but Quinn's costar, Gina Lollobrigida, would not allow it. She said that if anyone replaced Quinn they would also have to find someone to replace her! After a few more weeks Quinn went to see yet another doctor. The doctor told Quinn that he had been so worried about how to play a "monster" that he had turned himself into one. He gave Quinn a book called *The Saviors of God* by Nikos Kazantzakis and told him to wash his face with mineral water and spirit of camphor. Quinn read the entire book that night. The book dealt with the conscious and the subconscious. He awoke the next morning to find that his face had cleared up considerably. Quinn went back to work a few days later. Quinn became such a fan of Kazantzakis' that he made a film of one of his other books, *Zorba the Greek*.[110]

The Hunt for Red October (1990)

Sean Connery as Marko Ramius (Klaus Maria Brandauer, Harrison Ford)
Alec Baldwin as Jack Ryan (Kevin Costner, Harrison Ford)

Klaus Maria Brandauer was initially set to play submarine commander Marko Ramius. Soon after the producers learned that Sean Connery wanted the part. Brandauer agreed to relinquish the role for a sizable fee.[111]

Harrison Ford was offered the part of Jack Ryan. Ford considered it, but decided to make a counter offer. Ford said he would do the film, but only if he could play Ramius. Producer Mace Neufeld refused — he wanted to keep Sean Connery.[112] Kevin Costner was made an offer, which he rejected.[113] The role went to Alec Baldwin.

The Hurricane (1937)

Raymond Massey as Gov. Eugene De Laage (Basil Rathbone)

Basil Rathbone was sought for the role of Eugene De Laage. Rathbone was tired of playing the bad guy, and turned it down.[114]

Husbands and Wives (1992)

Judy Davis as Sally (Jane Fonda, Dianne Wiest)
Juliette Lewis as Rain (Emily Lloyd, Gwyneth Paltrow)

Writer/director Woody Allen asked Jane Fonda to play Sally. Fonda didn't want to change her hair style for the part. Allen also considered Dianne Wiest, but instead gave the part to Judy Davis. Davis was nominated for an Oscar for her work in the film.

Woody Allen saw Emily Lloyd in the film *Wish You Were Here*. He was impressed by her performance and cast her as Rain in *Husbands and Wives*. The English Lloyd was unable to conquer an American accent and Allen let her go.[115] Gwyneth Paltrow auditioned, but Allen chose Juliette Lewis instead.[116]

Hush ... Hush, Sweet Charlotte (1965)

Olivia De Havilland as Miriam Deering (Mary Astor, Joan Crawford, Vivien Leigh, Barbara Stanwyck, Loretta Young)
Mary Astor as Jewel Mayhew (Barbara Stanwyck)

After the success of *Whatever Happened to Baby Jane*, rivals Bette Davis and Joan Crawford agreed to reteam for the film, *Hush ... Hush, Sweet Charlotte*. They started work on the film and soon after the problems began. According to Len Baxter, a reporter on the set, Bette Davis made it her business to harass Crawford as often as possible. She complained about how long it took Crawford to get made up in the morning. She put down the way Crawford was playing her character. After work she would have parties for the cast and crew, everyone but Crawford. Co-star Agnes Moorehead even admitted that she and Bette Davis had ganged up on Crawford. It worked. Joan Crawford could not stand the pressure of this work situation and checked into the hospital claiming to be ill from extreme stress. She tried to rework the script to suit her better, but her suggestions were not accepted. She returned to the set, where nothing had changed. She quickly went back to the hospital, and director Robert Aldrich looked for a replacement. Aldrich considered Barbara Stanwyck and Loretta Young. Vivien Leigh was offered the part, but turned it down.[117] Mary Astor was also a possible choice, but the part ultimately went to Olivia De Havilland. Astor did appear in the film. Barbara Stanwyck was asked to play Jewel Mayhew. She said no, and the part went to Mary Astor.[118]

I Confess (1953)

Anne Baxter as Ruth Grandfort (Anita Bjork)

Director Alfred Hitchcock brought Anita Bjork to Hollywood from her home in Sweden

Warner Bros. prevented Alfred Hitchcock from casting Anita Bjork in the film *I Confess* because of her controversial lifestyle.

to play the part of Ruth Grandfort in *I Confess*. Warner Bros. balked at his choice when they learned that Bjork had an illegitimate child and a lover, and forced him to give the part to Anne Baxter instead.[1]

I Love Trouble (1994)
Nick Nolte as Peter Brackett (Harrison Ford)

Julia Roberts wanted Harrison Ford to star opposite her in *I Love Trouble*. He declined, and the part went to Nick Nolte.[2]

I Remember Mama (1948)
Irene Dunne as Mama Marta Hansen (Greta Garbo)

Greta Garbo turned down the title role of Mama.[3]

I Thank a Fool (1962)
Susan Hayward as Christine Allison (Ingrid Bergman)

Ingrid Bergman was considered to play Christine Allison early on. Later, when the film went into production, Susan Hayward had the part.[4]

I Wanna Hold Your Hand (1978)
Susan Kendall Newman as Janis Goldman (Carrie Fisher)

When Carrie Fisher dropped out of *I Wanna Hold Your Hand*, Susan Kendall Newman (daughter of Paul) replaced her.[5]

I Was a Male War Bride (1949)
Ann Sheridan as Catherine Gates (Ava Gardner)

Ava Gardner was considered for the part of Lt. Catherine Gates. Director Howard Hawks ultimately turned her down in favor of Ann Sheridan.[6]

Ice Age (2002)
Denis Leary as Diego (Philip Seymour Hoffman)

Philip Seymour Hoffman was a candidate for the part of Diego.[7]

The Ice Storm (1997)
Christina Ricci as Wendy Hood (Katie Holmes, Natalie Portman)

Director Ang Lee offered Natalie Portman the role of Wendy Hood in *The Ice Storm*. Portman felt the script was too dark and said no.[8] Katie Holmes auditioned but was told she was too old.[9] Holmes was switched over to the part of Libbets Casey. Lee cast Christina Ricci as Wendy.

I'd Climb the Highest Mountain (1951)
Susan Hayward as Mary Elizabeth Eden Thompson (Jeanne Crain)

The part of Mary Elizabeth Eden Thompson was originally to have been played by Jeanne Crain. Crain was pregnant, and Susan Hayward took the part.[10]

If ... Dog ... Rabbit (1999)
John Hurt as Sean Cooper (Harvey Keitel, Nick Nolte, Jon Voight, Christopher Walken, Treat Williams)
Kevin J. O'Connor as Jamie Cooper (Christian Bale, Jake Busey, Robert Carlyle, Simon Baker Denny, Matt

Dillon, Robert Downey, Jr., Christopher Eccleston, Ewan McGregor, Edward Norton)

Director Matthew Modine's first choices for the parts of his father and brother were Nick Nolte and Edward Norton. They passed on the project and Modine considered many other actors. For the father he thought of Jon Voight, John Hurt, Harvey, Keitel, Treat Williams, and Christopher Walken. For the brother he considered Matt Dillon, Ewan McGregor, Robert Downey, Jr., Christian Bale, Robert Carlyle, Jake Busey, Kevin J. O'Connor, Simon Baker Denny, and Christopher Eccleston. He eventually narrowed this list down to two possible families. Jon Voight, Modine, and Matt Dillon or John Hurt, Modine, and Robert Carlyle. Actually neither of these versions of the cast made the final cut. John Hurt won the role of the father, and Kevin J. O'Connor was cast as Modine's brother.[11]

I'll Be Seeing You (1944)

Ginger Rogers as Mary Marshall (Joan Fontaine)

Joan Fontaine was offered the part of Mary Marshall in *I'll Be Seeing You*. She turned it down, and it was played by Ginger Rogers instead.[12]

Imitation of Life (1959)

Sandra Dee as Susie, age 16 (Natalie Wood)

Natalie Wood was sought for *Imitation of Life*. Wood's fee was $200,000. Producer Ross Hunter decided he wasn't going to pay that much. He gave the part to Sandra Dee instead.[13]

The Impatient Years (1944)

Lee Bowman as Andy Anderson (Joel McCrea)

Joel McCrea was originally set to play Andy Anderson. He quit the film and was replaced by Lee Bowman.[14]

In a Lonely Place (1950)

Gloria Grahame as Laurel Gray (Lauren Bacall, Ginger Rogers)

Humphrey Bogart, who was the star of the film, tried to get the part of Laurel Gray for his wife, Lauren Bacall. Warner Bros. vetoed Bacall's participation. Columbia wanted Ginger Rogers but director Nicholas Ray gave the part to his wife, Gloria Grahame, instead.[15]

In & Out (1997)

Kevin Kline as Howard Brackett (Steve Martin)
Shalom Harlow as Sonya (Elizabeth Hurley)

Steve Martin considered playing Howard Brackett, but was unavailable when production started. The role went to Kevin Kline.[16]

Elizabeth Hurley was considered for the part of Sonya, eventually played by model Shalom Harlow.[17]

In Cold Blood (1967)

Robert Blake as Perry Smith (Paul Newman)
Scott Wilson as Dick Hickock (Steve McQueen)

Columbia wanted to have Paul Newman and Steve McQueen in the lead roles. But director Richards Brooks thought it was better to have lesser-known actors in the parts, that it would be more powerful if the strangers in the film were actually strangers to the audience.[18] He dropped the very famous Newman and McQueen in favor of Robert Blake and Scott Wilson.

In Love and War (1996)

Sandra Bullock as Agnes von Kurowsky (Julia Roberts)

Julia Roberts turned down the chance to star opposite Chris O'Donnell in *In Love and War*.[19] Sandra Bullock was cast instead. Roberts' decision turned out to be a good one; the film failed to excite both audiences and critics.

In Name Only (1939)

Carole Lombard as Julie Eden (Katharine Hepburn)

RKO bought the rights for *In Name Only* for Katharine Hepburn. When Hepburn failed to make the film, Carole Lombard won the role.[20]

In the Cool of the Day (1963)

Jane Fonda as Christine Bonner (Audrey Hepburn)

Audrey Hepburn declined an offer to star in *In the Cool of the Day*.[21]

In the Cut (2003)

Meg Ryan as Frannie (Nicole Kidman)
Mark Ruffalo as Detective Malloy (Kevin Bacon, Mickey Rourke)

Nicole Kidman owned the film rights for *In the Cut*. She decided that she would play the starring role of Frannie. However, Kidman's schedule was full, plus her marriage to Tom Cruise was dissolving. She decided to take herself out of the film. She did stay on as a producer though. Meg Ryan was very interested in playing Frannie. She asked director Jane Campion for an audition. Campion was impressed with Ryan and gave her the part.[22]

Jane Campion thought Kevin Bacon might be right for the part of Detective Malloy. She later reconsidered and gave Bacon the part of John Graham instead.[23] Campion was also interested in Mickey Rourke for the part of Detective Malloy. The studio intervened, and Mark Ruffalo played the part.[24]

In the Good Old Summertime (1949)

Judy Garland as Veronica Fisher (June Allyson)

June Allyson was originally cast as Veronica Fisher. When she learned that she was pregnant she backed out and was replaced by Judy Garland.[25]

In the Line of Fire (1993)

Clint Eastwood as Frank Horrigan (Dustin Hoffman, Nick Nolte)
John Malkovich as Mitch Leary (Robert Duvall, Jack Nicholson)
Rene Russo as Lilly Raines (Sharon Stone)

Dustin Hoffman had been attached to star in *In the Line of Fire* at one time.[26] Nick Nolte was also considered, but the part was played by Clint Eastwood instead.[27]

Jack Nicholson and Robert Duvall were discussed for the role of villain Mitch Leary.[28] John Malkovich was cast instead, and won an Oscar nomination for his performance.

Sharon Stone turned down the part of Lilly. Stone said that there wasn't anything to the part.[29]

Incognito (1997)

Jason Patric as Harry Donovan (Alec Baldwin)

Alec Baldwin was set to star in *Incognito* but changed his mind and left the film.[30]

Indecent Proposal (1993)

Demi Moore as Diana Murphy (Isabelle Adjani, Halle Berry, Lolita Davidovich, Nicole Kidman, Julia Roberts, Annabella Sciorra, Lisa Stansfield)
Woody Harrelson as David Murphy (Tom Cruise, Johnny Depp)

Many actresses wanted the part of Diana Murphy including Nicole Kidman and Annabella Sciorra.[31] Isabelle Adjani and Lolita Davidovich were also contenders.[32] Halle Berry wanted the part but was refused an interview. She was told that a black actress would not be considered; they didn't want the NAACP to complain about having a black woman have sex for money.[33] Singer Lisa Stansfield was also interested.[34] Julia Roberts was made an offer. She turned it down, clearing the way for Demi Moore.[35] Director Adrian Lyne had Moore audition. He was impressed with her reading, and he gave Moore the role.[36]

For the part of Diana's husband David, Adrian Lyne considered Johnny Depp. Tom Cruise was another possibility. Cruise had a problem with the idea of a man pimping his wife and, said no.[37]

Independence Day (1996)

Jeff Goldblum as David Levinson (Matthew Broderick)
Harry Connick, Jr., as Jimmy Wilder (Matthew Perry)

Scheduling problems prevented Matthew Broderick from starring in *Independence Day*.[38]

Writer/producer Dean Devlin wanted Matthew Perry to play Jimmy Wilder. Perry turned the role down, and it was played by Harry Connick, Jr., instead.[39]

Indiana Jones and the Last Crusade (1989)

Sean Connery as Henry Jones (Gregory Peck)
Michael Byrne as Vogel (Julian Glover)

George Lucas suggested that Gregory Peck play Indiana Jones' father. Steven Spielberg thought that Peck was a great choice for the part, but he had already decided on another actor: Sean Connery.[40]

Julian Glover was suggested to Spielberg for the part of Vogel. Spielberg liked the actor, but not for the part. He cast Michael Byrne as Vogel. Glover was given a part as well. He played Walter Donovan.[41]

Indiana Jones and the Temple of Doom (1984)
Kate Capshaw as Wilhelmina "Willie" Scott (Sharon Stone)

Sharon Stone auditioned to star opposite Harrison Ford in the sequel to *Raiders of the Lost Ark*. Steven Spielberg gave the part to Kate Capshaw instead. Capshaw and Spielberg met on the film and married in 1991.[42]

The Inn of the Sixth Happiness (1958)
Ingrid Bergman as Gladys Aylward (Audrey Hepburn)
Curt Jurgens as Lin Nan (Sean Connery)

Ingrid Bergman won the role of Gladys Aylward after it was rejected by Audrey Hepburn.[43]

Sean Connery was a possibility for the part of Capt. Lin Nan. The part went to Curt Jurgens instead.[44]

Inspector Clouseau (1968)
Alan Arkin as Inspector Clouseau (Peter Sellers)

Peter Sellers was offered the chance to reprise his role of Clouseau in the Pink Panther series with the film *Inspector Clouseau*. Sellers turned it down, and the part went to Alan Arkin.[45]

Interiors (1978)
Mary Beth Hurt as Joey (Diane Keaton)
Diane Keaton as Renata (Jane Alexander)
E.G. Marshall as Arthur (Denholm Elliott)
Sam Waterston as Mike (Harris Yulin)

Director Woody Allen had been an admirer of Denholm Elliott's work, so when he was casting his film, *Interiors*, he thought of the actor. He needed to hear the English Elliott try an American accent, which he did. Allen decided he was better off with an American actor and cast E.G. Marshall instead.[46]

Allen's original idea was for Diane Keaton to play Joey with Jane Alexander cast as Renata. Keaton persuaded him to give her the part of Renata. Mary Beth Hurt replaced Keaton as Joey.

Harris Yulin was cast as Mike. After a few days of rehearsal Yulin wanted out. Allen recast the role with Sam Waterston.[47]

Intermezzo (1939)
Leslie Howard as Holger Brandt (Ronald Colman, William Powell)

Both Ronald Colman and William Powell turned down the starring role of Holger Brandt.[48]

Intersection (1994)
Lolita Davidovich as Olivia Marshak (Sharon Stone)

Sharon Stone was initially asked to play the part of Richard Gere's mistress in *Intersection*. The actress wanted to break from this typecasting and wanted instead the role of the wife. Paramount Pictures couldn't see her in this role. They thought she was perfect to play the sexy Olivia. Stone wanted to play the wife so much that she asked to audition. Director Mark Rydell was impressed with her and gave her the part she wanted.[49]

Interview with the Vampire (1994)
Tom Cruise as Lestat de Lioncourt (Cher, Daniel Day-Lewis, Johnny Depp, Richard Gere, Mel Gibson, Jeremy Irons, John Travolta)
Christian Slater as Malloy (Leonardo DiCaprio, River Phoenix)
Kirsten Dunst as Claudia (Leelee Sobieski, Evan Rachel Wood)

There had been negotiations to make the novel *Interview with the Vampire* into a film for many years. John Travolta was mentioned as a leading man possibility in 1977. The plans fell through. In the mid–1980s Mel Gibson, Richard Gere, and even Cher were considered. Cher refused the part saying that she liked Anne Rice's novel too much to change it so drastically. Nothing much happened with the film until the '90s, when Daniel Day-Lewis was offered the part. He decided against it, and Jeremy Irons became a candidate.[50] Johnny Depp was another possibility.[51] Finally super star Tom Cruise signed on causing some controversy. Anne Rice felt that he was totally miscast and was very disappointed. Cruise remained calm and assured everyone she would change her mind after she saw his performance. Cruise was right. When Rice saw the finished product, she loved his performance.

River Phoenix was cast as Malloy. Sadly, Phoenix died of a drug overdose. Leonardo DiCaprio tried for the part, but it went, instead, to Christian Slater.[52] At the time Slater was a much bigger star than DiCaprio.

Kirsten Dunst beat out Leelee Sobieski[53] and Evan Rachel Wood[54] for the part of Claudia.

Invisible Stripes (1939)

William Holden as Tim Taylor (Wayne Morris)

William Holden, who was hot off the success of his star-making role in the film *Golden Boy*, went after the role of Tim Taylor in *Invisible Stripes*. The director of the film, Lloyd Bacon, didn't think the Hollywood newcomer was up to the challenge of the role. George Raft was the star of *Invisible Stripes*, and Bacon didn't think Holden would hold his own opposite such a powerful actor. He thought that Wayne Morris was better suited to the role. To prove him wrong, Holden took a small role in *Each Dawn I Die* where he would work with Raft. Bacon saw the film, realized he was wrong, and gave the part to Holden.[55]

The Ipcress File (1965)

Michael Caine as Harry Palmer (Christopher Plummer)

Christopher Plummer was the first choice for the lead role of Harry Palmer. He accepted the part, but was then offered the starring role in *The Sound of Music*. *The Sound of Music* was a hit Broadway play, and the film version was a very big deal. Plummer dropped out of *The Ipcress File* to accept the role, and Michael Caine was brought in as his replacement.[56]

Irma La Douce (1963)

Shirley MacLaine as Irma La Douce (Brigitte Bardot, Marilyn Monroe, Elizabeth Taylor)
Lou Jacobi as Moustache (Charles Laughton)

Marilyn Monroe was the front runner to star opposite Jack Lemmon in *Irma La Douce*. Monroe was unavailable and Elizabeth Taylor and Brigitte Bardot were mentioned as possible replacements. However, director Billy Wilder thought that Bardot's French accent was wrong for the part. He also thought that Taylor was wrong for Irma. MacLaine got the part.

Wilder thought that Charles Laughton was perfect to play the narrator and bartender Moustache. Sadly, Laughton died before shooting started. He was replaced by Lou Jacobi.[57]

Irreconcilable Differences (1984)

Ryan O'Neal as Albert Brodsky (John Travolta)
Shelley Long as Lucy Van Patten Brodsky (Marilu Henner)

Nancy Meyers and Charles Shyer wanted John Travolta and Marilu Henner to star in *Irreconcilable Differences*. Travolta wasn't interested, and they cast Ryan O'Neal and Shelley Long instead.[58]

The Island (1980)

Michael Caine as Blair Maynard (Anthony Hopkins)

Director Michael Ritchie wanted Anthony Hopkins to star in *The Island*. Hopkins was already doing a play, and so Michael Caine got the part instead.[59]

The Island of Dr. Moreau (1996)

David Thewlis as Edward Douglas (Val Kilmer, Rob Morrow)

Richard Stanley spent four years developing *The Island of Dr. Moreau*. He hired Val Kilmer to play the lead role of Edward Douglas. Shortly after, Kilmer decided that he wanted his role made smaller. Stanley told Kilmer that was a bad idea — he was the lead in the film. Stanley finally came up with the idea of replacing Kilmer as Douglas. Rob Morrow was the new lead. Kilmer was switched over to the part of Montgomery. The film's production company, New Line, agreed to the switch, and the company went to Queensland, Australia, for the shoot. On the first day of filming, Stanley and Kilmer clashed. According to Stanley, Kilmer threw his lines away, and said other actors' lines. He also insisted on costume pieces that Stanley found confusing. For example, Kilmer wanted a piece of blue material to wrap around his arm. The second day, Kilmer was very late to the set. In fact he arrived at three in the afternoon. Stanley also complained that Kilmer refused to rehearse his scenes. On day four New Line watched the dailies. They were unhappy with Kilmer's work. Kilmer was the main attraction of the film. Rather than replace him, Stanley was fired. Rob Morrow decided he no longer wanted to be involved and quit. David Thewlis was hired to replace him, although the character was totally rewritten.[60]

Islands in the Stream (1977)

George C. Scott as Thomas Hudson (Steve McQueen)

Steve McQueen considered playing the role of Thomas Hudson in *Islands in the Stream*, but he finally decided that he wasn't right for the part. He told director Franklin Schaffner to get a better actor that he. Schaffner gave the part to George C. Scott instead.[61]

It Could Happen to You (1994)

Bridget Fonda as Yvonne Biasi (Julia Roberts)

Julia Roberts was sought to star in *It Could Happen to You* as Yvonne Biasi. Roberts rejected the offer and Bridget Fonda won the role.[62]

It Happened One Night (1934)

Clark Gable as Peter Warne (Fredric March, Robert Montgomery)

Claudette Colbert as Ellie Andrews (Constance Bennett, Bette Davis, Miriam Hopkins, Carole Lombard, Myrna Loy, Margaret Sullavan, Loretta Young)

Fredric March[63] and Robert Montgomery turned down the male lead in *It Happened One Night*. Montgomery didn't like the script.[64] Myrna Loy rejected the female lead for the same reason. Loy claims that the script being shown around was very different from the final version we all know.[65] Margaret Sullavan, Constance Bennett, and Miriam Hopkins all rejected the role as well.[66] Studio head Harry Cohn suggested Loretta Young and Carole Lombard. Lombard was made an offer, but was already signed to star in *Bolero*.[67] Jack Warner refused to loan out Bette Davis.[68] Claudette Colbert won the role, and the film became a classic.

It's a Wonderful Life (1946)

James Stewart as George Bailey (Cary Grant)

Donna Reed as Mary Bailey (Jean Arthur, Olivia De Havilland, Ann Dvorak, Martha Scott)

Lionel Barrymore as Herbert Potter (Walter Abel, Leon Ames, Edward Arnold, George Bancroft, Edgar Barrier, Charles Bickford, Edgar Buchanan, Louis Calhern, Charles Coburn, Ray Collins, George Colouris, Albert Dekker, Charles Dingle, Dan Duryea, Richard Gaines, George Halton, Henry Hull, Victor Jory, Otto Kruger, Gene Lockhart, Raymond Massey, Thomas Mitchell, Vincent Price, Claude Rains, Stanley Ridges, Lee Tracy)

Thomas Mitchell as Uncle Billy (Walter Brennan, W.C. Fields, Barry Fitzgerald, Hugh Herbert, Edward Everett Horton, Adolphe Menjou, Victor Moore, Henry Travers, Roland Young)

Beulah Bondi as Ma Bailey (Kathleen Lockhart, Anne Revere, Selena Royle, Mary Young)

Frank Faylen as Ernie Bishop (Don Barclay, Steve Brodie, Edward Brophy, Alan Carney, Walter Catlett, William Demarest, Wally Ford, John Ireland, Frank Jenks, Red (Charles) Marshall, Frank McHugh, Walter Sande)

Ward Bond as Officer Bert (John Alexander, Irving Bacon, Wally Brown, James Burke, Sam Levene, Barton MacLane, Robert Mitchum, Walter Sande)

Gloria Grahame as Violet Bick (Myrna Dell, Jean Porter, Ann Sothern)

H.B. Warner as Mr. Gower (Irving Bacon, E. J. Ballantyne, Happy Cheshire, Jimmy Conlin, Harry Davenport, Charles Grapewin, Charles Halton, Jean Hersholt, Samuel Hinds, Guy Kibbee, Percy Kilbride, Donald Meek, Phillip Merivale, Reginald Owen, John Qualen, Erskine Sanford, Henry Travers)

Frank Albertson as Sam Wainwright (Bill Goodwin, Van Heflin, John Howard, Dean Jagger, Allyn Joslyn, Gordon

Oliver, Gene Raymond, Kent Smith, Phil Warren)
Samuel S. Hinds as Peter Bailey (Thurston Hall, Russell Hicks, Moroni Olsen, Henry Travers, Tom Tully)
William Edmunds as Mr. Martini (Louis Alberni, Fotunio Bononova, Joseph Calleia, Chef Milani, Nestor Paiva, Frank Puglie, Bob Vignola)
Lillian Randolph as Anne (Sara Allgood, Clara Blandioi, Helen Broderick, Jane Darwell, Ruth Donnelly, Connie Gilchrist, Hattie McDaniel, Una O'Connor, Irene Ryan

Most of the possibilities listed above are names director Frank Capra wrote down on his casting list.

It's hard to image anyone besides Jimmy Stewart as George Bailey. But originally, RKO bought the film with Cary Grant in mind. It sat on a shelf for years. By that time Grant had already made a Christmas movie—*The Bishop's Wife*. Director Frank Capra read the script and knew that it had potential. He bought the script from RKO. Capra had just formed Liberty Films with partner Sam Briskin, William Wyler, and George Stevens. *It's a Wonderful Life* was their first film.

Capra's only choice for the starring role of George Bailey was Jimmy Stewart. Stewart had just come out of the army. He wanted to make a film with Capra. Capra told Stewart about *It's a Wonderful Life*. Stewart eagerly signed on. He was the first actor to join the cast.

Jean Arthur (a common leading lady for Capra) was the first choice to play Mary. Capra, Stewart, and Arthur all worked together in *You Can't Take It with You* and *Mr. Smith Goes to Washington*. At the time Arthur was committed to a Broadway play and was unavailable. Capra also thought of Olivia De Havilland and Ann Dvorak. The part finally went to Donna Reed.

Alternate choices for Mr. Potter were Claude Rains, Vincent Price, Charles Coburn, and Edgar Buchanan.[69]

Gloria Grahame was cast as Violet Bick after Ann Sothern, Myrna Dell and Jean Porter were all considered.[70]

Anne Revere was considered for Ma Bailey.[71]

Capra considered W.C. Fields, Barry Fitzgerald, Adolphe Menjou, Walter Brennan, and Henry Travers for the part of George's Uncle Billy. Thomas Mitchell was cast instead. Travers was also considered for the parts of Peter Bailey and Mr. Gower.[72] Capra did find a part in the film for Travers—as the angel Clarence.

Ivanhoe (1952)
Joan Fontaine as Rowena (Elizabeth Taylor)

Elizabeth Taylor was offered the part of Rebecca. Taylor resisted; she wanted to play Rowena instead. But Joan Fontaine already had the part, and she wasn't going to give it up. Taylor ended up as Rebecca after all.[73]

Ivy (1947)
Joan Fontaine as Ivy Lexton (Olivia De Havilland)

Olivia De Havilland was offered the title role of Ivy. She turned it down, and it was played by her sister, Joan Fontaine, instead.[74]

J.F.K. (1991)
Kevin Costner as Jim Garrison (Alec Baldwin, Tom Berenger, Marlon Brando, Willem Dafoe, Robert De Niro, Michael Douglas, Harrison Ford, Mel Gibson, Gene Hackman, William Hurt, Michael Keaton, Kyle MacLachlan, John Malkovich, Matthew Modine, Jack Nicholson, Nick Nolte, Dennis Quaid, Robert Redford, Robin Williams)
Sissy Spacek as Liz Garrison (Elizabeth McGovern, Cybill Shepherd)
Kevin Bacon as Willie O'Keefe (Matt Dillon, Dennis Quaid, Tom Sizemore, James Spader, Michael Wincott)
Tommy Lee Jones as Clay Shaw (Michael Douglas, Martin Landau, Robert Loggia, Paul Newman, Peter O'Toole, Gregory Peck, Roy Scheider)
Gary Oldman as Lee Harvey Oswald (Alec Baldwin, Tom Cruise, Charlie Sheen, D.B. Sweeney)
Joe Pesci as David Ferrie (Willem Dafoe, Jeff Goldblum, Martin Landau, Gary Oldman, James Woods)
Donald Sutherland as X (Marlon Brando)
John Candy as Dean Andrews (Danny De Vito, Larry Drake, John Goodman)
Jack Lemmon as Jack Martin (Harry Dean Stanton)

Edward Asner as Guy Bannister (Brian Dennehy, Glenn Ford, Gene Hackman)

Jo Anderson as Julia Ann Mercer (Goldie Hawn)

Oliver Stone's long list for actors to possibly play Jim Garrison is shown above. Of those actors, at least two were offered the part. Mel Gibson and Harrison Ford both rejected the role. Ford thought that the Kennedy assassination was still too sensitive a topic for a film. Stone finally settled on Kevin Costner who was rewarded with an Oscar nomination.

Cybill Shepherd and Elizabeth McGovern were considered for Liz Garrison, but the role went to Sissy Spacek.

Other possibilities for Kevin Bacon's role of Willie O'Keefe include Dennis Quaid, Matt Dillon, James Spader, Tom Sizemore, and Michael Wincott.

Stone listed Michael Douglas, Paul Newman, Peter O'Toole, Gregory Peck, Roy Scheider, Martin Landau, and Robert Loggia as Clay Shaw candidates. He later chose Tommy Lee Jones to play the part.

Gary Oldman was cast as Lee Harvey Oswald after Tom Cruise, Alec Baldwin, Charlie Sheen, and D.B. Sweeney were considered. Besides Oswald, Gary Oldman was also considered for the Joe Pesci role of David Ferrie, along with James Woods, Jeff Goldblum, Willem Dafoe, and Martin Landau.

Marlon Brando was a possible X, but it went to Donald Sutherland instead.

Danny De Vito, John Goodman, and Larry Drake were possibilities for John Candy's small role of Dean Andrews.

Harry Dean Stanton almost got the part of Jack Martin, which went to Jack Lemmon instead.

Glenn Ford, Gene Hackman, and Brian Dennehy were on the list for the Guy Bannister role Ed Asner played.

Stone considered Goldie Hawn for witness Julia Ann Mercer, but eventually chose to cast Jo Anderson.[1]

Jack Frost (1998)

Michael Keaton as Jack Frost (George Clooney, John Travolta)

When Sam Raimi was going to direct *Jack Frost* he had George Clooney in mind to play the father turned snowman. Raimi left the project and was replaced by Troy Miller. Michael Keaton was cast as Jack Frost. Also considered was John Travolta.[2]

Jackie Brown (1997)

Samuel L. Jackson as Ordell Robbie (Quentin Tarantino)

Writer-director Quentin Tarantino had planned the part of Ordell for himself. He let the part go, although he claims it was extremely difficult for him.[3]

Jane Eyre (1944)

Orson Welles as Edward Rochester (Ronald Colman)

Ronald Colman was considered for Orson Welles' character, Edward Rochester.[4]

Jaws (1975)

Roy Scheider as Martin Brody (Joe Bologna, Robert Duvall, Charlton Heston)

Robert Shaw as Quint (Robert Duvall, Sterling Hayden, Lee Marvin)

Richard Dreyfuss as Matt Hooper (Timothy Bottoms, Jeff Bridges, Joel Grey, Jan-Michael Vincent, Jon Voight)

Lorraine Gary as Ellen Brody (Linda Harrison)

The actor Steven Spielberg most wanted to play Martin Brody was Joe Bologna. But the producers vetoed his choice. Robert Duvall was made an offer, which he turned down. He was more interested in the part of Quint, and even met with Spielberg to discuss it. The director says that at the time he couldn't see how good he might've been in the role.[5] Charlton Heston's name came up for Brody, but it was decided the part belonged to Roy Scheider.[6]

Sterling Hayden almost played the part of Quint. But Hayden had tax problems and couldn't do it.[7] Lee Marvin turned it down, and Robert Shaw was cast.[8]

Jon Voight was Spielberg's first choice to play Matt Hooper. Voight wasn't interested. Richard Dreyfuss won the role even though bigger stars such as Jeff Bridges,[10] Joel Grey,[11] Jan-Michael Vincent,[12] and Timothy Bottoms[13] were considered.

Producer Richard Zanuck's wife, Linda Harrison, wanted the part of Ellen Brody. Zanuck went to Spielberg on her behalf. At the same time Sid Sheinberg, the president of Universal Pictures, told Spielberg his wife, Lorraine Gary would be great in the part. Spielberg cast Gary, feeling she was better suited for the part.[14]

The Jazz Singer (1927)

Al Jolson as Jakie Rabinowitz/Jack Robin (Eddie Cantor, Buster Collier, Jr., George Jessel)

The Jazz Singer was originally supposed to have starred George Jessel rather than Al Jolson. Although he desperately wanted to play the part, Jessel left over a dispute about money.[15] It was reported that Jack Warner was offering him $30,000; Jessel wanted $40,000. Buster Collier, Jr., was a candidate, but Warner didn't like his voice.[16] The next offer was made to Eddie Cantor. Cantor refused, claiming that the part belonged to Jessel.[17] The part was finally taken by Al Jolson, who made motion picture history by speaking the first words ever heard on screen.

The Jazz Singer (1952)

Peggy Lee as Judy Lane (Doris Day)

Doris Day was the first choice for the part of Judy Lane. Day had no interest in remaking *The Jazz Singer* and turned it down. Singer Peggy Lee was brought in to replace her.[18]

Jealousy (1929)

Fredric March as Pierre (Anthony Bushell)

Jeanne Eagels and Anthony Bushell were cast in the lead roles of *Jealousy*. Shooting was completed, but Eagels was unhappy. She insisted that they re-shoot all of Bushell's scenes with Fredric March replacing him.[19]

Jerry Maguire (1996)

Tom Cruise as Jerry Maguire (Tom Hanks)
Renee Zellweger as Dorothy Boyd (Patricia Arquette, Bridget Fonda, Winona Ryder, Mira Sorvino, Marisa Tomei)
Kelly Preston as Avery Bishop (Diane Lane)
Cuba Gooding, Jr., as Rod Tidwell (Damon Wayans, Mykelti Williamson)
Jared Jussim as Dicky Fox (Billy Wilder)

The part of Jerry Maguire was written for Tom Hanks. Writer-director Cameron Crowe felt that because it had taken so long to finish the script, Hanks had aged too much for the part.[20] This was fine with Hanks who had problems with the script anyway.[21]

An unknown Renee Zellweger won the role of Dorothy over many famous actresses including

Anthony Bushell was replaced in the film *Jealousy* after shooting was completed.

Winona Ryder,[22] Bridget Fonda,[23] Marisa Tomei,[24] and Patricia Arquette.[25] Mira Sorvino, fresh from her Academy Award–winning performance in *Mighty Aphrodite*, was also interested. The deal fell through when Sorvino asked for too much money.[26]

Diane Lane tried for the role of Avery, but lost out to Kelly Preston.[27]

Damon Wayans and Mykelti Williamson were other possible choices for Rod Tidwell.[28] Cuba Gooding, Jr., was cast. The role earned Gooding an Academy Award.

Crowe offered director Billy Wilder the part of Cruise's mentor Dicky Fox. Wilder had zero interest in appearing in the film and turned it down.[29]

Jezebel (1938)

Bette Davis as Julia Marsden (Tallulah Bankhead, Miriam Hopkins, Barbara Stanwyck)
Henry Fonda as Preston Dillard (Jeffrey Lynn)

Bette Davis' role in *Jezebel* was coveted by several actresses. Miriam Hopkins had originated the role on Broadway. She owned the rights and intended to star in a film version. She was persuaded to sell to Warner Bros. on the promise that she would be considered before anyone else.

They considered her, and decided she was out. Hopkins was furious.[30] Barbara Stanwyck[31] and Tallulah Bankhead[32] also wanted the part, but it was Bette Davis who was chosen.

Jeffrey Lynn was a possibility to play Preston Dillard, but Davis herself liked Henry Fonda.[33] Fonda won the role.

Jimmy and Sally (1933)

Claire Trevor as Sally Johnson (Sally Eilers)

Sally Eilers was set for the lead role of Sally Johnson. Eilers quit, and was replaced by Claire Trevor.[34]

Johnny Belinda (1948)

Lew Ayres as Doctor Robert Richardson (Marlon Brando)
Jan Sterling as Stella McCormick (Janis Paige)

A 23-year-old Marlon Brando screen-tested for the part of Robert Richardson. Jack Warner didn't like Brando's voice; he complained that he mumbled. Lew Ayres won the part.[35]

Janis Paige was a strong contender to play Stella.[36]

Johnny Guitar (1954)

Mercedes McCambridge as Emma Small (Barbara Stanwyck)

Barbara Stanwyck was the first choice for the role that went to Mercedes McCambridge.[37]

Johnny Mnemonic (1995)

Keanu Reeves as Johnny Mnemonic (Val Kilmer)

Val Kilmer was signed to star in *Johnny Mnemonic*. He later decided there were problems with the script that should be worked out before filming. He left the film and was replaced by Keanu Reeves.[38]

Johnny Suede (1991)

Brad Pitt as Johnny Suede (Sam Rockwell)

Sam Rockwell auditioned for the role of Johnny Suede, but lost out to Brad Pitt.[39]

The Jolson Story (1946)

Larry Parks as Al Jolson (James Cagney, Richard Conte, Jose Ferrer, Al Jolson, Danny Thomas)

James Cagney was offered the title role of Al Jolson. Cagney wasn't interested in making *The Jolson Story* and turned it down. Danny Thomas was considered. He was told that if he accepted the part he would need to make his nose smaller. Thomas said to forget it. Jose Ferrer and Richard Conte were other possible choices.[40] Al Jolson wanted to play himself in the film, but Larry Parks was cast instead.[41]

Josie and the Pussycats (2001)

Rosario Dawson as Valerie Brown (Lisa "Left Eye" Lopes)

TLC singer Lisa "Left Eye" Lopes auditioned to play Valerie Brown. Lopes lost out to Rosario Dawson.[42]

Juarez (1939)

Bette Davis as Empress Carlotta von Habsburg (Kay Francis)

Kay Francis desperately wanted the part of Carlotta in *Juarez*. Warner Bros. turned her down in favor of Bette Davis.[43]

Judgment at Nuremberg (1961)

Burt Lancaster as Ernst Janning (Laurence Olivier)

Laurence Olivier was originally cast as Ernst Janning. He left at the last minute and was replaced by Burt Lancaster.[44]

Juke Girl (1942)

Ronald Reagan as Steve Talbot (George Raft)

George Raft was replaced by Ronald Reagan after not showing up for work on the film *Juke Girl*.[45]

Julia (1977)

Jane Fonda as Lillian Hellman (Faye Dunaway)
Vanessa Redgrave as Julia (Meryl Streep)

Faye Dunaway was offered the part of Lillian Hellman. She said no, and Jane Fonda got the role.[46]

Meryl Streep was asked to audition for the starring role in *Julia*. Before she got a chance to read, Vanessa Redgrave had been given the part. Instead Streep was cast in the smaller role of Anne Marie.[47]

Jumpin' Jack Flash (1986)
Whoopi Goldberg as Teresa "Terry" Dolittle (Shelley Long)

Shelley Long was originally supposed to star in *Jumpin' Jack Flash*. She and 20th Century–Fox had artistic differences, and Long dropped out. She was replaced by Whoopi Goldberg.[48]

June Bride (1948)
Robert Montgomery as Carey Jackson (Jack Carson, Dennis Morgan)

Dissatisfied with the choice of Robert Montgomery as her leading man, Bette Davis suggested either Dennis Morgan or Jack Carson to replace him. Warner Bros. ignored these suggestions, and stuck with Montgomery.[49]

Jungle Fever (1991)
Lonette McKee as Drew (Halle Berry)

Halle Berry auditioned to play Wesley Snipes' wife in *Jungle Fever*. Director Spike Lee didn't think she was right for that part, and cast her the crack addicted Vivian.[50]

Junior Bonner (1972)
Ida Lupino as Elvira Bonner (Jean Arthur)

Jean Arthur was offered the role of Elvira Bonner in *Junior Bonner*. Arthur had stopped making movies since 1953's *Shane*. She was not interested in making a comeback, and turned the part down.[51]

Jurassic Park (1993)
Sam Neill as Dr. Alan Grant (Richard Dreyfuss, Harrison Ford, William Hurt, Kurt Russell)
Laura Dern as Dr. Ellie Sattler (Robin Wright Penn)
Ariana Richards as Lex Murphy (Christina Ricci)

Harrison Ford was considered for the part of Dr. Alan Grant.[52] Other possibilities were Kurt Russell and Richard Dreyfuss. Both actors wanted too much money and Steven Spielberg continued his search. William Hurt turned the part down. Spielberg eventually gave the part to Sam Neill.[53]

Robin Wright Penn turned down the part of Ellie Sattler.[54] Laura Dern was cast instead.

Christina Ricci auditioned to play Lex Murphy, but lost out to Ariana Richards.[55]

Just for You (1952)
Natalie Wood as Barbara Blake (Margaret O'Brien)

Natalie Wood's main competition for the role of Barbara Blake, or "Babs," was child star Margaret O'Brien. Wood was 13 at the time and had been working in films steadily since the age of four. This part was important to her because it was the first part she was up for that was older. Babs was a teenager and Wood needed to make the difficult move into more adult roles. She worked very hard to prepare for her audition. Afterwards director Elliott Nugent enthusiastically gave her the role.[56]

Just Tell Me What You Want (1980)
Ali MacGraw as Bones Burton (Cybill Shepherd)

Cybill Shepherd flew out to California to audition for director Sidney Lumet's film, *Just Tell Me What You Want*. Shepherd arrived at Universal Studios and found Lumet. The director asked her why she was there. Shepherd told him that she was there to read for him. Lumet was confused as to why her agent didn't tell her that the part was already cast with Ali MacGraw. Shepherd fired her agent.[57]

The Karate Kid (1984)
Ralph Macchio as Daniel LaRusso (Kyle Eastwood)

Columbia Pictures approached Clint Eastwood to direct their film *The Karate Kid*. Eastwood was interested, but there was a catch. He insisted that his son Kyle be given the starring role of Daniel LaRusso. Kyle had acted in two films previously. He played Clint Eastwood's son in *The Outlaw Josey Wales* and then played his nephew in *Honkytonk Man*. The studio was not impressed. They refused to give Kyle the part. Not only did Eastwood not direct the film, he was so angry that he said he did not want to have any Coca-Cola in his sight since the company was linked to Columbia Pictures.[1] The studio hired John Avildsen to direct and gave the lead to Ralph Macchio.

Kathleen (1941)
Shirley Temple as Kathleen Davis (Kathryn Grayson)

In 1941 a teenage Kathryn Grayson was under contract to MGM. She was assigned to play the title role in *Kathleen*. To Grayson's surprise, MGM yanked her from the part in favor of another contract player — Shirley Temple. The 13-year-old Temple was one of the biggest stars in the world. Grayson had little experience at that point, although she would go on to star in many films including *Show Boat* and *Kiss Me Kate*. Temple was clearly the audience favorite, and she was cast in the role.[2]

The Keys of the Kingdom (1944)

Gregory Peck as Father Francis Chisholm (Gene Kelly)
Thomas Mitchell as Dr. Willie Tullock (Gene Kelly)
Jane Ball as Nora (Jennifer Jones)

Producer David O. Selznick was so fond of A.J. Cronin's novel, *The Keys of the Kingdom*, that he bought the film rights. Selznick planned to turn the story of missionary priest, Father Francis Chisholm, into a musical. Gene Kelly was very interested in nabbing a role. He called Selznick up to discuss the matter. At the time Kelly had not made any films. Selznick had seen him on Broadway, where Kelly was starring in *Pal Joey*. Kelly was signed to a contract. Kelly was eager to start working on a film. Selznick thought that the lead role of Father Francis Chisholm was right for Kelly. Kelly was apprehensive. He worried that he was not ready for a starring role yet. Selznick understood. He told Kelly that if he didn't think he could handle the lead, that the supporting role of Willie Tullock, the Scottish doctor, might be more to his liking. Kelly was relieved and started to work on the part. Selznick sent the young actor to a vocal coach to work on his Scottish accent. About ten days later Selznick told Kelly that he would be required to make a screen test. Kelly obliged. Selznick showed Kelly his test. There were technical problems. The picture and the sound were out of sync. Kelly also felt that his accent was not right and that it sounded silly. About a month later Kelly found out that Selznick sold the rights to 20th Century–Fox, who wanted it for Gregory Peck and Thomas Mitchell.[3]

Jennifer Jones was mentioned for the role of Nora, ultimately played by Jane Ball.[4]

Kill Bill: Vol. 1 (2003)

David Carradine as Bill (Warren Beatty)

Warren Beatty was director Quentin Tarantino's original choice for the part of Bill. Beatty dropped out, and David Carradine took the part.[5]

The Killers (1946)

Burt Lancaster as Ole "Swede" Anderson [aka Pete Lunn] (Wayne Morris, Sonny Tufts)

Wayne Morris and Sonny Tufts were both unable to appear in *The Killers* because of scheduling conflicts. The part was taken by Burt Lancaster.[6]

The Killing of Sister George (1968)

Beryl Reid as June Buckridge (Bette Davis)

Bette Davis sought the part of June Buckridge, and was very disappointed when she was turned down in favor of Beryl Reid.[7]

The King and I (1956)

Deborah Kerr as Anna Leonowens (Dinah Shore)
Yul Brynner as King Mongkut of Siam (Marlon Brando)
Rita Moreno as Tuptim (Dorothy Dandridge)

Dinah Shore was unsuccessful in her attempt to win the role of Anna.[8]

Yul Brynner had been interested in directing the film and thought Marlon Brando should play the King role Brynner had originated on Broadway.[9] Eventually Walter Lang was hired to direct and Brynner signed on to star.

Daryl F. Zanuck thought Dorothy Dandridge was the right choice to play Tuptim. Dandridge signed on for the film. Soon after Dandridge rethought her decision. She worried that the character was basically a slave. Her publicist, Orin Borsten, tried to assure her that this role had nothing to do with the slaves from Africa. Her boyfriend Otto Preminger thought that Dandridge should turn the part down because it wasn't a lead. Dandridge took his advice and refused the part. Zanuck was furious with her.[10] The part was recast with Rita Moreno.

King Kong (1976)

Jeff Bridges as Jack Prescott (Charles Grodin)
Jessica Lange as Dwan (Cher, Bette Midler, Valerie Perrine, Barbra Streisand)

Charles Grodin knew he would appear in the remake of *King Kong*, although he wasn't sure which role would be his.[11] Dino De Laurentiis eventually decided that Jeff Bridges should play the hero, Jack, which left the part of Fred Wilson for Grodin.

Barbra Streisand was the first choice for Dwan. Streisand would not be available when shooting was set to start, so another leading lady was needed. Valerie Perrine was a possibility. The problem with Perrine was that she was under contract to Universal. Universal was considering their own version of *King Kong*, and Perrine was out of the running. Bette Midler and Cher were considered, but the part was given to Jessica Lange instead.[12]

The King of Comedy (1983)

Jerry Lewis as Jerry Langford (Joey Bishop, Johnny Carson, Sammy Davis, Jr., Dean Martin, Frank Sinatra, Orson Welles)

Director Martin Scorsese's first choice for the role of Jerry Langford was Johnny Carson. The role was that of a late night talk show host, very much like Johnny Carson and the *Tonight Show*. Carson discussed the possibility with Scorsese. He told the director that he would only want to do one take. Scorsese couldn't guarantee that, and Carson passed. Scorsese's second choice was Frank Sinatra. After Sinatra said no he considered Joey Bishop, Sammy Davis, Jr., and Orson Welles. Welles was a contender, but in the end Scorsese decided he didn't have the quality he was looking for. Dean Martin was another possibility, which led Scorsese to think of Martin's former partner Jerry Lewis.[13] Lewis accepted Scorsese's offer, and gave one of his best performances to date.

The King of Marvin Gardens (1972)

Jack Nicholson as David Staebler (Bruce Dern)
Bruce Dern as Jason Staebler (Jack Nicholson)

Jack Nicholson and Bruce Dern were set to star as brothers in *The King of Marvin Gardens*. Nicholson was cast as Jason, the criminal scheming brother, while Dern was set to play David, the introverted radio host. Director Bob Rafelson decided that the film would work better if the two actors were cast against type and had the two actors switch roles.[14]

King Rat (1965)

George Segal as Corporal King (Steve McQueen, Paul Newman)

Neither Paul Newman nor Steve McQueen wanted the part of Corporal King. They both turned it down, and it went to George Segal.[15]

Kings Row (1942)

Robert Cummings as Parris Mitchell (Henry Fonda, Tyrone Power)
Ronald Reagan as Drake McHugh (Eddie Albert, Jack Carson, Robert Preston)
Betty Field as Cassandra Tower (Bette Davis, Olivia De Havilland, Ida Lupino)

Darryl F. Zanuck wouldn't loan out Henry Fonda or Tyrone Power to play Parris Mitchell in *Kings Row*. Eddie Albert, Robert Preston and Jack Carson tried to win the role of Drake McHugh, but Ronald Reagan was cast instead.[16]

Bette Davis and Olivia De Havilland sought the role of Cassandra. Warner Bros. wanted to cast Ida Lupino, but she wasn't interested.[17] Betty Field was finally chosen.

Kiss and Tell (1945)

Shirley Temple as Corliss Archer (Patricia Kirkland)

Patricia Kirkland was set to star in *Kiss and Tell* until David O. Selznick decided that he would rather see Shirley Temple play the role.[18]

Kiss Me Kate (1953)

Howard Keel as Fred Graham "Petruchio" (Laurence Olivier)

When MGM was planning to make *Kiss Me Kate* their first choice for the male lead was Laurence Olivier. His singing voice was going to be dubbed. Director George Sidney instead wanted Howard Keel.[19] Keel was cast and did his own singing.

Kiss Me Stupid (1964)

Ray Walston as Orville J. Spooner (Peter Sellers)

Peter Sellers was all set to star as Orville J. Spooner in *Kiss Me Stupid*. Sellers suffered a heart attack, and a replacement was needed.[20] The part was won by *My Favorite Martian's* Ray Walston.

Kiss of the Spider Woman (1985)

William Hurt as Luis Molina (Raul Julia, Burt Lancaster)
Raul Julia as Valentin Arregui (William Hurt)

Burt Lancaster was cast as Luis Molina. After he had a heart attack it became difficult to insure him.[21] Director Hector Babenco gave the role to William Hurt. Raul Julia was cast opposite Hurt. During rehearsals, Hurt thought that it might be a good idea if he and Julia switched roles. He asked Babenco, who decided it would not be a good idea.[22] Hurt won an Academy Award for his performance.

Kiss the Girls (1997)

Morgan Freeman as Alex Cross (Samuel L. Jackson)

Producer David Brown wanted Samuel L. Jackson to star as Alex Cross. Jackson thought the script was misogynistic and turned Brown down.[23] Morgan Freeman was cast in his place. Freeman reprised the role in the 2001 film *Along Came a Spider*.

Klute (1971)

Jane Fonda as Bree Daniels (Barbra Streisand)

Barbra Streisand rejected the role of call girl Bree Daniels.[24]

Knife in the Water (1962)

Zygmunt Malanowicz as Young Boy (Roman Polanski)

If director Roman Polanksi had had his way, he would have starred in *Knife in the Water*. Polanski had been an actor prior to becoming a director. The producers did not want Polanski in the film and Zygmunt Malanowicz was cast.[25]

Knight Without Armour (1937)

Robert Donat as A.J. Fothergill (Laurence Olivier)

Producer Alexander Korda wanted Laurence Olivier for the part of A.J. Fothergill. The part went not to Olivier, but to Robert Donat instead.[26]

Knute Rockne, All American (1940)

Pat O'Brien as Knute Rockne (James Cagney)

Warner Bros. initially wanted to cast James Cagney as Knute Rockne, feeling he would attract a bigger audience than Pat O'Brien.[27] They eventually reconsidered and the part went to O'Brien.

Kotch (1971)

Walter Matthau as Joseph P. Kotcher (Fredric March)

Jack Lemmon decided to make his directing debut with the film *Kotch*. Lemmon cast Fredric March as Joseph P. Kotcher. However March was sick, and Lemmon had trouble insuring him. Lemmon discussed the situation with his wife Felicia Farr and friend Carol Matthau. Matthau went home and told her husband Walter about Lemmon's problem. Matthau called Lemmon and offered to play the part himself. Matthau was nominated for an Oscar for his performance in the film.[28]

Kramer vs. Kramer (1979)

Dustin Hoffman as Ted Kramer (James Caan, Al Pacino)
Meryl Streep as Joanna Kramer (Kate Jackson, Susan Sarandon)
Jane Alexander as Margaret Phelps (Gail Strickland)
JoBeth Williams as Phyllis Bernard (Meryl Streep)

Al Pacino[29] and James Caan[30] turned down the starring role in *Kramer vs. Kramer*.

Kate Jackson was the first choice for the part of Joanna. At the time Jackson was starring on the hit television show, *Charlie's Angels*. Her schedule with the series did not allow her the time necessary to make the film.[31] Jackson left the series not long after. Susan Sarandon auditioned but was passed over.[32] Meryl Streep initially came in to read for the small role of Phyllis.[33] This character's most memorable scene is one in which, after sleeping with Dustin Hoffman's character, a naked Phyllis encounters his young son in the hallway. The producers realized that Streep would be perfect as Joanna Kramer, and gave the Phyllis part to JoBeth Williams.

Gail Strickland had been set for the part of Margaret Phelps. Strickland was unnerved by Dustin Hoffman. Her performance suffered as a result. She was eventually replaced by Jane Alexander.[34]

Kuffs (1992)

Milla Jovovich as Maya Carlton (Ashley Judd)

Ashley Judd won the part of Maya Carlton. The part required nudity, which Judd did not want to do. Milla Jovovich got the part. Judd briefly appears in the film as Wife of Paint Store Owner.[35]

The Lady Eve (1941)

Barbara Stanwyck as Jean Harrington/Lady Eve Sidwich (Madeleine Carroll, Claudette Colbert, Paulette Goddard)
Henry Fonda as Charles Pike [aka "Hopsie"] (Brian Aherne)

Writer/director Preston Sturges wrote *The Lady Eve* with Claudette Colbert in mind. The project was shelved for about two years. At that point Madeleine Carroll was suggested to him to star. Sturges didn't want to cast any contract players. He preferred Barbara Stanwyck and gave her the role.

Henry Fonda was pursued for the male lead. Sturges was told that Fonda might be unavailable. Brian Aherne was brought up as a replacement. Sturges insisted on Fonda. Darryl F. Zanuck finally agreed to loan out Fonda to Sturges.[1]

Lady for a Day (1933)

Warren William as Dave the Dude (James Cagney)
May Robson as Apple Annie (Marie Dressler)

James Cagney was a possibility to play Dave the Dude but was unavailable.[2] Marie Dressler's name came up when the part of Apple Annie was discussed. Louis B. Mayer was very opposed to the idea of using Dressler. Nevertheless, director Frank Capra mentioned her to Harry Cohn. Cohn told Capra to forget her; that there were plenty of "old dames," and to find one. Capra gave the part to May Robson.[3]

The Lady from Shanghai (1948)

Rita Hayworth as Elsa "Rosalie" Bannister (Barbara Laage, Ida Lupino)

When Orson Welles set out to make *The Lady from Shanghai*, he wanted the French actress Barbara Laage for the part of Elsa "Rosalie" Bannister.[4] Ida Lupino was also interested in this role, but she was not the only one.[5] Welles' estranged wife, Rita Hayworth, also wanted the part. Besides thinking the part was a good one, she saw this as a chance for her and Welles to reunite.[6] Hayworth's plan worked. The two got back together, but ultimately divorced in December of 1948.

Lady Godiva Rides Again (1951)

Pauline Stroud as Marjorie Clark (Joan Collins, Hazel Court, Jean Marsh, Joan Rice)

Joan Collins was asked to make a screen test for the part of Marjorie Clark. Collins arrived at the studio and reported to the makeup department. Collins hated the job they did on her. She felt the makeup was extremely unflattering.[7] Jean Marsh also tested,[8] as did Hazel Court and Joan Rice.[9] The part went to Pauline Stroud, making her film debut. Collins and Marsh were cast in the film as beauty pageant contestants.

Lady L (1965)

Sophia Loren as Lady L (Gina Lollobrigida)
Paul Newman as Armand (Tony Curtis)

In the early 1960s George Cukor was assigned to direct the film *Lady L*. He cast the lead roles with Tony Curtis and Gina Lollobrigida. Production began, and Cukor shot several scenes with the actors until suddenly, it was canceled. A few years later a studio executive decided that he wanted to have Paul Newman and Sophia Loren work together in a film version of Arthur Miller's play, *After the Fall*. The play dealt with the breakup of Miller's marriage to Marilyn Monroe. It didn't take long for the studio to realize that the Italian-born Loren was all wrong for this part. But the idea of Loren and Newman together was still something they wanted to make happen. At that point the script for Lady L came off the shelf. Peter Ustinov was chosen as the director and he was given the script to rewrite.[10] The leads vacated by Curtis and Lollobrigida were taken by Newman and Loren. Perhaps the script was better off on the shelf. *Lady L* turned out to be a flop at the box office.

The Lady Vanishes (1938)

Angela Lansbury as Miss Froy (Bette Davis)

Bette Davis turned down an offer to play the role of Miss Froy in *The Lady Vanishes*.[11]

Ladyhawke (1985)

Matthew Broderick as Phillipe Gaston (Dustin Hoffman)
Rutger Hauer as Etienne Navarre (Sean Connery)

A pairing of Dustin Hoffman and Sean Connery as the leads in *Ladyhawke* was considered. Connery chose another film instead, and director Richard Donner decided to go with Matthew Broderick and Rutger Hauer instead.[12]

Land of the Pharaohs (1955)

Jack Hawkins as Pharaoh Cheops (Sydney Chaplin)
Joan Collins as Princess Nellifer (Dee Hartford, Gina Lollobrigida, Ivy Nicholson)

Director Howard Hawks considered Sydney Chaplin for the part of Pharaoh Cheops. He eventually gave the part to Jack Hawkins instead. For the part of Princess Nellifer, Hawks' first choice was his wife, Dee Hartford. But she was pregnant and unable to play the part. He considered model Ivy Nicholson. Nicholson made a test with the star of the film, Jack Hawkins. During a seduction scene Nicholson bit Hawkins' hand extremely hard. The actor was incensed, and Nicholson lost the part. Gina Lollobrigida's name was mentioned, but the part went to Joan Collins instead.[13]

Lara Croft: Tomb Raider (2001)

Angelina Jolie as Lara Croft (Sandra Bullock, Jennifer Love Hewitt, Elizabeth Hurley, Ashley Judd, Denise Richards, Catherine Zeta-Jones)

Early on in development a list of possible Lara Crofts included Catherine Zeta-Jones, Sandra Bullock, Elizabeth Hurley, Ashley Judd, Denise Richards, and Jennifer Love Hewitt. Hewitt wanted very much to play the live action version of the video game adventurer. She lost the role, however, to Angelina Jolie, who everyone involved thought was the perfect choice.[14]

The Last Detail (1973)

Otis Young as Mule Mulhall (Rupert Crosse)
Randy Quaid as Seaman Meadows (John Travolta)
Carol Kane as Prostitute (Nancy Allen)

Rupert Crosse was originally cast as Mulhall in *The Last Detail*. Sadly, he was diagnosed with cancer and had to be replaced.[15] Director Hal Ashby gave the now-vacant role to Otis Young. An unknown John Travolta made it to the final round of auditions for Seaman Meadows, but lost the part to Randy Quaid. According to casting director Lynn Stalmaster, Ashby liked the offbeat quality Quaid was able to bring to the role.[16]

Nancy Allen was signed for the role of a prostitute, but didn't want to appear nude. Her part was given to Carol Kane and Allen ended up with another (smaller) role in the film.[17]

The Last of Mrs. Cheyney (1937)

Joan Crawford as Fay Cheyney (Myrna Loy)

Joan Crawford inherited the role of Mrs. Cheyney from Myrna Loy. The two actresses switched parts (in different films). Crawford traded Loy the role of Mrs. Cheyney for the role of Katie O'Shea in *Parnell*.[18]

The Last of the Dogmen (1995)

Barbara Hershey as Professor Lillian Stone (Mary McDonnell)

Mary McDonnell dropped out of *The Last of the Dogmen* because she was pregnant.[19]

The Last Picture Show (1971)

Cybill Shepherd as Jacy Farrow (Morgan Fairchild, Sissy Spacek)
Timothy Bottoms as Sonny Crawford (Jeff Bridges)
Ben Johnson as Sam the Lion (Tex Ritter)
Cloris Leachman as Ruth Popper (Ellen Burstyn)
Eileen Brennan as Genevieve (Ellen Burstyn)

When Jeff Bridges met with director Peter Bogdanovich for *The Last Picture Show*, he was interested in the part of Sonny. The director felt this part was wrong for him and cast him as Duane instead. Bogdanovich gave the part of Sonny to Timothy Bottoms.

A baby kept Mary McDonnell out of *Last of the Dogmen*.

Bogdanovich considered Tex Ritter for the role that went to Ben Johnson.

Ellen Burstyn read for the roles of Ruth Popper, Genevieve, and Lois Farrow. Burstyn was given her choice of the three roles and she picked Lois.[20]

Peter Bogdanovich originally considered Sissy Spacek and Morgan Fairchild for the pivotal role of Jacy Farrow. One day the director was on line in a Food Giant in the San Fernando Valley. He saw the cover of a *Glamour* magazine and was mesmerized by the model. He knew that she was perfect for the part. Her name was Cybill Shepherd. He contacted Shepherd and asked her to audition. Shepherd read with Jeff Bridges. She got the role as well as the director. She and Bogdanovich started an affair which lasted for about seven years.[21]

Last Summer (1969)

Barbara Hershey as Sandy (Sondra Locke)

Director Frank Perry wanted Sondra Locke to star as Sandy in the film *Last Summer*. Locke was shattered when she learned that her agent had turned it down without even consulting her. At the time Locke was awaiting the release of her first film, *The Heart Is a Lonely Hunter*, and her agent wanted to wait to see the reaction from it.[22] Turns out the agent was on to something. The film was a big hit, and Locke was nominated for an Oscar for her performance. As for *Last Summer*, the part of Sandy went to Barbara Hershey.

Last Tango in Paris (1973)

Marlon Brando as Paul (Warren Beatty, Jean-Louis Trintignant)
Maria Schneider as Jeanne (Catherine Deneuve, Dominique Sanda)

Warren Beatty and Jean-Louis Trintignant were approached for the role of Paul. Beatty turned it down.[23] Trintignant was paired with Dominique Sanda. Sanda was pregnant, and was unable to appear in the film. Trintignant was embarrassed by the steamy script, and turned the part down.[24] Catherine Deneuve was also considered, but the part of Jeanne went to Maria Schneider.[25] Paul was played by Marlon Brando.

The Last Temptation of Christ (1988)

Willem Dafoe as Jesus Christ (David Carradine, Robert De Niro, Aidan Quinn, Christopher Walken)
Barbara Hershey as Mary Magdalene (Cher)
David Bowie as Pontius Pilate (Sting)

According to David Carradine, he brought *The Last Temptation of Christ* to director Martin Scorsese's attention. Scorsese told the actor that he could play Jesus. However, Scorsese wasn't ready to make the film for another 15 years. By that time Carradine was too old for the part.[26] It almost went to Aidan Quinn. Quinn would have done the film, but production was postponed. When filming was finally ready to start, Quinn was working on another film and was unable to play the part.[27] Christopher Walken was mentioned as a possibility. The studio didn't want Walken in the role and he was passed over.[28] Martin Scorsese approached his good friend and frequent leading man, Robert De Niro. De Niro had no interest in playing the part. Besides that, De Niro had just finished shooting *Once Upon a Time in America*, for which he shaved his hair off. He did tell Scors-

Aidan Quinn almost played Jesus Christ (*The Last Temptation of Christ*).

ese that if he needed him, he would do it as a favor to him.[29] Scorsese didn't need to take him up on his offer. He cast Willem Dafoe in the role.

Cher turned down the part of Mary Magdalene.[30]

Rocker Sting was originally cast as Pontius Pilate opposite Aidan Quinn as Jesus. When production finally began Sting was replaced with another rock star — David Bowie.[31]

The Last Tycoon (1976)

Robert De Niro as Monroe Stahr (Dustin Hoffman, Jack Nicholson, Al Pacino)
Ingrid Boulting as Kathleen Moore (Cybill Shepherd)

Al Pacino and Dustin Hoffman were considered for the starring role of mogul Monroe Stahr in *The Last Tycoon*.[32] Producer Sam Spiegel thought the best choice was Jack Nicholson. At the time Mike Nichols was going to direct the film. When he dropped out, Elia Kazan took over. He took Nicholson out of the running, and gave the part to Robert De Niro instead. Nicholson was cast in the small role of communist union organizer Brimmer.[33]

Cybill Shepherd let it be known that she was very interested in the Norma Shearer–like role of Kathleen Moore. She met with director Elia Kazan and producer Sam Spiegel. Shepherd failed to impress them. She lost the role to Ingrid Boulting.[34]

Latin Lovers (1953)

Ricardo Montalban as Roberto Santos (Fernando Lamas)

Lana Turner and Fernando Lamas became romantically involved during the filming of the 1952 film, *The Merry Widow*. Both actors were signed to MGM, which got a great deal of publicity out of their affair. The studio decided to put them in a film together called *Latin Lovers*. Shooting began and everything was fine. One night Turner and Lamas attended a party given by Marion Davies and her husband Horace Brown. At the party Turner and Lamas were seated at a table with Ava Gardner, Arlene Dahl and husband Lex Barker, Esther Williams, and studio executive Benny Thau. Barker asked Turner to dance, and Lamas exploded. He told Barker that he knew that he really wanted to sleep with Turner. Turner was angry with Lamas, and refused to speak to him. At the end of the night the still feuding Turner and Lamas were walking to their car, when Broadway star Joan Diener advanced on Lamas. She told how great he looked. Lamas responded by throwing Diener into the pool. The couple drove off together. When they arrived home Turner turned on the television set. Lamas was so angry at being ignored that he kicked the screen. His foot was cut from the glass. Lamas left the house, but not before spraining his ankle on the stairs.

The next day Lamas arrived at the set limping. Turner showed up with a black eye and many bruises all over her body. In her autobiography, *The Million Dollar Mermaid*, Esther Williams said that Lana Turner had a history of hitting herself with a rope to inflict bruises. Although Lamas admitted that he had hit Turner, he also said that he wasn't responsible for most of her bruises. Turner went to Benny Thau and told him how Lamas had beaten her up. Thau fired Lamas and replaced him with Ricardo Montalban.[35]

Interestingly, Lex Barker and Arlene Dahl were divorced not long after the fateful party, at which point Barker and Lana Turner became involved. The two were married within a year. About 15 years later Esther Williams and Fernando Lamas were married.

Laughing Sinners (1931)

Clark Gable as Carl Loomis (Johnny Mack Brown)

Johnny Mack Brown landed the costarring role opposite Joan Crawford in *Complete Surrender*. The film was shot and screened for a preview audience. The audience found Brown inappropriately comical during the love scenes. Producer Irving Thalberg decided that Brown's scenes would be reshot, but with Clark Gable in the part. The film was retitled *Laughing Sinners*.[36]

Johnny Mack Brown's *Complete Surrender* became Clark Gable's *Laughing Sinners*.

Laughter in the Dark (1969)

Nicol Williamson as Sir Edward More (Richard Burton)

Director Tony Richardson cast Richard Burton as Sir Edward More. Very early into the filming Burton arrived to the set late. Burton was fired and replaced with Nicol Williamson.[37]

Laura (1944)

Gene Tierney as Laura Hunt (Jennifer Jones, Hedy Lamarr)
Dana Andrews as Mark McPherson (John Hodiak)
Clifton Webb as Waldo Lydecker (Laird Cregar, Monty Woolley)

Jennifer Jones and Hedy Lamarr turned down the title role in *Laura*.[38] Dana Andrews won the role of Mark McPherson over John Hodiak. Monty Woolley and Laird Cregar were considered for Waldo Lydecker, but Otto Preminger chose Clifton Webb instead.[39]

Lawrence of Arabia (1962)

Peter O'Toole as T.E. Lawrence (Marlon Brando, Richard Burton, Montgomery Clift, Albert Finney, Alec Guinness, Laurence Harvey, Anthony Perkins)
Omar Sharif as Sheik Ali (Alain Delon, Robert Evans, Maurice Ronet)
Arthur Kennedy as Jackson Bentley (Edmond O'Brien)

Marlon Brando turned down *Lawrence of Arabia* in order to star in *Mutiny on the Bounty*. Montgomery Clift wanted the part, but director David Lean didn't cast him. Richard Burton, Anthony Perkins and Laurence Harvey were all considered.[40] Alec Guinness was another possible choice.[41] Albert Finney actually had the role, but one of the conditions was that he had to sign a seven year contract. Finney changed his mind and quit in less than a week.[42] The role was finally filled by Peter O'Toole.

First choice Edmond O'Brien was unable to take the role of Jackson Bentley, so Lean cast Arthur Kennedy instead.[43]

Future producer Robert Evans auditioned to play Sheik Ali, as did Alain Delon.[44] Maurice Ronet was also up for the part. All of these men lost the role to Omar Sharif.[45]

A League of Their Own (1992)

Tom Hanks as Jimmy Duggan (James Belushi)
Geena Davis as Dottie Hinson (Demi Moore, Debra Winger)
Lori Petty as Kit Keller (Daryl Hannah)
Rosie O'Donnell as Doris Murphy (Camryn Manheim)

Before director Penny Marshall was involved, *A League of Their Own* was planned as a project for James Belushi and Demi Moore.⁴⁶ Plans fell through, and Marshall came on board. She cast Tom Hanks and Debra Winger in the leads. Madonna won a supporting role in the film, which reportedly upset Winger. She left the production and was replaced by Geena Davis.⁴⁷

Daryl Hannah was considered for the part of Kit Keller, but Penny Marshall hired Lori Petty.⁴⁸

Camryn Manheim auditioned to play Doris Murphy, but lost out to Rosie O'Donnell.

Legends of the Fall (1994)

Julia Ormond as Susannah Fincannon Ludlow (Gwyneth Paltrow)
Henry Thomas as Samuel Ludlow (Noah Wyle)

Gwyneth Paltrow tried for the part of Susannah. She lost out to Julia Ormond. Brad Pitt, the star of *Legends of the Fall*, was impressed with the actress. So much so that he suggested her for the part of his wife in his next film, *Seven*.⁴⁹ She was cast opposite Pitt and the two soon became a couple off screen as well. They were engaged, but eventually broke it off.

Noah Wyle auditioned for the part of Samuel Ludlow. He lost out to Henry Thomas.⁵⁰

Lenny (1974)

Dustin Hoffman as Lenny Bruce (Al Pacino)

Al Pacino was mentioned as a possibility for the starring role of comedian Lenny Bruce.⁵¹

The Leopard (1963)

Burt Lancaster as Prince Don Fabrizio Salina (Marlon Brando, Nicolai Cherkassov, Laurence Olivier, Gregory Peck, Anthony Quinn, Spencer Tracy)
Alain Delon as Tancredi Falconeri (Warren Beatty)

Director Luchino Visconti was interested in three actors for the starring role of Prince Don Fabrizio Salina: Nicolai Cherkassov, Marlon Brando and Laurence Olivier. Visconti was unable to sign any of these actors for the part. Twentieth Century–Fox wanted Spencer Tracy, Gregory Peck, Burt Lancaster or Anthony Quinn. The part was offered to Burt Lancaster, who accepted.⁵²

Warren Beatty was offered the supporting role of Tancredi. He wasn't interested and turned it down.⁵³

Let's Make Love (1960)

Yves Montand as Jean-Mark Clement (Yul Brynner, Cary Grant, Charlton Heston, Rock Hudson, Gregory Peck)

Gregory Peck was originally cast as Jean-Mark Clement in *Let's Make Love*. Peck later reconsidered his decision to do the film and dropped out.⁵⁴ Charlton Heston was offered the part. At the same time Heston had the opportunity to work with Laurence Olivier in the play *The Tumbler*. Heston chose the play, which meant he had to turn down the film.⁵⁵ Cary Grant and Yul Brynner were unsuccessfully courted for the role.⁵⁶ Rock Hudson was also sought, but the part finally ended up going to Yves Montand.⁵⁷

Letty Lynton (1932)

Robert Montgomery as Hale Darrow (Clark Gable)

Joan Crawford was signed for the lead in *Letty Lynton*. She went to Louis B. Mayer to request that her boyfriend, Clark Gable, be cast opposite her.⁵⁸ Mayer told her to forget it and put Gable in *Red Dust* instead.

The Liberation of L.B. Jones (1970)

Lee J. Cobb as Oman Hedgepath (Henry Fonda)

Director William Wyler's first choice for the part of Oman Hedgepath was Henry Fonda. Fonda was interested, but was unable to make the start date. Fonda's participation would have meant starting the filming a year later than the original date planned. Lee J. Cobb was cast instead.⁵⁹

The Lieutenant Wore Skirts (1956)

Sheree North as Katy Whitcomb (Betty Grable)

At one point it was announced that Betty Grable would star in *Mother Was a Marine*. The title was later changed to *The Lieutenant Wore Skirts* with Sheree North in the lead role.⁶⁰

The Life and Death of Colonel Blimp (1943)

Roger Livesey as General Clive Wynne-Candy (Laurence Olivier)

Deborah Kerr as Edith Hunter/Barbara Wynne/Angela Cannon (Wendy Hiller)

Laurence Olivier was considered for Roger Livesey's role of General Clive Wynne-Candy. Olivier was a member of the military, and required the permission from Britain's Ministry of War. The War Office was sent an outline of the script, which they disliked. The Ministry of War thought that the German characters were too soft. Olivier was not allowed to participate in the film.[61]

Wendy Hiller was unable to play the part that went to Deborah Kerr because she was pregnant.[62]

A Life Less Ordinary (1997)

Ewan McGregor as Robert Lewis (Brad Pitt)

Cameron Diaz as Celine Naville (Julia Roberts, Renee Zellweger)

Brad Pitt met with director Danny Boyle and producer Andrew Macdonald to discuss the starring role of Robert Lewis. Although Pitt was a superstar, the actor they really wanted was Ewan McGregor. In fact writer John Hodge wrote the part with McGregor in mind.[63]

Early on in the casting process Danny Boyle favored Cameron Diaz for the leading role of Celine. However, he also considered Julia Roberts and Renee Zellweger. Zellweger was very hot at the moment, having scored a major success with her breakthrough role opposite Tom Cruise in *Jerry Maguire*. The budget was a consideration, though. Boyle knew that either of these actresses would have been more than he could afford. He went back to his original choice, and gave Cameron Diaz the part.[64]

The Life of David Gale (2003)

Kevin Spacey as David Gale (George Clooney)

At one point George Clooney was attached to star in *The Life of David Gale*. Clooney fell through. Kevin Spacey was eventually cast instead.[65]

A Life of Her Own (1950)

Ray Milland as Steve Harleigh (Wendell Corey)

Lana Turner was cast in the starring role of Lily Brannel James. Part of her deal was that she had the right to participate in the casting. MGM

Wendell Corey was fired after insulting Lana Turner on the set of *A Life of Her Own*.

executive Dore Schary suggested Wendell Corey for the part of Steve Harleigh. Turner thought Corey was the wrong type. She refused to test with him. Schary hired him anyway. One day on the set there was a problem with one of Turner's costumes. The seams were pinned, but not sewn together. They were running late, so Turner wore the dress in the state it was in. She heard Corey remark, "It's interesting, you know. The wonderful Barbara Stanwyck never keeps us waiting. Not even for one minute." Turner was furious and refused to shoot the scene. She told director George Cukor that Corey had to be replaced. Dore Schary came to the set to speak with Turner. He told her that Corey was gone from the set. He went on to say that Turner was putting the studio in a bad situation since they didn't have a replacement for Corey. Turner told Schary that it was his own fault (she didn't want him cast in the first place). Production was stopped until a solution was found. Two days later Ray Milland was suggested. Turner thought he was a great choice. He charged the studio the large sum of $175,000 for his services. Corey was also paid for the part (even though he didn't play it). He was paid much less than the expensive Milland. Corey received $75,000.[66]

Life with Father (1947)
Irene Dunne as Vinnie Day (Bette Davis, Mary Pickford, Rosalind Russell)
William Powell as Clarence Day (Ronald Colman, Fredric March)
Elizabeth Taylor as Mary Skinner (Shirley Temple)

Life with Father was a hit Broadway play. It was written by Russell Crouse and Howard Lindsay, based on sketches by Clarence Day, Jr. Studio head Jack Warner bought the film rights, but Crouse, Lindsay and Day's widow had some creative control. Warner suggested either Fredric March or William Powell for the part of Clarence Day, with either Bette Davis, Rosalind Russell or Irene Dunne as his wife Vinnie. Day, Crouse and Lindsay brought up Ronald Colman as a possibility for Clarence Day and Mary Pickford for Vinnie. They also wanted Bette Davis to make a screen test. Davis, Colman and Pickford all tested, but lost out to William Powell and Irene Dunne.[67]

Shirley Temple was offered the role of Mary Skinner. She was unable to appear in the film, and Elizabeth Taylor was cast in her place.[68]

Lili (1953)
Leslie Caron as Lili Daurier (Pier Angeli)

Pier Angeli was originally announced as the lead in *Lili*. However, Angeli did not end up in the film. The part was played by Leslie Caron instead.[69]

Liliom (1930)
Rose Hobart as Julie (Janet Gaynor)

Janet Gaynor was originally scheduled to play Julie in *Liliom*. She was unhappy with the parts 20th Century–Fox was assigning her, and she left the studio. Fox recast the part with Rose Hobart.[70]

Lilith (1964)
Warren Beatty as Vincent Bruce (Peter Fonda)

In 1962 Peter Fonda read the book *Lilith*. He liked it so much that he wanted to buy the rights for the film version. His agents informed him that this was not possible; Robert Rossen had already done the same thing. His agents got a copy of the script and decided to submit Fonda for the male lead, Vincent Bruce. Fonda thought this was a bad choice. He told them he wanted to be considered for the part of Stephen Evshevsky. They only wanted Fonda to play leading men and refused. The resourceful actor went to New York and surprised Robert Rossen in his office. Rossen gave him an impromptu interview. Soon after Fonda learned he had won the part. The role of Vincent Bruce went to Warren Beatty.[71]

Little Big Man (1970)
Chief Dan George as Old Lodge Skins (Richard Boone, Laurence Olivier, Paul Scofield)

The role that went to Chief Dan George was turned down by Paul Scofield, Laurence Olivier, and Richard Boone.[72]

Little Caesar (1930)
Douglas Fairbanks, Jr., as Joe Massara (Clark Gable)
George E. Stone as Otero (Edward G. Robinson)

Clark Gable tested for the part of Joe Massara, but was turned down. Edward G. Robinson was offered the supporting role of Otero, but insisted on playing the title role instead.[73]

Little Egypt (1951)
Rhonda Fleming as Izora (Shelley Winters)

Shelley Winters was assigned the role of Izora in *Little Egypt*. Winters disliked the part so much that she purposely put on so much weight that she was replaced by Rhonda Fleming.[74]

The Little Foxes (1941)
Bette Davis as Regina Giddens (Tallulah Bankhead, Miriam Hopkins)
Teresa Wright as Alexandra Giddens (Bette Davis)

When *The Little Foxes* premiered on Broadway in 1939, the star was Tallulah Bankhead. Bankhead received wonderful notices for the play, and was considered for the part when the film version was planned. Miriam Hopkins was also a possibility, but director William Wyler only wanted to work with Bette Davis.[75]

An early suggestion was that Davis should not only play the role of Regina, but the part of Alexandra, her daughter, as well. Samuel Goldwyn rejected this idea and cast Teresa Wright as Alexandra.[76]

The Little Prince (1974)

Richard Kiley as The Pilot (Richard Burton, Jim Dale, Robert Goulet, Gene Hackman, Richard Harris, Frank Sinatra, Nicol Williamson)

The role of the Pilot proved difficult for director Stanley Donen to cast. Gene Hackman, Richard Harris, Robert Goulet, Nicol Williamson, and Jim Dale were all considered. Richard Burton made it known that he wanted the part. Instead Donen decided to go with the Broadway star, Richard Kiley. Everything was fine for a short time until Donen was informed by the studio that Frank Sinatra wanted to play the part. Donen was against the idea of hiring Sinatra. He felt that the superstar would soon change his mind, and he would be left without an actor in the part. Eventually Donen was able to convince the studio, although he had to put up quite a battle, and Richard Kiley was allowed to keep his job.[77]

The Little Shop of Horrors (1960)

Jonathan Haze as Seymour Krelboined (Jack Nicholson)

Jack Nicholson read the script to *The Little Shop of Horrors*, and decided that he wanted to play the starring role of Seymour Krelboined. He asked director Roger Corman for the chance to audition. Corman let him read for the role, but instead gave the part to Jonathan Haze.[78] At that time Corman and Haze had already made 13 films together, which probably went against Nicholson. Corman did think he had talent, however. As a consolation prize he offered Nicholson the featured role of Wilbur Force, a dental patient who turns out to be a masochist.

Little Women (1933)

Katharine Hepburn as Jo March (Constance Bennett)

Constance Bennett wanted to play the lead role of Jo in *Little Women*. RKO turned Bennett down in favor of their new star—Katharine Hepburn.[79]

The Living Daylights (1987)

Timothy Dalton as James Bond (Pierce Brosnan)

Pierce Brosnan was the first choice to play James Bond in *The Living Daylights*. At the time he was starring in the television series *Remington Steele*. His contract with the show was what prevented him from taking the role. Brosnan was very upset to have to lose out on the part.[80] He was later cast as Bond in the 1995 film *GoldenEye*. The role was eventually played by Timothy Dalton.

Living in Oblivion (1995)

Steve Buscemi as Nick Reve (Dermot Mulroney)

Dermot Mulroney told director Tom DiCillo that he was very interested in playing the part of director Nick Reve in *Living in Oblivion*. DiCillo thought Mulroney was too young, and cast him as Wolf instead. Mulroney recommended another actor to DiCillo for Nick Reve—Steve Buscemi. DiCillo liked the suggestion and gave Buscemi the part.[81]

Dermot Mulroney (pictured) helped get Steve Buscemi cast in *Living in Oblivion*.

Lloyd's of London (1936)

Madeleine Carroll as Lady Elizabeth Stacy (Loretta Young)

Tyrone Power as Jonathan Blake (Don Ameche)

Twentieth Century–Fox assigned Loretta Young the role of Lady Elizabeth Stacy in *Lloyd's of London*. Young didn't want to make the film. First of all, she was very angry that her friend Don Ameche was fired and replaced with Tyrone Power. Young also didn't think much of the script.[82] She wrote a letter to Darryl F. Zanuck informing him that she would not be appearing in the film. Furthermore, two times Young was scheduled for wardrobe fittings, and never showed up. Zanuck contacted her agent and told him that he still expected Young to play the part. Young did not budge, and was eventually suspended. Zanuck replaced her with Madeleine Carroll.[83]

Lolita (1962)

James Mason as Humbert Humbert (Noel Coward, Cary Grant, David Niven, Laurence Olivier)
Sue Lyon as Dolores "Lolita" Haze (Hayley Mills, Tuesday Weld)

Noel Coward was the first choice for the part of Humbert Humbert, but he turned it down.[84] Cary Grant disliked the script[85] and he, David Niven,[86] and Laurence Olivier[87] rejected the role, leaving it free for James Mason.

Tuesday Weld was considered for the title role of Lolita.[88] Squeaky clean child star Hayley Mills was another possibility. Mills' parents objected, and the part went to Sue Lyon.[89]

The Long Goodbye (1973)

Elliott Gould as Philip Marlowe (Lee Marvin, Steve McQueen, Robert Mitchum)

Robert Mitchum and Lee Marvin were considered for the starring role of Philip Marlowe.[90] Steve McQueen was offered the role. He was interested, but his asking price was too high, and director Robert Altman cast Elliott Gould instead.[91]

The Longest Day (1962)

John Wayne as Lieutenant Colonel Benjamin Vandervoort (Charlton Heston, William Holden)

William Holden[92] was considered for the role of Benjamin Vandervoort in *The Longest Day*, as was Charlton Heston. Superstar John Wayne also expressed interest, and producer Darryl F. Zanuck gave him the part.[93]

Look for the Silver Lining (1949)

June Haver as Marilyn Miller (Betty Grable)

Warner Bros. originally wanted Betty Grable to play Marilyn Miller. Darryl Zanuck, her boss at 20th Century–Fox, refused to loan her out.[94]

Looking for Mr. Goodbar (1977)

Tuesday Weld as Katherine Dunn (Cybill Shepherd)

Cybill Shepherd auditioned for the part of Katherine in *Looking for Mr. Goodbar*.[95]

Lord of the Rings: The Fellowship of the Ring (2001)

Elijah Wood as Frodo Baggins (Stuart Townsend)
Viggo Mortensen as Aragon (Stuart Townsend)
Hugo Weaving as Elrond (David Bowie)

Stuart Townsend was considered for Aragorn as well as Frodo. Director Peter Jackson liked Townsend very much and asked him to play Aragorn. A few days before filming was to begin, Townsend quit. According to New Line Cinema's Mark Ordesky, Townsend and Jackson had different ideas about who the character was. Unable to reach an agreement, Townsend left and was replaced by Viggo Mortensen.

David Bowie was interested in playing Elrond. He didn't secure the part; it went to Hugo Weaving instead.[96]

Lorenzo's Oil (1992)

Susan Sarandon as Michaela Odone (Michelle Pfeiffer)

Michelle Pfeiffer was signed to play Michaela Odone. However, Pfeiffer dropped out at the last minute. She was replaced by Susan Sarandon.[97]

Loser (2000)

Mena Suvari as Dora Diamond (Christina Ricci)

Christina Ricci was offered the part of Dora Diamond. Ricci read the script and turned the part down. According to her replacement, Mena Suvari, Ricci had a problem with the script, especially a line about oral sex.[98]

Lost Horizon (1937)
Sam Jaffe as High Lama (A.E. Anson, Walter Connolly, Henry B. Walthall)

Screenwriter Robert Riskin was interested in Walter Connolly for the part of High Lama. Director Frank Capra thought Connolly was the wrong type. He imagined either Henry B. Walthall or A.E. Anson. Unfortunately both actors died. Capra eventually cast Sam Jaffe.[99]

Lost in Space (1998)
Matt LeBlanc as Don West (Sean Patrick Flanery, Matthew Perry)

Matthew Perry's name was mentioned as a possible choice for the part of Don West.[100] Sean Patrick Flanery was eventually cast in the role. He started work on the film and was soon fired. The producers claimed Flanery did not have the right look for the part, and gave the role to the very popular Matt LeBlanc.[101]

Sean Patrick Flanery beat out one *Friends* cast member for *Lost in Space*, only to be replaced by another *Friends* cast member.

Lost Souls (2000)
Winona Ryder as Maya Larkin (Meg Ryan)

Meg Ryan was the original choice to play Maya Larkin. Ryan chose to make *City of Angels* instead. The part of Maya went to Winona Ryder.[102]

The Lost Weekend (1945)
Ray Milland as Don Birnam (Jose Ferrer)
Jane Wyman as Helen St. James (Jean Arthur, Barbara Stanwyck)

Director Billy Wilder considered Jose Ferrer and Barbara Stanwyck[103] for the leads in *The Lost Weekend*. Studio head Buddy DeSylva didn't think that Ferrer was good looking enough, and cast Ray Milland in the role.[104] Myrna Loy was asked to play Helen, but she said no. Jane Wyman played the part instead.[105]

Love and Pain (And the Whole Damn Thing) (1972)
Maggie Smith as Lila Fisher (Angela Lansbury)

Angela Lansbury lost the role of Lila Fisher to Maggie Smith.[106]

Love Field (1992)
Dennis Haysbert as Paul Cater (Denzel Washington)

Denzel Washington quit the film, *Love Field*. Co-star Michelle Pfeiffer tried to persuade him to stay, to no avail. Washington had serious problems with the script and refused to do the film.[107] He was replaced by Dennis Haysbert.

Love in the Afternoon (1957)
Gary Cooper as Frank Flannagan (Cary Grant)

Gary Cooper was cast in *Love in the Afternoon* after Cary Grant turned the part down. Grant felt he was too old to play opposite Audrey Hepburn.[108]

Love Me or Leave Me (1955)
Doris Day as Ruth Etting (Ava Gardner, Jane Russell)

Both Ava Gardner and Jane Russell turned down the role of Ruth Etting in *Love Me or Leave Me*. Russell wanted to make the film *I'll Cry Tomorrow* instead.[109] Unfortunately for Russell, she was not chosen for that film. Gardner later said that she regretted her decision to turn down *Love Me or Leave Me*.¹¹⁰

Love on the Run (1936)
Joan Crawford as Sally Parker (Jean Harlow, Myrna Loy)
Clark Gable as Michael Anthony (Robert Montgomery, Robert Taylor)

Love on the Run was purchased for Myrna Loy and Robert Taylor. The deal fell through and it was then considered for Jean Harlow and Robert Montgomery. The picture was finally made with Joan Crawford and Clark Gable in the leads.¹¹¹

Love Story (1970)
Ryan O'Neal as Oliver Barrett, IV (David Birney, Beau Bridges, Jeff Bridges, Keith Carradine, Michael Douglas, Peter Fonda, Ken Howard, Robert Redford, Michael Sarrazin, Jon Voight, Christopher Walken, Michael York)

The part of Oliver was turned down by Robert Redford.¹¹² Other rejections came from Michael Douglas, Jeff Bridges, Beau Bridges, Jon Voight, Peter Fonda, Michael York, Keith Carradine and Michael Sarrazin. Christopher Walken, David Birney, and Ken Howard were tested, but lost out to Ryan O'Neal.¹¹³

Love! Valour! Compassion! (1997)
Jason Alexander as Buzz Hauser (Tom Arnold, Nathan Lane, Cheech Marin)

Nathan Lane turned down the role of Buzz Hauser, which he created on the stage. Jason Alexander was cast after Cheech Marin and Tom Arnold were considered.¹¹⁴

Love with the Proper Stranger (1965)
Steve McQueen as Rocky Pampasano (Paul Newman)

Paul Newman was the first choice for the role of Rocky Pampasano in *Love with the Proper Stranger*. After Newman turned it down director Robert Mulligan cast Steve McQueen.¹¹⁵

The L-Shaped Room (1962)
Leslie Caron as Jane Fosset (Audrey Hepburn, Jean Simmons, Elizabeth Taylor)

Leslie Caron was chosen to star in *The L-Shaped Room* over hopefuls such as Elizabeth Taylor, Audrey Hepburn and Jean Simmons.¹¹⁶

Lucky Lady (1975)
Gene Hackman as Kibby (George Segal)

George Segal was originally set to play Kibby in *Lucky Lady*. Segal was replaced by Gene Hackman.¹¹⁷

Ludwig (1972)
Trevor Howard as Richard Wagner (Alec Guinness)

Alec Guinness' name was brought up as a possibility for the part of Richard Wagner. Guinness didn't participate in the film; the part went to Trevor Howard instead.¹¹⁸

Lumiere (1976)
Jeanne Moreau as Sarah (Audrey Hepburn)

Jeanne Moreau wrote the part of Sarah for Audrey Hepburn. Hepburn decided she didn't want to do the part, and Moreau ended up playing it herself.¹¹⁹

M. Butterfly (1993)
John Lone as Song Liling (B.D. Wong)

B.D. Wong originated the role of Song Liling in *M. Butterfly* on Broadway. He tried for the role in the film version, but felt the producers didn't really want him in the role. John Lone was eventually cast.

Mash (1970)
Sally Kellerman as Hot Lips Houlihan (Angie Dickinson, Elaine Stritch)
Gary Burghoff as Radar O'Reilly (Frankie Avalon)

Robert Altman offered the role of Hot Lips to Angie Dickinson.¹ She turned it down. He was also interested in Elaine Stritch, but the part eventually went to Sally Kellerman.²

Frankie Avalon was asked to play Radar. Avalon wasn't interested sine the character didn't have many lines. His agent told him that the part would be made bigger. Avalon still said no.³

Macao (1952)
Gloria Grahame as Margie (Jane Greer)

Jane Greer said no to the part of Margie in *Macao*. Gloria Grahame was cast in her place.⁴

B. D. WONG

B.D. Wong lost the part he originated on Broadway in *M. Butterfly*.

MacBeth (1948)

Jeanette Nolan as Lady MacBeth (Tallulah Bankhead, Geraldine Fitzgerald)

Director Orson Welles offered the starring role of Lady MacBeth to Tallulah Bankhead and Geraldine Fitzgerald. Fitzgerald was unavailable. Bankhead said no, and the part went to Jeanette Nolan instead.[5]

Mad City (1997)

Dustin Hoffman as Max Brackett (John Travolta)
Mia Kirshner as Lori (Ashley Judd, Mira Sorvino, Marisa Tomei)

John Travolta turned down the starring role in *Mad City*, but did agree to play the second lead.[6]

Relatively unknown Mia Kirshner won the role of Lori even though very famous actresses including Mira Sorvino, Ashley Judd, and Marisa Tomei were reportedly interested.[7]

Mad Dog and Glory (1993)

Bill Murray as Frank Milo (Robert De Niro)

In the early planning stages, Robert De Niro participated in a read through of the film for director John McNaughton and producers Martin Scorsese and Steven A. Jones. De Niro read the part of shy police photographer Wayne. That was the role he was interested in. However, he wanted to see what McNaughton thought. After the read through was over they decided to read it again. This time De Niro would read the part of crime boss Frank Milo. All involved thought that De Niro's first instinct was the right one; he should play Wayne. De Niro was glad, since he felt he had played the other type of role before.[8] Bill Murray was eventually cast as Frank.

The Mad Miss Manton (1938)

Barbara Stanwyck as Melsa Manton (Katharine Hepburn)

Katharine Hepburn was supposed to play the part of heiress Melsa Manton. However, Hepburn was working on the film *Bringing Up Baby*. Shooting on the film was taking longer than expected, and Hepburn had to relinquish the part of Melsa Manton to Barbara Stanwyck.[9]

Madame Bovary (1949)

Jennifer Jones as Emma Bovary (Lana Turner)

Lana Turner was assigned the role of Emma Bovary. Turner disliked the script and didn't want to do it. She informed MGM of this. She also told them that she was pregnant. MGM wasn't happy. They suspended her and kept her out of the public eye for most for the year.[10]

Madame Butterfly (1932)

Cary Grant as Lieutenant B.F. Pinkerton (Gary Cooper)

Gary Cooper turned down *Madame Butterfly*, and Cary Grant was cast as Lieutenant B.F. Pinkerton instead.[11]

The Madness of King George (1995)

Nigel Hawthorne as King George (Sean Connery, Dustin Hoffman, Anthony Hopkins)

Dustin Hoffman, Sean Connery, and Anthony Hopkins were all considered for the role of King

George.[12] Nigel Hawthorne won the part and earned an Oscar nomination for his performance.

Made in America (1993)
Whoopi Goldberg as Sarah Mathews (Jessica Lange)

Made in America was originally meant for Jessica Lange. She ultimately decided it was not for her and dropped out. Whoopi Goldberg was cast as her replacement.[13]

Magic (1978)
Anthony Hopkins as Corky/Voice of Fats the Dummy (Robert De Niro, Jack Nicholson)

Steven Spielberg considered making *Magic* with Robert De Niro in the lead. The project was eventually taken over by Richard Attenborough.[14] Attenborough's first choice was Jack Nicholson, but he eventually cast Anthony Hopkins instead.[15]

The Magic Bow (1947)
Stewart Granger as Nicolo Paganini (James Mason)
Jean Kent as Bianca (Margaret Lockwood)

James Mason was pursued to play Nicolo Paganini. Mason didn't want to make the film and turned down the offer. Stewart Granger replaced him.[16]

Margaret Lockwood rejected Jean Kent's role in *The Magic Bow*.[17]

The Magnificent Ambersons (1942)
Anne Baxter as Lucy (Jeanne Crain)

Jeanne Crain auditioned for the part of Lucy. She lost out to Anne Baxter.[18]

Maid in Manhattan (2002)
Jennifer Lopez as Marisa Ventura (Sandra Bullock, Julia Roberts, Hilary Swank)

Writer/director John Hughes and producer Joe Roth were looking for a leading lady for their film, *The Chambermaid*. Julia Roberts was contacted. The actress wasn't interested. Sandra Bullock was another possibility. Bullock wasn't happy with the script the way it was. However, Hughes didn't want to change it unless Bullock made a commitment to play the part. Bullock left the project. Hilary Swank was interested in the script. But Swank decided to make *Insomnia* instead. Roth gave the script to Elaine Goldsmith-Thomas to read. The former agent thought that the film was right for her former client Jennifer Lopez. Lopez wanted to do it. The script was rewritten to suit the actress.[19] The name of the film was eventually retitled *Maid In Manhattan*.

The Main Event (1979)
Barbra Streisand as Hillary Kramer (Jill Clayburgh, Diane Keaton, Diana Ross)
Ryan O'Neal as Eddie "Kid Natural" Scanlon (James Caan)
Paul Sand as David (Allan Miller)

Diana Ross was the intended star of *The Main Event*. She would play Hillary Kramer with James Caan opposite her as Eddie "Kid Natural" Scanlon. Caan eventually changed his mind about making the film.[20] Producer Jon Peters got a copy of the script. He thought it had potential and wanted to produce it. Instead of Diana Ross as Hillary, Peters thought that his girlfriend, Barbra Streisand, was the right choice. Streisand didn't think the script was all that great, but ultimately agreed to play the part. She asked Ryan O'Neal to be her costar. O'Neal, a former boxer himself, agreed. Peters ran into trouble negotiating a deal with executive producer Howard Rosenman. Rosenman owned the rights to the film. He claimed that Peters was only willing to give him half the amount of money that he had promised. Rosenman threatened to take Streisand out of the film, and give her part to Diane Keaton or Jill Clayburgh. Peters gave Rosenman what he asked for, and Streisand remained in the movie.[21]

Director Howard Zieff was interested in Allan Miller, Streisand's former acting teacher, for the part of Hillary's husband David. Miller told Zieff that Streisand would never agree to his casting. Zieff told Streisand of his intention to use Miller. She told Zieff that, although Miller was good, she didn't want him to play the part. Zieff cast Paul Sand instead.[22]

Maisie (1939)
Ann Sothern as Maisie Ravier (Jean Harlow)

Maisie was originally bought for Jean Harlow.[23] Harlow had died by the time *Maisie* started shooting, and the title role was taken by Ann Sothern.

Major Dundee (1965)

Richard Harris as Benjamin Tyreen (Steve McQueen, Anthony Quinn)
James Coburn as Samuel Potts (Lee Marvin)

Richard Harris was the first choice for the part of Captain Benjamin Tyreen. Harris and the producers tried to make a deal. At one point the negotiations were rocky, and Anthony Quinn and Steve McQueen were mentioned as possible replacements. In the end everything was ironed out, and Harris played the part.

Lee Marvin was asked to play Samuel Potts. Marvin didn't want to. The part then went to James Coburn.[24]

Major League 2 (1994)

Omar Epps as Willie Mays Hayes (Wesley Snipes)

Wesley Snipes decided against reprising his role of Willie Mays Hayes for the sequel to *Major League*.[25]

Malcolm X (1992)

Denzel Washington as Malcolm X (Richard Pryor, Dick Anthony Williams)
Delroy Lindo as West Indian Archie (Avery Brooks, Charles S. Dutton, Samuel L. Jackson)

Before Spike Lee and Denzel Washington came into the picture, Richard Pryor and Dick Anthony Williams had been considered to play Malcolm X. Samuel L. Jackson was director Lee's first choice for West Indian Archie.[26] Jackson felt he shouldn't have to audition for the film and refused. He was also wanted more money for the film (he was being offered scale — the lowest amount legally possible). He turned down the offer.[27] Lee's next choice was Charles S. Dutton. At the time Dutton was starring in a television series called *Roc*. The TV schedule could not be worked out for the film. Lee also considered Avery Brooks, but finally chose Delroy Lindo.[28]

Mallrats (1995)

Shannen Doherty as Rene Mosier (Joey Lauren Adams, Jenny McCarthy)
Jason Mewes as Jay (Seth Green)
Michael Rooker as Jared Svenning (William Atherton)

Director Kevin Smith's first film was *Clerks*. In the film Smith played the part of Silent Bob. His sidekick Jay was played by Jason Mewes. The independent film was a tremendous success. Smith's second film was *Mallrats*. The Jay and Silent Bob characters were also in this film. Smith assumed that Mewes would be back as Jay. But executives at Universal weren't sure about Mewes. The actor himself understood. He had no acting training. Smith insisted that Mewes be cast. The studio said okay, but there were conditions. They would not pay Mewes for traveling, hotels or rehearsal time. The also wanted other actors to be auditioned for the part. One of these actors was Seth Green. On Mewes' first day on the set executives from the studio were present to watch the actor and see if he would work out. After a short time they left. Mewes was allowed to remain in the film.[29]

A pre–*Singled Out* Jenny McCarthy auditioned for the role of Rene. According to McCarthy, director Kevin Smith was unimpressed with her reading, so much so that he laughed at her.[30] Joey Lauren Adams was a major contender, but Adams was eventually cast in the supporting role of Gwen Turner.[31] Smith chose *Beverly Hills 90210* star Shannen Doherty instead.

William Atherton was offered the chance to play Mr. Svenning. Atherton took another film instead (*Bio-Dome*). Michael Rooker got the part.[32]

The Maltese Falcon (1941)

Humphey Bogart as Sam Spade (Warner Baxter, Brian Donlevy, Melvyn Douglas, Henry Fonda, Preston Foster, Fred MacMurray, Fredric March, Robert Montgomery, Paul Muni, Lloyd Nolan, Anthony Quinn, George Raft, Edward G. Robinson, Franchot Tone, Richard Whorf)
Mary Astor as Brigid O'Shaughnessy (Annabella, Joan Bennett, Ingrid Bergman, Laraine Day, Frances Dee, Olivia De Havilland, Betty Field, Geraldine Fitzgerald, Janet Gaynor, Paulette Goddard, Rita Hayworth, Ruth Hussey, Dorothy Lamour, Brenda Marshall, Loretta Young)

The first choice to play Sam Spade was George Raft. Raft did not want to work with director John Huston in Huston's directorial debut.[33] Humphrey Bogart was cast after Melvyn Douglas, Henry Fonda, Fred MacMurray, Fredric

March, Paul Muni, Franchot Tone, Warner Baxter, Preston Foster, Lloyd Nolan, Brian Donlevy, Robert Montgomery, Edward G. Robinson, Richard Whorf, and Anthony Quinn were all considered.[34]

Geraldine Fitzgerald disliked the part of Brigid and turned it down.[35] The producers looked at Joan Bennett, Ingrid Bergman, Olivia De Havilland, Janet Gaynor, Paulette Goddard, Rita Hayworth, Ruth Hussey, Dorothy Lamour, Loretta Young, Laraine Day, Betty Field, Frances Dee, Brenda Marshall, and Annabella before deciding on Mary Astor.[36]

Mame (1974)

Lucille Ball as Mame Dennis (Angela Lansbury)
Beatrice Arthur as Vera Charles (Vivian Vance)
Robert Preston as Beauregard Burnside (Rory Calhoun, George Montgomery)
Jane Connell as Agnes Gooch (Madeline Kahn)

Angela Lansbury originated the role of Mame on Broadway. When Hollywood decided to make a film version Lansbury wasn't even a consideration. The studio wanted Lucille Ball. Gene Saks was hired to direct. Saks had also directed the Broadway version. Ball wanted Saks removed. The director spoke with Frank Wells, a Warner Bros. executive, and asked to have Ball replaced. Wells suggested Lansbury. Saks thought that was a great idea. Wells discussed the situation with the studio's board chairman Ted Ashley. Afterwards he informed Saks that Ball was not going anywhere.[37]

Ball's *I Love Lucy* co-star, Vivian Vance, was interested in playing opposite her. She thought that she was perfect for the part. In fact, 16 years earlier Vance campaigned for the role in the non-musical film version of *Auntie Mame*. Vance was unable to convince the producers to cast her. Vance said that they were concerned that people would see them as Lucy and Ethel rather than Mame and Vera. Beatrice Arthur, who created the role on Broadway, was cast instead.[38]

Even though Robert Preston was already cast as Beau, Ball arranged for George Montgomery and Rory Calhoun to audition. She felt either of the two would be better opposite her.[39] She was the only one who felt that way apparently, since Preston stayed in the role.

Madeline Kahn was the original choice to play frumpy Agnes Gooch. Lucille Ball thought that Kahn was too sexy for the part.[40] Kahn left the film and did *Blazing Saddles* instead. The part was then given to Jane Connell, who originated the role on Broadway.

Man About Town (1939)

Dorothy Lamour as Diana Wilson (Betty Grable)

Appendicitis forced Betty Grable to drop out of *Man About Town*. She was replaced by Dorothy Lamour.[41]

A Man for All Seasons (1966)

Susannah York as Margaret More (Vanessa Redgrave)

Vanessa Redgrave was cast as Margaret More in *A Man for All Seasons*. Soon after, she was offered the starring role in the play *The Prime of Miss Jean Brodie*. She asked to be let go from the film in order to do the film. Director Fred Zinnemann agreed. Her replacement in the film was Susannah York. Zinnemann asked Redgrave to play the part of Anne Boleyn. The part was very small, and he promised her that she would only be needed for one day. She agreed, but had two conditions: She didn't want to be paid, and she didn't want to be in the credits. Zinnemann agreed.[42]

The Man from Down Under (1943)

Binnie Barnes as Aggie Dawlins (Gracie Fields)

Charles Laughton, the star of *The Man from Down Under*, very much wanted Gracie Fields to take the role of Aggie Dawlins. Fields wasn't interested and turned it down. The part was played by Binnie Barnes instead.[43]

The Man in Grey (1943)

James Mason as Marquis of Rohan (Eric Portman)

Eric Portman was offered the lead in *The Man in Grey*. He turned it down and it was offered to James Mason.[44] *The Man in Grey* was Mason's breakthrough film. As a result Mason was signed to a four year contract with Gainsborough/Rank.

Man on the Moon (1999)

Jim Carrey as Andy Kaufman (Hank Azaria, Nicolas Cage, John Cusack, Edward Norton, Kevin Spacey)

Jim Carrey, Kevin Spacey, Edward Norton, Hank Azaria, and John Cusack all auditioned to play Andy Kaufman. Nicolas Cage wanted the role, but wouldn't audition. Jim Carrey's test was impressive. Director Milos Forman was also swayed by Carrey's moving performance in *The Truman Show*. It didn't hurt Carrey's chances that his films did huge box office business. Forman gave Carrey the role.[45]

Man Trouble (1992)

Jack Nicholson as Harry Bliss (Robert De Niro, Al Pacino)
Ellen Barkin as Joan Spruance (Diane Keaton, Jessica Lange, Jeanne Moreau, Meryl Streep)

In 1971 it was announced that Jack Nicholson and Jeanne Moreau would star in the film *Man Trouble*. Writer/director Carole Eastman had trouble getting the film made and it was shelved for about 20 years.[46]

For a time Jonathan Demme was going to direct the film. His choice for a leading lady was Diane Keaton. Another potential director was Lawrence Kasdan. He chose Jessica Lange who would have played Joan opposite Robert De Niro as Harry. Meryl Streep was finally cast. Al Pacino was the choice for Harry. Pacino asked for rewrites of the script. Eastman said okay, but even still Pacino decided against the film. Once again Jack Nicholson was sought to play Harry. Nicholson agreed. Bob Rafelson was brought in to direct. Then they found out that Streep was pregnant. Streep asked that the filming take place after her baby was born, but Nicholson was scheduled to make *Hoffa* then. Streep dropped out and was replaced by Ellen Barkin.[47]

The Man Who Came to Dinner (1941)

Bette Davis as Maggie Cutler (Olivia de Havilland)
Monty Woolley as Sheridan Whiteside (John Barrymore)

John Barrymore tested for the starring role of Sheridan Whiteside. Barrymore had a good chance but his memory was not good and he would have had to rely on cue cards.[48] Monty Woolley was given the part instead.

Olivia de Havilland was an early consideration for the role of secretary Maggie Cutler. The part was eventually taken by Bette Davis.[49]

The Man Who Would Be King (1975)

Sean Connery as Daniel Dravot (Clark Gable, Paul Newman)
Michael Caine as Peachy Carnehan (Humphrey Bogart, Robert Redford)
Shakira Caine as Roxanne (Tessa Dahl)

Director John Huston originally wanted Clark Gable and Humphrey Bogart to star in *The Man Who Would Be King*. The project was put on hold and the deal fell through. Huston later tried to make the film with Paul Newman and Robert Redford. Paul Newman advised Huston he would be better off with Sean Connery and Michael Caine. Huston took his advice and cast them. Newman and Redford made another film instead — *The Sting*.

Tessa Dahl was replaced by Shakira Caine, the wife of Michael Caine.[50]

The Manchurian Candidate (1962)

Angela Lansbury as Mrs. Iselin (Lucille Ball)

Frank Sinatra was set to star in *The Manchurian Candidate*. In his contract was a clause stating that he had casting approval. He wanted Lucille Ball to play Mrs. Iselin. Director John Frankenheimer had just completed work on the film *All Fall Down*, which starred Angela Lansbury. He felt that she would be right for the role of Mrs. Iselin. He arranged for Sinatra to see a rough cut of *All Fall Down*. After seeing her performance in the film Sinatra agreed that Lansbury was the right choice.[52]

Manhattan Melodrama (1934)

William Powell as Jim Wade (Robert Montgomery)

MGM's David O. Selznick considered contract player Robert Montgomery for the part of Jim Wade. Selznick dismissed Montgomery as too mild for the part. He hired William Powell instead.[55]

Manhattan Murder Mystery (1993)

Diane Keaton as Carol Lipton (Mia Farrow)

The role of Carol Lipton was written for Mia Farrow to play.[56] Farrow dropped out because of her tumultuous, very public breakup with director Woody Allen.[57] She was replaced by Allen's former leading lady (both on and off screen), Diane Keaton.

Manhunter (1986)

Brian Cox as Hannibal Lecter (Brian Dennehy, John Lithgow, Mandy Patinkin)

John Lithgow, Brian Dennehy and Mandy Patinkin were all considered for the part of Hannibal Lecter in 1986's *Manhunter*. Brian Cox was cast instead. The character of Hannibal Lecter became a household name five years later when Anthony Hopkins played it in *The Silence of the Lambs*. Hopkins won the Oscar for the role. He continued to play the character in the films *Hannibal* and *Red Dragon*.

Mannequin 2: On the Move (1991)

Jonathan Switcher—Andrew McCarthy

Andrew McCarthy vetoed the idea of reprising his role in the sequel to *Mannequin*.[58] His part was eliminated from the movie.

Man's Favorite Sport? (1964)

Rock Hudson as Roger Willoughby (Cary Grant)
Paula Prentiss as Abigail Page (Joanna Moore)
Maria Perschy as Isolde "Easy" Mueller (Ursula Andress)

The role that Rock Hudson played in *Man's Favorite Sport?* was originally intended for Cary Grant. Grant signed on for the part until he read the script. He didn't like it at all. He decided to drop out of the film, and signed on to make *Charade* instead.[53]

Director Howard Hawks thought that he would give the part of Abigail Page to Joanna Moore. He changed his mind when he saw Paula Prentiss. He went to Paramount with his decision. The studio didn't want Prentiss; they felt she wasn't a big enough star. Hawks was so impressed with Prentiss that he made the movie at Universal instead of Paramount for her.

Ursula Andress was pursued for the part of Isolde "Easy" Mueller. Andress turned the part down. It was played by Maria Perschy instead.[54]

Man's Genesis (1912)

Mae Marsh as Lillywhite (Mary Pickford)

Mary Pickford was offered the role of Lillywhite in director D.W. Griffith's *Man's Genesis*. The actress who was known as America's Sweetheart did not want to appear on film wearing a grass skirt. Mae Marsh was cast in her place. Although Pickford did not want to play the part herself, she objected to the casting of Marsh. She said that Marsh had no stage experience, and as a result Pickford left Griffith's studio Biograph.[51]

Marie (1985)

Sissy Spacek as Marie Ragghianti (Debra Winger)

Debra Winger was offered the title role of Marie. After she turned it down it went to Sissy Spacek.[59]

Marie Antoinette (1938)

Norma Shearer as Marie Antoinette (Marion Davies)

Marion Davies sought the title role of Marie Antoinette. Irving Thalberg turned her down in favor of Norma Shearer.[60]

Marie Galante (1934)

Spencer Tracy as Crawbett (Edmund Lowe)

Spencer Tracy was originally cast as Crawbett in *Marie Galante*. He later decided he didn't want to do the film, and dropped out. Edmund Lowe was hired to replace him. The film was started with Lowe in the lead. After a few days, Tracy had a change of heart. He wanted his part back. Since the had already started shooting with Lowe, they would lose money to start shooting all over again. Tracy paid with his own money for the reshoot, and Lowe was out of the movie.[61]

Marjorie Morningstar (1958)

Gene Kelly as Noel Airman (Paul Newman)
Natalie Wood as Marjorie Morgenstern (Elizabeth Taylor)

Elizabeth Taylor was considered for the lead in *Marjorie Morningstar*.[62] The role went to Natalie Wood instead.

Paul Newman was sought for the part of Noel Airman. Newman had problems with the script, and decided that he did not want to be in the film, and the part went to Gene Kelly instead.

158 Marnie

Spencer Tracy was the reason Edmund Lowe (pictured) didn't star in *Marie Galante*.

Newman filled the void in his schedule making *The Long Hot Summer*.[63]

Marnie (1964)
Tippi Hedren as Marnie Edgar (Grace Kelly)

When Grace Kelly married Prince Rainier and became the Princess of Monaco she retired from acting. However, after six years of marriage, Kelly thought she might like to return to films. She spoke to Alfred Hitchcock, who had Kelly in mind for the title role of *Marnie* all along. A deal was made and announced to the public. When the citizens of Monaco heard the news, they were upset. They did not want their princess to play a criminal. They had a vote, in which the outcome was that they wanted her to drop out of the film. Sadly, Kelly told Hitchcock the news. He was upset, and postponed the film for about two years, at which point he cast Tippi Hedren, his new leading lady from *The Birds*, in the title role.[64]

The Marrying Kind (1952)
Madge Kennedy as Judge Carroll (Ina Claire)

Screenwriter Garson Kanin did not want Ina Claire to play the judge and the role went to Madge Kennedy.[65]

Marty (1955)
Ernest Borgnine as Marty Pilletti (Rod Steiger)

Marty started out as a television movie in 1953. The stars were Rod Steiger and Nancy Marchand. When the feature film was planned Steiger was hurt to learn that he was replaced by Ernest Borgnine. He said that he thought Borgnine was very good, and that Borgnine's Marty Pilletti was very different from his own.[66] Ernest Borgnine won a an Oscar for his performance.

Mary of Scotland (1936)
Florence Eldridge as Queen Elizabeth (Bette Davis, Ginger Rogers)

Ginger Rogers desperately wanted to play Queen Elizabeth in Pandro S. Berman's *Mary of Scotland*. When Berman refused to test her, Rogers decided to take matters into her own hands. With the assistance of her agent Leland Hayward and director John Ford, Rogers was able to make a screen test under the alias Lady Ainsley. Ford had told Berman that Lady Ainsley was a British Shakespearean actress. The day of the screen test Rogers came to the studio in makeup and a wig. No one recognized her. Katharine Hepburn, who was already cast in the lead role, was to test with her. Ford had informed Hepburn as to whom Lady Ainsley really was. Hepburn did not appreciate the charade and did nothing to help Rogers out. After the test Rogers received a call telling her that they would like to make a second test with Lady Ainsley. Rogers was elated that she might actually get the part. Before the second test, Louella Parsons printed the story of the "practical joke" Rogers was playing. Her cover was blown. Later that day, Rogers ran into Berman at the racetrack. Although Berman was not angry, he would not allow Rogers to do another test.[67] Bette Davis wanted the part, but director John Ford was not interested in her.[68] He preferred Florence Eldridge instead, and gave her the part.

Mary Reilly (1996)
Julia Roberts as Mary Reilly (Uma Thurman)

Early on Uma Thurman was a contender for Julia Roberts' role of Mary Reilly.[69]

Mary Shelley's Frankenstein (1994)

Robert De Niro as The Monster (Gerard Depardieu)
Helena Bonham Carter as Elizabeth (Kate Winslet)

Gerard Depardieu was turned down for the role of the monster.[70]

Kate Winslet tried for the part of Elizabeth. Director Kenneth Branagh rejected her in favor of Helena Bonham Carter.[71]

Mask (1985)

Cher as Rusty Dennis (Jane Fonda)

Producer Martin Starger wanted Jane Fonda to play Rusty Dennis. He and director Peter Bogdanovich eventually decided that they couldn't see Fonda as a biker. Cher got the part instead.[72]

Mask of Zorro (1998)

Antonio Banderas as Alejandro Murietta/Zorro (Andy Garcia)
Anthony Hopkins as Don Diego de la Vega/Zorro (Sean Connery)

Andy Garcia was considered for the role of Zorro.

Sean Connery was mentioned for the role of older Zorro, but the part ultimately went to Anthony Hopkins.[73]

Masquerade (1965)

Cliff Robertson as David Frazer (Rex Harrison)

Rex Harrison was signed for the lead role of David Frazer in *Masquerade*. He later decided to leave the film, and was replaced by Cliff Robertson.[74]

The Matrix (1999)

Keanu Reeves as Thomas A. Anderson/Neo (Leonardo DiCaprio, Brad Pitt, Will Smith)
Laurence Fishburne as Morpheus (Val Kilmer)

Leonardo DiCaprio, Brad Pitt, and Will Smith were all considered for the Keanu Reeves role in *The Matrix*.

Val Kilmer rejected the role of Morpheus, which later went to Laurence Fishburne.[75]

The Matrix Reloaded (2003)
The Matrix Revolutions (2003)

Collin Chou as Seraph (Jet Li, Michelle Yeoh)
Nona M. Gaye as Zee (Aaliyah)

The role of Seraph was written for Jet Li. Li decided against doing the film, and Michelle Yeoh was considered. Yeoh fell through and the part went to Collin Chou instead.[76]

Singer Aaliyah made her film debut in 2000 with the film *Romeo Must Die*. Her performance was met with rave reviews. Directors Andy and Larry Wachowski cast her in the role of Zee in the upcoming two sequels to their mega-hit film, *The Matrix*. On August 25, 2001, Aaliyah was tragically killed in a plane crash.[77] She had not yet begun shooting the films.

Maverick (1994)

Jodie Foster as Annabelle Bransford (Julia Roberts, Meg Ryan)

Julia Roberts considered starring in *Maverick*, but ultimately turned the part down.[78] Meg Ryan signed on, but later changed her mind.[79] After she left the part was given to Jodie Foster.

McCabe & Mrs. Miller (1971)

Warren Beatty as John McCabe (Elliott Gould)

Elliott Gould was considered for John McCabe.[80]

McHale's Navy (1997)

Debra Messing as Lt. Penelope Carpenter (Cameron Diaz)

Cameron Diaz turned down the female lead of Lt. Penelope Carpenter in *McHale's Navy*.[81]

Mean Streets (1973)

Robert De Niro as John "Johnny Boy" Civello (Harvey Keitel)
Harvey Keitel as Charlie Cappa (Robert De Niro, Jon Voight)

Jon Voight was the first choice to star as Charlie in *Mean Streets*. When Voight rejected the role it was immediately offered to Harvey Keitel. Keitel had, up to this point, been the number one contender for the part of Johnny Boy. Keitel told his friend Robert De Niro about the film. De Niro told Keitel that he intended to ask

Meet John Doe (1941)

Gary Cooper as Long John Willoughby (Ronald Colman, James Stewart)
Barbara Stanwyck as Ann Mitchell (Jean Arthur, Olivia De Havilland, Ann Sheridan)

director Martin Scorsese for the part of Charlie. Scorsese kept Keitel. De Niro didn't mind. He was more interested in working with Scorsese than getting the lead. Scorsese cast De Niro in the supporting role of Johnny Boy instead.[82]

Ronald Colman, James Stewart and Jean Arthur were mentioned as possibilities for the lead roles in *Meet John Doe*. Both Olivia De Havilland and Ann Sheridan auditioned for the part of Ann Mitchell. Frank Capra wanted to cast Sheridan, but she was having trouble with Warner Bros. The studio refused to let her appear in the film, so Capra gave the part to Barbara Stanwyck instead.[83]

Meet Me After the Show (1951)

Macdonald Carey as Jeff Ames (Cary Grant)
Rory Calhoun as David Hemingway (Dale Robertson)

Cary Grant was offered the role of Jeff Ames. Grant's schedule did not allow him to do the film. Betty Grable wanted production to wait for Grant, but Darryl F. Zanuck gave the part to Macdonald Carey instead. Betty Grable wanted Dale Robertson to play David Hemingway, but Rory Calhoun was cast instead.[84]

Meet Me in St. Louis (1944)

Tom Drake as John Truett (Van Johnson)

Van Johnson was signed for the part of John Truett. At the last minute Johnson dropped out. He was replaced by Tom Drake.[85]

Meet the Parents (2000)

Ben Stiller as Greg Focker (Jim Carrey)
Teri Polo as Pamela "Pam" Martha Byrnes (Heather Graham)

Jim Herzfeld wrote the original draft of *Meet the Parents*. Jim Carrey was the front runner for the starring role of Greg Focker. Carrey eventually moved on, leaving the part of Greg open. The script went through many changes. One notable difference was that the role of the father was made more substantial. It was now such a good part that superstar Robert De Niro signed on to play it with Ben Stiller cast as Greg Focker opposite him.[86]

Heather Graham turned down the role of Pam.[87] Teri Polo was cast in her place, and had the biggest hit of her career to date.

Megaforce (1982)

Barry Bostwick as Ace Hunter (Tom Selleck)

Scheduling problems forced Tom Selleck to turn down the role of Ace Hunter in *Megaforce*.[88]

Men in Black (1997)

Tommy Lee Jones as Agent K (Clint Eastwood)
Will Smith as Agent J (Chris O'Donnell)

Executives from Columbia instructed director Barry Sonnenfeld to sign Chris O'Donnell for the part of Agent J. Sonnenfeld thought that O'Donnell was a good actor; he especially liked his performance in *Men Don't Leave*. However, Sonnenfeld's wife was a fan of Will Smith. She wanted her husband to give Smith the part. Sonnenfeld let O'Donnell get away to please his wife.

Clint Eastwood was a possible choice for agent K. But Sonnenfeld went to the studio to sing the praises of Tommy Lee Jones. The studio was so impressed that they became intent on Jones, while Sonnenfeld would only be hired if Jones approved him![89]

Men in Black II (2002)

Lara Flynn Boyle as Serleena (Famke Janssen)

[*Dr. Laurel Weaver/Agent L*— Linda Fiorentino]

Famke Janssen was originally cast as villain Serleena. After one day of filming Janssen had to drop out, due to an illness in her family. A replacement was needed in a hurry. An offer was made to Lara Flynn Boyle, star of the television series, *The Practice*. Boyle went to her boss, David E. Kelley, and asked for permission to do the film, despite the bad timing for the series. Kelley asked Boyle if it meant a lot to her. When Boyle said that it did, Kelley said yes.[90]

Linda Fiorentino was the female lead in *Men in Black*. Director Barry Sonnenfeld said that her character needed to be much smaller in the sequel to serve the story. Two scenes were written for the character. Fiorentino decided not to participate in the film, and the character was written out.[91]

Le Mepris (1963)
Michel Piccoli as Paul Javal (Raf Vallone)

Raf Vallone was originally cast as writer Paul Javal in director Jean-Luc Godard's *Le Mepris*. Vallone was busy working on *The Cardinal*, and the role of Paul had to be recast. Michel Piccoli was chosen to replace Vallone.[92]

Mermaids (1990)
Winona Ryder as Charlotte Flax (Emily Lloyd)

Emily Lloyd was originally cast as Charlotte Flax. Shortly afterwards she was fired and replaced by Winona Ryder.[93]

Emily Lloyd was fired from *Mermaids*.

The Merry Widow (1934)
Jeanette MacDonald as Sonia [aka Fifi] (Joan Crawford, Grace Moore, Lily Pons, Vivienne Segal, Gloria Swanson)

Gloria Swanson, Joan Crawford, Grace Moore, Lily Pons, and Vivienne Segal were all considered for the starring role of Sonia/Fifi in *The Merry Widow*. Moore came close to getting the part, but Jeanette MacDonald was deemed thinner and more photogenic.[94]

Meteor (1979)
Brian Keith as Dr. Alexei Dubov (Donald Pleasence)

Donald Pleasence had to drop out of *Meteor* because of a commitment to the film *Sergeant Pepper's Lonely Hearts Club Band*.[95]

Michael (1996)
John Travolta as Michael (Gerard Depardieu, Tom Hanks)

Director Nora Ephron offered the title role of Michael to Tom Hanks. Hanks turned it down, and Ephron continued her search for a leading man.[96] She briefly considered Gerard Depardieu before deciding to cast John Travolta.[97]

Micki & Maude (1984)
Amy Irving as Maude Salinger (Marilu Henner)

Marilu Henner was scheduled to audition for the film *Micki & Maude*. That same week the Academy Award nominations came out. Amy Irving was nominated for best supporting actress for her role in *Yentl*. Henner's audition was canceled because the role was given to Irving.[98]

Midnight Cowboy (1969)
Jon Voight as Joe Buck (Michael Sarrazin)

Director John Schlesinger's first choice for the role of Joe Buck was Michael Sarrazin. Sarrazin was working on the film *In Search of Gregory*, and couldn't get off to rehearse.[99] Schlesinger decided to go with another actor — Jon Voight.

Midnight Express (1978)
Brad Davis as Billy Hayes (Richard Gere, Dennis Quaid, John Savage, John Travolta)

John Travolta was offered the starring role of Billy Hayes in *Midnight Express*. He wasn't interested and turned it down.[100] Richard Gere and Brad Davis were up for the part. Gere and director Alan Parker didn't hit it off, which was good for Brad Davis. Davis auditioned with the other final candidates: Dennis Quaid and John Savage. Brad Davis won the part.[101]

Midnight Run (1988)
Charles Grodin as Jonathan Mardukas (Cher, Robin Williams)

When director Martin Brest told Paramount he wanted Charles Grodin to star opposite

Michael Sarrazin was the first choice for Joe Buck in *Midnight Cowboy*.

Robert De Niro in *Midnight Run*, the studio told him Grodin wasn't a big enough name. Brest contacted Cher, with the idea of changing the character to a female named Joanne. Cher had just won the Oscar for her performance in *Moonstruck*, and was very hot at the moment. Cher thought it wasn't a good idea and said no. Brest finally narrowed it down to a choice between two actors: Grodin and Robin Williams. Williams wanted the part so much he offered to audition for it, something an actor of his stature rarely does. Since the film had been transferred over to Universal Studios, there was no longer a problem with the casting of Charles Grodin. Brest thought he was the best choice, and gave him the part.[102]

A Midsummer Night's Dream (1935)

James Cagney as Bottom (Charlie Chaplin, Guy Kibbee)
Joe E. Brown as Flute (W.C. Fields)
Dick Powell as Lysander (Gary Cooper)
Mickey Rooney as Puck (Fred Astaire)
Victor Jory as Oberon (John Barrymore)
Ian Hunter as Theseus (Walter Huston)
Ross Alexander as Demetrius (Clark Gable)
Olivia De Havilland as Hermia (Joan Crawford)
Jean Muir as Helena (Myrna Loy)
Anita Louise as Titania (Greta Garbo)
Dewey Robinson as Snug (Wallace Beery)

Director Max Reinhardt's original wish list for *A Midsummer Night's Dream* consisted of Charlie Chaplin for Nick Bottom, W.C. Fields for Francis Flute, Gary Cooper for Lysander, Fred Astaire for Puck, John Barrymore for Oberon, Walter Huston for Theseus, Clark Gable for Demetrius, Joan Crawford for Hermia, Myrna Loy for Helena, Greta Garbo for Titania, and Wallace Beery for Snug. He asked his son Gottfried to try to get these actors to sign for the film. The problem he encountered was that these very famous actors were being offered much less money than they were accustomed to making. It was eventually clear to Reinhardt that he needed a cast of lesser known actors.[103]

Producer Hal B. Wallis wanted Guy Kibbee to play Nick Bottom. Reinhardt rejected the suggestion and cast James Cagney instead.[104]

Mildred Pierce (1945)

Joan Crawford as Mildred Pierce (Bette Davis, Rosalind Russell, Ann Sheridan, Barbara Stanwyck)
Ann Blyth as Veda Pierce (Shirley Temple, Virginia Weidler)
Bruce Bennett as Bert Pierce (Ralph Bellamy)

Both Shirley Temple and her mother Gertrude Temple thought that the part of Veda Pierce would be a great opportunity for Shirley. Shirley was the most popular child star of all time. Now, at age 16, Temple was eager to change her image. She and Gertrude thought that the part of the merciless Veda was the perfect vehicle to do just that. The producers liked the idea of using Temple. However, their first concern was finding an actress for the title role of Mildred Pierce.[105] Bette Davis was made an offer, which she turned down.[106] Warners was also rejected by Barbara Stanwyck,[107] Rosalind Russell and Ann Sheridan.[108] Joan Crawford was very eager to play the part. She campaigned heavily until the studio finally agreed. By this time Temple had moved on.[109] Virginia Weidler auditioned to play Veda, but lost out to Ann Blyth.[110]

Director Michael Curtiz and producer Jerry Wald liked Ralph Bellamy for the part of Mildred's first husband Bert Pierce. They didn't hire him, though. Just before shooting started the part was given to Bruce Bennett.¹¹¹

Miller's Crossing (1990)
Albert Finney as Leo (Trey Wilson)

The Coen brothers wrote the part of Leo for Trey Wilson. Wilson had worked with the Coens in their film *Raising Arizona*. Wilson was all set for the part. Sadly, he died a few days before they were to begin working on the film. The role was recast with Albert Finney.¹¹²

The Millionairess (1960)
Sophia Loren as Epifania Parerga (Ava Gardner)

Ava Gardner was the actress that executives at 20th Century–Fox wanted to play the part of Epifania Parerga. Producer Dimitri De Grunwald disagreed. He thought that Gardner was an awful choice, that Sophia Loren was much better for the part. He also said that Gardner had no chemistry with co-star Peter Sellers. De Grunwald was apparently persuasive; the role went to Loren.¹¹³

Minority Report (2002)
Colin Farrell as Ed Witwer (Matt Damon)

Minority Report was originally set to start shooting with Matt Damon as Ed Witwer. There were scheduling delays. First Tom Cruise was held back on *Mission: Impossible II*, and then *Eyes Wide Shut* went into overtime. Director Steven Spielberg was busy making *A.I.: Artificial Intelligence*. Damon couldn't wait any longer. He left and was replaced by Colin Farrell.¹¹⁴

The Miracle (1959)
Carroll Baker as Teresa (Natalie Wood)

Natalie Wood was asked to play Teresa. She turned the film down. Carroll Baker was cast instead.¹¹⁵

Miracle on 34th Street (1947)
John Payne as Fred Gailey (Mark Stevens)

Mark Stevens was considered for the part of attorney Fred Gailey. Studio head Darryl F. Zanuck thought that Stevens was all wrong. Zanuck also wanted a bigger box office name than Stevens and cast John Payne instead.¹¹⁶

Mark Stevens was not famous enough to star in *Miracle on 34th Street*.

The Miracle Worker (1962)
Anne Bancroft as Annie Sullivan (Ingrid Bergman)

Anne Bancroft originated the role of Annie Sullivan in *The Miracle Worker* on Broadway. When the role was being cast for the film version, it was offered to Ingrid Bergman. Bergman refused it, and insisted they give the part to Bancroft.¹¹⁷

The Mirror Crack'd (1980)
Elizabeth Taylor as Marina Rudd (Natalie Wood)

Natalie Wood dropped out of *The Mirror Crack'd*. Elizabeth Taylor went on to play the role.¹¹⁸

The Mirror Has Two Faces (1996)
George Segal as Henry Fine (Dudley Moore)

Dudley Moore left *The Mirror Has Two Faces* shortly after production started. Director Barbra Streisand replaced him with her old friend George Segal.¹¹⁹

Les Miserables (1998)
Geoffrey Rush as Javert (Anthony Hopkins)

Anthony Hopkins turned down the chance to play Javert in *Les Miserables*.[121]

Misery (1990)
James Caan as Paul Sheldon (Warren Beatty, Robert De Niro, Michael Douglas, Richard Dreyfuss, Harrison Ford, Gene Hackman, Dustin Hoffman, William Hurt, Kevin Kline, Al Pacino, Robert Redford)

Kathy Bates as Annie Wilkes (Bette Midler)

Director Rob Reiner offered the starring role of writer Paul Sheldon to William Hurt, who rejected it. Reiner was still interested in Hurt, and decided to submit the script to him once again. And once again Hurt said no. Reiner decided to move on. He offered the part to Kevin Kline, Michael Douglas, Harrison Ford, Robert De Niro, Dustin Hoffman and Al Pacino. None of them were interested. Reiner asked Richard Dreyfuss if he wanted to do it. Dreyfuss agreed to do the film without even reading the script. The problem of finding a leading man was solved. Reiner sent Dreyfuss a copy of the script. Dreyfuss changed his mind. He backed out of the project, leaving Reiner back in the search for a male lead.[121] Gene Hackman[122] and Robert Redford were both approached, and like all the others, both said no. Warren Beatty was interested in the role, but there was a scheduling problem with the film he was making at the time, *Dick Tracy*. Finally producer Andy Scheinman suggested James Caan. Reiner met with Caan, and decided to give him, the part.[123]

Reiner liked Bette Midler for the role of Annie Wilkes. They had lunch to discuss the film, and Midler decided she didn't want to do it. After this meeting Reiner decided that it would be wrong to have a star play the part of such a mysterious woman. A star would bring a familiar element into the role, which Reiner didn't want. He instead cast Broadway veteran Kathy Bates, who became a star, and wound up with an Oscar for her performance in the film.[124]

The Misfits (1961)
Clark Gable as Gay Langland (Robert Mitchum)

Robert Mitchum was the first choice to play Gay Langland, but Mitchum had problems with the script and the part went instead to Clark Gable.[125]

Missing (1982)
Jack Lemmon as Ed Horman (Paul Newman)

Paul Newman turned down the role of Ed Horman in *Missing*.[126] Jack Lemmon took the part. He was nominated for an Oscar for his performance. Lemmon lost the Academy Award to Ben Kingsley for *Gandhi*.

Mission to Mars (2000)
Connie Nielsen as Terri Fisher (Monica Potter)

Monica Potter dropped out of *Mission to Mars* in order to star in the film, *Head Over Heels*.[127]

Mississippi Burning (1988)
Willem Dafoe as Agent Ward (Kevin Costner)

The part of Agent Ward was offered to Kevin Costner; he declined. Willem Dafoe was cast.[128]

Mr. and Mrs. Smith (1941)
Robert Montgomery as David Smith (Cary Grant)

Carole Lombard wanted Cary Grant to star opposite her in *Mr. and Mrs. Smith*. Grant was unavailable, and Lombard asked for and got to work with Robert Montgomery.[156]

Mister Buddwing (1966)
James Garner as Mr. Buddwing (Jack Lemmon)

The first choice for the starring role of Mister Buddwing was Jack Lemmon. Lemmon, however, did not play the part. It went to James Garner instead.[129]

Mr. Majestyk (1974)
Charles Bronson as Vince Majestyk (Clint Eastwood)

Mr. Majestyk was originally intended for Clint Eastwood. The actor declined, and Charles Bronson was cast instead.[157]

Mister Roberts (1955)
Henry Fonda as Lieutenant Doug A. Roberts (Marlon Brando, William Holden)

Jack Lemmon as Frank Thurlowe Pulver (Frank Sinatra)

Marlon Brando and William Holden were approached before Henry Fonda signed on as Doug Roberts.[130]

Frank Sinatra was considered for the part of Ensign Frank Thurlowe Pulver. He lost the role because the producers wanted a younger actor. They cast Jack Lemmon. Lemmon is ten years younger than Frank Sinatra.[131]

Mr. Skeffington (1944)

Claude Rains as Job Skeffington (Paul Henreid)

Paul Henreid turned down the part of Job Skeffington. Henreid later said that he had no regrets about not taking the part.[158]

Mr. Smith Goes to Washington (1939)

James Stewart as Jefferson Smith (Gary Cooper)
Harry Carey as President of State (Edward Ellis)

When director Frank Capra first considered possibilities for the role of Mr. Smith, he thought of Gary Cooper. He later changed his mind, feeling the character was more Jimmy Stewart's style.[159]

Capra offered Edward Ellis a small part. Ellis was extremely insulted by this. He said that a third rate actor wouldn't accept such a small part. Ellis wanted an apology from Capra. Capra countered that he didn't want a star for the part. He looked through the Players Directory and saw Harry Carey's picture. Carey had no problem with the size of the role and signed on.[160]

Moby Dick (1956)

Gregory Peck as Captain Ahab (Gary Cooper, Errol Flynn, Walter Huston, Burt Lancaster, Fredric March, John Wayne, Orson Welles)

Director John Huston had wanted to make the film *Moby Dick* long before it actually went into production. His original plan was to have his father, actor Walter Huston, as Ahab.[132] He later considered Orson Welles and Fredric March for the part. Other actors mentioned for the role included Errol Flynn, John Wayne, Burt Lancaster, and Gary Cooper.[133]

The Mod Squad (1999)

Giovanni Ribisi as Peter Cochran (Casey Affleck)

Giovanni Ribisi and Casey Affleck were both contenders for the part of Peter Cochran. MGM president Michael Nathanson said that it would be a difficult decision, since both were very good actors.[134] Ribisi was ultimately chosen.

The Model Shop (1969)

Gary Lockwood as George Matthews (Harrison Ford)

Director Jacques Demy wanted an unknown actor for the starring role of George Matthews. *The Model Shop* was being produced by Columbia Pictures, where a young Harrison Ford was signed. Producer Gerry Ayres thought that Ford was right to play George. Ford was tested with Anouk Aimee, the film's leading lady. Demy and Ford became friends, and Demy was sure that Ford was the best actor for the role. Unfortunately for Ford, studio executive Jerry Tokovsky didn't think Ford had a future in films. He refused to let him star in the film. Demy fought the decision to no avail. He eventually gave up and cast Gary Lockwood instead.[135]

Mogambo (1953)

Ava Gardner as Eloise Y. "Honey Bear" Kelly (Lana Turner)
Grace Kelly as Linda Nordley (Deborah Kerr)

Lana Tuner was offered her choice of two scripts: *Mogambo* and *Flame and the Flesh*. Turner didn't especially like the *Mogambo* script. Her doctor also advised against going to Africa for the shoot because her blood type increased her risk of getting a rare infection. She made *Flame and the Flesh*. She later said that the finished script was different from the one that she read. She said that she made a mistake not doing the film. She also found out that her doctor might not have had much cause for concern, since the cast had all the comforts of home. Ava Gardner was cast in *Mogambo* instead.[136]

Dore Schary considered Deborah Kerr for the film, but director John Ford saw her as too proper. He cast Grace Kelly instead.[137]

Molly and Me (1945)

Gracie Fields as Molly Barry (Sophie Tucker)

At one time MGM planned to make Sophie Tucker a big movie star. One project they wanted her to do was *Molly and Me*. They eventually dropped the idea, and *Molly and Me* went to Gracie Fields instead.[138]

Mommie Dearest (1981)

Faye Dunaway as Joan Crawford (Anne Bancroft)

Anne Bancroft was initially cast as Joan Crawford. Bancroft was presented with numerous versions of the script. Bancroft was dissatisfied with every version and quit. She was replaced by Faye Dunaway.[139] The film was panned so much that Dunaway's career has never recovered.

Mona Lisa (1986)

Bob Hoskins as George (Sean Connery)

Sean Connery was director Neil Jordan's first choice to star as George. He was unavailable and the director met with Bob Hoskins. He thought the actor was right for the part and changed the script to suit Hoskins.

Monkey Business (1952)

Ginger Rogers as Edwina Fulton (Ava Gardner)

Director Howard Hawks was interested in Ava Gardner for the part of Edwina Fulton. Twentieth Century–Fox vetoed Gardner in favor of Ginger Rogers.[140]

Monsieur Verdoux (1947)

Isabel Elsom as Madame Grosnay (Edna Purviance)

Charlie Chaplin asked his former co-star Edna Purviance to audition for the part of Madame Grosnay. He had not seen the actress in twenty years. She read for the role, but ultimately Chaplin decided she was not right for the part and cast Isabel Elsom instead.[141]

Monster's Ball (2001)

Halle Berry as Leticia Musgrove (Angela Bassett, Vanessa Williams)

Both Angela Bassett and Vanessa Williams turned down Halle Berry's Academy Award winning role in *Monster's Ball*. Michael Paseornek, the president of Lion's Gate production, said that only Berry was officially offered the part. He claims that Bassett said she was unavailable before she ever saw the script. Bassett's agent, Peter

Charlie Chaplin thought of his old friend Edna Purviance for a part in *Monsieur Verdoux*.

Levine said that there wasn't a formal offer, but she did receive the script.[142]

The Moon and Sixpence (1942)

Elena Verdugo as Ata (Yvonne De Carlo)

Yvonne De Carlo was asked to make a screen test for the part of Ata in *The Moon and Sixpence*. Her audition went so well, that De Carlo thought the part was hers. She later received the heartbreaking news that she had lost out to Elena Verdugo.[143]

Moonstruck (1987)

Cher as Loretta Castorini (Sally Field)

Moonstruck was originally planned as a Sally Field film. Field eventually decided against doing the movie, and the role went to Cher, who won an Oscar for her performance.[144]

More American Graffiti (1979)

[*Curt*— Richard Dreyfuss]

Richard Dreyfuss wanted more money than George Lucas was willing to pay, so Dreyfuss turned down *More American Graffiti*.[145]

Morituri (1965)

Marlon Brando as Robert Crain (Charlton Heston)

Charlton Heston turned down Marlon Brando's role of Robert Crain in *Morituri*.[146]

Moscow on the Hudson (1984)

Robin Williams as Vladimir Ivanoff (Richard Dreyfuss)

Writer/director Paul Mazursky wanted Richard Dreyfuss to play Russian musician Vladimir Ivanoff in *Moscow on the Hudson*. Dreyfuss was unavailable.[147] Mazursky turned to Robin Williams. At the time Williams was best known for starring in the television series *Mork & Mindy*. Williams' performance in *Moscow on the Hudson* was critically acclaimed, earning him a Golden Globe nomination.

The Mosquito Coast (1986)

Harrison Ford as Allie Fox (Robert De Niro)

Robert De Niro considered playing Allie Fox, but eventually passed. Harrison Ford was then considered. Ford took the part against the advice of his agent Patricia McQueeney. *The Mosquito Coast* was not a hit, but Ford has said that he has never regretted his decision to play the part of Allie Fox.[148]

Mother (1996)

Debbie Reynolds as Beatrice Henderson (Doris Day, Nancy Reagan, Esther Williams)

Director Albert Brooks knew he wanted a legendary leading lady to star opposite him in his film, *Mother*. He offered the part to Doris Day. Day didn't want to come out of retirement. He approached Esther Williams and Nancy Reagan, before deciding on Debbie Reynolds.[149]

Mother Carey's Chickens (1938)

Anne Shirley as Nancy Carey (Joan Bennett, Katharine Hepburn, Ginger Rogers)

Katharine Hepburn, Ginger Rogers, and Joan Bennett all turned down the part of Nancy Carey.[150]

Mother Wore Tights (1947)

Dan Dailey as Frank Burt (Fred Astaire, James Cagney, John Payne)

Fred Astaire and James Cagney were sought for the lead role of Frank Burt in *Mother Wore Tights*. Cagney was interested, but Warner Bros. refused to loan him out. Astaire wanted the script changed to make his character stronger. Darryl Zanuck wanted to keep the script the way it was. Astaire took himself out of consideration. Betty Grable, who was the star of the film wanted John Payne to costar with her instead of Dan Dailey, who the studio was interested in. It was in her contract that she had approval over her leading man. After rehearsing with Dailey she changed her mind and he was given the role.[151]

Moulin Rouge (2001)

Ewan McGregor as Christian (Heath Ledger)

Nicole Kidman as Satine (Courtney Love, Renee Zellweger, Catherine Zeta-Jones)

Director Baz Luhrmann thought that Heath Ledger and Catherine Zeta-Jones might be right for the leads in *Moulin Rouge*. He eventually decided that Zeta-Jones didn't have the right quality for the part. He passed Ledger over because he thought he was too young.[152] Renee Zellweger auditioned.[153] Courtney Love was considered but was turned down in favor of Nicole Kidman. Later on Luhrmann wanted to use a cover version of Nirvana's "Smells Like Teen Spirit" for the film. He needed Love's permission in order to use the song. She agreed. Luhrmann was impressed that, even though she didn't get the part she was still open to helping him. He said that it showed her integrity and character.[154]

Mourning Becomes Electra (1947)

Rosalind Russell as Lavinia Mannon (Greta Garbo)

Greta Garbo rejected the role of Lavinia Mannon.[155]

Mrs. Miniver (1942)

Greer Garson as Kay Miniver (Ann Harding, Norma Shearer)

Norma Shearer and Ann Harding were the first choices to play Mrs. Miniver. Both actresses felt the character was older than they were comfortable playing and said no.[161]

Mrs. Soffel (1984)
Mel Gibson as Ed Biddle (Kevin Costner, Tom Cruise)

Producer Scott Rudin's first choice to play opposite Diane Keaton was Mel Gibson. Director Gillian Armstrong wanted to find an American actor for the part. Tom Cruise screen tested, as did Kevin Costner. Armstrong finally agreed with Rudin that Gibson was the best choice, and gave him the part.[162]

Mrs. Winterbourne (1996)
Brendan Fraser as Hugh/Bill Winterbourne (Matthew McConaughey)

An unknown Matthew McConaughey auditioned for *Mrs. Winterbourne*, but lost out to Brendan Fraser.[163]

The Mummy (1999)
Brendan Fraser as Richard "Rick" O'Connell (Ben Affleck)

Executives at Universal Studios wanted either Ben Affleck or Brendan Fraser to star in *The Mummy*. They got what they wanted. Fraser played the part. The film was a such a big success that a sequel was made two years later called *The Mummy Returns*.[164]

Murder by Death (1976)
Maggie Smith as Dora Charleston (Myrna Loy)

Myrna Loy felt that doing the role of Dora Charleston would have been a poor imitation of her role of Nora Charles in *The Thin Man* movies. She turned the part down and it went to Maggie Smith.[165]

Murder, Inc. (1960)
Peter Falk as Abe "Kid Twist" Peters (Robert Evans)

Robert Evans was offered the role of Peters. He rejected the part, feeling that it wasn't important enough. Peter Falk took the role and was nominated for an Academy Award.[166]

Murder on the Orient Express (1974)
Wendy Hiller as Princess Dragomiroff (Ingrid Bergman, Marlene Dietrich)

Marlene Dietrich and Ingrid Bergman were considered for the role of Princess Dragomiroff. Dietrich was passed over,[167] and Bergman asked for a different role instead.[168] The part she wanted was the dim maid Greta Ohlsson. Director Sidney Lumet wanted Ingrid Bergman in the film, and so he let her play the role she wanted, and gave Princess Dragomiroff to Wendy Hiller instead. Turns out, it was a good move. Ingrid Bergman won the Oscar for her performance in the film.

Music for the Millions (1944)
June Allyson as Barbara Ainsworth (Donna Reed)

Donna Reed was a possibility for the part of musician Barbara Ainsworth in *Music for the Millions*. She was making *The Picture of Dorian Gray*, and shooting was taking a very long time. She had to let the part go to June Allyson.[169]

The Music Man (1962)
Robert Preston as Harold Hill (Cary Grant)

Cary Gant was offered the starring role of Harold Hill. Grant turned it down, and it was played by Robert Preston.[170] Preston originated the role in the Broadway production.

Music of the Heart (1999)
Meryl Streep as Roberta Tzavaras (Madonna)

Madonna was the original choice to play Roberta Tzavaras. In preparing for the film, Madonna spent time with her and learned to play the violin. She dropped out of the project because of creative differences. Madonna was disappointed to not have been in the film, but stated that she was happy she had become friends with Tzavaras.[171] Meryl Streep replaced Madonna.

Mutiny on the Bounty (1935)
Charles Laughton as Captain William Bligh (Wallace Beery)
Franchot Tone as Roger Byam (Robert Montgomery)

Wallace Beery was the original choice for Captain William Bligh with Robert Montgomery playing Roger Byam opposite him. It was soon decided that Beery was too American, and he was replaced with Charles Laughton.[172] Robert Montgomery didn't want to do the film, and the role was taken by Franchot Tone.[173]

My Best Friend's Wedding (1997)

Dermot Mulroney as Michael O'Neal (Matthew Perry)
Cameron Diaz as Kimberly Wallace (Drew Barrymore)

Drew Barrymore was interested in the supporting part of Kimberly Wallace in *My Best Friend's Wedding*. Barrymore didn't get the part. It went to Cameron Diaz instead.[174]

Matthew Perry was considered for the part of Michael, eventually played by Dermot Mulroney.[175]

My Cousin Vinny (1992)

Marisa Tomei as Mona Lisa Vito (Geena Davis)

Geena Davis was asked to play the part of Mona Lisa Vito in *My Cousin Vinny*. Davis didn't think the part was for her and declined.[176] Marisa Tomei was cast instead. At the time, Tomei was mostly unknown. Her biggest part to date was a costarring role on the first season of the NBC sitcom *A Different World*.

Tomei's performance in *My Cousin Vinny* was so good that she was nominated for an Oscar for Best Supporting Actress. Her competition was Judy Davis (*Husbands and Wives*), Joan Plowright (*Enchanted April*), Vanessa Redgrave (*Howards End*) and Miranda Richardson (*Damage*). Jack Palance presented the award. Tomei was the surprise winner. Her victory was so unexpected that a rumor spread that Palance read the wrong name, and that Tomei was not really the winner. There was no truth to the rumor. Tomei was again nominated for Best Supporting Actress nine years later for her performance in *In the Bedroom*.

My Darling Clementine (1946)

Victor Mature as Doc Holliday (James Stewart)
Cathy Downs as Clementine Carter (Jeanne Crain)

James Stewart was the first choice for the part of Doc Holliday. Twentieth Century–Fox later reconsidered, and gave the part to Victor Mature.

Jeanne Crain was sought for the role of Clementine. However, at the time Crain was such a popular actress that Darryl F. Zanuck refused to put her in the small role. He thought that the backlash from the public as well as critics would be too great, and instead gave the part to the much lesser-known Cathy Downs.[177]

My Fair Lady (1964)

Rex Harrison as Prof. Henry Higgins (Richard Burton, Cary Grant, Trevor Howard, Rock Hudson, Laurence Olivier, Peter O'Toole
Audrey Hepburn as Eliza Doolittle (Julie Andrews)
Stanley Holloway as Alfred Doolittle (James Cagney)

Warner Bros. honcho Jack Warner offered Cary Grant the part of Professor Henry Higgins. Alan Jay Lerner told Warner that although he liked Grant, his accent was a Cockney accent — the kind he was trying to rid Eliza Doolittle of! Warner didn't care. Grant did, however.[178] He turned it down, insisting the part should go to Rex Harrison.[179] Harrison had originated the role in the Broadway production. Warner then suggested Rock Hudson, citing that he wasn't a Cockney. Lerner nixed the idea.[180] Another actor Warner was interested in was Trevor Howard, but the actor had little interest in the film.[181]

George Cukor thought that Peter O'Toole was the actor for the part. Alan Jay Lerner suggested a meeting between Cukor, O'Toole, and O'Toole's manager, Jules Buck. Buck made so many demands during negotiations that Jack Warner took O'Toole out of the running.[182]

Richard Burton was considered along with Laurence Olivier, who turned it down.[183]

The casting of Eliza Doolittle caused quite a controversy. Everyone assumed that the part would go to Julie Andrews. Andrews became a Broadway star when she created the role of Eliza in the original production. But studio boss Jack Warner wanted a movie star in the role. He chose Audrey Hepburn over Andrews even though Andrews would have been able to do all her own singing.[184] With Hepburn in the role, Marni Nixon was hired to dub her vocals.

Warner wanted to cast James Cagney as Alfred Doolittle, but he turned it down, and the part went to Stanley Holloway.[185]

My Forbidden Past (1951)

Robert Mitchum as Mark Lucas (Mel Ferrer)
Ava Gardner as Barbara Beaurevel (Ann Sheridan)

Ann Sheridan was promised the role of Barbara Beaurevel in *My Forbidden Past*. Part of her contract stipulated that she had casting approval. However, she and RKO head Howard Hughes clashed over who would be her costar. Sheridan liked Robert Mitchum. Hughes disagreed; he was interested Mel Ferrer. After much trying Hughes and Sheridan were unable to agree. He dropped her from the film and cast Ava Gardner instead. Sheridan sued RKO for breach of contract. She won, and was awarded $55,000. Gardner's costar, ironically, was Robert Mitchum.[186]

My Gal Sal (1942)

Rita Hayworth as Sally Elliott (Alice Faye, Betty Grable)

Alice Faye was first offered the part of Sally Elliott. She was pregnant, and had to turn it down.[187] Betty Grable was also considered.[188] The part went to Rita Hayworth instead.

My Man Godfrey (1936)

William Powell as Godfrey "Duke" Parke (Ronald Colman)

Carole Lombard as Irene Bullock (Constance Bennett, Joan Bennett)

Charles R. Rogers bought the rights to *My Man Godfrey*. He imagined Constance Bennett starring as Irene Bullock. He was interested in having Gregory LaCava direct the film. LaCava and Bennett worked together previously on the film *The Affairs of Cellini*. He wasn't all that interested in working with Bennett again. He suggested that either she or her sister Joan Bennett would be right for the part. LaCava favored Joan Bennett. He thought that she was the superior actress and more pleasant of the two. Ronald Colman wanted the title role of Godfrey, but LaCava wanted to cast William Powell. Powell requested that his ex-wife, Carole Lombard, be cast as Irene. Lombard accepted the job, and the Bennett sisters were out.[189]

My Own Private Idaho (1991)

River Phoenix as Mike Waters (Michael Parker)

Keanu Reeves as Scott Favor (Rodney Harvey)

Writer/director Gus Van Sant initially wanted to use unknown actors for the starring roles in *My Own Private Idaho*. To play narcoleptic Mike Waters, Van Sant chose Michael Parker. Parker appeared in a bit part in Van Sant's earlier film,

Rodney Harvey almost got to play hustler Scott Favor in *My Own Private Idaho*.

Drugstore Cowboy. Parker had once been homeless, and was Van Sant's inspiration for the character. For the part of Scott Van Sant wanted Rodney Harvey. Harvey was also cast in *Drugstore Cowboy*, but had to be replaced due to a drug problem. Since that time, Harvey landed a co-starring role on the television series *The Outsiders*. After a while, Van Sant reconsidered his decision to use unknowns. His career had just started to take off, and he was now in the position of being able to get actors for his films that he never could before. He submitted his script to both River Phoenix's and Keanu Reeves' agents. Reeves loved the script so much that he decided to talk to Phoenix himself to urge him to sign on. After much consideration Phoenix agreed to play the part. Van Sant recast Michael Parker as Digger, and moved Rodney Harvey to the part of Gary.[190]

Myra Breckinridge (1970)

Raquel Welch as Myra Breckinridge (Anne Bancroft, Elizabeth Taylor)

Raquel Welch was cast as Myra Breckinridge after both Elizabeth Taylor and Anne Bancroft turned it down.[191]

Nashville (1975)

Henry Gibson as Haven Hamilton (Robert Duvall)
Ronee Blakely as Barbara Jean (Susan Anspach)
Keith Carradine as Tom Frank (Gary Busey)
Allan Nicholls as Bill (Keith Carradine)
Lily Tomlin as Linnea Reese (Louise Fletcher)
Barbara Harris as Albuquerque (Bette Midler, Bernadette Peters)
David Hayward as Kenny Fraiser (Michael Burns)

The role of Haven Hamilton was turned down by Robert Duvall.

Susan Anspach was set for Barbara Jean, but dropped out. She was replaced by Ronee Blakely.

Director Robert Altman initially had Keith Carradine in mind to play Bill, with Gary Busey cast as Tom. Busey chose to instead make a television pilot called *The Texas Wheelers*. Altman decided that Carradine would switch roles and cast him as ladies' man Tom. Carradine hated being seen in that manner, but agreed to the switch anyway. Carradine recommended Allan Nicholls to Altman to replace him as Bill. The two actors worked together in *Hair* in New York. When Nicholls arrived at his interview with Altman, Altman asked him one question, "Want to be in our movie?" Nicholls said, "Sure." Altman gave him the part.

Louise Fletcher was married to producer Jerry Bick. Fletcher helped create the character of Linnea Reese. The character was a housewife who was the mother of deaf children. In real life Fletcher's parents are deaf. Fletcher planned to play the part, but Altman and Bick had a falling out. Altman gave the part to Lily Tomlin instead.

Altman considered Bernadette Peters and Bette Midler for the part of Albuquerque. Midler was made an offer, but turned Altman down. The role was played by Barbara Harris instead.

Altman considered Michael Burns for the part of Kenny Fraiser, but eventually opted for David Hayward instead.[1]

National Velvet (1944)

Donald Crisp as Mr. Brown (Spencer Tracy)

At one time Spencer Tracy was a contender for the part of Mr. Brown. Tracy's participation with the film fell through, and the part went to Donald Crisp instead.[2]

Natural Born Killers (1994)

Woody Harrelson as Mickey Knox (Kevin Costner, Mel Gibson, Ray Liotta, Michael Madsen, Tom Sizemore)
Robert Downey, Jr., as Wayne Gayle (Geraldo Rivera)
Tommy Lee Jones as Dwight McClusky (Jack Palance)

Michael Madsen was director Oliver Stone's first choice for the role of Mickey Knox.[3] Madsen claims he turned down the role,[4] although Stone says the decision was made by Warner Bros. The studio didn't have confidence that Madsen would bring audiences in and told Stone that if he were cast, the budget would be $10 million. Stone felt that that wasn't enough money for the film, and Madsen was out. Stone was asked to consider more bankable stars including Mel Gibson and Kevin Costner.[5] Ray Liotta was suggested to Stone. Stone didn't think that Liotta was sexy enough to play Mickey. Tom Sizemore wanted the part, but Stone thought he was better suited for the part of Jack Scagnetti.[6] Another actor that Warner Bros. liked was Woody Harrelson. Stone met with Harrelson and decided that he was the right actor for the role.[7]

Stone considered casting Geraldo Rivera in the role of tabloid journalist Wayne Gayle, but decided to go with an actor instead. He wanted someone who would be able to bring a Geraldo-like quality to the part. Stone knew that Robert Downey, Jr., could do just that, and gave him the part.[8]

Jack Palance was offered the part of Warden McClusky. Palance thought the film was too violent and said no. Stone tried to convince him to change his mind to no avail. Tommy Lee Jones was eventually cast in his place.[9]

Neighbors (1981)

John Belushi as Earl Keese (Dan Aykroyd)
Kathryn Walker as Enid Keese (Penny Marshall)

Director John Avildsen had a meeting with John Belushi to discuss the film *Neighbors*. Avildsen told Belushi he was thinking of him for the part of Earl Keese. Belushi told Avildsen that he thought he should play the abrasive Vic. The director told Belushi that he had played parts similar to Vic before. Belushi wasn't opposed to repeating himself, but Avildsen convinced him to try the other part. Belushi's friend Dan Aykroyd was cast as Vic.

Penny Marshall auditioned for the part of Enid, but lost out to Kathryn Walker.[10]

Network (1976)

William Holden as Max Schumacher (Peter Finch, Robert Mitchum)
Faye Dunaway as Diana Christensen (Jane Fonda)
Peter Finch as Howard Beale (John Chancellor, Walter Cronkite, Henry Fonda, Glenn Ford, William Holden, George C. Scott)

The list of possible Diana Christensens was narrowed down to two actresses: Jane Fonda and Faye Dunaway. Fonda decided she didn't want it, and Dunaway was cast.[11] She went on to win an Oscar for her performance.

Dunaway suggested Robert Mitchum to director Sidney Lumet for the role of Max Schumacher.[12] Lumet nixed the idea and explored the possibility of Peter Finch playing Max with William Holden cast opposite him as Howard Beale.[13] Holden preferred the character of Max Schumacher.[14] He was cast in the role after Sidney Lumet was convinced that the Australian Peter Finch could play Howard Beale with a believable American accent.

Real-life newscasters Walter Cronkite and John Chancellor were thought of to play Howard Beale, but the idea was scrapped.[15] First choice Henry Fonda rejected the role along with George C. Scott and Glenn Ford.[16]

Never on Sunday (1960)

Jules Dassin as Homer (Henry Fonda, Van Johnson, Jack Lemmon)

After being unable to get Henry Fonda, Jack Lemmon, or Van Johnson for *Never on Sunday*, director Jules Dassin gave himself the part.[17]

Never So Few (1959)

Steve McQueen as Bill Ringa (Sammy Davis, Jr.)

According to Sammy Davis, Jr., he was too busy to take the role of Corporal Ringa in *Never So Few*. However, Davis' former manager Hilly Elkins disputed this. He claims that it was the star of the film, Frank Sinatra, that was the reason for Davis' departure form the film. During an interview, Davis was asked who the bigger star was: him or Sinatra. Davis said that he was bigger than Sinatra. Shortly afterwards, Davis was off the film. He was replaced by another one of Hilly Elkins' clients, Steve McQueen.[18]

Next Stop, Greenwich Village (1976)

Lenny Baker as Larry Lapinsky (Richard Dreyfuss)

Writer/director Paul Mazursky wanted Richard Dreyfuss to star as Larry Lapinsky in his semi autobiographical film, *Next Stop, Greenwich Village*. Dreyfuss turned him down, and Lenny Baker was cast instead.[19]

Niagara (1953)

Marilyn Monroe as Rose Loomis (Anne Baxter)

Niagara was announced as an Anne Baxter vehicle at one time. Baxter fell through, and the starring role of Rose Loomis was played by Marilyn Monroe.[20]

Niagara Falls (1933)

Shirley Temple as Child (Cora Sue Collins)

Cora Sue Collins was cast as a young child in *Niagara Falls*. The five-year-old Collins was too big for the part and she was replaced by a four-year-old Shirley Temple.[21]

Nicholas and Alexandra (1971)

Janet Suzman as Alexandra (Audrey Hepburn, Grace Kelly)

Audrey Hepburn felt that she too old to play the role of Alexandra.[22] Hepburn was around 40 at the time. Grace Kelly was offered the part. She wasn't impressed with the script and said no. Janet Suzman was cast instead. Suzman earned an Oscar nomination for her work in the film.[23]

Nick of Time (1995)

Johnny Depp as Gene Watson (John Travolta)

Johnny Depp was given the lead role of Gene Wilson after it had been turned down by John Travolta.[24]

The Night of the Following Day (1969)

Richard Boone as Leer (Marlon Brando)

Marlon Brando was cast as Leer in *The Night of the Following Day*. He had problems with director Hubert Cornfield and was replaced by Richard Boone.[27]

The Night of the Iguana (1964)

Richard Burton as The Rev. T. Lawrence Shannon (Marlon Brando, Richard Harris, William Holden)

Ava Gardner as Maxine Faulk (Bette Davis)

William Holden, Marlon Brando, and Richard Harris were all thought of for the role that went to Richard Burton.[28]

Bette Davis originated the role of Maxine Faulk on Broadway. She lost out to Ava Gardner for the film version. Davis was very disappointed to lose the part.[29]

Night Shift (1982)

Michael Keaton as Bill Blazejowski (John Travolta, Henry Winkler)

Director Ron Howard considered John Travolta for the part of Bill Blazejowski in *Night Shift*.[30] He decided that Michael Keaton was better suited to the part.

9½ Weeks (1986)

Kim Basinger as Elizabeth (Lonette McKee)

Lonette McKee went after the starring role of Elizabeth. The biracial McKee was told she was too exotic for the part. Kim Basinger was cast instead.[31]

1941 (1979)

Robert Stack as Joseph W. Stilwell (John Wayne)

John Wayne was offered the part of Maj. Gen. Joseph W. Stilwell. The patriotic Wayne didn't like that there was a scene in which two American aircraft crashed, and turned the part down. Robert Stack was hired for the role.[32]

Ninotchka (1939)

Melvyn Douglas as Count Leon D'Algout (Cary Grant, William Powell)

At the age of five Cora Sue Collins lost a part to a younger actress (*Niagara Falls*).

Nickelodeon (1976)

Brian Keith as H.H. Cobb (Orson Welles)

Jane Hitchcock as Kathleen Cooke (Cybill Shepherd)

Writer/director Peter Bogdanovich wanted his girlfriend Cybill Shepherd to play the role of Kathleen Cooke in his upcoming movie *Nickelodeon*. At the same time Shepherd was offered the part of Betsy in Martin Scorsese's *Taxi Driver*. Columbia Pictures was producing both films. David Begelman, the president of Columbia Pictures, told Shepherd that she would not be able to do both films. She had to make a choice. Bogdanovich wrote the part of Kathleen specifically for Shepherd. However, she also thought that she would not be taken seriously if she were to work with Bogdanovich again. Their last film, *At Long Last Love*, bombed. Shepherd was not well respected in the industry, and couldn't afford more criticism.[25] She chose *Taxi Driver*. Shepherd had good instincts. *Nickelodeon* was a flop, while *Taxi Driver* has become a classic.

Orson Welles was considered for the part of H.H. Cobb.[26]

Lonette McKee tried to win the starring role in *9½ Weeks*.

William Powell didn't want to play second banana to leading lady Greta Garbo, and turned down the role of Count Leon D'Algout.[33] Cary Grant was a candidate, but the part was eventually played by Melvyn Douglas.[34]

Nixon (1995)

Anthony Hopkins as Richard Nixon (Warren Beatty, Gee Hackman, Tom Hanks, Dustin Hoffman, Tommy Lee Jones, John Malkovich, Jack Nicholson, Robin Williams)
Joan Allen as Pat Nixon (Jessica Lange)
Paul Sorvino as Henry Kissinger (John Turturro)

Director Oliver Stone's first choice to play Richard Nixon was Tom Hanks. Hanks had previously been involved with Disney for a film titled *The Passion of Richard Nixon*. Stone offered Hanks the part, but he wasn't interested and turned him down. Turndowns also came from Dustin Hoffman and Jack Nicholson. Gene Hackman was a possibility as was Robin Williams. Williams read the script and decided he didn't want to do it. Tommy Lee Jones met with Stone to discuss playing the part. He persuaded Stone to give him a painting that was on the wall. Stone agreed, but Jones still refused to do the film. Stone was interested in Warren Beatty. Beatty wanted to make many changes in the script. Stone decided to move on. Stone discussed the part with John Malkovich. Malkovich got the false impression that Stone had made him an offer. At the same time Stone was also considering Anthony Hopkins, who he decided to give the part to. When Malkovich found out he was upset. He spoke to Stone about the situation. Stone stuck to his guns. Anthony Hopkins was nominated for an Oscar for his performance in the film.

Stone considered Jessica Lange to play Pat Nixon. However when Warren Beatty was involved with the project he wanted to do a reading. Joan Allen played Pat. Her reading was so good Stone cast her in the film.[35]

John Turturro rejected the role of Henry Kissinger.[36]

No Man of Her Own (1932)

Clark Gable as Babe Stewart (George Raft)
Carole Lombard as Connie Randall (Miriam Hopkins)

George Raft was an early consideration to star in *No Man of Her Own*. Eventually Clark Gable and Miriam Hopkins were set for the leads. When Hopkins found out that Gable was going to be billed first she demanded to be released from the film. Her replacement was Carole Lombard.[37]

No Small Affair (1984)

Jon Cryer as Charles Cummings (Matthew Broderick)
Demi Moore as Laura Victor (Sally Field)

Sally Field and Matthew Broderick were signed for the leads in *No Small Affair*. The film started production in early 1981. It became clear soon after that director Martin Ritt was suffering from exhaustion. He became unable to continue with the film, and production was put on hold. Mark Rydell considered replacing Ritt. However, Rydell was still working on *On Golden Pond* and wanted to delay shooting *No Small Affair* until that summer. The problem with that was that the footage Ritt already shot was shot during the winter! The studio shut down the film for three years. Jerry Schatzberg directed with Demi Moore and Jon Cryer in the lead roles.[38]

No Way Out (1950)
Linda Darnell as Edie Johnson (Anne Baxter)

Linda Darnell was chosen over Anne Baxter for the role of Edie Johnson.[39]

Noises Off (1992)
Carol Burnett as Dotty Otley (Audrey Hepburn)

Director Peter Bogdanovich wanted Audrey Hepburn for his leading lady. Hepburn considered the offer, but eventually said no. Bogdanovich gave the part to Carol Burnett.[40]

Norma Rae (1979)
Sally Field as Norma Rae (Jill Clayburgh, Faye Dunaway, Jane Fonda, Marsha Mason, Tuesday Weld)

Tuesday Weld was one of the first choices for the title role of Norma Rae. Weld didn't want the part and said no.[41] Director Martin Ritt offered the part to Jane Fonda. Fonda turned him down.[42] Ritt went on to offer the part to Faye Dunaway[43] and Jill Clayburgh,[44] who also rejected the role. Marsha Mason was another possibility. Mason wanted to play the part very much. The problem was that if she took the job she would be away from her husband, playwright Neil Simon, for two months. Not wanting to put a strain on her marriage, Mason declined the offer.[45] At that point Ritt met with Sally Field, who wanted the part terribly. She was so persuasive in her interview that by the end of it Ritt decided that she was the best choice.

Norma Rae was both a commercial and critical hit. Field won an Oscar for her performance. Oddly enough, her competition included Jill Clayburgh for *Starting Over*, Jane Fonda for *The China Syndrome*, and Marsha Mason for *Chapter Two*.

North by Northwest (1959)
Cary Grant as Roger O. Thornhill (James Stewart)
Eva Marie Saint as Eve Kendall (Cyd Charisse, Sophia Loren)

The lead role was initially supposed to be played by Jimmy Stewart. Director Alfred Hitchcock gave the part to Cary Grant, feeling he was more suited to the film.

Schedule conflicts prevented Sophia Loren from taking the part of Eve. Cyd Charisse was considered by MGM, but Hitchcock preferred Eva Marie Saint.[46]

The North Star (1943)
Anne Baxter as Marina (Teresa Wright)

Teresa Wright dropped out of *The North Star* because she was pregnant.[47] Anne Baxter stepped in as her replacement.

Northwest Passage (1940)
Robert Young as Langdon Towne (Robert Taylor)

Robert Taylor decided against appearing in *Northwest Passage*. He was replaced by Robert Young.[48]

Nothing in Common (1986)
Jackie Gleason as Max Basner (Sid Caesar, Dick Van Dyke)

Possible choices for the role of Max included Dick Van Dyke and Sid Caesar. Director Garry Marshall offered the role to Jackie Gleason. At first Gleason turned him down. Marshall told Gleason that if he didn't do the film his last movie would be *Smokey and the Bandit III*. Gleason agreed to do *Nothing in Common*.[49]

Notorious (1946)
Claude Rains as Alexander Sebastian (Clifton Webb)
Leopoldine Konstantin as Madame Sebastian (Ethel Barrymore)

Alfred Hitchcock's first choice for the role that Claude Rains played was Clifton Webb.

Ethel Barrymore was wanted for Leopoldine Konstantin's part, but she turned it down.[50]

Now, Voyager (1942)
Bette Davis as Charlotte Vale (Irene Dunne, Ginger Rogers, Norma Shearer)
Paul Henreid as Jerry D. Durance (Charles Boyer, George Brent, Henry Fonda, Fredric March)

Irene Dunne and Charles Boyer were the first choices to star in *Now, Voyager*. When Norma Shearer hinted that she might want the part, Dunne was put on the back burner. When Shearer finally moved on, Dunne was unavailable.[51] Bette Davis was signed for the role. Problems arose and Davis left the film. She found out that Ginger Rogers was being considered as a replacement and returned to the role.[52]

Henry Fonda, Fredric March, and George Brent were all considered to play Jerry, but the role went to Paul Henreid instead.[53]

Nurse Betty (2000)

Renee Zellweger as Betty Sizemore (Jodie Foster)

Jodie Foster was interested in the title role of Betty. Her interest waned when she was offered $15 million to star in *Anna and the King*. Foster signed on for the part of Anna, and Renee Zellweger was cast as Betty.[54]

Nuts (1987)

Barbra Streisand as Claudia Draper (Bette Midler, Debra Winger)
Richard Dreyfuss as Aaron Levinsky (Alan Arkin, Marlon Brando, Jeff Bridges, Robert De Niro, Robert Duvall, Peter Falk, Richard Gere, Elliott Gould, Dustin Hoffman, Bob Hoskins, Kevin Kline, Ron Leibman, John Malkovich, Paul Newman, Al Pacino, Sean Penn)
Karl Malden as Arthur Kirk (Richard Basehart, Kirk Douglas, Jose Ferrer, Ben Gazzara, Burt Lancaster, Robert Mitchum, Gregory Peck, George C. Scott, Richard Widmark)

Bette Midler was considered for the lead role of Claudia Draper.[55] Debra Winger was offered the part. She turned it down.[56] Director Mark Rydell knew that Barbra Streisand was interested in the film. She was sent a copy of the script and eventually agreed to take the part. Rydell clashed with Warner Bros. and he was replaced with Martin Ritt.[57]

The role of Aaron Levinsky was rejected by Paul Newman, Al Pacino, Robert De Niro, Marlon Brando, Robert Duvall, Jeff Bridges, Kevin Kline, Elliott Gould, and Richard Gere. For a short time it looked as if Dustin Hoffman might play the part, but a deal wasn't made. Sean Penn, John Malkovich, Peter Falk, Alan Arkin, Bob Hoskins, and Ron Leibman all wanted the part, but lost out to Richard Dreyfuss.

Gregory Peck, George C. Scott, Burt Lancaster, Kirk Douglas, Robert Mitchum, Jose Ferrer, and Richard Widmark were all approached for the part of Arthur Kirk, but none of these actors were interested. Ben Gazzara was considered, as was Richard Basehart. Basehart was pursued until the producers found out he was dead. The role went instead to Karl Malden.[58]

O (2001)

Julia Stiles as Desi Brable (Natasha Lyonne, Mena Suvari)

Mena Suvari and Natasha Lyonne were both considered for the part of Desi Brable. Instead the part went to Julia Stiles.[1]

The Object of My Affection (1998)

Jennifer Aniston as Nina Borowski (Sarah Jessica Parker, Winona Ryder, Kyra Sedgwick, Uma Thurman, Debra Winger)
Paul Rudd as George Hanson (Robert Downey, Jr., Matthew Modine, Keanu Reeves)

Very early on, Debra Winger and Matthew Modine had been considered for the leads.[2] Another possible pair was former couple Sarah Jessica Parker and Robert Downey, Jr.[3] Winona Ryder, Uma Thurman, and Kyra Sedgwick were all connected to the project at various times.[4] Keanu Reeves came close to playing George,[5] but ultimately the parts went to Jennifer Aniston and Paul Rudd.

Ocean's 11 (2001)

Matt Damon as Linus Zerga (Mark Wahlberg)
Andy Garcia as Harry Benedict (Ralph Fiennes)
Vladimir Klitschko as Himself (Mike Tyson)

Mark Wahlberg turned down the supporting part of Linus Zerga to star in the remake of *Planet of the Apes*.[6]

Director Steven Soderbergh talked with Ralph Fiennes about the role of Harry Benedict. Soderbergh cast Andy Garcia instead, and was happy with his choice. Says Soderbergh, "I love Andy Garcia in this. He's not afraid to play the role."[7]

Soderbergh initially wanted Mike Tyson to play himself. In the film he would have boxed against Lennox Lewis. The two real life boxers were not on good terms. Soderbergh thought that having them both on the set might be very tense. Tyson wanted to make the film, but Soderbergh felt he could only have one of them and chose Lewis instead. He replaced Tyson with Vladimir Klitschko.[8]

Octopussy (1983)
Roger Moore as James Bond (James Brolin)

Roger Moore was not sure whether or not he was interested in reprising his role as James Bond for *Octopussy*. Producer Cubby Broccoli screen tested James Brolin. Brolin auditioned alongside Maud Adams. Ultimately, Roger Moore decided to return to the role.[9]

Of Human Bondage (1934)
Bette Davis as Mildred Rogers (Irene Dunne, Ann Harding, Katharine Hepburn)

Bette Davis was cast as Mildred Rogers after the part had been turned down by Katharine Hepburn, Irene Dunne, and Ann Harding.[10]

Of Mice and Men (1939)
Betty Field as Curley's Wife (Evelyn Keyes)

Evelyn Keyes screen tested for the role of Curley's wife, but lost the part to Betty Field.[11]

Office Space (1999)
Ron Livingston as Peter Gibbons (Ben Affleck)

Ben Affleck was offered the starring role of Peter Gibbons in *Office Space*.[12] Affleck decided not to take the part. Ron Livingston was cast instead.

An Officer and a Gentleman (1982)
Richard Gere as Zack Mayo (Kevin Costner, John Denver, Dennis Quaid, Eric Roberts, John Travolta)
Louis Gossett, Jr., as Sgt. Emil Foley (Scott Glenn, Jack Nicholson, Mandy Patinkin)

Producer Jerry Weintraub planned to make *An Officer and a Gentleman* with John Denver cast as Zack Mayo. Weintraub eventually sold the rights to the film.[13] The role of Zack Mayo was first offered to John Travolta. At the time Travolta was enrolled in a 21-day flying course and didn't want to have his lessons interrupted.[14] Kevin Costner, Dennis Quaid and Eric Roberts all auditioned. Roberts made a good impression. He was made an offer which he rejected. His former agent, Gary Lucchesi, said that Roberts wanted to make an after school special instead. Richard Gere was asked to play Mayo. He turned the part down at first, but eventually changed his mind and signed for the film.[15]

Scott Glenn rejected the supporting role of Sgt. Foley.[16] Jack Nicholson was considered, as was Mandy Patinkin. Producer Martin Elfand thought that Patinkin's audition was outstanding, but director Taylor Hackford didn't want to cast him. The part went to Louis Gossett, Jr. Gossett won an Oscar for his performance in the film.[17]

Oklahoma! (1955)
Gordon MacRae as Curly McClain (Montgomery Clift, James Dean, Paul Newman)
Shirley Jones as Laurey Williams (Eva Marie Saint, Joanne Woodward)
Rod Steiger as Jud Fry (Eli Wallach)
Gloria Grahame as Ado Annie Carnes (Debbie Reynolds)

Real-life husband and wife Paul Newman and Joanne Woodward were briefly considered for the leads in the film version of *Oklahoma!*[18] Montgomery Clift was a possibility for Curly, while Eva Marie Saint was a potential Laurey. Rod Steiger and Eli Wallach competed for the part of Jud Fry. Steiger was to test with Paul Newman. However Newman was late so director Fred Zinnemann had him test with James Dean.[19] Dean sang "Poor Jud Is Dead" with Rod Steiger playing Jud. His voice wasn't extremely strong, but Zinnemann calls the test a classic.[20]

Debbie Reynolds tried for the part of Ado Annie but lost out to non-singer Gloria Grahame.[21]

Old Acquaintance (1943)
Miriam Hopkins as Mildred Drake (Constance Bennett, Janet Gaynor, Norma Shearer, Margaret Sullavan)

Bette Davis wanted Norma Shearer to play her rival, Mildred Drake. Shearer didn't want to play the mother of an adult child. She also refused to accept second billing to Davis.[22] The part was given to Miriam Hopkins instead. When Miriam Hopkins proved to be trouble on the set, director Edmund Goulding considered Margaret Sullavan, Constance Bennett, or Janet Gaynor as a replacement if necessary. Hopkins stayed in line and Goulding allowed her to stay with the film.[23]

Old Gringo (1989)

Gregory Peck as Ambrose Bierce (Burt Lancaster, Paul Newman)

Paul Newman was the first actor who was supposed to play the role of Ambrose Bierce. Newman unexpectedly left the film. He was replaced by Burt Lancaster. Lancaster had a history of heart problems, and the studio decided it would be too expensive to insure him. They dropped him and cast Gregory Peck instead.[24]

The Old Maid (1939)

George Brent as Clem Spender (Humphrey Bogart)

Humphrey Bogart was set to play Clem Spender, but was fired early in the filming.[25] The part went to George Brent instead.

Oliver! (1968)

Ron Moody as Fagin (Peter Sellers)
Shani Wallis as Nancy (Shirley Bassey)

Peter Sellers was initially cast as Fagin. Sellers later decided against doing the film. The part was recast with Ron Moody. Moody originated the role in the stage version of *Oliver!*

Shirley Bassey was director Carol Reed's first choice for the part of Nancy. Columbia Pictures worried that having a black actress in the role wouldn't go over well in the South. The studio had Reed give the part to another actress. His choice was Shani Wallis.[26]

The Omega Man (1971)

Rosalind Cash as Lisa (Diahann Carroll)

Director Boris Sagal ignored Warner Bros.' choice of Diahann Carroll for the part of Lisa in *The Omega Man*. Sagal cast the unknown Rosalind Cash instead.[27]

The Omen (1976)

Gregory Peck as Robert Thorn (Charlton Heston)

Charlton Heston was offered the starring role of Robert Thorn in *The Omen*. Heston didn't want to go to Europe where the film was being shot and turned the part down.[28] Gregory Peck was signed for the role. The film was a big hit. Heston later said that he was sorry he had turned it down.[29]

On a Clear Day You Can See Forever (1970)

Barbra Streisand as Daisy Gamble (Audrey Hepburn)
Yves Montand as Dr. Marc Chabot (Richard Harris, Gregory Peck, Frank Sinatra)

The role of Daisy Gamble was first offered to Barbra Streisand. Streisand had just given birth to her son Jason and was not ready to go back to work. Audrey Hepburn was next on the list. Hepburn said that some of the scenes reminded her of *My Fair Lady*. Not wanting to repeat herself, she said no. Streisand was contacted again. She was offered $350,000. In addition she would have a say on who was hired in any creative position. Streisand couldn't resist, and signed on.[30]

Richard Harris was just about set for the part of Dr. Marc Chabot. Suddenly Harris decided he didn't want to do it after all. Producer Howard W. Koch said that Harris had gotten a better offer somewhere else.[31] Gregory Peck and Frank Sinatra were both asked to play the role. Neither wanted it.[32] Koch then remembered Yves Montand. He thought that the French actor would be perfect. He arranged for Streisand to meet him. Montand turned on the charm, and Streisand gave her approval.[33]

On Golden Pond (1981)

Katharine Hepburn as Ethel Thayer (Greer Garson, Barbara Stanwyck)

Greer Garson and Barbara Stanwyck both tried to get the role Katharine Hepburn played in *On Golden Pond*.[34]

On Her Majesty's Secret Service (1969)

George Lazenby as James Bond (Robert Campbell, Sean Connery, Hans de Vries, John Richardson, Anthony Rogers)
Diana Rigg as Tracy (Brigitte Bardot, Catherine Deneuve)

When Sean Connery decided not to reprise his role as James Bond, a search was on for a new leading man. Producers Albert "Cubby" Broccoli and Harry Saltzman narrowed the competition down to five actors: George Lazenby, Robert Campbell, Hans de Vries, John Richardson and Anthony Rogers. Lazenby did well in a screen test in which the character fights, and was chosen as the new James Bond.[35]

Director Peter Hunt wanted Brigitte Bardot to play Tracy. He and Harry Saltzman went to France to see her. She was already committed to the film *Shalako* and had to turn them down. Catherine Deneuve was the second choice. Deneuve said no. Diana Rigg was cast as Tracy.[36]

On the Waterfront (1954)

Marlon Brando as Terry Molloy (Montgomery Clift, Frank Sinatra)
Rod Steiger as Charley Molloy (Lawrence Tierney)
Eva Marie Saint as Edie Doyle (Grace Kelly)

Montgomery Clift was considered for the role of Terry Molloy, but director Elia Kazan had another actor in mind — Frank Sinatra. Kazan liked Sinatra, and, since Montgomery Clift had turned the part down, Sinatra was cast.[37] Shortly after, producer Sam Spiegel decided he would rather have Marlon Brando in the role. Sinatra was let go, and promptly sued Spiegel for breach of contract.[38]

Lawrence Tierney was an early choice for the part of Charley Molloy. Tierney asked for a large amount of money. Elia Kazan was no longer interested. Rod Steiger made a splash on television with the film *Marty*. Kazan saw Steiger a few days after it aired. He hadn't seen *Marty*, but had heard so many great things about Steiger's performance. He suggested that Steiger go up for the part of Charley. Steiger won the part, and was nominated for an Oscar for his performance.[39]

Grace Kelly had a choice to make. She was offered the female lead in two films, and she had to choose between them. One was *On the Waterfront*, the other *Rear Window*. She opted for *Rear Window* and the part of Edie Doyle went to Eva Marie Saint.[40]

Once in a Lifetime (1932)

Aline MacMahon as May Daniels (Barbara Stanwyck)

Barbara Stanwyck coveted the role of May Daniels, but lost out to Aline MacMahon.[41]

Once Upon a Dream (1947)

Googie Withers as Carol Gilbert (Margaret Lockwood)

The part of Carol Gilbert was assigned to Margaret Lockwood. She refused to play it, and was suspended by Rank, her studio. Googie Withers was brought in as her replacement.[42]

One Desire (1955)

Anne Baxter as Tacey Cromwell (Jeanne Crain)

Jeanne Crain was once set for the part of Tacey Cromwell in *One Desire*. Crain's participation with the film fell through, and the role was played instead by Anne Baxter.[43]

One Flew Over the Cuckoo's Nest (1975)

Jack Nicholson as Randle McMurphy (Marlon Brando, James Caan, Kirk Douglas, Gene Hackman, Burt Reynolds)
Louise Fletcher as Nurse Mildred Ratched (Anne Bancroft, Ellen Burstyn, Colleen Dewhurst, Jane Fonda, Angela Lansbury, Geraldine Page, Lily Tomlin)

Kirk Douglas starred in *One Flew Over the Cuckoo's Nest* on Broadway. He wanted very much to reprise his role in on screen. He bought the rights and tried to get a film made. He ran into difficulties and eventually outgrew the role. At that point he gave the project to his son, Michael Douglas, to produce. Douglas wanted either Marlon Brando or Gene Hackman to star, but was turned down by both of them.[44] James Caan was also offered the chance to star, but decided against making the film.[45] Douglas and director Milos Forman searched for a leading man, and finally narrowed it down to a choice between two actors: Burt Reynolds and Jack Nicholson. Reynolds wanted the part very, very much. Director Milos Forman met with him to discuss it. He told Reynolds that it was between him and Nicholson. Reynolds knew this was trouble. Nicholson was cast as Randle McMurphy.[46] The film was a huge hit, and Nicholson won the Oscar for his performance.

Finding an actress to play Nurse Ratched proved just as difficult as the search for a male lead. Jane Fonda was made an offer, but the actress wasn't interested.[47] Further rejections came from Anne Bancroft, Angela Lansbury, Geraldine Page, Ellen Burstyn and Colleen Dewhurst.[48] Lily Tomlin was considered,[49] but finally the part went to Louise Fletcher. Fletcher's portrayal of Nurse Ratched was critically acclaimed. She won the Academy Award for her performance in the film.

One Glorious Day (1922)
Will Rogers as Ezra Botts (Fatty Arbuckle)

The part of Ezra Botts was originally planned for Fatty Arbuckle. On Labor Day in 1921 Arbuckle attended a party. A young actress named Virginia Rappe crashed the party. During the party Rappe drank heavily and became gravely ill. Arbuckle tried to help her. Rappe died a few days later, and Arbuckle was accused of manslaughter. His career was severely damaged. Will Rogers took the part that had been his in *One Glorious Day*. Arbuckle was later acquitted of all charges, but his career never fully recovered.[50]

One Million B.C. (1940)
Carole Landis as Loana (Evelyn Keyes)

Evelyn Keyes auditioned for the role of Loana, but lost out to Carole Landis.[51]

One Million Years B.C. (1966)
Raquel Welch as Loana (Ursula Andress)

Ursula Andress was the first choice for the part of Loana. She turned it down, and Raquel Welch was cast instead.[52]

One Minute to Zero (1952)
Ann Blyth as Linda Day (Claudette Colbert)

Claudette Colbert was originally scheduled to star in *One Minute to Zero* as Linda Day. Production began, but soon after Colbert became ill with pneumonia. She was unable to finish the film and was replaced with Ann Blyth.[53]

One Tough Cop (1998)
Stephen Baldwin as Bo Dietl (Robert De Niro, Matt Dillon, Andy Garcia, Al Pacino, Eric Roberts, Sylvester Stallone, Mark Wahlberg)

Among the actors considered at various times to star were Al Pacino, Robert De Niro, Sylvester Stallone, Andy Garcia, Mark Wahlberg, and Eric Roberts.[54] Finally it came down to two actors: Stephen Baldwin and Matt Dillon. Baldwin was chosen over the better known Dillon.

Only Angels Have Wings (1939)
Rita Hayworth as Judith "Judy" MacPherson (Dorothy Comingore, Beverly Holden)

Dorothy Comingore, then known as Linda Winters, was supposed to be set for the part of Judy MacPherson. However, agent George Chasin convinced director Howard Hawks to give Rita Hayworth a shot at the part. Beverly Holden was also a contender, but Hawks thought that Hayworth was the right actress for the part.[55]

The Only Game in Town (1970)
Warren Beatty as Joe Grady (Frank Sinatra)

Frank Sinatra was signed to play Joe Grady opposite Elizabeth Taylor in *The Only Game in Town*. Taylor fell ill, and production on the film was delayed. The actress had to have a hysterectomy. Sinatra had another commitment at Caesar's Palace in Las Vegas. He could not wait for Taylor to recover. Sinatra quit and was replaced by Warren Beatty.[56]

Only Yesterday (1933)
Margaret Sullavan as Mary Lane (Claudette Colbert, Irene Dunne)

Claudette Colbert and Irene Dunne both turned down the lead role of Mary Lane in *Only Yesterday*.[57]

Only You (1994)
Marisa Tomei as Faith Horvath (Demi Moore, Michelle Pfeiffer, Susan Sarandon)

Michelle Pfeiffer, Demi Moore, and Susan Sarandon had all been mentioned for the part of Faith Horvath at various times.[58]

Operation Petticoat (1959)
Cary Grant as Commander Matt Sherman (Jeff Chandler, Robert Taylor)

Jeff Chandler was supposed to play Commander Matt Sherman. He was sick and could not stay in the film.[59] Executives at Universal suggested Robert Taylor for the part. Tony Curtis, the star of the film, had only one actor in mind—Cary Grant. Still, Universal talked with Taylor. Taylor was so interested that he offered to give Curtis five percent of the ten percent of the gross he was promised. Curtis wouldn't bend. Universal finally gave in and Curtis got the opportunity to co-star with the legendary Grant.[60]

Ordinary People (1980)

Donald Sutherland as Calvin Jarrett (Robert Redford)
Mary Tyler Moore as Beth Jarrett (Ann-Margret, Lee Remick, Natalie Wood)
Judd Hirsch as Berger (Donald Sutherland)

The producers tried to persuade director Robert Redford into taking the role of Calvin Jarrett. He resisted and continued to search for an actor. He found one among the cast members. Donald Sutherland, who had originally been set for the part of the psychiatrist Berger, went to Redford and asked for the role.[61] Judd Hirsch replaced him as Berger, and filmed the part in ten days. For his brief stint, Hirsch was nominated for an Oscar, but ultimately lost out to co-star Timothy Hutton.

Natalie Wood,[62] Ann-Margret[63] and Lee Remick[64] were considered for the part of Beth. Redford decided to instead cast Mary Tyler Moore against type. Moore's dramatic performance was critically acclaimed, and won the actress an Oscar nomination.

Out of Africa (1985)

Meryl Streep as Karen Blixen (Audrey Hepburn)

In the late 1970s producer Anna Cataldi contacted Audrey Hepburn for the starring role of Karen Blixen in *Out of Africa*. Hepburn was enthusiastic and sent Cataldi to see Fred Zinnemann. She also suggested that Cataldi speak to her agent Kurt Frings. Frings thought it was a terrible idea and tried to discourage Cataldi. The determined producer called Frings back a day later at which point he informed her that Hepburn was otherwise engaged. *Out of Africa* was finally made in the mid–1980s with Meryl Streep in the lead.[65]

Out of Sight (1998)

Albert Brooks as Richard Ripley (Danny DeVito, Garry Shandling)

Danny De Vito and Garry Shandling considered playing the part of Richard Ripley. They both decided against making the film. Albert Brooks didn't feel the same way. He was offered the part, and accepted it.[66]

Out of the Fog (1941)

John Garfield as Harold Goff (Humphrey Bogart

Humphrey Bogart was very enthusiastic about starring as Harold Goff in *Out of the Fog*. He approached studio head Jack Warner, but was denied. The part was instead played by John Garfield.[67]

Out of the Past (1947)

Robert Mitchum as Jeff Bailey (Humphrey Bogart, John Garfield, Dick Powell)

Humphrey Bogart had been the first choice for the role of Jeff Bailey. Warner Bros. denied him permission to do the film, and he was forced to turn it down. Robert Mitchum was cast after John Garfield and Dick Powell both said no.[68]

Outcast Lady (1934)

Constance Bennett as Iris March (Norma Shearer)

Norma Shearer was the early choice to star in *Outcast Lady*. When she fell through Constance Bennett was hired to replace her.[69]

The Outlaw (1943)

Jack Buetel as Billy the Kid (Will Fowler, Wallace Reid, Jr.)
Jane Russell as Rio (Beverly Holden)

Will Fowler and Wallace Reid, Jr., were both considered for the part of outlaw Billy the Kid. Jack Buetel was given the part instead.

Beverly Holden lost out to Jane Russell for the part of Rio.[70]

The Outrage (1964)

Paul Newman as Juan Carrasco (Marlon Brando)

Paul Newman initially turned down *The Outrage*. When he heard that Marlon Brando was interested in starring he changed his mind and signed on.[71]

The Outsiders (1983)

Matt Dillon as Dallas Winston (Nicolas Cage)

An unknown Nicolas Cage auditioned for the role of Dallas Winston in his uncle's (Francis Ford Coppola) film, *The Outsiders*. He was beaten out by the very popular Matt Dillon.[72]

The Owl and the Pussycat (1970)

Barbra Streisand as Doris Wilgus (Abbey Lincoln, Elizabeth Taylor)
George Segal as Felix Sherman (Richard Burton, William Holden, Sidney Poitier, Rod Taylor)

The Owl and the Pussycat began as a Broadway play in 1964. Originally the role of Doris was a black character. The play centered on an interracial romance with Diana Sands and Alan Alda in the leads. Producer Ray Stark bought the rights for the film version. His plan was to star husband and wife Elizabeth Taylor and Richard Burton. Richard Burton wasn't interested and turned Stark down. Stark then offered the role of Felix to Rod Taylor. He negotiated with Stark, but eventually took himself out of the running.[73] William Holden was another contender.[74] Unable to find a leading man, Elizabeth Taylor dropped out.[75] Abbey Lincoln was asked to play Doris, but Lincoln said no. Finally Stark realized that Barbra Streisand owed him a film. He gave her $1 million to play the part.[76]

Sidney Poitier was considered to co-star with Streisand, but the idea was dropped and George Segal got the part.[77]

PT 109 (1963)

Cliff Robertson as John F. Kennedy (Warren Beatty, Peter Fonda, Frank Sinatra)

Peter Fonda was set to screen test for the part of John F. Kennedy in *PT 109*. He was asked to take voice lessons in order to master Kennedy's Boston accent. Fonda thought this was unnecessary, that there was more to Kennedy than just his accent. He refused to do the accent for the audition. Producer Bryan Foy was upset by this, and wanted someone to tell Fonda's father (legendary actor Henry Fonda) about his son's behavior. Fonda told Foy that his father had given him the advice in the first place! Foy called Fonda's agents who said that Fonda must comply with Foy's wishes, which he did. Studio head Jack Warner saw the screen test and noticed that on the slate that Fonda had the cameraman write Under Protest, Actor. Warner was so mad he vowed that Fonda would never work in Hollywood. The next day it was front page news in *The Hollywood Reporter* and *Daily Variety*.[1] Despite Warner's promise Fonda has had a very successful career.

First lady Jacqueline Kennedy saw *Splendor in the Grass*. She told her husband, John F. Kennedy, that there was an actor in the film who might be the right person to play him. Kennedy agreed with his wife and Beatty was offered the part. Beatty declined telling press secretary Pierre Salinger that he didn't want to work with producer Bryan Foy. Frank Sinatra was considered, but Cliff Robertson won the part.[2]

Paid (1930)

Joan Crawford as Mary Turner (Norma Shearer)

Norma Shearer was set for the lead role of Mary Turner in *Paid*. When she learned that she was pregnant the part was recast with Joan Crawford.[3]

Paint Your Wagon (1969)

Lee Marvin as Ben Rumson (Bing Crosby)

Bing Crosby was offered the part of Ben Rumson in the musical *Paint Your Wagon*. Crosby did not want to go on location, and turned the part down. Lee Marvin was cast in his place.[4]

The Pajama Game (1957)

John Raitt as Sid Sorokin (Marlon Brando, Bing Crosby, Stephen Douglass, Howard Keel, Gordon MacRae, Dean Martin, Frank Sinatra)

Director George Abbott's first choice for the lead role of Sid Sorokin in the film version of the Broadway musical, *The Pajama Game*, was Marlon Brando. Brando wasn't interested, and Warner Bros. considered Bing Crosby, Frank Sinatra as well as Howard Keel. Abbott liked John Raitt, and arranged for him to make a screen test. Abbott was also considering another actor, Stephen Douglass. At the time, Douglass was starring as Joe Hardy in Abbott's current Broadway hit, *Damn Yankees*. Doris Day had already been cast as Babe, the female lead. She saw Raitt's test and was not impressed. She asked Abbott's co-director Stanley Donen to consider casting Dean Martin or Gordon MacRae. Abbott felt strongly about John Raitt. He decided that Raitt should fly to California to make another test, this time with Doris Day. Day changed her position on the actor, and he was given the role.[5]

Pal Joey (1957)

Frank Sinatra as Joey Evans (Marlon Brando, Gene Kelly)
Kim Novak as Linda English (Rita Hayworth)
Rita Hayworth as Vera Simpson (Marlene Dietrich, Barbara Stanwyck)

Gene Kelly played the role of Joey Evans on Broadway. Columbia studio head Harry Cohn bought the film rights. He contacted MGM, Kelly's studio, to arrange a loan-out. Cohn called Kelly to inform him that Kelly would be bringing the role to the big screen. Kelly was thrilled. The problem was that a deal had not been worked out yet. Kelly called Cohn over and over. Cohn told Kelly that he would need more time to make a deal. MGM was asking too much money for Kelly, and Cohn was trying to work it out. Cohn even offered to trade Rita Hayworth to MGM in exchange for Kelly, but Louis B. Mayer wasn't interested in the actress. Mayer eventually told Cohn to forget it and assigned Kelly to another film, *Anchors Aweigh*.[6] Marlon Brando was considered, but Harry Cohn gave the part to Frank Sinatra instead.[7]

Harry Cohn wanted Marlene Dietrich for the role of Vera Simpson in *Pal Joey*. Dietrich was unavailable. Barbara Stanwyck let it be known that she was interested in the part, but Cohn chose Rita Hayworth instead.[8] Incidentally, Hayworth had originally been considered for the part of Linda English.[9]

The Panic Room (2002)

Jodie Foster as Meg Altman (Nicole Kidman)

During the filming of *Moulin Rouge* Nicole Kidman suffered a knee injury. The injury caused her to drop out of her next film, *The Panic Room*. Jodie Foster stepped in as a replacement.[10]

Paper Moon (1973)

Ryan O'Neal as Moses Pray (Warren Beatty, Paul Newman, Jack Nicholson)
Tatum O'Neal as Addie Pray (Nell Potts Newman)

Paper Moon was, at one point, intended to star Paul Newman and his daughter, Nell Potts Newman, with John Huston as director. Huston left the project and the Newmans followed.[11] Peter Bodganovich was brought in to direct. He told the executives at Paramount Pictures that he wanted Ryan O'Neal to star as scam artist Moses Pray, with O'Neal's daughter Tatum cast as Addie Pray. Robert Evans was head of production at the studio. Evans' former wife, Ali MacGraw, had an affair with O'Neal during the filming of *Love Story*. Evans did not want to work with O'Neal. He suggested that Bogdanovich consider either Warren Beatty or Jack Nicholson. However, Evans eventually relented and the O'Neals were cast.[12]

Paper Moon was Tatum O'Neal's film debut. She won an Academy Award for her performance in the film, and made Oscar history as the youngest winner ever.

Papillon (1973)

Steve McQueen as Henri "Papillon" Charriere (Jean-Paul Belmondo)

Producer Robert Dorfman bought the rights to *Papillon* with Jean-Paul Belmondo in mind as its star. He changed his mind when he realized that there was more money to be made with a big American star in the lead. He gave the role to the biggest star at the time, Steve McQueen.[13]

The Paradine Case (1947)

Gregory Peck as Anthony Keane, Council for the Defense (Ronald Colman, Laurence Olivier)
Alida Valli as Mrs. Maddalena Anna Paradine (Ingrid Bergman, Greta Garbo, Vivien Leigh)

While working at MGM, producer David O. Selznick bought the rights to *The Paradine Case* with Greta Garbo in mind to star. He presented the idea to her, but she wasn't interested.[14] Selznick later formed his own production company. He still owned the rights, and once again went to Garbo. She could not be persuaded, and Selznick considered both Ingrid Bergman and Vivien Leigh, but neither actress was cast.[15] Selznick decided at that point to cast an unknown in the part. The actress he found was Alida Valli.

Director Alfred Hitchcock wanted Laurence Olivier to play Anthony Keane, but he was unattainable.[16] Ronald Colman was also considered, but Gregory Peck was given the part instead.[17]

Parnell (1937)

Myrna Loy as Katie O'Shea (Joan Crawford)

Joan Crawford was scheduled to play Katie O'Shea until the last minute when she and

Myrna Loy traded roles; Crawford gave Loy *Parnell* in exchange for the title role in *The Last of Mrs. Cheyney*.[18]

Parrish (1961)

Troy Donahue as Parrish McLean (Warren Beatty)

Warren Beatty tried for the starring role of Parrish McLean. He was beaten out by Troy Donahue.[19]

Pat Garrett and Billy the Kid (1973)

James Coburn as Patrick J. Garrett (Henry Fonda, Charlton Heston, Robert Mitchum, Paul Newman, Rod Steiger)
Kris Kristofferson as William H. "Billy the Kid" Bonney (Peter Fonda, Don Johnson, Malcolm McDowell, Jon Voight)
Bob Dylan as Alias (Jackson Browne, Johnny Crawford, Bo Hopkins)

Henry Fonda, Paul Newman, Robert Mitchum and Rod Steiger were all considered for the part of Pat Garrett. Charlton Heston was made an offer, which he rejected. The part went to James Coburn.

Jon Voight, Peter Fonda, Malcolm McDowell and Don Johnson were all possible choices for Billy the Kid. Director Sam Peckinpah knew he found the right actor when he saw the film *Cisco Pike*. Kris Kristofferson played the title role. Peckinpah hired him to play Billy the Kid.

Rocker Jackson Browne was mentioned as a possibility for the part of Alias, along with Bo Hopkins. Johnny Crawford auditioned but failed to win the part. The part went to singer Bob Dylan.[20]

Patriot Games (1992)

Harrison Ford as Jack Ryan (Alec Baldwin)

Alec Baldwin planned to reprise his role as Jack Ryan (from *The Hunt for Red October*) in the sequel, *Patriot Games*. Production was postponed and Baldwin took another job—starring in *A Streetcar Named Desire* on Broadway. Baldwin would not break his commitment to the play and Harrison Ford was cast as Jack Ryan.[21]

Patton (1970)

George C. Scott as General George S. Patton, Jr. (Burt Lancaster, Lee Marvin, Robert Mitchum, Rod Steiger, Spencer Tracy, John Wayne)
Karl Malden as General Omar N. Bradley (Jimmy Stewart)

The first choice for the role of Patton was Lee Marvin. Marvin turned it down, and it was offered to Rod Steiger.[22] Steiger thought the film glorified war and turned it down. He later said that that was the biggest business mistake he ever made.[23] Spencer Tracy was considered,[24] as was John Wayne. Wayne was eager to play the part, but the producers decided his style of acting wasn't right for the role. Burt Lancaster and Robert Mitchum both had the chance to play the part, but turned it down.[25] George C. Scott accepted the role and won an Oscar.

Jimmy Stewart was considered for the role of General Bradley, later played by Karl Malden.[26]

Paulie (1998)

Jay Mohr as Voice of Paulie (Buddy Hackett)

Jay Mohr beat out Buddy Hackett to do the voice of Paulie. Buddy Hackett was cast in the supporting part of Artie. The two actors met at the audition and became friends. They later starred on the short lived television series *Action* together.[27]

Paycheck (2003)

Ben Affleck as Michael Jennings (Matt Damon)

Matt Damon was asked to star in *Paycheck* as amnesiac Michael Jennings. Damon had recently made the film *The Bourne Identity*. His character in that film, Jason Bourne, also had amnesia. Damon didn't want to repeat himself and said no. He suggested they cast his friend Ben Affleck instead.[28]

Pearl Harbor (2001)

Josh Hartnett as Danny Walker (James Caviezel, Ashton Kutcher)
Kate Beckinsale as Evelyn Johnson (Charlize Theron)
Jon Voight as Franklin Delano Roosevelt (Gene Hackman)

Ashton Kutcher and James Caviezel auditioned to play Danny Walker. Caviezel didn't think he would be cast. He turned out to be right.²⁹ Producer Jerry Bruckheimer gave the part to Josh Hartnett instead.³⁰

Charlize Theron was asked to play nurse Evelyn Johnson. Theron took a pass, and made *Sweet November* with Keanu Reeves instead.³¹

Gene Hackman was an early choice for the part of Franklin Delano Roosevelt in *Pearl Harbor*.³²

Peggy Sue Got Married (1986)

Kathleen Turner as Peggy Sue (Debra Winger)
Nicolas Cage as Charlie Bodell (Judge Reinhold, Martin Short)

Debra Winger was originally thought of to play Peggy Sue. She was all set to star, but then she started to have back problems. Her doctor recommended that she not work for about six months, so Winger was out and Kathleen Turner was in.³³

Director Francis Ford Coppola cast his nephew, Nicolas Cage as Charlie Bodell after considering Martin Short and Judge Reinhold.³⁴

The People vs. Larry Flynt (1996)

Woody Harrelson as Larry Flynt (Tom Arnold, Jim Carrey, Tom Hanks, Bill Murray)
Courtney Love as Althea Leasure (Patricia Arquette, Georgina Cates, Rachel Griffiths, Ashley Judd, Parker Posey, Mira Sorvino)

Bill Murray was the first choice for Larry Flynt. Producer Oliver Stone claims that Murray did not respond to their offer, and they moved on. Names such as Tom Hanks, Tom Arnold, and Jim Carrey were brought up before Woody Harrelson was cast.³⁵

Candidates for the role of Althea Leasure included Parker Posey, Rachel Griffiths, Georgina Cates and Patricia Arquette.³⁶ Ashley Judd and Oscar winner Mira Sorvino also wanted the part. However, it was rock star Courtney Love who beat everyone out when she was cast as Althea.³⁷

People Will Talk (1951)

Jeanne Crain as Deborah Higgins (Anne Baxter)

Anne Baxter was the main candidate for the part of Deborah Higgins. Jeanne Crain was cast after Baxter revealed she was pregnant.³⁸

The Perez Family (1995)

Marisa Tomei as Dottie Perez (Maria Conchita Alonso, Rosie Perez)
Alfred Molina as Juan Raul Perez (Al Pacino)

Rosie Perez met with director Mira Nair to discuss *The Perez Family*. Perez was angry when she lost the role of a Latina to (American) Marisa Tomei. Maria Conchita Alonso says she went after the part, but wasn't even given an audition.

Al Pacino was Nair's first choice for the role that went to Alfred Molina.³⁹

Maria Conchita Alonso couldn't even get an audition for *The Perez Family*.

The Perfect Storm (2000)

George Clooney as Billy Tyne (Harrison Ford, Mel Gibson)
Mark Wahlberg as Bobby Shatford (George Clooney)

Harrison Ford was offered the starring role of Billy Tyne.⁴⁰ Ford wasn't interested. Mel Gibson was considered. Gibson asked for more money than the studio wanted to pay.⁴¹ George Clooney wanted to play the supporting part of Bobby Shatford. Director Wolfgang Petersen told Clooney that he shouldn't play Bobby; he was better for the lead role. Clooney agreed to take the part, and Mark Wahlberg was cast as Bobby.[42]

A Perfect World (1993)

Linda Hart as Eileen (Park Overall)

Park Overall was disappointed that she was unable to appear with Kevin Costner in *A Perfect World*.[43] Overall was starring on the sitcom *Empty Nest* at the time.

A sitcom prevented Park Overall from making *A Perfect World*.

The Petrified Forest (1936)

Humphey Bogart as Duke Mantee (Edward G. Robinson)

Leslie Howard and Humphrey Bogart appeared together in the stage version of *The Petrified Forest*. Howard was an established star, while Bogart was an up and coming young actor. Warner Bros. decided to make a film of the play. Howard was secured to reprise his role. However, Warner Bros. was not interested in Humphrey Bogart. They wanted to replace him with Edward G. Robinson. Leslie Howard wouldn't hear of it. Howard threatened that if Bogart did not appear in the film, than he would quit. The studio gave in and Bogart got the part.[44] *The Petrified Forest* turned out to be Bogart's big break. Bogart was so grateful to Howard that he and wife Lauren Bacall named their daughter Leslie after him.

The Phantom (1996)

Catherine Zeta-Jones as Sala (Jenny McCarthy)

Jenny McCarthy auditioned, and was called back for the role of Sala. She eventually lost out to Catherine Zeta-Jones.[45]

Phantom of the Paradise (1974)

William Finley as Winslow Leach (Paul Williams)
Jessica Harper as Phoenix (Sissy Spacek)

Singer/composer Paul Williams was hired to write the music for *Phantom of the Paradise*. Williams felt a kinship with the part of Phantom Winslow Leach. Both Williams and the character had had negative dealings with the music industry. Director Brian De Palma cast Williams in the film, but not as Leach. He gave that part to William Finley. Williams was cast as the duplicitous Swan.

Sissy Spacek auditioned to play singer Phoenix. De Palma didn't think her voice was good enough. She lost out to Jessica Harper.[46] Spacek and her husband Jack Fisk worked on the film — he as production designer, she as set dresser.

Phffft! (1954)

Kim Novak as Janis (Sheree North)

Columbia Pictures intended to cast Sheree North as Janis. Those plans were abandoned and the part went to Kim Novak instead.[47]

Philadelphia (1993)

Tom Hanks as Andrew Beckett (Daniel Day-Lewis)
Denzel Washington as Joe Miller (Tom Hanks)

Daniel Day-Lewis was director Jonathan Demme's first choice for the role of Andrew Beckett. Tom Hanks was asked to play lawyer Joe Miller.[48] Hanks was more interested in playing Andrew Beckett. Since Day-Lewis turned the part down, it was free for Hanks to take.[49]

Hanks won an Oscar for his performance in the film.

The Philadelphia Story (1940)
Cary Grant as C.K. Dexter Haven (Clark Gable)

James Stewart as Macaulay Connor (Spencer Tracy)

Katharine Hepburn owned the rights to *The Philadelphia Story*. She wanted Spencer Tracy and Clark Gable to co-star. Neither actor wanted to commit, and the parts went to James Stewart and Cary Grant.[50]

Phone Booth (2002)
Colin Farrell as Stuart Shepard (Jim Carrey)

Kiefer Sutherland as The Caller (Ron Eldard)

Jim Carrey was supposed to play the part of Stuart Shepard, but he eventually changed his mind and dropped out.[51]

Ron Eldard was originally supposed to be The Caller. However the sound of his voice was not exactly what was needed. Kiefer Sutherland's voice was deemed more menacing. Sutherland replaced Eldard.[52]

Pickup on South Street (1953)
Jean Peters as Candy (Ava Gardner, Betty Grable, Marilyn Monroe, Shelley Winters)

Marilyn Monroe, Ava Gardner, Betty Grable and Shelley Winters all wanted the part of Candy. Betty Grable wanted the character to have a dance number. Writer/director Samuel Fuller thought this was a terrible idea. Plus he wanted a plain looking actress for the part. He saw Grable as too glamorous. He thought Ava Gardner was too beautiful, and Shelley Winters also wasn't right. Marilyn Monroe read for Fuller. He told her that she too was the wrong type. Monroe was very disappointed. Fuller gave the part to Jean Peters.[53]

Picnic (1955)
William Holden as Hal Carter (Marlon Brando, Paul Newman)

Kim Novak as Madge Owens (Carroll Baker, Janice Rule)

Marlon Brando rejected the role of Hal.[54] Paul Newman tested, but lost out to William Holden.[55]

Janice Rule played the part of Madge on Broadway. Director Joshua Logan wanted her for the film.[56] Also considered was Carroll Baker. Baker screen tested, but failed to win the part.[57] Producer Harry Cohn decided the right actress was Kim Novak.[58]

Picnic at Hanging Rock (1975)
Rachel Roberts as Mrs. Appleyard (Vivien Merchant)

Director Peter Weir cast Vivien Merchant as Mrs. Appleyard. Merchant was having personal problems, and eventually quit to be replaced by Rachel Roberts.[59]

Picture Mommy Dead (1966)
Zsa Zsa Gabor as Jessica Shelley (Hedy Lamarr, Gene Tierney)

Gene Tierney was originally cast as Jessica. She left the film and the role went to Hedy Lamarr.[60] On January 28, 1966 Lamarr was charged with shoplifting. Lamarr said that she was innocent. She insisted on a trial. The jury found Lamarr not guilty. Soon after Lamarr went into the hospital. Her part in the film was recast with Zsa Zsa Gabor. Producer Bert I. Gordon said that her arrest had nothing to do with her leaving the film. He only had Lamarr's scenes left to shoot. Waiting for her to be released would be too costly. Lamarr agreed with his decision.[61]

The Picture of Dorian Gray (1945)
Hurd Hatfield as Dorian Gray (Michael Dyne)

Michael Dyne screen-tested for the title role of Dorian Gray. Dyne recommended an actress to the casting people for the role of Sibyl Vane. Her name was Angela Lansbury.[62] Lansbury tested and was chosen for the part, while Dyne was left out in the cold. Dyne, a relative newcomer, continued to make mostly forgettable films, until he retired from acting two years later.

Pillow Talk (1959)
Nick Adams as Tony Walters (Dwayne Hickman)

Dwayne Hickman became ill and was unable to appear in *Pillow Talk*. He was replaced by Nick Adams.[63]

The Pink Panther (1964)

Peter Sellers as Inspector Jacques Clouseau (Peter Ustinov)
Capucine as Simone Clouseau (Ava Gardner)

Peter Ustinov was the first choice for the role of Inspector Clouseau. He declined and the part of Clouseau went to Peter Sellers. Sellers' portrayal of the bumbling inspector became of the most famous in film history.

Ava Gardner was asked to play Simone Clouseau. Gardner didn't think much of the part. She turned it down. Capucine was given the part.[64]

Pinky (1949)

Jeanne Crain as Patricia "Pinky" Johnson (Dorothy Dandridge)

Dorothy Dandridge was considered to play the title role of Pinky. Pinky is a light skinned black woman who passes for white. Darryl F. Zanuck eventually decided the safest bet was to turn the black Dandridge down and cast the white Jeanne Crain instead.[65]

Pirates (1986)

Walter Matthau as Captain Thomas Bartholomew Red (Jack Nicholson)
Cris Campion as The Frog (Dustin Hoffman, Roman Polanski)

Writer/director Roman Polanski originally intended to have Jack Nicholson star in *Pirates* as Captain Red with himself as the Frog. Nicholson appeared interested, but according to Polanski kept asking for more money. Finally Paramount Pictures grew tired of this and canceled the project entirely. Polanski took the film to United Artists. This new studio didn't want Polanski in the co-starring role, feeling they needed a star in the part. Polanski pursued Dustin Hoffman, but was unsuccessful. Hoffman, a star in his own right, did not want to be the sidekick to Nicholson. Nicholson's agent continued to demand more money for his client, until Polanski canceled the whole thing. He did make the movie, ten years later, but without Jack Nicholson. The role of Captain Red was given to Walter Matthau.[66] *Pirates* might have been better off on Polanski's shelf. The film opened to poor reviews, and was a flop at the box office as well.

Planet of the Apes (1968)

Roddy McDowall as Cornelius (Rock Hudson)
Kim Hunter as Zira (Julie Harris)
Maurice Evans as Dr. Zaius (Edward G. Robinson)

Rock Hudson was a contender for the part of Cornelius. It was eventually decided that Hudson was too big a star and the star of the film, Charlton Heston, might be overshadowed.

Julie Harris was sent a copy of the script. She couldn't imagine how the apes were going to appear, so producer Mort Abrahams showed her a test film which was made earlier. Harris liked the film, but didn't think she could work with the ape makeup. Abrahams asked her to think about it, which she did. Harris called Abrahams the next day to say no. The next choice was Kim Hunter. Hunter initially had the same concerns as Harris, and Abrahams offered to show her the test film. Hunter didn't feel it was necessary. She met with Abrahams and director Franklin Schaffner. Hunter signed for the film soon after.[67]

Edward G. Robinson played Dr. Zaius in the test film. He was supposed to reprise the role in *Planet of the Apes*, but bowed out because he felt that he could not go through the hours long process of having the ape makeup applied every day.[68]

Platoon (1986)

Tom Berenger as Bob Barnes (Kevin Costner, Willem Dafoe, Michael Pare)
Charlie Sheen as Chris Taylor (Emilio Estevez)
Francesco Quinn as Rhah (Willem Dafoe)

Charlie Sheen auditioned for the part of Chris Taylor in 1983. Writer/director Oliver Stone thought that the 18-year-old Sheen was too skinny, and not the right type. He did offer the role to Sheen's brother Emilio Estevez. Stone had Michael Pare lined up to play Bob Barnes. There was a problem getting money to make the film and plans were put on hold for about three years. At that point Sheen was brought in to audition once more. Stone thought the actor was much improved and offered him the part.[69]

Kevin Costner tuned down the part of Sgt. Barnes. Costner's brother had been in Vietnam, which made Costner not want to do the film.[70]

Oliver Stone considered Willem Dafoe for the parts of Sgt. Barnes, Elias Gordon and Rhah.

After seeing Dafoe in a trailer for the film *To Live and Die in L.A.* Stone decided to cast him as Elias.[71]

Play Dirty (1968)

Nigel Davenport as Cyril Leech (Richard Harris)

Richard Harris was originally cast as Capt. Cyril Keech in *Play Dirty*. Harris reconsidered, and quit just before shooting was to start. Nigel Davenport was brought in as a replacement.[72]

Play It Again, Sam (1972)

Woody Allen as Allan Felix (Richard Benjamin, Dustin Hoffman)
Diane Keaton as Linda Christie (Paula Prentiss)

Play It Again, Sam started as a Broadway play in 1969 starring Woody Allen and Diane Keaton. When the film version was being planned Dustin Hoffman was mentioned for Allen's stage role, Allan Felix. However, Woody Allen had other ideas. He thought that Richard Benjamin was a good choice, with Benjamin's wife, Paula Prentiss, cast as Linda Christie. During the planning stages of the film Allen's movie *Bananas* was released. It was a big hit, and producer Arthur Jacobs decided that Allen should star in this film as well. He gave the part of Linda to the woman who created it on stage — Diane Keaton.[73]

Play Misty for Me (1971)

Clint Eastwood as Dave Garver (Steve McQueen)

Steve McQueen was offered the part of Dave Garver in *Play Misty for Me*. He liked the script very much, but turned it down because the female lead was a better role than the part of Dave Garver.[74]

The Player (1992)

Tim Robbins as Griffin Mill (John Travolta)

Director Robert Altman considered casting John Travolta (before his big comeback) as Griffin Mill. But Altman felt that the audience might associate Travolta with his old characters and might soften the character too much. He instead cast the lesser known Tim Robbins as the murdering movie executive, Griffin Mill.[75]

Playing by Heart (1998)

Angelina Jolie as Joan (Gillian Anderson)

When Gillian Anderson first heard about *Playing by Heart* she was interested in the part of Joan. At the time Anderson was starring on the television series *The X-Files*. Joan was completely different from her TV character Dana Scully. However Angelina Jolie was chosen to play Joan. Anderson still made the film; she costarred as Meredith.[76]

Plaza Suite (1971)

Maureen Stapleton as Karen Nash (Vivian Vance)

Vivian Vance was intent on landing the role of Karen Nash in the film version of Neil Simon's *Plaza Suite*. She tried to convince the producers she was the right actress for the part to no avail. She was turned down in favor of Maureen Stapleton.[77]

Pocketful of Miracles (1961)

Bette Davis as Apple Annie (Jean Arthur, Shirley Booth, Helen Hayes, Katharine Hepburn)
Glenn Ford as Dave the Dude (Kirk Douglas, Jackie Gleason, Dean Martin, Steve McQueen, Frank Sinatra)
Hope Lange as Queenie Martin (Shirley Jones)

Shirley Booth was offered the role of Apple Annie in *Pocketful of Miracles*. The movie was a remake of the 1933 film, *Lady for a Day*, which starred May Robson. Booth felt that Robson's performance was so good in the original, her own performance would not have measured up. She turned it down and it was offered to Helen Hayes. Hayes wanted to do the film a great deal. There was a conflict in her schedule and she was forced to say no.[78] Director Frank Capra was extremely disappointed to lose such a great actress for the role. Offers were made to Katharine Hepburn and Jean Arthur, but neither actress wanted to do it.[79] Capra approached Bette Davis, and she said yes.

Capra considered Jackie Gleason and Kirk Douglas,[80] as well as Frank Sinatra and Dean Martin[81] for the part of Dave the Dude. All were offered the part, but turned it down. Capra wanted Steve McQueen for the part, but United Artists didn't think he was a big enough star.[82]

Capra wanted Shirley Jones to play Queenie Martin. The role was hers until co-star Glenn

Ford got involved. He insisted that Hope Lange be given the role or else he would quit the picture. Lange was in, and Jones was out.[83]

Point Break (1991)
Patrick Swayze as Bodhi (Johnny Depp)

Johnny Depp turned down the role of surfer Bodhi.[84]

Pontiac Moon (1994)
Mary Steenburgen as Katherine Bellamy (Whoopi Goldberg)

When they were still romantically involved, Whoopi Goldberg and Ted Danson planned to star in *Pontiac Moon* together. Other commitments forced Goldberg out of the film, and she was replaced by Mary Steenburgen. Steenburgen and Danson fell in love and were married.[85]

Popeye (1980)
Robin Williams as Popeye (Dustin Hoffman)
Shelley Duvall as Olive Oyl (Gilda Radner)

Dustin Hoffman was originally cast as Popeye. When he and screenwriter Jules Feiffer could not work together producer Robert Evans got involved. Hoffman gave him an ultimatum — either Feiffer be fired or he would walk. Evans chose Feiffer and cast Robin Williams as Popeye.[86]

Gilda Radner was offered $850,000 to play Olive Oyl. The actress was famous for starring on the groundbreaking late night show *Saturday Night Live*. Many of her close friends thought it was a great offer and encouraged her to take the job. Her *SNL* producer Lorne Michaels thought that if she did the film it would detract from her work on the show. Radner said no to the part and Shelley Duvall was cast in her place.[87]

Porgy and Bess (1959)
Sidney Poitier as Porgy (Harry Belafonte)
Sammy Davis, Jr., as Sportin' Life (Cab Calloway)

Harry Belafonte rejected the role of Porgy which was eventually played by Sidney Poitier.

When first choice Cab Calloway was unavailable, Sammy Davis, Jr., was cast as Sportin' Life.[88]

Portrait of Jennie (1948)
Jennifer Jones as Jennie Appleton (Shirley Temple)

Producer David O. Selznick considered casting a 16-year-old Shirley Temple in the title role of Jennie.[89] Unfortunately for Temple, Selznick fell in love with actress Jennifer Jones. He gave her the part of Jennie, and the two were married about a year later.

The Poseidon Adventure (1972)
Shelley Winters as Belle Rosen (Esther Williams)

Director Ronald Neame called Esther Williams to offer her the role of Belle Rosen in *The Poseidon Adventure*. This angered Williams' husband Fernando Lamas, who blew up at Neame.[90] Williams lost the role to Shelley Winters, who was nominated for an Oscar for her performance.

Posse (1993)
Salli Richardson as Lana (Stacey Dash)

Stacey Dash lost out to Salli Richardson for the role of Lana in Posse.

Possession (2002)
Jennifer Ehle as Christabel LaMotte (Gwyneth Paltrow)

At one point director Neil LaBute considered having Gwyneth Paltrow play both female leads in *Possession*. But LaBute and Paltrow both felt that it would take the audience out of the story of the film, that they would be seeing the actor rather than the character. He cast Paltrow as Maud Bailey, while Jennifer Ehle played Christabel LaMotte.[91]

The Postman Always Rings Twice (1946)
John Garfield as Frank Chambers (Cameron Mitchell)

Cameron Mitchell was considered as a replacement for John Garfield. Garfield was in the military, and the producers thought he would be unavailable. When he was released, he got the role he was originally considered for, and Mitchell was out.[92]

The Postman Always Rings Twice (1981)

Jessica Lange as Cora Papadakis (Kim Basinger, Lindsay Crouse, Michelle Phillips, Meryl Streep, Raquel Welch

There was an attempt to make *The Postman Always Rings Twice* in the mid-1970s. Raquel Welch was a contender for the part of Cora Papadakis. Jack Nicholson wanted to star with his then girlfriend Michelle Phillips. The studio preferred Welch, and Nicholson wouldn't make the film. He and Phillips broke up, but Nicholson wasn't available to make the film until 1981.[93] Meryl Streep was interested in playing the part of Cora. The film contained steamy sex scenes between Cora and Frank Chambers. Jack Nicholson had been cast as Chambers. Streep had no problem with the sex scenes if Nicholson was just as explicit as she would be. The producers decided to keep searching for a leading lady.[94] Jessica Lange won the role of Cora over Lindsay Crouse[95] and Kim Basinger.[96]

Practical Magic (1998)

Nicole Kidman as Gillian Owens (Sandra Bullock)

Before Nicole Kidman was involved with *Practical Magic*, Sandra Bullock had her choice of either of the two starring roles. She chose to play Sally, and Kidman was cast as Gillian.

Presenting Lily Mars (1943)

Judy Garland as Lily Mars (Kathryn Grayson, Lana Turner)

Presenting Lily Mars was originally planned for Lana Turner. The studio didn't think that the finished script was right for Turner. They gave the property to producer Joseph Pasternak. He considered both Kathryn Grayson and Judy Garland.[97] Garland, the bigger star, got the part.

Presumed Innocent (1990)

Harrison Ford as Rusty Sabich (Kevin Costner, Robert Redford)

Kevin Costner turned down the role of Rusty Sabich.[98] Robert Redford was also considered, but producer Sydney Pollack decided to go with a younger actor. He decided that the right choice was Harrison Ford.[99]

Pretty Baby (1978)

Brooke Shields as Violet (Diane Lane, Dana Plato)

Dana Plato and Diane Lane[100] turned down the role of Violet that later went to Brooke Shields.

Pretty Woman (1990)

Richard Gere as Edward Lewis (Albert Brooks, Sean Connery, Charles Grodin, Al Pacino, Sting
Julia Roberts as Vivian Ward (Laura Dern, Bridget Fonda, Valeria Golino, Daryl Hannah, Jennifer Jason Leigh, Madonna, Mary Stuart Masterson, Michelle Pfeiffer, Molly Ringwald, Madeleine Stowe, Lea Thompson)

Charles Grodin auditioned for the starring role of Edward Lewis but was not selected.[101] Albert Brooks was sought, but he wasn't interested. He thought the script was silly.[102] Sean Connery and Sting were considered, as well as Al Pacino.[103] The actor director Garry Marshall finally chose was Richard Gere.

The original script for *Pretty Woman* was much darker than the Cinderella story eventually filmed. At the end of this version Edward and Vivian did not end up together, and Vivian was a cocaine addict.[104] Garry Marshall had a long list of actresses as possible Vivians, including Michelle Pfeiffer, Laura Dern, Bridget Fonda, Lea Thompson, Daryl Hannah, Madeleine Stowe, Mary Stuart Masterson, and Valeria Golino.[105] Molly Ringwald was another possibility.[106] Jennifer Jason Leigh met with Marshall to discuss the part. Marshall told Leigh that Vivian had only been a hooker for a few weeks, and that she thought it was exciting. Leigh had a more cynical view of the part, and was out of the running.[107] Marshall wanted to cast Madonna, but Madonna told him that a younger actress would be better casting. Marshall took her advice and cast an unknown Julia Roberts.[108]

Pride and Prejudice (1940)

Greer Garson as Elizabeth Bennet (Vivien Leigh, Norma Shearer)
Laurence Olivier as Mr. Darcy (Robert Donat, Melvyn Douglas, Clark Gable)

Pride and Prejudice was acquired by Irving Thalberg. He planned for his wife, Norma Shearer, to star. Thalberg's death caused the project to be shelved. When MGM decided to resume production they were still interested in Shearer. Clark Gable, Melvyn Douglas, and Robert Donat were mentioned as possible co-stars. Eventually Shearer left the film.[109] Laurence Olivier was cast as Mr. Darcy. When he learned that the part of Elizabeth Bennet was open he suggested his then-wife Vivien Leigh for it. She was turned down in favor of Greer Garson.[110]

The Pride and the Passion (1957)

Sophia Loren as Juana (Ava Gardner)

Ava Gardner turned down the part of Juana in *The Pride and the Passion*. The role was later taken by Sophia Loren.[111]

Primal Fear (1996)

Edward Norton as Aaron Stampler/Roy (Matt Damon, Leonardo DiCaprio, James Marsden, Danny Masterson, James Van Der Beek)

Leonardo DiCaprio was originally offered the role of Aaron, but turned it down.[112] James Marsden auditioned for the part,[113] as well as James Van Der Beek. Van Der Beek was called back, but was so nervous he felt he blew the audition.[114] Danny Masterson came close to landing the part. He auditioned six times.[115] According to Matt Damon, he and Edward Norton were the last two contenders.[116] Norton beat out Damon, and was nominated for an Oscar for his performance.

Primary Colors (1998)

John Travolta as Jack Stanton (Mel Gibson, Tom Hanks, Liam Neeson)

Director Mike Nichols' first choice for the part of Clintonesque Jack Stanton was Tom Hanks. Hanks wanted to do it, but his schedule was booked up. He told Nichols to find someone else. He considered Mel Gibson and Liam Neeson, but realized he would rather have an American actor in the role. John Travolta fit the bill, and he was cast.[117]

The Prime of Miss Jean Brodie (1969)

Maggie Smith as Jean Brodie (Julie Andrews, Angela Lansbury)
Celia Johnson as Miss Mackay (Wendy Hiller)
Diane Grayson as Jenny (Angela Cartwright)

Angela Lansbury tried to buy the rights for *The Prime of Miss Jean Brodie* and planned to star in the film. She lost the rights and was out of the project.[118] Julie Andrews was made an offer but turned it down.[119] The role was finally played by Maggie Smith.

Celia Johnson was mentioned as a possible choice to play the part of Miss Mackay. Twentieth Century–Fox had another actress in mind, Wendy Hiller. They opposed Johnson's casting at first. Eventually they came round, and Johnson was given the part.[120]

Child star Angela Cartwright screen-tested for the role of Jenny in *The Prime of Miss Jean Brodie*, but lost out to Diane Grayson.

Prince of the City (1981)

Treat Williams as Danny Ciello (Al Pacino, John Travolta)

Treat Williams was cast as Danny Ciello after Al Pacino[121] and John Travolta[122] were considered.

The Prince of Tides (1991)

Nick Nolte as Tom Wingo (Warren Beatty, Tom Berenger, Jeff Bridges, Kevin Costner, Don Johnson, Dennis Quaid, Robert Redford)
Blythe Danner as Sallie Wingo (Kate Nelligan)
Kate Nelligan as Lila Wingo Newbury (Irene Worth)
Jason Gould as Bernard Woodruff (Chris O'Donnell)
Brad Sullivan as Henry Wingo (Lloyd Bridges)

Robert Redford[123] and Warren Beatty[124] were both early choices for the part of Tom Wingo. Redford, at one point, was also attached to produce the film. Eventually Redford dropped out of the project and Barbra Streisand came aboard. Streisand planned to direct, as well as play the role of Susan Lowenstein. For the part of Tom, she considered casting her then boyfriend Don Johnson. Eventually their relationship cooled and Johnson was no longer in the running. Streisand asked Redford, but he did not want her as the director.[125] Kevin Costner was offered the part but turned it down.[126] Streisand wanted Jeff Bridges to play Tom, with his father, Lloyd Bridges, as Tom's father Henry Wingo. Jeff said no. Lloyd was very disappointed. Streisand met with Dennis Quaid and Tom Berenger to no avail.[127] The role was finally taken by Nick Nolte, who was nominated for an Academy Award for his performance.

Streisand interviewed Kate Nelligan for the part of Tom's wife Sallie. After meeting the actress Streisand realized that the role she was perfect for was the young version of Tom's mother Lila. Streisand initially considered having two actresses play the role of Lila. A younger actress would play her in flashbacks, and an older actress would play the present day Lila.[128] Irene Worth would have played the other Lila,[129] but Streisand eventually decided that Nelligan was such a good actress that she should play both parts.[130]

Chris O'Donnell was hired to play Bernard, Streisand's character's son. When writer Pat Conroy saw O'Donnell, he told Streisand he wasn't right for the part. Bernard is supposed to be awkward, not athletic. O'Donnell has the opposite appearance. Streisand showed Conroy another actor. Conroy loved him. He told her this actor was exactly right. It turned out to be her son, Jason Gould.[131] She told O'Donnell his mother would understand, and paid him anyway.[132]

The Princess Bride (1987)

Andre the Giant as Fezzik (Bubba Smith)
Robin Wright as Princess Buttercup (Whoopi Goldberg)

Former football star Bubba Smith lost the role of Fezzik because he was too small. The part was given to professional wrestler Andre the Giant, who was 7'5" and weighed over 500 pounds.

Whoopi Goldberg's agent tried to convince director Rob Reiner that his client was perfect for the role of Princess Buttercup, the most beautiful girl in the world. Reiner politely tried to explain to him that Goldberg was not the type he had in mind, that he wanted an actress in her 20s. Robin Wright auditioned. Wright was then starring on the soap opera *Santa Barbara*.[133] The American born Wright did a very convincing English accent. Reiner was impressed with her, and gave her the part.

The Princess Comes Across (1936)

Fred MacMurray as King Mantell (George Raft)

George Raft was originally cast as King Mantell in *The Princess Comes Across*. His leading lady was Carole Lombard. Lombard selected a cameraman, and Raft was upset. He only wanted to work with who he considered was the best cameraman. He said that he wasn't a good enough actor to trust anyone but the best. He quit the film and was replaced by Fred MacMurray.[134]

The Private Lives of Elizabeth and Essex (1939)

Bette Davis as Elizabeth (Geraldine Fitzgerald)
Errol Flynn as Earl of Essex (Laurence Olivier)

Geraldine Fitzgerald auditioned to play Elizabeth, but Bette Davis ended up in the role. Davis wanted Laurence Olivier to play opposite her,[135] but Errol Flynn was cast instead.

Private Parts (1997)

Howard Stern as Howard Stern (Jeff Goldblum)
Carol Alt as Gloria (Sandra Taylor)
John Stamos as Himself (Luke Perry)

Originally, producers did not want Howard Stern to play himself, in the autobiographical film *Private Parts*. They suggested Jeff Goldblum play the part, but Stern would not agree. When the film came out everyone agreed that Stern's acting was very natural.

Sandra Taylor, an actress and frequent guest of Howard Stern's show, auditioned for the role of Gloria. She didn't get it, and was told they were looking for a supermodel for the part.

The opening scene of the film is a reenactment of an MTV award show. Stern was developing a character for a movie. The character was called Fartman. In real life Luke Perry introduced Stern. However, in the film John Stamos replaced Perry. Incidentally, don't look for the Fartman movie. Stern later decided to scrap the idea.

The Prizefighter and the Lady (1933)

Max Baer as Steven "Steve" Morgan (Clark Gable)

Very early on Clark Gable was announced as the leading man for the film *The Prizefighter and the Lady*. Gable was eventually dropped, and the role went to real-life boxer Max Baer.[136]

Prizzi's Honor (1985)

William Hickey as Don Corrado Prizzi (Sam Jaffe)

Sam Jaffe was director John Huston's first

choice for his film, *Prizzi's Honor*. Jaffe died, and the part went to William Hickey.[137]

The Producers (1968)

Gene Wilder as Leo Bloom (Peter Sellers)
Kenneth Mars as Franz Liebkind (Mel Brooks, Dustin Hoffman)

Peter Sellers was considered for the role of Leo Bloom. Instead of Sellers, the part was eventually played by Gene Wilder.[138]

Director Mel Brooks originally saw himself playing Franz Liebkind. He changed his mind and offered the part to his neighbor Dustin Hoffman. Hoffman turned it down because he had been offered another film, *The Graduate*.[139] Hoffman took *The Graduate* and played opposite Brooks' wife, Anne Bancroft.

Proof of Life (2000)

Russell Crowe as Terry Thorne (Mel Gibson)

Mel Gibson was offered the part of Terry Thorne. Gibson decided against it, and Russell Crowe was cast instead.[140]

Psycho (1960)

Janet Leigh as Marion Crane (Martha Hyer, Shirley Jones, Hope Lange, Piper Laurie, Eva Marie Saint, Lana Turner)
Vera Miles as Lila Crane (Caroline Kurney)
John Gavin as Sam Loomis (Richard Basehart, Brian Keith, Tom Laughlin, Robert Loggia, Jack Lord, Leslie Nielsen, Cliff Robertson, Rod Taylor, Tom Tryon, Stuart Whitman)
Frank Albertson as Tom Cassidy (Alan Reed)
Jeanette Nolan as Voice of Mother (Norma Varden)

Janet Leigh became Marion Crane after Lana Turner, Eva Marie Saint, Piper Laurie, Shirley Jones, Martha Hyer, and Hope Lange were all considered.

Director Alfred Hitchcock looked at Caroline Kurney for the part of Lila, but instead chose Vera Miles.[141]

Hitchcock's list of possible Sam Loomis' included: Cliff Robertson, Robert Loggia, Leslie Nielsen, Jack Lord, Brian Keith, Rod Taylor, Tom Laughlin, Stuart Whitman and Tom Tryon.[142] Richard Basehart was another contender, but Hitchcock chose John Gavin instead.[143]

Hitchcock was interested in Alan Reed for the part of Tom Cassidy, but ultimately cast Frank Albertson.

Norma Varden was turned down for the voice of Norman Bates' mother.[144]

Psycho (1998)

Vince Vaughn as Norman Bates (Matt Damon, Leonardo DiCaprio, Joaquin Phoenix)
Anne Heche as Marion Crane (Drew Barrymore, Claire Danes, Nicole Kidman, Julianne Moore, Winona Ryder)

Director Gus Van Sant considered casting Leonardo DiCaprio or Matt Damon as Norman Bates. Neither actor was really into doing it, and Van Sant went to Joaquin Phoenix. Phoenix wanted the part, but his schedule did not work with the production schedule. Van Sant finally cast Vince Vaughn.

Nicole Kidman was offered the part of Marion Crane. She was unavailable, and Van Sant looked at other actresses including Winona Ryder, Julianne Moore, Claire Danes, and Drew Barrymore. He felt that both Barrymore and Ryder were too young. One actresses audition stood out in his mind—Anne Heche's. He felt that she was different from Janet Leigh, but very interesting. He gave her the part and cast Marion contender Julianne Moore as Marion's sister Lila Crane.[145]

The Public Enemy (1931)

James Cagney as Tom Powers (Edward Woods)
Edward Woods as Matt Doyle (James Cagney)
Jean Harlow as Gwen Allen (Louise Brooks)
Mae Clarke as Kitty (Louise Brooks)

Edward Woods was originally cast as Tom Powers with James Cagney as Matt Doyle. Director William Wellman decided the two actors should switch roles.[146] Louise Brooks was slated to play Kitty, but left the film and was replaced by Mae Clarke.[147] Brooks was also offered the part of Gwen Allen, but chose instead to go to New York. The role was then given to Jean Harlow.[148]

Pulp Fiction (1994)

John Travolta as Vincent Vega (Daniel Day-Lewis)
Samuel L. Jackson as Jules Winnfield (Paul Tagliore)
Uma Thurman as Mia Wallace (Rosanna Arquette, Holly Hunter, Kelly Lynch, Meg Ryan, Meg Tilly, Alfre Woodard)
Bruce Willis as Butch Coolidge (Matt Dillon)
Amanda Plummer as Honey Bunny (Uma Thurman)
Rosanna Arquette as Jody (Ellen DeGeneres, Pam Grier)

[*Vic Vega*—Michael Madsen]

Daniel Day-Lewis was interested in the role of Vincent Vega. Director Quentin Tarantino bravely turned down the Oscar winning actor in favor of John Travolta, and restarted Travolta's career.[149]

Samuel L. Jackson was given the role of Jules. He went in to read as a matter of procedure. He later found out that Paul Tagliore had also auditioned. Tagliore was initially called in to read for a small role that didn't have a lot of lines. He asked if he could read Jules as his audition. His reading was so powerful that Jackson was now in danger of losing the part. Jackson's manager and agent quickly called Tarantino, producers Danny DeVito and Lawrence Bender, as well as the heads of Miramax, brothers Bob and Harvey Weinstein. Weinstein acknowledged that Jackson had been told the part was already his, but that Jackson's reading had been less than what was expected. Ultimately, Jackson was allowed to go in and audition. Jackson was not going to make the same mistake as last time, when he was secure the role was his.[150] He auditioned for Tarantino, DeVito, Bender, and the casting director. Jackson read for Jules opposite a reader who was hired to assist at the audition by reading the role of Vincent Vega. Jackson went all out. During his reading, Jackson noticed that the reader was so caught up in Jackson's performance, that he lost his place in the script. At that point Jackson knew that he was doing well. He ended the audition by reading Jules' final speech in the movie. Tarantino and company were extremely impressed with Jackson. They gave him the role and dropped the idea of Tagliore.[151]

Meg Ryan, Meg Tilly and Alfre Woodard[152] were all up for the part of Mia, as well as Holly Hunter and Rosanna Arquette.[153] Kelly Lynch auditioned to play Mia. Uma Thurman had originally been considered for the part of Honey Bunny.[154] But Tarantino liked her better as Mia and gave her the role. Kelly Lynch was told she had been the second choice.[155]

Matt Dillon was an early candidate for the part of Butch.[156]

Ellen De Generes[157] and Pam Grier[158] both auditioned for the part of Jody, but lost out to Mia-candidate Rosanna Arquette.

The part of Vincent Vega was originally intended to be Vic Vega, a character previously played by Michael Madsen in *Reservoir Dogs*. Madsen chose to do the film *Wyatt Earp* instead. Tarantino eliminated Vic, and had his brother Vincent as the lead character.[159]

The Purple Rose of Cairo (1985)

Jeff Daniels as Tom Baxter/Gil Shepherd (Woody Allen, Michael Keaton, Kevin Kline)

Michael Keaton was originally cast as the male lead. After ten days of filming Allen decided that Keaton was not working out. The problem was that *The Purple Rose of Cairo* is set in the 1930s. Keaton was not believable as being of that era.[160] Allen thought he might take the part himself, but later changed his mind. Kevin Kline was considered, but Allen decided to go with Jeff Daniels.[161]

Queen Christina (1933)

John Gilbert as Don Antonio de la Prada (John Barrymore, Ronald Colman, Leslie Howard, Laurence Olivier)

Laurence Olivier was originally cast opposite Greta Garbo. Garbo insisted that Olivier be fired.[1] It might have been for the best. Reportedly Olivier later said that he couldn't hold a candle to Garbo.[2] John Barrymore's name was mentioned for the part, but Garbo didn't want him.[3] Ronald Colman's name was bandied about, but MGM continued to search for a leading man.[4] Leslie Howard rejected an offer, feeling he wouldn't get much attention.[5] The role was finally played by John Gilbert.

Queen of the Damned (2002)

Stuart Townsend as Lestat (Wes Bentley)

On March 2, 2000, the *New York Daily News* reported that Wes Bentley was in final talks for the part of Lestat. However, Bentley's participation with the film fell through, and Stuart Townsend was cast instead.[6]

The Queen's Affair (1934)

Anna Neagle as Queen Nadina (Jeanette MacDonald)

Jeanette MacDonald was cast as Queen Nadina in *The Queen's Affair*. Early in rehearsals and with no reason given, MacDonald quit. She was replaced by Anna Neagle.[7]

The Quick and the Dead (1995)

Leonardo DiCaprio as The Kid (Matt Damon)

Matt Damon turned down the part of The Kid in *The Quick and the Dead*. Damon later said he didn't regret his decision.[8]

Quigley Down Under (1990)

Tom Selleck as Matthew Quigley (Steve McQueen)

Steve McQueen briefly discussed the possibility in starring in *Quigley Down Under*. The film was made about ten years later with Tom Selleck in the lead role of Matthew Quigley.[9]

Quo Vadis? (1951)

Robert Taylor as Marcus Vincius (Clark Gable, Gregory Peck)
Deborah Kerr as Lygia (Audrey Hepburn, Elizabeth Taylor)
Finlay Currie as Peter (Walter Huston)

John Huston was the first director assigned to *Quo Vadis?* His cast included Gregory Peck, Elizabeth Taylor, and Walter Huston. Production was stalled, and Huston was taken off the film. The new director, Mervyn LeRoy, contacted the actors. They had taken other projects and LeRoy looked to replace them. He cast Robert Taylor as Marcus Vincius (a part rejected by Clark Gable[10]) and Finlay Currie as Peter. He wanted to use Audrey Hepburn for Lygia, but the studio insisted on Deborah Kerr.[11]

The Rack (1956)

Paul Newman as Captain Edward W. Hall, Jr. (Glenn Ford)

Director Arnold Laven's choice for the role of Captain Edward W. Hall, Jr., was Glenn Ford. Ford was unavailable, and Laven had to come up with another choice.[1] He decided that instead of an established star like Ford, he would give the part to a newcomer. His search ended with an unknown actor by the name of Paul Newman.

Radio Flyer (1992)

Lorraine Bracco as Mary (Rosanna Arquette)

Production on *Radio Flyer* started with Rosanna Arquette. She ultimately left the film and was replaced by Lorraine Bracco.[2]

Raffles (1930)

Kay Francis as Gwen Manders (Bette Davis)

Bette Davis auditioned for the film. Studio boss Samuel Goldwyn thought that Davis was unattractive and gave the part to Kay Francis instead.[3]

Raffles (1940)

David Niven as A.J. Raffles (Cary Grant)

MGM's Samuel Goldwyn's first choice for the part of A.J. Raffles was Cary Grant. However, David Niven's contract with the studio was about to expire. Goldwyn worried that Niven would leave MGM, and in order to keep him gave him the part instead of Grant.[4]

Raging Bull (1980)

Cathy Moriarty as Vickie La Motta (Jodie Foster)

Jodie Foster's mother Brandy wanted the role of Vickie La Motta for her 16-year-old daughter. Brandy Foster insisted that Jodie be auditioned. Director Martin Scorsese agreed to see Foster. Brandy Foster had sexy photos taken of her daughter, but it was obvious that she was too young for the part. Foster was about 17 at the time. Scorsese cast 19-year-old Cathy Moriarty instead.[5]

Ragtime (1981)

Howard E. Rollins as Coalhouse Walker (O.J. Simpson)
James Olson as Father (George C. Scott)

O.J. Simpson went after the part of Coalhouse Walker. Director Milos Forman thought Howard Rollins, Jr., was the better actor for the part.
James Olson was chosen over George C. Scott for the role of Father.[6]

Raiders of the Lost Ark (1981)

Harrison Ford as Dr. Henry "Indiana Jones" Jones, Jr. (John Beck, Nick Mancuso, Tom Selleck)
Karen Allen as Marian Ravenwood (Janice Dickinson, Amy Irving, Debra Winger, Sean Young)
Paul Freeman as Rene Belloq (Jacques Dutronc, Giancarlo Giannini)
John Rhys-Davies as Sallah (Kevork Malikyan)

The number one choice for the role of Indiana Jones was Tom Selleck. Selleck had the role, but his commitment to the television series *Magnum, P.I.* made him unavailable. Selleck was extremely upset to have lost the role. Ironically, a writers strike delayed production on *Magnum, P.I.* so long that *Raiders* was finished filming before Selleck was ever needed for the series.[7] John Beck[8] and Nick Mancuso[9] auditioned, but lost the part to Harrison Ford.

Model Janice Dickinson[10] and Amy Irving[11] were considered for the part of Marion Ravenwood, as well as Sean Young and Debra Winger.[12] The actress Steven Spielberg wanted was Karen Allen. Spielberg did an experiment to make sure he was making the right choice. Spielberg showed about 60 people the Marion screen tests. Afterwards they voted on their favorite for the part. About 80 percent of the people liked Allen. Spielberg happily gave her the part.[13]

Jacques Dutronc was considered for the part of Rene Belloq.[14] Giancarlo Giannini came close to landing the part, but ultimately Spielberg and director George Lucas cast Paul Freeman instead.[15]

Kevork Malikyan was a contender to play Sallah. The actor had an interview with Spielberg. He got stuck in traffic on the way there. He showed up an hour late. Spielberg gave the part to John Rhys-Davies instead.[16]

Rain Man (1988)

Dustin Hoffman as Raymond Babbitt (Bill Murray, Randy Quaid)
Tom Cruise as Charlie Babbitt (Dustin Hoffman, Dennis Quaid)

Real life brothers Dennis and Randy Quaid were considerations for the parts of the Babbitt brothers.[17] When Dustin Hoffman was first offered the film *Rain Man*, it was the part of Charlie that the actor was told to look at.[18] The idea was to have Bill Murray star opposite him. Murray wasn't interested in making *Rain Man*. Hoffman decided he would much rather play the other brother, Raymond. Tom Cruise was given a copy of the script. Cruise was very enthusiastic about the film, and signed up for the part of Charlie Babbitt.[19] *Rain Man* was a hit with the critics as well as at the box office. The film was nominated for eight Academy Awards. It won four: Best Picture, Best Director (Barry Levinson), Best Original Screenplay (Ronald Bass and Barry Morrow) and Best Actor (Dustin Hoffman).

Rainbow Island (1944)

Dorothy Lamour as Lona (Yvonne De Carlo)

When *Rainbow Island* went into production Dorothy Lamour was cast in the starring role of Lona. Soon after, Lamour decided that the part was not substantial enough and walked out. A replacement was needed. Yvonne De Carlo was brought in for a screen test. Shortly after, De Carlo heard through the grapevine that Lamour had changed her mind and was back in the film. De Carlo was awarded with a very small role as a handmaiden.[20]

The Rainmaker (1956)

Burt Lancaster as Bill Starbuck (William Holden, Elvis Presley)

Elvis Presley screen tested for the role of Starbuck in the film version of *The Rainmaker*.[21] Producer Hal B. Wallis originally planned to have William Holden play part. Burt Lancaster had other ideas. He went to Wallis and told him he wanted the part. Wallis was persuaded, and Lancaster won the role.[22]

The Rainmaker (1997)

Matt Damon as Rudy Baylor (Stephen Dorff, Edward Norton, Sean Penn)

Sean Penn was director Francis Ford Coppola's first choice for the role of lawyer Rudy Baylor. Penn was unavailable, and turned it down. Coppola looked at Edward Norton and Stephen Dorff, but instead chose a pre–*Good Will Hunting* Matt Damon instead.[23]

The Rains Came (1939)

Myrna Loy as Lady Edwina Esketh (Tallulah Bankhead, Ina Claire, Marlene Dietrich, Kay Francis, Rosalind Russell)

Myrna Loy was cast as Lady Edwina Esketh, beating out Marlene Dietrich, Tallulah Bankhead, Rosalind Russell, Ina Claire, and Kay Francis.[24]

Raise the Titanic (1980)

Jason Robards as Adm. James Sandecker (Steve McQueen)

Steve McQueen turned down a $3 million offer to star in *Raise the Titanic*. He didn't think the script was very good. Jason Robards was cast in his place.[25]

Rally Round the Flag, Boys (1958)

Joan Collins as Angela Hoffa (Jayne Mansfield)

Jayne Mansfield was originally set for the role of Angela. Co-stars Paul Newman and Joanne Woodward campaigned to director Leo McCarey in favor of Joan Collins. They thought that Mansfield was wrong for the part. They said that she was too common for the role. They felt that Collins had the right qualities for the part. McCarey was eventually persuaded and gave the part to Collins.[26]

Ramona (1936)

Loretta Young as Ramona (Rita Hayworth)

Ramona started out as a project for the Fox Film Corporation. Studio head Winfield Sheehan had an actress in mind to play the title role — a 16-year-old Rita Hayworth. However, Fox was having financial troubles. In order to save the studio, they merged with another company — 20th Century — and became 20th Century–Fox. Unfortunately for Hayworth, Sheehan lost his job as a result of the merger. His replacement was the legendary Darryl F. Zanuck. Zanuck saw the screen test Hayworth made for *Ramona*. He decided that she wasn't right for the part at all, and cast Loretta Young instead.[27]

The Razor's Edge (1946)

Anne Baxter as Sophie MacDonald (Alice Faye, Judy Garland, Betty Grable, Bonita Granville, Susan Hayward, Maureen O'Hara)

Judy Garland was sought for the part of Sophie. She went to her studio, MGM, who refused to loan her out.[28] Betty Grable was offered the part. Grable felt her audience would not accept her in such a dramatic role and said no.[29] The role was also rejected by Maureen O'Hara, Alice Faye, Susan Hayward, and Bonita Granville.[30]

Reap the Wild Wind (1942)

Paulette Goddard as Loxi Claiborne (Katharine Hepburn)

Katharine Hepburn was the first choice to star as Loxi Claiborne. She turned it down, and it was played by Paulette Goddard instead.[31]

Rebecca (1940)

Laurence Olivier as Maxim de Winter (Ronald Colman, Leslie Howard, David Niven, William Powell)

Joan Fontaine as The second Mrs. de Winter (Kathryn Aldrich, Heather Angel, Katharine Bard, Anne Baxter, Betty Campbell, Louise Campbell, Marion Clayton, Joyce Coad, Augusta Dabney, Frances Dee, Olivia De Havilland, Mary Kay Dodson, Ellen Drew, Lucille Fairbanks, Geraldine Fitzgerald, Sidney Fox, Agnes Fraser, Virginia Gilmore, Julie Haydon, Susan Hayward, Fay Helm, Mary Howard, Dorothy Hyson, Evelyn Keyes, Margaret Lang, Andrea Leeds, Vivien Leigh, Shirley Logan, Anita Louise, Pauline Moore, Patricia Morison, Jean Muir, Miriam Patty, Nova Pilbeam, Maevis Raeburn, Rene Ray, Frances Reid, Audrey Reynolds, Marjorie Reynolds, Alicia Rhett, Lynn Roberts, Jean Rouvenol, Ann Rutherford, Jo Ann Sayres, Anne Shirley, Margaret Sullavan, Mary Taylor, Helen Terry, Joan Tetzel, Sylvia Weld, Carolyn Whittingham, Loretta Young)

Judith Anderson as Mrs. Danvers (Nazimova, Flora Robson)

Florence Bates as Edythe Van Hopper (Mary Boland, Alice Brady, Laura Hope Crews, Lucile Watson, Cora Witherspoon)

Ronald Colman was the first choice to play Maxim de Winter. Producer David O. Selznick suggested Leslie Howard if Colman said no.[32] David Niven's name was brought up, but Alfred Hitchcock thought that Niven was too shallow.[33] It turned out that Colman wasn't interested, and eventually it came down to a choice between Laurence Olivier and William Powell. Powell was not available, and the role went to Olivier.³⁴

Olivier and his real life leading lady Vivien Leigh thought Leigh would be the perfect co-star. She persuaded Selznick to let her audition. He allowed her to test twice. He informed Leigh she did not get the part because she was completely wrong for it. He also went on to say that he felt that had she played the part, the criticism might have been damaging to her career. He also told Olivier he felt that Leigh was only interested in playing the role because it was opposite him. When he had first mentioned it to her, she wasn't interested. It was only after learning that Olivier was cast that she wanted in.³⁵ Loretta Young and Susan Hayward screen tested,³⁶ as did Joan Fontaine, Margaret Sullavan and Anne Baxter. Other actresses considered included Marjorie Reynolds, Betty Campbell, Mary Howard, Sidney Fox, Mary Taylor, Anne Shirley, Andrea Leeds, Kathryn Aldrich, Audrey Reynolds, Jo Ann Sayres, Alicia Rhett, Geraldine Fitzgerald, Jean Rouvenol, Ann Rutherford, Evelyn Keyes, Lynn Roberts, Carolyn Whittingham, Joyce Coad, Marion Clayton, Shirley Logan and Patricia Morison.³⁷ Jean Muir, Sylvia Weld, Julie Haydon, Mary Kay Dodson, Virginia Gilmore, Lucille Fairbanks, Dorothy Hyson, Augusta Dabney, Helen Terry, Heather Angel, Ellen Drew, Frances Dee, Margaret Lang, Frances Reid, Pauline Moore, Joan Tetzel, Maevis Raeburn, Katharine Bard, Louise Campbell, Agnes Fraser, Rene Ray, Fay Helm, Miriam Patty, Anita Louise, and Nova Pilbeam were all screen tested. The director especially disliked Pilbeam for the part.³⁸ Hitchcock narrowed the choice down to three actresses: Fontaine, Baxter, and Sullavan.³⁹ Director Alfred Hitchcock chose Baxter. But Selznick felt that at age 16, Baxter was too young for the part, and she was out. Many other actresses were considered including Olivia De Havilland, who had just worked with Selznick in *Gone with the Wind*. She thought about it briefly, but then took herself out of the running to insure that her sister, Joan Fontaine, would get the part, which she did.⁴⁰

Nazimova and Flora Robson were possibilities for the part of Mrs. Danvers, eventually played by Judith Anderson.

Hitchcock considered Laura Hope Crews, Alice Brady, Lucile Watson, Cora Witherspoon and Mary Boland to play Mrs. Van Hopper until he saw Florence Bates in a play at the Pasadena Playhouse. He told Selznick about her. Selznick gave her the part.⁴¹

Rebecca of Sunnybrook Farm (1932)

Marian Nixon as Rebecca (Janet Gaynor)

Janet Gaynor was offered the title role of Rebecca. She turned it down, and it went to Marian Nixon instead.⁴²

Rebel Without a Cause (1955)

James Dean as Jim Stark (Tab Hunter, John Kerr, Robert Wagner)
Natalie Wood as Judy (Carroll Baker, Gloria Castillo, Patricia Crowley, Kathryn Grant, Beverly Long, Jayne Mansfield, Terry Moore, Lori Nelson, Margaret O'Brien, Lee Remick, Debbie Reynolds)
Sal Mineo as John "Plato" Crawford (Bobby Hyatt)

James Dean was cast as Jim Stark. A month before production was set to star Dean disappeared. Unable to locate their leading man, Warner Bros. considered Tab Hunter, Robert Wagner and John Kerr as possible replacements. This turned out to be unnecessary. Dean suddenly returned in time to start shooting.⁴³

Director Nicholas Ray's first choice for the part of Judy was former child star Margaret O'Brien. O'Brien's mother didn't think the film was right for her daughter and said no. O'Brien made the film *Glory* instead. Also considered were Jayne Mansfield,⁴⁴ Lori Nelson, and Terry Moore. When Natalie Wood heard of this she decided that she would do whatever was necessary to win the role. Wood made sure that she would run into Ray by spending much of her time at the Warner Bros. commissary. Her plan worked. Ray noticed her one day and invited her to have lunch with him. He soon asked her to audition for the part. Before long the 16-year-old Wood and the 43-year-old Ray were having an affair. This did not secure the part for her. Other actresses were considered including Debbie Reynolds, Lee Remick, Patricia Crowley, Gloria Castillo, and Kathryn Grant.⁴⁵ Beverly Long auditioned. She said that Ray didn't have her read anything; he just asked her questions about her home and school life.⁴⁶ Wood made a screen test, but Ray was very interested in Carroll Baker. She came quite close to landing the part. Eventually Ray decided against Baker and gave the part to Natalie Wood.⁴⁷

Bobby Hyatt auditioned for the role of Plato, but lost out to Sal Mineo.⁴⁸

Reckless (1935)

Jean Harlow as Mona Leslie (Joan Crawford)
Rosalind Russell as Josephine Mercer (Myrna Loy)

Joan Crawford accepted the starring role of Mona Leslie, and all was set until Louis B. Mayer decided that Jean Harlow was more suited to the part.[49]

For the role of Josephine Mercer, Myrna Loy was sought. Loy said no, and Rosalind Russell was cast instead.[50]

The Red Danube (1949)

Ethel Barrymore as the Mother Superior (Deborah Kerr)

Deborah Kerr told MGM's Dore Schary that she was interested in starring in *The African Queen*. Schary told her that another studio already owned the rights. He went on to say that if she wanted to make a film in Africa she could play the Mother Superior in *The Red Danube*. Kerr said to forget it and Ethel Barrymore was cast instead.[51]

Red Dragon (2002)

Ralph Fiennes as Francis Dolarhyde (Paul Bettany, Nicolas Cage, Philip Seymour Hoffman, Sean Penn)

Director Brett Ratner met with Nicolas Cage, Sean Penn and Paul Bettany for the part of Francis Dolarhyde. He also considered Philip Seymour Hoffman, but instead gave him the part of reporter Freddy Lounds. Ratner's search ended with Ralph Fiennes.[52]

Red Dust (1932)

Clark Gable as Dennis Carson (John Gilbert)
Jean Harlow as Vantine (Joan Crawford, Greta Garbo, Norma Shearer)

The lead in *Red Dust* was originally intended for John Gilbert. It was later decided that Gilbert's drinking was too much of a problem. Another sticking point was that Gilbert was contractually required to make $250,000 a film. The decision was made to replace him with Clark Gable.[53]

Greta Garbo, Joan Crawford, and Norma Shearer were all considered for the part that went to Jean Harlow.[54]

Red Garters (1954)

Jack Carson as Jason Carberry (Don Taylor)
Pat Crowley as Susan Martinez De La Cruz (Anna Maria Alberghetti)

Mitchell Leisen was originally slated to direct *Red Garters*. In the part of Jason Carberry was Don Taylor, while Anna Maria Alberghetti was cast as Susan Martinez De La Cruz. Alberghetti left the film and was replaced by Pat Crowley. Not long after Leisen also left. George Marshall signed on as the new director. He got rid of the footage that was already shot of Don Taylor. He recast the role with Jack Carson.[55]

Red Line 7000 (1965)

Marianna Hill as Gabrielle (Francoise Dorleac)

Francoise Dorleac was offered the part of Gabrielle in *Red Line 7000*. Director Howard Hawks was so intent on having her in the film he offered her seven times the amount of money James Caan, the star of the film, was making. Dorleac decided to make the movie *Genghis Khan* instead. Gabrielle was played by Marianna Hill.[56]

A big payday could not persuade Francoise Dorleac to take a part she didn't want (*Red Line 7000*).

Red River (1948)

John Wayne as Thomas Dunson (Gary Cooper)
Montgomery Clift as Matthew "Matt" Garth (Jack Buetel, Casey Tibbs)
Joanne Dru as Tess Millay (Margaret Sheridan)
John Ireland as Cherry Valance (Cary Grant)

Gary Cooper was the first choice for Thomas Dunson. He thought that audiences wouldn't like the character. Cooper turned it down and made the film *Unconquered* instead.

Director Howard Hawks thought that champion rodeo rider Casey Tibbs would be ideal to play Matt Garth. Hawks later worried that since Tibbs wasn't an actor he might not fare well opposite John Wayne. The decision was final when Tibbs fell and broke his arm rendering him unavailable. Jack Buetel came close to landing the part. His lost out when Howard Hughes refused to loan him out. Hawks gave the part to Montgomery Clift instead.[57]

Margaret Sheridan was cast as Tess, but pregnancy forced her to be replaced by Joanne Dru.[58]

Cary Grant was offered the role of Cherry Valance. Grant didn't think the part was substantial enough and turned it down. John Ireland was cast in his place.[59]

Red Sonja (1985)

Brigitte Nielsen as Red Sonja (Sandahl Bergman)

Sandahl Bergman was first cast as Red Sonja. Bergman didn't want to be typecast and asked for the part of Queen Gedren. Brigitte Nielsen was brought in to play Red Sonja.[60]

The Red-Headed Woman (1932)

Jean Harlow as Lillian "Lil"/"Red" Andrews Legendre (Clara Bow, Joan Crawford, Norma Shearer)

The lead role in *The Red-Headed Woman* was offered to Joan Crawford and Norma Shearer.[61] Neither of these actresses wanted to play the trampy character and passed. Clara Bow was another consideration, but Jean Harlow was cast instead.[62]

Originally cast in the title role in *Red Sonja*, Sandahl Bergman asked for a different part.

The Ref (1994)

Judy Davis as Caroline Chausseur (Cybill Shepherd)

Cybill Shepherd coveted the role of Caroline. Shepherd didn't have any hard feelings about losing the part to Judy Davis because she thought that Davis was wonderful in the film.[63]

Reflections in a Golden Eye (1967)

Marlon Brando as Maj. Weldon Penderton (Montgomery Clift)

Montgomery Clift was cast as Penderton. Clift died suddenly of a heart attack before production began.[64] Director John Huston brought in Marlon Brando as a replacement.

The Reluctant Widow (1951)

Jean Kent as Helena (Margaret Lockwood)

The role of Helena was offered to Margaret Lockwood. She turned it down and it was played by Jean Kent instead.[65]

Rendezvous (1935)
Rosalind Russell as Joel Carter (Myrna Loy)

The role of Joel Carter was originally planned for Myrna Loy. Loy refused to appear, and Rosalind Russell was brought in to replace her.[66]

Reservoir Dogs (1992)
Tim Roth as Mr. Orange (Steve Buscemi)
Michael Madsen as Mr. Blonde/Vic (Lawrence Bender, George Clooney, Harvey Keitel, Tim Roth)
Chris Penn as Nice Guy Eddie (Steve Buscemi)
Steve Buscemi as Mr. Pink (Harvey Keitel, Michael Madsen, Tim Roth, Quentin Tarantino)
Randy Brooks as Holdaway (Samuel L. Jackson, Ving Rhames)

When Steve Buscemi was given the script he was told to look at the parts of Mr. Orange and Nice Guy Eddie. Buscemi read it and decided the part he wanted was Mr. Pink.[67] Writer/director Quentin Tarantino had intended to play that part himself. Harvey Keitel also considered playing Mr. Pink, as did Tim Roth and Michael Madsen. Tarantino cast Buscemi. Tim Roth was chosen to play Mr. Orange, but was considered for Mr. Blonde as well. Keitel, also thought about playing Mr. Blonde.[68] Producer Lawrence Bender was considered,[69] as well as George Clooney. Clooney auditioned, but Tarantino preferred Michael Madsen. A gracious loser, Clooney later said that had he gotten the role, he probably would have been awful in it, and that Madsen did a great job.[70] Samuel L. Jackson and Ving Rhames auditioned for Holdaway, but lost out to Randy Brooks.[71]

Return of the Seven (1966)
Robert Fuller as Vin (Steve McQueen)

Steve McQueen refused to reprise his role of Vin in *Return of the Seven*, the sequel to the hit film, *The Magnificent Seven*. He didn't like the script, and said that he was unavailable.[72]

The Revengers (1972)
Susan Hayward as Elizabeth Reilly (Mary Ure)

Mary Ure was wanted for the part of Elizabeth Reilly in *The Revengers*. Ure chose to do a play on Broadway instead. The part of Elizabeth Reilly went to Susan Hayward.[73]

Reversal of Fortune (1990)
Ron Silver as Alan Dershowitz (Woody Allen)

Woody Allen was the first choice to play real life lawyer Alan Dershowitz. Allen proved unavailable, and Ron Silver was subsequently cast.[74]

Revolution (1985)
Al Pacino as Tom Dobb (Robert Duvall, Harrison Ford, Richard Gere)

Harrison Ford turned down the role of Tom Dobb in *Revolution*.[75] Al Pacino was cast after Robert Duvall and Richard Gere were both considered.[76]

Rich and Famous (1981)
David Selby as Doug Blake (Tom Selleck)

Tom Selleck was offered the part of Doug Blake in *Rich and Famous*. Selleck was unable to make the film because of his shooting schedule for his hit series *Magnum, P.I.* Doug Blake was played by David Selby.[77]

Richard III (1955)
Claire Bloom as Lady Anne (Vivien Leigh)

Vivien Leigh lost the role of Lady Anne to Claire Bloom in her then-husband Laurence Olivier's film version of *Richard III* to Claire Bloom.[78]

Richard's Things (1980)
Liv Ullman as Kate Morris (Audrey Hepburn)

Audrey Hepburn said no to the part of Kate Morris.[79]

Ride the High Country (1962)
Joel McCrea as Steve Judd (Randolph Scott)
Randolph Scott as Gil Westrum (Joel McCrea)
Ron Starr as Heck Longtree (Wayne Rogers)
James Drury as Billy Hammond (Robert Culp)

Originally Randolph Scott was hired to play Steve Judd. Joel McCrea was offered the role of Westrum. McCrea would only do the film if he were cast as Judd. Scott said okay, and they switched roles.[80]

Wayne Rogers made a screen test for the part of Heck Longtree. He lost out to Ron Starr.

Director Sam Peckinpah offered Robert Culp the part of Billy Hammond. Culp was only interested in leading man parts and turned Peckinpah down. Culp said that Peckinpah never forgave him for rejecting his offer, and that he never asked him to be in another film. Culp regretted his decision. Peckinpah gave the part to James Drury.[81]

The Ring (2002)

Naomi Watts as Rachel Keller (Kate Beckinsale, Jennifer Connelly, Gwyneth Paltrow)

Jennifer Connelly was the first choice for the part of Rachel.[82] Connelly had problems with the character. She didn't like the fact that Rachel was a negligent parent. She wanted changes made in the script. The producers started to have second thoughts about Connelly.[83] Gwyneth Paltrow was the second choice. She wasn't interested and turned the part down. Naomi Watts and Kate Beckinsale were both up for the part. DreamWorks said that although the studio was fond of Beckinsale, Watts won the part because DreamWorks executive Walter Parkes was extremely impressed with her performance in David Lynch's *Mulholland Drive*.[84]

Rio Bravo (1959)

John Wayne as John T. Chance (Kirk Douglas, Sterling Hayden, Burt Lancaster, Gregory Peck)

Dean Martin as Dude [aka "Borachon"] (James Cagney, John Cassavetes, Montgomery Clift, Tony Curtis, Kirk Douglas, Henry Fonda, Glenn Ford, Cary Grant, William Holden, John Ireland, Van Johnson, Burt Lancaster, Ray Milland, Robert Mitchum, Edmond O'Brien, Frank Sinatra, Rod Steiger, Spencer Tracy, Richard Widmark)

Ricky Nelson as Colorado Ryan (Lloyd Bridges, Chuck Connors, Tony Curtis, James Garner, Frank Gifford, Michael Landon, Jack Lemmon, Lee Marvin, Robert Mitchum, Jack Palance, Rod Taylor, Stuart Whitman)

Angie Dickinson as Feathers (Mari Blanchard, Diane Brewster, Rhonda Fleming, Beverly Garland, Jane Greer, Martha Hyer, Carolyn Jones, Piper Laurie, Julie London, Sheree North, Janis Paige, Donna Reed)

Walter Brennan as Stumpy (Lee J. Cobb, William Demarest, Buddy Ebsen, Gabby Hayes, Arthur Hunnicutt, Burl Ives, Lee Marvin)

In the original *Rio Bravo* script the sheriff was named John Wayne. The first choice for the part was John Wayne (the actor). Just in case Wayne didn't work out other actors such as Gregory Peck, Burt Lancaster, Kirk Douglas and Sterling Hayden were possible replacements. Wayne eventually signed for the film, and no other actor was needed to play the sheriff.

Montgomery Clift was the actor that director Howard Hawks wanted to play Dude. Clift wasn't interested and turned the part down. Other possibilities were Frank Sinatra, James Cagney, Edmond O'Brien, Robert Mitchum, Glenn Ford, Cary Grant, John Cassavetes, Rod Steiger, Spencer Tracy, William Holden, Richard Widmark, John Ireland, Tony Curtis, Henry Fonda, Burt Lancaster, Van Johnson and Ray Milland. Studio head Jack Warner thought that James Cagney was a good choice, but Hawks wasn't sold. Dean Martin was interested in the part. He arranged a meeting with Hawks. Martin had to leave Las Vegas the morning after a show. He chartered a plane to meet Hawks. The director thought that if Martin went to that much trouble to get the job that he would work out fine. He gave Martin the part that day.

The original list of candidates for the part of Colorado Ryan included Robert Mitchum, Jack Lemmon, Jack Palance, James Garner, Tony Curtis, Lloyd Bridges, Lee Marvin and Chuck Connors. It was eventually decided that a younger actor should play the part and a new list of possible choice was made up. Hawks considered Michael Landon, Stuart Whitman, Rod Taylor and football player Frank Gifford before settling on Ricky Nelson.

Martha Hyer, Piper Laurie, Donna Reed, Jane Greer, Carolyn Jones, Janis Paige, Rhonda Fleming, Beverly Garland, Sheree North, Diane Brewster, Julie London and Mari Blanchard all lost out to Angie Dickinson for the part of Feathers.

William Demarest, Lee J. Cobb, Burl Ives, Buddy Ebsen, Gabby Hayes, Lee Marvin and Arthur Hunnicutt were all considered to play Stumpy. The part went to Walter Brennan instead.[85]

Rio Lobo (1970)

Jennifer O'Neill as Shasta Delaney (Katrine Schaake)

Director Howard Hawks was interested in Katrine Schaake for the part of Shasta Delaney. The German actress was not able to obtain a work permit in time. Hawks recast the part with Jennifer O'Neill.[86]

Risky Business (1983)

Tom Cruise as Joel Goodson (Timothy Hutton)
Rebecca DeMornay as Lana (Megan Mullally)

Timothy Hutton was offered the starring role of Joel Goodson in *Risky Business*. Hutton's agents and manager thought that this film was a great choice for the 23-year-old actor. Hutton turned it down, and his *Taps* co-star Tom Cruise was cast. *Risky Business* made Tom Cruise a superstar.[87]

Megan Mullally auditioned for the lead. She didn't get the part, but was cast in a role which turned out to basically be an extra.

The Robe (1953)

Richard Burton as Marcellus Gallio (Tyrone Power)
Victor Mature as Demetrius (Burt Lancaster)

Tyrone Power was the first choice to play Marcellus Gallio. He was unavailable; Richard Burton was cast.

Burt Lancaster was cast as Demetrius. When he left the film, he was replaced by Victor Mature.[88]

Robin and Marian (1976)

Nicol Williamson as Little John (Sean Connery)

Sean Connery was first considered for the role of Little John, until director Richard Lester decided he would make a much better Robin Hood. The part of Little John went to Nicol Williamson.[89]

Robin Hood: Prince of Thieves (1991)

Mary Elizabeth Mastrantonio as Maid Marian (Robin Wright Penn)
Alan Rickman as Sheriff of Nottingham (John Malkovich)

Robin Wright Penn was unable to play Maid Marian because she was pregnant.[90] Mary Elizabeth Mastrantonio replaced her.

John Malkovich turned down the chance to play the Sheriff of Nottingham.[91]

Rock Star (2001)

Mark Wahlberg as Chris "Izzy" Cole (Brad Pitt)

Brad Pitt was originally slated for the starring role of Chris "Izzy" Cole. But Pitt and the studio couldn't agree on who should direct the film. Pitt finally walked away. Mark Wahlberg came in to replace him.[92] Wahlberg's costar was Jennifer Aniston — Brad Pitt's wife.

Rocky (1976)

Sylvester Stallone as Rocky Balboa (James Caan, Gene Hackman, Paul Newman, Jack Nicholson, Ryan O'Neal, Al Pacino, Robert Redford, Burt Reynolds)
Talia Shire as Adrian (Susan Sarandon, Carrie Snodgress)
Carl Weathers as Apollo Creed (Ken Norton)
Burgess Meredith as Mickey (Lee J. Cobb, Lee Strasberg)

An unknown Sylvester Stallone wrote the screenplay for *Rocky*. He shopped the script around to various studios, with the condition that he play the title role of underdog boxer Rocky Balboa. United Artists liked the script but wanted James Caan in the lead.[93] Also considered were Paul Newman,[94] Burt Reynolds,[95] Robert Redford,[96] Ryan O'Neal,[97] Al Pacino,[98] Jack Nicholson[99] and Gene Hackman.[100] Stallone refused to let anyone play the part. Universal liked the project so much that they gave in. *Rocky* won the Oscar for best picture of 1976, while Stallone was nominated for Best Actor.

To play Rocky's love interest Adrian, Stallone envisioned Carrie Snodgress. The budget wasn't high enough to pay Snodgress the amount she wanted. Stallone even offered to give her his salary. She refused the part. Susan Sarandon was then considered. She was eliminated because she came off as too sophisticated for the mousy Adrian. She was also too pretty. Talia Shire auditioned. Her looks were considered too pretty also. However, at her audition Shire came dressed very plainly. Her audition was extremely impressive, and she won the part.

Real life heavyweight boxer Ken Norton was originally cast as Apollo Creed. At the last minute he informed Stallone that he was offered a spot on television on ABC's *The Superstars*. On the program professional athletes competed for a cash prize. Norton was dropping out of *Rocky* to appear on the show. Carl Weathers auditioned for the part. Stallone was introduced to Weathers as the writer of the film. Weathers had no idea that Stallone was also starring. The two read together. Weathers stopped early in the scene and said that he would do better if there was an actor available to read with him. Stallone was surprised, but didn't hold it against Weathers. He was cast as the arrogant boxer.

Stallone pictured Lee J. Cobb as Mickey while he was writing the screenplay. Director John Avildsen insisted that everyone audition for the film. Cobb refused, saying, "The last prick I auditioned for was Arthur Miller and I ain't gonna read for anyone else!" Lee Strasberg was made an offer. Strasberg wanted $75,000, which was too much money. Burgess Meredith auditioned. After going through the lines a few times Avildsen asked him to improvise with Stallone. Meredith, as Mickey, said, "Hey Rocky, ever think about retiring? Well, start thinking about it!" Avildsen was won over, and gave him the part.[101]

Rocky III (1982)

Mr. T as Clubber Lang (Joe Frazier, Ernie Shavers)

Boxers Joe Frazier and Ernie Shavers auditioned for the role of Clubber Lang. An unknown Mr. T auditioned and won the role that made him a star.[102]

Roman Holiday (1953)

Audrey Hepburn as Princess Ann [aka Anya Smith] (Jean Simmons, Elizabeth Taylor)
Gregory Peck as Joe Bradley (Cary Grant)

An early candidate for the lead in *Roman Holiday* was Elizabeth Taylor. Frank Capra was set to direct and wanted to cast Cary Grant opposite Taylor. Capra eventually gave the film over to William Wyler. Wyler wanted Jean Simmons to star, but Howard Hughes, owner of RKO, reused to loan her out for the film.[103]

The Romance of Rosy Ridge (1947)

Janet Leigh as Lissy Anne MacBean (Beverly Tyler)

The part of Lissy Anne was originally intended for Beverly Tyler, until an unknown Janet Leigh came on the scene. Both actresses tested, and Leigh won the role over the well known actress.[104]

Romance on the High Seas (1948)

Doris Day as Georgia Garrett (Lauren Bacall)

Lauren Bacall was put on suspension for turning down the role of Georgia Garrett.[105]

Rome Adventure (1962)

Suzanne Pleshette as Prudence Bell (Natalie Wood)

Natalie Wood was signed for the role of Prudence Bell in *Lovers Must Learn*. Wood was taking pills at the time which made her sick. The story she told the press, however, was that she had the flu. At the time Wood was going through a breakup with her husband Robert Wagner. She asked Warner Bros. for a leave of absence, which they granted her. *Lovers Must Learn* was retitled *Rome Adventure* and Wood was replaced by Suzanne Pleshette.[106]

Romeo and Juliet (1936)

Leslie Howard as Romeo Montague (Clark Gable, Fredric March)
John Barrymore as Mercutio (William Powell)

Director George Cukor wanted Fredric March to play the role of Romeo. March turned it down.[107] Irving Thalberg wanted Clark Gable for Romeo. Gable refused and Leslie Howard was cast instead.[108]

Cukor cast John Barrymore in the supporting role of Mercutio. Shortly after it became apparent that Barrymore's drinking was interfering with the film. The role was then offered to William Powell. Powell quickly turned it down; he was loyal to Barrymore, who had given him a chance when he was starting out as an actor.

Romeo and Juliet (1954)

Cukor and MGM then decided to stick it out with Barrymore.[109]

Romeo and Juliet (1954)

Susan Shentall as Juliet Capulet (Joan Collins)
John Gielgud as Chorus (Laurence Olivier)

Joan Collins screen tested for the role of Juliet. Director Renato Castellani felt that Collins didn't have the right look for the role. He suggested to the actress that she should have a nose job in order to play the part. Collins declined, and newcomer Susan Shentall was cast instead.[110]

Laurence Olivier was asked to play the Chorus. Olivier turned the part down, saying, "I'm too fucking grand."[111]

Romeo and Juliet (1968)

Leonard Whiting as Romeo Montague (Paul McCartney)

Paul McCartney was offered the starring role of Romeo. McCartney was in The Beatles at the time. The band had made the films *A Hard Day's Night* and *Help!* In both films McCartney played himself. McCartney was uneasy about tackling Shakespeare for his first try at playing someone else. He turned the film down. Leonard Whiting was cast instead.[112]

The Roots of Heaven (1958)

Trevor Howard as Morel (William Holden)

William Holden's busy schedule prevented him from taking the role of Morel in *The Roots of Heaven*. The part was eventually played by Trevor Howard.[113]

Rope (1948)

James Stewart as Rupert Cadell (Cary Grant)
John Dall as Brandon Shaw (Montgomery Clift)

Director Alfred Hitchcock's first choices for *Rope* were Cary Grant, Montgomery Clift, and Farley Granger. Both Grant and Clift turned down the parts. Clift was wary about playing a homosexual, fearing the public's reaction. Cary Grant also said no. Hitchcock instead cast Jimmy Stewart and John Dall.[114]

Rose Marie (1936)

Jeanette MacDonald as Marie De Flor (Grace Moore)

Singer Grace Moore was the first choice for the part of Marie De Flor. Due to a contract dispute Moore quit, and the part was recast with Jeanette MacDonald.[115]

The Rose Tattoo (1955)

Anna Magnani as Serafina Delle Rose (Maureen Stapleton)
Marisa Pavan as Rosa Delle Rose (Pier Angeli)

Maureen Stapleton won a Tony award for *The Rose Tattoo* on Broadway. She lost out on the film, though, when Anna Magnani was cast in her place.[116]

Pier Angeli was considered for the part of Rosa Delle Rose. She was pregnant, and the part was played by her sister Marisa Pavan.[117]

Rosebud (1975)

Peter O'Toole as Larry Martin (Burt Lancaster, Robert Mitchum, Donald Sutherland)
Claude Dauphin as Charles-Andre Fargeau (Charles Boyer, Jean Gabin, Louis Jourdan)

Donald Sutherland and Burt Lancaster were suggested for the starring role of Larry Martin. Instead director Otto Preminger gave the part to Robert Mitchum. Shortly after production began Preminger had a problem with Mitchum. The actor was drinking heavily and causing trouble on the set. Tension grew between the two men and they started to argue. Preminger fired Mitchum and replaced him with Peter O'Toole.

Otto Preminger considered Louis Jourdan for the part of Charles-Andre Fargeau. Preminger thought that his acting was great, but he was too young for the part. Jean Gabin was offered the part. The French actor said the film would be too much work and turned the part down. Charles Boyer was considered, but the part went to Claude Dauphin instead.[118]

Rosemary's Baby (1968)

Mia Farrow as Rosemary Woodhouse (Jane Fonda, Sharon Tate, Tuesday Weld, Natalie Wood)
John Cassavetes as Guy Woodhouse (Warren Beatty, Laurence Harvey, Jack Nicholson, Robert Redford)

Director Roman Polanski thought of his wife, Sharon Tate, for the part of Rosemary Woodhouse. The studio felt she wasn't the right choice and told Polanski to keep looking.[119] Jane Fonda was made an offer, but she didn't want the part.[120] Natalie Wood was a possible choice,[121] as was Tuesday Weld. Weld was a strong contender,[122] but the studio felt she wasn't established enough.[123] The role went instead to Mia Farrow.

Warren Beatty turned down the role of Rosemary's husband Guy Woodhouse.[124] Robert Redford was mentioned, but the actor was unavailable. Redford made the film *Blue* instead.[125] Jack Nicholson and Laurence Harvey wanted the part, but it went, instead, to John Cassavetes.[126]

Roughshod (1949)

Gloria Grahame as Mary Wells (Anne Jeffreys)

Anne Jeffreys was sought for the part of Mary Wells. Jeffreys chose not to do the film and the part went to Gloria Grahame.[127]

Rounders (1998)

Gretchen Mol as Jo (Neve Campbell)

The role of Jo was first offered to Neve Campbell. She turned down the part and it went to Gretchen Mol.[128]

Royal Wedding (1951)

Jane Powell as Ellen Bowen (June Allyson, Judy Garland)
Sarah Churchill as Anne Ashmond (Moira Shearer)

June Allyson was originally set to star in *Royal Wedding*. When she became pregnant, the role went to Judy Garland. Garland started work on the film. She was suffering migraine headaches and nausea which caused her to report for work late, or not at all. The studio replaced her with Jane Powell.[129]

Moira Shearer was a contender for the role of Anne Ashmond, eventually played by Sarah Churchill.[130]

Ruggles of Red Gap (1935)

ZaSu Pitts as Prunella Judson (Ruth Gordon)

Charles Laughton was hired for the starring role of Marmaduke "Bill" Ruggles in *Ruggles of Red Gap*. He suggested Ruth Gordon for the part of Prunella Judson. Paramount agreed to test her. Gordon didn't think her test went especially well. She was shown the test, which confirmed what she thought. The part went to ZaSu Pitts.[131]

The Rules of Attraction (2002)

Shannyn Sossamon as Lauren Hynde (Jessica Biel)

Jessica Biel first read *The Rules of Attraction* with the thought of playing the lead role of Lauren Hynde. Biel had a problem with a scene in the film in which Lauren is raped and then vomited on. Shannyn Sossamon was cast as Lauren. Biel instead auditioned for, and won, the supporting part of Lara Holleran.[132]

Jessica Biel passed on a starring role rather than be vomited on in *The Rules of Attraction*.

The Running Man (1987)

Arnold Schwarzenegger as Ben Richards (Christopher Reeve)

Early on in production, George Pan Cosmatos was set to direct *The Running Man*. He cast Christopher Reeve in the lead role of Ben Richards. After financial and creative problems arose, Cosmatos left the project. Other directors were associated with the film, but none stayed very long. Finally former actor Paul Michael Glaser (*Starsky and Hutch*) was hired to direct. Instead of Reeve, he gave the lead role of Ben to action star Arnold Schwarzenegger.[133]

Rush (1991)

Jason Patric as Raynor (Tom Cruise)

Tom Cruise considered starring in *Rush* as Raynor.[134] Cruise decided to pass, and Jason Patric was cast instead.

Ruthless People (1986)

Bette Midler as Barbara Stone (Madonna)

Madonna was a strong contender for the role of Barbara Stone. She met with producer Jon Peters, but Bette Midler was eventually cast instead.[135]

Sabotage (1936)

John Loder as Ted Spencer (Robert Donat)

Director Alfred Hitchcock's first choice for the part of Ted Spencer was Robert Donat. Hitchcock couldn't get him, and he cast John Loder instead.[1]

Saboteur (1942)

Robert Cummings as Barry Kane (Gary Cooper)
Priscilla Lane as Patricia Martin (Barbara Stanwyck)
Otto Kruger as Robert Tobin (Harry Carey)

Director Alfred Hitchcock envisioned Gary Cooper, Barbara Stanwyck, and Harry Carey for the lead roles in *Saboteur*. They all turned the parts down, and Hitchcock had to settle for other actors, who he felt were not right for the parts. Hitchcock thought that his leading man, Robert Cummings, was physically the wrong type for the part. Universal Studios, and not Hitchcock, cast Priscilla Lane as Patricia Martin. Harry Carey's wife would not allow her husband to take the role of a bad guy, and so Hitchcock cast Otto Kruger as Robert Tobin instead.[2]

Sabrina (1954)

Humphey Bogart as Linus Larrabee (Cary Grant)

Cary Grant dropped out of *Sabrina* at the last minute. He was replaced by Humphrey Bogart.[3]

Sabrina (1995)

Julia Ormond as Sabrina Fairchild (Juliette Binoche, Sandra Bullock, Darcey Bussell, Julie Delpy, Demi Moore, Gwyneth Paltrow, Julia Roberts, Meg Ryan, Winona Ryder, Robin Wright Penn)
Greg Kinnear as David Larrabee (Tom Cruise)

The first name brought up to reprise Audrey Hepburn's role of Sabrina was Julia Roberts. Roberts passed on it as did Sandra Bullock and Robin Wright Penn.[4] Ballerina Darcey Bussell went after the part, as did Winona Ryder.[5] Meg Ryan and Demi Moore were considered, as well as lesser known actresses Julie Delpy and Gwyneth Paltrow.[6] Juliette Binoche tried for the part, but lost out to Julia Ormond.[7]

Tom Cruise considered playing David Larrabee. The ever popular actor found that his schedule was full and eventually passed.[8] Sydney Pollack had a hunch that television talk show host Greg Kinnear might be right. He called up the acting novice to see if he was interested. Kinnear jumped at the chance to work with Pollack. On top of that, he would be playing veteran actor Harrison Ford's brother. Pollack turned out to be right about Kinnear. Not only was his performance in *Sabrina* well reviewed, two years later Kinnear was nominated for a Best Supporting Actor Oscar for *As Good as It Gets*. He lost the award to Robin Williams for *Good Will Hunting*.

The Saint (1997)

Val Kilmer as Simon Templar (Ralph Fiennes, Mel Gibson, Hugh Grant, Brad Pitt)

The role of Simon Templar was turned down by Mel Gibson, Brad Pitt and Ralph Fiennes.[9] An offer also went out to Hugh Grant. Like the others, Grant wasn't interested. He said no.[10] The search was over when Val Kilmer said yes.

Saint Joan (1957)

John Gielgud as Warwick (Richard Burton)
Kenneth Haigh as Martin Ladvenu (Paul Scofield)
Jean Seberg as Joan of Arc (Audrey Hepburn, Barbra Streisand)

Richard Burton was courted for the part of Warwick. Burton considered it, but was unable to make a deal. The part was eventually played by John Gielgud.

Paul Scofield was cast as Brother Martin Ladvenu. He suddenly withdrew from the film. Kenneth Haigh was brought in to replace him.[11]

Audrey Hepburn was courted for the title role of Saint Joan. Hepburn said no, and director Otto Preminger continued to search for a leading lady.[12] A teenage Barbra Streisand went to an open call to audition for the lead in *Saint Joan*. She and her mother, Diana Kind, arrived at the audition to find hundreds of girls all waiting to read. Streisand was told by Preminger's assistant that her reading was very good. Streisand was encouraged by the remark. For weeks she waited to hear if she won the role. One day she read Walter Winchell's column. He reported that Otto Preminger had chosen another newcomer for the part — Jean Seberg.[13]

Salvador (1986)

James Woods as Richard Boyle (Richard Boyle, Martin Sheen
James Belushi as Dr. Rock (James Woods)
John Savage as John Cassady (Willem Dafoe)

Salvador tells the story of real life journalist Richard Boyle. Writer/director Oliver Stone briefly considered having Boyle play himself in the film. He shot a test with Boyle which wasn't very good. He went on to consider Martin Sheen for the part, and James Woods in the supporting role of Dr. Rock. After Woods read the script he went after the lead role. He was able to persuade Stone that he was a better choice than Martin Sheen. James Belushi was brought in to play Dr. Rock.

Stone's first choice for the part of John Cassady was John Savage. However Stone asked Willem Dafoe to be ready to take the part in case Savage turned him down.[14]

Samson and Delilah (1949)

Hedy Lamarr as Delilah (Betty Hutton)

Betty Hutton was pursued for the part of Delilah. When Hedy Lamarr learned of this she got in touch with her agent who arranged a meeting with director Cecil B. DeMille for the next day. At the meeting she learned that the movie would be in color. This made Lamarr want the part even more, since she had yet to make a film in color. At the end of the meeting DeMille offered Lamarr the part.[15]

The Sand Pebbles (1966)

Steve McQueen as Jake Holman (Paul Newman)

Director Robert Wise's first choice for the starring role of Jake Holman in *The Sand Pebbles* was Paul Newman. Newman turned down the film, and practically did Wise a favor.[16] Wise's second choice was Steve McQueen. Since the time Wise had offered the part to Newman, *The Great Escape* had come out. It was a big hit, and made the star of the film, McQueen, the number one box office attraction in the world. Wise offered the part to McQueen, and he accepted. McQueen was nominated for an Oscar for his performance in the film.

Saratoga (1937)

Jean Harlow as Carol Clayton (Joan Crawford)

Saratoga was originally conceived as a vehicle for Joan Crawford. Louis B. Mayer had other ideas. He removed Crawford and gave the part to Jean Harlow instead.[17]

Saratoga Trunk (1945)

Ingrid Bergman as Clio Dulaine (Olivia De Havilland)

Olivia De Havilland was originally cast as Clio Dulaine. Soon after she was fired by Warner Bros.[18] The part was played by Ingrid Bergman instead.

Saturday Night Fever (1977)

Karen Lyn Gorney as Stephanie Mangano (Marilu Henner, Amy Irving, Jessica Lange)

Amy Irving auditioned to play Tony Manero's dance partner Stephanie. Jessica Lange was also a contender but John Travolta, the star of the film, had another idea. He wanted his old friend (and former girlfriend) Marilu Henner to be cast opposite him. Director John Badham allowed Henner to interview, but instead cast his girlfriend Karen Lyn Gorney.[19]

Saving Private Ryan (1998)

Tom Sizemore as Sergeant Horvath (Pete Postlethwaite)

Pete Postlethwaite turned down the role of Sergeant Horvath in *Saving Private Ryan*.[20]

The relatively unknown Karen Lyn Gorney beat out established actresses for the lead in *Saturday Night Fever*.

Say Anything (1989)

John Cusak as Lloyd Dobler (Peter Berg, Robert Downey, Jr., Todd Field, Christian Slater)
Ione Skye as Diane Court (Jennifer Connelly, Elisabeth Shue)
John Mahoney as James Court (Rob Reiner, Dick Van Dyke)

Robert Downey, Jr., was offered the starring role of kickboxer Lloyd Dobler in *Say Anything*. Downey didn't like the script and passed. Christian Slater and Todd Field both cane close to landing the part, as well as Peter Berg. According to writer/director Cameron Crowe, Berg gave a great audition. However the actor Crowe really wanted was John Cusack. Cusack and Crowe had a meeting in a diner in Cusack's home town of Chicago. They discussed the character. They both agreed on how the character should be portrayed. At the end of the meeting Cusack was hesitant to commit to the film. Instead, he agreed to go to some rehearsals. Cusack eventually made a deal for the film.

Elisabeth Shue auditioned for Diane Court. Crowe thought that her reading of the graduation speech was extremely good. Jennifer Connelly was also a contender. According to Crowe, Connelly was the runner up for the part. The actress he was intent on casting was Ione Skye.

Rob Reiner was the first choice to play James Court. Reiner wasn't interested in acting at the time. Cameron Crowe considered Dick Van Dyke, and thought that the actor was very good. But he preferred John Mahoney.[21] Mahoney later went on to fame as Frasier Crane's father Martin on NBC's *Frasier*.

Sayonara (1957)

Marlon Brando as Major Lloyd Gruver (Montgomery Clift, Barry Coe, Kirk Douglas, Glenn Ford, James Garner, William Holden, Rock Hudson, Tab Hunter, Don Murray, Paul Newman, Lee Phillips, Cornel Wilde, Gig Young)
James Garner as Mike Bailey (David Ford, David Janssen, Darren McGavin, Gary Merrill, Ronald Reagan, John Smith, Robert Sterling, Efrem Zimbalist, Jr.)
Miiko Taka as Hana-Ogi (Audrey Hepburn)

Rock Hudson, Paul Newman, William Holden, Montgomery Clift, Kirk Douglas, Tab Hunter, Glenn Ford, Gig Young, Don Murray, Barry Coe and Cornel Wilde were all considered for the starring role of Lloyd Gruver.[22] Rock Hudson was offered the part. At the same time he was also asked to star in the remake of *A Farewell to Arms*. Hudson chose the latter.[23] James Garner went after the part, but Marlon Brando was cast instead.[24]

The candidates for the supporting part of Mike Bailey included David Janssen, Ronald Reagan, John Smith, Efrem Zimbalist, Jr., Gary Merrill, David Ford, Darren McGavin, Robert Sterling and James Garner. Garner appealed to Solly Biano, the casting director, personally. Biano sent him to Josh Logan. Garner also spoke to producer William Goetz. He was obviously persuasive; Garner won the part.[25]

Audrey Hepburn turned down the part of Hana-Ogi, later played by Miiko Taka.[26]

Scarface (1932)

Paul Muni as Tony Camonte (Clark Gable)

Clark Gable was suggested for the part of Tony "Scarface" Camonte. Director Howard

Hawks saw Gable as more of a personality than an actor and rejected him. Hawks met with Paul Muni to discuss the part. Muni didn't think that he was right for the part. Hawks convinced him to make a test. After seeing the test Muni agreed to play the part.[27]

Scarface (1983)

Al Pacino as Tony Montana (John Travolta)

Director Brian De Palma wanted John Travolta for the starring role of Tony Montana. Travolta didn't want to play the drug addicted mobster. Al Pacino was cast after Travolta said no.[28]

Scary Movie (2000)

Carmen Electra as Drew Decker (Melissa Joan Hart, Jenny McCarthy)

Jenny McCarthy was offered the part of Drew Decker. McCarthy turned it down in order to do the film *Scream 3*. Next on the list was Melissa Joan Hart. Hart signed on and went for a costume fitting. She was suddenly fired, although the reason why was not given publicly. Carmen Electra was finally cast in the role.[29]

Scary Movie 2 (2001)

James Woods as Father McFeely (Marlon Brando, Charlton Heston)

Charlton Heston was approached for the part of Father McFeely. When Heston declined Marlon Brando was contacted. Brando had a meeting with director Keenen Ivory Wayans to discuss the film. Brando agreed to play the cameo role for $2 million.[30] However Brando became ill and had to drop out. He was replaced with James Woods.

Scent of a Woman (1992)

Chris O'Donnell as Charlie Simms (Stephen Dorff)

Stephen Dorff auditioned for the part of Charlie Simms.[31] Director Martin Brest instead chose Chris O'Donnell. *Scent of a Woman* was a big hit, making O'Donnell a star.

Schindler's List (1993)

Liam Neeson as Oskar Schindler (Kevin Costner, Daniel Day-Lewis, Robert Duvall, Harrison Ford, Mel Gibson, Jack Thompson)

Harrison Ford, Robert Duvall, Jack Thompson, Daniel Day-Lewis, Mel Gibson and Kevin Costner were all considered for the starring role of Oskar Schindler.[32] However director Steven Spielberg thought that Liam Neeson gave a great audition. Spielberg also liked that Neeson wasn't a big star like some of the others.[33] Neeson was awarded the part. The film won seven Academy Awards, including Best Picture and Best Director. Neeson was nominated for the Oscar, but lost out to Tom Hanks (for *Philadelphia*).

School Daze (1988)

Tisha Campbell as Jane Toussaint (Vanessa L. Williams)
Kyme as Rachel Meadows (Phyllis Yvonne Stickney)
Spike Lee as Half-Pint (Larry B. Scott)
Leonard Thomas as Big Brother General George Patton (Laurence Fishburne)
Tyra Ferrell as Tasha (Eartha Robinson)
Jasmine Guy as Dina (Tisha Campbell)
Frances Morgan as Frances (Cheryl Burr, Erica Gimpel)

Spike Lee considered Vanessa Williams for the part of Jane Toussaint. Tisha Campbell auditioned for the same part. Casting director Robi Reed was so impressed with her audition (especially when she sang "God Bless the Child") that if Lee didn't accept her as Jane she would submit her to play the supporting role of Dina. When Lee met Campbell he was just as impressed as Reed. Campbell won the part of Jane and Jasmine Guy was cast as Dina.

Very early on Lee told Laurence Fishburne that he was considering him for the supporting role of Big Brother General George Patton. Fishburne's ego was bruised, since he would have liked a larger part in the film. Later on, Lee changed his mind and gave Fishburne the starring role of Dap Dunlap instead.

Lee considered Larry B. Scott for the role of Half-Pint before ultimately deciding to play the part himself.

Eartha Robinson auditioned and won the part of Tasha. At the time Robinson was a dancer on a TV show called *Dancing with the Hits*. She still had five months left on her contract. Her agent requested that Lee buy out her contract for $5000. Lee debated the issue. Robinson's agent finally said that unless he agreed, Robinson would not appear in the film. Lee said to forget it. He recast the role with Tyra Ferrell. Robinson's agent called back to say that Lee didn't have to buy out the contract after all. Lee explained that the role was no longer available. He agreed

Erica Gimpel couldn't decide whether or not she was willing to take a supporting role in *School Daze*; the decision was eventually made for her.

to give Robinson a part in the ensemble as Eartha.

Lee wanted Erica Gimpel for the part of Frances. Gimpel is best known for her portrayal of Coco on the television series *Fame*. Since Frances wasn't a leading role Gimpel wasn't sure if she would take it or not. At the same time her agent was asking for more money. Lee decided to move on. He gave the part to Cheryl Burr instead. On the second day of rehearsal Burr broke her foot and had to drop out. She was replaced by the assistant choreographer Frances Morgan.[34]

The Score (2001)
Robert De Niro as Nick Wells (Michael Douglas)
Edward Norton as Jack Teller (Ben Affleck, Brad Pitt)

Michael Douglas was originally supposed to play Nick Wells. Douglas' participation fell through and Robert De Niro was hired to replace him.[35]

Ben Affleck was all set to star in *The Score*. However Affleck unexpectedly dropped out. Affleck's representatives didn't give any reason for his leaving the film. Brad Pitt was asked to step in. The part went to Edward Norton instead.[36]

The Scout (1994)
Albert Brooks as Al Percolo (Walter Matthau)

In the late 1970s Andrew Bergman wrote the screenplay for *The Scout*. Walter Matthau was considered for the title role of Al Percolo. Matthau was very fond of the script.[37] Over 20 years later Bergman passed the script along to Albert Brooks and Monica Johnson. Brooks and Johnson tailored the script for Brooks, who was now set to play Al Percolo, the scout.

Scream (1996)
Neve Campbell as Sidney Prescott (Drew Barrymore)

Drew Barrymore was originally offered the part of Sidney. She read the script and decided it would be more fun to play Casey, a character who dies ten minutes into the film, à la Janet Leigh in *Psycho*.[38]

Scrooge (1970)
Albert Finney as Ebeneezer Scrooge (Richard Harris, Rex Harrison)

Scrooge was a musical version of Charles Dickens' *A Christmas Carol*. Rex Harrison and Richard Harris were both mentioned for the title role of Scrooge. Neither actor signed on for the film. Instead, the part was played by Albert Finney.[39]

Scudda-Hoo! Scudda-Hay! (1948)
Natalie Wood as Bean McGill (Connie Marshall)

Writer/director F. Hugh Herbert thought that child actress Connie Marshall was perfect for the role of Bean McGill. She auditioned for the part and came quite close to landing it. Her main competition was nine-year-old Natalie Wood. Marshall, also nine, was already a film veteran, but still no competition for Wood.[40]

Connie Marshall lost out on the role of Bean McGill in *Scudda-Hoo! Scudda-Hay!*

Sea of Grass (1947)

Katharine Hepburn as Lutie Cameron (Myrna Loy)

Sea of Grass was originally scheduled to star Myrna Loy and Spencer Tracy. Production was postponed many times until it finally went into production with Loy replaced by Katharine Hepburn.[41]

The Sea Wolf (1941)

Edward G. Robinson as Wolf Larsen (Paul Muni)
John Garfield as George Leach (George Raft)

The Sea Wolf was scheduled to go into production in 1937. Paul Muni was sought to star, but he turned it down. The project was stalled. Three years later the film was made with Edward G. Robinson as the star. George Raft turned down the chance to play George Leach. John Garfield took the role.[42]

Seconds (1966)

Rock Hudson as Antiochus "Tony" Wilson (Laurence Olivier)

Director John Frankenheimer thought that Laurence Olivier was the right actor for the starring role in *Seconds*. He was unable to sign Olivier, and gave the part to the popular Rock Hudson.[43]

The Secret Call (1931)

Peggy Shannon as Wanda Kelly (Clara Bow)

Clara Bow was cast in the role of Wanda Kelly in *The Secret Call*. Soon after Bow suffered a nervous breakdown and was replaced by Peggy Shannon.[44]

Selena (1997)

Jennifer Lopez as Selena Quintanilla Perez (Salma Hayek)

Salma Hayek claims she was offered the role of Selena. Star of the film, Jennifer Lopez, says this was an outright lie.[45]

Separate Tables (1958)

Burt Lancaster as John Malcolm (Laurence Olivier)
Rita Hayworth as Ann Shankland (Vivien Leigh)
David Niven as Major Pollock (Laurence Olivier)
Deborah Kerr as Sibyl Railton-Bell (Vivien Leigh)

Laurence Olivier and Vivien Leigh were originally cast in dual roles in *Separate Tables*. When the studio decided to split the parts, they quit. Their replacements were Burt Lancaster, David Niven, Rita Hayworth, and Deborah Kerr.[46]

September (1987)

Denholm Elliott as Howard (Charles Durning)
Elaine Stritch as Diane (Maureen O'Sullivan, Gena Rowlands)
Sam Waterston as Peter (Sam Shepard, Christopher Walken)
Jack Warden as Lloyd (Denholm Elliott)

Director Woody Allen shot the film *September* with two different casts. Originally, Charles Durning played Howard, Maureen O'Sullivan was Diane, Sam Shepard played Peter, and Denholm Elliott was cast as Lloyd. Allen later decided this was not the cast he wanted and decided to reshoot the film. He felt Denholm Elliott would be better in the role of Howard, and got Jack Warden to take Elliott's original role of Lloyd. When first casting the film Allen had asked Gena Rowlands to play Diane. Rowlands turned it down, and Allen cast Maureen O'Sullivan, the mother of his then-girlfriend Mia Farrow. But he later decided that O'Sullivan's performance wasn't what he was looking for and in the second cast the part went to Elaine Stritch. Christopher Walken was the first actor to play Peter. Walken and Allen had worked together previously on *Annie Hall*. The director later realized Walken was not right for the part, and replaced him with Sam Shepard. For the reshoot Allen decided not to ask Shepard to come back (he felt Shepard would not want to do it) and cast Sam Waterston instead.[47]

Serenade (1956)
Joan Fontaine as Kendall Hale (Tallulah Bankhead)

Tallulah Bankhead was offered the part of Kendall Hale in *Serenade*. She turned it down, and it was played by Joan Fontaine instead.[48]

Sergeant York (1941)
Gary Cooper as Alvin C. York (Henry Fonda, Ronald Reagan, James Stewart)

Although Warner Bros. announced Gary Cooper as the lead in their upcoming film *Sergeant York*, it didn't stop them from continuing to search for a leading man. Henry Fonda and James Stewart were possible choices. Ronald Reagan was another candidate; he made a screen test for the part. Howard Hawks eventually signed on as director, and Gary Cooper was cast in the title role, as previously announced.[49]

Serial Mom (1994)
Kathleen Turner as Beverly Sutphin (Julie Andrews, Sally Field, Goldie Hawn, Jessica Lange, Mary Tyler Moore, Susan Sarandon, Cybill Shepherd, Tracey Ullman, Tuesday Weld)
Sam Waterston as Eugene Sutphin (Chevy Chase)

Director John Waters' original list of possible serial moms included Mary Tyler Moore, Tuesday Weld, and Julie Andrews. Producers urged him to consider other actresses such as Goldie Hawn, Jessica Lange, and Susan Sarandon. Sarandon was contacted but asked for too much money.[50] Cybill Shepherd was interested in starring. She begged Waters for an audition, but he said that she didn't look anything like Ricki Lake. Lake was already cast to play Beverly's daughter. Waters refused to let Shepherd audition.[51] Sally Field and Tracey Ullman were considered before Kathleen Turner was cast. Chevy Chase was suggested for the role eventually played by Sam Waterston.[52]

The Servant (1963)
James Fox as Tony (Jean-Louis Trintignant)

French actor Jean-Louis Trintignant was offered the part of bachelor Tony. Trintignant didn't speak English and refused the part. James Fox was ultimately cast.[53]

Set It Off (1996)
Queen Latifah as Cleopatra "Cleo" Sims (Jada Pinkett Smith)
Vivica A. Fox as Francesca "Frankie" Sutton (Rosie Perez)

Jada Pinkett Smith thought she might like to play against type and play the butch Cleo. Director F. Gary Gray said no, gave the part to Queen Latifah, and cast Pinkett Smith in another role. Rosie Perez turned down the role of Frankie, which later went to Vivica A. Fox.[54]

Seven Brides for Seven Brothers (1954)
Jane Powell as Milly Pontipee (Vera-Ellen)

Vera-Ellen was announced for the part of Milly Pontipee in *Seven Brides for Seven Brothers*. She didn't make the film though. When production started Jane Powell had the part.[55]

7 Women (1966)
Anne Bancroft as Dr. D.R. Cartwright (Patricia Neal)

Patricia Neal was initially cast as Dr. D.R. Cartwright. During the filming Neal suffered a stroke. She was unable to complete the film, and Anne Bancroft replaced her.[56]

The Seven Year Itch (1955)
Tom Ewell as Richard Sherman (Gary Cooper, William Holden, Walter Matthau, James Stewart)

Walter Matthau screen tested for the starring role of Richard Sherman. Director Billy Wilder thought Matthau was great. He told the actor that he was 83 percent sure that Matthau would be cast. There was a problem, though: Matthau was not well known. Big stars such as James Stewart and William Holden were considered. Wilder was very interested in Gary Cooper. Darryl F. Zanuck thought that Tom Ewell was a good actor. Ewell originated the role of Richard Sherman in the Broadway production. Ewell got the part. He won a Golden Globe award for his performance.[57]

Seven Years in Tibet (1997)
Brad Pitt as Heinrich Harrer (Daniel Day-Lewis, Ralph Fiennes)

Both Daniel Day-Lewis and Ralph Fiennes were briefly considered to star in *Seven Years in Tibet*. Director Jean-Jacques Annuad eventually gave the part to Brad Pitt.[58]

Seventh Heaven (1937)
Simone Simon as Diane (Janet Gaynor)

Janet Gaynor was offered the part of Diane in *Seventh Heaven*. She turned it down, and it went to Simone Simon instead.[59]

Sex, Lies, and Videotape (1989)
James Spader as Graham Dalton (Brad Greenquist, Kyle MacLachlan, Aidan Quinn)
Andie MacDowell as Ann Millaney (Linda Kozlowski, Elizabeth McGovern)
Peter Gallagher as John Millaney (Tim Daly, Ron Vawter)
Laura San Giacomo as Cynthia Bishop (Jennifer Jason Leigh, Helen Slater)

The role of Graham Dalton was turned down by Kyle MacLachlan and Aidan Quinn. Director Steven Soderbergh thought Brad Greenquist was great for the part, but the producers wanted an actor people were more familiar with, and Soderbergh cast James Spader.

Elizabeth McGovern and Linda Kozlowski's agents both disliked the script so much, it might not have ever been passed along to their clients. Both actresses were being considered for the part of Ann, which was taken by Andie MacDowell.

Tim Daly was the first choice for the character of John Millaney. Daly chose to do the television series *Almost Grown* instead, and ended up passing on the film. Ron Vawter was considered before Peter Gallagher was cast.

Jennifer Jason Leigh turned down the role of Cynthia. Helen Slater was mentioned, but the part went to Laura SanGiacomo.[60]

Shadows and Fog (1992)
Donald Pleasence as Doctor (Bob Balaban)

Bob Balaban won the part of the doctor in Woody Allen's *Shadows and Fog*. After a week of filming Balaban was fired. Allen replaced him with Donald Pleasence.[61]

A young Bob Balaban, many years before Woody Allen fired him from the film *Shadows and Fog*.

Shaft (2000)
Samuel L. Jackson as John Shaft (Don Cheadle, Wesley Snipes)
Jeffrey Wright as Peoples Hernandez (John Leguizamo)

Director John Singleton thought that Don Cheadle would be good for the title role of Shaft in his upcoming film. Producer Scott Rudin disagreed, but it had nothing to do with Cheadle's acting ability. Rudin felt that the part called for a star, and that although Cheadle was known, he simply was not famous enough. Wesley Snipes was considered, but Singleton decided to cast Samuel L. Jackson instead.

John Leguizamo was cast in the role of Peoples Hernandez. He dropped out when he was offered the part of Toulouse-Lautrec in the film *Moulin Rouge*. Rudin was not upset about this; he has said that Leguizamo did the movie a big favor. Rudin, and many others working on the film, thought that Leguizamo's replacement, Jeffrey Wright, was outstanding in the part.[62]

Shakespeare in Love (1998)

Joseph Fiennes as William Shakespeare (Daniel Day-Lewis, Ralph Fiennes, Colin Firth, Mel Gibson, Hugh Grant, Paul McGann)

Gwyneth Paltrow as Viola de Lesseps (Jodie Foster, Julia Roberts, Meg Ryan, Winona Ryder)

About five years before *Shakespeare in Love* actually went into production, Universal planned to make the film with Julia Roberts in the lead. One potential co-star for her was Hugh Grant,[63] who was rejected in favor of Daniel Day-Lewis. Meanwhile, Day-Lewis wasn't interested. Ralph Fiennes, Colin Firth and Paul McGann were possibilities, but Roberts wasn't happy with any of them. Unable to find a costar she found suitable, Roberts left the project. Mel Gibson briefly considered playing Shakespeare on the condition that his production company rewrite the script. Writer Marc Norman refused and Gibson withdrew. Without any stars on board, Universal decided to sell the film to Miramax.[64] Winona Ryder,[65] Jodie Foster[66] and Meg Ryan[67] were all considered. Gwyneth Paltrow was cast. She won an Oscar for her performance and joined the elite circle of actresses whose asking price is about $12 million a film.

Shalako (1968)

Honor Blackman as Julia Baggett (Claire Bloom)

Claire Bloom was cast as Lady Julia Baggett in *Shalako*. Soon after, Bloom learned that Anne Heywood was dropping out of *Charly*. Bloom dropped out of *Shalako* and replaced Heywood in *Charly*.[68]

Shallow Grave (1994)

Ewan McGregor as Alex Law (Robert Carlyle)

Ewan McGregor beat out Robert Carlyle to win the role of Alex Law.[69]

Shallow Hal (2001)

Jack Black as Hal Larson (Tom Cruise, Ben Stiller)

Writer/directors Bobby and Peter Farrelly's dream choice for the title role of Hal was Tom Cruise. Their second choice was Ben Stiller. Rather than Cruise or Stiller the part was finally played by Jack Black.[70]

The Shawshank Redemption (1994)

Tim Robbins as Andy Dufresne (Tom Cruise)

Bob Gunton as Samuel Norton (Harvey Keitel)

Gil Bellows as Tommy Williams (Brad Pitt)

Tom Cruise was asked to star in *The Shawshank Redemption*. After some deliberation, he passed. On the first day of shooting he sent director Frank Darabont a gift basket for good luck on the project.[71]

Harvey Keitel was considered to play the warden, but lost out to Bob Gunton.[72]

Due to a scheduling problem, Brad Pitt was unable to appear in the film. His part was recast with Gil Bellows.[73]

She-Devil (1989)

Roseanne Barr as Ruth Patchett (Cher)
A Martinez as Garcia (Maurice Benard)

Cher lost out to Roseanne Barr for the starring role in *She-Devil*.[74]

Maurice Benard auditioned and was called back for the role of Garcia, Meryl Streep's butler.[75] He eventually lost the role to A Martinez. The two later starred on the soap *General Hospital* together.

The Sheltering Sky (1990)

Debra Winger as Kit Moresby (Ellen Barkin, Melanie Griffith)

Ellen Barkin was very interested in playing Kit Moresby in *The Sheltering Sky*. Barkin said that the part of Kit was the only part she was even interested in playing at the time.[76] Director Bernardo Bertolucci didn't think she was right for it, and turned her down. He offered the part to Melanie Griffith. Griffith was unable to do the film because she was pregnant.[77]

Maurice Bernard lost out on the role of Garcia the butler in *She-Devil* to a future *General Hospital* cast mate.

She's Gotta Have It (1986)

John Canada Terrell as Greer Childs (Ruben Hudson, Eriq La Salle, Eric Payne)
Raye Dowell as Opal Gilstrap (Renata Cobbs, Elaine Graham, Sanett White)

Spike Lee considered Ruben Hudson, Eric Payne and Eriq La Salle for the part of Greer Childs. Hudson told Lee he wasn't interested. La Salle had problems with the way the character was written, but auditioned anyway. Lee was impressed with his reading, but eventually cast John Canada Terrell instead.

Elaine Graham, Sanett White and Renata Cobbs were originally considered for Opal. Lee thought that Raye Dowell was the right actress for the part. He liked Renata Cobbs and gave her the part of Shawn.[78]

Ship of Fools (1965)

Vivien Leigh as Mary Treadwell (Katharine Hepburn)

Katharine Hepburn turned down *Ship of Fools* in order to be with an ailing Spencer Tracy.[79]

The Shipping News (2001)

Kevin Spacey as Quoyle (John Travolta)
Julianne Moore as Wavey Prowse (Kelly Preston)

Husband and wife John Travolta and Kelly Preston were set to star in *The Shipping News* for director Fred Schepisi. Schepisi planned to shoot the film near the couple's home in Maine. The plans fell through however, and Lasse Hallstrom directed the film. It was shot in Canada with Kevin Spacey and Julianne Moore in the leads.[80]

Shock Treatment (1981)

Jessica Harper as Janet Weiss (Susan Sarandon)

Susan Sarandon turned down the chance to reprise the role of Janet Weiss in this sequel to the cult hit, *The Rocky Horror Picture Show*.[81] Jessica Harper was cast in her place. Sarandon's judgment turned out to be good; the sequel lacked the charm of the original, and was a critical and financial flop.

Shopworn (1932)

Barbara Stanwyck as Kitty Lane (Lila Lee)

The part of Kitty Lane was offered to Lila Lee. Lee turned down the offer. Barbara Stanwyck won the role.[82]

Short Cuts (1993)

Julianne Moore as Marian Wyman (Madeleine Stowe)

Director Robert Altman first asked Madeleine Stowe to play the part of artist Marian Wyman. He warned her that she would be required to play an entire scene nude from the waist down. Stowe declined. He then offered the part to Julianne Moore, who accepted.[83]

Show Boat (1951)

Ava Gardner as Julie LaVerne (Judy Garland, Lena Horne)

Lena Horne was a contender for the part of the biracial singer Julie LaVerne. MGM dropped Horne and gave the part to Judy Garland. Garland was unable to perform and Ava Gardner stepped in as a replacement.[84]

Showgirls (1995)

Elizabeth Berkley as Nomi Malone (Drew Barrymore, Jenny McCarthy, Denise Richards, Charlize Theron)
Gina Gershon as Cristal Conners (Madonna, Debi Mazar)
Kyle MacLachlan as Zack Carey (Dylan McDermott)

Drew Barrymore considered starring in *Showgirls*. She later decided against doing the film.[85] Charlize Theron auditioned[86] along with Denise Richards[87] and Jenny McCarthy. McCarthy had been called back several times, but finally lost the role to Elizabeth Berkley.[88]

Madonna's name was mentioned for the part of Cristal Conners,[89] as was Madonna's former make-up artist, Debi Mazar. Although Mazar didn't think much of the script, she still auditioned, but eventually lost the role to Gina Gershon.[90]

Dylan McDermott turned down the part of Zack Carey which ended up going to Kyle MacLachlan.[91]

Shrek (2001)

Mike Myers as Shrek (Chris Farley)

Chris Farley was originally going to supply the voice of Shrek. Farley had problems with drugs and alcohol. The head of DreamWorks, Jeffrey Katzenberg, had a bodyguard for him 24 hours a day to make sure the actor stayed sober. Farley started to work on the film. Sadly, Farley died of a drug overdose. At that time the studio wasn't sure whether or not they would replace him.[92] They eventually gave the part to Mike Myers. *Shrek* was an enormous hit which spawned the sequel, *Shrek 2*.

Signs (2002)

Joaquin Phoenix as Merrill Hess (Mark Ruffalo, Peter Sarsgaard)

Peter Sarsgaard tried for the part of Merrill Hess, but was passed over.[93] Mark Ruffalo was cast. A cyst in his inner ear forced him to drop out, and he was replaced by Joaquin Phoenix.[94]

The Silence of the Lambs (1991)

Jodie Foster as Clarice Starling (Andie MacDowell, Michelle Pfeiffer, Meg Ryan)
Anthony Hopkins as Hannibal Lecter (Robert Duvall, John Hurt)
Scott Glenn as Jack Crawford (Robert Duvall, Gene Hackman)

Michelle Pfeiffer was director Jonathan Demme's first choice for the role of Clarice Starling. She considered the offer, but finally decided it wasn't the kind of film she wanted to make.[95] Demme had recently seen *When Harry Met Sally* and loved Meg Ryan.[96] Andie MacDowell was another possibility. MacDowell wasn't interested and said no.[97] Jodie Foster felt much differently about the character. She campaigned heavily for the role. Her hard work paid off. Foster won her second Academy Award for playing Clarice Starling.

Gene Hackman was originally to play Jack Crawford. John Hurt would be cast as Hannibal Lecter opposite him. Hackman ultimately decided he didn't want to do the film. Demme considered Robert Duvall for the parts of Lecter and Jack Crawford.[98] He eventually decided on Anthony Hopkins for Lecter and Scott Glenn for Crawford.

The Silence of the Lambs was a major hit. The film was nominated for seven Oscars. It won five including Best Picture, Best Actor (Hopkins), Best Actress (Foster), Best Director and Best Adapted Screenplay. It was only the third film to ever win all of the five major Academy Awards. The other two were *It Happened One Night* (1934) and *One Flew Over the Cuckoo's Nest* (1975).

A Simple Plan (1998)

Bridget Fonda as Sarah Mitchell (Anne Heche)

Producer Scott Rudin thought that Anne Heche was a great choice for the part of Sarah Mitchell. However, the idea of Heche fell through. Bridget Fonda was eventually cast.[99]

Since You Went Away (1944)

Claudette Colbert as Anne Hilton (Katharine Cornell)
Agnes Moorehead as Emily Hawkins (Ruth Gordon)

Producer David O. Selznick turned down Katharine Cornell for the part of Anne Hilton. It was eventually played by Claudette Colbert. Selznick felt Cornell was not right for the role.[100]

Ruth Gordon was asked to take the supporting role of Emily Hawkins. Gordon declined, and it was taken by Agnes Moorehead.[101]

Singin' in the Rain (1952)
Gene Kelly as Don Lockwood (Howard Keel)
Donald O'Connor as Cosmo Brown (Oscar Levant)
Jean Hagen as Lina Lamont (Nina Foch)

It's hard to picture anyone but Gene Kelly singing and dancing in the rain, but before he was cast, Howard Keel had been mentioned as a possibility for the part of Don Lockwood. Oscar Levant was producer Arthur Freed's first choice for Cosmo Brown. It was later decided that Brown was going to dance, and they hired Donald O'Connor instead.[102] Nina Foch made a screen test but failed to win the part of Lina Lamont.[103] It went instead to Jean Hagen.

Single White Female (1992)
Bridget Fonda as Allison Jones (Whoopi Goldberg)

Whoopi Goldberg tried for the lead role in *Single White Female*. Goldberg went in knowing that she was not the traditional leading lady that was wanted for the film. For that reason she was not surprised when director Barbet Schroeder turned her down.[104]

Sister Act (1992)
Whoopi Goldberg as Deloris Van Cartier (Bette Midler)

Bette Midler was the first choice for the starring role in *Sister Act*. She declined the offer, and the part went to Whoopi Goldberg.[105]

The Sisters (1938)
Bette Davis as Louise Elliott Medlin (Kay Francis)

Warner Bros. bought *The Sisters* for Kay Francis. Francis fell through, and the part of Louise was played by Bette Davis.[106]

Six Days, Seven Nights (1998)
Anne Heche as Robin Monroe (Sandra Bullock, Minnie Driver, Elizabeth Hurley, Nicole Kidman)
Jacqueline Obradors as Angelica (Melanie Griffith)

Nicole Kidman and Sandra Bullock were considered for the part of Robin Monroe.[107] Minnie Driver took herself out of the running by refusing to audition. Elizabeth Hurley read with Harrison Ford but lost the part to Anne Heche.[108] Melanie Griffith turned down the part of Angelica.[109]

Six Degrees of Separation (1993)
Will Smith as Paul (Courtney B. Vance)

Courtney B. Vance originated the role of Paul in the stage version of *Six Degrees of Separation*. When the film was being made, Vance's name came up. It was decided that on screen he looked too old for the character.[110] He lost the part to Will Smith.

The Skulls (2000)
Joshua Jackson as Luke McNamara (James Van Der Beek)

According to Joshua Jackson, the only two actors director Rob Cohen and writer John Pogue seriously considered for the lead in *The Skulls* were James Van Der Beek and Joshua Jackson. The two actors starred in the television show *Dawson's Creek*. Van Der Beek was also offered *Texas Rangers*. He was more interested in that film, and Jackson got the part in *The Skulls*.[111]

Sleepers (1996)
Minnie Driver as Carol Martinez (Sandra Bullock)

Sandra Bullock was interested in the role of Carol but couldn't fit it into her schedule.[112] Minnie Driver took the part instead.

Sleeping with the Enemy (1991)
Julia Roberts as Sara/Laura Burney (Kim Basinger)

Kim Basinger was cast in the starring role of Sara/Laura Burney. However, Basinger had started a relationship with Alec Baldwin, who was set to make the film *The Marrying Man*. The female lead in *The Marrying Man* was still open, and Basinger dropped out of *Sleeping with the Enemy* to work with Baldwin.[113]

Sleepless in Seattle (1993)
Tom Hanks as Sam Baldwin (Dennis Quaid)
Meg Ryan as Annie Reed (Kim Basinger, Demi Moore, Julia Roberts)
Rosie O'Donnell as Becky (Camryn Manheim, Rita Wilson)

Husband and wife team Dennis Quaid and Meg Ryan were the first actors attached to *Sleepless in Seattle*. When nothing seemed to be happening with the project the actors moved on.[114] Kim Basinger was interested in the role,[115] as was Julia Roberts. Roberts considered the project, but decided to pass on it.[116] Demi Moore did what she could to convince the studio she was right for the part, but they disagreed.[117] Meg Ryan came back on board and instead of Dennis Quaid, Tom Hanks was cast opposite her.

Hanks' wife Rita Wilson expressed interest in the role of Becky.[118] Camryn Manheim auditioned, but director Nora Ephron felt Rosie O'Donnell was better for the character. Ephron did find a part for Wilson. She cast her as Suzy, and Wilson had a memorable crying scene. Her performance was singled out as one of the film's funniest. *Sleepless in Seattle* brought Wilson out of the shadow of her famous husband.

Sleuth (1972)

Michael Caine as Milo Tindle (Alan Bates, Albert Finney)

After Albert Finney and Alan Bates proved unavailable, Michael Caine was cast in *Sleuth*.[119]

Sliding Doors (1998)

Gwyneth Paltrow as Helen Quilley (Gillian Anderson)

Gillian Anderson lost out to Gwyneth Paltrow for the part of Helen in *Sliding Doors*.[120]

Small Time Crooks (2000)

Tracey Ullman as Frances "Frenchy" Winkler (Madonna, Meryl Streep, Barbra Streisand)

Writer/director Woody Allen asked Barbra Streisand to be his costar in *Small Time Crooks*. Streisand was unavailable and had to turn Allen down. Madonna and Meryl Streep were considered, but Allen chose Tracey Ullman instead.[121]

Smiles of a Summer Night (1955)

Ulla Jacobsson as Annie Egerman (Bibi Andersson)

Ulla Jacobsson was cast as Annie Egerman. She became pregnant, and if she was unable to finish the film, Bibi Andersson was ready to step in.[122] That didn't happen, and Andersson's services were not needed.

Smilin' Through (1932)

Norma Shearer as Kathleen Sheridan/Moonyeen Clare (Joan Bennett)

United Artists wanted to make *Smilin' Through* with Joan Bennett in the lead. However, MGM acquired it and gave the part to Norma Shearer.[123]

The Snake Pit (1948)

Olivia De Havilland as Virginia Stuart Cunningham (Ingrid Bergman, Ginger Rogers)

Ginger Rogers[124] and Ingrid Bergman turned down Olivia De Havilland's Academy Award winning role in *The Snake Pit*. Bergman wrote in her autobiography that if she had taken the part, she wouldn't have won the Oscar.[125]

So I Married an Axe Murderer (1993)

Nancy Travis as Harriet Michaels (Sharon Stone)

Amanda Plummer as Rose Michaels (Sharon Stone)

Sharon Stone was offered the chance to star opposite Mike Myers in *So I Married an Axe Murderer* as Harriet Michaels. Stone was interested, but only if she could play both Harriet and her sister Rose. TriStar didn't want that, so Stone passed on the film.[126]

Soapdish (1991)

Kevin Kline as Jeffrey Anderson (Burt Reynolds)

Burt Reynolds was offered the part of soap opera actor Jeffrey Anderson in *Soapdish*. Reynolds' former girlfriend Sally Field was already signed to star. Reynolds would have played opposite her. The characters in the film are also former lovers. According to Reynolds, Loni Anderson (his wife at the time) didn't want him to work with Field. Reynolds turned the part down.[127]

A Soldier's Daughter Never Cries (1998)

Kris Kristofferson as Bill Willis (Nick Nolte)

Nick Nolte, who was originally cast as Bill Willis, dropped out to star in *The Thin Red Line*.[128]

The Solid Gold Cadillac (1956)

Judy Holliday as Laura Partridge (Shirley Booth, Marilyn Monroe)
Paul Douglas as Edward L. McKeever (Rod Steiger)

Competing studios were interested in buying *The Solid Gold Cadillac* for their own stars. Twentieth Century–Fox wanted it for Marilyn Monroe. Paramount wanted to buy it for Shirley Booth. Instead it went to Columbia, and starred Judy Holliday.[129]

Rod Steiger auditioned to play Edward L. McKeever. He lost out to Paul Douglas.[130]

Solomon and Sheba (1959)

Yul Brynner as Solomon (Tyrone Power)

Tyrone Power was originally cast as Solomon. Sadly, he died while the film was in production. Yul Brynner was brought in to play the part.[131]

Some Came Running (1958)

Shirley MacLaine as Ginny Moorhead (Shelley Winters)

Shelley Winters was pursued for the part of Ginny Moorhead. Unable to sign Winters, the part was played by Shirley MacLaine.[132]

Some Like It Hot (1959)

Jack Lemmon as Jerry (Danny Kaye, Anthony Perkins, Frank Sinatra)
Tony Curtis as Joe (Bob Hope, Frank Sinatra)
Marilyn Monroe as Sugar Kane (Mitzi Gaynor)

Several pairings of leading men were considered for the leads in *Some Like It Hot*. United Artists considered casting Danny Kaye as Jerry opposite Bob Hope as Joe.[133] Director Billy Wilder wanted Anthony Perkins as Jerry with Frank Sinatra as Joe.[134] The idea to have Sinatra play Jerry was also a possibility.[135] The Hope/Kaye idea fell through, as did Sinatra's involvement. Anthony Perkins' schedule was booked up with the film *Green Mansions*.[136] Tony Curtis played Joe, and Wilder called in Jack Lemmon to play Jerry.

Mitzi Gaynor was considered for the role of Sugar Kane. However, Marilyn Monroe was too big a star to ignore. Billy Wilder gave up his first choice (Gaynor) and gave the part to Monroe.[137]

Somebody Up There Likes Me (1956)

Paul Newman as Rocky Graziano/Rocco Barbella (Montgomery Clift, James Dean)

The lead role in *Somebody Up There Likes Me* was turned down by Montgomery Clift.[138] Had James Dean not been killed in a car crash, the role would have been his. He had discussed doing the film with MGM, and he was all set to do it.[139] The part was eventually played by Paul Newman.

Someone Like You (2001)

Ashley Judd as Jane Goodale (Julia Roberts)

Julia Roberts was offered the starring role of Jane Goodale. Roberts said yes and then no. When she dropped out Ashley Judd was brought in as a replacement.[140]

Something's Gotta Give (2003)

Keanu Reeves as Julian Mercer (Matthew Perry)

Matthew Perry auditioned for the part of Julian Mercer. He was told that he lost the part because he was too closely identified with the character of Chandler Bing from the television series *Friends*. Perry was on the show for ten years. The part of Julian Mercer was eventually taken by film star Keanu Reeves.[141]

Somewhere I'll Find You (1942)

Clark Gable as Jonathon "Jonny" Davis (Robert Taylor)
Lana Turner as Paula Lane (Esther Williams)

Clark Gable was cast in the lead in *Somewhere I'll Find You*. After the first day of shooting Gable's wife, Carole Lombard, was killed in a plane crash. The film was put on hold. If Gable decided not to make the movie, Robert Taylor was a possible replacement. Gable finally decided that he would need a month off, but then he would continue with the film.[142]

Lana Turner was originally cast as Paula Lane in *Somewhere I'll Find You*. During the shooting Turner became AWOL. She had gone to New York to marry bandleader Artie Shaw. MGM gave Esther Williams a screen test as a possible replacement. It turned out to be unnecessary. Turner soon returned and was allowed to remain in the film.[143]

The Song of Bernadette (1943)
Jennifer Jones as Bernadette Soubirous (Anne Baxter, Teresa Wright)

Jennifer Jones, Anne Baxter and Teresa Wright all auditioned for the starring role of Bernadette Soubirous. Director Henry King was extremely impressed with Jones' reading and gave her the part.[144]

Sonny (2002)
James Franco as Sonny Phillips (Mark Ruffalo)

Mark Ruffalo was director Nicolas Cage's first choice for the starring role of Sonny Phillips. Ruffalo said no, and Cage gave the part to James Franco.[145]

Sons and Lovers (1960)
Mary Ure as Clara Dawes (Joan Collins)

Joan Collins was dating Warren Beatty when she was offered the part of Clara Dawes in *Sons and Lovers*. The actress read the script and was ready to sign on for the film. Beatty didn't like the script. He also didn't want Collins to go on location to England without him. Beatty pleaded with her to turn the part down. Collins complied, and Mary Ure played Clara.[146] Collins regretted her decision once she saw the film. Not only was the film better than she had anticipated, but Mary Ure was nominated for an Oscar for her performance.[147] On top of that, Collins' career was floundering, while Beatty's was taking off. Collins and Beatty broke up not long after.

Sons of the Desert (1933)
Dorothy Christy as Mrs. Betty Laurel (Patsy Kelly)

Patsy Kelly was unable to appear in *Sons of the Desert* and was replaced by Dorothy Christy.[148]

Sorcerer (1977)
Roy Scheider as Scanlon/Dominguez (Clint Eastwood, Steve McQueen, Jack Nicholson)

Bruno Cremer as Victor Manzon/"Serrano" (Lino Ventura)

Director William Friedkin asked Steve McQueen to star in *Sorcerer*. McQueen agreed on the condition that his wife, Ali MacGraw, was also cast in the film. Friedkin did not have a part for her. McQueen said he would still do the film, but only if it were shot in the U.S. so that he could still see MacGraw. Friedkin insisted that South America was the location for the shoot. Finally McQueen asked if MacGraw could be hired as an associate producer. Again Friedkin told him no. McQueen decided not to do the film. Friedkin later admitted that he made a very big mistake letting McQueen go, and that he should have done whatever McQueen asked of him.[149]

Friedkin pursued Jack Nicholson and Clint Eastwood, but neither actor wanted to do it. Friedkin finally gave the part to Roy Scheider. Friedkin later said that casting Scheider was a mistake, that he was wrong for the part. He went on to say that the problem was that the part needed to be played by a star. He said that Scheider was not a star.

Friedkin wanted Lino Ventura to play Victor Manzon/"Serrano." Ventura was interested, but only if Steve McQueen or Clint Eastwood played Scanlon/Dominguez. Friedkin gave the part to Bruno Cremer instead.[150]

The Sound of Music (1965)
Julie Andrews as Maria (Anne Bancroft, Leslie Caron, Doris Day, Angie Dickinson, Audrey Hepburn, Shirley Jones, Grace Kelly, Carol Lawrence)

Christopher Plummer as Captain Von Trapp (Stanley Baker, Stephen Boyd, Yul Brynner, Richard Burton, Sean Connery, Jerome Courtland, Michael Craig, Bing Crosby, Anton Diffring, Peter Finch, Vittorio Gassman, Louis Jourdan, John Justin, Brian Keith, Walter Matthau, Keith Michell, David Niven, Patrick O'Neal, Eric Porter, Denis Quilley, Maximilian Schell, Paul Scofield, Massimo Serato, Carlos Thompson)

Eleanor Parker as Baroness Schraeder (Dawn Adams, Anouk Aimee, Elizabeth Allen, Anna-Lisa, Martine Bartlett, Capucine, Cyd Charisse, Diane Cilento, Jan Clayton, Hazel Court, Yvonne Furneaux, Eva Gabor, Rita Gam, Jane Greer, Grace Kelly, Viveca Lindfors, Ida Lupino, Vera Miles, Patricia Owen, Lillie Palmer, Joyce

Redman, Raby Rodgers, Eva Marie Saint, Elizabeth Sellars, Victoria Shaw, Joan Tetzel, Mary Ure, Christine White, Nancy Wickwire, Irene Worth, Dana Wynter)

Peggy Wood as Mother Abbess (Peggy Ashcroft, Hermione Baddeley, Fay Bainter, Cicely Courtneidge, Lillie Darvas, Irene Dunne, Edith Evans, Isabel Jeans, Jeanette MacDonald, Anna Neagle, Cathleen Nesbitt, Atheny Seyler, Lilia Skala, Mona Washbourne)

Richard Haydn as Max Detweiler (Fred Astaire, Edgar Bergen, Hershel Bernardi, Sorrell Booke, Victor Borge, Roger C. Carmor, Robert Coote, Noel Coward, Claude Dauphin, Hal Holbrook, Kurt Kasznar, John McGiver, Burgess Meredith, Robert Morley, Louis Nye, Cesar Romero, George Rose, Heinz Ruhmann, Walter Slezak, George Voscover, Emlyn Williams)

Norma Varden as Frau Schmidt (Eleanor Audley, Isobel Elsom, Kathryn Givney, Hilda Plowright)

Charmian Carr as Liesl Von Trapp (Melanie Alexander, Geraldine Chaplin, Kathy Dunn, Shelley Fabares, Mia Farrow, Teri Garr, Tish Sterling, Sharon Tate, Lesley Ann Warren)

Nicholas Hammond as Friedrich Von Trapp (Doug Chapin)

Heather Menzies as Louisa Von Trapp (Carole Lyons, Ave Maria Megna, Christopher Norris, Monique Vermont)

Duane Chase as Kurt Von Trapp (Jack Jones, Jay North)

Angela Cartwright as Brigitta Von Trapp (Andrea Darvi, Renee Dudley, Lisa Jager, Joy Stark)

Debbie Turner as Marta Von Trapp (Diane Higgins, Frances McKenna, Tracy Stratford, Melody Thomas)

Kym Karath as Gretl Von Trapp (Eileen Baral, Cynthia Grover, Susie Higgins, Pamie Lee, Wendy Muldoon)

Ben Wright as Herr Zeller (Robert Ellenstein, Robert Gist, Gavin MacLeod, Alfred Ryder, Fritz Weaver)

Daniel Truhitte as Rolfe (Jerry Bono, Mart Hulswitt, Danny Lockin, Mike Toren)

Gilchrist Stuart as Franz (Eric Berry, Leslie Bradley, Edward Colmans, Eduard Franz, Gavin Gordon, Jonathan Harris, Hedley Mattingly, Shepperd Strudwick)

Doris Day's husband, Martin Melcher, tried unsuccessfully to land Day the role of Maria in *The Sound of Music*. Although Julie Andrews was eventually cast, many actresses were also considered. Among them were Angie Dickinson, Grace Kelly, Audrey Hepburn, Shirley Jones, Carol Lawrence, Anne Bancroft, and Leslie Caron.

Director Robert Wise's first choice for the role of Captain Von Trapp was Christopher Plummer. Plummer wasn't interested, and Wise turned to Peter Finch, who was unavailable. Richard Burton's name was brought up, but Wise decided to keep looking. Yul Brynner went out for the part. Wise felt he had already played a role similar to Von Trapp in *The King and I*. He also thought Brynner's accent was wrong for the character and turned him down. Wise was somewhat interested in Keith Michell, but not enough to be persuaded he was the ultimate choice. Walter Matthau and Patrick O'Neal met Wise to interview. Sean Connery, David Niven, and Stephen Boyd were all mentioned. Wise continued his exhaustive search by considering Stanley Baker, Bing Crosby, Maximilian Schell, Jerome Courtland, Anton Diffring, Louis Jourdan, Eric Porter, Paul Scofield, Michael Craig, Vittorio Gassman, Brian Keith, Denis Quilley, Massimo Serato, John Justin and Carlos Thompson. Wise was still interested in Plummer. He flew to England to discuss the film with him. Plummer was so impressed with Wise that he changed his mind and agreed to take the part.

All of the actresses listed above were considered for the role of Baroness Schraeder, eventually played by Eleanor Parker.[151]

Lilia Skala tried to win the role of Mother Abbess, but was turned down.[152] Jeanette MacDonald's name was brought up, but producer Saul Chaplin said that she never came close to landing the part.[153] Peggy Wood was cast after Peggy Ashcroft, Fay Bainter, Irene Dunne, Anna Neagle, Mona Washbourne, Edith Evans, Hermione Baddeley, Cathleen Nesbitt, Isabel Jeans, Lillie Darvas, Cicely Courtneidge, and Atheny Seyler were all considered.[154]

Wise chose Richard Haydn, Norma Varden, Gilchrist Stuart, Daniel Truhitte, and Ben

Wright for their roles after discussing the many candidates listed above.

Both veteran child actors and unknowns auditioned to play the children. Shelley Fabares was a Liesl contender. Fabares was best known for playing Mary on *The Donna Reed Show* for five years. One of the stars of *The Beverly Hillbillies*, Sharon Tate, auditioned as well. Charlie Chaplin's daughter Geraldine Chaplin was up for it, as was Maureen O'Sullivan and John Farrow's daughter Mia Farrow. Robert Wise liked Chaplin very much, but was concerned that her father might interfere with the negotiations. Wise thought that Farrow's reading was good, but the 19-year-old actress lacked energy and didn't dance well enough. Wise thought that Teri Garr was too old; that Sharon Tate didn't dance; and that Lesley Ann Warren was excellent. Other actresses such as Tish Sterling, Melanie Alexander, and Kathy Dunn auditioned, but lost out to newcomer Charmian Carr. *The Sound of Music* was Carr's only film. She retired from show business shortly after.

Nicholas Hammond beat out Doug Chapin for the part of Friedrich Von Trapp.

Broadway actress Christopher Norris tried out for Louisa. Norris came to fame in the late 1970s as Nurse Gloria "Ripples" Brancusi on the TV series *Trapper John, M.D.* Also considered were Carole Lyons, Monique Vermont, and Ave Maria Megna. The role was won by newcomer Heather Menzies. Surprisingly (for one of the kids from *The Sound of Music*), Menzies later posed for *Playboy*. She continued to act until the late 1980s. In 1974 she married actor Robert Urich.

Newcomer Duane Chase beat out *Dennis the Menace* star Jay North and Jack Jones for the part of Kurt. Jack Jones is well known as the singer of the theme song for *The Love Boat*.

Make Room for Daddy star Angela Cartwright was cast as Brigitta after Joy Stark, Andrea Darvi, Lisa Jager, and Renee Dudley were all considered.

Diane Higgins, Frances McKenna, Tracy Stratford, and Melody Thomas went out for the part of Marta. Wise instead gave the part to Debbie Turner. Shortly after Stratford became the voice of Lucy Van Pelt in many of the Charlie Brown cartoons. Although Melody Thomas played the Tippi Hedren as a young girl in director Alfred Hitchcock's *Marnie*, she is best known for her starring role of Nikki on *The Young and the Restless*. Thomas joined the cast in 1979 and as of 2004 is still on the show.

Kym Karath won the role of Gretl, beating out contenders such as Wendy Muldoon, Pamie Lee, Eileen Baral, Cynthia Grover, and Susie Higgins.[155]

South Pacific (1958)

Mitzi Gaynor as Nellie Forbush (Doris Day, Judy Garland, Mary Martin, Elizabeth Taylor)

When *South Pacific* was being made into a movie, Mary Martin, the original Broadway Nellie Forbush, was considered too old to play the part on screen. Director Joshua Logan wanted to see Elizabeth Taylor as Nellie, but her singing prevented a deal.[156] Doris Day was considered,[157] as was Judy Garland,[158] but the part finally went to Mitzi Gaynor.

Sparkle (1976)

Phillip Michael Thomas as Stix (Lawrence Hilton-Jacobs)

In his pre–*Welcome Back Kotter* years, Lawrence Hilton-Jacobs auditioned for the film *Sparkle*. He lost out to Phillip Michael Thomas.[159]

Speed (1994)

Keanu Reeves as Jack Traven (Johnny Depp)

Johnny Depp turned down the starring role of Jack Traven.[160]

Speed 2: Cruise Control (1997)

[Jack Travern—Keanu Reeves]

Keanu Reeves turned down the chance to reprise his role of Jack Traven in the sequel to the blockbuster film *Speed*. According to *Speed 2: Cruise Control* star Sandra Bullock, at that time Reeves didn't want to do a film on such a large scale.[161] His character was written out and replaced by a new character, Alex Shaw.

Spider-Man (2002)

Tobey Maguire as Peter Parker/Spiderman (Jim Carrey, Leonardo DiCaprio, Jude Law, Chris O'Donnell, Freddie Prinze, Jr.)

Willem Dafoe as Norman Osborn/The Green Goblin (Nicolas Cage)

Kirsten Dunst as Mary Jane Watson (Alicia Witt)

Freddie Prinze, Jr., wanted the role of Spiderman very much. He said he grew up reading the

Spiderman comics.[162] Jude Law,[163] Chris O'Donnell,[164] and Jim Carrey's[165] names were bandied about as possible choices. Leonardo DiCaprio was a possible choice. His representative Ken Sunshine said that the actor would have to see the script.[166] Director Sam Raimi's wife, Gillian Green, was impressed with Tobey Maguire's performance in *The Cider House Rules*.[167] She showed the film to her husband, who thought he was perfect for Spiderman. Sam Raimi finally gave the part to Tobey Maguire.

Nicolas Cage expressed interest in playing the Green Goblin. Negotiations fell through when Cage realized that he would be unavailable due to the filming of *Windtalkers*.[168]

Alicia Witt was a candidate for the role of Mary Jane Watson.[169] The part was eventually played by Kirsten Dunst.

Splash (1984)

Tom Hanks as Allen Bauer (Chevy Chase, Michael Keaton, Dudley Moore, Bill Murray, Burt Reynolds, John Travolta)
John Candy as Freddie Bauer (Tom Hanks)

The starring role of Allen Bauer was turned down by John Travolta,[170] Michael Keaton,[171] Chevy Chase,[172] Burt Reynolds,[173] Dudley Moore[174] and Bill Murray.[175] Director Ron Howard worked with Tom Hanks on an episode of Howard's television series, *Happy Days*. Howard was impressed with Hanks' performance, and asked him to audition for the film. Hanks read for the part of Allen's brother Freddie. However Howard recognized that Hanks was right for the lead. He gave Hanks the part, and brought in John Candy for the part of Freddie.[176]

Splendor in the Grass (1961)

Natalie Wood as Wilma Dean Loomis (Jane Fonda, Lee Remick)
Warren Beatty as Bud Stamper (Troy Donahue)

Lee Remick and Troy Donahue[177] were considered for the leads in *Splendor in the Grass*. Remick became pregnant and had to withdraw.[178] Director Elia Kazan also considered Jane Fonda.[179] The leads finally went to Natalie Wood and Warren Beatty.

The Spy Who Loved Me (1977)

Richard Kiel as Jaws (Will Sampson)

Will Sampson competed for the part of Jaws in *The Spy Who Loved Me*.

Producer Albert "Cubby" Broccoli considered Will Sampson for the part of Jaws, but eventually chose Richard Kiel. Sampson is best known as the Indian in *One Flew Over the Cuckoo's Nest*.[180]

St. Louis Blues (1939)

Lloyd Nolan as Dave Guerney (George Raft)

The role of Dave Guerney was initially assigned to George Raft. Raft refused to play the part, and he was replaced by Lloyd Nolan.[181]

The St. Valentine's Day Massacre (1967)

Jason Robards as Al Capone (Orson Welles)
Ralph Meeker as Bugs Moran (Marlon Brando)

Director Roger Corman hoped to sign Orson Welles for the part of Al Capone with Marlon

Brando playing Bugs Moran. He was unable to get these actors. The roles were played by Jason Robards and Ralph Meeker instead.[182]

Stagecoach (1939)

Claire Trevor as Dallas (Marlene Dietrich)
John Wayne as Ringo Kid (Gary Cooper)

Marlene Dietrich and Gary Cooper were the first choices for *Stagecoach*.[183] At his wife Rocky's urging, Cooper turned down the film. The parts went instead to Claire Trevor and John Wayne.[184]

Stalag 17 (1953)

William Holden as J.J. Sefton (Kirk Douglas, Charlton Heston)

Writer/director Billy Wilder wrote the part of Sefton with Charlton Heston in mind. Wilder offered Heston the part, but he turned it down.[185] Wilder also considered Kirk Douglas before approaching William Holden.[186] Holden recognized that this was a very good script and accepted the part.[187]

Stallion Road (1947)

Alexis Smith as Rory Teller (Lauren Bacall)

Lauren Bacall turned down the role of Rory Teller in *Stallion Road*. She was put on suspension and replaced with Alexis Smith.[188]

Stand Up and Be Counted (1972)

Jacqueline Bisset as Sheila Hammond (Sally Kellerman)
Gary Lockwood as Eliot Travis (Alan Alda)

Former child star Jackie Cooper was hired to direct the feature film *Stand Up and Be Counted*. He considered Alan Alda for the part of Eliot Travis. He sent a copy of the script to Alda. The two later had a meeting to discuss the film. Alda had problems with the script. He thought it ridiculed the women's movement. Cooper agreed that Alda had a point and said that perhaps the script could be changed. Producer Mike Frankovich didn't want the script altered, and Alda passed on the part.

Sally Kellerman was offered the part of Sheila Travis. She wasn't interested and it was played by Jacqueline Bisset instead.[189]

Star 80 (1983)

Eric Roberts as Paul Snider (Richard Gere)

Director Bob Fosse chose Eric Roberts over Richard Gere to play Paul Snider in *Star 80*.[190]

A Star Is Born (1954)

James Mason as Norman Maine (Humphrey Bogart, Marlon Brando, Richard Burton, Montgomery Clift, Gary Cooper, Glenn Ford, Stewart Granger, Cary Grant, Ray Milland, Laurence Olivier, Gregory Peck, Tyrone Power, Frank Sinatra, James Stewart, Robert Taylor)
Charles Bickford as Oliver Niles (William Powell)

The list of possible Norman Maines included Laurence Olivier, Richard Burton, Tyrone Power, Cary Grant, Humphrey Bogart, Marlon Brando, James Stewart, Frank Sinatra, Gregory Peck, Montgomery Clift, Stewart Granger, Ray Milland, Robert Taylor, and Glenn Ford. Jack Warner turned down Frank Sinatra, but liked Humphrey Bogart. The problem was that producer Sid Luft thought he was too old for the role. Stewart Granger was interested for a while, but eventually took himself out of the running. Cary Grant was offered $450,000 for the role and almost took it. He finally decided it wasn't for him. Judy Garland was very upset when she found out Grant would not be playing opposite her. Richard Burton might have played the part, but a commitment to *The Robe* forced him out. The role was finally taken by James Mason.

William Powell rejected the part of Oliver Niles which was eventually played by Charles Bickford.[191]

A Star Is Born (1976)

Barbra Streisand as Esther Hoffman (Cher, Bianca Jagger, Liza Minnelli, Diana Ross, Cybill Shepherd, Carly Simon)
Kris Kristofferson as John Norman Howard (Gregg Allman, Sonny Bono, Marlon Brando, Mick Jagger, Jon Peters, Elvis Presley, Alan Price, James Taylor)

Several real life couples were considered for the leads in *A Star Is Born*. James Taylor and Carly Simon turned it down. It was rumored that the film too closely mirrored their lives.[192] Mick and Bianca Jagger[193] were considered as were Sonny and Cher[194] and Cher and Gregg Allman.[195] Non-couple Elvis Presley and Liza Minnelli were another possible pair, as well as Diana Ross who was to be teamed with Alan Price.[196] Cybill Shepherd was also considered for Esther Hoffman.[197] Superstar Barbra Streisand was interested and the part was hers. She and her boyfriend, hairdresser-turned-producer Jon Peters went to Las Vegas to offer Elvis Presley the part of John Norman Howard. Presley told Streisand that she was the only one whom he was intimidated by and declined the offer. Streisand even considered making the film less of a musical with Marlon Brando as her co-star. Kris Kristofferson was made an offer, which he turned down. Jon Peters decided that he himself would be perfect for the part. Streisand backed him up. When Peters tried to sing all involved realized he wouldn't be able to pull it off. Kristofferson reconsidered his decision, and the part was his.[198]

Star Trek: Generations (1994)

[*Mr. Spock*—Leonard Nimoy]

[*Dr. McCoy*—DeForest Kelley]

Leonard Nimoy and De Forest Kelley did not want to appear in *Star Trek: Generations*. They felt that their roles were only included for name value, but served no real purpose in the story. Both characters were eliminated from the film.[199]

Star Wars (1977)

Mark Hamill as Luke Skywalker (Will Seltzer)

Harrison Ford as Han Solo (Richard Dreyfuss, William Katt, Nick Nolte, Al Pacino, John Travolta, Glynn Turman, Christopher Walken)

Carrie Fisher as Princess Leia Organa (Jodie Foster, Amy Irving, Terri Nunn, Cindy Williams)

Alec Guinness as Ben Kenobi (Toshiro Mifune)

Peter Mayhew as Chewbacca (David Prowse)

Director George Lucas and casting director Fred Roos auditioned many young actors for the three lead roles in *Star Wars*. Brian De Palma was at the casting sessions. De Palma was looking for actors for his upcoming film *Carrie*. Will Seltzer auditioned for the part of Luke Skywalker, but lost out to Mark Hamill.[200]

Lucas considered casting an established star as Han Solo. Al Pacino's name was mentioned.[201] Richard Dreyfuss was considered for the part. However the actor Lucas was really interested in was Christopher Walken. Casting director Dianne Crittenden thought John Travolta was the right choice, but Lucas disagreed. At one point Lucas thought about having a black actor play Han Solo. The actor he had in mind was Glynn Turman. He later realized that having an interracial romance between Han Solo and Princess Leia might take away from the story, and he dropped the idea. Nick Nolte and William Katt both auditioned and were called back.[202] Harrison Ford was working at the casting sessions as a carpenter. Lucas knew him from *American Graffiti*. Lucas had Ford read with some of the actresses auditioning for Princess Leia. Even though Ford wasn't there to audition Lucas was impressed with his reading.[203]

Jodie Foster auditioned for Princess Leia, as well as Amy Irving, Carrie Fisher and Cindy Williams. Williams worked with Lucas on *American Graffiti*. Williams wanted the part very much, but George Lucas thought that, at age 29, she was too old. He wanted to find a "young Cindy Williams." The choices were finally narrowed down to Mark Hamill and Will Seltzer for Luke Skywalker, Harrison Ford and Christopher Walken for Han Solo, and Terri Nunn and Amy Irving for Princess Leia.[204] Lucas chose Hamill, Ford, and Fisher. Christopher Walken's career was not hurt by not appearing in *Star Wars*. He made *The Deer Hunter* the following year, for which he won the Best Supporting Academy Award. George Lucas apparently liked Will Seltzer enough to cast him in his film, *More American Graffiti* as Andy Henderson. Terri Nunn quit acting around 1982. She is best known for being the lead singer of the band Berlin. Brian DePalma got three of his leads for *Carrie* from those not chosen by George Lucas: John Travolta, William Katt, and Amy Irving.

Toshiro Mifune was considered for Ben Kenobi, but Lucas eventually cast Alec Guinness instead.

David Prowse was up for Chewbacca.[205] Prowse was instead cast as Darth Vader, although the voice was supplied by James Earl Jones.

Star Wars: Episode I—The Phantom Menace (1999)

Jake Lloyd as Anakin Skywalker (Haley Joel Osment)

Haley Joel Osment auditioned for the role of Anakin Skywalker very early in the casting process. He was turned down.[206] The part went to Jake Lloyd instead. The same year *Phantom Menace* was released, Osment had a major success with a film of his own — *The Sixth Sense*.

Star Wars: Episode II — Attack of the Clones (2002)

Hayden Christensen as Anakin Skywalker (Leonardo DiCaprio, Jeff Garner, Colin Hanks, Jonathan Jackson, Chris Klein, Ryan Phillippe, James Van Der Beek, Erik von Detten)

Leonardo DiCaprio was mentioned for the part of Anakin Skywalker. Producer Rick McCallum said that he liked the actor. However, DiCaprio did not end up with the part.[207] Lucasfilm requested newcomer Jeff Garner's picture to be sent.[208] Ryan Phillippe, Chris Klein and Colin Hanks were all possibilities,[209] as were James Van Der Beek and Erik von Detten.[210] *Newsweek* reported that Jonathan Jackson was close to getting the part. Jackson's agent said that Jackson previously had a good chance at getting the part, but the article ruined his chances.[211] George Lucas ended his exhaustive search when he chose relative newcomer Hayden Christensen.

Stargate (1994)

Kurt Russell as Colonel Jonathan "Jack" O'Neil (Sean Connery, Wesley Snipes)

James Spader as Dr. Daniel Jackson (Matthew Broderick)

Sean Connery was first offered the role of Jack O'Neil. When he said no, Wesley Snipes was approached. Like Connery, he also turned the part down.[212] Matthew Broderick was offered the role of Daniel Jackson, but was unavailable.[213]

Starship Troopers (1997)

Casper Van Dien as Johnny Rico (Jonathon Schaech, Mark Wahlberg)

Casper Van Dien won the role of Johnny Rico over such contenders as Mark Wahlberg and Jonathon Schaech.[214]

Starsky & Hutch (2004)

Owen Wilson as Ken Hutchinson (Vince Vaughn)

Vince Vaughn was a consideration for the part of Hutch in the film version of *Starsky & Hutch*.[215] Owen Wilson was eventually cast alongside Ben Stiller as Starsky. Stiller and Wilson worked together many times before in films such as *Meet the Parents*, *Zoolander* and *The Royal Tenenbaums*.

Start the Revolution Without Me (1970)

Donald Sutherland as Charles/Pierre (Charles Grodin)

Gene Wilder arranged for Charles Grodin to be offered a role in his film, *Start the Revolution Without Me*. Grodin was already committed to do a play, and was forced to pass on the film.[216]

Starting Over (1979)

Jill Clayburgh as Marilyn Holmberg (Candice Bergen)

Candice Bergen was interested in playing the role of Marilyn Holmberg. Director Alan J. Pakula offered that part to Jill Clayburgh. Pakula was interested in Bergen, but for the supporting role of Jessica Potter. Bergen didn't like the part of the shallow Jessica. She worried that people might think that she was just like the character in real life. But Bergen was eager to work with Pakula and loved the script. She accepted the part. Bergen was glad she did; she was nominated for an Oscar for her performance.[217]

State Fair (1962)

Pamela Tiffin as Margy Frake (Ann-Margret)

Although Ann-Margret originally auditioned for the role of Margy, she was ultimately cast as Emily Porter. The producers felt she was too alluring for the ingénue role, and cast Pamela Tiffin instead.[218]

Steel Magnolias (1989)

Julia Roberts as Shelby Eatenton Latcherie (Laura Dern, Meg Ryan, Winona Ryder)

Laura Dern auditioned for the part of Shelby. Dern's reading was good, but she looked nothing like Sally Field. Field was already cast to play Shelby's mother. Producer Ray Stark suggested Julia Roberts. He knew the actress from working with her on *Baja Oklahoma*. Stark thought director Herbert Ross should watch it. After viewing *Baja Oklahoma* Ross concluded that Roberts looked bad, and was bad in it. Ross really wanted Meg Ryan to play the part. Ryan had another offer, which she took. The film was *When Harry Met Sally*. The movie made Ryan a star. Winona Ryder was considered, but Ross thought she was too young. Sally Field liked Julia Roberts. Field told Ross so. He gave Roberts an audition. Ross was so impressed with her that she got the part.[219]

Steelyard Blues (1973)
John Savage as The Kid (Keith Carradine)

Keith Carradine auditioned for the role of The Kid. In producer Julia Phillips' autobiography, *You'll Never Eat Lunch in This Town Again*, Phillips claims that the star of the film — Donald Sutherland — was threatened by Carradine. This resulted in his losing the role to John Savage.[220]

Stella Dallas (1937)
Barbara Stanwyck as Stella Dallas (Ruth Chatterton, Gladys George)

Ruth Chatterton and Gladys George were considered for the lead.[221] Barbara Stanwyck was eventually cast and was nominated for an Academy Award for her performance.

The Sterile Cuckoo (1969)
Liza Minnelli as Pookie (Mary Ann) Adams (Sondra Locke)

Sondra Locke wanted very much to play the part of Pookie Adams. Her agent contacted the director, Alan J. Pakula, and arranged a meeting. Locke had heard rumors that Liza Minnelli was set for the part, but figured if he wanted to meet her, she had a chance. Locke met the director and did a reading for him. Afterwards Pakula told her that her audition was the best one. He also went on to say that it was too bad he had not met her six months ago when the film was being cast. Locke lost out to Liza Minnelli.[222]

The Sting (1973)
Paul Newman as Henry Gondorff (Peter Boyle)
Robert Redford as Johnny Hooker (Warren Beatty)
Robert Shaw as Doyle Lonigan (Richard Boone, Stephen Boyd, Laurence Olivier)

Peter Boyle was considered for the role of Gondorff.[223] Warren Beatty rejected the role of Johnny Hooker.[224]

Richard Boone was offered the part of Doyle Lonigan, but turned it down.[225] Robert Shaw was cast after Laurence Olivier and Stephen Boyd were both considered.[226]

Storm Center (1956)
Bette Davis as Alicia Hull (Mary Pickford)

In 1952 Mary Pickford considered starring in *Storm Center*. Pickford dropped the project at the last minute. She said that she thought the movie was going to be in color.[227] Bette Davis eventually signed on as the star.

Stormy Monday (1988)
Sean Bean as Brendan (Tim Roth)

Writer/director Mike Figgis' choice for the starring role of Brendan was Tim Roth. Melanie Griffith was set for the female lead, Kate. Griffith's manager, Phyllis Carlisle, had a problem with Roth's looks. She didn't think he was good looking enough to be matched with Griffith. Sean Bean, however, was another story. Figgis appeased them and gave Bean the part, but only because he thought Bean was a very good actor.[228]

The Story of Dr. Wassell (1944)
Carol Thurston as Tremartini (Yvonne De Carlo, Simone Simon, Elena Verdugo)

Yvonne De Carlo auditioned for director Cecil B. De Mille to play the role of Tremartini in *The Story of Dr. Wassell*. De Mille thought that De Carlo's acting was fine, but questioned if she was the right physical type. He thought that she did not have the right build to play a native girl, such as Tremartini. Another problem was De Carlo's blue eyes. As far as De Carlo was concerned, the actress she had to look out for was Elena Verdugo. Verdugo had already beaten her out for a role in *The Moon and Sixpence*. Verdugo also had brown eyes, which were a plus for the part in question. De Mille was also interested in Simone Simon, who came very close to landing the part. Eventually, he decided the best actress for the part was Carol Thurston.[229]

The Story of Three Loves (1953)

Kirk Douglas as Pierre Narval (Ricardo Montalban)

Ricardo Montalban originally had the part of Pierre Narval in *The Story of Three Loves*. Montalban's costar, Pier Angeli, broke her wrist on the set. Shooting had to be rescheduled. When they resumed filming, Montalban was no longer in the cast. His part was taken by Kirk Douglas.[230]

The Stranger (1946)

Edward G. Robinson as Wilson (Agnes Moorehead)

Director Orson Welles wanted Agnes Moorehead for the lead role of War Crimes Commission agent Wilson. Producer Sam Spiegel rejected the non-traditional casting idea, and instead gave the part to Edward G. Robinson.[231]

Strangers on a Train (1951)

Farley Granger as Guy Haines (William Holden)

William Holden was director Alfred Hitchcock's number one choice for the part of Guy Haines.[232] When he was unavailable Hitchcock cast Farley Granger.

The Stratton Story (1949)

James Stewart as Monty Stratton (Van Johnson)
June Allyson as Ethel Stratton (Donna Reed)

Van Johnson and Donna Reed were originally set to star in *The Stratton Story*. The choice of Johnson was later in question. It was determined that he wasn't right for the part of Monty Stratton. James Stewart was signed to replace him. Stewart and Reed starred in *It's a Wonderful Life* together. The film has since become a classic, but at the time of its release it was not popular. Stewart was aware of this, and had Reed replaced. June Allyson got the part. Reed was very hurt for years by this rejection.[233]

Straw Dogs (1971)

Dustin Hoffman as David Sumner (Beau Bridges, Elliott Gould, Stacy Keach, Jack Nicholson, Sidney Poitier, Donald Sutherland)
Susan George as Amy Sumner (Judy Geeson, Carol White)

Jack Nicholson, Sidney Poitier, Donald Sutherland, Beau Bridges and Stacy Keach were all mentioned for the part of David Sumner.[234] Elliott Gould was another contender, but the role was won by Dustin Hoffman instead.[235]

Judy Geeson and Carol White auditioned to play Amy Sumner. Director Sam Peckinpah liked another actress: Susan George. Dustin Hoffman and producer Daniel Melnick both questioned his decision. They thought that George was not the right choice. Peckinpah refused to change his mind. He gave the part to Susan George.[236]

The Strawberry Blonde (1941)

Rita Hayworth as Virginia Brush (Ann Sheridan)

Ann Sheridan was cast in the role of Virginia Brush in *The Strawberry Blonde*. She was fighting with the studio over a contract problem. Warner Bros. agreed to pay her $600 a week, but Sheridan felt it wasn't enough. She was a very popular star and had made the studio a considerable amount of money. She wanted $2000 a week. Jack Warner said no and suspended her, which caused her to lose the part of Virginia to Rita Hayworth.[237] *The Strawberry Blonde* was Hayworth's first big hit.

Street Scene (1931)

Sylvia Sidney as Rose Maurrant (Nancy Carroll)

Nancy Carroll was announced as the star of the upcoming film *Street Scene*. Paramount later decided they would rather have Sylvia Sidney in the part and dropped Carroll.[238]

A Streetcar Named Desire (1951)

Vivien Leigh as Blanche Du Bois (Anne Baxter, Olivia de Havilland, Jennifer Jones, Jessica Tandy)

Jessica Tandy originated the role of Blanche Du Bois on Broadway but was turned down for the film version. Tandy was very upset to lose the part. She was the only one of the four lead actors from the original Broadway cast to not reprise their role on the film.[239] Jennifer Jones was a contender, but failed to win the part.[240] Anne Baxter was another possibility.[241] Olivia De Havilland was considered, but the actress just

Strictly Dishonorable (1931)
Sidney Fox as Isabelle Perry (Bette Davis)

Early on Bette Davis was promised the part of Isabelle Perry. Davis made a screen test, and was offered a contract with Universal Studios. There was one thing in her way to getting the part of Isabelle: Producer Carl Laemmle, Jr., thought that Davis was plain looking, that she had no sex appeal. He wanted a more glamorous type for the part and Davis lost the role of Isabelle to Sidney Fox.[243]

The Stripper (1963)
Richard Beymer as Kenny (Warren Beatty)

Richard Beymer was cast as Kenny after the part had been turned down by Warren Beatty.[244]

Striptease (1996)
Burt Reynolds as David Dilbeck (Michael Caine, Gene Hackman)

Burt Reynolds won the role of David Dilbeck over contenders Gene Hackman and Michael Caine.[245]

The Student Prince (1954)
Ann Blyth as Kathie (Jane Powell)
Edmund Purdom as Prince Karl (Mario Lanza)

Jane Powell was chosen for the part of Kathie. Powell wouldn't make the film. Ann Blyth signed on instead.[246]

Mario Lanza was originally cast in the role of Prince Karl. Lanza quit, and MGM sued him for $5 million. They settled by using Lanza's voice. Edmund Purdom replaced Lanza. Purdom lip-synched to Lanza's voice.[247]

Studs Lonigan (1960)
Christopher Knight as Studs Lonigan (Warren Beatty, Jack Nicholson)

Writer/producer Philip Yordan had Warren Beatty in mind for the title role of Studs Lonigan. Beatty was interested and read the script. He told director Irving Lerner that he thought the script needed to be changed. At that time Beatty was known only for the role of Milton Armitage on the television series *The Many Loves of Dobie Gillis*. Lerner had no way of knowing that Beatty would go on to become an acclaimed actor/writer/producer. He decided that he didn't want to put up with Beatty and he lost the role. Jack Nicholson was a contender, but he was given the smaller role of Weary Reilly. Lerner gave the starring role to Christopher Knight.[248]

Suddenly, Last Summer (1959)
Elizabeth Taylor as Catherine Holly (Marilyn Monroe, Patricia Neal)
Montgomery Clift as Dr. Cukrowicz (Peter O'Toole)

Patricia Neal played the part of Catherine Holly in the London stage production of *Suddenly, Last Summer*. One night producer Sam Spiegel was in the audience. He thought that Neal's performance was so good that he bought the rights for the film. Spiegel thought that Neal was wonderful in the play, which made her feel confident she would reprise the role in the film version. Neal was stunned when one day she picked up a newspaper to find that the part was to be played by Elizabeth Taylor. Neal has said that it was the biggest disappointment of her career.[249] Marilyn Monroe tried to win the part, but Spiegel stuck with Elizabeth Taylor.[250]

Peter O'Toole was tested for the role of Dr. Cukrowicz but lost out to Montgomery Clift.[251]

Sullivan's Travels (1941)
Veronica Lake as The Girl (Lucille Ball, Frances Farmer, Betty Field, Ruby Keeler, Ida Lupino, Claire Trevor

Preston Sturges wanted Veronica Lake to play the Girl in *Sullivan's Travels*. Producer Buddy DeSylva disagreed with Sturges' choice. He suggested the director cast any of the following actresses instead: Lucille Ball, Frances Farmer, Ruby Keeler, Ida Lupino, Claire Trevor and Betty Field. Sturges wouldn't hear of it. He gave the part to Lake.[252]

The Sum of All Fears (2002)
Ben Affleck as Jack Ryan (Harrison Ford)

The Sum of All Fears was the fourth installment of the Jack Ryan films. Alec Baldwin originated the part in the first film, *The Hunt for Red October*. When Baldwin decided against signing on for the sequel, *Patriot Games*, Harrison Ford

232 Summer and Smoke

was brought in as a replacement. Ford starred in the third movie, *Clear and Present Danger*, and intended to return for the fourth, *The Sum of All Fears*. After Ford read a copy of the screenplay there was a problem. He thought that there were problems with the story structure and told Paramount Pictures CEO Sherry Lansing to get another writer to fix the script. The first draft was written by Akiva Goldsman along with a second draft, at which point Paul Attanasio was brought in to polish it up. According to producer Mace Neufeld, Ford had a problem with the fact that his character, who had previously been a CIA executive, was now working in the field. He felt it wasn't believable. At this point Lansing went to Ford's writer of choice, Steven Zaillian. Zaillian was already working on another film, *Hannibal*, and turned it down. Lansing decided that before she went any further she told Ford that he must commit to a start date for the film. Ford refused to do so and consequently left the project entirely. When the news broke Ben Affleck's agent Patrick Whitesell arranged a deal for his client with Paramount.[253]

Summer and Smoke (1961)

Laurence Harvey as John Buchanan, Jr. (Mel Ferrer)
Geraldine Page as Alma Winemiller (Audrey Hepburn)

Producer Hal Wallis and writer Tennessee Williams wanted Audrey Hepburn for the part of Alma Winemiller. Hepburn met with the pair in Switzerland to discuss the film. Hepburn wanted her husband Mel Ferrer to be cast opposite her as John Buchanan, Jr. On top of that, she wanted Givenchy to design her costumes. Wallis and Williams were not interested in accommodating her requests and cast Geraldine Page and Laurence Harvey instead.[254]

Summer of Sam (1999)

Mira Sorvino as Dionna (Jennifer Esposito)
Adrien Brody as Ritchie (Leonardo DiCaprio)

Jennifer Esposito was originally cast in the Mira Sorvino role of Dionna. There were scheduling problems and director Spike Lee was forced to switch her over to the smaller role of Ruby.[255]

Leonardo DiCaprio was asked to join the cast as punk rocker Ritchie.[256] He declined and Lee cast Adrien Brody instead.

Scheduling problems affected Jennifer Esposito's role in *Summer of Sam*.

The Sun Also Rises (1957)

Tyrone Power as Jake Barnes (Marlon Brando, Montgomery Clift)
Ava Gardner as Lady Brett Ashley (Gene Tierney)
Robert Evans as Pedro Romero (John Gavin)

Director Howard Hawks decided that he would make *The Sun Also Rises*. He planned to have Gene Tierney and Montgomery Clift star as Lady Brett Ashley and Jake Barnes. Hawks later changed his mind and was planning to use Marlon Brando in the Jake Barnes role. He eventually sold the rights to 20th Century–Fox. Henry King was hired to direct.[257]

John Gavin lost the role of Pedro to future producer Robert Evans.[258]

Sunday, Bloody Sunday (1971)

Glenda Jackson as Alex Greville (Vanessa Redgrave)
Peter Finch as Dr. Daniel Hirsh (Ian Bannen, Sean Connery)

Vanessa Redgrave turned down the part of Alex in order to star in *The Devils*.[259]

Ian Bannen was cast as Daniel Hirsh until he developed pneumonia.[260] Sean Connery wanted to replace him, but the part had already been taken by Peter Finch.[261]

Sunset (1988)

Kathleen Quinlan as Nancy Shoemaker (Marilu Henner)

Marilu Henner auditioned for the role of Nancy Shoemaker. Director Blake Edwards assured her she would be cast, but later gave the role to Kathleen Quinlan.[262]

Sunset Boulevard (1950)

Gloria Swanson as Norma Desmond (Pola Negri, Mary Pickford, Mae West)
William Holden as Joe Gillis (Marlon Brando, Montgomery Clift, Gene Kelly, Fred MacMurray)

Director Billy Wilder's first choice for the legendary role of Norma Desmond was Mae West. West felt she was too young for the part and turned it down.[263] Mary Pickford was interested, but only if she were allowed to make changes in the script. She wasn't, and an offer was made to Pola Negri. Negri didn't want the part, but there was an actress who did: Gloria Swanson.[264]

Montgomery Clift was offered and accepted the role of Joe. He later reconsidered and dropped out. He told Wilder that he was quitting because he did not think he would be convincing making love to a much older woman. Wilder said that that was bullshit, and if he was a good actor he could be convincing making love to any woman.[265] Fred MacMurray was offered the role, but had serious problems with the character. He turned it down telling Wilder that playing a kept man offended his morals.[266] Marlon Brando was considered as was Gene Kelly. Kelly's studio, MGM, refused to loan him out.[267] Wilder finally thought about William Holden. His decision was made; Holden was cast as Joe Gillis.

Superman (1978)

Christopher Reeve as Clark Kent/Superman (Warren Beatty, Charles Bronson, James Caan, Clint Eastwood, Bruce Jenner, Steve McQueen, Nick Nolte, Robert Redford, Burt Reynolds, Sylvester Stallone)
Margot Kidder as Lois Lane (Anne Archer, Susan Blakely, Stockard Channing, Deborah Raffin, Lesley Ann Warren)
Jackie Cooper as Perry White (Eddie Albert, Jack Klugman, Keenan Wynn)
Phyllis Thaxter as Ma Kent (Joan Crawford)

Burt Reynolds,[268] James Caan,[269] and Nick Nolte all turned down the chance to star as Superman. Nolte considered accepting the part. He spoke with the producers and told them that he saw the character as a schizophrenic. The producers balked at this suggestion, and Nolte took himself out of the running.[270] Robert Redford was made an offer of $2 million. Redford said it would take too much time to shoot, and passed on the part.[271] Warren Beatty was also asked to play Superman. He even took a costume home to try on. He wore it around his house for a very short time, at which point he decided to pass on the film.[272] Sylvester Stallone tried out. However, Stallone didn't have the all–American look necessary for the part.[273] Olympian Bruce Jenner was certainly all–American. He had the right look, but his acting wasn't up to par.[274] Steve McQueen was a possibility, but was ruled out after the producers decided that he had gotten too fat.[275] After considering other actors such as Clint Eastwood and Charles Bronson, the producers decided to go with an unknown Christopher Reeve.[276]

Barbra Streisand was a very early consideration for reporter Lois Lane. Susan Blakely screen tested for Lois Lane in a dark wig, as did Deborah Raffin. Stockard Channing tested. Her Lois was in the style of the 1940s female reporter that actress Barbara Stanwyck specialized in. Anne Archer auditioned as well as Lesley Ann Warren. Casting director Lynn Stalmaster thought that Kidder was clearly the best choice.

Three actors were cast as Perry White prior to Jackie Cooper. Jack Klugman and Eddie Albert both dropped out. Keenan Wynn became sick and was unable to perform in the film.

Joan Crawford was considered to play Clark Kent's mother. When the actress died, the part went to Phyllis Thaxter.[277]

Superman II (1980)

Sarah Douglas as Ursa (Dana Gillespie, Rohan McCullogh, Marilu Tulo, Carinthia West)

Dana Gillespie, Rohan McCullogh, Carinthia West and Marilu Tulo all screen tested for the part of Ursa. Sarah Douglas was cast instead.

Susan Lennox (Her Fall and Rise) (1931)
Clark Gable as Rodney (John Gilbert)

The role of Rodney was originally planned for John Gilbert. However, Greta Garbo, the star of the film, refused to work with Gilbert. Gilbert was removed from the film, and replaced by Clark Gable.[278]

Sweet Bird of Youth (1962)
Geraldine Page as Alexandra del Lago (Ava Gardner)

Ava Gardner was the first choice for the part of Alexandra del Lago. She said no, and the part went to Geraldine Page. Page created the role in the original Broadway production.[279]

The Sweet Hereafter (1997)
Ian Holm as Mitchell Stephens (Donald Sutherland)

Donald Sutherland was set to play Mitchell Stephens in *The Sweet Hereafter*. When he dropped out, director Atom Egoyan replaced him with Ian Holm.[280]

Switch Back (1997)
Dennis Quaid as Frank Lacrosse (Steven Seagal)
R. Lee Ermey as Buck Olmstead (Danny Glover)

Steven Seagal was considered for the part of Frank Lacrosse.

Danny Glover was offered the role of Buck. He didn't want that role, but was interested in playing Bob Goodall. He got the part, and Buck was played by R. Lee Ermey.[281]

Switching Channels (1988)
Burt Reynolds as John L. Sullivan, IV (Michael Caine)

Michael Caine was originally scheduled to star in *Switching Channels*. When Caine left the film, Burt Reynolds was brought in as a replacement.[282]

Sylvia Scarlett (1936)
Brian Aherne as Michael Fane (Errol Flynn)

Producer Pandro S. Berman thought that Errol Flynn should play the part of Michael Fane. Director George Cukor met with Flynn. The meeting lasted five minutes. Cukor didn't want Flynn. He gave the part to Brian Aherne instead.[283]

Tai-Pan (1986)
Bryan Brown as Dick Straun (Steve McQueen)

Steve McQueen and producer Georges-Alain Vuille arranged a deal in which McQueen was to receive $10 million to star in *Tai-Pan*. One million was to be paid up front (for signing the contract), with the rest of the money paid in installments. Vuille was late with the first installment. McQueen dropped out of the film without doing any work, but the $1 million signing fee was his to keep.[1]

Take a Letter, Darling (1942)
Rosalind Russell as A.M. MacGregor (Katharine Hepburn)

Katharine Hepburn was offered the role of A.M. MacGregor in *Take a Letter, Darling*. She turned it down and it was played by Rosalind Russell instead.[2]

Take Me Out to the Ball Game (1949)
Esther Williams as K.C. Higgins (June Allyson, Judy Garland, Kathryn Grayson)

The role of K.C. Higgins was written with Kathryn Grayson in mind. Although Grayson wanted to play the part, producer Arthur Freed decided that he didn't want her and instead gave the part to Judy Garland. However, Garland was unable to make the movie due to her ongoing problems with substance abuse. June Allyson was set to replace Garland, but Allyson found out that she was pregnant. Arthur Freed finally gave the part to Esther Williams.[3]

A Tale of Two Cities (1935)
Ronald Colman as Sydney Carton (Brian Aherne)

Brian Aherne was offered the leading role of Sydney Carton in MGM's *A Tale of Two Cities*. Once the studio heard that Ronald Colman was also available, they forgot all about Aherne, and gave Colman the part instead.[4]

Tales That Witness Madness (1973)

Kim Novak as Auriol Pageant (Rita Hayworth)

Rita Hayworth was originally cast in the role of Auriol Pageant. Hayworth disappeared from the set during shooting and was replaced by Kim Novak. It was not known at the time, but the problem was that Hayworth was suffering from Alzheimer's disease.[5]

The Talented Mr. Ripley (1999)

Matt Damon as Tom Ripley (Christian Bale, Leonardo DiCaprio)

Christian Bale was interested in the starring role of Tom Ripley but was unsuccessful in getting the part.[6] Director Anthony Minghella was very interested in Leonardo DiCaprio. The two spoke about DiCaprio's participation in the film, but Minghella became convinced that another actor was the right choice. He met with Matt Damon to discuss the film. Minghella said that Damon was desperate for the part, and Minghella felt he was the best possible choice.[7]

Tall Story (1960)

Anthony Perkins as Ray Blent (Warren Beatty)

Director Joshua Logan's first choice to play Ray was Warren Beatty. When the studio learned of Logan's choice, they became involved. They told Logan that no one knew who Warren Beatty was, and that he had no choice but to give the part to Anthony Perkins instead.[8]

Tarzan (1999)

Tony Goldwyn as Tarzan (Brendan Fraser)
Rosie O'Donnell as Terkoz "Terk" (Chris Rock)

Brendan Fraser auditioned to be the voice of Tarzan, but Tony Goldwyn was cast instead.[9]

Chris Rock rejected the role of Terk, which went to Rosie O'Donnell.[10]

Tarzan, the Ape Man (1932)

Johnny Weissmueller as Tarzan (Charles Bickford, Herman Brix, Johnny Mack Brown, Buster Crabbe, Clark Gable, Joel McCrea, Tom Tyler)

Johnny Weissmueller won the role of Tarzan after Herman Brix, Charles Bickford, Buster Crabbe and Joel McCrea were considered.[11] Tom Tyler and Johnny Mack Brown were also mentioned as possible choices to play Tarzan, as well as Clark Gable. Gable participated in a camera test in which he had to wear swim trunks. It was decided that he didn't have the physique the part called for. Olympian Johnny Weissmueller was cast instead.[12]

Tarzan, the Ape Man (1981)

Miles O'Keeffe as Tarzan (Lee Canalito)

Lee Canalito was originally cast as Tarzan. He left the film and was replaced by Miles O'Keeffe.[13]

A Taste of Honey (1961)

Rita Tushingham as Jo (Audrey Hepburn)

Audrey Hepburn rejected the part of Jo in *A Taste of Honey*.[14]

Taxi (1953)

Constance Smith as Mary (Grace Kelly)

Grace Kelly auditioned for the role of Mary in *Taxi* but lost out to Constance Smith. John Ford saw the screen test Kelly made and cast her as Linda Nordley in *Mogambo*. As a result, Kelly was signed to a seven year contract with MGM.[15]

Taxi Driver (1976)

Robert De Niro as Travis Bickle (Jeff Bridges)
Cybill Shepherd as Betsy (Farrah Fawcett, Meryl Streep)
Martin Scorsese as Passenger Watching Silhouette (George Memmoli)

Director Martin Scorsese had the opportunity to direct *Taxi Driver* with Jeff Bridges as Travis Bickle. He decided to postpone the film until it was possible to have Robert De Niro star as Travis.[16]

Cybill Shepherd beat out Meryl Streep[17] and Farrah Fawcett[18] for the role of Betsy.

George Memmoli was scheduled to be De Niro's passenger. Memmoli was injured while making another film, and was unable to appear in the movie. Martin Scorsese decided to take the role himself.[19]

Tea with Mussolini (1999)
Cher as Elsa Morganthal Strauss-Armistan (Glenn Close, Diane Keaton, Susan Sarandon)

Director Franco Zeffirelli's original list of actresses for the role of Elsa included Susan Sarandon, Diane Keaton, and Glenn Close. As an afterthought he checked to see if Cher was available. Cher was sent a copy of the screenplay, which she loved. She agreed to take the role. Although the film opened to favorable reviews, Cher wasn't entirely pleased. She complained that many of her scenes were edited in a disjointed manner. She was also able to acknowledge that she may have been overly critical by only looking at her own performance.[20]

The Teahouse of the August Moon (1956)
Marlon Brando as Sakini (Gene Kelly)

Gene Kelly was the first choice for the starring role of Sakini in the film version of *The Teahouse of the August Moon*. Kelly was interested, but then Marlon Brando let it be known that he too wanted to play the part. Kelly was quickly pushed aside and Brando was cast.[21]

Tempest (1982)
John Cassavettes as Philip (Paul Newman)

Paul Stewart as Philip's father (Elia Kazan)

Writer/director Paul Mazursky and casting director Juliet Taylor thought that Elia Kazan would be perfect for the part of Philip's father. Kazan was known as a renowned director, but he did have some acting experience. He appeared in 1940's *City for Conquest* and 1941's *Blues in the Night*. Mazursky approached Kazan, who responded by asking to see the script. A week went by and Kazan contacted Mazursky. Kazan told him that although he liked the script, he was too busy writing to commit his time. Mazursky promised to shoot his entire role very quickly, in a matter of days, to accommodate him. Kazan said he would consider the offer some more. He invited Mazursky to his home to discuss it. Mazursky happily agreed to meet him. At their meeting Kazan again told the director that he was busy writing and would not be available. Mazursky accepted the rejection and started to leave. Kazan became enraged. He told Mazursky that if he were really interested in him for the part that he would not have given up so easily. Later in the week Mazursky cast the role with Paul Stewart.

Mazursky offered Paul Newman the role of Philip. Newman turned Mazursky down, and John Cassavetes was hired for the part.[22]

10 (1979)
Dudley Moore as George Webber (George Segal)

Writer/director Blake Edwards cast George Segal in the starring role of George Webber. Segal reconsidered making the film and dropped out at the last minute.[23] Edwards soon found Dudley Moore and was able to start filming. *10* turned out to be a huge hit and Edwards was given the Writers Guild Award for Best Screenplay (Comedy).

Tender Is the Night (1962)
Jennifer Jones as Nicole Diver (Elizabeth Taylor)

Jason Robards as Dr. Dick Diver (Warren Beatty, Dirk Bogarde, Richard Burton, Montgomery Clift, Peter Finch, Glenn Ford, Cary Grant, Paul Newman, Christopher Plummer)

Producer David O. Selznick thought that Cary Grant should star as Dick Diver opposite his wife Jennifer Jones as Nicole Diver. Grant wasn't overly enthusiastic. Selznick also considered John Frankenheimer to direct the film. Both men thought that Montgomery Clift was perfectly suited for the part of Diver. George Cukor was another possibility to direct. Cukor wanted Glenn Ford to play Diver. But Cukor turned the project down. Meanwhile, Frankenheimer was making plans for Christopher Plummer to take the lead. The studio didn't like his choice. Peter Finch, Paul Newman and Dirk Bogarde were all considered as was Warren Beatty. It was eventually decided that at 27 he was too young.[24] Jennifer Jones had some competition for her part. Elizabeth Taylor was a possibility with Richard Burton playing Diver. Selznick explained that the only reason he wanted to make the film was for his wife. Twentieth Century–Fox kept her in the part. The studio eventually dropped Selznick from the film, although he was paid. Henry Weinstein replaced Selznick as producer while Henry King was hired to direct. King cast Jason Robards as Dick Diver.[25]

Tequila Sunrise (1988)

Mel Gibson as Dale McKussic (Harrison Ford)
Kurt Russell as Nick Frescia (Pat Riley)

Harrison Ford briefly considered starring in *Tequila Sunrise*. The producers were enthusiastic to have a star of his stature. However, Ford was on the fence about playing a drug dealer and eventually pulled out. Writer/director Robert Towne's wife suggested that Towne think about Mel Gibson. Towne watched Gibson's film *Lethal Weapon* and became enthused. He sent a copy of the script to Gibson, who accepted.

Los Angeles Lakers coach Pat Riley was approached for the part of Nick Frescia. Riley was good friends with Robert Towne. Riley said that he was too busy with his coaching job. Towne gave the part to Kurt Russell.[26]

The Terminator (1984)

Arnold Schwarzenegger as the Terminator (O.J. Simpson)
Michael Biehn as Kyle Reese (Arnold Schwarzenegger)

The first choice for the part of the Terminator was O.J. Simpson. Arnold Schwarzenegger was originally considered to play the hero, Kyle Reese. Schwarzenegger read the script and decided he would rather play the Terminator. He got the part and Michael Biehn was brought in to play Kyle Reese.[27]

Terminator 2: Judgment Day (1991)

Robert Patrick as T-1000 (Billy Idol)

Robert Patrick beat out rocker Billy Idol for the part of T-1000.[28]

Terminator 3: Rise of the Machines (2003)

Claire Danes as Kate Brewster (Sophia Bush)
Kristanna Loken as T-X (Joanie Laurer)
[*Sarah Connor*— Linda Hamilton]

Sophia Bush was hired to play Kate Brewster. After a week of filming director Jonathan Mostow fired her. Mostow said that Bush was two years too young. Her replacement was Claire Danes.[29] Danes is three years older than Bush.

Joanie Laurer was considered for the part of T-X. Laurer came to fame known as the wrestler Chyna.[30]

Linda Hamilton starred in the first two Terminator movies with Arnold Schwarzenegger. She read the script for the third installment and decided not to make the film. The role was not recast.[31]

Terms of Endearment (1983)

Shirley MacLaine as Aurora Greenway (Jennifer Jones, Diane Keaton)
Debra Winger as Emma Horton (Sissy Spacek, Mary Steenburgen)
Jack Nicholson as Garrett Breedlove (Harrison Ford, Paul Newman, Burt Reynolds)
Lisa Hart Carroll as Patsy Clark (Kim Basinger)

Originally Diane Keaton had the inside track on playing Aurora Greenway in *Terms of Endearment*. Jennifer Jones purchased the rights to the film with the idea of playing Aurora Greenway. She approached several directors including James L. Brooks. Brooks loved the script and had the rights bought from Jones.[32] Brooks decided Shirley MacLaine was the best choice for Aurora.

Mary Steenburgen was considered for the part of Emma. Sissy Spacek was made an offer, but she said no. Debra Winger was cast instead.[33]

Brooks offered Burt Reynolds the part of Garrett Breedlove. Reynolds was already committed to star in *Stroker Ace* and turned the part down.[34] Another rejection came from Paul Newman.[35] Harrison Ford was also offered the part. Ford knew that it was a good role, a potential award-winning role, but just didn't think he was the right actor for it. He turned it down, and Jack Nicholson was cast.[36] Nicholson won rave reviews for his performance, and many awards including the Academy Award, Golden Globe Award, Los Angeles Film Critics Award, National Board of Review Award, National Society of Film Critics Award, and the New York Film Critics Award.

Brooks was interested in Kim Basinger for the part of Emma's best friend Patsy Clark. He, Shirley MacLaine and Debra Winger called her at home to discuss the film. She was upset that they didn't go through her agent. She told them that she wasn't going to do the film. Patsy was a supporting character. She was offered a lead role in *The Man Who Loved Women* with Burt Reynolds. She was going to take that part instead. *Terms of Endearment* was a huge hit, both critically and financially. It won five Oscars including Best Picture. *The Man Who Loved Women* flopped.³⁷

Texas Rangers (2001)
Leonor Varela as Perdita (Laetitia Casta, Patricia Manterola)

Laetitia Casta and Patricia Manterola lost out to Leonor Varela for the role of Perdita in *Texas Rangers*.³⁸

That Certain Feeling (1956)
Eva Marie Saint as Dunreath Henry (June Allyson)

June Allyson was considered to play Dunreath Henry. The role was eventually taken by Eva Marie Saint.³⁹

That Kind of Woman (1959)
Barbara Nichols as Jane (Shirley MacLaine)

Paramount Pictures wanted Shirley MacLaine to play the supporting role of Jane in *That Kind of Woman*. Director Carlo Ponti thought that MacLaine was too big a star, and might overshadow the film's leading lady — his wife, Sophia Loren. He turned down MacLaine, and instead gave the part to Barbara Nichols.⁴⁰

That Old Feeling (1997)
Dennis Farina as Dan DeMauro (Richard Dreyfuss, Gene Hackman)

Richard Dreyfuss and Bette Midler were scheduled for the leads in *That Old Feeling*. Reportedly, Dreyfuss was upset with the amount of money he was being paid, and left the film. Gene Hackman considered taking the part, but it went instead to Dennis Farina.⁴¹

Thelma & Louise (1991)
Susan Sarandon as Louise Sawyer (Cher)
Geena Davis as Thelma (Melanie Griffith)
Brad Pitt as J.D. (William Baldwin, George Clooney)

Melanie Griffith was offered the part of Thelma. She didn't like the character and said no.⁴² Cher turned down the role of Louise, a decision she later regretted.⁴³

William Baldwin decided he would rather appear in *Backdraft* than play J.D.⁴⁴ George Clooney auditioned. Clooney came close, making it all the way down to the final callbacks. He eventually lost the role to Brad Pitt. At the time Clooney was upset and refused to see the film. About a year later he changed his mind, and watched it on video. Clooney was amazed at what Brad Pitt had done with the character. At that point he realized that Ridley Scott had made the right decision in turning him down in favor of Pitt.⁴⁵

There's Something About Mary (1998)
Cameron Diaz as Mary Jensen Matthews (Courteney Cox)

Directors Bobby and Peter Farrelly considered casting either Cameron Diaz or Courteney Cox as Mary. They decided on Diaz after seeing her performance in *My Best Friend's Wedding*.⁴⁶

They All Kissed the Bride (1942)
Joan Crawford as Margaret Drew (Carole Lombard)

Carole Lombard was scheduled to star as Margaret Drew in *They All Kissed the Bride*. Lombard was killed in a plane crash, and the part was recast with Joan Crawford. Crawford gave her entire salary to the Red Cross (who had found Lombard's body) in the name of Carole Lombard.⁴⁷

They All Laughed (1981)
Linda MacEwen as Amy Lester (Dorothy Stratten)

Dorothy Stratten was originally set to play Amy Lester. Director Peter Bogdanovich felt the part was too small for her. He cast her in a larger role and gave the part of Amy to Linda MacEwen.⁴⁸

They Died with Their Boots On (1941)
Olivia De Havilland as Elizabeth Bacon (Joan Fontaine)

Olivia de Havilland played the role of Elizabeth Bacon, which was turned down by her sister, Joan Fontaine.⁴⁹

Thieves (1977)
Charles Grodin as Martin Cramer (Peter Falk, Gene Hackman)

Charles Grodin was cast as Martin Cramer after Peter Falk and then Gene Hackman turned it down.⁵⁰

Thieves Like Us (1974)
Louise Fletcher as Mattie (Joan Tewkesbury)

Writer Joan Tewkesbury was briefly considered to play Mattie.[51] The part went to Louise Fletcher instead. Tewkesbury had a cameo in the film under the name Joan Maguire.

The Thin Man (1934)
Myrna Loy as Nora Charles (Laura La Plante)

MGM boss Louis B. Mayer thought Laura La Plante was the best choice to play Nora Charles. Director W.S. Van Dyke disagreed, and cast Myrna Loy instead.[52]

The Third Man (1949)
Orson Welles as Harry Lime (Noel Coward)
Joseph Cotten as Holly Martins (Cary Grant)

Producer David O. Selznick wanted Noel Coward for the part of Harry Lime. Director Carol Reed preferred Orson Welles. Welles was eventually cast.

For the Holly Martins role, Selznick was interested in Cary Grant. Grant asked for too much money. Ultimately Joseph Cotten was cast, reuniting him with Orson Welles, his costar from *Citizen Kane*.[53]

This Boy's Life (1993)
Ellen Barkin as Caroline Wolff (Debra Winger)

Debra Winger was cast as Caroline Wolff in *This Boy's Life*. She eventually left the cast and was replaced by Ellen Barkin.[54]

This Could Be the Night (1957)
Paul Douglas as Rocco (James Cagney)

James Cagney was the first choice for the part of Rocco. Cagney didn't take the part, and Paul Douglas was cast in his place.[55]

This Earth Is Mine (1959)
Dorothy McGuire as Martha Fairon (Barbara Stanwyck)

Barbara Stanwyck was offered the part of Martha Fairon in *This Earth Is Mine*. Stanwyck turned it down, and Dorothy McGuire was cast instead.[56]

This Gun for Hire (1942)
Alan Ladd as Philip Raven (Robert Preston)

Robert Preston was the first choice to play Raven. When it was decided that the 5'10" Preston was too tall, Alan Ladd (5'6") won the role.[57]

This Is My Affair (1937)
Barbara Stanwyck as Lil Duryea (Alice Faye)

Alice Faye was originally set to star in *This Is My Affair*. When it came time to start shooting Faye had scheduling problems. On top of that she fell ill. Twentieth Century–Fox's boss, Darryl F. Zanuck, decided the best thing to do was to replace her with Barbara Stanwyck.[58]

This Way Please (1937)
Betty Grable as Jane Morrow (Shirley Ross)

Shirley Ross quit *This Way Please* because she felt that her part was being cut down while costar Mary Livingstone's part was expanding. Betty Grable took her place.[59]

Shirley Ross thought her part in *This Way Please* was becoming too small.

The Thomas Crown Affair (1968)
Faye Dunaway as Vicki Anderson (Eva Marie Saint)

Eva Marie Saint was originally announced as the costar of *The Thomas Crown Affair*. Saint didn't make the film, though. The part was recast with Faye Dunaway.[60]

A Thousand Acres (1997)
Jason Robards as Larry Cook (Paul Newman)

Paul Newman was a possibility for the part of Larry Cook. Newman didn't sign for the film. The part went to Jason Robards instead.[61]

365 Nights in Hollywood (1934)
Alice Faye as Alice Perkins (Lilian Harvey)

Alice Faye has Lilian Harvey to thank for her career. First Harvey dropped out of *George White's Scandals*, and Faye was cast in her place. Then, another role originally intended for Harvey went to Faye: the part of Alice Perkins in *365 Nights in Hollywood*.[62]

Three Kings (1999)
George Clooney as Archie Gates (Nicolas Cage, Clint Eastwood, Mel Gibson)
Mark Wahlberg as Troy Barlow (George Clooney)

Mel Gibson was the studio's choice to star in *Three Kings*. However, director David O. Russell wanted Nicolas Cage. Clint Eastwood was another possibility. Eastwood was going to do it, but he decided to make the film *True Crime* instead.[63] George Clooney was originally considered for Troy Barlow,[64] but went after the part of Archie Gates. At the time Clooney was primarily known for starring in *ER* on television. Clooney wrote to Russell, and even showed up at his home in order to win the role. Meanwhile, Nicolas Cage was offered the film *Bringing Out the Dead*, which was to be directed by Martin Scorsese. Cage chose that film, and Russell gave Clooney the starring role in his film.[65]

The Three Musketeers (1948)
Lana Turner as Lady DeWinter (Angela Lansbury)

Angela Lansbury tried for the role of Lady DeWinter, but Louis B. Mayer preferred Lana Turner. Lansbury was cast as Queen Anne instead.[66]

The Three Musketeers (1973)
Oliver Reed as Athos (Charlton Heston)
Simon Ward as Duke of Buckingham (Charlton Heston)

Director Richard Lester offered the role of Athos to Charlton Heston. Heston liked the script, just not necessarily the part. He decided he'd rather play a cameo role than sign on for a major role.[67] He suggested to Lester that he might be interested in the part of the Duke of Buckingham.[68] Lester instead offered Heston the part of Cardinal Richelieu.[69] Heston liked the idea of being cast against type, as a bad guy.[70] He agreed to do the part. Oliver Reed was cast as Athos, and Simon Ward got the part of the Duke of Buckingham.

Three of Hearts (1993)
William Baldwin as Joe (Robert Downey, Jr.)

Robert Downey, Jr., was cast as Joe, but dropped out. He was replaced by William Baldwin.[71]

The Thrill of It All (1963)
Edward Andrews as Gardiner Fraleigh (Walter Matthau)

Walter Matthau was offered the role of Gardiner Fraleigh. He asked for the (then) large salary of $100,000 to appear in the film. Producer Ross Hunter was annoyed by this and said so publicly. Matthau explained that there was not much to the part, and he was insulted. Edward Andrews was cast instead.[72]

Thunderball (1965)
Sean Connery as James Bond (Richard Burton)
Claudine Auger as Domino Derval (Maria Grazia Buccella, Julie Christie, Faye Dunaway, Raquel Welch)

Early on, it seemed that Sean Connery would not be able to reprise the role of James Bond. Richard Burton was considered as a replacement.[73] Sean Connery was eventually signed for the film.

Faye Dunaway was considered for the role of Domino Derval, but the actress chose to do the film *The Happening* instead. Producer Cubby Broccoli saw Julie Christie on television. He thought she was beautiful and brought her in for an interview. She showed up to meet Broccoli and director Terence Young in jeans. Broccoli thought she looked sloppy, not at all the way she did on television. Christie's small bustline was one of the reasons she lost the part. Raquel Welch came very close to landing the part. She chose to do the film *Fantastic Voyage* instead. Maria Grazia Buccella auditioned, but the role went to Claudine Auger.[74]

Tightrope (1984)
Genevieve Bujold as Beryl Thibodeaux (Susan Sarandon)

Susan Sarandon was the first choice for the role of Beryl Thibodeaux. She turned it down, and it went to Genevieve Bujold instead.[75]

'Til We Meet Again (1940)
Merle Oberon as Joan Ames (Bette Davis)

Bette Davis was an early choice for Merle Oberon's part of Joan Ames in *'Til We Meet Again*.[76]

Time Bandits (1981)
David Warner as Evil Genius (Jonathan Pryce)
Katherine Helmond as Mrs. Ogre (Ruth Gordon)

Jonathan Pryce was considered for the part of the Evil Genius. He decided to do another movie instead, and David Warner got the part.

Gilliam's first choice for Mrs. Ogre was Katherine Helmond. Helmond was primarily known for starring in the television series *Soap*. This hurt her chances; she was considered a television actress. Ruth Gordon was sought. She broke her leg making the film *Every Which Way but Loose* and was unable to appear. Helmond was under consideration once again, and this time ended up with the part.[77]

A Time to Kill (1996)
Matthew McConaughey as Jake Brigance (Alec Baldwin, Kevin Costner, Ralph Fiennes, Woody Harrelson, Val Kilmer, Bill Paxton, Brad Pitt, Aidan Quinn)
Donald Sutherland as Lucien Wilbanks (Paul Newman)
Kiefer Sutherland as Freddie Cobb (Matthew McConaughey)

Initially, Kevin Costner was set for the role of lawyer Jake Brigance. The actor wanted to have complete creative control of the project, which proved to be a deal-breaker. Brad Pitt was considered, as well as Alec Baldwin, Ralph Fiennes, and Val Kilmer. John Grisham, the author of the novel the film was based on, pictured either Bill Paxton or Aidan Quinn in the role. Woody Harrelson went after the role, but Grisham decided against him. He felt Harrelson was the wrong type to play Jake. Matthew McConaughey was already in the cast as Freddie Cobb. Grisham saw him on film and okayed him for Jake. His role went to Kiefer Sutherland. Sutherland's father Donald Sutherland was cast as Lucien Wilbanks after Paul Newman's name was mentioned.[78]

Tin Cup (1996)
Cheech Marin as Romeo Posar (Garth Brooks)

Singer Garth Brooks went up for the part of Romeo Posar, but director Ron Shelton decided to cast Cheech Marin instead.[79]

Titanic (1997)
Leonardo DiCaprio as Jack Dawson (Billy Crudup, Tom Cruise, Matthew McConaughey, Chris O'Donnell, Brad Pitt)
Kate Winslet as Rose De Witt Bukater (Gabrielle Anwar, Claire Danes, Gwyneth Paltrow)
Billy Zane as Caledon "Cal" Hockley (Nicholas Lea, Matthew McConaughey)
Kathy Bates as Molly Brown (Linda Hamilton, Reba McEntire)

Director James Cameron worked with casting director Mali Finn to find the leads for his upcoming film, *Titanic*. Finn recommended Billy Crudup for the starring role of Jack Dawson. Crudup auditioned, but ultimately decided that he wasn't interested in making such a big effects-driven film. Tom Cruise expressed interest. Cameron was tempted by the thought of having Cruise star in his film. He ultimately decided that the thirtysomething Cruise was too old for the part. Matthew McConaughey and Chris O'Donnell were suggested. Like Cruise, Cameron felt they were too old. He liked McConaughey's work though, and offered him the supporting part of Cal Hockley. McConaughey turned it down in favor of Steven Spielberg's film, *Amistad*. Brad Pitt was also considered. Mali Finn suggested Leonardo DiCaprio. Di-

Caprio auditioned for Cameron. The director liked his reading so much that he brought him in for a call back where he would read with Rose contender Kate Winslet. DiCaprio's audition was so good that even Winslet told Cameron to hire him. Cameron went to 20th Century–Fox and told them that DiCaprio was going to star. Executives at the studio were not thrilled. They wanted a big star for the part. Cameron insisted and DiCaprio was cast.[80]

Claire Danes and Gabrielle Anwar were possible choices to play Rose.[81] Gwyneth Paltrow met with Cameron to discuss the role. The actress ultimately decided the project was not for her. She felt that it was too big a movie for her. She was more interested in character driven stories and saw this as an action movie. The part went to Kate Winslet. Winslet was nominated for an Oscar for her performance.

Nicholas Lea auditioned to play Cal Hockley, but Cameron chose Billy Zane instead.[82]

Cameron's first choice for Molly Brown was his wife, Linda Hamilton. Hamilton turned it down and Cameron auditioned country singer Reba McEntire. McEntire's audition impressed the director, but he was more interested in Academy Award winner Kathy Bates. Cameron wanted actors who resembled the real life figures in the movie. Not only was Bates a great actress, but she actually looked like the real Molly Brown. The studio did not want to pay Bates what she was asking. The actress agreed on a lower price, and the studio still said no. James Cameron wanted her so badly that he made up the difference with his own money.[83]

To Be or Not to Be (1942)

Carole Lombard as Maria Tura (Miriam Hopkins)

Miriam Hopkins was originally set to play Maria Tura. When she quit, she was replaced by Carole Lombard.[84]

To Die For (1995)

Nicole Kidman as Suzanne Stone Marretto (Patricia Arquette, Bridget Fonda, Jodie Foster, Holly Hunter, Jennifer Jason Leigh, Kelly Lynch, Mary-Louise Parker, Meg Ryan, Susan Sarandon)

Joaquin Phoenix as Jimmy Emmett (Matt Damon)

Director Gus Van Sant's list of possible Suzannes included Jodie Foster, Meg Ryan, Nicole Kidman, Holly Hunter, Bridget Fonda, Patricia Arquette, Susan Sarandon, Jennifer Jason Leigh, and Mary-Louise Parker. Van Sant was interested in Sarandon, who committed for a brief period. When she left the project the top two contenders became Meg Ryan and Patricia Arquette. At the time Ryan was signed for the lead in John Boorman's film, *Beyond Rangoon*. Ryan ultimately decided to drop out of the film. Boorman offered the part to Patricia Arquette who accepted. This took her out of the running to play Suzanne Stone Marretto. Van Sant offered Ryan the part, which was against type for the typically sunny actress. Ryan decided she didn't want to do it and told Van Sant no.[85] Van Sant's former leading lady (*Drugstore Cowboy*) Kelly Lynch was interested. She went after the part to no avail.[86] Nicole Kidman called Van Sant personally to campaign for the role. She told Van Sant that she loved the script and that she was destined to play the part. He had liked her work in the film *Malice*, and figured that if she was so intent on winning the part she would work very hard. Without an audition the part was hers.[87]

Matt Damon auditioned for Jimmy. Van Sant liked his audition so much that he was one of the two final contenders for the part. The other was Joaquin Phoenix. According to Van Sant, it was a very close race, but that Phoenix was the better choice for him.[88]

To Each His Own (1946)

Olivia De Havilland as Miss Josephine Norris (Ginger Rogers)

Ginger Rogers, in her mid-thirties, turned down the lead role of Josephine Norris because she didn't want to play the mother of a twenty year old.[89] Olivia de Havilland got the part and an Academy Award for her portrayal.

To Wong Foo Thanks for Everything, Julie Newmar (1995)

Patrick Swayze as Vida Boheme (Viggo Mortensen)

Viggo Mortensen auditioned to play drag queen Vida Boheme, but lost the role to Patrick Swayze.[90]

Tom Horn (1979)

Steve McQueen as Tom Horn (Robert Redford)

Both Robert Redford and Steve McQueen wanted to play the title role of Tom Horn. McQueen, who eventually won the role, felt a strong tie to this character. He later said that out of all the characters he ever played, Tom Horn was the one he identified with the most.[91]

Too Late Blues (1961)

Bobby Darin as John "Ghost" Wakefield (Montgomery Clift)
Stella Stevens as Jess Polanski (Gena Rowlands)

Writer/director John Cassavetes wanted Montgomery Clift and Gena Rowlands to star in *Too Late Blues*. Paramount Pictures' Marty Racklin didn't want either of them for the film. He insisted that Cassavetes give the parts to Bobby Darin and Stella Stevens.[92]

Tootsie (1982)

Dustin Hoffman as Michael Dorsey (Chevy Chase, Elliott Gould, George Hamilton, George Segal)
Jessica Lange as Julie Nichols (Cher, Goldie Hawn)
Dabney Coleman as Ron (Peter Bogdanovich)
Sydney Pollack as George Fields (Dabney Coleman, Buddy Hackett)
Doris Belack as Rita (Polly Holliday)

George Hamilton was originally set to star as Michael Dorsey in *Tootsie*. Executive producer Charles Evans had the script rewritten. Evans liked the new version of the script much more than the original. He started to have second thoughts about Hamilton. He considered George Segal, but decided that Segal was too old. Elliott Gould was another possibility, but he thought that Gould would be funny looking as a nurse (the character plays a female nurse on a soap opera). Evans also considered Chevy Chase. However, he had a deal with Bob Kaufman. Kaufman was going to act as an executive producer. Kaufman and Hamilton were a package deal. Hamilton lost the part when Evans' brother, producer Robert Evans, became involved. Robert Evans wanted the script changed. If Charles Evans went along with his brother's ideas then Kaufman and Hamilton would be out of the picture and he could cast anyone he liked. After Kaufman and Hamilton's departure, Dustin Hoffman was shown the script. Hoffman accepted the part.[93]

Hoffman wanted Goldie Hawn to play opposite him, but the actress declined.[94] Cher was interested,[95] but lost out to Jessica Lange. Lange won a Best Supporting Actress Oscar for her performance.

Director Sydney Pollack offered the role of Ron, director of a soap opera, to real life director Peter Bogdanovich. Bogdanovich felt the part should go to an actor.[96] Buddy Hackett wanted to play agent George Fields, but Dabney Coleman was Pollack's choice. But Dustin Hoffman thought Pollack should play the part. Hoffman said that he saw Coleman as a peer, while he was intimidated by Pollack. Pollack resisted, but Hoffman kept after him until Pollack finally decided to play the part. He gave Coleman the part of Ron.[97]

Dustin Hoffman wanted his friend Polly Holliday to play Rita, the soap opera producer. Pollack felt differently, and gave the part to Doris Belack instead.[98]

Top Gun (1986)

Tom Cruise as Lt. Peter Mitchell "Maverick" (Matthew Modine)
Kelly McGillis as Charlotte "Charlie" Blackwood (Linda Fiorentino, Ally Sheedy)

Matthew Modine was offered the part of Maverick, but had problems with the script and turned it down.[99] Tom Cruise was cast. *Top Gun* turned the popular Cruise into a superstar.

Linda Fiorentino was sought for the role of Charlie. She chose instead to do another film, which was ultimately canceled.[100] Ally Sheedy was also asked to play Charlie. She said no, thinking it would flop. The same year Sheedy made the films *Blue City* and *Short Circuit*. *Blue City* was a bomb, while *Short Circuit* was a modest success. However, neither film even came close to being the enormous success *Top Gun* was.

Topaz (1969)

Roberto Contreras as Munoz (Aram Katcher)

Aram Katcher was cast in the role of Munoz in director Alfred Hitchcock's *Topaz*. He shot all his scenes, and therefore when the film opened he was surprised to find that he was not in it! Now this was not a case of being left on the cutting room floor. After his scenes were filmed, Hitchcock decided that he didn't like Katcher's interpretation of the role, and had replaced him with Roberto Contreras.[101]

Topkapi (1964)
Peter Ustinov as Arthur Simpson (Peter Sellers)

Jules Dassin spoke with Peter Sellers about the possibility of him playing the role of Arthur Simpson in Dassin's upcoming film, *Topkapi*. Sellers was interested until he found out that Dassin was also considering Maximilian Schell for a role in the film.[102] Sellers turned Dassin down, and Dassin gave the part of Arthur Simpson to Peter Ustinov. Interestingly, Sellers took over a role Peter Ustinov dropped the very same year. The part was Inspector Clouseau in *The Pink Panther*, which became one of Sellers' most identifiable roles.

Topper (1937)
Constance Bennett as Marian Kirby (Jean Harlow)
Cary Grant as George Kirby (W.C. Fields)
Roland Young as Topper (W.C. Fields)

Producer Hal Roach first envisioned Jean Harlow as Marian Kirby[103] and W.C. Fields as either George[104] or Topper.[105] Neither actor signed for the film, and the parts went to Constance Bennett, Cary Grant, and Roland Young.

Torrent (1926)
Greta Garbo as Leonora Moreno/La Brunna (Norma Shearer)

Norma Shearer was considered for the lead in *The Torrent*. She turned it down and it was played by Greta Garbo.[106]

Tortilla Flat (1942)
John Garfield as Danny (Ricardo Montalban)

Mexican born Ricardo Montalban screentested for the role of Danny.[107] Danny was a Mexican-American. It was common practice in Hollywood at the time for white actors to play characters of all ethnicities in makeup rather than hire minority actors. *Tortilla Flat* was no exception. Montalban lost the role to John Garfield.

Total Recall (1990)
Arnold Schwarzenegger as Douglas Quaid (Richard Dreyfuss, Patrick Swayze)

Total Recall was in development for ten years before it was made. During that time several actors were attached to star including Richard Dreyfuss and Patrick Swayze.[108]

Tovarich (1937)
Claudette Colbert as Grand Duchess Tatiana Petrovna (Kay Francis)

Warner Bros. bought the rights to *Tovarich* with Kay Francis in mind. Francis had recently had a bad time at the box office, and so the studio gave the part to Claudette Colbert instead.[109]

The Towering Inferno (1974)
Steve McQueen as Michael O'Hallorhan (Ernest Borgnine)
Paul Newman as Doug Roberts (Steve McQueen)

In the early stages of production Steve McQueen was considered for the part of architect Doug Roberts opposite Ernest Borgnine as fire chief Michael O'Hallorhan. McQueen preferred the role of the fire chief, but it was a small part and his first scene wasn't until the middle of the movie. Not wanting to drop the project, he spoke to screenwriter Sterling Silliphant and told him his concerns. McQueen thought the film would work better if the fire chief and the architect were comparable parts, and wanted an actor of his caliber to play opposite him. His sometime rival (for roles) Paul Newman was cast as Doug Roberts. McQueen kept in very close contact with Silliphant to make sure that the roles were even down to the number of lines they had. (At one point McQueen complained that Newman had 12 more lines of dialogue than him, and Silliphant was forced to leave a vacation to remedy the situation.)[110]

Tracks (1976)
Dennis Hopper as Sgt. Jack Falen (Jack Nicholson)

Bob Rafelson was originally supposed to direct the film *Tracks*. He and writer Henry Jaglom discussed the type of film they wanted to make, and Jaglom wrote the script based on their conversations. Rafelson planned to have Jack Nicholson play the starring role. Jaglom completed the script and gave it to Rafelson to read, at which point the director decided to drop out of the project entirely. The script was shelved for years, when Jaglom decided to direct it himself, and gave the lead role to Dennis Hopper instead of Jack Nicholson.[111]

Trading Places (1983)

Charles Brown as Officer Reynolds (Count Stovall)
Maurice Woods as Duke & Duke Employee (Count Stovall)

Broadway actor Count Stovall came in to audition for two small roles in the film. He read for director John Landis, who then asked the casting director next to him if Stovall was black. He was looking for black actors, and Stovall did not look black enough for him. He went on to say that maybe Stovall could pass for Hawaiian, but not black. Stovall was embarrassed to have Landis say this in front of the casting director. He felt that Landis might be blowing his chance at future roles. If this casting director became convinced that Stovall did not look black, would he be called in to read for other parts? Landis was unaware of the possible damage he was doing to this actor and continued. Stovall endured as much of this humiliation as he could, but finally went over to Landis. He got very close to the director and asked him if he looked black then. Stovall lost both roles in the film.

Traffic (2000)

Michael Douglas as Judge Robert Lewis (Harrison Ford)

Harrison Ford almost starred in *Traffic* as Judge Robert Lewis. However, Ford ultimately decided he didn't want to make the film.[112] Michael Douglas stepped in as a replacement. Douglas' co-star was his pregnant fiancée, Catherine Zeta-Jones, although the two had no scenes together.

Training Day (2001)

Scott Glenn as Roger (Mickey Rourke)

Director Antoine Fuqua's first choice to play Roger was Mickey Rourke. The studio didn't want him in the role, and he was out of the running. Scott Glenn won the part instead.[113]

Travels with My Aunt (1972)

Maggie Smith as Aunt Augusta (Katharine Hepburn, Angela Lansbury)
Cindy Williams as Tooley (Cybill Shepherd)

Katharine Hepburn was the original choice for the role of Aunt Augusta. Hepburn had problems with the script and was fired. Angela Lansbury was considered for her replacement, but the part went instead to Maggie Smith.[114]

Cybill Shepherd auditioned for the part of Tooley. Director George Cukor told her that her reading was bad and told her to take the script home to prepare. He invited her to come back the next day and audition again. Shepherd worked all night on the script. She returned the next day and read again. She was pleased at how improved she was. Cukor told Shepherd that she had no talent as a comedienne, and advised her to never try comedy again.[115]

The Treasure of the Sierra Madre (1948)

Humphey Bogart as Fred C. Dobbs (John Garfield, Walter Huston, Edward G. Robinson)
Walter Huston as Howard (Lewis Stone)
Tim Holt as Bob Curtin (John Garfield, Ronald Reagan)
Bruce Bennett as James Cody (Ronald Reagan, Zachary Scott)

Director John Huston started working on *The Treasure of the Sierra Madre* about six years before the film went into production. At that time he considered Edward G. Robinson, John Garfield and his father Walter Huston (Warner Bros.' first choice) for the starring role of Fred Dobbs. The role was eventually played by Humphrey Bogart.

B. Traven, who wrote the novel on which the film was based, wanted Lewis Stone to play Howard. It went to Walter Huston instead. Huston won the Best Supporting Actor Academy Award for his work in the film.[116]

Ronald Reagan had been a possible choice for the part of Curtin.[117] The actor was also interested in the part of Cody.[118] The studio took Reagan out of the running by putting him in another movie.[119] John Garfield was approached, but was not obtainable.[120]

Zachary Scott was thought of for Cody, but the role went instead to Bruce Bennett.[121]

A Tree Grows in Brooklyn (1945)

Joan Blondell as Aunt Cissy (Alice Faye)
James Dunn as Johnny Nolan (Fred MacMurray)

Alice Faye was considered for the part of Aunt Cissy in *A Tree Grows in Brooklyn*, which was eventually played by Joan Blondell.[122]

Fred MacMurray was announced for the part

of Johnny Nolan. However when the camera rolled it was James Dunn playing the part.[123]

Tribute to a Bad Man (1956)

James Cagney as Jeremy Roderick (Spencer Tracy)
Irene Papas as Jocasta Constantine (Grace Kelly)

Spencer Tracy was unhappy working on *Tribute to a Bad Man*. He would often argue with director Robert Wise. He was eventually fired and replaced by James Cagney.[124]

When Tracy was still involved his then girlfriend Grace Kelly was going to play opposite him. Kelly dropped out and was replaced by Irene Papas.[125]

Les Tricheurs (1958)

Jacques Charrier as Bob Letellier (Jean-Claude Belmondo)

Director Marcel Carne was interested in Jean-Paul Belmondo for the part of Bob Letellier in *Les Tricheurs*. He gave Belmondo a screen test. Carne eventually decided that Jacques Charrier was the better choice. He liked Belmondo enough to give him another part in the movie. Belmondo was cast in the part of Lou.[126]

Trick or Treat (1986)

Tony Fields as Sammi Curr (Gene Simmons)

Gene Simmons was asked to play to lead role of Sammi Curr. Simmons didn't want this part; he felt that the small role of Nuke was more suited to him. He played Nuke, while Tony Fields was cast as Sammi Curr.[127]

The Trip (1967)

Bruce Dern as John (Jack Nicholson)

Jack Nicholson wrote the screenplay for *The Trip*, and decided that he wanted to play the part of John. Obviously being the writer doesn't guarantee you a part! When Nicholson told director Roger Corman that he wanted the part Corman said no and cast Bruce Dern instead.[128]

True Grit (1969)

Kim Darby as Mattie Ross (Mia Farrow, Sally Field, Sondra Locke)

Many actresses were considered for the coveted role of Mattie Ross opposite John Wayne in *True Grit*. Sally Field, then the star of the television series *The Flying Nun*, went after it. The producers thought she was the wrong type for it and refused to even let her audition.[129] Producer Hal Wallis heard about a brand new actress who was making her film debut in the upcoming film *The Heart Is a Lonely Hunter*. Her name was Sondra Locke. Wallis contacted Locke's agent. Locke read the script and decided that the character of Mattie Ross was very much like the character she had just finished playing. Locke also felt that the film version would not capture the book it was based on and told her agent she would rather not audition.[130] Finally Mia Farrow was chosen. Farrow soon changed her mind and dropped out. Kim Darby was cast in her place. Many years later Farrow said that she made a very big mistake by not making the film.[131]

True Romance (1993)

Bronson Pinchot as Elliot Blitzer (Steve Buscemi)
Chris Penn as Nicky Dimes (Steve Buscemi)

Steve Buscemi was considered for the roles of Elliot Blitzer and Nicky Dimes but lost out to Bronson Pinchot and Chris Penn respectively.[132]

The Truman Show (1998)

Ed Harris as Christof (Dennis Hopper)

After a single day of shooting, Dennis Hopper left *The Truman Show* over creative differences with director Peter Weir. Weir admits that his ideas for the character of Christof had changed from when he originally cast Hopper in the role. Weir has said that Hopper was sympathetic to him and handled the situation with much grace.[133]

Tucker: The Man and His Dream (1988)

Jeff Bridges as Preston Tucker (Jack Nicholson, Burt Reynolds)

Jack Nicholson and Burt Reynolds were early considerations for the starring role of Preston Tucker.[134] Instead director Francis Ford Coppola decided to cast the younger Jeff Bridges.

The Turning Point (1977)

Shirley MacLaine as Didi (Grace Kelly)
Anne Bancroft as Emma Jacklin (Audrey Hepburn, Grace Kelly)

Director Herbert Ross wanted Grace Kelly for the part of former dancer Didi. Didi gave up her career as a dancer to marry and raise a family. In real life Kelly gave up her acting career to marry Prince Rainier of Monaco and raise a family. Kelly loved the script, but thought that the part of Didi might be too much like her own story. She wanted to play Emma Jacklin. Ross had no problem with the switch; he just wanted Kelly in the movie. Kelly discussed the prospect with her husband. Prince Rainier thought that Kelly needed to be with her family. Kelly agreed and turned the film down.[135] The part went to Shirley MacLaine.

When Audrey Hepburn learned of the film, she tried for the role of Emma Jacklin. Hepburn was too late; Anne Bancroft had already been signed for the part.[136]

24-Hour Woman (1999)
Marianne Jean-Baptiste as Madeline Labelle (Rosie Perez)

Rosie Perez was initially approached to play the part of Madeline in *24-Hour Woman*. Perez said she would prefer to play the lead role, and director Nancy Savoca agreed to give her the part.[137] The part of Madeline was then taken by Marianne Jean-Baptiste.

21 Grams (2003)
Charlotte Gainsbourg as Mary Rivers (Katrin Cartlidge)

Katrin Cartlidge was originally cast as Mary Rivers. Sadly, Cartlidge died suddenly. Charlotte Gainsbourg was brought in to play the part.[138]

20,000 Years in Sing Sing (1933)
Spencer Tracy as Tom "Tommy" Connors (James Cagney)

James Cagney was originally set to star in *20,000 Years in Sing Sing*. Cagney was involved in a battle with Warner Bros. and was replaced by Spencer Tracy.[139]

Two for the Road (1967)
Albert Finney as Mark Wallace (Steve McQueen)

After Albert Finney was cast Steve McQueen found out that the producer of the film had tried unsuccessfully to contact McQueen about playing the role of Mark Wallace. McQueen was annoyed that he didn't know about this sooner. He knew that the female lead was being played by Audrey Hepburn, a woman who McQueen was interested in becoming romantically linked with.[140]

The Two Jakes (1990)
Jack Nicholson as Jake Gittes (Harrison Ford, Roy Scheider)
Harvey Keitel as Jake Berman (Robert Evans, Dustin Hoffman)
Richard Farnsworth as Earl Rawley (Budd Boetticher)

Actor-turned-producer Robert Evans was initially set to play the role of Jake Berman opposite Jack Nicholson in *The Two Jakes*, a sequel to the classic film, *Chinatown*. Nicholson was reprising his role of detective Jake Gittes from the original, while Evans would be playing the other Jake. The news of Evans' casting was quite a surprise, since his last acting job was about 35 years prior in *The Best of Everything*. Also in the cast was Budd Boetticher in the role of Earl Rawley.[141] Production started in April of 1985. Early on writer/director Robert Towne began to have second thoughts about his old friend Robert Evans. He was worried that Evans was not up to the part. He expressed his feelings to Jack Nicholson, who disagreed. Shortly after, Towne and Evans had an argument, which led to a meeting between the three men. Nicholson told Robert Towne that his friendship with Robert Evans was more important to him than the movie, and that if Evans wasn't in the film, he wouldn't be either.[142] Now, losing Jack Nicholson in the sequel to *Chinatown* is a very big deal. Towne's hands were tied, and Evans was allowed to stay, while Towne resigned as director.[143] A new director was sought, but eventually Paramount Pictures decided that this tumultuous movie was costing them too much money, and they cancelled production. Robert Towne tried to make the film on his own, without Nicholson. He wanted Harrison Ford or Roy Scheider in Nicholson's role with Dustin Hoffman co-starring as the second Jake.[144] He was ultimately not able to get the film off the ground, and the project was put to rest for about three years. Jack Nicholson was still interested in making the film, and after some time had passed, Evans and Towne came on board. This time around, Evans would produce the film, and Harvey Keitel stepped into his former role of Jake Berman. Budd Boetticher was replaced by former stuntman Richard Farnsworth.

2001: A Space Odyssey (1968)
Douglas Rain as Voice of HAL (Martin Balsam, Nigel Davenport)

Douglas Rain had originally been hired to do narration for *2001: A Space Odyssey*. Nigel Davenport had the part of the voice of HAL. Director Stanley Kubrick decided that Davenport's English accent was wrong for the part. He gave the part to Martin Balsam. Like Davenport, Balsam's voice was deemed unsuitable. Balsam's performance was too American and emotional. He was let go. Kubrick dropped the narration from the film and gave Douglas Rain the part of HAL.[145]

Typhoon (1940)
Robert Preston as Johnny Potter (Jon Hall)

Jon Hall was sought for the part of Johnny Potter in *Typhoon*. Hall was unavailable, and the part was played by Robert Preston instead.[146]

U-571 (2000)
Bill Paxton as Captain Dahlgren (Michael Douglas)

Michael Douglas signed on to play Captain Dahlgren in *U-571*. However Douglas decided to drop out of the film. He was replaced by Bill Paxton.[1]

U-Turn (1997)
Sean Penn as John Stewart (Bill Paxton)
Jennifer Lopez as Grace McKenna (Sharon Stone)

Director Oliver Stone's first choice for the part of John Stewart was Sean Penn. When the actor's schedule proved to be full, Stone offered the part to Bill Paxton. Paxton accepted, but soon changed his mind. He felt uncomfortable with the character and asked Stone if he would replace him. Stone contacted Penn again, and found out his schedule had become clear. Paxton was released from the film and Stone got his first choice of a leading man.

Sharon Stone thought about playing the part of Grace. She negotiated, but ultimately decided against it. Oliver Stone gave the part to Jennifer Lopez instead.[2]

Ulee's Gold (1997)
Peter Fonda as Ulee Jackson (Nick Nolte)

Nick Nolte was offered the role of Ulee Jackson. Nolte wasn't interested and turned it down.[3]

Ulysses (1967)
Milo O'Shea as Leopold Bloom (Peter Sellers)

The first time *Ulysses* was being planned was in 1962. At that time Peter Sellers was the choice for the part of Leopold Bloom.[4] The film was put on hold until 1966. Joseph Strick was hired to direct. He gave the part of Leopold Bloom to Milo O'Shea.

Unbreakable (2000)
Robin Wright Penn as Audrey Dunn (Julianne Moore)

Julianne Moore agreed to play Audrey Dunn for director M. Night Shyamalan. Soon after, Moore got a call to interview for the starring role of Clarice Starling in *Hannibal*. Moore met with *Hannibal* director Ridley Scott and was offered the part the next day. *Hannibal* was pay-or-play, which meant that Moore would be paid for the film even if it never got made. This became her priority. The shooting schedules for both films interfered. Moore dropped out of *Unbreakable*. Shyamalan recast the role with Robin Wright Penn.[5]

Unconquered (1947)
Howard Da Silva as Martin Garth (Robert Preston)

Robert Preston turned down the chance to play Martin Garth in *Unconquered*. Howard Da Silva was cast in his place.[6]

Under Siege 2: Dark Territory (1995)
Sandra Taylor as Kelly (Jenny McCarthy)

According to Jenny McCarthy, she auditioned for the supporting role of Kelly in *Under Siege 2*. She says that the only person in the room with her was the star of the film, Steven Seagal. She was prepared to read from the script, but Seagal instead asked her to take off her dress. He said that the character needed to be sexy, and the dress she was wearing was not revealing enough. McCarthy told him that she didn't want to take any clothes off; there was no nudity required for the part. Seagal told her she was wrong. McCarthy was a former *Playboy* playmate, but was looking for a change. She would not have auditioned if there was any nudity. Seagal continued to ask her to disrobe. McCarthy refused, telling him to rent her *Playboy* video instead. She left in tears, and Seagal told her not to tell the story to anyone. McCarthy has told it in print and on television many times because she felt it was important to bring out in the open.[7]

Unfaithful (2002)

Richard Gere as Edward Sumner (George Clooney)

George Clooney was in talks for the part of Edward Sumner. Clooney's participation fell through, and Richard Gere was cast instead.[8]

Union Pacific (1939)

Barbara Stanwyck as Mollie Monahan (Claudette Colbert, Vivien Leigh)

Vivien Leigh was a candidate to play Mollie Monahan. Had she taken the job, she would have been unavailable to play Scarlett O'Hara in *Gone With the Wind*. Claudette Colbert was also considered, but the part went to Barbara Stanwyck instead.[9]

An Unmarried Woman (1978)

Jill Clayburgh as Erica Benton (Jane Fonda)

Jane Fonda was offered the starring role in *An Unmarried Woman*. Political activist Fonda said the movie was not relevant and turned it down.[10]

The Unsinkable Molly Brown (1964)

Debbie Reynolds as Molly Brown (Shirley MacLaine)

Shirley MacLaine was a candidate to play Molly Brown. She and MGM were unable to make a deal, and the part went to Debbie Reynolds.[11]

Untamed Heart (1993)

Marisa Tomei as Caroline (Geena Davis, Madonna)

Madonna was the first actress attached to star in *Untamed Heart* as Caroline.[12] Geena Davis was also sought for the role which was eventually played by Marisa Tomei.[13]

The Untouchables (1987)

Kevin Costner as Eliot Ness (Harrison Ford, Mel Gibson, Don Johnson)
Robert De Niro as Al Capone (Bob Hoskins, Al Pacino)

Director Brian De Palma considered Kevin Costner for the starring role of Eliot Ness. However, Costner was basically a newcomer at this point. De Palma considered such heavy hitters like Harrison Ford and Mel Gibson. Gibson met with De Palma to discuss the film. He ultimately decided against it and made *Lethal Weapon* instead. Don Johnson was another possibility, but De Palma chose Costner instead.[14]

De Palma's first choice for the part of Al Capone was Robert De Niro. De Niro was unavailable and Al Pacino[15] and Bob Hoskins were up for it. Hoskins was eventually chosen. De Palma later learned that the situation with De Niro had changed and he wanted to do the film. He paid Hoskins $200,000 and gave his part to Robert De Niro.[16]

Urban Cowboy (1980)

John Travolta as Buford "Bud" Uan Davis (Dennis Quaid)
Debra Winger as Sissy Davis (Michelle Pfeiffer, Sissy Spacek)

Dennis Quaid was an early consideration for the role of Bud. When the red hot John Travolta became interested, Quaid lost the role.[17]

Sissy Spacek was considered for the part of Sissy.[18] Ultimately the producers decided to go with an unknown actress instead. It was narrowed down to two actresses: Michelle Pfeiffer and Debra Winger. Winger won the role, but both actresses became stars.[19]

The VIPs (1963)

Elizabeth Taylor as Frances Andros (Sophia Loren)

Sophia Loren lost the role of Frances Andros when Elizabeth Taylor asked to do the part. What sealed the deal for Taylor was that she was willing to be paid much less money than Loren was asking for.[1]

The Valley of Decision (1945)

Marshall Thompson as Ted Scott (Hume Cronyn)

Hume Cronyn was cast to play Gregory Peck's brother. When Cronyn showed up for work director Tay Garnett realized that Peck was much larger than Cronyn. Cronyn was replaced with Marshall Thompson.[2]

Valley of the Dolls (1967)

Barbara Parkins as Anne Welles (Natalie Wood)

Sharon Tate as Jennifer North (Jane Fonda, Raquel Welch)
Patty Duke as Neely O'Hara (Petula Clark, Barbara Harris)
Susan Hayward as Helen Lawson (Bette Davis, Judy Garland)

The original choices to star in *Valley of the Dolls* included Natalie Wood as Anne, Jane Fonda as Jennifer, Barbara Harris as Neely, and Bette Davis as Helen. This cast never materialized and Barbara Parkins, Sharon Tate, Patty Duke, and Judy Garland were cast instead. Soon after filming began Judy Garland was fired for her uncooperative and erratic behavior on the set.[3] Susan Hayward was hired as a replacement.

Raquel Welch was offered the part of Jennifer North, but turned it down.[4]

Petula Clark was asked to play Neely O'Hara. Clark wasn't interested. The part was played by Patty Duke instead.[5]

Valley of the Kings (1954)

Robert Taylor as Mark Brandon (Vittorio Gassman)

Vittorio Gassman was announced as the star of *Valley of the Kings*. However, Gassman decided against the film. Robert Taylor was brought in to replace him.[6]

Valmont (1989)

Annette Bening as Madame de Merteuil (Michelle Pfeiffer)

Director Milos Forman wanted Michelle Pfeiffer for the part of Madame de Merteuil. Pfeiffer turned him down, and Annette Bening was cast in her place.[7]

The Verdict (1982)

Paul Newman as Frank Galvin (Cary Grant, Dustin Hoffman, Robert Redford, Roy Scheider, Frank Sinatra)

The role of Frank Galvin interested many hard-to-get actors. Cary Grant, Frank Sinatra, Dustin Hoffman, and Roy Scheider all wanted the part. It went instead to Robert Redford. Soon after a problem arose. Redford was not happy with the script. He didn't want to play Galvin as gritty as the character was written by screenwriter Jay Presson Allen. The script was rewritten about ten times. Producer Richard Zanuck decided he no longer wanted Redford involved with the project. Director Sidney Lumet gave the role to Paul Newman.[8]

Vertigo (1958)

Kim Novak as Madeleine Elster/Judy Barton (Vera Miles)

Vera Miles was director Alfred Hitchcock's first choice to star in *Vertigo*. When she became pregnant she was forced to drop out of the film. Hitchcock replaced her with Kim Novak.[9]

Victor/Victoria (1982)

James Garner as King Marchand (Tom Selleck)

James Garner was cast as King Marchand after the part had been turned down by Tom Selleck.[10]

Virtuosity (1995)

Denzel Washington as Parker Barnes (Michael Douglas)

Michael Douglas was courted to star in *Virtuosity*. When he said no, the part went to Denzel Washington.[11]

Viva Zapata! (1952)

Marlon Brando as Emiliano Zapata (Tyrone Power)
Jean Peters as Josefa Zapata (Julie Harris)

Darryl F. Zanuck wanted Tyrone Power for the male lead. It was director Elia Kazan who wanted Marlon Brando and got him.[12] Julie Harris screen tested with Brando, but Jean Peters was chosen instead.[13]

Volcano (1997)

Tommy Lee Jones as Mike Roark (Bill Pullman)

Bill Pullman was considered for the part of Mike Roark. Pullman wanted more money than the studio wanted to pay, and they got Tommy Lee Jones to star instead.[14]

Wabash Avenue (1950)

Betty Grable as Ruby Summers (June Haver)
Victor Mature as Andy Clark (Dan Dailey)

Dan Dailey was the first choice to star in *Wabash Avenue*. He was unable to appear because he was already making the film *A Ticket to Tomahawk*.

June Haver was considered for the role of Ruby Summers, ultimately played by Betty Grable.[1]

Waiting to Exhale (1995)

Loretta Devine as Gloria Johnson (Ellia English)

Ellia English was up for the role of Gloria Johnson. English gained about 70 pounds before her audition. She lost the role to Loretta Devine.[2]

A Walk in the Clouds (1995)

Aitana Sanchez-Gijon as Victoria Aragon (Penelope Cruz, Winona Ryder)

Penelope Cruz auditioned for the part of Victoria Aragon. Cruz, who is from Madrid, Spain, didn't speak English at the time and was turned down.[3] Director Alfonso Arau also considered Winona Ryder for the lead role, before deciding on Aitana Sanchez-Gijon.[4]

A Walk on the Moon (1999)

Liev Schreiber as Marty Kantrowitz (Dustin Hoffman)

Dustin Hoffman was considered for the role of the husband in *A Walk on the Moon*. He thought the part was too young for him, and produced the film instead.

Wall Street (1987)

Charlie Sheen as Bud Fox (Tom Cruise)
Michael Douglas as Gordon Gekko (Warren Beatty, Richard Gere, Al Pacino)
Daryl Hannah as Darien Taylor (Sean Young)
Sean Young as Kate Gekko (Daryl Hannah)

Richard Gere turned down the role in *Wall Street* for which Michael Douglas won an Academy Award.

Tom Cruise was interested in playing Bud Fox. Cruise was a much bigger star than Charlie Sheen, but Oliver Stone had already promised Sheen the part and wanted to honor that commitment.

Sean Young thought that she was being wasted in the small role of Kate Gekko. She informed Oliver Stone that she would be better cast as Darien Taylor. According to Stone, Young said that she and Daryl Hannah should switch roles. She then moved her stuff into Hannah's trailer. The shy Hannah was so intimidated by Young that she allowed it. Although Stone thought that Young had a point, he refused to change his casting.[5]

War and Peace (1956)

Henry Fonda as Pierre Bezukhov (Marlon Brando, Gregory Peck, Peter Ustinov)

Gregory Peck turned down the Henry Fonda role in *War and Peace* because his schedule was already full.[6] Peter Ustinov was a contender but producer Dino De Laurentiis wanted a bigger star. Marlon Brando was also considered, but Henry Fonda won the part.[7]

The War Lover (1962)

Steve McQueen as Buzz Rickson (Warren Beatty)
Robert Wagner as Ed Bolland (Warren Beatty)

Warren Beatty was offered the roles of Buzz Rickson and Ed Bolland in *The War Lover*. He wasn't interested in doing the film and passed on both parts.[8]

WarGames (1983)

Matthew Broderick as David Lightman (Kevin Costner)

Kevin Costner was offered parts in both *WarGames* and *The Big Chill*. It was not possible to appear in both films, so Costner had to pick one. The role in *WarGames* was the lead role; the part in *The Big Chill* was a supporting role in an ensemble cast with established stars in the roles. Costner felt *The Big Chill* was the move, and turned down the lead in *WarGames*. He accepted the role of Alex in *The Big Chill*. Alex is the friend of the group who has committed suicide. Costner was to appear in flashback scenes. However, while in the editing room, director Lawrence Kasdan felt the film would be better without those scenes. Costner's entire role was cut from the film. Kasdan felt so bad about cutting Costner, he promised the actor he would cast him in his next film. That film turned out to be *Silverado*.[9] Matthew Broderick had a big hit with the role Costner rejected in *WarGames*.

The War of the Roses (1989)

Kathleen Turner as Barbara Rose (Cher, Barbra Streisand)

Cher turned down the part of Barbara Rose.[10] Barbra Streisand wanted the part, but director Danny De Vito preferred Kathleen Turner instead.[11]

Watch on the Rhine (1943)
Bette Davis as Sara Muller (Irene Dunne)
Paul Lukas as Kurt Muller (Charles Boyer, Paul Henreid)

The leads in *Watch on the Rhine* were first offered to Irene Dunne and Charles Boyer. They turned them down.[12] Paul Henreid was asked to play Kurt Muller, but he too said no. Henreid later regretted his decision. Paul Lukas took the part of Kurt, while Bette Davis was cast as Sara Muller.[13]

Way Down East (1935)
Rochelle Hudson as Anna Moore (Janet Gaynor)

Janet Gaynor was cast in the role of Anna Moore in *Way Down East*. She had an accident and was unable to appear in the film. Gaynor was replaced by Rochelle Hudson.[14]

The Way to Love (1933)
Ann Dvorak as Madeleine (Sylvia Sidney)

Sylvia Sidney was scheduled to play the part of Madeleine in *The Way to Love*. After about a week and a half of filming, Sidney dropped out.[15] It was said that she was sick, although there was some speculation as to whether or not this was true. She was replaced by Ann Dvorak.[16]

The Way We Were (1973)
Robert Redford as Hubbell Gardner (Warren Beatty, Dennis Cole, Ken Howard, Ryan O'Neal)

Barbra Streisand was cast in the starring role of Katie Morosky. At the time Streisand was dating her *What's Up, Doc?* co-star Ryan O'Neal. It was expected that O'Neal would play opposite Streisand in *The Way We Were* as well. When the film was ready to begin production the romance was over, and a new leading man was needed.[17] Streisand was interested in Warren Beatty. Beatty wasn't overly enthusiastic.[18] Ken Howard wanted the part. Writer Arthur Laurents arranged a tennis match for Howard and Streisand to meet. They played doubles with Laurents and director Herb Ross' wife, Nora Kaye. According to Laurents the two actors got along just fine. At the end of the day a very pretty girl met Howard to drive him home. Laurents said that Streisand was affected by this, and told Laurents that they had no chemistry. Ken Howard was out.[19] Dennis Cole auditioned but was not what they were looking for.[20] Streisand and producer Ray Stark

Barbra Streisand nixed Ken Howard as her leading man in *The Way We Were*.

both thought Robert Redford would be ideal. Stark decided to hire Sydney Pollack to direct the film. Stark had ulterior motives; Pollack and Redford were good friends. Pollack liked the script immediately and agreed to direct. He sent Redford the script. Redford was not impressed. Changes were made to the script, which was again submitted to the actor. Redford remained unmoved. Pollack tried and tried to convince his friend to take the part. He worried that there wasn't enough to the character. He finally agreed to do the film. According to Redford his reason was that he trusted Pollack.[21]

The Wedding Planner (2001)
Matthew McConaughey as Steven James Edison (Brendan Fraser)

Brendan Fraser dropped out of *The Wedding Planner*. His replacement was Matthew McConaughey.[22]

Welcome to Mooseport (2004)
Gene Hackman as Monroe "The Eagle" Cole (Dustin Hoffman)

Director Rod Lurie had the idea of casting Dustin Hoffman opposite Ray Romano in *Wel-*

come to Mooseport. The three took a meeting together. Romano said that he was intimidated by Hoffman. Lurie said that Hoffman was very fond of Romano. Lurie and Hoffman eventually decided against the film. Donald Petrie signed to direct, and Hoffman's old friend Gene Hackman was cast as Monroe Cole. Romano stayed with the film as Handy Harrison.[23]

Welcome to Sarajevo (1997)

Stephen Dillane as Michael Henderson (Jeremy Irons)

Jeremy Irons was a possibility for the part of Michael Henderson. Miramax boss Harvey Weinstein preferred the lesser-known Stephen Dillane.[24]

West Side Story (1961)

Natalie Wood as Maria (Anna Maria Alberghetti, Denise Alexander, Pier Angeli, Ann-Margret, Elizabeth Ashley, Diane Baker, Yvonne Craig, Angie Dickinson, Elinor Donahue, Gloria Ellis, Jane Fonda, Ann Helm, Audrey Hepburn, Susan Kohner, Hope Lange, Carol Lawrence, Barbara Luna, Sharon Nugent, Millie Perkins, Suzanne Pleshette, Jill St. John, Dodie Stevens)

Richard Beymer as Tony (John Alderman, Warren Beatty, Alan Case, Richard Chamberlain, Mark Goddard, Robert Harland, Christopher Knight, Michael Landon, Scott Marlowe, Ron Nicholas, George Peppard, Elvis Presley, Robert Redford, Burt Reynolds, Tommy Sands, Russ Tamblyn)

George Chakiris as Bernardo (Gus Trikonis)

Susan Oakes as Anybodys (Bonnie Franklin)

Gina Trikonis as Graziella (Joey Heatherton)

Co-director Robert Wise originally made a list of preliminary considerations for the starring roles of Tony and Maria. On the list for Maria were Suzanne Pleshette, Susan Kohner, Elinor Donahue, Barbara Luna, Millie Perkins, Diane Baker, Yvonne Craig, Ann Helm, Denise Alexander, Sharon Nugent, Dodie Stevens, and Gloria Ellis.

The Tony list included Warren Beatty, Richard Chamberlain, Michael Landon, George Peppard, Russ Tamblyn, Robert Harland, Tommy Sands, Christopher Knight, Ron Nicholas, Alan Case, John Alderman, Scott Marlowe, and Mark Goddard.

Carol Lawrence originated the role of Maria on Broadway. Wise's co-director Jerome Robbins directed and choreographed the Broadway show. He pushed for Lawrence to be cast in the film. After viewing her test it was obvious that at 25, she was too old for the part. Lawrence's name was dropped from consideration.[25] Susan Kohner auditioned, as did Pier Angeli, Hope Lange, Anna Maria Alberghetti, Angie Dickinson, and Jane Fonda.[26] Suzanne Pleshette gave a very good reading. According to Wise, Jill St. John was lovely, but not what they were looking for. Ann-Margret had brown hair at the time she was sent to audition. The actress was grateful for the chance, but knew she wouldn't get the job.[27] An offer went out to Audrey Hepburn, who was pregnant and eventually passed.[28] Elizabeth Ashley was a serious contender, but was eventually rejected.

Executive producer Walter Mirisch wanted Elvis Presley to play Tony. Jerome Robbins eventually convinced him that Presley was not the right choice.[29] Burt Reynolds was briefly considered. He lost the part because he looked too tough.[30] Richard Chamberlain read well, but came off as too mature. Robert Wise thought Russ Tamblyn gave an excellent reading. He lost the role of Tony, but landed the supporting part of gang leader Riff instead. Wise liked Robert Redford's reading, as well as Warren Beatty's. Beatty was in the middle of making his first film, *Splendor in the Grass*. Wise went to Warner Bros. to look at some of the footage Beatty had shot. Co-starring with Beatty was Natalie Wood. As soon as Wise saw Wood he realized that she was the perfect choice for Maria. Wood won the part, but Beatty did not fare as well. He was passed over in favor of Richard Beymer.

Gus Trikonis auditioned to play Bernardo, the leader of the Sharks. He lost the role to George Chakiris. Robbins and Wise liked him and cast him in the smaller role of Indio. His sister Gina Trikonis beat out a 15-year-old Joey Heatherton for the part of Graziella, even though Wise thought Heatherton's reading was very good.

Bonnie Franklin read for tomboy Anybodys, but the directors chose Susan Oakes instead.

The Westerner (1940)

Doris Davenport as Jane-Ellen Mathews (Margaret Tallichet)

Director William Wyler's first choice for the female lead was his wife, Margaret Tallichet. He was unable to cast her because the studio preferred Doris Davenport.[31]

When a Man Loves a Woman (1994)

Andy Garcia as Michael Green (Tom Hanks)
Meg Ryan as Alice Green (Michelle Pfeiffer, Debra Winger)

Tom Hanks and Michelle Pfeiffer were set to star in *When a Man Loves a Woman*. However Pfeiffer changed her mind and left the film. Debra Winger was to replace her, but then she too changed her mind and dropped out. At that point Hanks decided to move on. The parts were finally cast with Andy Garcia and Meg Ryan.[32]

When Harry Met Sally (1989)

Billy Crystal as Harry Burns (Albert Brooks, Richard Dreyfuss)

Director Rob Reiner offered his old friend Richard Dreyfuss the part of Harry in *When Harry Met Sally*. Dreyfuss declined.[33] Albert Brooks was approached, but he too said no.[34] The role of Harry went to another of Reiner's old friends — Billy Crystal.

Where the Heart Is (1990)

Dabney Coleman as Stewart McBain (Sean Connery)

Exhaustion forced Sean Connery to drop out of *Where the Heart Is*.[35] He was replaced by Dabney Coleman.

White Christmas (1954)

Danny Kaye as Phil Davis (Fred Astaire, Donald O'Connor)

Fred Astaire was asked to play the part of Phil Davis. Astaire said no and Donald O'Connor was cast instead. Soon after O'Connor suffered an injury and had to bow out. He was replaced by Danny Kaye.[36]

The White Sister (1923)

Ronald Colman as Captain Giovanni Severini (Humphrey Bogart)

Humphrey Bogart made a screen test for the role of Captain Giovanni Severini in *The White Sister*. He lost the part to Ronald Colman. Bogart believed that a scar on his lip was partly to blame. After losing the role in *The White Sister* Bogart had an operation on his lip. It seems as though he was right. Soon after his operation he was offered a studio contract for $400 a week.[37]

White Witch Doctor (1953)

Susan Hayward as Ellen Burton (Anne Baxter)

Anne Baxter's name was mentioned for the part of Ellen Burton. Susan Hayward was the bigger star, and Baxter lost the film.[38]

Who's Afraid of Virginia Woolf (1966)

Elizabeth Taylor as Martha (Ingrid Bergman, Bette Davis, Patricia Neal)
Richard Burton as George (Henry Fonda, Glenn Ford, Cary Grant, Jack Lemmon, James Mason)
George Segal as Nick (Warren Beatty, Jim Hutton, Robert Redford)
Sandy Dennis as Honey (Connie Stevens, Pamela Tiffin)

Ingrid Bergman was the first choice for the role of Martha. Bergman wasn't particularly interested and turned down the film. Patricia Neal was offered the part, but turned it down in order to star as Mrs. Robinson in *The Graduate*. Neal was eventually replaced in that film by Anne Bancroft. Bette Davis was interested in the part. Playwright Edward Albee thought that Davis was right for the part but Jack Warner disagreed, and cast Elizabeth Taylor instead.[39]

The first choice to play George was Cary Grant. Grant turned it down, feeling the part was too much of a departure for him. Albee wanted James Mason as George; Jack Warner disagreed.[40] Warner offered the role to Glenn Ford and Jack Lemmon, who both turned it down.[41] Henry Fonda was considered, but Warner finally gave the part to Richard Burton, the husband of his leading lady.[42]

A pairing of Warren Beatty and Pamela Tiffin as Nick and Honey was considered. The actor director Mike Nichols really wanted for the part of Nick was Robert Redford. Redford turned the film down. He wanted to make *This Property Is Condemned* instead. Jim Hutton and Connie Stevens tried to win the roles, but lost out to George Segal and Sandy Dennis.[43]

Why Do Fools Fall in Love (1998)

Halle Berry as Zola Taylor (Vivica A. Fox)
Lela Rochon as Emira Eagle (Halle Berry)

Vivica A. Fox was originally cast as Zola Taylor with Halle Berry as Emira Eagle. The parts were later switched around and Berry became Zola, with Lela Rochon as Emira. The third female lead, Elizabeth, went to Fox.

The Wild Angels (1966)

Peter Fonda as Heavenly Blues (George Chakiris)
Bruce Dern as Loser (Peter Fonda)

When casting *The Wild Angels*, director Roger Corman cast George Chakiris in the lead role of Heavenly Blues with Peter Fonda in the supporting role of the Loser. Corman wanted the actors to ride their own motorcycles, which Chakiris couldn't do. Corman called Fonda in to replace him. Bruce Dern filled in as the Loser.[44]

George Chakiris' inability to ride a motorcycle lost him the lead in *The Wild Angels*.

The Wild Bunch (1969)

William Holden as Pike Bishop (Richard Boone, Sterling Hayden, Charlton Heston, Burt Lancaster, Lee Marvin, Robert Mitchum, Gregory Peck, James Stewart)
Robert Ryan as Deke Thornton (Henry Fonda, Glenn Ford, Richard Harris, Van Heflin, Ben Johnson, Brian Keith, Arthur Kennedy)
Ernest Borgnine as Dutch Engstrom (Charles Bronson, James Brown, Alex Cord, Robert Culp, Sammy Davis, Jr., Richard Jaeckel, Steve McQueen, George Peppard)
Edmond O'Brien as Freddie Sykes (Walter Brennan, Andy Clyde, Lee J. Cobb, William Demarest, Paul Fix, Jason Robards)
Jaime Sanchez as Angel (Robert Blake)

Director Sam Peckinpah's first choice for the part of Pike Bishop was Lee Marvin. Marvin was unable to take the part because of his role in *Paint Your Wagon*.[45] William Holden was cast after the part was considered by Richard Boone, James Stewart, Burt Lancaster, Robert Mitchum, Charlton Heston, Gregory Peck, and Sterling Hayden.[46]

Brian Keith was offered the role of Deke Thornton. The actor turned Peckinpah down. Also considered were Richard Harris, Arthur Kennedy, Henry Fonda, Van Heflin and Ben Johnson.[47] Another possibility was Glenn Ford.[48] Robert Ryan was ultimately cast.

The list of possible Dutches included Steve McQueen, Charles Bronson, Sammy Davis, Jr., Robert Culp, George Peppard, Richard Jaeckel, Alex Cord and James Brown. Ernest Borgnine was suggested to Peckinpah. At first the director was against Borgnine; he had never worked with him before. He soon changed his mind and gave Borgnine the part.

Peckinpah cast Edmond O'Brien as Freddie Sykes after considering Jason Robards, William Demarest, Walter Brennan, Lee J. Cobb, Andy Clyde and Paul Fix.

Robert Blake was offered $75,000 to play Angel. Blake didn't want to play a part as small as Angel and turned it down. Jaime Sanchez was cast instead.[49]

Wild Orchid (1990)

Carre Otis as Emily Reed (Cindy Crawford)

Cindy Crawford and Carre Otis were the two major contenders for the part of Emily.[50] *Wild*

Orchid was Otis' first film. She was primarily known as a model. She and co-star Mickey Rourke were married two years after the film was released.

Wild River (1960)

Montgomery Clift as Chuck Glover (Ben Gazzara)

Ben Gazzara was very enthusiastic about re-teaming with director Elia Kazan for the film *Wild River*. The director instead chose Montgomery Clift to star in the film. When Gazzara learned of this, he was extremely upset and angry with Kazan.[51]

Will Success Spoil Rock Hunter? (1957)

Joan Blondell as Violet (Thelma Ritter)

Thelma Ritter was set for the part of Violet in *Will Success Spoil Rock Hunter?* At the same time Ritter was in rehearsals for *New Girl in Town* on Broadway. Ritter had to bow out of the film. Joan Blondell stepped in as her replacement.[52]

Willard (2003)

Crispin Glover as Willard Stiles (Joaquin Phoenix, Mark Ruffalo)

Director Glen Morgan wanted Crispin Glover for the title role for Willard. Glover's reputation as being unusual worked against him. The production company, New Line Cinema, wanted Morgan to cast more popular actors like Joaquin Phoenix or Mark Ruffalo. Morgan eventually got his way and signed Glover for the part.[53]

William Shakespeare's Romeo + Juliet (1996)

Claire Danes as Juliet Capulet (Jennifer Love Hewitt, Christina Ricci, Kate Winslet)
Harold Perrineau, Jr., as Mercutio (Christian Bale)

Kate Winslet, Jennifer Love Hewitt and Christina Ricci all auditioned for the role of Juliet. Ricci was told she lost the part because of her height and her age.[54] Winslet knew that she was too old for the part. Even if director Baz Luhrmann thought she could pass physically for Juliet, Winslet knew that emotionally she was too mature for the girlish character.[55] Hewitt was turned down because Luhrmann didn't think she was modern enough for his updated version of the classic story.[56] Luhrmann chose Claire Danes instead.

Christian Bale auditioned to play Mercutio. Bale was called back numerous times, but finally lost out to Harold Perrineau, Jr.[57]

Willow (1988)

Val Kilmer as Madmartigan (John Cusack)

John Cusack auditioned for the part of Madmartigan. He lost out to Val Kilmer.[58]

Win a Date with Tad Hamilton! (2004)

Josh Duhamel as Tad Hamilton (Ben Affleck, Hugh Grant)

Ben Affleck and Hugh Grant were mentioned for the title role of Tad Hamilton. However, when the producers saw footage of former soap star (*All My Children*) Josh Duhamel at a Super Soap Weekend, they knew they had their man.[59]

The Winning of Barbara Worth (1926)

Gary Cooper as Abe Lee (Harold Goodwin)

Harold Goodwin was cast as Abe Lee. Due to scheduling problems on *The Honeymoon Express* he was not able to show up for filming. Bit player Gary Cooper was his replacement.[60]

The Witches of Eastwick (1987)

Jack Nicholson as Daryl Van Horne (Bill Murray)
Cher as Alexandra Medford (Susan Sarandon)
Susan Sarandon as Jane Spofford (Cher)

Bill Murray was the first choice for the devilish Daryl Van Horne. Murray wasn't interested, and Jack Nicholson was cast in his place.[61]

Susan Sarandon was originally scheduled to play the part of Alexandra, with Cher cast as Jane. However, the studio decided they wanted Cher in the larger role and told Sarandon she would have to switch roles with Cher. Sarandon was very unhappy with this decision. She was also under the false impression that it was Cher's idea to swap roles. Cher was unaware of the details of the situation, and had no problem with the switch.[62]

Without Limits (1998)

Billy Crudup as Steve Prefontaine (Tom Cruise, Leonardo DiCaprio, Ethan Hawke)

Donald Sutherland as Bill Bowerman (Harrison Ford, Tommy Lee Jones)

Tom Cruise was originally interested in starring as Steve Prefontaine. Once he read the script, he realized he was too old for the part. He dropped the idea of acting in the film, and instead took a job as a producer. Ethan Hawke and Leonardo DiCaprio were discussed as possibilities for the part. Director Robert Towne felt that DiCaprio physically didn't resemble Prefontaine enough. He instead gave the part to Billy Crudup.

Towne considered Harrison Ford and Tommy Lee Jones for the part of Bill Bowerman before deciding on Donald Sutherland.[63]

The Wizard of Oz (1939)

Judy Garland as Dorothy Gale (Deanna Durbin Shirley Temple)

Ray Bolger as The Scarecrow (Buddy Ebsen)

Jack Haley as The Tin Woodsman (Ray Bolger, Buddy Ebsen)

Frank Morgan as The Wizard of Oz (W.C. Fields, Hugh Herbert, Victor Moore, Ed Wynn)

Billie Burke as Glinda the Good Witch (Fanny Brice, Constance Collier, Helen Gilbert, Beatrice Lillie, Una Merkel, Edna May Oliver, Cora Witherspoon)

Margaret Hamilton as Miss Almira Gulch/The Wicked Witch of the West (Edna May Oliver, Gale Sondergaard)

Clara Blandick as Aunt Emily "Auntie Em" Gale (Janet Beecher, May Robson)

MGM boss Louis B. Mayer originally wanted Shirley Temple to star as Dorothy in *The Wizard of Oz*. According to Temple, Mayer called Darryl F. Zanuck, the head of 20th Century–Fox to discuss a possible trade.[64] Mayer would get Temple, and in exchange, he would loan out Jean Harlow and Clark Gable to Fox. Jean Harlow's death prevented this deal,[65] and Zanuck decided against loaning Temple to MGM.[66] Deanna Durbin's name was discussed, but Durbin left MGM for Universal Studios.[67] The role ultimately went to Judy Garland.

Gale Sondergaard wanted to play the Wicked Witch of the West as a beautiful woman in *The Wizard of Oz*.

The supporting cast consisted of Bert Lahr as the Cowardly Lion, Buddy Ebsen as the Scarecrow, and Ray Bolger as the Tin Woodsman. This casting did not make Bolger happy. He had always wanted to play the part of the Scarecrow. After meeting with Mayer, it was decided that Bolger and Ebsen would switch parts. Early into the filming Ebsen had a severe allergic reaction to the silver makeup he wore as the character. He was hospitalized, and later replaced by Jack Haley. If you watch the film closely, you can still see Buddy Ebsen in some long shots as the Tin Woodsman![68]

Ed Wynn was the first choice for the Wizard.[69] He felt the part was too small and turned it down.[70] W.C. Fields was offered $75,000 to play the part. The actor wanted to be paid about $100,000 for his services. Mayer said no to this, and kept looking for a Wizard.[71] He considered Hugh Herbert and Victor Moore, but Mayer instead chose Frank Morgan.[72]

Helen Gilbert was the first choice to play Glinda the Good Witch. The actress was interested and it seemed the deal would be made. After she ran off with Howard Hughes, the role was up for grabs.[73] Billie Burke was cast after Fanny Brice,[74] Beatrice Lillie,[75] Una Merkel,[76] Edna May Oliver,[77] Cora Witherspoon,[78] and Constance Collier[79] were all considered.

The original concept for the Wicked Witch character was as a glamorous, sexy woman. Gale Sondergaard was the first choice for this role. Soon after, the idea for the character changed. The Wicked Witch would now be portrayed as an ugly hag. Sondergaard was not interested in the character this way. She took herself out of the running.[80] Edna May Oliver was considered. The actress was unable to appear because of a commitment to the film *Drums Along the Mohawk*.[81]

May Robson was an early choice for the part of Aunt Em. She felt the role wasn't substantial enough, and turned it down. Janet Beecher was briefly considered, but the part went to Clara Blandick.[82]

A Woman Rebels (1936)

Katharine Hepburn as Pamela Thistlewaite (Ann Harding)

A Woman Rebels as originally planned for Ann Harding. Harding ended up not making the film, and Katharine Hepburn was brought in to star.[83]

Working Girl (1988)

Harrison Ford as Jack Trainer (Alec Baldwin)

Alec Baldwin was considered for the starring role of Jack, but was eventually cast in a smaller role. The lead role went to Harrison Ford instead. Baldwin didn't mind the demotion, saying that he understood why they would want Harrison Ford instead of him to star.[84]

The World of Suzie Wong (1960)

Nancy Kwan as Suzie Wong (France Nuyen)

France Nuyen was originally cast as Suzie Wong, a role she created on Broadway. At the time Nuyen was dating Marlon Brando, who was in California. Nuyen was filming in Hong Kong, and then London. She missed Brando, and when she learned that he was seeing another actress, Barbara Luna, she became alarmed. She was so upset that she left the film and was replaced by Nancy Kwan.[85]

Wrestling Ernest Hemingway (1993)

Richard Harris as Frank (Kirk Douglas)

Director Randa Haines insisted that Kirk Douglas audition for the part of Frank in *Wrestling Ernest Hemingway*. For a star as big as Kirk Douglas, being asked to test for a role is highly unusual. Because he liked the part so much, he reluctantly agreed. After the test was completed Douglas was informed that Haines preferred Richard Harris for the part.[86]

Wuthering Heights (1939)

Merle Oberon as Cathy Earnshaw (Bette Davis, Katharine Hepburn, Sylvia Sidney)
Laurence Olivier as Heathcliff (Charles Boyer, Douglas Fairbanks, Jr., Robert Newton)

Sylvia Sidney and Charles Boyer were the first choices for the leads in *Wuthering Heights*. The studio also wanted Sidney to appear in the film *Algiers*. When Sidney refused to appear in *Algiers*, she lost the lead role in *Wuthering Heights*. Katharine Hepburn was the next name on the list, but was never more than a consideration. Bette Davis was interested in the role, but lost out to Merle Oberon.

Robert Newton was considered for Heathcliff. Studio boss Samuel Goldwyn didn't think Newton was handsome enough and rejected him. Merle Oberon wanted Douglas Fairbanks, Jr., to play opposite her. He made a test, which Goldwyn decided was unsatisfactory.[87]

Xanadu (1980)

Michael Beck as Sonny Malone (John Travolta)

Olivia Newton-John tried to lure her old *Grease* star John Travolta into co-starring with her in the roller disco film *Xanadu*. Travolta turned her down.[1] *Xanadu* was not a hit, but it was a blockbuster compared to the film he later agreed to work on with Newton-John: *Two of a Kind*.

X-Men (2000)

Hugh Jackman as Logan/Wolverine (Russell Crowe, Dougray Scott)
Halle Berry as Storm (Angela Bassett)

Dougray Scott was cast as Wolverine. Scott was scheduled to start work on *X-Men* just after he finished shooting *Mission: Impossible 2*. Production was delayed on *Mission: Impossible 2*, and it became clear that Scott would not be ready in time for the *X-Men* start date. Hugh Jackman was brought in to replace him.[2]

A Yank at Oxford (1938)

Maureen O'Sullivan as Molly Beaumont (Vivien Leigh)

Vivien Leigh was originally set to play the female lead in *A Yank at Oxford*. However, Louis B. Mayer had her replaced by Maureen O'Sullivan. Leigh remained in the film, but in a supporting role.[1]

Year of the Comet (1992)

Timothy Daly as Oliver Plexico (Robert Redford)

In the early 1980s Joseph E. Levine had a deal with screenwriter William Goldman to produce his screenplay, *Year of the Comet*. For the leading man role of Oliver Plexico, Levine wanted Robert Redford. Redford was never contacted because of financial reasons. Levine had to let the project go, and his deal with Goldman was over.[2] About ten years later the movie was finally made, with Timothy Daly (best known for his work in the TV series *Wings*) as Oliver.

The Yearling (1946)

Gregory Peck as Pa Baxter (Spencer Tracy)
Jane Wyman as Ma Baxter (Anne Revere)
Claude Jarman, Jr., as Jody Baxter (Gene Eckman)

The Yearling was originally intended to star Spencer Tracy, Anne Revere, and Gene Eckman with King Vidor directing. Filming began, but then was postponed for four years.[3] When production resumed the original cast was no longer an option.

Yentl (1983)

Mandy Patinkin as Avigdor (Michael Douglas, Richard Gere, Kevin Kline, Enrico Marcias, John Shea)
Nehemiah Persoff as Yentl's father (Norbert Auerbach, Morris Carnovsky)

Richard Gere was director Barbra Streisand's first choice for the role of Avigdor. Gere thought that Streisand couldn't handle both acting and directing in the film. He offered to take the role if she would just either let someone else play her part or have someone else direct. Gere also wanted $5 million. Streisand refused.[4] She made an offer to Michael Douglas, which he turned down.[5] Enrico Marcias[6] was mentioned as a possibility as were John Shea[7] and Kevin Kline.[8] Shea auditioned for Streisand, but she picked Broadway star Mandy Patinkin instead.

United Artists president Norbert Auerbach claimed that Barbra Streisand asked him to play Yentl's father. Auerbach was very excited at this offer. He was from Prague, where Streisand planned to film. About a month later Auerbach and other UA executives had dinner with Streisand. He brought up Streisand's offer to him. She seemed confused. She told Auerbach that she intended to have Morris Carnovsky play her father. The Carnovsky deal was never finalized, and Nehemiah Persoff ended up with the part.[9]

You Can Count on Me (2000)

Mark Ruffalo as Terry Prescott (Peter Sarsgaard)

Peter Sarsgaard wanted the role of Terry Prescott very badly. According to the actor, he begged for the part. He was not persuasive enough, and Mark Ruffalo got the part instead.[10]

You Can't Take It with You (1938)

Jean Arthur as Alice Sycamore (Olivia De Havilland)
Spring Byington as Penny Sycamore (Fay Bainter)

Director Frank Capra was set to make *You Can't Take It with You* for Columbia Pictures. At the time actress Jean Arthur was involved in a feud with the studio. Studio head Harry Cohn ordered her to report for work at another studio (Warner Bros.). Arthur refused, and Cohn put her on suspension. Unable to work, Arthur hatched a plot to kill Cohn. When her husband, Frank Ross, learned of this he whisked Arthur away to Carmel. Not long after, Cohn decided he wanted Arthur back for *You Can't Take It with You*. Arthur was a favorite of Capra's. He assumed that she would be unattainable and planned to cast Olivia De Havilland as Alice Sycamore. His plans changed when De Havilland's studio (Warner Bros.) refused to loan her out. Capra convinced Cohn to buy the rights to *Golden Boy* for Arthur to star in (those plans eventually fell through). Arthur was convinced and signed on to play Alice.[11]

Capra wanted Fay Bainter to play the role of Penny in *You Can't Take It with You*. She wasn't available, and he cast Spring Byington instead.[12]

You Only Live Twice (1967)
Donald Pleasence as Ernst Stavro Blofeld
(Jan Werich)

Jan Werich was supposed to ply the part of Blofeld. An illness forced him to drop out. Donald Pleasence was his replacement.[13]

Young Bess (1953)
Jean Simmons as Queen Elizabeth I
(Deborah Kerr, Elizabeth Taylor)

Elizabeth Taylor was a possibility to play Queen Elizabeth I, as was Deborah Kerr. Kerr made a test, but lost out to Jean Simmons.[14] Her consolation prize was the smaller role of Catherine Parr.

Young Cassidy (1965)
Rod Taylor as John Cassidy (Sean Connery)

Sean Connery turned down the role of John Cassidy.[15]

The Young in Heart (1938)
Paulette Goddard as Leslie Saunders
(Vivien Leigh)

Vivien Leigh was up for the role of Leslie Saunders in *The Young in Heart*. Producer David O. Selznick didn't think she was right for the role, and cast Paulette Goddard instead.[16] Coincidentally, Goddard was the number two choice for the role of Scarlett O'Hara in *Gone with the Wind*. She lost the part to Vivien Leigh.

The Young Lions (1958)
Dean Martin as Michael Whiteacre (Tony Randall)

Tony Randall was originally signed for the part of Michael Whiteacre. Dean Martin was also interested in the role. Martin's agency, MCA, also had Marlon Brando and Montgomery Clift as clients. Both actors were also signed for *The Young Lions*. The agency threatened to remove them if Martin was not cast. The studio gave in and gave Martin the role already promised to Randall.

The Young Mr. Pitt (1942)
Phyllis Calvert as Eleanor Eden
(Margaret Lockwood)

Margaret Lockwood was originally cast as Eleanor Eden in *The Young Mr. Pitt*. Shortly after she found out that she was pregnant, and

Margaret Lockwood's pregnancy prevented her from making *The Young Mr. Pitt*.

gave up the part. Phyllis Calvert was brought in as her replacement.[17]

Youngblood Hawke (1964)
James Franciscus as Youngblood Hawke
(Warren Beatty)

Warren Beatty was cast in the title role of Youngblood Hawke. Beatty was somewhat demanding and Warner Bros. replaced him with James Franciscus.[18]

Zabiskie Point (1970)
Mark Frechette as Mark (Harrison Ford)

Casting director Fred Roos brought Harrison Ford in to audition for the lead role of Mark in *Zabriskie Point*. Roos thought that Ford gave a great audition but director Michelangelo Antonioni was unimpressed. Roos was unable to convince the director to cast Ford. Antonioni gave the part to Mark Frechette instead. Roos liked Ford so much that he gave him a small role as an airport worker.[1]

Zardoz (1974)
Sean Connery as Zed (Burt Reynolds)

Burt Reynolds was originally cast as Zed. He had back problems and had to leave the film. Sean Connery was his replacement.[2]

Zee and Co. (1972)

Michael Caine as Robert Blakeley (Peter O'Toole)

Susannah York as Stella (Anouk Aimee, Faye Dunaway, Lee Remick, Romy Schneider)

Peter O'Toole was the first choice for the starring role of Robert Blakeley. When he said no it went to Michael Caine.

Anouk Aimee was considered for the part of Stella. Aimee had had problems with a former agent who was one of the producers of the film. That took her out of the running. Faye Dunaway was made an offer, but she was already busy. Lee Remick said she would do it, but later changed her mind and dropped out. Romy Schneider was considered, but the role eventually went to Susannah York.[3]

Ziegfeld Follies (1946)

Judy Garland as Great Lady (Greer Garson)

Greer Garson was offered the Great Lady role. She thought it was degrading, and turned it down.[4]

Zorba the Greek (1964)

Lila Kedrova as Madame Hortense (Stella Adler, Tallulah Bankhead, Simone Signoret, Ann Sothern, Barbara Stanwyck)

Simone Signoret was offered the role of Madame Hortense. Signoret was fond of the script, but had reservations about playing the part. She told director Michael Cacoyannis that she didn't think it was "her." He assured her that he would spend as much time as she needed rehearsing, and that if she was uncomfortable with anything he would take care of it. Signoret told Cacoyannis that she didn't like to rehearse; she would rather play the part spontaneously. Cacoyannis, an advocate of rehearsing, reluctantly agreed to do it Signoret's way. The actress finally agreed to take the part. Signoret flew to Crete to begin filming. The very first scene that she was to shoot was a difficult scene in which Madame Hortense makes a fool of herself. Signoret's discomfort was obvious. Cacoyannis did take after take for four hours. Signoret's confidence was shot. She started to cry, and told Cacoyannis and co-star Anthony Quinn that there was no way she could play this part. They tried to console her, to no avail. Finally Signoret admitted that she was uncomfortable playing a character that was older than she was. The fortysomething actress did not want her husband to see her that way. Signoret left Crete the next day. Anthony Quinn personally made phone calls to Barbara Stanwyck, Tallulah Bankhead, Stella Adler, and Ann Sothern. No one was able to come to Crete soon enough. Finally Cacoyannis remembered an actress who he thought would be perfect — Lila Kedrova. He told United Artists his choice. The studio was not pleased. They wanted a star for the part, and Kedrova was an unknown. Anthony Quinn stepped in and called 20th Century–Fox boss Darryl F. Zanuck. He told Zanuck the situation, and Zanuck immediately agreed to finance the film.[5]

Zulu (1964)

James Booth as Private Henry Hook (Michael Caine)

Actor Stanley Baker was set to play the lead role in *Zulu*, which he was also producing. Baker went to see a play in London called *Next Time I'll Sing to You*, which had a young actor named Michael Caine in the cast. Baker went backstage after the show and asked Caine to audition for the role of Private Henry Hook the next morning. When Caine arrived the next day, director Cy Endfield told him that the part had already been given to another actor, James Booth! Endfield explained that the character was Cockney, and Booth looked the part more than Caine. Although he was disappointed by the news, Caine agreed that based on looks alone, Booth was the better choice. Caine started to leave until Endfield called him back. He asked Caine if he would stay to read for another part, Gonville Bromhead. Caine agreed, and he won the role.[6]

NOTES

A

1. Bob Woodward, *Wired: The Short Life & Fast Times of John Belushi* (New York: Simon and Schuster, 1984), 210.
2. Warren G. Harris, *Clark Gable: A Biography* (New York: Harmony Books, 2002), 259.
3. James Robert Parish and Ronald L. Bowers, *The MGM Stock Company: The Golden Era* (New Rochelle: Arlington House, 1973), 482.
4. Lawrence J. Quirk, *Paul Newman* (Dallas: Taylor, 1996), 271.
5. Karen Valby, "The Actress: Diane Keaton" *Entertainment Weekly*, 14 November 2003, 44.
6. William Goldman, *Which Lie Did I Tell?* (New York: Pantheon Books, 2000), 109–111.
7. Stephen Rebello, "Born to Be Bad" *Movieline*, May 1992, 77.
8. Roger Friedman, "Sex & Sensibility" *Entertainment Weekly*, 3 May 1991, 23.
9. Ron Base, *"If the Other Guy Isn't Jack Nicholson, I've Got the Part"* (Chicago: Contemporary Books, 1994), 243, 277.
10. Rachel Abramowitz, *Is That a Gun in Your Pocket?: Women's Experience of Power in Hollywood* (New York: Random House, 2000), 269–272.
11. Martin Knelman, *Jim Carrey: The Joker Is Wild* (Buffalo: Firefly Books, 1996), 148.
12. Anthony Quinn with Daniel Paisner, *One Man Tango* (New York: HarperCollins, 1995), 352–353.
13. John Parker, *Warren Beatty: The Last Great Lover of Hollywood* (New York: Carroll & Graf, 1993), 88.
14. Patrick McGilligan, *A Double Life: George Cukor* (New York: St. Martin's Press, 1991), 210.
15. Emanuel Levy, *George Cukor, Master of Elegance: Hollywood's Legendary Director and His Stars* (New York: William Morrow, 1994), 210.
16. Maureen Stapleton and Jane Scovell, *A Hell of a Life* (New York: Simon & Schuster, 1995), 149.
17. Lawrence J. Quirk, *Totally Uninhibited: The Life and Wild Times of Cher* (New York: William Morrow, 1991), 231.
18. Andrew Yule, *Sean Connery: From 007 to Hollywood Icon* (New York: Donald I. Fine, 1992), 239–241.
19. Arthur Marx, *Goldwyn: A Biography of the Man Behind the Myth* (New York: W. W. Norton, 1976), 254.
20. A. Scott Berg, *Goldwyn: A Biography* (New York: Alfred A. Knopf, 1989), 317.
21. *New York Daily News* (New York), 15 March 2000.
22. Frank Miller, *Movies We Love* (Atlanta: Turner, 1996), 13.
23. David Shipman, *The Great Movie Stars: The Golden Years* (New York: Crown, 1970), 417.
24. Charles Higham, *Sisters: The Story of Olivia De Havilland & Joan Fontaine* (New York: Coward-McCann, 1984), 121.
25. Jeff Burkhart and Bruce Stuart, *Hollywood's First Choices* (New York: Crown Trade Paperbacks, 1994), 204.
26. Eric Braun, *Deborah Kerr* (New York: St. Martin's Press, 1977), 121.
27. John Huston, *An Open Book* (New York: Alfred A. Knopf, 1980), 187.
28. Peter Bart and Peter Guber, *Shoot Out: Surviving Fame and (Mis)Fortune in Hollywood* (New York: G. P. Putnam's Sons, 2002), 124.
29. Josh Young, "Texas Two-Step" *Entertainment Weekly*, 23 August, 2002, 8–9.
30. Joe Eszterhas, "Mr. Smithee Goes to Hollywood" *Entertainment Weekly*, 6 March, 1998, 31, 32.
31. Chris Nashawaty, "Chow Time" *Entertainment Weekly*, 13 February, 1998, 18.
32. Joe Eszterhas, "Mr. Smithee Goes to Hollywood" *Entertainment Weekly*, 6 March, 1998, 31, 32.
33. Ron Base, *"If the Other Guy Isn't Jack Nicholson, I've Got the Part"* (Chicago: Contemporary Books, 1994), 135–136.
34. John Eastman, *Retakes: Behind the Scenes of 500 Classic Movies* (New York: Ballantine Books, 1989), 8.
35. Matthew Bernstein, *Walter Wanger: Hollywood Independent* (Berkeley/Los Angeles/London: University of California Press, 1994), 143.
36. Randall Riese, *Her Name Is Barbra: An Intimate Portrait of the Real Barbra Streisand* (New York: St. Martin's Paperbacks, 1993), 385.
37. William Donati, *Ida Lupino: A Biography* (Lexington: The University Press of Kentucky, 1996), 23–26.
38. John Eastman, *Retakes: Behind the Scenes of 500 Classic Movies* (New York: Ballantine Books, 1989), 9.
39. Brantley Bardin, "Idol Chatter: Jill Clayburgh" *Premiere*, August 2002, 92.
40. Susan Bluestein Davis, *After Midnight: The Life and Death of Brad Davis* (New York: Pocket Books, 1997), 87.
41. Sam Staggs, *All About "All About Eve": The Complete Behind-the-Scenes Story of the Bitchiest Film Ever Made* (New York: St. Martin's Press, 2000), 6–8, 11, 61–64.

42. George F. Custen, *Twentieth Century's Fox* (New York: BasicBooks, 1997), 339, 340.
43. Rudy Behlmer, *Memo from Darryl F. Zanuck: The Golden Years at Twentieth Century–Fox* (New York: Grove Press, 1993), 165, 167.
44. Steven Bach, *Marlene Dietrich: Life and Legend* (New York: William Morrow, 1992), 349.
45. Sam Staggs, *All About "All About Eve": The Complete Behind-the-Scenes Story of the Bitchiest Film Ever Made* (New York: St. Martin's Press, 2000), 6–8, 11, 61–64.
46. George F. Custen, *Twentieth Century's Fox* (New York: BasicBooks, 1997), 339, 340.
47. George F. Custen, *Twentieth Century's Fox* (New York: BasicBooks, 1997), 339, 340.
48. Sam Staggs, *All About "All About Eve": The Complete Behind-the-Scenes Story of the Bitchiest Film Ever Made* (New York: St. Martin's Press, 2000), 6–8, 11, 61–64.
49. Sam Staggs, *All About "All About Eve": The Complete Behind-the-Scenes Story of the Bitchiest Film Ever Made* (New York: St. Martin's Press, 2000), 6–8, 11, 61–64.
50. Rudy Behlmer, *Memo from Darryl F. Zanuck: The Golden Years at Twentieth Century–Fox* (New York: Grove Press, 1993), 165, 167.
51. Sam Staggs, *All About "All About Eve": The Complete Behind-the-Scenes Story of the Bitchiest Film Ever Made* (New York: St. Martin's Press, 2000), 6–8, 11, 61–64.
52. William Goldman, *Adventures in the Screen Trade* (New York: Warner Books, 1983), 55.
53. James Spada, *Streisand: Her Life* (New York: Ivy Books, 1995), 426–428.
54. John Eastman, *Retakes: Behind the Scenes of 500 Classic Movies* (New York: Ballantine Books, 1989), 11.
55. Martin Gottfried, *All His Jazz: The Life and Death of Bob Fosse* (New York: Bantam Books, 1990), 371–378.
56. Martin Gottfried, *All His Jazz: The Life and Death of Bob Fosse* (New York: Bantam Books, 1990), 371–378.
57. Shirley MacLaine, *My Lucky Stars: A Hollywood Memoir* (New York: Bantam Books, 1995), 188.
58. David Shipman, *The Great Movie Stars: The International Years* (New York: St. Martin's Press, 1972), 102.
59. Rebecca Ascher-Walsh, "5 Card Stud" *Entertainment Weekly*, 18 September 1998, 38.
60. Hollywood Kids, "Q&A" *Movieline*, August 1998, 38.
61. Ron Base, *"If the Other Guy Isn't Jack Nicholson, I've Got the Part"* (Chicago: Contemporary Books, 1994), 62.
62. Ileane Rudolph, "Roy Story" *TV Guide*, 17 February 2001, 47.
63. Tricia Johnson, "The Entertainers: Breakouts" *Entertainment Weekly*, 22–29 December 2000, 44.
64. Jared Brown, *Zero Mostel: A Biography* (New York: Atheneum, 1989), 215.
65. Frank Sanello, *Spielberg: The Man, the Movies, the Mythology* (Dallas: Taylor, 1996), 200–202.
66. Rob Edelman and Audrey Kupferberg, *Matthau: A Life* (Lanham: Taylor Trade, 2002), 236.
67. John Eastman, *Retakes: Behind the Scenes of 500 Classic Movies* (New York: Ballantine Books, 1989), 14.
68. Stephen Rebello, "Leelee Land" *Movieline*, March 2000, 54.
69. *The Observer* (London), 15 October 2000.
70. Nigel Andrews, *Travolta: The Life* (New York: Bloomsbury, 1998), 107–108.
71. Chris Nickson, *Superhero: An Unauthorized Biography of Christopher Reeve* (New York: St. Martin's Paperbacks, 1998), 57.
72. Dale Pollock, *Skywalking: The Life and Films of George Lucas* (New York: Harmony Books, 1983), 110.
73. Marilu Henner with Jim Jerome, *By All Means Keep on Moving* (New York: Pocket Books, 1994), 113.
74. Clive Hirschhorn, *Gene Kelly* (Chicago: Henry Regnery, 1974), 196, 198.
75. Clive Hirschhorn, *Gene Kelly* (Chicago: Henry Regnery, 1974), 196, 198.
76. John Eastman, *Retakes: Behind the Scenes of 500 Classic Movies* (New York: Ballantine Books, 1989), 16.
77. *New York Daily News* (New York), 25 August 1998.
78. Raymond Strait, *James Garner: A Biography* (New York: St. Martin's Press, 1985), 199–205.
79. Ty Burr, "America's Most Wanted" *Entertainment Weekly*, 20 July 2001, 29–30.
80. Maximillian Potter, "A Man, a Plan, a Van" *Premiere*, December 1997, 100.
81. Jill Nelson, "No More Mr. Nice Guy?" *USA Weekend*, 9–11 January 1998, 5.
82. Roy Pickard, *Jimmy Stewart: A Life in Film* (New York: St. Martin's Press, 1992), 140–141.
83. John Eastman, *Retakes: Behind the Scenes of 500 Classic Movies* (New York: Ballantine Books, 1989), 17.
84. Arthur Marx, *The Nine Lives of Mickey Rooney* (Briarcliff Manor: Stein and Day, 1986), 217.
85. *New York Daily News* (New York), 13 April 2000.
86. Fred Schreurs, "De Niro" *Rolling Stone*, 25 August 1988, 74.
87. Jeff Gordinier, "ReelWorld" *Entertainment Weekly*, 31 July 1998, 45.
88. David Shipman, *The Great Movie Stars: The Golden Years* (New York: Crown, 1970), 271.
89. Ron Base, *"If the Other Guy Isn't Jack Nicholson, I've Got the Part"* (Chicago: Contemporary Books, 1994), 285–286.
90. Chris Nashawaty, "Building Animal House" *Entertainment Weekly*, 9 October 1998, 46.
91. James Kotsilibas-Davis and Myrna Loy, *Myrna Loy: Being and Becoming* (New York: Alfred A. Knopf, 1987), 76.
92. Rudy Behlmer, *Memo from Darryl F. Zanuck: The Golden Years at Twentieth Century–Fox* (New York: Grove Press, 1993), 88–90.
93. John Eastman, *Retakes: Behind the Scenes of 500 Classic Movies* (New York: Ballantine Books, 1989), 19.
94. R. Dixon Smith, *Ronald Colman, Gentleman of the Cinema* (Jefferson: McFarland, 1991), 140.
95. John Eastman, *Retakes: Behind the Scenes of 500 Classic Movies* (New York: Ballantine Books, 1989), 19.
96. C. David Heymann, *Liz: An Intimate Biography of Elizabeth Taylor* (New York: Birch Lane Press, 1995), 294.
97. Andrew Yule, *Sean Connery: From 007 to Hollywood Icon* (New York: Donald I. Fine, 1992), 195.
98. J. Randy Taraborrelli, *Laughing Till It Hurts: The Complete Life and Career of Carol Burnett* (New York: William Morrow, 1988), 388.
99. Tom McGee, *Betty Grable: The Girl with the Million Dollar Legs* (Vestal: The Vestal Press, 1995), 155.
100. David Shipman, *Judy Garland: The Secret Life of an American Legend* (New York: Hyperion, 1992), 234–241.
101. Ginger Rogers, *Ginger: My Story* (New York: HarperCollins, 1991), 247.
102. David Shipman, *The Great Movie Stars: The Golden Years* (New York: Crown, 1970), 403.

103. John Baxter, *Woody Allen: A Biography* (New York: Carroll & Graf, 1998), 248–249.
104. Peter Biskind, "The Crucible: An Oral History" *Premiere*, Special Issue 1994, 120.
105. Axel Madsen, *Stanwyck* (New York: HarperCollins, 1994), 107.
106. Eric Lax, *Woody Allen: A Biography* (New York: Alfred A. Knopf, 1991), 301.
107. Dave Karger, "The Entertainers" *Entertainment Weekly*, 20/27 December, 2002, 15.
108. Lawrence Grobel, "Coming & Going" *Movieline*, April 2000, 56.
109. *New York Daily News* (New York), 13 August 1999.
110. Daniel Davis, "Slow Daddy" *Movieline*, July 2002, 58.
111. *New York Daily News* (New York), 7 February 1999.
112. John Eastman, *Retakes: Behind the Scenes of 500 Classic Movies* (New York: Ballantine Books, 1989), 22.
113. Ron Base, *"If the Other Guy Isn't Jack Nicholson, I've Got the Part"* (Chicago: Contemporary Books, 1994), 192–195.
114. Michael Schumacher, *Francis Ford Coppola: A Filmmaker's Life* (New York: Crown, 1999), 197–198.
115. Richard Schickel, *Clint Eastwood: A Biography* (New York: Alfred A. Knopf, 1996), 361.
116. Christopher Silvester, *The Grove Book of Hollywood* (New York: Grove Press, 1998), 544.
117. Michael Schumacher, *Francis Ford Coppola: A Filmmaker's Life* (New York: Crown, 1999), 197–198.
118. Peter Cowie, *The Apocalypse Now Book* (New York: Da Capo Press, 2000, 2001), 17–18.
119. Ron Base, *"If the Other Guy Isn't Jack Nicholson, I've Got the Part"* (Chicago: Contemporary Books, 1994), 192–195.
120. Patrick Goldstein, "Fly Me to the Moon" *Premiere*, June 1995, 87.
121. Bruce Fretts, "Robert Duvall" *Entertainment Weekly*, 13 February 1998, 26.
122. Dave Karger, "King's Cursed Movie" *Entertainment Weekly*, 13 December 1996, 21.
123. Warren G. Harris, *Sophia Loren: A Biography* (New York: Simon & Schuster, 1998), 208.
124. Bob Thomas, *Golden Boy: The Untold Story of William Holden* (New York: St. Martin's Press, 1983), 39.
125. Graham McCann, *Cary Grant: A Class Apart* (New York: Columbia University Press, 1996), 323.
126. David Shipman, *The Great Movie Stars: The International Years* (New York: St. Martin's Press, 1972), 147–148.
127. Jay Fultz, *In Search of Donna Reed* (Iowa City: University of Iowa Press, 1998), 107.
128. John Eastman, *Retakes: Behind the Scenes of 500 Classic Movies* (Chicago: Ballantine Books, 1989), 24.
129. Nellie Bly, *Marlon Brando: Larger Than Life* (New York: Pinnacle Books, 1994), 140–141.
130. John Eastman, *Retakes: Behind the Scenes of 500 Classic Movies* (New York: Ballantine Books, 1989), 24–25.
131. Dave Thompson, *Travolta* (Dallas: Taylor, 1996), 149.
132. Ron Base, *"If the Other Guy Isn't Jack Nicholson, I've Got the Part"* (Chicago: Contemporary Books, 1994), 279.
133. Marilu Henner with Jim Jerome, *By All Means Keep on Moving* (New York: Pocket Books, 1994), 246.
134. Michael Fleming, "The Hunt Is On" *Movieline*, November 2000, 58.
135. Stephen Rebello, "The Unsinkable Melanie Griffith" *Movieline*, April 1999, 56.
136. David Shipman, *The Great Movie Stars: The International Years* (New York: St. Martin's Press, 1972), 449.
137. Jeff Burkhart and Bruce Stuart, *Hollywood's First Choices* (New York: Crown Trade Paperbacks, 1994), 210.
138. Esther Williams with Digby Diehl, *The Million Dollar Mermaid* (New York: Simon & Schuster, 1999), 257–258.
139. David Shipman, *The Great Movie Stars: The International Years* (New York: St. Martin's Press, 1972), 528.
140. Frank Castelluccio and Alvin Walker, *The Other Side of Ethel Mertz: The Life Story of Vivian Vance* (Manchester: Knowledge, Ideas & Trends, 1998), 217.
141. Stephen Rebello, "Elizabeth's Reign" *Movieline*, September 1998, 56.
142. *New York Daily News* (New York), 19 April 1998.
143. Matt Mueller, "Sliding Doors" *Movieline*, March 1998, 20.
144. Michael Fleming, "Casting Glances" *Movieline*, June 1997, 94.
145. Andy Dougan, *Robin Williams* (New York: Thunder's Mouth Press, 1998), 171.
146. Trish Deitch Rohrer, "Fade-In: Auditions" *Premiere*, September 1992, 99.
147. John Eastman, *Retakes: Behind the Scenes of 500 Classic Movies* (New York: Ballantine Books, 1989), 26.

B

1. Damien Bona, *Starring John Wayne as Genghis Khan* (Secaucus: Citadel Press, 1996), 4–5.
2. Anne Edwards, *Shirley Temple: American Princess* (New York: Berkley Books, 1988), 119.
3. Jim Calio, "The Player" *Entertainment Weekly*, 16 July 2001, 38.
4. Lawrence J. Quirk, *Totally Uninhibited: The Life and Wild Times of Cher* (New York: William Morrow, 1991), 229.
5. Jeff Burkhart and Bruce Stuart, *Hollywood's First Choices* (New York: Crown Trade Paperbacks, 1994), 195.
6. Gavin Smith, *Sayles on Sayles* (London: Faber and Faber, 1998), 80.
7. Lee Pfeiffer and Michael Lewis, *The Films of Tom Hanks* (Secaucus: Citadel Press, 1996), 26.
8. Frank Sanello, *Spielberg: The Man, the Movies, the Mythology* (Dallas: Taylor, 1996), 166–167.
9. Tom Russo, "What If...?" *Premiere*, February 2004, 86.
10. Frank Sanello, *Spielberg: The Man, the Movies, the Mythology* (Dallas: Taylor, 1996), 166–167.
11. Andrew Yule, *Picture Shows: The Life and Films of Peter Bogdanovich* (New York: Limelight Editions, 1992), 187.
12. Rachel Abramowitz, "Studios Ignoring You? Quick, Make an Indie!" *New York Times Magazine*, 16 November 1997, 100.
13. Chris Nashawaty, "Star Spelled Backward" *Entertainment Weekly*, 28 March 2003, 31.
14. Aljean Harmetz, *Round Up the Usual Suspects: The Making of Casablanca* (New York: Hyperion, 1992), 87.

15. Yvonne De Carlo with Doug Warren, *Yvonne: An Autobiography* (New York: St. Martin's Press, 1987), 145.
16. James Robert Parish, *Whoopi Goldberg: Her Journey from Poverty to Megastardom* (Secaucus: Birch Lane Press, 1996), 223.
17. Ginger Rogers, *Ginger: My Story* (New York: HarperCollins, 1991), 245–246.
18. Axel Madsen, *Stanwyck* (New York: HarperCollins, 1994), 202.
19. Todd McCarthy, *Howard Hawks: The Grey Fox of Hollywood* (New York: Grove Press, 1997), 324–325.
20. Kathleen Brady, *Lucille: The Life of Lucille Ball* (New York: Hyperion, 1994), 123.
21. Marshall Fine, *Bloody Sam: The Life and Films of Sam Peckinpah* (New York: Donald I. Fine, 1991), 163–164.
22. John Eastman, *Retakes: Behind the Scenes of 500 Classic Movies* (New York: Ballantine Books, 1989), 29.
23. David Shipman, *The Great Movie Stars: The Golden Years* (New York: Crown, 1970), 239.
24. Richard Fleischer, *Just Tell Me When to Cry: A Memoir* (New York: Carroll & Graf, 1993), 220–222.
25. Christopher Andersen, *Citizen Jane: The Turbulent Life of Jane Fonda* (New York: Henry Holt, 1990), 156.
26. Jane Ellen Wayne, *The Golden Girls of MGM* (New York: Carroll & Graf, 2002), 334.
27. John Eastman, *Retakes: Behind the Scenes of 500 Classic Movies* (New York: Ballantine Books, 1989), 30.
28. Warren G. Harris, *Natalie & R.J.: Hollywood's Star-Crossed Lovers* (New York: A Dolphin Book, 1988), 146.
29. David Shipman, *Judy Garland: The Secret Life of an American Legend* (New York: Hyperion, 1992), 225.
30. Gary Carey, *All the Stars in Heaven: Louis B. Mayer's M-G-M* (New York: E. P. Dutton, 1981), 358.
31. David Shipman, *The Great Movie Stars: The Golden Years* (New York: Crown, 1970), 142–143.
32. Marion Davies, *The Times We Had: Life with William Randolph Hearst* (Indianapolis/New York: Bobbs-Merrill, 1975), 254.
33. Robert Lacey, *Grace* (New York: G.P. Putnam's Sons, 1994), 197.
34. Michael Fleming, "Casting Glances" *Movieline*, June 1997, 65.
35. Michael Munn, *The Sharon Stone Story* (London: Robson Books, 1997), 65, 67.
36. Michael Munn, *The Sharon Stone Story* (London: Robson Books, 1997), 65, 67.
37. Michael Fleming, "Casting Glances" *Movieline*, June 1997, 65.
38. Michael Munn, *The Sharon Stone Story* (London: Robson Books, 1997), 65, 67.
39. Stephen Rebello, "The Unsinkable Melanie Griffith" *Movieline*, April 1999, 56.
40. Michael Sauter, "Sexual Dealings" *Entertainment Weekly*, 22 March 2002, 116.
41. Michael Sauter, "Sexual Dealings" *Entertainment Weekly*, 22 March 2002, 116.
42. Alec Foege and Bryan Alexander, "Epic Effort" *People*, 12 May 1997, 212.
43. Ron Base, *"If the Other Guy Isn't Jack Nicholson, I've Got the Part"* (Chicago: Contemporary Books, 1994), 286.
44. Lyall Bush, "Waiting for Hitchcock" *MovieMaker*, May/June/July 1997, 36.
45. Stephen Rebello, "Born to be Bad" *Movieline*, May 1992, 77.
46. Michael Fleming, "Casting Glances" *Movieline*, June 1997, 65.
47. Holly Sorensen, "Linda Fiorentino" *Us*, July 1997, 60.
48. *New York Post* (New York), 11 February 1998.
49. Adam West with Jeff Rovin, *Back to the Batcave* (New York: Berkley Books, 1994), 206.
50. Peter Gerstenzang, "Issues of Character" *Entertainment Weekly*, 2 June 1995, 63.
51. Damien Bona, *Starring John Wayne as Genghis Khan* (Secaucus: Citadel Press, 1996), 118.
52. Damien Bona, *Starring John Wayne as Genghis Khan* (Secaucus: Citadel Press, 1996), 118.
53. Damien Bona, *Starring John Wayne as Genghis Khan* (Secaucus: Citadel Press, 1996), 118.
54. Damien Bona, *Starring John Wayne as Genghis Khan* (Secaucus: Citadel Press, 1996), 118.
55. Peter Gerstenzang, "Issues of Character" *Entertainment Weekly*, 2 June 1995, 63.
56. Nancy Griffin and Kim Masters, *Hit & Run: How Jon Peters and Peter Guber Took Sony for a Ride in Hollywood* (New York: Simon & Schuster, 1996), 167.
57. Larry Grobel, "Dr. Michael & Mr. Keaton" *Movieline*, August 1997, 52.
58. Michael Munn, *The Sharon Stone Story* (London: Robson Books, 1997), 43–44.
59. Jeffrey Lantos, "Sela Under Covers" *Movieline*, February 2000, 65.
60. Nancy Griffin and Kim Masters, *Hit & Run: How Jon Peters and Peter Guber Took Sony for a Ride in Hollywood* (New York: Simon & Schuster, 1996), 167.
61. Rebecca Ascher-Walsh, "Psycho Kilmer" *Entertainment Weekly*, 31 May 1996, 35.
62. Michael Fleming, "Casting Glances" *Movieline*, June 1997, 64.
63. Ryan Murphy, "No Comment" *Us*, September 1994, 34.
64. Stephen Rebello, "The Boogie Man" *Movieline*, June 1997, 86.
65. Benjamin Svetkey, "Seeing Red" *Entertainment Weekly*, 9 June 1995, 22.
66. Lawrence Grobel, "There's Something About Sandy" *Movieline*, April 1999, 51.
67. Michael Fleming, "Casting Glances" *Movieline*, June 1997, 66.
68. Stephen Rebello, "The Next McCarthy Era" *Movieline*, August 1998, 56.
69. Gene Brown, *Movie Time: A Chronology of Hollywood and the Movie Industry from Its Beginnings to the Present* (New York: Macmillan, 1995), 393–394.
70. Ron Base, *"If the Other Guy Isn't Jack Nicholson, I've Got the Part"* (Chicago: Contemporary Books, 1994), 287.
71. Ron Base, *"If the Other Guy Isn't Jack Nicholson, I've Got the Part"* (Chicago: Contemporary Books, 1994), 287.
72. Michael Fleming, "Casting Glances" *Movieline*, June 1997, 64.
73. Gene Brown, *Movie Time: A Chronology of Hollywood and the Movie Industry from Its Beginnings to the Present* (New York: Macmillan, 1995), 393–394.
74. Stephen Rebello, "Born to be Bad" *Movieline*, May 1992, 77.
75. Michael Munn, *The Sharon Stone Story* (London: Robson Books, 1997), 124.
76. David Shipman, *The Great Movie Stars: The International Years* (New York: St. Martin's Press, 1972), 6.

77. Joe Russo and Larry Landsman with Edward Gross, *Planet of the Apes Revisited: The Behind-The Scenes Story of the Classic Science Fiction Saga* (New York: Thomas Dunne Books, 2001), 210.
78. Jeffrey Ressner, "In the Swim Again" *Time*, 1 March 1999, 66–67.
79. Garry Marshall with Lori Marshall, *Wake Me When It's Funny* (Holbrook: Adams, 1995), 206.
80. David Shipman, *The Great Movie Stars: The International Years* (New York: St. Martin's Press, 1972), 214.
81. Rebecca Ascher-Walsh, "Reel World" *Entertainment Weekly*, 31 March 2000, 37.
82. John Eastman, *Retakes: Behind the Scenes of 500 Classic Movies* (New York: Ballantine Books, 1989), 33.
83. John Baxter, *Woody Allen: A Biography* (New York: Carroll & Graf, 1998), 90–91.
84. Robert Edelman and Audrey Kupferberg, *Angela Lansbury: A Life on Stage and Screen* (Thorndike: G.K. Hall, and Bath: Chivers Press, 1996), 242.
85. Steve Daly, "Night Writer" *Entertainment Weekly*, 19 January 2001, 47.
86. *New York Daily News* (New York), 17 December 2000.
87. Steve Daly, "Night Writer" *Entertainment Weekly*, 19 January 2001, 47.
88. John Eastman, *Retakes: Behind the Scenes of 500 Classic Movies* (New York: Ballantine Books, 1989), 34.
89. David Shipman, *The Great Movie Stars: The International Years* (New York: St. Martin's Press, 1972), 146.
90. David Shipman, *Judy Garland: The Secret Life of an American Legend* (New York: Hyperion, 1992), 175, 184–185.
91. Jill Nelson, "No More Mr. Nice Guy?" *USA Weekend*, 9–11 January 1998, 5.
92. Joe Russo and Larry Landsman with Edward Gross, *Planet of the Apes Revisited: The Behind-The Scenes Story of the Classic Science Fiction Saga* (New York: Thomas Dunne Books, 2001), 117–121, 124, 126.
93. James Kotsilibas-Davis and Myrna Loy, *Myrna Loy: Being and Becoming* (New York: Alfred A. Knopf, 1987), 40.
94. Frank Miller, *Movies We Love* (Atlanta: Turner, 1996), 27.
95. Ron Base, *"If the Other Guy Isn't Jack Nicholson, I've Got the Part"* (Chicago: Contemporary Books, 1994), 115–116.
96. Kate Buford, *Burt Lancaster: An American Life* (New York: Alfred A. Knopf, 2000), 189–190.
97. Ron Base, *"If the Other Guy Isn't Jack Nicholson, I've Got the Part"* (Chicago: Contemporary Books, 1994), 115–116.
98. David Shipman, *The Great Movie Stars: The International Years* (New York: St. Martin's Press, 1972), 222.
99. Frank Miller, *Movies We Love* (Atlanta: Turner, 1996), 27.
100. Ryan Murphy, "A Perfect Mismatch" *Entertainment Weekly*, 7 May 1993, 21.
101. Michael Viner and Terrie Maxine Frankel, *Tales from Casting Couch: An Unprecedented Candid Collection of Stories, Essays, and Anecdotes by and About Legendary Hollywood Stars, Starlets, and Wanna-bees...* (Beverly Hills: Dove Books, 1995), 88–89.
102. Joan Wester Anderson, *Forever Young: The Life, Loves and Enduring Faith of a Hollywood Legend* (Edinburgh: Mainstream, 1998), 61.
103. Kathleen Brady, *Lucille: The Life of Lucille Ball* (Allen: Thomas More, 2000), 140.
104. Burt Reynolds, *My Life* (New York: Hyperion, 1994), 252–253.
105. David Shipman, *The Great Movie Stars: The International Years* (New York: St. Martin's Press, 1972), 183.
106. Steve Daly, "Wyler" *Entertainment Weekly*, Special Oscar Guide 1997, 120.
107. A. Scott Berg, *Goldwyn: A Biography* (New York: Alfred A. Knopf, 1989), 410.
108. Ron Base, *"If the Other Guy Isn't Jack Nicholson, I've Got the Part"* (Chicago: Contemporary Books, 1994), 243, 280.
109. Todd Keith, *Kevin Costner: The Unauthorized Biography* (London: ikonprint, 1991), 52.
110. Marshall Terrill, *Steve McQueen: Portrait of an American Rebel* (New York: Donald I. Fine, 1993), 425.
111. Ron Base, *"If the Other Guy Isn't Jack Nicholson, I've Got the Part"* (Chicago: Contemporary Books, 1994), 222–223.
112. Peter Bart and Peter Guber, *Shoot Out: Surviving Fame and (Mis)Fortune in Hollywood* (New York: G. P. Putnam's Sons, 2002), 116–119.
113. Susan Sackett, *The Hollywood Reporter Book of Box Office Hits* (New York: Billboard Books, 1990), 186.
114. Lawrence Grobel, *The Hustons* (New York: Scribner's, 1989), 549.
115. Ava Gardner, *Ava: My Story* (Thorndike: Thorndike Press, 1990), 443–444.
116. *New York Daily News* (New York), 30 March 1999.
117. John Eastman, *Retakes: Behind the Scenes of 500 Classic Movies* (New York: Ballantine Books, 1989), 36.
118. Frank Sanello, *Spielberg: The Man, the Movies, the Mythology* (Dallas: Taylor, 1996), 184.
119. Benjamin Svetkey, "Clown Jewel" *Entertainment Weekly*, 30 May 2003, 67.
120. Lee Pfeiffer and Michael Lewis, *The Films of Tom Hanks* (Secaucus: Citadel Press, 1996), 82.
121. Rachel Abramowitz, *Is That a Gun in Your Pocket?: Women's Experience of Power in Hollywood* (New York: Random House, 2000), 300–301.
122. Lawrence J. Quirk, *Bob Hope: The Road Well-Traveled* (New York: Applause Books, 2000), 107.
123. Jeff Gordinier, "A Time to Chill" *Entertainment Weekly*, 6 November 1998, 38.
124. Todd McCarthy, *Howard Hawks: The Grey Fox of Hollywood* (New York: Grove Press, 1997), 486.
125. Jeff Burkhart and Bruce Stuart, *Hollywood's First Choices* (New York: Crown Trade Paperbacks, 1994), 28.
126. Patrick McGilligan, *George Cukor: A Double Life* (New York: St. Martin's Press, 1991), 81.
127. Jan Herman, *A Talent for Trouble: The Life of Hollywood's Most Acclaimed Director, William Wyler* (New York: G. P. Putnam's Sons, 1995), 422.
128. Ron Base, *"If the Other Guy Isn't Jack Nicholson, I've Got the Part"* (Chicago: Contemporary Books, 1994), 143–144.
129. Andy Dougan, *Robin Williams* (New York: Thunder's Mouth Press, 1998), 219.
130. Evan Hunter, *Me and Hitch* (London: Faber and Faber, 1997), 14–15.

131. Donald Spoto, *The Dark Side of Genius: The Life of Alfred Hitchcock* (Boston, Toronto: Little, Brown, 1983), 454.
132. David Shipman, *The Great Movie Stars: The Golden Years* (New York: Crown, 1970), 359.
133. Ian Woodward, *Glenda Jackson: A Study in Fire and Ice* (New York: St. Martin's Press, 1985), 89.
134. Clive Hirschhorn, *Gene Kelly* (Chicago: Henry Regnery, 1974), 188.
135. Alvin Yudkoff, *Gene Kelly: A Life of Dance and Dreams* (New York: Back Stage Books, 1999), 203–204.
136. *New York Daily News* (New York), 27 April 2000.
137. Warren G. Harris, *Sophia Loren: A Biography* (New York: Simon & Schuster, 1998), 114.
138. Marilu Henner with Jim Jerome, *By All Means Keep on Moving* (New York: Pocket Books, 1994), 247.
139. Lawrence J. Quirk, *Totally Uninhibited: The Life and Wild Times of Cher* (New York: William Morrow, 1991), 228.
140. Paul M. Sammon, *Future Noir: The Making of Blade Runner* (New York: HarperPrism, 1996), 82–85, 91.
141. Simon Banner, "Easy Doesn't Do It" *Movieline*, July 1997, 12.
142. Lawrence J. Quirk, *Paul Newman* (Dallas: Taylor, 1996), 312.
143. Christopher Connelly, "You're So Square: Baby, I Don't Care" *Premiere*, September 1992, 77.
144. Maurice Yacowar, *Method in Madness: The Comic Art of Mel Brooks* (New York: St. Martin's Press, 1981), 117.
145. Doug Warren with James Cagney, *James Cagney: The Authorized Biography* (New York: St. Martin's Press, 1983), 88.
146. Christopher Andersen, *Madonna Unauthorized* (New York: Simon & Schuster, 1991), 196, 221.
147. David Shipman, *The Great Movie Stars: The International Years* (New York: St. Martin's Press, 1972), 4.
148. James Kotsilibas-Davis and Myrna Loy, *Myrna Loy: Being and Becoming* (New York: Alfred A. Knopf, 1987), 192.
149. David Shipman, *The Great Movie Stars: The International Years* (New York: St. Martin's Press, 1972), 355–356.
150. Barbara Leaming, *If This Was Happiness: A Biography of Rita Hayworth* (New York: Viking, 1989), 54.
151. Ronald Bergan, *The Coen Brothers* (New York: Thunder's Mouth Press, 2000), 80.
152. Warren G. Harris, *Audrey Hepburn: A Biography* (New York: Simon & Schuster, 1994), 259.
153. James Spada, *Streisand: Her Life* (New York: Ivy Books, 1995), 125.
154. Laurent Bouzereau, *The DePalma Cut: The Films of America's Most Controversial Director* (New York: Dembner Books, 1988), 66.
155. Axel Madsen, *Stanwyck* (New York: HarperCollins, 1994), 300.
156. Ron Base, *"If the Other Guy Isn't Jack Nicholson, I've Got the Part"* (Chicago: Contemporary Books, 1994), 166.
157. Ron Base, *"If the Other Guy Isn't Jack Nicholson, I've Got the Part"* (Chicago: Contemporary Books, 1994), 166.
158. John Eastman, *Retakes: Behind the Scenes of 500 Classic Movies* (New York: Ballantine Books, 1989), 39.
159. Donald Spoto, *Blue Angel: The Life of Marlene Dietrich* (New York: Doubleday, 1992), 55–56.
160. Rachel Abramowitz, *Is That a Gun in Your Pocket?: Women's Experience of Power in Hollywood* (New York: Random House, 2000), 117.
161. *New York Daily News* (New York), 21 March 1999.
162. David Shipman, *Judy Garland: The Secret Life of an American Legend* (New York: Hyperion, 1992), 185.
163. *New York Daily News* (New York), 10 December 2000.
164. Anthony Quinn with Daniel Paisner, *One Man Tango* (New York: HarperCollins, 1995), 166–167.
165. Paul Mazursky, *Show Me the Magic* (New York: Simon & Schuster, 1999), 178.
166. Paul Mazursky, *Show Me the Magic* (New York: Simon & Schuster, 1999), 157.
167. Elena Oumano, *Paul Newman* (New York: St. Martin's Press, 1994), 178.
168. Laurent Bouzereau, *The De Palma Cut: The Films of America's Most Controversial Director* (New York: Dembner Books, 1988), 70.
169. Chris Nickson, *Superhero: An Unauthorized Biography of Christopher Reeve* (New York: St. Martin's Paperbacks, 1998), 57.
170. Ron Base, *"If the Other Guy Isn't Jack Nicholson, I've Got the Part"* (Chicago: Contemporary Books, 1994), 243.
171. Marshall Terrill, *Steve McQueen: Portrait of an American Rebel* (New York: Donald I. Fine, 1993), 427.
172. Ron Base, *"If the Other Guy Isn't Jack Nicholson, I've Got the Part"* (Chicago: Contemporary Books, 1994), 243.
173. Julie Salamon, *The Devil's Candy: The Bonfire of the Vanities Goes to Hollywood* (Boston: Houghton Mifflin, 1991), 4–9, 11–18.
174. Ron Base, *"If the Other Guy Isn't Jack Nicholson, I've Got the Part"* (Chicago: Contemporary Books, 1994), 244.
175. Chris Nickson, *Superhero: An Unauthorized Biography of Christopher Reeve* (New York: St. Martin's Paperbacks, 1998), 151–152.
176. Julie Salamon, *The Devil's Candy: The Bonfire of the Vanities Goes to Hollywood* (Boston: Houghton Mifflin, 1991), 4–9, 11–18.
177. Julie Salamon, *The Devil's Candy: The Bonfire of the Vanities Goes to Hollywood* (Boston: Houghton Mifflin, 1991), 4–9, 11–18.
178. Benjamin Svetkey, "Spider Man" *Entertainment Weekly*, 20 April 2001, 40.
179. John Parker, *Warren Beatty: The Last Great Lover of Hollywood* (New York: Carroll & Graf, 1993), 122–123.
180. Jeff Burkhart and Bruce Stuart, *Hollywood's First Choices* (New York: Crown Trade Paperbacks, 1994), 176–177.
181. Faye Dunaway with Betsy Sharkey, *Looking for Gatsby: My Life* (New York: Simon & Schuster, 1995), 120.
182. Ellis Amburn, *The Sexiest Man Alive: A Biography of Warren Beatty* (New York: HarperCollins, 2002), 97.
183. Jeff Burkhart and Bruce Stuart, *Hollywood's First Choices* (New York: Crown Trade Paperbacks, 1994), 176–177.
184. Chris Nashawaty, "The Warren Report" *Entertainment Weekly*, Special Oscar Guide March 2000, 77.
185. Scott Brown, Clarissa Cruz, Daniel Fierman, Dave Karger, William Keck, Brian M. Raftery, Joshua Rich, Noah Robischon, Evan Serpick, Benjamin Svetkey, Karen Valby, Chris Willman, "How They Did That" *Entertainment Weekly*, 3 August 2001, 24.
186. David Thomson, "The Comeback Kids" *Movieline's Hollywood Life*, November 2003, 55.

187. Valerie Milano, *Gwyneth Paltrow* (Toronto: ECW Press, 2000), 88.
188. Meredith Berkman, "Alternate Roots" *Entertainment Weekly*, 22 October 1993, 57.
189. Patrick McGilligan, *Jack's Life: A Biography of Jack Nicholson* (New York, London: W. W. Norton, 1994), 317.
190. Jeff Burkhart and Bruce Stuart, *Hollywood's First Choices* (New York: Crown Trade Paperbacks, 1994), 197.
191. James Riordan, *Stone: The Controversies, Excesses, and Exploits of a Radical Filmmaker* (New York: Hyperion, 1995), 276.
192. Joan Wester Anderson, *Forever Young: The Life, Loves and Enduring Faith of a Hollywood Legend* (Edinburgh: Mainstream, 1998), 91–92.
193. Garson Kanin, *Hollywood* (New York: The Viking Press, 1967, 1974), 315–317.
194. Jeff Burkhart and Bruce Stuart, *Hollywood's First Choices* (New York: Crown Trade Paperbacks, 1994), 22, 24.
195. Emanuel Levy, *George Cukor, Master of Elegance: Hollywood's Legendary Director and His Stars* (New York: William Morrow, 1994), 190.
196. Jeff Burkhart and Bruce Stuart, *Hollywood's First Choices* (New York: Crown Trade Paperbacks, 1994), 22, 24.
197. Kathleen Brady, *Lucille: The Life of Lucille Ball* (New York: Hyperion, 1994), 167.
198. David Shipman, *The Great Movie Stars: The International Years* (New York: St. Martin's Press, 1972), 229.
199. Gary Carey, *Judy Holliday: An Intimate Life Story* (New York: Seaview Books, 1982), 96–98.
200. Andy Dougan, *Untouchable: A Biography of Robert De Niro* (New York: Thunder's Mouth Press, 1996), 96.
201. Chris Nickson, *Superhero: An Unauthorized Biography of Christopher Reeve* (New York: St. Martin's Paperbacks, 1998), 107.
202. *New York Daily News* (New York), 21 June 2000.
203. Giselle Benatar, "Out on a Limb" *Entertainment Weekly*, 9 April 1993, 28, 31.
204. Jessica Shaw, "Monitor" *Entertainment Weekly*, 22 December 1995, 16.
205. Julie Poll, *As the World Turns: The Complete Family Scrapbook* (Los Angeles: General, 1996), 268–269.
206. Michael Schumacher, *Francis Ford Coppola* (New York: Crown, 1999), 440–442.
207. Stephen Rebello, "Imitation of Love" *Movieline*, July 2000, 70.
208. Ronald Bergan, *Francis Ford Coppola Close Up: The Making of His Movies* (New York: Thunder's Mouth Press, 1998), 94.
209. Michael Schumacher, *Francis Ford Coppola* (New York: Crown, 1999), 440–442.
210. *New York Daily News* (New York), 12 March 1999.
211. Ian Christie, *Gilliam on Gilliam* (London: Faber and Faber, 1999), 113–114.
212. Jack Mathews, *The Battle of Brazil* (New York: Crown, 1987), 29.
213. Jack Mathews, *The Battle of Brazil* (New York: Crown, 1987), 29.
214. Ian Christie, *Gilliam on Gilliam* (London: Faber and Faber, 1999), 113–114.
215. Ian Christie, *Gilliam on Gilliam* (London: Faber and Faber, 1999), 113–114.
216. Warren G. Harris, *Audrey Hepburn: A Biography* (New York: Simon & Schuster, 1994), 171.
217. Marshall Terrill, *Steve McQueen: Portrait of an American Rebel* (New York: Donald I. Fine, 1993), 420.
218. Michael Sauter, "Elemental, This Dear Watson" *Entertainment Weekly*, 6 December 1996, 47.
219. Sondra Locke, *The Good, the Bad & the Very Ugly: A Hollywood Journey* (New York: William Morrow, 1997), 131, 138.
220. Andrew Yule, *Picture Shows: The Life and Films of Peter Bogdanovich* (New York: Limelight Editions, 1992), 179.
221. Jay Fultz, *In Search of Donna Reed* (Iowa City: University of Iowa Press, 1998), 80.
222. John Eastman, *Retakes: Behind the Scenes of 500 Classic Movies* (New York: Ballantine Books, 1989), 46.
223. Ron Base, *"If the Other Guy Isn't Jack Nicholson, I've Got the Part"* (Chicago: Contemporary Books, 1994), 123.
224. Jeff Burkhart and Bruce Stuart, *Hollywood's First Choices* (New York: Crown Trade Paperbacks, 1994), 211.
225. Ron Base, *"If the Other Guy Isn't Jack Nicholson, I've Got the Part"* (Chicago: Contemporary Books, 1994), 123.
226. Jeff Burkhart and Bruce Stuart, *Hollywood's First Choices* (New York: Crown Trade Paperbacks, 1994), 211.
227. Jeff Burkhart and Bruce Stuart, *Hollywood's First Choices* (New York: Crown Trade Paperbacks, 1994), 211.
228. William Goldman, *Adventures in the Screen Trade* (New York: Warner Books, 1983), 283–285.
229. Frank Spotnitz, "Star Search" *Entertainment Weekly*, 16 July 1993, 6–7.
230. Kelli Pryor, "Flashes" *Entertainment Weekly*, 11 June 1993, 11.
231. Mitchell Fink, "The Insider" *People*, 25 July 1994, 29.
232. James Kaplan, "Susan Lucci's Fatal Attraction" *TV Guide*, 22 April 1995, 16.
233. David Hochman, "Reel World" *Entertainment Weekly*, 17 December 1999, 56.
234. Axel Madsen, *Stanwyck* (New York: HarperCollins, 1994), 100.
235. Leslie Van Buskirk, "Tom Cruise and His Movie Machine" *Us*, 6 August 1990, 25.
236. Marshall Fine, *Bloody Sam: The Life and Films of Sam Peckinpah* (New York: Donald I. Fine, 1991), 268–270.
237. Todd McCarthy, *Howard Hawks: The Grey Fox of Hollywood* (New York: Grove Press, 1997), 247.
238. Frank Miller, *Movies We Love* (Atlanta: Turner, 1996), 44.
239. Jeff Burkhart and Bruce Stuart, *Hollywood's First Choices* (New York: Crown Trade Paperbacks, 1994), 207.
240. John Eastman, *Retakes: Behind the Scenes of 500 Classic Movies* (New York: Ballantine Books, 1989), 47.
241. John Baxter, *Woody Allen: A Biography* (New York: Carroll & Graf, 1998), 322.
242. David Shipman, *The Great Movie Stars: The Golden Years* (New York: Crown, 1970), 439.
243. Axel Madsen, *Stanwyck* (New York: HarperCollins, 1994), 29.
244. Stephen Rebello, "One Hundred Percent from the Heart" *Movieline*, November 1998, 81.
245. Judy Brennan and Bret Watson, "News & Notes" *Entertainment Weekly*, 17 November 1995, 6.
246. Dan Snierson, "Fast 'Friends'" *Entertainment Weekly*, 21 April 1995, 16.
247. David Shipman, *The Great Movie Stars: The Golden Years* (New York: Crown, 1970), 156.

248. Patrick McGilligan, *Jack's Life: A Biography of Jack Nicholson* (New York, London: W. W. Norton, 1994), 125.
249. Sondra Locke, *The Good, the Bad & the Very Ugly: A Hollywood Journey* (New York: William Morrow, 1997), 193.
250. Andy Dougan, *Untouchable: A Biography of Robert De Niro* (New York: Thunder's Mouth Press, 1996), 240–241.
251. David Shipman, *The Great Movie Stars: The Golden Years* (New York: Crown, 1970), 344.
252. Anthony Quinn with Daniel Paisner, *One Man Tango* (New York: HarperCollins, 1995), 133–134.
253. Rebecca Ascher-Walsh, "Miracle Worker" *Entertainment Weekly*, 13 February 2004, 45.
254. Paul Rosenfield, *The Club Rules: Power, Money, Sex, and Fear–How It Works in Hollywood* (New York: Warner Books, 1992), 241.
255. Marc Shapiro, *Susan Sarandon: Actress-Activist* (Amherst: Prometheus Books, 1983, 2001), 127–128.
256. James Robert Parish, *Whoopi Goldberg: Her Journey from Poverty to Megastardom* (Secaucus: Birch Lane Press, 1996), 153.
257. John Eastman, *Retakes: Behind the Scenes of 500 Classic Movies* (New York: Ballantine Books, 1989), 47–48.
258. Donald Bogle, *Dorothy Dandridge: A Biography* (New York: Amistad Press, 1997), 330, 332–334, 339.
259. John Eastman, *Retakes: Behind the Scenes of 500 Classic Movies* (New York: Ballantine Books, 1989), 47–48.
260. Ron Base, *"If the Other Guy Isn't Jack Nicholson, I've Got the Part"* (Chicago: Contemporary Books, 1994), 231.
261. Susan Sackett, *The Hollywood Reporter Book of Box Office Hits* (New York: Billboard Books, 1990), 64.
262. William Goldman, *Adventures in the Screen Trade* (New York: Warner Books, 1983), 13.
263. Elena Oumano, *Paul Newman* (New York: St. Martin's Press, 1994), 123.
264. William Goldman, Hype and Glory (New York: Villard Books, 1990), 54, 112–114.
265. Ron Base, *"If the Other Guy Isn't Jack Nicholson, I've Got the Part"* (Chicago: Contemporary Books, 1994), 169.
266. William Goldman, Hype and Glory (New York: Villard Books, 1990), 54, 112–114.
267. C. David Heymann, *Liz: An Intimate Biography of Elizabeth Taylor* (New York: Birch Lane Press, 1995), 209.

C

1. Randall Riese, *Her Name Is Barbra* (New York: St. Martin's Paperbacks, 1993), 385.
2. Jeff Burkhart and Bruce Stuart, *Hollywood's First Choices* (New York: Crown Trade Paperbacks, 1994), 198.
3. Martin Gottfried, *All His Jazz: The Life and Death of Bob Fosse* (New York: Bantam Books, 1990), 225.
4. Lauren Bacall, *By Myself* (New York: Ballantine Books, 1978), 448.
5. Kathleen Brady, *Lucille: The Life of Lucille Ball* (New York: Hyperion, 1994), 320.
6. David Shipman, *The Great Movie Stars: The International Years* (New York: St. Martin's Press, 1972), 190.
7. James Robert Parish and Ronald L. Bowers, *The MGM Stock Company: The Golden Era* (New Rochelle: Arlington House, 1973), 359.
8. Patrick McGilligan, *Robert Altman: Jumping Off the Cliff* (New York: St. Martin's Press, 1989), 377.
9. Robert Windeler, *Julie Andrews: A Life on Stage and Screen* (Secaucus: Birch Lane Press, 1997), 134.
10. David Shipman, *The Great Movie Stars: The Golden Years* (New York: Crown, 1970), 44–45.
11. Gene Brown, *Movie Time: A Chronology of Hollywood and the Movie Industry from Its Beginnings to the Present* (New York: Macmillan, 1995), 350.
12. Burt Reynolds, *My Life* (New York: Hyperion, 1994), 135.
13. Gene Brown, *Movie Time: A Chronology of Hollywood and the Movie Industry from Its Beginnings to the Present* (New York: Macmillan, 1995), 350.
14. Jason Bonderoff, *Tom Selleck: An Unauthorized Biography* (New York: Signet, 1983), 129.
15. *Sydney Morning Herald* (Sydney), 24 June 2002.
16. David Hochman, "Bohemian Rhapsody" *Premiere*, May 2003, 81.
17. Ron Base, *"If the Other Guy Isn't Jack Nicholson, I've Got the Part"* (Chicago: Contemporary Books, 1994), 71.
18. Gene Brown, *Movie Time: A Chronology of Hollywood and the Movie Industry from Its Beginnings to the Present* (New York: Macmillan, 1995), 142.
19. Jeffrey Meyers, *Inherited Risk: Errol and Sean Flynn in Hollywood and Vietnam* (New York: Simon & Schuster, 2002), 117.
20. Frank Miller, *Movies We Love* (Atlanta: Turner, 1996), 53, 55.
21. Gregory Speck, *Hollywood Royalty: Hepburn, Davis, Stewart & Friends at the Dinner Party of the Century* (New York: Birch Lane Press, 1992), 242.
22. Frank Miller, *Movies We Love* (Atlanta: Turner, 1996), 53, 55.
23. John Eastman, *Retakes: Behind the Scenes of 500 Classic Movies* (New York: Ballantine Books, 1989), 52.
24. Michael Fleming, "The Treasure from Toledo" *Movieline*, October 2002, 90.
25. Damien Bona, *Starring John Wayne as Genghis Khan* (Secaucus: Citadel Press, 1996), 203.
26. Yvonne De Carlo with Doug Warren, *Yvonne: An Autobiography* (New York: St. Martin's Press, 1987), 174.
27. Barry Paris, *Audrey Hepburn* (New York: G. P. Putnam's Sons, 1996), 168–169.
28. Christopher Andersen, *Citizen Jane: The Turbulent Life of Jane Fonda* (New York: Henry Holt, 1990), 188.
29. J. Randy Taraborrelli, *Sinatra: Behind the Legend* (Secaucus: Birch Lane Press, 1997), 187.
30. Jan Herman, *A Talent for Trouble: The Life of Hollywood's Most Acclaimed Director, William Wyler* (New York: G. P. Putnam's Sons, 1995), 321–323.
31. Laurent Bouzereau, *The DePalma Cut: The Films of America's Most Controversial Director* (New York: Dembner Books, 1988), 43.
32. Jeff Burkhart and Bruce Stuart, *Hollywood's First Choices* (New York: Crown Trade Paperbacks, 1994), 86–87, 90.
33. Aljean Harmetz, *Round Up the Usual Suspects: The Making of Casablanca* (New York: Hyperion, 1992), 72–73, 88–90, 95, 140–142.
34. Jeff Siegel, *The Casablanca Companion: The Movie and More* (Dallas: Taylor, 1992), 39, 42.
35. James C. Robertson, *The Casablanca Man: The Cinema of Michael Curtiz* (London, New York: Routledge, 1993), 77.

36. Aljean Harmetz, *Round Up the Usual Suspects: The Making of Casablanca* (New York: Hyperion, 1992), 72–73, 88–90, 95, 140–142.
37. John Eastman, *Retakes: Behind the Scenes of 500 Classic Movies* (New York: Ballantine Books, 1989), 53.
38. Jeff Burkhart and Bruce Stuart, *Hollywood's First Choices* (New York: Crown Trade Paperbacks, 1994), 86–87, 90.
39. Aljean Harmetz, *Round Up the Usual Suspects: The Making of Casablanca* (New York: Hyperion, 1992), 72–73, 88–90, 95, 140–142.
40. Jeff Siegel, *The Casablanca Companion: The Movie and More* (Dallas: Taylor, 1992), 39, 42.
41. James C. Robertson, *The Casablanca Man: The Cinema of Michael Curtiz* (London, New York: Routledge, 1993), 77.
42. James Spada, *More Than a Woman: An Intimate Biography of Bette Davis* (New York: Bantam Books, 1993), 108.
43. Stephen Rebello, "The Unsinkable Melanie Griffith" *Movieline*, April 1999, 56.
44. Michael Fleming, "Casting Glances" *Movieline*, June 1997, 94.
45. Eliza Bergman Krause, Kristen O'Neill, Maximillian Potter and Christine Spines, "The Ultimate Fall Preview" *Premiere*, October 1995, 113.
46. Esther Williams with Digby Diehl, *The Million Dollar Mermaid* (New York: Simon & Schuster, 1999), 153–154.
47. Gary Fishgall, *Against Type: The Biography of Burt Lancaster* (New York: Scribner, 1995), 310.
48. Jeff Burkhart and Bruce Stuart, *Hollywood's First Choices* (New York: Crown Trade Paperbacks, 1994), 189.
49. Peter Harry Brown and Patte B. Barham, *Marilyn: The Last Take* (New York: Signet, 1993), 99.
50. Charles Grodin, Jr., *It Would Be So Nice If You Weren't Here...* (New York: Vintage Books, 1989), 168–179.
51. Douglas Fairbanks, Jr., *A Hell of a War* (New York: St. Martin's Press, 1993), 35.
52. Ryan Murphy, "No Comment" *Us*, August 1995, 24.
53. Todd McCarthy, *Howard Hawks: The Grey Fox of Hollywood* (New York: Grove Press, 1997), 219.
54. *New York Daily News* (New York), 15 November 1998.
55. Michael Fleming, "Daisies and Butterflies" *Movieline*, April 1998, 54.
56. Stephen Rebello, "Kiss Us Kate" *Movieline*, March 1998, 118–119.
57. Degen Pener, "Playing the No-Name Game" *Entertainment Weekly*, 12 April 1996, 18.
58. Jeff Burkhart and Bruce Stuart, *Hollywood's First Choices* (New York: Crown Trade Paperbacks, 1994), 197.
59. Stephen M. Silverman, *Dancing on the Ceiling: Stanley Donen and His Movies* (New York: Alfred A. Knopf, 1996), 287–288.
60. Andrew Yule, *Sean Connery: From 007 to Hollywood Icon* (New York: Donald I. Fine, 1992), 275.
61. *New York Daily News* (New York), 30 September 1999.
62. David Hochman, "News & Notes" *Entertainment Weekly*, 26 March 1999, 11.
63. *New York Daily News* (New York), 30 September 1999.
64. *New York Daily News* (New York), 1 May 2000.
65. David Shipman, *The Great Movie Stars: The International Years* (New York: St. Martin's Press, 1972), 53–54.
66. David Shipman, *The Great Movie Stars: The International Years* (New York: St. Martin's Press, 1972), 438.
67. Stephen Rebello, "Through the Eyes of Faye Dunaway" *Movieline*, June 2002, 91.
68. Tag Gallagher, *John Ford: The Man and His Films* (Berkeley and Los Angeles: University of California Press, 1986), 429–430.
69. Steve Daly, "Chicago's Hope" *Entertainment Weekly*, 17 January 2003, 22, 24–25, 28.
70. Steve Daly, "Chicago's Hope" *Entertainment Weekly*, 17 January 2003, 22, 24–25, 28.
71. Stephen Rebello, "Getting Moore" *Movieline*, March 2003, 38.
72. Suzanne Finstad, *Natasha: The Biography of Natalie Wood* (New York: Harmony Books, 2001), 62.
73. Steve Daly, "Fowl Play" *Entertainment Weekly*, 23 June 2000, 62.
74. David Shipman, *Judy Garland: The Secret Life of an American Legend* (New York: Hyperion, 1992), 419.
75. Warren G. Harris, *Audrey Hepburn: A Biography* (New York: Simon & Schuster, 1994), 181–182.
76. David Shipman, *The Great Movie Stars: The International Years* (New York: St. Martin's Press, 1972), 425.
77. Michael Freedland, *Jane Fonda: A Biography* (New York: St. Martin's Press, 1988), 217.
78. Cybill Shepherd, *Cybill Disobedience* (New York: HarperCollins, 2000), 133.
79. Ron Base, *"If the Other Guy Isn't Jack Nicholson, I've Got the Part"* (Chicago: Contemporary Books, 1994), 151.
80. Rachel Abramowitz, *Is That a Gun in Your Pocket?: Women's Experience of Power in Hollywood* (New York: Random House, 2000), 80.
81. John Eastman, *Retakes: Behind the Scenes of 500 Classic Movies* (New York: Ballantine Books, 1989), 58.
82. Nigel Andrews, *Travolta: The Life* (New York: Bloomsbury, 1998), 155.
83. Gary Stevens and Alan George, *The Longest Line, Broadway's Most Singular Sensation: A Chorus Line* (New York, London: Applause Books, 1995), 35.
84. Tom Hutchinson, *Rod Steiger* (New York: Fromm International, 2000), 149.
85. Joe Rhodes, "Everybody Loves Ralphie" *TV Guide*, 22 December 2001, 28.
86. David Shipman, *The Great Movie Stars: The Golden Years* (New York: Crown, 1970), 278.
87. Charlton Heston, *In the Arena: An Autobiography* (New York: Simon & Schuster, 1995), 244.
88. John Irving, *My Movie Business: A Memoir* (New York: Ballantine Books, 1999), 55, 112.
89. Barbara Leaming, *Katharine Hepburn* (New York: Crown, 1995), 490.
90. Marshall Terrill, *Steve McQueen: Portrait of an American Rebel* (New York: Donald I. Fine, 1993), 113.
91. Daniel Bubbeo, *The Women of Warner Brothers: The Lives and Careers of 15 Leading Ladies* (Jefferson: McFarland, 2002), 196.
92. Marilu Henner with Jim Jerome, *By All Means Keep on Moving* (New York: Pocket Books, 1994), 214.
93. Richard Schickel, *Clint Eastwood* (New York: Alfred A. Knopf, 1996), 396.
94. Sondra Locke, *The Good, the Bad & the Very Ugly:*

A Hollywood Journey (New York: William Morrow, 1997), 189–190.
95. Marilu Henner with Jim Jerome, *By All Means Keep on Moving* (New York: Pocket Books, 1994), 214.
96. Sondra Locke, *The Good, the Bad & the Very Ugly: A Hollywood Journey* (New York: William Morrow, 1997), 189–190.
97. John Eastman, *Retakes: Behind the Scenes of 500 Classic Movies* (New York: Ballantine Books, 1989), 61.
98. David Shipman, *The Great Movie Stars: The Golden Years* (New York: Crown, 1970), 495.
99. James Spada, *Julia: Her Life* (New York: St. Martin's Press, 2004), 137–138.
100. David Shipman, *The Great Movie Stars: The International Years* (New York: St. Martin's Press, 1972), 45.
101. James Robert Parish and Ronald L. Bowers, *The MGM Stock Company: The Golden Era* (New Rochelle: Arlington House, 1973), 714.
102. John Baxter, *Woody Allen: A Biography* (New York: Carroll & Graf, 1998), 52–61.
103. James Earl Jones and Penelope Niven, *James Earl Jones: Voices and Silences* (New York: Scribner's, 1989, 1993), 314.
104. Steve Daly, "Encore" *Entertainment Weekly*, 14 June 1996, 76.
105. Matthew Bernstein, *Walter Wanger: Hollywood Independent* (Berkeley/Los Angeles/London: University of California Press, 1994), 353.
106. Barry Paris, *Audrey Hepburn* (New York: G. P. Putnam's Sons, 1996), 168–169.
107. Peter Harry Brown and Patte B. Barham, *Marilyn: The Last Take* (New York: Signet, 1993), 98.
108. Joan Collins, *Past Imperfect: An Autobiography* (New York: Berkley Books, 1985), 164–166.
109. Gene Brown, *Movie Time: A Chronology of Hollywood and the Movie Industry from Its Beginnings to the Present* (New York: Macmillan, 1995), 257.
110. Stephen Lowenstein, *My First Movie: Twenty Celebrated Directors Talk About Their First Film* (New York: Pantheon Books, 2000), 78–79.
111. David Shipman, *Judy Garland: The Secret Life of an American Legend* (New York: Hyperion, 1992), 164–165.
112. James Robert Parish and Ronald L. Bowers, *The MGM Stock Company: The Golden Era* (New Rochelle: Arlington House, 1973), 154.
113. Marshall Fine, *Harvey Keitel: The Art of Darkness* (New York: Fromm International, 1998), 235.
114. Frank Sanello, *Spielberg: The Man, the Movies, the Mythology* (Dallas: Taylor, 1996), 59, 67.
115. Marshall Terrill, *Steve McQueen: Portrait of an American Rebel* (New York: Donald I. Fine, 1993), 428.
116. Frank Sanello, *Spielberg: The Man, the Movies, the Mythology* (Dallas: Taylor, 1996), 59, 67.
117. Julia Phillips, *You'll Never Eat Lunch in This Town Again* (New York: Signet, 1992), 240–241.
118. Frank Sanello, *Spielberg: The Man, the Movies, the Mythology* (Dallas: Taylor, 1996), 59, 67.
119. John Baxter, *Steven Spielberg: The Unauthorized Biography* (London: HarperCollins, 1997), 157–158.
120. James Kotsilibas-Davis and Myrna Loy, *Myrna Loy: Being and Becoming* (New York: Alfred A. Knopf, 1987), 38–39.
121. Donald Spoto, *Rebel: The Life and Legend of James Dean* (New York: HarperCollins, 1996), 188–189.

122. Nancy Griffin, "Making Love & War" *Premiere*, December 2003/January 2004, 105.
123. James Robert Parish, *Whoopi Goldberg: Her Journey from Poverty to Megastardom* (Secaucus: Birch Lane Press, 1996), 119–120.
124. Frank Sanello, *Spielberg: The Man, the Movies, the Mythology* (Dallas: Taylor, 1996), 160.
125. James Robert Parish, *Whoopi Goldberg: Her Journey from Poverty to Megastardom* (Secaucus: Birch Lane Press, 1996), 119–120.
126. A. Scott Berg, *Goldwyn: A Biography* (New York: Alfred A. Knopf, 1989), 275–276.
127. Whitney Stine, *"I'd Love to Kiss You...": Conversations with Bette Davis* (New York: Pocket Books, 1990), 79.
128. Lawrence J. Quirk, *Totally Uninhibited: The Life and Wild Times of Cher* (New York: William Morrow, 1991), 157.
129. Warren G. Harris, *Sophia Loren: A Biography* (New York: Simon & Schuster, 1998), 279.
130. James Spada, *More Than a Woman: An Intimate Biography of Bette Davis* (New York: Bantam Books, 1993), 140.
131. Ty Burr, "Good at What Ails Them" *Entertainment Weekly*, Special Oscar Guide March 1997, 11.
132. Oliver Jones, "Furious George?" *Premiere*, September 2002, 24.
133. Damien Bona, *Starring John Wayne as Genghis Khan* (Secaucus: Citadel Press, 1996), 30.
134. Charles Higham, *Sisters: The Story of Olivia De Havilland & Joan Fontaine* (New York: Coward-McCann, 1984), 110, 112.
135. Bob Woodward, *Wired: The Short Life & Fast Times of John Belushi* (New York: Simon and Schuster, 1984), 160.
136. Michael Schumacher, *Francis Ford Coppola* (New York: Crown, 1999), 98.
137. Garry Jenkins, *Harrison Ford: Imperfect Hero* (Secaucus: Birch Lane Press, 1998), 317.
138. Warren G. Harris, *Audrey Hepburn: A Biography* (New York: Simon & Schuster, 1994), 247.
139. Marshall Terrill, *Steve McQueen: Portrait of an American Rebel* (New York: Donald I. Fine, 1993), 310–311, 427, 428.
140. Michael Grant Jaffe, "'Dry Spell" *Entertainment Weekly*, 12 March 1999, 16.
141. Robert Edelman and Audrey Kupferberg, *Angela Lansbury: A Life on Stage and Screen* (Thorndike: G.K. Hall, and Bath: Chivers Press, 1996), 93.
142. Michael Schumacher, *Francis Ford Coppola* (New York: Crown, 1999), 338.
143. Robert Evans, *Francis The Kid Stays in the Picture* (New York: Hyperion, 1994), 393–394.
144. Jan Herman, *A Talent for Trouble: The Life of Hollywood's Most Acclaimed Director, William Wyler* (New York: G. P. Putnam's Sons, 1995), 115.
145. John Eastman, *Retakes: Behind the Scenes of 500 Classic Movies* (New York: Ballantine Books, 1989), 69.
146. John Eastman, *Retakes: Behind the Scenes of 500 Classic Movies* (New York: Ballantine Books, 1989), 69.
147. David Shipman, *The Great Movie Stars: The International Years* (New York: St. Martin's Press, 1972), 267–268.
148. Arthur Marx, *The Nine Lives of Mickey Rooney* (Briarcliff Manor: Stein and Day, 1986), 113

149. Stephen M. Silverman, *Dancing on the Ceiling: Stanley Donen and His Movies* (New York: Alfred A. Knopf, 1996), 54.
150. Lauren Bacall, *By Myself* (New York: Ballantine Books, 1978), 91–93, 108.
151. Stig Bjorkman and Alfabeta Bokforlag, *Woody Allen on Woody Allen* (New York: Grove Press, 1993), 214.
152. Jeff Burkhart and Bruce Stuart, *Hollywood's First Choices* (New York: Crown Trade Paperbacks, 1994), 200.
153. Susan Bluestein Davis, *After Midnight: The Life and Death of Brad Davis* (New York: Pocket Books, 1997), 175–176.
154. Ari Posner, "The Princes of 'Tide'" *Premiere,* March 1995, 100.
155. Stephen Rebello, "Nowhere to Hide" *Movieline,* May 1995, 41–42.
156. Yvonne De Carlo with Doug Warren, *Yvonne: An Autobiography* (New York: St. Martin's Press, 1987), 140.
157. Frank Sanello, *Eddie Murphy: The Life and Times of a Comic on the Edge* (Secaucus: Birch Lane Press, 1997), 121.
158. Mark Harris, "The Brief Life and Unnecessary Death of Brandon Lee" *Entertainment Weekly,* 16 April 1993, 20.
159. Anne Thompson, "Next in Line" *Entertainment Weekly,* 26 May 1995, 8.
160. Jeff Gordinier, "Joan Allen" *Entertainment Weekly,* Special Oscar Guide March 1997, 62.
161. Stephen Rebello, "Kiss Us Kate" *Movieline,* March 1998, 118.
162. Stephen Rebello, "One Hundred Percent from the Heart" *Movieline,* November 1998, 81.
163. Michael Fleming, "Casting Glances" *Movieline,* June 1997, 11.
164. Thomas D. Clagett, *William Friedkin: Films of Aberration, Obsession and Reality* (Jefferson: McFarland, 1990), 191–192.
165. Patrick McGilligan, *Jack's Life: A Biography of Jack Nicholson* (New York, London: W. W. Norton, 1994), 102.
166. Barbara Leaming, *Polanski: A Biography, The Filmmaker as Voyeur* (New York: Simon and Schuster, 1981), 67.
167. David Shipman, *The Great Movie Stars: The Golden Years* (New York: Crown, 1970), 211.

D

1. David Shipman, *The Great Movie Stars: The International Years* (New York: St. Martin's Press, 1972), 112.
2. Christopher Petkanas, "Looking Good" *Us,* January 1994, 42.
3. Graham McCann, *Cary Grant: A Class Apart* (New York: Columbia University Press, 1996), 323.
4. David Shipman, *The Great Movie Stars: The Golden Years* (New York: Crown, 1970), 206.
5. Warren G. Harris, *Clark Gable: A Biography* (New York: Harmony Books, 2002), 108, 109–110.
6. David Shipman, *The Great Movie Stars: The International Years* (New York: St. Martin's Press, 1972), 534.
7. Raymond Strait, *James Garner: A Biography* (New York: St. Martin's Press, 1985), 62–63, 65–67.
8. Christine Spines, "Sympathy for the Daredevil" *Premiere,* February 2003, 52.
9. Steve Daly, "Dare-Devil" *Entertainment Weekly,* 7 February 2003, 23.
10. Michael Munn, *Burt Lancaster: The Terrible-Tempered Charmer* (London: Robson Books, 1995), 53.
11. Rudy Behlmer, *Memo from David O. Selznick* (New York: The Viking Press, 1972), 79.
12. Frank Miller, *Movies We Love* (Atlanta: Turner, 1996), 74.
13. John Eastman, *Retakes: Behind the Scenes of 500 Classic Movies* (New York: Ballantine Books, 1989), 76.
14. John Parker, *Warren Beatty: The Last Great Lover of Hollywood* (New York: Carroll & Graf, 1993), 150.
15. John Eastman, *Retakes: Behind the Scenes of 500 Classic Movies* (New York: Ballantine Books, 1989), 77.
16. David Shipman, *The Great Movie Stars: The Golden Years* (New York: Crown, 1970), 57.
17. David Shipman, *The Great Movie Stars: The International Years* (New York: St. Martin's Press, 1972), 40.
18. Gary Fishgall, *Gregory Peck: A Biography* (New York: Scribner, 2002), 160.
19. David Shipman, *The Great Movie Stars: The International Years* (New York: St. Martin's Press, 1972), 40.
20. Frank Miller, *Movies We Love* (Atlanta: Turner, 1996), 77, 79.
21. Cybill Shepherd, *Cybill Disobedience* (New York: HarperCollins, 2000), 143.
22. John Eastman, *Retakes: Behind the Scenes of 500 Classic Movies* (New York: Ballantine Books, 1989), 80.
23. George F. Custen, *Twentieth Century's Fox* (New York: BasicBooks, 1997), 330.
24. Garry Jenkins, *Harrison Ford: Imperfect Hero* (Secaucus: Birch Lane Press, 1998), 302.
25. Josh Young, "In the Line of Fire" *Entertainment Weekly,* 5 September 1997, 44.
26. Josh Young, "Days of Hell" *Entertainment Weekly,* 15 January 1999, 31.
27. Peter Biskind, *Easy Riders, Raging Bulls* (New York: Simon & Schuster, 1998), 296.
28. A. Scott Berg, *Goldwyn: A Biography* (New York: Alfred A. Knopf, 1989), 291–292.
29. David Gardner, *Tom Hanks: The Unauthorized Biography* (London: Blake, 1999), 118.
30. Jeff Burkhart and Bruce Stuart, *Hollywood's First Choices* (New York: Crown Trade Paperbacks, 1994), 201.
31. Stephen Jones, *Creepshows: The Illustrated Stephen King Movie Guide* (New York: Billboard Books, 2002), 31.
32. Teresa Carpenter, "Hope I Die Before I Get Old" *Premiere,* September 1992, 76.
33. Cybill Shepherd, *Cybill Disobedience* (New York: HarperCollins, 2000), 142–143.
34. Kate Buford, *Burt Lancaster: An American Life* (New York: Alfred A. Knopf, 2000), 274.
35. Gavin Lambert, *Norma Shearer* (New York: Alfred A. Knopf, 1990), 318.
36. Stephen M. Silverman, *Dancing on the Ceiling: Stanley Donen and His Movies* (New York: Alfred A. Knopf, 1996), 201.
37. Shawn Levy, *King of Comedy: The Life and Art of Jerry Lewis* (New York: St. Martin's Press, 1996), 209.
38. Charlton Heston, *In the Arena: An Autobiography* (New York: Simon & Schuster, 1995), 446–447.
39. Burt Reynolds, *My Life* (New York: Hyperion, 1994), 151.
40. Jeffrey Wells and Heidi Siegmund, "News & Notes" *Entertainment Weekly,* 23 April 1993, 10.

41. David Shipman, *The Great Movie Stars: The Golden Years* (New York: Crown, 1970), 185.
42. Gregory Speck, *Hollywood Royalty: Hepburn, Davis, Stewart & Friends At the Dinner Party of the Century* (New York: Birch Lane Press, 1992), 25, 28.
43. David Shipman, *The Great Movie Stars: The Golden Years* (New York: Crown, 1970), 399.
44. Mark Bego, *Madonna: Blonde Ambition* (New York: Harmony Books, 1992), 107–108.
45. J. Randy Taraborrelli, *Madonna: An Intimate Biography* (New York: Simon & Schuster, 2001), 86.
46. Christopher Andersen, *Madonna Unauthorized* (New York: Simon & Schuster, 1991), 123.
47. John Parker, *Bruce Willis: The Unauthorized Biography* (London: Virgin Books, 1997), 28.
48. Roy Pickard, *Jimmy Stewart: A Life in Film* (New York: St. Martin's Press, 1992), 36.
49. Robert Evans, *The Kid Stays in the Picture* (New York: Hyperion, 1994), 138–139.
50. Beverly Linet, *Ladd: The Life, The Legend, The Legacy of Alan Ladd* (New York: Arbor House, 1979), 143–144.
51. Charlton Heston, *In the Arena: An Autobiography* (New York: Simon & Schuster, 1995), 102, 492.
52. A. Scott Berg, *Goldwyn: A Biography* (New York: Alfred A. Knopf, 1989), 193–194.
53. John Eastman, *Retakes: Behind the Scenes of 500 Classic Movies* (New York: Ballantine Books, 1989), 330.
54. Minty Clinch, *Burt Lancaster* (Briarcliff Manor: Stein and Day, 1985), 83.
55. David Shipman, *The Great Movie Stars: The Golden Years* (New York: Crown, 1970), 353.
56. Degen Pener, "Dealing with the Devil" *Entertainment Weekly*, 11 April 1997, 34.
57. Charlton Heston, *In the Arena: An Autobiography* (New York: Simon & Schuster, 1995), 274.
58. Steven Jay Rubin, *The James Bond Films* (Westport: Arlington House, 1981), 100–101.
59. Steven Jay Rubin, *The Complete James Bond Movie Encyclopedia* (Chicago: Contemporary Books, 1990), 156, 357–358.
60. Jeff Burkhart and Bruce Stuart, *Hollywood's First Choices* (New York: Crown Trade Paperbacks, 1994), 207.
61. Garry Jenkins, *Harrison Ford: Imperfect Hero* (Secaucus: Birch Lane Press, 1998), 251.
62. John Parker, *Warren Beatty: The Last Great Lover of Hollywood* (New York: Carroll & Graf, 1993), 297.
63. Michael Munn, *The Sharon Stone Story* (London: Robson Books, 1997), 44.
64. John Parker, *Warren Beatty: The Last Great Lover of Hollywood* (New York: Carroll & Graf, 1993), 297.
65. Ellis Amburn, *The Sexiest Man Alive: A Biography of Warren Beatty* (New York: HarperCollins, 2002), 277.
66. John Parker, *Bruce Willis: The Unauthorized Biography* (London: Virgin Books, 1997), 76.
67. Warren G. Harris, *Clark Gable: A Biography* (New York: Harmony Books, 2002), 102.
68. Linda Gottlieb, "Singin' in the Rain" *Premiere*, September 1992, 89.
69. Frank Miller, *Movies We Love* (Atlanta: Turner, 1996), 86.
70. Gene Brown, *Movie Time: A Chronology of Hollywood and the Movie Industry from Its Beginnings to the Present* (New York: Macmillan, 1995), 286.
71. Jeff Burkhart and Bruce Stuart, *Hollywood's First Choices* (New York: Crown Trade Paperbacks, 1994), 189.
72. Marshall Terrill, *Steve McQueen: Portrait of an American Rebel* (New York: Donald I. Fine, 1993), 423.
73. Rob Edelman and Audrey Kupferberg, *Matthau: A Life* (Lanham: Taylor Trade, 2002), 235.
74. Richard Schickel, *Clint Eastwood* (New York: Alfred A. Knopf, 1996), 257.
75. George Eells, *Robert Mitchum: A Biography* (New York, Toronto: Franklin Watts, 1984), 261.
76. Kate Buford, *Burt Lancaster: An American Life* (New York: Alfred A. Knopf, 2000), 269.
77. Michael Caine, *What's It All About?: An Autobiography* (New York: Turtle Bay Books, 1992), 499.
78. Casey Davidson and Anne Thompson, "News & Notes" *Entertainment Weekly*, 1 April 1994, 10.
79. Ari Posner, "The Princes of Tide" *Premiere*, June 1995, 100.
80. Spike Lee with Lisa Jones, *Do the Right Thing: A Spike Lee Joint* (New York: Fireside, 1989), 58, 75, 77, 81, 82, 84, 92.
81. Tom McGee, *Betty Grable: The Girl with the Million Dollar Legs* (Vestal: The Vestal Press, 1995), 133.
82. Kevin Brownlow, *David Lean: A Biography* (New York: Wyatt Book for St. Martin's Press, 1996), 499, 508–513.
83. Jan Herman, *A Talent for Trouble: The Life of Hollywood's Most Acclaimed Director, William Wyler* (New York: G. P. Putnam's Sons, 1995), 152–153.
84. John Kenneth Muir, *An Askew View: The Films of Kevin Smith* (New York: Applause Theatre & Cinema Books, 2002), 114.
85. John Eastman, *Retakes: Behind the Scenes of 500 Classic Movies* (New York: Ballantine Books, 1989), 94.
86. John Eastman, *Retakes: Behind the Scenes of 500 Classic Movies* (New York: Ballantine Books, 1989), 94.
87. John Eastman, *Retakes: Behind the Scenes of 500 Classic Movies* (New York: Ballantine Books, 1989), 94.
88. Gregory Speck, *Hollywood Royalty: Hepburn, Davis, Stewart & Friends At the Dinner Party of the Century* (New York: Birch Lane Press, 1992), 183–184.
89. David Shipman, *The Great Movie Stars: The Golden Years* (New York: Crown, 1970), 43.
90. Nigel Andrews, *Travolta: The Life* (New York: Bloomsbury, 1998), 267.
91. Maurice Zolotow, *Billy Wilder in Hollywood* (New York: G.P. Putnam's Sons, 1977), 117.
92. Ed Sikov, *On Sunset Boulevard: The Life and Times of Billy Wilder* (New York: Hyperion, 1998), 202.
93. Yvonne De Carlo with Doug Warren, *Yvonne: An Autobiography* (New York: St. Martin's Press, 1987), 81.
94. James L. Dickerson, *Ashley Judd: Crying on the Inside* (New York: Schirmer Trade Books, 2002), 145.
95. Anita M. Busch, "Reel World" *Entertainment Weekly*, 29 May 1998, 50.
96. Patrick McGilligan, *George Cukor: A Double Life* (New York: St. Martin's Press, 1991), 194.
97. Yvonne De Carlo with Doug Warren, *Yvonne: An Autobiography* (New York: St. Martin's Press, 1987), 122–123.
98. Shelley Winters, *Shelley: Also Known as Shirley* (New York: Ballantine Books, 1980), 167.
99. Paul Mazursky, *Show Me the Magic* (New York: Simon & Schuster, 1999), 176–180.

100. Jane Lenz Elder, *Alice Faye* (Jackson: University Press of Mississippi, 2002), 134, 139.
101. *New York Daily News* (New York), 15 April 1999.
102. John Eastman, *Retakes: Behind the Scenes of 500 Classic Movies* (New York: Ballantine Books, 1989), 91.
103. Andrew Yule, *Sean Connery: From 007 to Hollywood Icon* (New York: Donald I. Fine, 1992), 54.
104. Steven Jay Rubin, *The Complete James Bond Movie Encyclopedia* (Chicago: Contemporary Books, 1990), 91.
105. Jill Bernstein, Vianney Brandicourt, Jay A. Fernandez, Gregg Goldstein, Susannah Gora, Timothy Gunatilaka, Brooke Hauser, Kristin Hohenadel, Oliver Jones, Kerrie Mitchell, Laura Morice, Tom Roston, Josh Rottenberg, Tom Russo, Mark Salisbury, Amanda Volper, "Fall Movie Preview" *Premiere*, September, 2003, 58.
106. John Eastman, *Retakes: Behind the Scenes of 500 Classic Movies* (New York: Ballantine Books, 1989), 92.
107. Ed Sikov, *Mr. Strangelove: A Biography of Peter Sellers* (New York: Hyperion, 2002), 192–193.
108. John Eastman, *Retakes: Behind the Scenes of 500 Classic Movies* (New York: Ballantine Books, 1989), 95.
109. Lee Pfeiffer and Michael Lewis, *The Films of Tom Hanks* (Secaucus: Citadel Press, 1996), 74.
110. Mark Harris, "The Brief Life and Unnecessary Death of Brandon Lee" *Entertainment Weekly*, 16 April 1993, 20.
111. Robert Draper, "The Tao of Dennis" *Premiere*, February 1995, 72.
112. Laurent Bouzereau, *The DePalma Cut: The Films of America's Most Controversial Director* (New York: Dembner Books, 1988), 59.
113. Patrick McGilligan, *Jack's Life: A Biography of Jack Nicholson* (New York, London: W. W. Norton, 1994), 177, 214.
114. Marshall Terrill, *Steve McQueen: Portrait of an American Rebel* (New York: Donald I. Fine, 1993), 428.
115. Shirley MacLaine, *My Lucky Stars: A Hollywood Memoir* (New York: Bantam Books, 1995), 366.
116. James Robert Parish, *Gus Van Sant: An Unauthorized Biography* (New York: Thunder's Mouth Press, 2001), 88–91.
117. Ian Woodward, *Glenda Jackson: A Study in Fire and Ice* (New York: St. Martin's Press, 1985), 89.
118. David Thomson, *Showman: The Life of David O. Selznick* (New York: Alfred A. Knopf, 1992), 448–449.
119. *New York Daily News* (New York), 12 June 1997.
120. Mitchell Fink, "The Insider" *Entertainment Weekly*, 16 January 1995, 39.
121. Michel Chion, *David Lynch* (London: British Film Institute, 1995), 74.

E

1. John Baxter, *Steven Spielberg: The Unauthorized Biography* (London: HarperCollins, 1996), 235.
2. David Shipman, *The Great Movie Stars: The International Years* (New York: St. Martin's Press, 1972), 410.
3. Elia Kazan, *Elia Kazan: A Life* (New York: Alfred A. Knopf, 1988), 534.
4. William Goldman, *Adventures in the Screen Trade* (New York: Warner Books, 1983), 14.
5. Lawrence J. Quirk, *Paul Newman* (Dallas: Taylor, 1996), 44.
6. Axel Madsen, *Stanwyck* (New York: HarperCollins, 1994), 262.
7. Gregory Speck, *Hollywood Royalty: Hepburn, Davis, Stewart & Friends At the Dinner Party of the Century* (New York: Birch Lane Press, 1992), 59.
8. Arthur Laurents, *Original Story By: A Memoir of Broadway and Hollywood* (New York: Alfred A. Knopf, 2000), 95–96.
9. Frank Miller, *Movies We Love* (Atlanta: Turner, 1996), 96.
10. Patrick McGilligan, *Jack's Life: A Biography of Jack Nicholson* (New York, London: W. W. Norton, 1994), 20, 22.
11. Peter Fonda, *Don't Tell Dad: A Memoir* (New York: Hyperion, 1998), 248.
12. Dan Snierson, "Filling in LeBlanc" *Entertainment Weekly*, 3 May 2002, 42.
13. Elaine Gallagher, *Candidly Caine* (London: Robson Books, 1990), 197.
14. Mark Salisbury, *Burton on Burton* (London: Faber and Faber, 2000), 91.
15. Nellie Bly, *Marlon Brando: Larger Than Life* (New York: Pinnacle Books, 1994), 59.
16. Gene Brown, *Movie Time: A Chronology of Hollywood and the Movie Industry from Its Beginnings to the Present* (New York: Macmillan, 1995), 222.
17. Peter Harry Brown and Patte B. Barham, *Marilyn: The Last Take* (New York: Signet, 1993), 97.
18. Patrick McGilligan, *Clint: The Life and Legend* (New York: St. Martin's Press, 1999), 241.
19. Gavin Smith, *Sayles on Sayles* (London: Faber and Faber, 1998), 143.
20. Karen Valby, "The Actress: Diane Keaton" *Entertainment Weekly*, 14 November 2003, 44.
21. Elaine Dundy, *Finch, Bloody Finch: A Life of Peter Finch* (New York: Holt, Rinehart and Winston, 1980), 178.
22. Anne Edwards, *Vivien Leigh* (New York: Pocket Books, 1977), 233–237.
23. David Shipman, *The Great Movie Stars: The International Years* (New York: St. Martin's Press, 1972), 502.
24. Robyn Karney, "Making History" *Movieline*, December/January 1999, 18.
25. Tom Sinclair, "Elizabeth" *Entertainment Weekly*, 1 March 1999, 127.
26. Jeff Burkhart and Bruce Stuart, *Hollywood's First Choices* (New York: Crown Trade Paperbacks, 1994), 200–201.
27. Paul Mazursky, *Show Me the Magic* (New York: Simon & Schuster, 1999), 233–235.
28. Marshall Terrill, *Steve McQueen: Portrait of an American Rebel* (New York: Donald I. Fine, 1993), 293, 295.
29. Jessica Shaw, "Will Power" *Entertainment Weekly*, 20 June, 1997, 9.
30. *New York Daily News* (New York), 28 February 2000.
31. Jeff Gordinier, "What Pryce Glory" *Entertainment Weekly*, 17 November 1995, 36.
32. James Kotsilibas and Myrna Loy, *Myrna Loy: Being and Becoming* (New York: Alfred A. Knopf, 1987), 98–100.
33. Joe Russo and Larry Landsman with Edward Gross, *Planet of the Apes Revisited: The Behind-The-Scenes Story of the Classic Science Fiction Saga* (New York: Thomas Dunne Books, 2001), 152.

34. James Robert Parish, *Gus Van Sant: An Unauthorized Biography* (New York: Thunder's Mouth Press, 2001), 173, 177.
35. Rebecca Ascher-Walsh, Kristen Baldwin, Anita M. Busch, Steve Daly, Andrew Essex, Daniel Fierman, Jeff Gordinier, David Hochman, Dave Karger, Tricia Laine, Chris Nashawaty, Joe Neumaier, Degen Pener, Megan Quitkin, Jessica Shaw, Tom Sinclair, Benjamin Svetkey, "The Following Summer Movie Preview Has Been Approved for All Audiences by the Editors of Entertainment Weekly" *Entertainment Weekly*, 15 May 1998, 64, 67.
36. Ron Base, *"If the Other Guy Isn't Jack Nicholson, I've Got the Part"* (Chicago: Contemporary Books, 1994), 243.
37. Michael Logan, "Breaking the Soap Barrier" *TV Guide*, 18 October 1997, 49.
38. Randall Riese, *Her Name Is Barbra* (New York: St. Martin's Paperbacks, 1993), 471.
39. Christopher Andersen, *Madonna Unauthorized* (New York: Simon & Schuster, 1991), 318.
40. J. Randy Taraborrelli, *Madonna: An Intimate Biography* (New York: Simon & Schuster, 2001), 244.
41. Eric Hamburg, *JFK, Nixon, Oliver Stone & Me: An Idealist's Journey from Capitol Hill to Hollywood Hell* (New York: Public Affairs, 2002), 88.
42. James Riordan, *Stone: The Controversies, Excesses, and Exploits of a Radical Filmmaker* (New York: Hyperion, 1995), 309–310.
43. Christopher Andersen, *Madonna Unauthorized* (New York: Simon & Schuster, 1991), 318.
44. Stephen Rebello, "The New Divas" *Movieline*, October 1997, 70.
45. Ryan Murphy, "No Comment" *Us*, August 1994, 28.
46. Frank Miller, *Movies We Love* (Atlanta: Turner, 1996), 98.
47. Thomas D. Clagett, *William Friedkin: Films of Aberration, Obsession and Reality* (Jefferson: McFarland, 1990), 110–111, 113.
48. Nat Segaloff, *Hurricane Billy: The Stormy Life and Films of William Friedkin* (New York: William Morrow, 1990), 134.
49. Peter Biskind, *Easy Riders, Raging Bulls* (New York: Simon & Schuster, 1998), 199.
50. Jeff Burkhart and Bruce Stuart, *Hollywood's First Choices* (New York: Crown Trade Paperbacks, 1994), 108–109.
51. Thomas D. Clagett, *William Friedkin: Films of Aberration, Obsession and Reality* (Jefferson: McFarland, 1990), 110–111, 113.
52. Thomas D. Clagett, *William Friedkin: Films of Aberration, Obsession and Reality* (Jefferson: McFarland, 1990), 110–111, 113.
53. Eric Braun, *Deborah Kerr* (New York: St. Martin's Press, 1977), 198.
54. Randall Riese, *Her Name Is Barbra* (New York: St. Martin's Paperbacks, 1993), 434–435.
55. Benjamin Svetkey, "Eyes of the Storm" *Entertainment Weekly*, 23 July 1999, 34.
56. Josh Young, "Mystery Movie" *Entertainment Weekly*, 2 October 1998, 19.
57. Michael Fleming, "Fearless Leigh" *Movieline*, April 1999, 62.

F

1. Ellis Amburn, *The Sexiest Man Alive: A Biography of Warren Beatty* (New York: HarperCollins, 2002), 279.
2. John Parker, *Warren Beatty: The Last Great Lover of Hollywood* (New York: Carroll & Graf, 1993), 117.
3. John Russell Taylor, *Hitch: The Life and Times of Alfred Hitchcock* (New York: Pantheon Books, 1978), 291.
4. Cybill Shepherd, *Cybill Disobedience* (New York: HarperCollins, 2000), 143.
5. Donald Spoto, *The Dark Side of Genius: The Life of Alfred Hitchcock* (Boston, Toronto: Little, Brown, 1983), 531.
6. Donald Spoto, *The Dark Side of Genius: The Life of Alfred Hitchcock* (Boston, Toronto: Little, Brown, 1983), 531.
7. Mitchell Fink, "The Insider" *People*, 24 July 1995, 35.
8. Cindy Pearlman, "News & Notes" *Entertainment Weekly*, 1 December 1995, 13.
9. Christopher Andersen, *Citizen Jane: The Turbulent Life of Jane Fonda* (New York: Henry Holt, 1990), 85–86.
10. David Shipman, *The Great Movie Stars: The International Years* (New York: St. Martin's Press, 1972), 78.
11. John Eastman, *Retakes: Behind the Scenes of 500 Classic Movies* (New York: Ballantine Books, 1989), 104.
12. Tom Hutchinson, *Rod Steiger* (New York: Fromm International, 2000), 97.
13. Dave Karger, "Best Supporting Actor: William H. Macy" *Entertainment Weekly*, Special Oscar Guide March 1997, 76.
14. John Springer, *The Fondas: The Films and Careers of Henry, Jane and Peter Fonda* (New York: The Citadel Press, 1970), 52.
15. Donald Spoto, *Notorious: The Life of Ingrid Bergman* (New York: HarperCollins, 1997), 194.
16. Joan Wester Anderson, *Forever Young: The Life, Loves and Enduring Faith of a Hollywood Legend* (Edinburgh: Mainstream, 1998), 149.
17. Stuart Kaminsky, *John Huston: Maker of Magic* (Boston: Houghton Mifflin, 1978), 188.
18. Chris Nashawaty, "American Graffiti" *Entertainment Weekly*, 1 March 1999, 97.
19. Jeff Burkhart and Bruce Stuart, *Hollywood's First Choices* (New York: Crown Trade Paperbacks, 1994), 215.
20. Michael Munn, *The Sharon Stone Story* (London: Robson Books, 1997), 37.
21. James Robert Parish, *Whoopi Goldberg: Her Journey from Poverty to Megastardom* (Secaucus: Birch Lane Press, 1996), 164–165.
22. Frank Miller, *Movies We Love* (Atlanta: Turner, 1996), 99.
23. Stephen M. Silverman, *Dancing on the Ceiling: Stanley Donen and His Movies* (New York: Alfred A. Knopf, 1996), 172.
24. Nigel Goodall, *Demi Moore: The Most Powerful Woman in Hollywood* (Edinburgh: Mainstream, 2000), 93–94.
25. Betsy Israel, "Kevin Bacon" *Us*, December 1992, 68.
26. Jared Brown, *Zero Mostel: A Biography* (New York: Atheneum, 1989), 289.
27. David Gardner, *Tom Hanks: The Unauthorized Biography* (London: Blake, 1999), 118.
28. Charlton Heston, *The Actor's Life: Journals 1956–1976* (New York: E. P. Dutton, 1976, 1978), 144.

29. Charlton Heston, *In the Arena: An Autobiography* (New York: Simon & Schuster, 1995), 280–281.
30. James Kotsilibas-Davis and Myrna Loy, *Myrna Loy: Being and Becoming* (New York: Alfred A. Knopf, 1987), 76.
31. Benjamin Svetkey, "Blood, Sweat, & Fears" *Entertainment Weekly*, 15 October 1999, 27.
32. Peter Cowie, *Coppola: A Biography* (New York: Scribner's, 1989, 1990), 43.
33. Michael Munn, *Burt Lancaster: The Terrible-Tempered Charmer* (London: Robson Books, 1995), 233.
34. Gregg Kilday, "A Film So Nice They Rewrote It Twice" *Entertainment Weekly*, 23 July 1993, 36–37.
35. Shelley Levitt, Karen G. Jackovich and Joyce Wagner, *People*, 8 February 1993, 68.
36. Michael Fleming, "Casting Glances" *Movieline*, June 1997, 66.
37. Frank Spotnitz, "News & Notes" *Entertainment Weekly*, 30 July 1993, 10.
38. Ron Base, *"If the Other Guy Isn't Jack Nicholson, I've Got the Part"* (Chicago: Contemporary Books, 1994), 208–214, 218.
39. Bob Thomas, *Golden Boy: The Untold Story of William Holden* (New York: St. Martin's Press, 1983), 229–230.
40. Stephen Rebello, "The Next McCarthy Era" *Movieline*, August 1998, 56.
41. Ian Christie, *Gilliam on Gilliam* (London: Faber and Faber, 1999), 198.
42. Stephen Schaefer, "Mick's Flick Flop" *Us*, 29 September 1981, 15.
43. David Shipman, *The Great Movie Stars: The International Years* (New York: St. Martin's Press, 1972), 397–398.
44. Garry Marshall with Lori Marshall, *Wake Me When It's Funny* (Holbrook: Adams, 1995), 206.
45. David Shipman, *The Great Movie Stars: The International Years* (New York: St. Martin's Press, 1972), 204.
46. Michael Fleming, "Casting Glances" *Movieline*, June 1997, 63.
47. 2Dale Sherman, *Black Diamond: The Unauthorized Biography of Kiss* (London: CG, 1997), 169.
48. Michael Fleming, "Radiance & Shadow" *Movieline*, February 1999, 69.
49. James Robert Parish, *Rosie: Rosie O'Donnell's Biography* (New York: Carroll & Graf, 1997), 146, 148–149.
50. *New York Daily News* (New York), 30 August 1998.
51. Michael Musto, "A Woman of Substance" *Entertainment Weekly*, 28 May 1993, 15.
52. James Robert Parish, *Rosie: Rosie O'Donnell's Biography* (New York: Carroll & Graf, 1997), 146, 148–149.
53. Ginger Rogers, *Ginger: My Story* (New York: HarperCollins, 1991), 125.
54. John Eastman, *Retakes: Behind the Scenes of 500 Classic Movies* (New York: Ballantine Books, 1989), 107.
55. Stephen Rebello, "The Wow" *Movieline*, February 1998, 53.
56. Rachel Abramowitz, *Is That a Gun in Your Pocket?: Women's Experience of Power in Hollywood* (New York: Random House, 2000), 202–203.
57. J. Randy Taraborrelli, *Madonna: An Intimate Biography* (New York: Simon & Schuster, 2001), 49.
58. David Shipman, *Judy Garland: The Secret Life of an American Legend* (New York: Hyperion, 1992), 128–129.
59. Alvin Yudkoff, *Gene Kelly: A Life of Dance and Dreams* (New York: Back Stage Books, 1999), 103–105.
60. Ingrid Bergman and Alan Burgess, *Ingrid Bergman: My Story* (New York: Dell, 1980), 139.
61. Donald Spoto, *Notorious: The Life of Ingrid Bergman* (New York: HarperCollins, 1997), 103, 129–130.
62. Donald Spoto, *Notorious: The Life of Ingrid Bergman* (New York: HarperCollins, 1997), 103, 129–130.
63. John Russell Taylor, *Hitch: The Life and Times of Alfred Hitchcock* (New York: Pantheon Books, 1978), 166.
64. John Eastman, *Retakes: Behind the Scenes of 500 Classic Movies* (New York: Ballantine Books, 1989), 108.
65. Leonard J. Leff, *Hitchcock & Selznick: The Rich and Strange Collaboration of Alfred Hitchcock and David O. Selznick in Hollywood* (New York: Weidenfeld & Nicolson, 1987), 94.
66. Susan Sackett, *The Hollywood Reporter Book of Box Office Hits* (New York: Billboard Books, 1990), 71.
67. David Shipman, *The Great Movie Stars: The International Years* (New York: St. Martin's Press, 1972), 111.
68. David Shipman, *The Great Movie Stars: The International Years* (New York: St. Martin's Press, 1972), 111.
69. Susan Sackett, *The Hollywood Reporter Book of Box Office Hits* (New York: Billboard Books, 1990), 71.
70. David Shipman, *The Great Movie Stars: The International Years* (New York: St. Martin's Press, 1972), 111.
71. Susan Sackett, *The Hollywood Reporter Book of Box Office Hits* (New York: Billboard Books, 1990), 71.
72. Robert Edelman and Audrey Kupferberg, *Angela Lansbury: A Life on Stage and Screen* (Thorndike: G.K. Hall, and Bath: Chivers Press, 1996), 97.
73. Michael Logan, "Here, Try This!" *Soap Opera Digest*, 5 September 1989, 119.
74. Elena Oumano, *Paul Newman* (New York: St. Martin's Press, 1994), 171.
75. Lawrence J. Quirk, *Paul Newman* (Dallas: Taylor, 1996), 267.
76. Lawrence J. Quirk, *Totally Uninhibited: The Life and Wild Times of Cher* (New York: William Morrow, 1991), 227.
77. Ellis Amburn, *The Sexiest Man Alive: A Biography of Warren Beatty* (New York: HarperCollins, 2002), 199–200.
78. Warren G. Harris, *Audrey Hepburn: A Biography* (New York: Simon & Schuster, 1994), 243.
79. John Horn, "Signed, Sealed, and Delivered" *Premiere*, January, 2001, 48.
80. Axel Madsen, *Stanwyck* (New York: HarperCollins, 1994), 317.
81. Peter Bart and Peter Guber, *Shoot Out: Surviving Fame and (Mis)Fortune in Hollywood* (New York: G. P. Putnam's Sons, 2002), 120–121.
82. David Shipman, *The Great Movie Stars: The Golden Years* (New York: Crown, 1970), 67.
83. Frank Miller, *Movies We Love* (Atlanta: Turner, 1996), 113–114.
84. David Shipman, *The Great Movie Stars: The Golden Years* (New York: Crown, 1970), 211.
85. Frank Miller, *Movies We Love* (Atlanta: Turner, 1996), 113–114.
86. Jeff Burkhart and Bruce Stuart, *Hollywood's First Choices* (New York: Crown Trade Paperbacks, 1994), 215.
87. Axel Madsen, *Stanwyck* (New York: HarperCollins, 1994), 226, 228–230.
88. Jami Bernard, *Quentin Tarantino: The Man and His Movies* (New York: HarperPerennial, 1995), 223–224.
89. Marc Shapiro, *Sarah Jessica Parker* (Toronto: ECW Press, 2001), 96.

90. Buddy Foster and Leon Wagener, *Foster Child: A Biography of Jodie Foster* (New York: Dutton, 1997), 118–119.
91. David Hochman, "Next of Kim" *Entertainment Weekly*, 3 October 1997, 43.
92. Arthur Marx, *The Nine Lives of Mickey Rooney* (Briarcliff Manor: Stein and Day, 1986), 165.
93. Jeff Burkhart and Bruce Stuart, *Hollywood's First Choices* (New York: Crown Trade Paperbacks, 1994), 96–97.
94. Garry Marshall with Lori Marshall, *Wake Me When It's Funny* (Holbrook: Adams, 1995), 206.
95. David Stenn, *Bombshell: The Life and Death of Jean Harlow* (New York: Doubleday, 1993), 67–68.
96. Warren G. Harris, *Clark Gable: A Biography* (New York: Harmony Books, 2002), 72.
97. Michael Sauter, "Gene Hackman" *Entertainment Weekly*, Special Oscar Guide March 1997, 84.
98. Steve Lopez, "Sweet and Sourpuss" *Entertainment Weekly*, 12 January 2001, 49.
99. Nat Segaloff, *Hurricane Billy: The Stormy Life and Films of William Friedkin* (New York: William Morrow, 1990), 112.
100. Kent Jones, *Memorable Movie Roles: And the Actors Who Played Them* (Avenel: Crescent Books, 1992), 79.
101. Marshall Terrill, *Steve McQueen: Portrait of an American Rebel* (New York: Donald I. Fine, 1993), 423.
102. Jeff Burkhart and Bruce Stuart, *Hollywood's First Choices* (New York: Crown Trade Paperbacks, 1994), 192.
103. Michael Sauter, "Gene Hackman" *Entertainment Weekly*, Special Oscar Guide March 1997, 84.
104. John Eastman, *Retakes: Behind the Scenes of 500 Classic Movies* (New York: Ballantine Books, 1989), 113.
105. B.J. Sigesmund, "Who Were Those Masked Men?" *Entertainment Weekly*, 20 August, 1993, 17.
106. Jeff Burkhart and Bruce Stuart, *Hollywood's First Choices* (New York: Crown Trade Paperbacks, 1994), 194.
107. Jan Herman, *A Talent for Trouble: The Life of Hollywood's Most Acclaimed Director, William Wyler* (New York: G. P. Putnam's Sons, 1995), 372–373.
108. Jan Herman, *A Talent for Trouble: The Life of Hollywood's Most Acclaimed Director, William Wyler* (New York: G. P. Putnam's Sons, 1995), 372–373.
109. Mark Salisbury, "Hell Raisers" *Premiere*, November 2001, 41.
110. Susan Sackett, *The Hollywood Reporter Book of Box Office Hits* (New York: Billboard Books, 1994), 107.
111. Jeff Burkhart and Bruce Stuart, *Hollywood's First Choices* (New York: Crown Trade Paperbacks, 1994), 118–119.
112. Jeff Burkhart and Bruce Stuart, *Hollywood's First Choices* (New York: Crown Trade Paperbacks, 1994), 118–119.
113. Robert LaGuardia, *Monty: A Biography of Montgomery Clift* (New York: Arbor House, 1977), 109.
114. Jay Fultz, *In Search of Donna Reed* (Iowa City: University of Iowa Press, 1998), 88–89.
115. Shelley Winters, *Shelley II: The Middle of My Century* (New York: Simon and Schuster, 1989), 72.
116. Rob Edelman and Audrey Kupferberg, *Matthau: A Life* (Lanham: Taylor Trade, 2002), 82.
117. Steven Jay Rubin, *The Complete James Bond Movie Encyclopedia* (Chicago: Contemporary Books, 1990), 11, 62, 238.
118. John Eastman, *Retakes: Behind the Scenes of 500 Classic Movies* (New York: Ballantine Books, 1989), 116.
119. Yvonne De Carlo with Doug Warren, *Yvonne: An Autobiography* (New York: St. Martin's Press, 1987), 102.
120. Ron Base, *"If the Other Guy Isn't Jack Nicholson, I've Got the Part"* (Chicago: Contemporary Books, 1994), 265–166.
121. *The New York Times* (New York), 3 November 1996.
122. Barry Paris, *Audrey Hepburn* (New York: G. P. Putnam's Sons, 1996), 124–125.
123. Warren G. Harris, *Audrey Hepburn: A Biography* (New York: Simon & Schuster, 1994), 136.
124. Barry Paris, *Audrey Hepburn* (New York: G. P. Putnam's Sons, 1996), 124–125.
125. Randall Riese, *Her Name Is Barbra* (New York: St. Martin's Paperbacks, 1993), 259, 288.
126. Randall Riese, *Her Name Is Barbra* (New York: St. Martin's Paperbacks, 1993), 259, 288.
127. James Spada, *Streisand: Her Life* (New York: Ivy Books, 1995), 208–209.
128. James Spada, *Streisand: The Woman and the Legend* (Garden City: Dolphin Books, 1981), 98.
129. James Spada, *Streisand: Her Life* (New York: Ivy Books, 1995), 208–209.
130. Randall Riese, *Her Name Is Barbra* (New York: St. Martin's Paperbacks, 1993), 259, 288.
131. James Spada, *Streisand: Her Life* (New York: Ivy Books, 1995), 357–358.
132. Randall Riese, *Her Name Is Barbra* (New York: St. Martin's Paperbacks, 1993), 391.
133. Randall Riese, *Her Name Is Barbra* (New York: St. Martin's Paperbacks, 1993), 391.
134. Randall Riese, *Her Name Is Barbra* (New York: St. Martin's Paperbacks, 1993), 391.
135. James Spada, *Streisand: Her Life* (New York: Ivy Books, 1995), 357–358.
136. Jane Russell, *Jane Russell: An Autobiography* (New York: Franklin Watts, 1985), 174–175.

G

1. Marshall Terrill, *Steve McQueen: Portrait of an American Rebel* (New York: Donald I. Fine, 1993), 421, 427.
2. Damien Bona, *Starring John Wayne as Genghis Khan* (Secaucus: Citadel Press, 1996), 8–9.
3. Damien Bona, *Starring John Wayne as Genghis Khan* (Secaucus: Citadel Press, 1996), 8–9.
4. Andy Dougan, *Untouchable: A Biography of Robert De Niro* (New York: Thunder's Mouth Press, 1996), 91.
5. Michael Feeney Callan, *Anthony Hopkins: The Unauthorized Biography* (New York: Scribner's, 1993), 223–225.
6. Jeff Burkhart and Bruce Stuart, *Hollywood's First Choices* (New York: Crown Trade Paperbacks, 1994), 221.
7. Robert Evans, *Francis The Kid Stays in the Picture* (New York: Hyperion, 1994), 222–224.
8. *New York Daily News* (New York), 7 June 2000.
9. David Thomson, *Showman: The Life of David O. Selznick* (New York: Alfred A. Knopf, 1992), 206.
10. Donald Spoto, *Blue Angel: The Life of Marlene Dietrich* (New York: Doubleday, 1992), 130.
11. Steven Bach, *Marlene Dietrich: Life and Legend* (New York: William Morrow, 1992), 212.
12. Steven Bach, *Marlene Dietrich: Life and Legend* (New York: William Morrow, 1992), 212.

13. James Spada, *More Than a Woman: An Intimate Biography of Bette Davis* (New York: Bantam Books, 1993), 140.
14. Stephen Lowenstein, *My First Movie: Twenty Celebrated Directors Talk About Their First Film* (New York: Pantheon Books, 2000), 63–64.
15. Donald Spoto, *Notorious: The Life of Ingrid Bergman* (New York: HarperCollins, 1997), 146.
16. Frank Miller, *Movies We Love* (Atlanta: Turner, 1996), 119.
17. Jeff Lantos, "Brave New World" *Movieline*, March 1997, 104.
18. Marshall Terrill, *Steve McQueen: Portrait of an American Rebel* (New York: Donald I. Fine, 1993), 428.
19. Axel Madsen, *Stanwyck* (New York: HarperCollins, 1994), 208.
20. *New York Daily News* (New York), 19 May 2000.
21. John Eastman, *Retakes: Behind the Scenes of 500 Classic Movies* (New York: Ballantine Books, 1989), 281–282.
22. Tom McGee, *Betty Grable: The Girl with the Million Dollar Legs* (Vestal: The Vestal Press, 1995), 193, 196, 197.
23. Robert Evans, *Francis The Kid Stays in the Picture* (New York: Hyperion, 1994), 76.
24. David Shipman, *The Great Movie Stars: The Golden Years* (New York: Crown, 1970), 189.
25. Anne Thompson, "News & Notes" *Entertainment Weekly*, 12 March 1993, 12.
26. Cybill Shepherd, *Cybill Disobedience* (New York: HarperCollins, 2000), 132–133.
27. Marshall Terrill, *Steve McQueen: Portrait of an American Rebel* (New York: Donald I. Fine, 1993), 224–227.
28. Marshall Fine, *Bloody Sam: The Life and Films of Sam Peckinpah* (New York: Donald I. Fine, 1991), 227.
29. Michael Viner and Terrie Maxine Frankel, *Tales from Casting Couch: An Unprecedented Candid Collection of Stories, Essays, and Anecdotes by and About Legendary Hollywood Stars, Starlets, and Wanna-bees...* (Beverly Hills: Dove Books, 1995), 48, 171–172.
30. John Parker, *Bruce Willis: The Unauthorized Biography* (London: Virgin Books, 1997), 129.
31. Michael Fleming, "Casting Glances" *Movieline*, June 1997, 94.
32. Michael Viner and Terrie Maxine Frankel, *Tales from Casting Couch: An Unprecedented Candid Collection of Stories, Essays, and Anecdotes by and About Legendary Hollywood Stars, Starlets, and Wanna-bees...* (Beverly Hills: Dove Books, 1995), 48, 171–172.
33. Suzanne Finstad, *Natasha: The Biography of Natalie Wood* (New York: Harmony Books, 2001), 48.
34. George F. Custen, *Twentieth Century's Fox* (New York: BasicBooks, 1997), 332.
35. Rudy Behlmer, *Memo from Darryl F. Zanuck: The Golden Years at Twentieth Century–Fox* (New York: Grove Press, 1993), 111.
36. William Goldman, *Which Lie Did I Tell?* (New York: Pantheon Books, 2000), 73–77, 89–90.
37. Joshua Rich, "High Spirits" *Entertainment Weekly*, 9 June 2000, 49.
38. Frank Sanello, *Eddie Murphy: The Life and Times of a Comic on the Edge* (Secaucus: Birch Lane Press, 1997), 98.
39. Beverly Linet, *Ladd: The Life, The Legend, The Legacy of Alan Ladd* (New York: Arbor House, 1979), 187–188.
40. Jerry Oppenheimer and Jack Vitek, *Idol: Rock Hudson, The True Story of an American Film Hero* (New York: Villard Books, 1986), 53.
41. Bob Thomas, *Golden Boy: The Untold Story of William Holden* (New York: St. Martin's Press, 1983), 39.
42. Jane Ellen Wayne, *The Golden Girls of MGM* (New York: Carroll & Graf, 2002), 334–335.
43. David Shipman, *The Great Movie Stars: The International Years* (New York: St. Martin's Press, 1972), 122.
44. Warren G. Harris, *Audrey Hepburn: A Biography* (New York: Simon & Schuster, 1994), 144–145.
45. Frank Miller, *Movies We Love* (Atlanta: Turner, 1996), 124.
46. Edward Baron Turk, *Hollywood Diva: A Biography of Jeanette MacDonald* (Berkeley and Los Angeles: University of California Press, 1998), 150.
47. John Eastman, *Retakes: Behind the Scenes of 500 Classic Movies* (New York: Ballantine Books, 1989), 124.
48. Alan Jay Lerner, *On the Street Where I Live* (New York: Da Capo Press, 1994), 152, 157.
49. Kathleen Brady, *Lucille: The Life of Lucille Ball* (New York: Hyperion, 1994), 111.
50. Joan Collins, *Past Imperfect: An Autobiography* (New York: Berkley Books, 1985), 64.
51. Holly Millea, "Love Is a Battlefield" *Entertainment Weekly*, 29 March 2002, 36.
52. Tom McGee, *Betty Grable: The Girl with the Million Dollar Legs* (Vestal: The Vestal Press, 1995), 185, 187–188.
53. Edward Baron Turk, *Hollywood Diva: A Biography of Jeanette MacDonald* (Berkeley and Los Angeles: University of California Press, 1998), 221.
54. Andy Dougan, *Untouchable: A Biography of Robert De Niro* (New York: Thunder's Mouth Press, 1996), 204.
55. A.M. Sperber and Eric Lax, *Bogart* (New York: William Morrow, 1997), 268–269.
56. Robert Evans, *Francis The Kid Stays in the Picture* (New York: Hyperion, 1994), 219, 221.
57. Harlan Lebo, *The Godfather Legacy* (New York: Fireside, 1997), 46.
58. Peter Biskind, *The Godfather Companion* (New York: Harper Perennial, 1990), 10–16.
59. Peter Biskind, *The Godfather Companion* (New York: Harper Perennial, 1990), 10–16.
60. Susan Sackett, *The Hollywood Reporter Book of Box Office Hits* (New York: Billboard Books, 1990), 222.
61. Peter Biskind, *The Godfather Companion* (New York: Harper Perennial, 1990), 10–16.
62. Peter Biskind, *The Godfather Companion* (New York: Harper Perennial, 1990), 10–16.
63. Peter Biskind, *The Godfather Companion* (New York: Harper Perennial, 1990), 10–16.
64. Peter Biskind, *Easy Riders, Raging Bulls* (New York: Simon & Schuster, 1998), 153.
65. Peter Biskind, *The Godfather Companion* (New York: Harper Perennial, 1990), 10–16.
66. Peter Biskind, *The Godfather Companion* (New York: Harper Perennial, 1990), 10–16.
67. Jeff Burkhart and Bruce Stuart, *Hollywood's First Choices* (New York: Crown Trade Paperbacks, 1994), 148.
68. Jeff Burkhart and Bruce Stuart, *Hollywood's First Choices* (New York: Crown Trade Paperbacks, 1994), 148.

69. Peter Biskind, *The Godfather Companion* (New York: Harper Perennial, 1990), 10–16.
70. Peter Biskind, *The Godfather Companion* (New York: Harper Perennial, 1990), 10–16.
71. Peter Biskind, *The Godfather Companion* (New York: Harper Perennial, 1990), 10–16.
72. Jeff Burkhart and Bruce Stuart, *Hollywood's First Choices* (New York: Crown Trade Paperbacks, 1994), 148.
73. Peter Biskind, *The Godfather Companion* (New York: Harper Perennial, 1990), 10–16.
74. John Eastman, *Retakes: Behind the Scenes of 500 Classic Movies* (New York: Ballantine Books, 1989), 127.
75. Peter Biskind, *The Godfather Companion* (New York: Harper Perennial, 1990), 10–16.
76. Peter Biskind, *The Godfather Companion* (New York: Harper Perennial, 1990), 10–16.
77. Peter Biskind, *The Godfather Companion* (New York: Harper Perennial, 1990), 10–16.
78. Peter Biskind, *The Godfather Companion* (New York: Harper Perennial, 1990), 10–16.
79. Peter Biskind, *The Godfather Companion* (New York: Harper Perennial, 1990), 83–86.
80. Peter Biskind, *The Godfather Companion* (New York: Harper Perennial, 1990), 142–146, 151.
81. Dave Thompson, *Travolta* (Dallas: Taylor, 1996), 125.
82. Peter Biskind, *The Godfather Companion* (New York: Harper Perennial, 1990), 142–146, 151.
83. Peter Biskind, *The Godfather Companion* (New York: Harper Perennial, 1990), 142–146, 151.
84. Jeff Burkhart and Bruce Stuart, *Hollywood's First Choices* (New York: Crown Trade Paperbacks, 1994), 153.
85. Chris Nashawaty, "Stomp the World" *Entertainment Weekly*, 22 May 1998, 27.
86. "Casting About" *Movieline*, 9 June 2000, 30.
87. Donald Shepherd, *Jack Nicholson: An Unauthorized Biography* (New York: St. Martin's Press, 1991), 123.
88. Susan Sackett, *The Hollywood Reporter Book of Box Office Hits* (New York: Billboard Books, 1990), 48–49.
89. Wes D. Gehring, *Carole Lombard* (Indianapolis: Indiana Historical Society Press, 2003), 39–40.
90. John Oller, *Jean Arthur: The Actress Nobody Knew* (New York: Limelight Editions, 1997), 113.
91. Bob Thomas, *Golden Boy: The Untold Story of William Holden* (New York: St. Martin's Press, 1983), 25.
92. Axel Madsen, *Stanwyck* (New York: HarperCollins, 1994), 165.
93. Edward Baron Turk, *Hollywood Diva: A Biography of Jeanette MacDonald* (Berkeley and Los Angeles: University of California Press, 1998), 240.
94. Bob Thomas, *Golden Boy: The Untold Story of William Holden* (New York: St. Martin's Press, 1983), 25.
95. Beverly Linet, *Ladd: The Life, The Legend, The Legacy of Alan Ladd* (New York: Arbor House, 1979), 42.
96. Ryan Murphy, "No Comment" *Us*, August 1994, 28.
97. Benjamin Svetkey, "The Spy Who Came Back from the Cold" *Entertainment Weekly*, 20 November 1995, 20.
98. Steven Jay Rubin, *The Complete James Bond Movie Encyclopedia* (Chicago: Contemporary Books, 1990), 238.
99. Gerald Gardner and Harriet Modell Gardner, *Pictorial History of Gone with the Wind* (Avenel: Wings Books, 1996), 12–23, 39–42, 129–132.
100. Jeff Burkhart and Bruce Stuart, *Hollywood's First Choices* (New York: Crown Trade Paperbacks, 1994), 129–134, 136–138.
101. Ron Base, *"If the Other Guy Isn't Jack Nicholson, I've Got the Part"* (Chicago: Contemporary Books, 1994), 86–87.
102. Jeff Burkhart and Bruce Stuart, *Hollywood's First Choices* (New York: Crown Trade Paperbacks, 1994), 129–134, 136–138.
103. Gerald Gardner and Harriet Modell Gardner, *Pictorial History of Gone with the Wind* (Avenel: Wings Books, 1996), 12–23, 39–42, 129–132.
104. Barbara Leaming, *Katharine Hepburn* (New York: Crown, 1995), 353, 359–360, 368.
105. Jeff Burkhart and Bruce Stuart, *Hollywood's First Choices* (New York: Crown Trade Paperbacks, 1994), 129–134, 136–138.
106. Ronald Haver, *David O. Selznick's Hollywood* (New York: Alfred A. Knopf, 1980), 260–262.
107. Gerald Gardner and Harriet Modell Gardner, *Pictorial History of Gone with the Wind* (Avenel: Wings Books, 1996), 12–23, 39–42, 129–132.
108. Joe Morella and Edward Z. Epstein, *Forever Lucy: The Life of Lucille Ball* (Secaucus: Lyle Stuart, 1986), 49–51.
109. Kathleen Brady, *Lucille: The Life of Lucille Ball* (New York: Hyperion, 1994), 81.
110. Joe Morella and Edward Z. Epstein, *Forever Lucy: The Life of Lucille Ball* (Secaucus: Lyle Stuart, 1986), 49–51.
111. Gerald Gardner and Harriet Modell Gardner, *Pictorial History of Gone with the Wind* (Avenel: Wings Books, 1996), 12–23, 39–42, 129–132.
112. Ronald Haver, *David O. Selznick's Hollywood* (New York: Alfred A. Knopf, 1980), 260–262.
113. Gerald Gardner and Harriet Modell Gardner, *Pictorial History of Gone with the Wind* (Avenel: Wings Books, 1996), 12–23, 39–42, 129–132.
114. Ronald Haver, *David O. Selznick's Hollywood* (New York: Alfred A. Knopf, 1980), 260–262.
115. Jeff Burkhart and Bruce Stuart, *Hollywood's First Choices* (New York: Crown Trade Paperbacks, 1994), 129–134, 136–138.
116. Gerald Gardner and Harriet Modell Gardner, *Pictorial History of Gone with the Wind* (Avenel: Wings Books, 1996), 12–23, 39–42, 129–132.
117. Beverly Linet, *Susan Hayward: Portrait of a Survivor* (New York: Atheneum, 1980), 34–37, 39–40.
118. Gerald Gardner and Harriet Modell Gardner, *Pictorial History of Gone with the Wind* (Avenel: Wings Books, 1996), 12–23, 39–42, 129–132.
119. Ronald Haver, *David O. Selznick's Hollywood* (New York: Alfred A. Knopf, 1980), 260–262.
120. Jeff Burkhart and Bruce Stuart, *Hollywood's First Choices* (New York: Crown Trade Paperbacks, 1994), 129–134, 136–138.
121. Gerald Gardner and Harriet Modell Gardner, *Pictorial History of Gone with the Wind* (Avenel: Wings Books, 1996), 12–23, 39–42, 129–132.
122. Shelley Winters, *Shelley: Also Known as Shirley* (New York: Ballantine Books, 1980), 22–23.
123. Ronald Haver, *David O. Selznick's Hollywood* (New York: Alfred A. Knopf, 1980), 260–262.
124. Jeff Burkhart and Bruce Stuart, *Hollywood's First Choices* (New York: Crown Trade Paperbacks, 1994), 129–134, 136–138.

125. Gerald Gardner and Harriet Modell Gardner, *Pictorial History of Gone with the Wind* (Avenel: Wings Books, 1996), 12–23, 39–42, 129–132.
126. David Thomson, *Showman: The Life of David O. Selznick* (New York: Alfred A. Knopf, 1992), 249, 287.
127. Jeff Burkhart and Bruce Stuart, *Hollywood's First Choices* (New York: Crown Trade Paperbacks, 1994), 129–134, 136–138.
128. Gerald Gardner and Harriet Modell Gardner, *Pictorial History of Gone with the Wind* (Avenel: Wings Books, 1996), 12–23, 39–42, 129–132.
129. Jeff Burkhart and Bruce Stuart, *Hollywood's First Choices* (New York: Crown Trade Paperbacks, 1994), 129–134, 136–138.
130. Gerald Gardner and Harriet Modell Gardner, *Pictorial History of Gone with the Wind* (Avenel: Wings Books, 1996), 12–23, 39–42, 129–132.
131. Jeff Burkhart and Bruce Stuart, *Hollywood's First Choices* (New York: Crown Trade Paperbacks, 1994), 129–134, 136–138.
132. Rudy Behlmer, *Memo from David O. Selznick* (New York: The Viking Press, 1972), 141, 158, 177, 179, 187, 189.
133. Gerald Gardner and Harriet Modell Gardner, *Pictorial History of Gone with the Wind* (Avenel: Wings Books, 1996), 12–23, 39–42, 129–132.
134. Jeff Burkhart and Bruce Stuart, *Hollywood's First Choices* (New York: Crown Trade Paperbacks, 1994), 129–134, 136–138.
135. Rudy Behlmer, *Memo from David O. Selznick* (New York: The Viking Press, 1972), 141, 158, 177, 179, 187, 189.
136. Jeff Burkhart and Bruce Stuart, *Hollywood's First Choices* (New York: Crown Trade Paperbacks, 1994), 129–134, 136–138.
137. David Thomson, *Showman: The Life of David O. Selznick* (New York: Alfred A. Knopf, 1992), 249, 287.
138. Gregory Speck, *Hollywood Royalty: Hepburn, Davis, Stewart & Friends at the Dinner Party of the Century* (New York: Birch Lane Press, 1992), 124–125.
139. Gerald Gardner and Harriet Modell Gardner, *Pictorial History of Gone with the Wind* (Avenel: Wings Books, 1996), 12–23, 39–42, 129–132.
140. Rudy Behlmer, *Memo from David O. Selznick* (New York: The Viking Press, 1972), 141, 158, 177, 179, 187, 189.
141. Herb Bridges and Terryl C. Boodman, *Gone with the Wind: The Definitive Illustrated History of the Book, the Movie, and the Legend* (New York: Simon and Schuster/Fireside, 1989), 40.
142. Rudy Behlmer, *Memo from David O. Selznick* (New York: The Viking Press, 1972), 141, 158, 177, 179, 187, 189.
143. Rudy Behlmer, *Memo from David O. Selznick* (New York: The Viking Press, 1972), 141, 158, 177, 179, 187, 189.
144. Rudy Behlmer, *Memo from David O. Selznick* (New York: The Viking Press, 1972), 141, 158, 177, 179, 187, 189.
145. Jeff Burkhart and Bruce Stuart, *Hollywood's First Choices* (New York: Crown Trade Paperbacks, 1994), 129–134, 136–138.
146. Jeff Burkhart and Bruce Stuart, *Hollywood's First Choices* (New York: Crown Trade Paperbacks, 1994), 129–134, 136–138.
147. Rudy Behlmer, *Memo from David O. Selznick* (New York: The Viking Press, 1972), 141, 158, 177, 179, 187, 189.
148. Gerald Gardner and Harriet Modell Gardner, *Pictorial History of Gone with the Wind* (Avenel: Wings Books, 1996), 12–23, 39–42, 129–132.
149. Gerald Gardner and Harriet Modell Gardner, *Pictorial History of Gone with the Wind* (Avenel: Wings Books, 1996), 12–23, 39–42, 129–132.
150. Rudy Behlmer, *Memo from David O. Selznick* (New York: The Viking Press, 1972), 141, 158, 177, 179, 187, 189.
151. Gerald Gardner and Harriet Modell Gardner, *Pictorial History of Gone with the Wind* (Avenel: Wings Books, 1996), 12–23, 39–42, 129–132.
152. Paul Rosenfield, *The Club Rules: Power, Money, Sex, and Fear-How It Works in Hollywood* (New York: Warner Books, 1992), 239.
153. Ryan Murphy, "No Comment" *Us*, January 1996, 28.
154. James Robert Parish, *Gus Van Sant: An Unauthorized Biography* (New York: Thunder's Mouth Press, 2001), 232.
155. Robert Evans, *Francis The Kid Stays in the Picture* (New York: Hyperion, 1994), 150–151.
156. Warren G. Harris, *Natalie & R.J.: Hollywood's Star-Crossed Lovers* (New York: A Dolphin Book, 1988), 146.
157. Ron Base, *"If the Other Guy Isn't Jack Nicholson, I've Got the Part"* (Chicago: Contemporary Books, 1994), 189–190.
158. Marsha Mason, *Journey: A Personal Odyssey* (New York: Simon & Schuster, 2000), 284–285, 290, 293.
159. Andy Dougan, *Untouchable: A Biography of Robert De Niro* (New York: Thunder's Mouth Press, 1996), 82–84.
160. Marsha Mason, *Journey: A Personal Odyssey* (New York: Simon & Schuster, 2000), 284–285, 290, 293.
161. John Eastman, *Retakes: Behind the Scenes of 500 Classic Movies* (New York: Ballantine Books, 1989), 132.
162. Warren G. Harris, *Audrey Hepburn: A Biography* (New York: Simon & Schuster, 1994), 218.
163. Stephen Rebello, "Born to be Bad" *Movieline*, May 1992, 77.
164. Marshall Terrill, *Steve McQueen: Portrait of an American Rebel* (New York: Donald I. Fine, 1993), 426.
165. Jeff Burkhart and Bruce Stuart, *Hollywood's First Choices* (New York: Crown Trade Paperbacks, 1994), 182–183, 185.
166. Tom Russo, "What If...?" *Premiere*, February 2004, 88.
167. Peter Thompson, *Jack Nicholson: The Life and Times of an Actor on the Edge* (Secaucus: Birch Lane Press, 1997), 41.
168. Garry Jenkins, *Harrison Ford: Imperfect Hero* (Secaucus: Birch Lane Press, 1998), 81.
169. Charles Grodin, Jr., *It Would Be So Nice If You Weren't Here...* (New York: Vintage Books, 1989), 147–151.
170. Ron Base, *"If the Other Guy Isn't Jack Nicholson, I've Got the Part"* (Chicago: Contemporary Books, 1994), 156.
171. Jeff Burkhart and Bruce Stuart, *Hollywood's First Choices* (New York: Crown Trade Paperbacks, 1994), 182–183, 185.
172. Ava Gardner, *Ava: My Story* (Thorndike: Thorndike Press, 1990), 482.

173. Patricia Neal, *As I Am* (New York: Simon and Schuster, 1988), 290–291.
174. Jeff Burkhart and Bruce Stuart, *Hollywood's First Choices* (New York: Crown Trade Paperbacks, 1994), 182–183, 185.
175. Jason Bonderoff, *Sally Field: A Biography* (New York: St. Martin's Press, 1987), 20.
176. Ron Base, *"If the Other Guy Isn't Jack Nicholson, I've Got the Part"* (Chicago: Contemporary Books, 1994), 156.
177. Allan Hunter, *Gene Hackman* (New York: St. Martin's Press, 1987), 121–122.
178. John Eastman, *Retakes: Behind the Scenes of 500 Classic Movies* (New York: Ballantine Books, 1989), 133–134.
179. David Shipman, *The Great Movie Stars: The Golden Years* (New York: Crown, 1970), 309.
180. Lawrence J. Quirk, *Totally Uninhibited: The Life and Wild Times of Cher* (New York: William Morrow, 1991), 228.
181. Tag Gallagher, *John Ford: The Man and His Films* (Berkeley and Los Angeles: University of California Press, 1986), 180.
182. John Eastman, *Retakes: Behind the Scenes of 500 Classic Movies* (New York: Ballantine Books, 1989), 135.
183. George F. Custen, *Twentieth Century's Fox* (New York: BasicBooks, 1997), 232–233.
184. Wensley Clarkson, *John Travolta: Back in Character* (Woodstock: The Overlook Press, 1996), 119–120.
185. Didi Conn, *Frenchy's Grease Scrapbook: "We'll Always Be Together!"* (New York: Hyperion, 1998), 22–26, 30, 36–37.
186. Didi Conn, *Frenchy's Grease Scrapbook: "We'll Always Be Together!"* (New York: Hyperion, 1998), 22–26, 30, 36–37.
187. Rebecca Ascher-Walsh, "Grease Lightning Strikes Twice" *Entertainment Weekly*, 20 March 1998, 47, 49.
188. Nigel Andrews, *Travolta: The Life* (New York: Bloomsbury, 1998), 86.
189. Didi Conn, *Frenchy's Grease Scrapbook: "We'll Always Be Together!"* (New York: Hyperion, 1998), 22–26, 30, 36–37.
190. *New York Daily News* (New York), 26 March 1998.
191. Didi Conn, *Frenchy's Grease Scrapbook: "We'll Always Be Together!"* (New York: Hyperion, 1998), 22–26, 30, 36–37.
192. Rebecca Ascher-Walsh, "Grease Lightning Strikes Twice" *Entertainment Weekly*, 20 March 1998, 47, 49.
193. Didi Conn, *Frenchy's Grease Scrapbook: "We'll Always Be Together!"* (New York: Hyperion, 1998), 22–26, 30, 36–37.
194. David Shipman, *The Great Movie Stars: The Golden Years* (New York: Crown, 1970), 282.
195. Robert Evans, *The Kid Stays in the Picture* (New York: Hyperion, 1994), 241, 250–253.
196. Peter Thompson, *Jack Nicholson: The Life and Times of an Actor on the Edge* (Secaucus: Birch Lane Press, 1997), 116.
197. Edward Z. Epstein and Joe Morella, *Mia: The Life of Mia Farrow* (New York: Dell, 1991), 207–208.
198. Robert Evans, *The Kid Stays in the Picture* (New York: Hyperion, 1994), 241, 250–253.
199. Edward Z. Epstein and Joe Morella, *Mia: The Life of Mia Farrow* (New York: Dell, 1991), 207–208.
200. Cybill Shepherd, *Cybill Disobedience* (New York: HarperCollins, 2000), 142.
201. Robert Evans, *The Kid Stays in the Picture* (New York: Hyperion, 1994), 241, 250–253.
202. Peter Thompson, *Jack Nicholson: The Life and Times of an Actor on the Edge* (Secaucus: Birch Lane Press, 1997), 116.
203. Jeff Burkhart and Bruce Stuart, *Hollywood's First Choices* (New York: Crown Trade Paperbacks, 1994), 198.
204. Hedy Lamarr, *Ecstasy and Me: My Life as a Woman* (U.S.A.: Bartholomew House, 1966), 179.
205. Minty Clinch, *Burt Lancaster* (New York: Stein and Day, 1984), 40.
206. Joe Morella and Edward Z. Epstein, *Forever Lucy: The Life of Lucille Ball* (Secaucus: Lyle Stuart, 1986), 87–91.
207. Roy Pickard, *Jimmy Stewart: A Life in Film* (New York: St. Martin's Press, 1992), 102.
208. Damien Bona, *Starring John Wayne as Genghis Khan* (Secaucus: Citadel Press, 1996), 85.
209. A. Scott Berg, *Goldwyn: A Biography* (New York: Alfred A. Knopf, 1989), 215–216.
210. Warren G. Harris, *Audrey Hepburn: A Biography* (New York: Simon & Schuster, 1994), 161.
211. David Hochman, "'Green' Acher" *Entertainment Weekly*, 23 July 1999, 16.
212. Tom Roston, "The Hero Returns" *Movieline*, January 2003, 88.
213. Ned Zeman, "Jeanne Makes the Scene" *Entertainment Weekly*, 23 July 1993, 34.
214. Stephen Rebello, "Through the Eyes of Faye Dunaway" *Movieline*, June 2002, 91.
215. Beverly Gray, *Ron Howard: From Mayberry To the Moon ... and Beyond* (Nashville: Rutledge Hill Press, 2003), 124.
216. Todd McCarthy, *Howard Hawks: The Grey Fox of Hollywood* (New York: Grove Press, 1997), 246.
217. Frank Miller, *Movies We Love* (Atlanta: Turner, 1996), 145.
218. Douglas Fairbanks, Jr., *A Hell of a War* (New York: St. Martin's Press, 1993), 46.
219. Edward Z. Epstein and Joe Morella, *Mia: The Life of Mia Farrow* (New York: Dell, 1991), 65.
220. Gary Carey, *Marlon Brando: The Only Contender* (New York: St. Martin's Press, 1985), 112–113.
221. Alvin Yudkoff, *Gene Kelly: A Life of Dance and Dreams* (New York: Back Stage Books, 1999), 233.
222. A. Scott Berg, *Goldwyn: A Biography* (New York: Alfred A. Knopf, 1989), 471–472.
223. Tom McGee, *Betty Grable: The Girl with the Million Dollar Legs* (Vestal: The Vestal Press, 1995), 243.
224. A. Scott Berg, *Goldwyn: A Biography* (New York: Alfred A. Knopf, 1989), 471–472.
2225. Tom McGee, *Betty Grable: The Girl with the Million Dollar Legs* (Vestal: The Vestal Press, 1995), 243.
226. John Eastman, *Retakes: Behind the Scenes of 500 Classic Movies* (New York: Ballantine Books, 1989), 142.
227. A. Scott Berg, *Goldwyn: A Biography* (New York: Alfred A. Knopf, 1989), 471–472.

H

1. Anne Edwards, *Vivien Leigh* (New York: Pocket Books, 1977), 187.
2. Daniel Fierman, "The Dane Event" *Entertainment Weekly*, 2 June 2000, 42.

3. James Riordan, *Stone: The Controversies, Excesses, and Exploits of a Radical Filmmaker* (New York: Hyperion, 1995), 121.
4. John Baxter, *Woody Allen: A Biography* (New York: Carroll & Graf, 1998), 332–333.
5. Jill Bernstein, "Eat Drink Man Woman" *Premiere*, February 2001, 61, 106.
6. Sean M. Smith, "Jodie's Choice" *Premiere*, March 2002, 47–48.
7. Jill Bernstein, "Eat Drink Man Woman" *Premiere*, February 2001, 61, 106.
8. Daniel Fierman, "Killer Instinct" *Entertainment Weekly*, 17 March 2000, 26–27.
9. Jill Bernstein, "Eat Drink Man Woman" *Premiere*, February 2001, 61, 106.
10. Ron Base, *"If the Other Guy Isn't Jack Nicholson, I've Got the Part"* (Chicago: Contemporary Books, 1994), 231.
11. Carol Easton, *The Search for Sam Goldwyn: A Biography* (New York: William Morrow, 1976), 461, 273.
12. Richard Fleischer, *Just Tell Me When To Cry: A Memoir* (New York: Carroll & Graf, 1993), 30–31.
13. John Parker, *Warren Beatty: The Last Great Lover of Hollywood* (New York: Carroll & Graf, 1993), 226–227.
14. Karen S. Schneider and Lois Armstrong, "Born to be Bad" *People*, 26 October 1992, 43.
15. Gene Brown, *Movie Time: A Chronology of Hollywood and the Movie Industry from Its Beginnings to the Present* (New York: Macmillan, 1995), 282.
16. Ruth Gordon, *My Side: The Autobiography of Ruth Gordon* (New York: Donald I. Fine, 1976), 389–399.
17. John Eastman, *Retakes: Behind the Scenes of 500 Classic Movies* (New York: Ballantine Books, 1989), 146.
18. Joe Morella and Edward Z. Epstein, *Paul and Joanne: A Biography of Paul Newman and Joanne Woodward* (New York: Delacorte Press, 1988), 277.
19. Elena Oumano, *Paul Newman* (New York: St. Martin's Press, 1994), 225–226.
20. Steve Wulf, "But Seriously, Folks!" *Entertainment Weekly*, 6 February 2004, 40.
21. Michael Seth Starr, *Art Carney: A Biography* (New York: Fromm International, 1997), 172–174.
22. Paul Mazursky, *Show Me the Magic* (New York: Simon & Schuster, 1999), 69–71.
23. Michael Seth Starr, *Art Carney: A Biography* (New York: Fromm International, 1997), 172–174.
24. Jeff Jensen, "Secrets Revealed" *Entertainment Weekly*, 7 June 2002, 25.
25. *New York Daily News* (New York), 20 June 2000.
26. Daniel Fierman, "Indecision 2000" *Entertainment Weekly*, 1 December 2000, 13.
27. Stephen Schaefer, "Flashes" *Entertainment Weekly*, 1 March 2002, 12.
28. David Shipman, *Judy Garland: The Secret Life of an American Legend* (New York: Hyperion, 1992), 174.
29. Martin Gottfried, *Balancing Act: The Authorized Biography of Angela Lansbury* (Boston, New York, London: Little, Brown, 1999), 71.
30. Todd McCarthy, *Howard Hawks: The Grey Fox of Hollywood* (New York: Grove Press, 1997), 576–577.
31. David Shipman, *The Great Movie Stars: The International Years* (New York: St. Martin's Press, 1972), 272.
32. Barry Paris, *Audrey Hepburn* (New York: G. P. Putnam's Sons, 1996), 154.
33. Chris Nashawaty, "Hoops to Conquer" *Entertainment Weekly*, 22 May 1998, 46.
34. Rebecca Ascher-Walsh, "Reel World" *Entertainment Weekly*, 23 July 1999, 42.
35. Sondra Locke, *The Good, the Bad & the Very Ugly: A Hollywood Journey* (New York: William Morrow, 1997), 67, 70, 74–75, 79, 81.
36. *New York Daily News* (New York), 20 January 1999.
37. Patrick McGilligan, *Jack's Life: A Biography of Jack Nicholson* (New York, London: W. W. Norton, 1994), 347.
38. Mark Harris, "Depth Becomes Her" *Entertainment Weekly*, 24 March 2000, 54.
39. John Parker, *Warren Beatty: The Last Great Lover of Hollywood* (New York: Carroll & Graf, 1993), 233.
40. Ellis Amburn, *The Sexiest Man Alive: A Biography of Warren Beatty* (New York: HarperCollins, 2002), 225.
41. Barbara Siegel and Scott Siegel, *Susan Lucci: The Woman Behind Erica Kane* (New York: St. Martin's Press, 1986), 45.
42. Graham McCann, *Cary Grant: A Class Apart* (New York: Columbia University Press, 1996), 199.
43. Jeff Burkhart and Bruce Stuart, *Hollywood's First Choices* (New York: Crown Trade Paperbacks, 1994), 215.
44. Jay Fultz, *In Search of Donna Reed* (Iowa City: University of Iowa Press, 1998), 100.
45. Lawrence Grobel, *The Hustons* (New York: Scribner's, 1989), 435.
46. Steven Bach, *Final Cut* (New York: Onyx, 1985), 126, 146–147.
47. Yvonne De Carlo with Doug Warren, *Yvonne: An Autobiography* (New York: St. Martin's Press, 1987), 199.
48. David Shipman, *The Great Movie Stars: The Golden Years* (New York: Crown, 1970), 527.
49. James Spada, *Streisand: Her Life* (New York: Ivy Books, 1992), 233.
50. Susan Sackett, *The Hollywood Reporter Book of Box Office Hits* (New York: Billboard Books, 1990), 207.
51. Randall Riese, *Her Name Is Barbra* (New York: St. Martin's Paperbacks, 1993), 297.
52. Anne Edwards, *Streisand: A Biography* (Boston, New York, Toronto, London: Little, Brown, 1997), 259.
53. David Stenn, *Bombshell: The Life and Death of Jean Harlow* (New York: Doubleday, 1993), 37–38.
54. Ron Base, *"If the Other Guy Isn't Jack Nicholson, I've Got the Part"* (Chicago: Contemporary Books, 1994), 146.
55. Anthony Holden, *Laurence Olivier: A Biography* (New York: Atheneum, 1988), 178.
56. John Eastman, *Retakes: Behind the Scenes of 500 Classic Movies* (New York: Ballantine Books, 1989), 148.
57. Michael Viner and Terrie Maxine Frankel, *Tales from Casting Couch: An Unprecedented Candid Collection of Stories, Essays, and Anecdotes by and About Legendary Hollywood Stars, Starlets, and Wanna-bees...* (Beverly Hills: Dove Books, 1995), 28–29.
58. Ronald L. Davis, *Duke: The Life and Image of John Wayne* (Norman: University of Oklahoma Press, 1998), 142.
59. Axel Madsen, *Stanwyck* (New York: HarperCollins, 1994), 296.
60. Ron Base, *"If the Other Guy Isn't Jack Nicholson, I've Got the Part"* (Chicago: Contemporary Books, 1994), 108.
61. Jason Bonderoff, *Tom Selleck: An Unauthorized Biography* (New York: Signet, 1983), 142.
62. John Eastman, *Retakes: Behind the Scenes of 500 Classic Movies* (New York: Ballantine Books, 1989), 150.
63. Lawrence Grobel, *The Hustons* (New York: Scribner's, 1989), 210–211.

64. John Eastman, *Retakes: Behind the Scenes of 500 Classic Movies* (New York: Ballantine Books, 1989), 150.
65. Lawrence Grobel, *The Hustons* (New York: Scribner's, 1989), 210–211.
66. Lawrence Grobel, *The Hustons* (New York: Scribner's, 1989), 210–211.
67. *New York Daily News* (New York), 29 December 1998.
68. Peter Fonda, *Don't Tell Dad: A Memoir* (New York: Hyperion, 1998), 300, 303.
69. John Eastman, *Retakes: Behind the Scenes of 500 Classic Movies* (New York: Ballantine Books, 1989), 152.
70. Clive Hirschhorn, *The Columbia Story* (London: Hamlyn, 1999), 95.
71. Lee Server, *Robert Mitchum: "Baby, I Don't Care"* (New York: St. Martin's Press, 2001), 213.
72. David Shipman, *The Great Movie Stars: The International Years* (New York: St. Martin's Press, 1972), 528.
73. John Eastman, *Retakes: Behind the Scenes of 500 Classic Movies* (New York: Ballantine Books, 1989), 152.
74. James Robert Parish, *Rosie: Rosie O'Donnell's Biography* (New York: Carroll & Graf, 1997), 145.
75. Tom McGee, *Betty Grable: The Girl with the Million Dollar Legs* (Vestal: The Vestal Press, 1995), 44.
76. Frank Capra, *The Name Above the Title: An Autobiography* (New York: Macmillan, 1971), 463.
77. Clive Hirschhorn, *The Columbia Story* (London: Hamlyn, 1999), 81.
78. David Shipman, *The Great Movie Stars: The Golden Years* (New York: Crown, 1970), 271.
79. Shirley Temple Black, *Child Star: An Autobiography* (New York: McGraw-Hill, 1988), 390–391.
80. Christopher Connelly, "You're So Square Baby, I Don't Care" *Premiere*, September 1992, 126.
81. Marshall Terrill, *Steve McQueen: Portrait of an American Rebel* (New York: Donald I. Fine, 1993), 68.
82. John Baxter, *Steven Spielberg: The Unauthorized Biography* (London: HarperCollins, 1996), 366, 378.
83. Rebecca Ascher-Walsh, "Redford Rides Again" *Entertainment Weekly*, 5 September 1997, 35.
84. *New York Daily News* (New York), 1 December 1996.
85. David Shipman, *The Great Movie Stars: The International Years* (New York: St. Martin's Press, 1972), 440.
86. David Shipman, *The Great Movie Stars: The Golden Years* (New York: Crown, 1970), 255.
87. *New York Daily News* (New York), 21 March 1999.
88. Daniel Fierman, "Counting Down the Hours" *Entertainment Weekly*, 10 January 2003, 27.
89. James Spada, *More Than a Woman: An Intimate Biography of Bette Davis* (New York: Bantam Books, 1993), 134–135.
90. Warren G. Harris, *Sophia Loren: A Biography* (New York: Simon & Schuster, 1998), 93, 102–103.
91. Rudy Behlmer, *Memo from Darryl F. Zanuck: The Golden Years at Twentieth Century–Fox* (New York: Grove Press, 1993), 41, 43.
92. George F. Custen, *Twentieth Century's Fox* (New York: BasicBooks, 1997), 241, 246–247, 248.
93. George F. Custen, *Twentieth Century's Fox* (New York: BasicBooks, 1997), 241, 246–247, 248.
94. Rudy Behlmer, *Memo from Darryl F. Zanuck: The Golden Years at Twentieth Century–Fox* (New York: Grove Press, 1993), 41, 43.
95. George F. Custen, *Twentieth Century's Fox* (New York: BasicBooks, 1997), 241, 246–247, 248.
96. Rudy Behlmer, *Memo from Darryl F. Zanuck: The Golden Years at Twentieth Century–Fox* (New York: Grove Press, 1993), 41, 43.
97. Rudy Behlmer, *Memo from Darryl F. Zanuck: The Golden Years at Twentieth Century–Fox* (New York: Grove Press, 1993), 41, 43.
98. George F. Custen, *Twentieth Century's Fox* (New York: BasicBooks, 1997), 241, 246–247, 248.
99. Jeff Jensen, "Green Wiseacre" *Entertainment Weekly*, 17 November, 2000, 50.
100. Peter Harry Brown and Patte B. Barham, *Marilyn: The Last Take* (New York: Signet, 1993), 28.
101. Gene Brown, *Movie Time: A Chronology of Hollywood and the Movie Industry from Its Beginnings to the Present* (New York: Macmillan, 1995), 226.
102. Rebecca Ascher-Walsh, "Reel World" *Entertainment Weekly*, 4 August 2000, 52.
103. David Shipman, *The Great Movie Stars: The International Years* (New York: St. Martin's Press, 1972), 73, 470.
104. David Shipman, *The Great Movie Stars: The Golden Years* (New York: Crown, 1970), 218.
105. John Parker, *Bruce Willis: The Unauthorized Biography* (London: Virgin Books, 1997), 123.
106. Ronald Bergan, *The Coen Brothers* (New York: Thunder's Mouth Press, 2000), 158.
107. Michael Fleming, "Casting Glances" *Movieline*, June 1997, 66.
108. Shawna Malcom, "Busting Out All Over" *TV Guide*, 21–27 June 2003, 26.
109. Vincent Curcio, *Suicide Blonde: The Life of Gloria Grahame* (New York: William Morrow, 1989), 161.
110. Anthony Quinn with Daniel Paisner, *One Man Tango* (New York: HarperCollins, 1995), 252–254.
111. Garry Jenkins, *Harrison Ford: Imperfect Hero* (Secaucus: Birch Lane Press, 1998), 260–261.
112. Garry Jenkins, *Harrison Ford: Imperfect Hero* (Secaucus: Birch Lane Press, 1998), 260–261.
113. Todd Keith, *Kevin Costner: The Unauthorized Biography* (London: ikonprint, 1991), 52.
114. David Shipman, *The Great Movie Stars: The Golden Years* (New York: Crown, 1970), 456.
115. John Baxter, *Woody Allen: A Biography* (New York: Carroll & Graf, 1998), 395.
116. Valerie Milano, *Gwyneth Paltrow* (Toronto: ECW Press, 2000), 40.
117. James Spada, *More Than a Woman: An Intimate Biography of Bette Davis* (New York: Bantam Books, 1993), 380–383.
118. Axel Madsen, *Stanwyck* (New York: HarperCollins, 1994), 332–333.

I

1. Michael Haley, *The Alfred Hitchcock Album* (Englewood Cliffs: Prentice-Hall, 1981), 74.
2. Shelley Levitt, Kasren G. Jackovich and Joyce Wagner, "Hidden Star" *People*, 8 February 1993, 65.
3. Frank Miller, *Movies We Love* (Atlanta: Turner, 1996), 156.
4. David Shipman, *The Great Movie Stars: The International Years* (New York: St. Martin's Press, 1972), 216.
5. Joe Morella and Edward Z. Epstein, *Paul and*

Joanne: A Biography of Paul Newman and Joanne Woodward (New York: Delacorte Press, 1988), 228.

6. Todd McCarthy, *Howard Hawks: The Grey Fox of Hollywood* (New York: Grove Press, 1997), 452.

7. Steve Daly, "The Uncommon Cold" *Entertainment Weekly*, 15 March 2002, 40.

8. Stephen Rebello, "Girl We Love" *Movieline*, April 1998, 94.

9. Michael Fleming, "The Treasure from Toledo" *Movieline*, October 2002, 54.

10. David Shipman, *The Great Movie Stars: The International Years* (New York: St. Martin's Press, 1972), 215.

11. Rachel Abramowitz, "Studios Ignoring You? Quick, Make an Indie!" *The New York Times Magazine*, 16 November 1997, 98–100.

12. David Shipman, *The Great Movie Stars: The Golden Years* (New York: Crown, 1970), 207.

13. David Shipman, *The Great Movie Stars: The International Years* (New York: St. Martin's Press, 1972), 122.

14. John Oller, *Jean Arthur: The Actress Nobody Knew* (New York: Limelight Editions, 1997), 146.

15. Vincent Curcio, *Suicide Blonde: The Life of Gloria Grahame* (New York: William Morrow, 1989), 161.

16. Steve Daly, "In the Money" *Entertainment Weekly*, 3 October 1997, 21.

17. Stephen Rebello, "Elizabeth's Reign" *Movieline*, September 1998, 56.

18. Jeff Burkhart and Bruce Stuart, *Hollywood's First Choices* (New York: Crown Trade Paperbacks, 1994), 205.

19. Michael Fleming, "Casting Glances" *Movieline*, June 1997, 66.

20. Larry Swindell, *Screwball: The Life of Carole Lombard* (New York: William Morrow, 1975), 252.

21. Ian Woodward, *Audrey Hepburn* (New York: St. Martin's Press, 1984), 192.

22. Josh Rottenberg, "Sex Ed" *Premiere*, November, 2003, 88.

23. Josh Rottenberg, "Sex Ed" *Premiere*, November, 2003, 88.

24. Holly Millea, "The Second Coming of Mickey Rourke" *Premiere*, February 2003, 75.

25. David Shipman, *Judy Garland: The Secret Life of an American Legend* (New York: Hyperion, 1992), 229.

26. Patrick McGilligan, *Clint: The Life and Legend* (New York: St. Martin's Press, 1999), 477.

27. Richard Schickel, *Clint Eastwood* (New York: Alfred A. Knopf, 1996), 475.

28. Ron Base, *"If the Other Guy Isn't Jack Nicholson, I've Got the Part"* (Chicago: Contemporary Books, 1994), 261.

29. Michael Munn, *The Sharon Stone Story* (London: Robson Books, 1997), 95.

30. Rebecca Ascher-Walsh, Steve Daly, Jeff Gardinier, David Hochman, Dave Karger, Dana Kennedy, Gregg Kilday, Tricia Laine, Chris Nashawaty, Degen Pener, Erin Richter, Jessica Shaw, Benjamin Svetkey, Caren Weiner, Chris Willman, "Fall Movie Guide" *Entertainment Weekly*, 22/29 August 1997, 58.

31. Nigel Goodall, *Demi Moore: The Most Powerful Woman in Hollywood* (Edinburgh: Mainstream, 2000), 112–113.

32. Ron Base, *"If the Other Guy Isn't Jack Nicholson, I've Got the Part"* (Chicago: Contemporary Books, 1994), 288.

33. Lawrence Grobel, "Glory, Glory, Halle-Lujah" *Movieline*, December/January 2002, 56, 98.

34. Nigel Goodall, *Demi Moore: The Most Powerful Woman in Hollywood* (Edinburgh: Mainstream, 2000), 112–113.

35. Ryan Murphy, "Desperately Seeking Next Julia Roberts" *Us,* January 1994, 21.

36. Ron Base, *"If the Other Guy Isn't Jack Nicholson, I've Got the Part"* (Chicago: Contemporary Books, 1994), 288.

37. Ron Base, *"If the Other Guy Isn't Jack Nicholson, I've Got the Part"* (Chicago: Contemporary Books, 1994), 288.

38. Chris Nashawaty, "Stomp the World: I Want to Get Off" *Entertainment Weekly*, 22 May 1998, 25–26.

39. David Hochman and Dave Karger, "Fools Paradise" *Entertainment Weekly*, 24 January, 1997, 23.

40. Jason Matloff, "Serial Thrillers" *Premiere*, October 2003, 80.

41. John Baxter, *Steven Spielberg: The Unauthorized Biography* (London: HarperCollins, 1996), 336.

42. Jason Matloff, "Serial Thrillers" *Premiere*, October 2003, 78.

43. Barry Paris, *Audrey Hepburn* (New York: G. P. Putnam's Sons, 1996), 124.

44. David Shipman, *The Great Movie Stars: The International Years* (New York: St. Martin's Press, 1972), 94.

45. Ed Sikov, *Mr. Strangelove: A Biography of Peter Sellers* (New York: Hyperion, 2002), 282.

46. Eric Lax, *Woody Allen: A Biography* (New York: Alfred A. Knopf, 1991), 302–303.

47. John Baxter, *Woody Allen: A Biography* (New York: Carroll & Graf, 1998), 265.

48. R. Dixon Smith, *Ronald Colman, Gentleman of the Cinema* (Jefferson: McFarland, 1991), 143.

49. Michael Munn, *The Sharon Stone Story* (London: Robson Books, 1997), 110–111.

50. Richard Natale, Pat H. Broeske and Casey Davidson, "Outvamped" *Entertainment Weekly*, 30 July 1993, 7.

51. Tom Russo, "What If…?" *Premiere*, February 2004, 87.

52. Erin Culley, "The Young Leonardo" *Us*, January 1994, 85.

53. Stephen Rebello, "Leelee Land" *Movieline*, March 2000, 56.

54. Susan Spillman, "Starving for Attention" *TV Guide*, 18 November 2000, 31.

55. Bob Thomas, *Golden Boy: The Untold Story of William Holden* (New York: St. Martin's Press, 1983), 33.

56. Michael Caine, *What's It All About?: An Autobiography* (New York: Turtle Bay Books, 1992), 194.

57. Charlotte Chandler, *Nobody's Perfect: Billy Wilder: A Personal Biography* (New York: Simon & Schuster, 2002), 243–244.

58. Marilu Henner with Jim Jerome, *By All Means Keep on Moving* (New York: Pocket Books, 1994), 250.

59. Michael Feeney Callan, *Anthony Hopkins: The Unauthorized Biography* (New York: Scribner's, 1993), 233–234.

60. Rebecca Ascher-Walsh, "Psycho Kilmer" *Entertainment Weekly*, 31 May 1996, 35–36.

61. Marshall Terrill, *Steve McQueen: Portrait of an American Rebel* (New York: Donald I. Fine, 1993), 425.

62. Ryan Murphy, "Desperately Seeking Next Julia Roberts" *Us,* January 1994, 21.

63. David Shipman, *The Great Movie Stars: The Golden Years* (New York: Crown, 1970), 216.

64. Jeff Burkhart and Bruce Stuart, *Hollywood's First Choices* (New York: Crown Trade Paperbacks, 1994), 205.

65. James Kotsilibas-Davis and Myrna Loy, *Myrna Loy: Being and Becoming* (New York: Alfred A. Knopf, 1987), 94.
66. Jeff Burkhart and Bruce Stuart, *Hollywood's First Choices* (New York: Crown Trade Paperbacks, 1994), 205.
67. Joseph McBride, *Frank Capra: The Catastrophe of Success* (New York: Simon & Schuster, 1992), 304.
68. Ron Base, *"If the Other Guy Isn't Jack Nicholson, I've Got the Part"* (Chicago: Contemporary Books, 1994), 80.
69. Jeanine Basinger, *The It's a Wonderful Life Book* (New York: Alfred A. Knopf, 1986), 7–9, 77.
70. Vincent Curcio, *Suicide Blonde: The Life of Gloria Grahame* (New York: William Morrow, 1989), 161.
71. Joseph McBride, *Frank Capra: The Catastrophe of Success* (New York: Simon & Schuster, 1992), 517–518.
72. Jeanine Basinger, *The It's a Wonderful Life Book* (New York: Alfred A. Knopf, 1986), 7–9, 77.
73. C. David Heymann, *Liz: An Intimate Biography of Elizabeth Taylor* (New York: Birch Lane Press, 1995), 108.
74. David Shipman, *The Great Movie Stars: The Golden Years* (New York: Crown, 1970), 207.

J

1. James Riordan, *Stone: The Controversies, Excesses, and Exploits of a Radical Filmmaker* (New York: Hyperion, 1995), 361–363.
2. Kristen Baldwin and Shirley Fung, "Where Are They Now?" *Entertainment Weekly*, 22/29 August 1997, 12–13.
3. Lynn Hirschberg, "The Two Hollywoods: The Man Who Changed Everything," *The New York Times Magazine*, 16 November 1997, 115.
4. R. Dixon Smith, *Ronald Colman, Gentleman of the Cinema* (Jefferson: McFarland, 1991), 143.
5. Nancy Griffin, "In the Grip of 'Jaws'" *Premiere*, October 1995, 92.
6. Frank Sanello, *Spielberg: The Man, the Movies, the Mythology* (Dallas: Taylor, 1996), 51, 256.
7. John Eastman, *Retakes: Behind the Scenes of 500 Classic Movies* (New York: Ballantine Books, 1989), 166.
8. Frank Sanello, *Spielberg: The Man, the Movies, the Mythology* (Dallas: Taylor, 1996), 51, 256.
9. Frank Sanello, *Spielberg: The Man, the Movies, the Mythology* (Dallas: Taylor, 1996), 51, 256.
10. Frank Sanello, *Spielberg: The Man, the Movies, the Mythology* (Dallas: Taylor, 1996), 51, 256.
11. Ron Base, *"If the Other Guy Isn't Jack Nicholson, I've Got the Part"* (Chicago: Contemporary Books, 1994), 186.
12. Peter Biskind, *Easy Riders, Raging Bulls* (New York: Simon & Schuster, 1998), 266.
13. Frank Sanello, *Spielberg: The Man, the Movies, the Mythology* (Dallas: Taylor, 1996), 51, 256.
14. Nancy Griffin, "In the Grip of 'Jaws'" *Premiere*, October 1995, 92.
15. George Burns with David Fisher, *All My Best Friends* (New York: Perigee Books, 1990), 148.
16. Jack L. Warner, *My First Hundred Years in Hollywood: An Autobiography* (New York: Random House, 1964, 1965), 175.
17. Susan Sackett, *The Hollywood Reporter Book of Box Office Hits* (New York: Billboard Books, 1990), 64.
18. James C. Robertson, *The Casablanca Man: The Cinema of Michael Curtiz* (London and New York: Routledge, 1993), 114.
19. David Shipman, *The Great Movie Stars: The Golden Years* (New York: Crown, 1970), 366.
20. Benjamin Svetkey, "The Cruisible" *Entertainment Weekly*, 20 December 1996, 24.
21. Steve Daly, "A Kwan-Do Kind of Guy" *Entertainment Weekly*, 30 May 1997, 76.
22. Michael Fleming, "Casting Glances" *Movieline*, June 1997, 65.
23. Degen Pener, "Playing the No-Name Game" *Entertainment Weekly*, 12 April 1996, 18.
24. Michael Fleming, "Casting Glances" *Movieline*, June 1997, 65.
25. Degen Pener, "Playing the No-Name Game" *Entertainment Weekly*, 12 April 1996, 18.
26. Michael Fleming, "Casting Glances" *Movieline*, June 1997, 65.
27. Stephen Rebello, "Sudden Lane Changes" *Movieline's Hollywood Life*, October, 2003, 75.
28. Ty Burr, "Good at What Ails Them" *Entertainment Weekly*, Special Oscar Guide March 1997, 71.
29. Steve Daly, "A Kwan-Do Kind of Guy" *Entertainment Weekly*, 30 May 1997, 76.
30. James Spada, *More Than a Woman: An Intimate Biography of Bette Davis* (New York: Bantam Books, 1993), 158.
31. Axel Madsen, *Stanwyck* (New York: HarperCollins, 1994), 158.
32. John Eastman, *Retakes: Behind the Scenes of 500 Classic Movies* (New York: Ballantine Books, 1989), 167–168.
33. John Eastman, *Retakes: Behind the Scenes of 500 Classic Movies* (New York: Ballantine Books, 1989), 167–168.
34. David Shipman, *The Great Movie Stars: The Golden Years* (New York: Crown, 1970), 532.
35. Ron Base, *"If the Other Guy Isn't Jack Nicholson, I've Got the Part"* (Chicago: Contemporary Books, 1994), 99.
36. John Eastman, *Retakes: Behind the Scenes of 500 Classic Movies* (New York: Ballantine Books, 1989), 168.
37. Axel Madsen, *Stanwyck* (New York: HarperCollins, 1994), 308.
38. John Clark, "Good-Bye, Mr. Chip" *Premiere*, June 1995, 110.
39. Lisa Schwarzbaum, "Cardboard 'Box'" *Entertainment Weekly*, 1 August 1997, 46.
40. Clive Hirschhorn, *The Columbia Story* (London: Hamlyn, 1999), 141.
41. David Shipman, *The Great Movie Stars: The Golden Years* (New York: Crown, 1970), 302.
42. Daniel Fierman, "The Sound & the Fury" *Entertainment Weekly*, 16 February 2001, 37.
43. David Shipman, *The Great Movie Stars: The Golden Years* (New York: Crown, 1970), 213.
44. David Shipman, *The Great Movie Stars: The International Years* (New York: St. Martin's Press, 1972), 277.
45. Ron Base, *"If the Other Guy Isn't Jack Nicholson, I've Got the Part"* (Chicago: Contemporary Books, 1994), 63.
46. Faye Dunaway with Betsy Sharkey, *Looking for Gatsby: My Life* (New York: Simon & Schuster, 1995), 321.
47. Peter Biskind, "The Crucible" *Premiere*, Special Issue 1994, 119.
48. James Robert Parish, *Whoopi Goldberg: Her Journey*

from Poverty to Megastardom (Secaucus: Birch Lane Press, 1996), 143–144.
49. James Spada, *More Than a Woman: An Intimate Biography of Bette Davis* (New York: Bantam Books, 1993), 256.
50. *New York Daily News* (New York), 30 August 1998.
51. John Oller, *Jean Arthur: The Actress Nobody Knew* (New York: Limelight Editions, 1997), 256.
52. Douglas Brode, *The Films of Steven Spielberg* (New York: Citadel Press, 1995, 2000), 220.
53. John Baxter, *Steven Spielberg: The Unauthorized Biography* (London: HarperCollins, 1996), 377.
54. Michael Fleming, "Casting Glances" *Movieline*, June 1997, 66.
55. Stephen Rebello, "Girl We Love" *Movieline*, April 1998, 94.
56. Suzanne Finstad, *Natasha: The Biography of Natalie Wood* (New York: Harmony Books, 2001), 93.
57. Cybill Shepherd, *Cybill Disobedience* (New York: HarperCollins, 2000), 181–182.

K

1. Sondra Locke, *The Good, the Bad & the Very Ugly: A Hollywood Journey* (New York: William Morrow, 1997), 247.
2. Shirley Temple Black, *Child Star: An Autobiography* (New York: McGraw-Hill, 1988), 331.
3. Alvin Yudkoff, *Gene Kelly: A Life of Dance and Dreams* (New York: Back Stage Books, 1999), 99–101.
4. John Baxter, *Woody Allen: A Biography* (New York: Carroll & Graf, 1998), 61.
5. Daniel Fierman, "Blood Work" *Entertainment Weekly*, 20 September, 2002, 30.
6. John Eastman, *Retakes: Behind the Scenes of 500 Classic Movies* (New York: Ballantine Books, 1989), 170.
7. David Shipman, *The Great Movie Stars: The Golden Years* (New York: Crown, 1970), 43.
8. Eric Braun, *Deborah Kerr* (New York: St. Martin's Press, 1977), 153.
9. Jeff Burkhart and Bruce Stuart, *Hollywood's First Choices* (New York: Crown Trade Paperbacks, 1994), 216.
10. Donald Bogle, *Dorothy Dandridge: A Biography* (New York: Amistad Press, 1997), 330, 332–334, 336–338.
11. Charles Grodin, Jr., *It Would Be So Nice If You Weren't Here...* (New York: Vintage Books, 1989), 234.
12. Bruce Bahrenburg, *The Creation of Dino De Laurentiis' King Kong* (London: Star, 1976), 4.
13. Shawn Levy, *King of Comedy: The Life and Art of Jerry Lewis* (New York: St. Martin's Press, 1996), 419.
14. Peter Biskind, *Easy Riders, Raging Bulls* (New York: Simon & Schuster, 1998), 176.
15. Marshall Terrill, *Steve McQueen: Portrait of an American Rebel* (New York: Donald I. Fine, 1993), 421.
16. Frank Miller, *Movies We Love* (Atlanta: Turner, 1996), 176–177.
17. John Eastman, *Retakes: Behind the Scenes of 500 Classic Movies* (New York: Ballantine Books, 1989), 176.
18. Anne Edwards, *Shirley Temple: American Princess* (New York: Berkley Books, 1988), 130–131.
19. James Robert Parish and Ronald L. Bowers, *The MGM Stock Company: The Golden Era* (New Rochelle: Arlington House, 1973), 391.

20. Ed Sikov, *On Sunset Boulevard: The Life and Times of Billy Wilder* (New York: Hyperion, 1998), 483, 486–487.
21. Jeff Burkhart and Bruce Stuart, *Hollywood's First Choices* (New York: Crown Trade Paperbacks, 1994), 191.
22. John Eastman, *Retakes: Behind the Scenes of 500 Classic Movies* (New York: Ballantine Books, 1989), 176–177.
23. James L. Dickerson, *Ashley Judd: Crying on the Inside* (New York: Schirmer Trade Books, 2002), 124.
24. Randall Riese, *Her Name Is Barbra* (New York: St. Martin's Paperbacks, 1993), 385.
25. John Eastman, *Retakes: Behind the Scenes of 500 Classic Movies* (New York: Ballantine Books, 1989), 178.
26. Roger Lewis, *The Real Life of Laurence Olivier* (New York: Applause Books, 1996), 11.
27. Gene Brown, *Movie Time: A Chronology of Hollywood and the Movie Industry from Its Beginnings to the Present* (New York: Macmillan, 1995), 150.(Cagney)
28. Rob Edelman and Audrey Kupferberg, *Matthau: A Life* (Lanham: Taylor Trade, 2002), 200–201.
29. Andrew Yule, *Life on the Wire: The Life and Art of Al Pacino* (New York: Donald I. Fine, 1991), 160.
30. *New York Daily News* (New York), 20 August 2001.
31. Jeff Burkhart and Bruce Stuart, *Hollywood's First Choices* (New York: Crown Trade Paperbacks, 1994), 195.
32. Tom Russo, "What If...?" *Premiere*, February 2004, 87.
33. 5John Eastman, *Retakes: Behind the Scenes of 500 Classic Movies* (New York: Ballantine Books, 1989), 178.
34. Jeff Burkhart and Bruce Stuart, *Hollywood's First Choices* (New York: Crown Trade Paperbacks, 1994), 195.
35. James L. Dickerson, *Ashley Judd: Crying on the Inside* (New York: Schirmer Trade Books, 2002), 63–64.

L

1. James Curtis, *Between Flops: A Biography of Preston Sturges* (New York: Harcourt Brace Jovanovich, 1982), 145.
2. Joseph McBride, *Frank Capra: The Catastrophe of Success* (New York: Simon & Schuster, 1992), 299.
3. Frank Capra, *Frank Capra: The Name Above the Title* (New York: Macmillan, 1971), 148–149.
4. Orson Welles and Peter Bogdanovich, *This Is Orson Welles* (New York: Da Capo, 1998), 193.
5. John Eastman, *Retakes: Behind the Scenes of 500 Classic Movies* (New York: Ballantine Books, 1989), 179.
6. Barbara Leaming, *Orson Welles: A Biography* (New York: Viking, 1983, 1985), 332.
7. Joan Collins, *Past Imperfect: An Autobiography* (New York: Berkley Books, 1985), 12–13.
8. Joan Collins, *Past Imperfect: An Autobiography* (New York: Berkley Books, 1985), 12–13.
9. David Shipman, *The Great Movie Stars: The International Years* (New York: St. Martin's Press, 1972), 216.
10. Lawrence J. Quirk, *Paul Newman* (Dallas: Taylor, 1996), 136.
11. Robert Edelman and Audrey Kupferberg, *Angela Lansbury: A Life on Stage and Screen* (Thorndike: G.K. Hall, and Bath: Chivers Press, 1996), 315–316.
12. Damien Bona, *Starring John Wayne as Genghis Khan* (Secaucus: Citadel Press, 1996), 146.
13. Todd McCarthy, *Howard Hawks: The Grey Fox of Hollywood* (New York: Grove Press, 1997), 521, 526–527.

14. Christine Spines, "Tomb with a View" *Premiere*, July 2001, 37–38.
15. Peter Biskind, *Easy Riders, Raging Bulls* (New York: Simon & Schuster, 1998), 178.
16. Nigel Andrews, *Travolta: The Life* (New York: Bloomsbury, 1998), 30.
17. The Hollywood Kids, "Q&A: Nancy Allen" *Movieline*, July 1998, 32.
18. Lawrence J. Quirk and William Schoell, *Joan Crawford: The Essential Biography* (Lexington: The University Press of Kentucky, 2002), 85.
19. Anne Thompson, "News & Notes" *Entertainment Weekly*, 1 April 1994, 66.
20. Andrew Yule, *Picture Shows: The Life and Films of Peter Bogdanovich* (New York: Limelight Editions, 1992), 40.
21. Cybill Shepherd, *Cybill Disobedience* (New York: HarperCollins, 2000), 88.
22. Sondra Locke, *The Good, the Bad & the Very Ugly: A Hollywood Journey* (New York: William Morrow, 1997), 101.
23. John Parker, *Warren Beatty: The Last Great Lover of Hollywood* (New York: Carroll & Graf, 1993), 195.
24. Gary Carey, *Marlon Brando: The Only Contender* (New York: St. Martin's Press, 1985), 221.
25. John Eastman, *Retakes: Behind the Scenes of 500 Classic Movies* (New York: Ballantine Books, 1989), 182–183.
26. Jennifer Armstrong, Rebecca Ascher-Walsh, Sumeet Bal, Mandi Bierly, Ben Brashares, Scott Brown, Tim Carvell, Steve Daly, Michael Endelman, Amy Feitelberg, Daniel Fierman, Raymond Fiore, Gillian Flynn, Nicholas Fonseca, Henry Goldblatt, Nisha Gopalan, Brian Hiatt, Jeff Jensen, Dave Karger, Gregory Kirschling, Alice M. Lee, Allyssa Lee, Nancy Miller, Troy Patterson, Kimberly Reyes, Lynette Rice, Joshua Rich, Dalton Ross, Missy Schwartz, Jessica Shaw, Dan Snierson, Ken Tucker, Karen Valby, Alynda Wheat, Chris Willman, Josh Wolk, "Forecast 2004" *Entertainment Weekly*, 23/30 January 2004, 29.
27. Andy Dougan, *Untouchable: A Biography of Robert De Niro* (New York: Thunder's Mouth Press, 1996), 172–173.
28. Mary Pat Kelly, *Martin Scorsese: A Journey* (New York: Thunder's Mouth Press, 1991), 172–173.
29. Andy Dougan, *Untouchable: A Biography of Robert De Niro* (New York: Thunder's Mouth Press, 1996), 172–173.
30. Lawrence J. Quirk, *Totally Uninhibited: The Life and Wild Times of Cher* (New York: William Morrow, 1991), 230.
31. Mary Pat Kelly, *Martin Scorsese: A Journey* (New York: Thunder's Mouth Press, 1991), 172–173.
32. Andrew Yule, *Life on the Wire: The Life and Art of Al Pacino* (New York: Donald I. Fine, 1991), 124–125.
33. Elia Kazan, *Elia Kazan: A Life* (New York: Alfred A. Knopf, 1988), 765.
34. Cybill Shepherd, *Cybill Disobedience* (New York: HarperCollins, 2000), 143–144.
35. Esther Williams with Digby Diehl, *The Million Dollar Mermaid* (New York: Simon & Schuster, 1999), 234–236.
36. Warren G. Harris, *Clark Gable: A Biography* (New York: Harmony Books, 2002), 75–76.
37. Melvyn Bragg, *Richard Burton: A Life* (Boston: Little, Brown, 1988), 254.
38. John Eastman, *Retakes: Behind the Scenes of 500 Classic Movies* (New York: Ballantine Books, 1989), 184.
39. George F. Custen, *Twentieth Century's Fox* (New York: BasicBooks, 1997), 289.
40. Jeff Burkhart and Bruce Stuart, *Hollywood's First Choices* (New York: Crown Trade Paperbacks, 1994), 42–43.
41. John Eastman, *Retakes: Behind the Scenes of 500 Classic Movies* (New York: Ballantine Books, 1989), 185.
42. Jeff Burkhart and Bruce Stuart, *Hollywood's First Choices* (New York: Crown Trade Paperbacks, 1994), 42–43.
43. L. Robert Morris and Lawrence Raskin, *Robert Mitchum: "Baby, I Don't Care"* (New York: Anchor Books, 1992), 41, 68–71.
44. Robert Evans, *Francis Lawrence of Arabia: The 30th Anniversary Pictorial History* (New York: Hyperion, 1994), 78–81.
45. L. Robert Morris and Lawrence Raskin, *Robert Mitchum: "Baby, I Don't Care"* (New York: Anchor Books, 1992), 41, 68–71.
46. Ron Base, *"If the Other Guy Isn't Jack Nicholson, I've Got the Part"* (Chicago: Contemporary Books, 1994), 281.
47. Lee Pfeiffer and Michael Lewis, *The Films of Tom Hanks* (Secaucus: Citadel Press, 1996), 141–142.
48. James Robert Parish, *Rosie: Rosie O'Donnell's Biography* (New York: Carroll & Graf, 1997), 83.
49. Valerie Milano, *Gwyneth Paltrow* (Toronto: ECW Press, 2000), 40, 55.
50. Steven Goldman, "Young Doctor in Love" *Premiere*, September 1997, 85.
51. Andrew Yule, *Life on the Wire: The Life and Art of Al Pacino* (New York: Donald I. Fine, 1991), 145.
52. Kate Buford, *Burt Lancaster: An American Life* (New York: Alfred A. Knopf, 2000), 222.
53. John Parker, *Warren Beatty: The Last Great Lover of Hollywood* (New York: Carroll & Graf, 1993), 88.
54. Patrick McGilligan, *George Cukor: A Double Life* (New York: St. Martin's Press, 1991), 257–258.
55. Charlton Heston, *In the Arena: An Autobiography* (New York: Simon & Schuster, 1995), 217–218.
56. Peter Harry Brown and Patte B. Barham, *Marilyn: The Last Take* (New York: Signet, 1993), 36.
57. Patrick McGilligan, *George Cukor: A Double Life* (New York: St. Martin's Press, 1991), 257–258.
58. Jane Ellen Wayne, *The Golden Girls of MGM* (New York: Carroll & Graf, 2002), 142–143.
59. Jan Herman, *A Talent for Trouble: The Life of Hollywood's Most Acclaimed Director, William Wyler* (New York: G. P. Putnam's Sons, 1995), 451–452.
60. Tom McGee, *Betty Grable: The Girl with the Million Dollar Legs* (Vestal: The Vestal Press, 1995), 215.
61. Roger Lewis, *The Real Life of Laurence Olivier* (New York: Applause Books, 1996), 82.
62. Eric Braun, *Deborah Kerr* (New York: St. Martin's Press, 1977), 66.
63. Billy Adams, *Ewan McGregor: The Unauthorized Biography* (Woodstock: The Overlook Press, 1999), 184.
64. Benjamin Svetkey, "Ordinary People" *Entertainment Weekly*, 24 October 1997, 26.
65. Michael Fleming, "The Thinking Person's Sex Symbol" *Movieline*, February 2003, 44.
66. Lana Turner, *Lana: The Lady, the Legend, the Truth* (New York: E. P. Dutton, 1982), 150–152.
67. James C. Robertson, *The Casablanca Man: The*

Cinema of Michael Curtiz (London, New York: Routledge, 1993), 95–96.
68. Anne Edwards, *Shirley Temple: American Princess* (New York: Berkley Books, 1988), 146–147.
69. David Shipman, *The Great Movie Stars: The International Years* (New York: St. Martin's Press, 1972), 77.
70. David Shipman, *The Great Movie Stars: The Golden Years* (New York: Crown, 1970), 238.
71. Peter Fonda, *Don't Tell Dad: A Memoir* (New York: Hyperion, 1998), 172–173.
72. John Eastman, *Retakes: Behind the Scenes of 500 Classic Movies* (New York: Ballantine Books, 1989), 191.
73. Frank Miller, *Movies We Love* (Atlanta: Turner, 1996), 179–181.
74. Shelley Winters, *Shelley II: The Middle of My Century* (New York: Simon and Schuster, 1989), 60.
75. James Spada, *More Than a Woman: An Intimate Biography of Bette Davis* (New York: Bantam Books, 1993), 180–182.
76. A. Scott Berg, *Goldwyn: A Biography* (New York: Alfred A. Knopf, 1989), 358
77. Stephen M. Silverman, *Dancing on the Ceiling: Stanley Donen and His Movies* (New York: Alfred A. Knopf, 1996), 324–325.
78. Patrick McGilligan, *Jack's Life: A Biography of Jack Nicholson* (New York, London: W. W. Norton, 1994), 114.
79. David Shipman, *The Great Movie Stars: The Golden Years* (New York: Crown, 1970), 57.
80. Kim Cunningham, "Chatters" *People*, 20 November 1995, 198.
81. Steve Pond, "Dermot Mulroney" *Us,* July 1997, 66.
82. Joan Wester Anderson, *Forever Young: The Life, Loves and Enduring Faith of a Hollywood Legend* (Edinburgh: Mainstream, 1998), 92.
83. Rudy Behlmer, *Memo from Darryl F. Zanuck: The Golden Years at Twentieth Century-Fox* (New York: Grove Press, 1993), 8–12.
84. Jeff Burkhart and Bruce Stuart, *Hollywood's First Choices* (New York: Crown Trade Paperbacks, 1994), 190, 209.
85. Jeff Burkhart and Bruce Stuart, *Hollywood's First Choices* (New York: Crown Trade Paperbacks, 1994), 190, 209.
86. Ed Sikov, *Mr. Strangelove: A Biography of Peter Sellers* (New York: Hyperion, 2002), 159.
87. Frank Miller, *Movies We Love* (Atlanta: Turner, 1996), 185–186.
88. Frank Miller, *Movies We Love* (Atlanta: Turner, 1996), 185–186.
89. Jeff Burkhart and Bruce Stuart, *Hollywood's First Choices* (New York: Crown Trade Paperbacks, 1994), 190, 209.
90. Patrick McGilligan, *Robert Altman: Jumping Off the Cliff* (New York: St. Martin's Press, 1989), 360.
91. Marshall Terrill, *Steve McQueen: Portrait of an American Rebel* (New York: Donald I. Fine, 1993), 424.
92. John Eastman, *Retakes: Behind the Scenes of 500 Classic Movies* (New York: Ballantine Books, 1989), 195.
93. Charlton Heston, *In the Arena: An Autobiography* (New York: Simon & Schuster, 1995), 270.
94. Tom McGee, *Betty Grable: The Girl with the Million Dollar Legs* (Vestal: The Vestal Press, 1995), 166.
95. Andrew Yule, *Picture Shows: The Life and Films of Peter Bogdanovich* (New York: Limelight Editions, 1992), 111.
96. Gillian Flynn, "Ring Masters" *Entertainment Weekly*, 16 November 2001, 41.
97. A. Harvey Baker, "Star Turn" *Queens College Report,* Spring 1993, 10.
98. *New York Daily News* (New York), 14 June 2000.
99. Joseph McBride, *Frank Capra: The Catastrophe of Success* (New York: Simon & Schuster, 1992), 358.
100. Mitchell Fink, "The Insider" *People*, 28 April 1997, 45.
101. Tricia Laine, "News & Notes" *Entertainment Weekly*, 4 April 1997, 19.
102. Gillian Flynn, "Raising Hell" *Entertainment Weekly*, 20 October 2000, 22.
103. Axel Madsen, *Stanwyck* (New York: HarperCollins, 1994), 220.
104. Maurice Zolotow, *Billy Wilder in Hollywood* (New York: G.P. Putnam's Sons, 1977), 130.
105. Ed Sikov, *On Sunset Boulevard: The Life and Times of Billy Wilder* (New York: Hyperion, 1998), 218.
106. Robert Edelman and Audrey Kupferberg, *Angela Lansbury: A Life on Stage and Screen* (Thorndike: G.K. Hall, and Bath: Chivers Press, 1996), 240.
107. Stephen Rebello, "Nowhere to Hide" *Movieline*, May 1995, 85.
108. Warren G. Harris, *Audrey Hepburn: A Biography* (New York: Simon & Schuster, 1994), 142.
109. Jane Russell, *Jane Russell: An Autobiography* (New York: Franklin Watts, 1985), 175.
110. Gregory Speck, *Hollywood Royalty: Hepburn, Davis, Stewart & Friends At the Dinner Party of the Century* (New York: Birch Lane Press, 1992), 164.
111. James Kotsilibas-Davis and Myrna Loy, *Myrna Loy: Being and Becoming* (New York: Alfred A. Knopf, 1987), 119–120.
112. John Eastman, *Retakes: Behind the Scenes of 500 Classic Movies* (New York: Ballantine Books, 1989), 197.
113. Robert Evans, *Francis the Kid Stays in the Picture* (New York: Hyperion, 1994), 177, 180.
114. Steve Daly, "Love! Valour! Costanza!" *Entertainment Weekly*, 23 May 1997, 20.
115. Marshall Terrill, *Steve McQueen: Portrait of an American Rebel* (New York: Donald I. Fine, 1993), 100.
116. Ian Woodward, *Audrey Hepburn* (New York: St. Martin's Press, 1984), 192.
117. Allan Hunter, *Gene Hackman* (New York: St. Martin's Press, 1987), 131.
118. David Shipman, *The Great Movie Stars: The International Years* (New York: St. Martin's Press, 1972), 235.
119. Barry Paris, *Audrey Hepburn* (New York: G. P. Putnam's Sons, 1996), 254.

M

1. John Eastman, *Retakes: Behind the Scenes of 500 Classic Movies* (New York: Ballantine Books, 1989), 208.
2. Patrick McGilligan, *Robert Altman: Jumping Off the Cliff* (New York: St. Martin's Press, 1989), 300, 302.
3. Patrick McGilligan, *Robert Altman: Jumping Off the Cliff* (New York: St. Martin's Press, 1989), 300, 302.
4. Vincent Curcio, *Suicide Blonde: The Life of Gloria Grahame* (New York: William Morrow, 1989), 161.
5. Barbara Leaming, *Orson Welles: A Biography* (New York: Viking, 1983, 1985), 346.

6. Nigel Andrews, *Travolta: The Life* (New York: Bloomsbury, 1998), 293–294.
7. Michael Fleming, "Casting Glances" *Movieline*, June 1997, 65–66.
8. Andy Dougan, *Untouchable: A Biography of Robert De Niro* (New York: Thunder's Mouth Press, 1996), 239.
9. Todd McCarthy, *Howard Hawks: The Grey Fox of Hollywood* (New York: Grove Press, 1997), 257–258.
10. Lana Turner, *Lana: The Lady, the Legend, the Truth* (New York: E. P. Dutton, 1982), 140.
11. David Shipman, *The Great Movie Stars: The Golden Years* (New York: Crown, 1970), 255.
12. Ty Burr, "Good at What Ails Them" *Entertainment Weekly*, Special Oscar Guide March 1997, 41.
13. James Robert Parish, *Whoopi Goldberg: Her Journey from Poverty to Megastardom* (Secaucus: Birch Lane Press, 1996), 269.
14. Andy Dougan, *Untouchable: A Biography of Robert De Niro* (New York: Thunder's Mouth Press, 1996), 227.
15. Michael Feeney Callan, *Anthony Hopkins: The Unauthorized Biography* (New York: Scribner's, 1993), 217.
16. David Shipman, *The Great Movie Stars: The International Years* (New York: St. Martin's Press, 1972), 190.
17. David Shipman, *The Great Movie Stars: The Golden Years* (New York: Crown, 1970), 344.
18. David Shipman, *The Great Movie Stars: The International Years* (New York: St. Martin's Press, 1972), 100.
19. Gregg Goldstein, "Suite Dreams" *Premiere*, January 2003, 38.
20. Randall Riese, *Her Name Is Barbra* (New York: St. Martin's Paperbacks, 1993), 439.
21. James Spada, *Streisand: Her Life* (New York: Ivy Books, 1995), 416–417.
22. James Spada, *Streisand: Her Life* (New York: Ivy Books, 1995), 416–417.
23. David Shipman, *The Great Movie Stars: The Golden Years* (New York: Crown, 1970), 498.
24. Marshall Fine, *Bloody Sam: The Life and Films of Sam Peckinpah* (New York: Donald I. Fine, 1991), 85.
25. Anne Thompson, "News & Notes" *Entertainment Weekly*, 11 June 1993, 11.
26. Spike Lee with Ralph Wiley, *By Any Means Necessary: The Trials and Tribulations of the Making of Malcolm X...* (New York: Hyperion, 1992), 25–26, 93.
27. Claudia Dreifus, "Sam I Am" *Premiere*, June 1995, 95.
28. Spike Lee with Ralph Wiley, *By Any Means Necessary: The Trials and Tribulations of the Making of Malcolm X...* (New York: Hyperion, 1992), 25–26, 93.
29. John Kenneth Muir, *An Askew View: The Films of Kevin Smith* (New York: Applause Theatre & Cinema Books, 2002), 65.
30. Stephen Rebello, "The Next McCarty Era" *Movieline*, August 1998, 56.
31. John Kenneth Muir, *An Askew View: The Films of Kevin Smith* (New York: Applause Theatre & Cinema Books, 2002), 65.
32. John Kenneth Muir, *An Askew View: The Films of Kevin Smith* (New York: Applause Theatre & Cinema Books, 2002), 65.
33. William Goldman, *Adventures in the Screen Trade* (New York: Warner Books, 1983), 14.
34. Ron Base, *"If the Other Guy Isn't Jack Nicholson, I've Got the Part"* (Chicago: Contemporary Books, 1994), 58–59.
35. Jeff Burkhart and Bruce Stuart, *Hollywood's First Choices* (New York: Crown Trade Paperbacks, 1994), 217.
36. Ron Base, *"If the Other Guy Isn't Jack Nicholson, I've Got the Part"* (Chicago: Contemporary Books, 1994), 58–59.
37. Martin Gottfried, *Balancing Act: The Authorized Biography of Angela Lansbury* (Boston, New York, London: Little, Brown, 1999), 191–192.
38. Frank Castelluccio and Alvin Walker, *The Other Side of Ethel Mertz: The Life Story of Vivian Vance* (Manchester: Knowledge, Ideas & Trends, 1998), 286.
39. Kathleen Brady, *Lucille: The Life of Lucille Ball* (New York: Hyperion, 1994), 322.
40. Kathleen Brady, *Lucille: The Life of Lucille Ball* (New York: Hyperion, 1994), 322.
41. Tom McGee, *Betty Grable: The Girl with the Million Dollar Legs* (Vestal: The Vestal Press, 1995), 62–63.
42. Fred Zinnemann, *A Life in the Movies* (New York: Scribner's, 1992), 205–206.
43. David Shipman, *The Great Movie Stars: The Golden Years* (New York: Crown, 1970), 193.
44. David Shipman, *The Great Movie Stars: The Golden Years* (New York: Crown, 1970), 379.
45. Jennifer Pendleton, "Landing 'The Moon'" *Entertainment Weekly*, 13 March 1998, 9.
46. Patrick McGilligan, *Jack's Life: A Biography of Jack Nicholson* (New York, London: W. W. Norton, 1994), 269.
47. Jay Boyer, *Bob Rafelson* (New York: Twayne, 1996), 117–118.
48. Whitney Stine, *"I'd Love to Kiss You...": Conversations with Bette Davis* (New York: Pocket Books, 1990), 251.
49. Charles Higham, *Sisters: The Story of Olivia De Havilland & Joan Fontaine* (New York: Coward-McCann, 1984), 125.
50. Andrew Yule, *Sean Connery: From 007 to Hollywood Icon* (New York: Donald I. Fine, 1992), 151.
51. David Shipman, *The Great Movie Stars: The Golden Years* (New York: Crown, 1970), 429.
52. Martin Gottfried, *Balancing Act: The Authorized Biography of Angela Lansbury* (Boston, New York, London: Little, Brown, 1999), 128.
53. Stephen M. Silverman, *Dancing on the Ceiling: Stanley Donen and His Movies* (New York: Alfred A. Knopf, 1996), 287–288.
54. Todd McCarthy, *Howard Hawks: The Grey Fox of Hollywood* (New York: Grove Press, 1997), 597.
55. Warren G. Harris, *Clark Gable: A Biography* (New York: Harmony Books, 2002), 120.
56. Stig Bjorkman and Alfabeta Bokforlag, *Woody Allen on Woody Allen* (New York: Grove Press, 1993), 257.
57. Jeff Burkhart and Bruce Stuart, *Hollywood's First Choices* (New York: Crown Trade Paperbacks, 1994), 209.
58. Murgatroyd, "This and That" *Movieline*, May 1992, 9.
59. Paul Rosenfield, *The Club Rules: Power, Money, Sex, and Fear-How It Works in Hollywood* (New York: Warner Books, 1992), 241.
60. Warren G. Harris, *Clark Gable: A Biography* (New York: Harmony Books, 2002), 134.
61. David Shipman, *The Great Movie Stars: The Golden Years* (New York: Crown, 1970), 211.
62. Suzanne Finstad, *Natasha: The Biography of Natalie Wood* (New York: Harmony Books, 2001), 204.

63. Lawrence J. Quirk, *Paul Newman* (Dallas: Taylor, 1996), 74.
64. John Russell Taylor, *Hitch: The Life and Times of Alfred Hitchcock* (New York: Pantheon Books, 1978), 265.
65. Patrick McGilligan, *George Cukor: A Double Life* (New York: St. Martin's Press, 1991), 208.
66. Tom Hutchinson, *Rod Steiger* (New York: Fromm International, 2000), 75.
67. Ginger Rogers, *Ginger: My Story* (New York: HarperCollins, 1991), 170–175.
68. David Shipman, *The Great Movie Stars: The Golden Years* (New York: Crown, 1970), 145.
69. Michael Fleming, "Casting Glances" *Movieline*, June 1997, 94.
70. Melina Gerosa, "News & Notes" *Entertainment Weekly*, 23 April 1993, 10.
71. Stephen Rebello, "Kiss Us, Kate" *Movieline*, March 1998, 109.
72. J. Randy Taraborrelli, *Cher: A Biography* (New York: St. Martin's Press, 1986), 306.
73. Rebecca Ascher-Walsh, Kristen Baldwin, Anita M. Busch, Steve Daly, Andrew Essex, Daniel Fierman, Jeff Gardinier, David Hochman, Dave Karger, Tricia Laine, Chris Nashawaty, Joe Neumaier, Degen Pener, Megan Quitkin, Jessica Shaw, Tom Sinclair, Benjamin Svetkey, "The Following Summer Movie Preview Has Been Approved for All Audiences by the Editors of Entertainment Weekly" *Entertainment Weekly*, 15 May 1998, 49.
74. William Goldman, *Adventures in the Screen Trade* (New York: Warner Books, 1983), 170.
75. Rebecca Ascher-Walsh, "Reality Bytes" *Entertainment Weekly*, 9 April 1999, 30, 31
76. Mark Salisbury, "Rage Against the Machines" *Premiere*, 7 May, 2003, 49.
77. Tom Sinclair, "Mourning Aaliyah" *Entertainment Weekly*, 7 September, 2001, 24.
78. Ryan Murphy, "Desperately Seeking Next Julia Roberts" *Us*, January 1994, 21.
79. Buddy Foster and Leon Wagener, *Foster Child: A Biography of Jodie Foster* (New York: Dutton, 1997), 222.
80. Patrick McGilligan, *Robert Altman: Jumping Off the Cliff* (New York: St. Martin's Press, 1989), 339.
81. Brantley Bardin, "Who Says Comedy Can't Be Pretty?" *Premiere*, October 2001, 62.
82. Mary Pat Kelly, *Martin Scorsese: A Journey* (New York: Thunder's Mouth Press, 1991), 73–74.
83. Joseph McBride, *Frank Capra: The Catastrophe of Success* (New York: Simon & Schuster, 1992), 49–430.
84. Tom McGee, *Betty Grable: The Girl with the Million Dollar Legs* (Vestal: The Vestal Press, 1995), 181–182.
85. David Shipman, *Judy Garland: The Secret Life of an American Legend* (New York: Hyperion, 1992), 155.
86. Steve Daly, "In-Laws & Disorder" *Entertainment Weekly*, 13 October 2000, 30.
87. Michael Fleming, "The Heat on Heather" *Movieline*, September 2001, 52.
88. Jason Bonderoff, *Tom Selleck: An Unauthorized Biography* (New York: Signet, 1983), 142.
89. Tom Russo, "What If…?" *Premiere*, February 2004, 88.
90. Fred Schruers, "Black Magic" *Premiere*, July 2002, 61.
91. Dave Karger, "Aliens, Smith, and Jones" *Entertainment Weekly*, 12 July 2002, 36.
92. David Shipman, *The Great Movie Stars: The International Years* (New York: St. Martin's Press, 1972), 525.
93. Lawrence J. Quirk, *Totally Uninhibited: The Life and Wild Times of Cher* (New York: William Morrow, 1991), 249.
94. Edward Baron Turk, *Hollywood Diva: A Biography of Jeanette MacDonald* (Berkeley and Los Angeles: University of California Press, 1998), 142–143.
95. Andrew Yule, *Sean Connery: From 007 to Hollywood Icon* (New York: Donald I. Fine, 1992), 179.
96. Benjamin Svetkey, "Mail Bonding" *Entertainment Weekly*, 18 December 1998, 28.
97. Nigel Andrews, *Travolta: The Life* (New York: Bloomsbury, 1998), 279.
98. Marilu Henner with Jim Jerome, *By All Means Keep on Moving* (New York: Pocket Books, 1994), 215.
99. Peter Biskind, "The Crucible" *Premiere*, Special Issue 1994, 115.
100. Dave Thompson, *Travolta* (Dallas: Taylor, 1996), 69.
101. Susan Bluestein Davis, *After Midnight: The Life and Death of Brad Davis* (New York: Pocket Books, 1997), 58–62.
102. Charles Grodin, Jr., *It Would Be So Nice If You Weren't Here…* (New York: Vintage Books, 1989), 285–286.
103. Arthur Marx, *The Nine Lives of Mickey Rooney* (Briarcliff Manor: Stein and Day, 1986), 46.
104. John McCabe, *Cagney* (New York: Alfred A. Knopf, 1997), 139.
105. Shirley Temple Black, *Child Star: An Autobiography* (New York: McGraw-Hill, 1988), 336.
106. John Eastman, *Retakes: Behind the Scenes of 500 Classic Movies* (New York: Ballantine Books, 1989), 211.
107. John Eastman, *Retakes: Behind the Scenes of 500 Classic Movies* (New York: Ballantine Books, 1989), 211.
108. Axel Madsen, *Stanwyck* (New York: HarperCollins, 1994), 222.
109. Shirley Temple Black, *Child Star: An Autobiography* (New York: McGraw-Hill, 1988), 336.
110. James C. Robertson, *The Casablanca Man: The Cinema of Michael Curtiz* (London, New York: Routledge, 1993), 89.
111. James C. Robertson, *The Casablanca Man: The Cinema of Michael Curtiz* (London, New York: Routledge, 1993), 89.
112. Ronald Bergan, *The Coen Brothers* (New York: Thunder's Mouth Press, 2000), 115.
113. Warren G. Harris, *Sophia Loren: A Biography* (New York: Simon & Schuster, 1998), 145–146.
114. Fred Schruers, "It's About Tom" *Premiere*, July 2002, 88.
115. David Shipman, *The Great Movie Stars: The International Years* (New York: St. Martin's Press, 1972), 28.
116. Rudy Behlmer, *Memo from Darryl F. Zanuck: The Golden Years at Twentieth Century-Fox* (New York: Grove Press, 1993), 119.
117. Ingrid Bergman and Alan Burgess, *Ingrid Bergman: My Story* (New York: Dell, 1980), 513.
118. Jeff Burkhart and Bruce Stuart, *Hollywood's First Choices* (New York: Crown Trade Paperbacks, 1994), 204.
119. Jeffrey Wells, "Mirror, Mirror" *Entertainment Weekly*, 12 April 1996, 8.
120. Murgatroyd, "Hollywood Ink" *Movieline*, March 1997, 22.
121. William Goldman, *Which Lie Did I Tell?* (New York: Pantheon Books, 2000), 41–43.

122. Stephen Jones, *Creepshows: The Illustrated Stephen King Movie Guide* (New York: Billboard Books, 2002), 67.
123. William Goldman, *Which Lie Did I Tell?* (New York: Pantheon Books, 2000), 41–43.
124. William Goldman, *Which Lie Did I Tell?* (New York: Pantheon Books, 2000), 41–43.
125. Lee Server, *Robert Mitchum: "Baby, I Don't Care"* (New York: St. Martin's Press, 2001), 380.
126. Joe Morella and Edward Z. Epstein, *Paul and Joanne: A Biography of Paul Newman and Joanne Woodward* (New York: Delacorte Press, 1988), 256.
127. Rebecca Ascher-Walsh, "Reel World" *Entertainment Weekly*, 23 July 1999, 42.
128. Todd Keith, *Kevin Costner: The Unauthorized Biography* (London: ikonprint, 1991), 52.
129. Raymond Strait, *James Garner: A Biography* (New York: St. Martin's Press, 1985), 224.
130. David Shipman, *The Great Movie Stars: The Golden Years* (New York: Crown, 1970), 204.
131. David Shipman, *The Great Movie Stars: The International Years* (New York: St. Martin's Press, 1972), 491.
132. John Eastman, *Retakes: Behind the Scenes of 500 Classic Movies* (New York: Ballantine Books, 1989), 218.
133. Damien Bona, *Starring John Wayne as Genghis Khan* (Secaucus: Citadel Press, 1996), 205–206.
134. Anita M. Busch, "Reel World" *Entertainment Weekly*, 3 April 1998, 65.
135. Garry Jenkins, *Harrison Ford: Imperfect Hero* (Secaucus: Birch Lane Press, 1998), 82, 84.
136. Lana Turner, *Lana: The Lady, the Legend, the Truth* (New York: E. P. Dutton, 1982), 176–177.
137. Warren G. Harris, *Clark Gable: A Biography* (New York: Harmony Books, 2002), 328.
138. David Shipman, *The Great Movie Stars: The Golden Years* (New York: Crown, 1970), 193.
139. Faye Dunaway with Betsy Sharkey, *Looking for Gatsby: My Life* (New York: Simon & Schuster, 1995), 329.
140. Todd McCarthy, *Howard Hawks: The Grey Fox of Hollywood* (New York: Grove Press, 1997), 496.
141. Charles Chaplin, *My Autobiography* (New York: Simon and Schuster, 1964), 493.
142. Nancy Miller, "'Ball' Games" *Entertainment Weekly*, 19 July 2002, 9.
143. Yvonne De Carlo with Doug Warren, *Yvonne: An Autobiography* (New York: St. Martin's Press, 1987), 69.
144. Michael Viner and Terrie Maxine Frankel, *Tales from Casting Couch: An Unprecedented Candid Collection of Stories, Essays, and Anecdotes by and About Legendary Hollywood Stars, Starlets, and Wanna-bees...* (Beverly Hills: Dove Books, 1995), 169.
145. Dale Pollock, *Skywalking: The Life and Films of George Lucas* (New York: Harmony Books, 1983), 201.
146. Charlton Heston, *In the Arena: An Autobiography* (New York: Simon & Schuster, 1995), 310.
147. Paul Mazursky, *Show Me the Magic* (New York: Simon & Schuster, 1999), 177.
148. Garry Jenkins, *Harrison Ford: Imperfect Hero* (Secaucus: Birch Lane Press, 1998), 208.
149. Benjamin Svetkey, "Clown Jewel" *Entertainment Weekly*, 30 May 2003, 68.
150. David Shipman, *The Great Movie Stars: The Golden Years* (New York: Crown, 1970), 313.
151. Tom McGee, *Betty Grable: The Girl with the Million Dollar Legs* (Vestal: The Vestal Press, 1995), 138–140.
152. James L. Dickerson, *Nicole Kidman* (New York: Citadel Press, 2003), 134.
153. Steve Daly, "Chicago's Hope" *Entertainment Weekly*, 17 January 2003, 25.
154. Holly Millea, "Love Is a Battlefield" *Entertainment Weekly*, 29 March 2002, 38.
155. James Robert Parish and Ronald L. Bowers, *The MGM Stock Company: The Golden Era* (New Rochelle: Arlington House, 1973), 238.
156. Warren G. Harris, *Clark Gable: A Biography* (New York: Harmony Books, 2002), 228.
157. Patrick McGilligan, *Clint: The Life and Legend* (New York: St. Martin's Press, 1999), 228–229.
158. Michael Freedland, *The Warner Brothers* (New York: St. Martin's Press, 1983), 145.
159. Roy Pickard, *Jimmy Stewart: A Life in Film* (New York: St. Martin's Press, 1992), 33.
160. Frank Capra, *The Name Above the Title: An Autobiography* (New York: Macmillan, 1971), 262–263.
161. Frank Miller, *Movies We Love* (Atlanta: Turner, 1996), 202, 204.
162. Rachel Abramowitz, *Is That a Gun in Your Pocket?: Women's Experience of Power in Hollywood* (New York: Random House, 2000), 218.
163. Maximillian Potter, "A Man a Plan a Van" *Premiere*, December 1997, 100.
164. John Brodie, "The Wild Bunch" *Premiere*, March 1998, 65.
165. James Kotsilibas-Davis and Myrna Loy, *Myrna Loy: Being and Becoming* (New York: Alfred A. Knopf, 1987), 346.
166. Robert Evans, *Francis The Kid Stays in the Picture* (New York: Hyperion, 1994), 77.
167. Jeff Burkhart and Bruce Stuart, *Hollywood's First Choices* (New York: Crown Trade Paperbacks, 1994), 199.
168. John Eastman, *Retakes: Behind the Scenes of 500 Classic Movies* (New York: Ballantine Books, 1989), 224.
169. Jay Fultz, *In Search of Donna Reed* (Iowa City: University of Iowa Press, 1998), 61.
170. Graham McCann, *Cary Grant: A Class Apart* (New York: Columbia University Press, 1996), 323.
171. *New York Daily News* (New York), 9 September 1998.
172. Frank Miller, *Movies We Love* (Atlanta: Turner, 1996), 208.
173. James Robert Parish and Ronald L. Bowers, *The MGM Stock Company: The Golden Era* (New Rochelle: Arlington House, 1973), 725.
174. Mitchell Fink, "The Insider" *People*, 13 November 1995, 51.
175. James Spada, *Julia: Her Life* (New York: St. Martin's Press, 2004), 242.
176. Ron Base, *"If the Other Guy Isn't Jack Nicholson, I've Got the Part"* (Chicago: Contemporary Books, 1994), 284.
177. Rudy Behlmer, *Memo from Darryl F. Zanuck: The Golden Years at Twentieth Century-Fox* (New York: Grove Press, 1993), 101, 103.
178. Alan Jay Lerner, *On the Street Where I Live* (New York: Da Capo Press, 1994), 130–131.
179. Patrick McGilligan, *George Cukor: A Double Life* (New York: St. Martin's Press, 1991), 281–282.
180. Alan Jay Lerner, *On the Street Where I Live* (New York: Da Capo Press, 1994), 130–131.

181. Patrick McGilligan, *George Cukor: A Double Life* (New York: St. Martin's Press, 1991), 281–282.
182. Emanuel Levy, *George Cukor, Master of Elegance: Hollywood's Legendary Director and His Stars* (New York: William Morrow, 1994), 276.
183. Warren G. Harris, *Audrey Hepburn: A Biography* (New York: Simon & Schuster, 1994), 198.
184. Alan Jay Lerner, *On the Street Where I Live* (New York: Da Capo Press, 1994), 130–131.
185. Patrick McGilligan, *George Cukor: A Double Life* (New York: St. Martin's Press, 1991), 281–282.
186. Daniel Bubbeo, *The Women of Warner Brothers: The Lives and Careers of 15 Leading Ladies* (Jefferson: McFarland, 2002), 205.
187. Jane Lenz Elder, *Alice Faye* (Jackson: University Press of Mississippi, 2002), 159.
188. Tom McGee, *Betty Grable: The Girl with the Million Dollar Legs* (Vestal: The Vestal Press, 1995), 100.
189. Larry Swindell, *Screwball: The Life of Carole Lombard* (New York: William Morrow, 1975), 184–185.
190. James Robert Parish, *Gus Van Sant: An Unauthorized Biography* (New York: Thunder's Mouth Press, 2001), 126, 130–133.
191. Jason Bonderoff, *Tom Selleck: An Unauthorized Biography* (New York: Signet, 1983), 41.

N

1. Jan Stuart, *The Nashville Chronicles: The Making of Robert Altman's Masterpiece* (New York: Simon & Schuster, 2000), 85–86, 89, 92, 102.
2. Frank Miller, *Movies We Love* (Atlanta: Turner, 1996), 212.
3. James Riordan, *Stone: The Controversies, Excesses, and Exploits of a Radical Filmmaker* (New York: Hyperion, 1995), 491, 494.
4. Jane Hamsher, *Killer Instinct: How Two Young Producers Took on Hollywood and Made the Most Controversial Film of the Decade* (New York: Broadway Books, 1997), 102, 109.
5. James Riordan, *Stone: The Controversies, Excesses, and Exploits of a Radical Filmmaker* (New York: Hyperion, 1995), 491, 494.
6. Jane Hamsher, *Killer Instinct: How Two Young Producers Took on Hollywood and Made the Most Controversial Film of the Decade* (New York: Broadway Books, 1997), 102, 109.
7. James Riordan, *Stone: The Controversies, Excesses, and Exploits of a Radical Filmmaker* (New York: Hyperion, 1995), 491, 494.
8. Jane Hamsher, *Killer Instinct: How Two Young Producers Took on Hollywood and Made the Most Controversial Film of the Decade* (New York: Broadway Books, 1997), 102, 109.
9. James Riordan, *Stone: The Controversies, Excesses, and Exploits of a Radical Filmmaker* (New York: Hyperion, 1995), 491, 494.
10. Bob Woodward, *Wired: The Short Life & Fast Times of John Belushi* (New York: Simon and Schuster, 1984), 188–189, 192.
11. Ron Base, *"If the Other Guy Isn't Jack Nicholson, I've Got the Part"* (Chicago: Contemporary Books, 1994), 152.
12. Stephen Rebello, "Through the Eyes of Faye Dunaway" *Movieline*, June 2002, 91.
13. John Eastman, *Retakes: Behind the Scenes of 500 Classic Movies* (New York: Ballantine Books, 1989), 230–231.
14. Jeff Burkhart and Bruce Stuart, *Hollywood's First Choices* (New York: Crown Trade Paperbacks, 1994), 221.
15. Frank Miller, *Movies We Love* (Atlanta: Turner, 1996), 215.
16. Jeff Burkhart and Bruce Stuart, *Hollywood's First Choices* (New York: Crown Trade Paperbacks, 1994), 221.
17. John Eastman, *Retakes: Behind the Scenes of 500 Classic Movies* (New York: Ballantine Books, 1989), 231.
18. Marshall Terrill, *Steve McQueen: Portrait of an American Rebel* (New York: Donald I. Fine, 1993), 53–54.
19. Paul Mazursky, *Show Me the Magic* (New York: Simon & Schuster, 1999), 177.
20. David Shipman, *The Great Movie Stars: The International Years* (New York: St. Martin's Press, 1972), 40.
21. Shirley Temple Black, *Child Star: An Autobiography* (New York: McGraw-Hill, 1988), 331.
22. Warren G. Harris, *Audrey Hepburn: A Biography* (New York: Simon & Schuster, 1994), 243.
23. J. Randy Taraborrelli, *Once Upon a Time: Behind the Fairy Tale of Princess Grace and Prince Rainier* (New York: Warner Books, 2003), 352.
24. Nigel Andrews, *Travolta: The Life* (New York: Bloomsbury, 1998), 267.
25. Cybill Shepherd, *Cybill Disobedience* (New York: HarperCollins, 2000), 153–154.
26. Andrew Yule, *Picture Shows: The Life and Films of Peter Bogdanovich* (New York: Limelight Editions, 1992), 99.
27. Nellie Bly, *Marlon Brando: Larger Than Life* (New York: Pinnacle Books, 1994), 140.
28. Lawrence Grobel, *The Hustons* (New York: Scribner's, 1989), 530.
29. David Shipman, *The Great Movie Stars: The Golden Years* (New York: Crown, 1970), 151.
30. Dave Thompson, *Travolta* (Dallas: Taylor, 1996), 149.
31. Steve Dougherty, Lorna Grisby, "Her Dream Boat" *People*, 28 November 1994, 159.
32. John Baxter, *Steven Spielberg: The Unauthorized Biography* (London: HarperCollins, 1996), 181.
33. Jeff Burkhart and Bruce Stuart, *Hollywood's First Choices* (New York: Crown Trade Paperbacks, 1994), 196–197.
34. Paul Rosenfield, *The Club Rules: Power, Money, Sex, and Fear-How It Works in Hollywood* (New York: Warner Books, 1992), 157.
35. Eric Hamburg, *JFK, Nixon, Oliver Stone & Me: An Idealist's Journey from Capitol Hill to Hollywood Hell* (New York: Public Affairs, 2002), 117–120.
36. Eliza Bergman Krause, Kristen O'Neill, Maximillian Potter and Christine Spines, "The Ultimate Fall Preview" *Premiere*, October 1995, 114.
37. Warren G. Harris, *Clark Gable: A Biography* (New York: Harmony Books, 2002), 95, 97.
38. Jason Bonderoff, *Sally Field: A Biography* (New York: St. Martin's Press, 1987), 118–120.
39. George F. Custen, *Twentieth Century's Fox* (New York: BasicBooks, 1997), 335.
40. Barry Paris, *Audrey Hepburn* (New York: G. P. Putnam's Sons, 1996), 285.
41. Paul Rosenfield, *The Club Rules: Power, Money, Sex, and Fear-How It Works in Hollywood* (New York: Warner Books, 1992), 182.

42. Ron Base, *"If the Other Guy Isn't Jack Nicholson, I've Got the Part"* (Chicago: Contemporary Books, 1994), 152.
43. Ron Base, *"If the Other Guy Isn't Jack Nicholson, I've Got the Part"* (Chicago: Contemporary Books, 1994), 152.
44. Brantley Bardin, "Idol Chatter: Jill Clayburgh" *Premiere*, August 2002, 92.
45. Marsha Mason, *Journey: A Personal Odyssey* (New York: Simon & Schuster, 2000), 208–209.
46. Frank Miller, *Movies We Love* (Atlanta: Turner, 1996), 226.
47. A. Scott Berg, *Goldwyn: A Biography* (New York: Alfred A. Knopf, 1989), 375–376.
48. Ron Base, *"If the Other Guy Isn't Jack Nicholson, I've Got the Part"* (Chicago: Contemporary Books, 1994), 37.
49. Garry Marshall with Lori Marshall, *Wake Me When It's Funny* (Holbrook: Adams, 1995), 191.
50. John Eastman, *Retakes: Behind the Scenes of 500 Classic Movies* (New York: Ballantine Books, 1989), 238–239.(Webb, Barrymore)
51. Frank Miller, *Movies We Love* (Atlanta: Turner, 1996), 229, 231.
52. Ginger Rogers, *Ginger: My Story* (New York: HarperCollins, 1991), 248.
53. Frank Miller, *Movies We Love* (Atlanta: Turner, 1996), 229, 231.
54. Steve Daly, "Daze of Her Lives" *Entertainment Weekly*, 15 September 2000, 41.
55. Randall Riese, *Her Name Is Barbra* (New York: St. Martin's Paperbacks, 1993), 475–479.
56. Ron Base, *"If the Other Guy Isn't Jack Nicholson, I've Got the Part"* (Chicago: Contemporary Books, 1994), 279.
57. Randall Riese, *Her Name Is Barbra* (New York: St. Martin's Paperbacks, 1993), 475–479.
58. Randall Riese, *Her Name Is Barbra* (New York: St. Martin's Paperbacks, 1993), 475–479.

O

1. Daniel Fierman, "The Story of O" *Entertainment Weekly*, 10 August 2001, 22.
2. Rebecca Ascher-Walsh, "Boy Meets Girl, Boy Meets Boy…" *Entertainment Weekly*, 24 April 1998, 40–41.
3. Jess Cagle, "Sarah Jessica Parker … What Kind of Household Name Is That?" *Entertainment Weekly*, 1 October 1993, 46.
4. Rebecca Ascher-Walsh, "Boy Meets Girl, Boy Meets Boy…" *Entertainment Weekly*, 24 April 1998, 40–41.
5. Scott Brown, "The Man Who Would Be Keanu" *Entertainment Weekly*, 7 November 2003, 27.
6. Daniel Fierman, "Indecision 2000" *Entertainment Weekly*, 1 December 2000, 13.
7. Stephen Rebello, "Steven Soderbergh Is So Money" *Movieline*, December/January 2002, 60.
8. *New York Daily News* (New York), 7 March 2001.
9. Mark Schwed, "Licensed to Still Thrill" *TV Guide*, 13 November 1999, 28.
10. John Eastman, *Retakes: Behind the Scenes of 500 Classic Movies* (New York: Ballantine Books, 1989), 240.
11. Evelyn Keyes, *Scarlett O'Hara's Younger Sister* (New York: Fawcett Crest Books, 1977), 34.
12. Gary Socol, "Ron Livingston" *Movieline*, March 1999, 22.
13. Charles Fleming, *High Concept: Don Simpson and the Hollywood Culture of Excess* (New York: Doubleday, 1998), 35–36.
14. Nigel Andrews, *Travolta: The Life* (New York: Bloomsbury, 1998), 123.
15. Charles Fleming, *High Concept: Don Simpson and the Hollywood Culture of Excess* (New York: Doubleday, 1998), 35–36.
16. Ron Base, *"If the Other Guy Isn't Jack Nicholson, I've Got the Part"* (Chicago: Contemporary Books, 1994), 244.
17. Charles Fleming, *High Concept: Don Simpson and the Hollywood Culture of Excess* (New York: Doubleday, 1998), 35–36.
18. John Eastman, *Retakes: Behind the Scenes of 500 Classic Movies* (New York: Ballantine Books, 1989), 241–242.
19. Tom Hutchinson, *Rod Steiger* (New York: Fromm International, 2000), 91.
20. Fred Zinnemann, *A Life in the Movies* (New York: Scribner's, 1992), 117.
21. Vincent Curcio, *Suicide Blonde: The Life of Gloria Grahame* (New York: William Morrow, 1989), 165.
22. Gavin Lambert, *Norma Shearer* (New York: Alfred A. Knopf, 1990), 311.
23. James Spada, *More Than a Woman: An Intimate Biography of Bette Davis* (New York: Bantam Books, 1993), 196.
24. Gary Fishgall, *Gregory Peck: A Biography* (New York: Scribner, 2002), 316–318.
25. Damien Bona, *Starring John Wayne as Genghis Khan* (Secaucus: Citadel Press, 1996), 103.
26. Robert F. Moss, *The Films of Carol Reed* (New York: Columbia University Press, 1987), 248, 250, 251.
27. Charlton Heston, *In the Arena: An Autobiography* (New York: Simon & Schuster, 1995), 438.
28. Charlton Heston, *The Actor's Life: Journals 1956–1976* (New York: E. P. Dutton, 1976, 1978), 453.
29. Charlton Heston, *In the Arena: An Autobiography* (New York: Simon & Schuster, 1995), 310.
30. James Spada, *Streisand: Her Life* (New York: Ivy Books, 1995), 254.
31. James Spada, *Streisand: Her Life* (New York: Ivy Books, 1995), 254.
32. Randall Riese, *Her Name Is Barbra* (New York: St. Martin's Paperbacks, 1993), 317.
33. James Spada, *Streisand: Her Life* (New York: Ivy Books, 1995), 254.
34. Axel Madsen, *Stanwyck* (New York: HarperCollins, 1994), 348.
35. Steven Jay Rubin, *The James Bond Films* (Westport: Arlington House, 1981), 86.
36. Steven Jay Rubin, *The Complete James Bond Movie Encyclopedia* (Chicago: Contemporary Books, 1990), 27, 104–105.
37. William Goldman, *Adventures in the Screen Trade* (New York: Warner Books, 1983), 14.
38. Nellie Bly, *Marlon Brando: Larger Than Life* (New York: Pinnacle Books, 1994), 58.
39. Tom Hutchinson, *Rod Steiger* (New York: Fromm International, 2000), 80–81.
40. John Eastman, *Retakes: Behind the Scenes of 500 Classic Movies* (New York: Ballantine Books, 1989), 246.
41. Axel Madsen, *Stanwyck* (New York: HarperCollins, 1994), 100.
42. David Shipman, *The Great Movie Stars: The Golden Years* (New York: Crown, 1970), 344.

43. David Shipman, *The Great Movie Stars: The International Years* (New York: St. Martin's Press, 1972), 101.
44. John Eastman, *Retakes: Behind the Scenes of 500 Classic Movies* (New York: Ballantine Books, 1989), 247.
45. *New York Daily News* (New York), 20 August 201.
46. Ron Base, *"If the Other Guy Isn't Jack Nicholson, I've Got the Part"* (Chicago: Contemporary Books, 1994), 175–176.
47. Peter Thompson, *Jack Nicholson: The Life and Times of an Actor on the Edge* (Secaucus: Birch Lane Press, 1997), 196–197.
48. John Eastman, *Retakes: Behind the Scenes of 500 Classic Movies* (New York: Ballantine Books, 1989), 247.
49. Jan Stuart, *The Nashville Chronicles: The Making of Robert Altman's Masterpiece* (New York: Simon & Schuster, 2000), 92.
50. David Shipman, *The Great Movie Stars: The Golden Years* (New York: Crown, 1970), 20, 476.
51. Evelyn Keyes, *Scarlett O'Hara's Younger Sister* (New York: Fawcett Crest Books, 1977), 34.
52. Peter Haining, *Raquel Welch: Sex Symbol to Super Star* (New York: St. Martin's Press 1984), 47.
53. Lee Server, *Robert Mitchum: "Baby, I Don't Care"* (New York: St. Martin's Press, 2001), 223.
54. *New York Daily News* (New York), 7 October 1998.
55. Todd McCarthy, *Howard Hawks: The Grey Fox of Hollywood* (New York: Grove Press, 1997), 270–271, 294.
56. John Parker, *Warren Beatty: The Last Great Lover of Hollywood* (New York: Carroll & Graf, 1993), 157.
57. David Shipman, *The Great Movie Stars: The Golden Years* (New York: Crown, 1970), 510.
58. Ryan Murphy, "Happily Ever Oscar" *Entertainment Weekly*, 16 April 1993, 13.
59. David Shipman, *The Great Movie Stars: The International Years* (New York: St. Martin's Press, 1972), 85
60. Tony Curtis and Barry Paris, *Tony Curtis: The Autobiography* (New York: William Morrow, 1993), 172.
61. John Eastman, *Retakes: Behind the Scenes of 500 Classic Movies* (New York: Ballantine Books, 1989), 248.
62. Suzanne Finstad, *Natasha: The Biography of Natalie Wood* (New York: Harmony Books, 2001), 319–320.
63. Jeff Burkhart and Bruce Stuart, *Hollywood's First Choices* (New York: Crown Trade Paperbacks, 1994), 206.
64. John Eastman, *Retakes: Behind the Scenes of 500 Classic Movies* (New York: Ballantine Books, 1989), 248.
65. Barry Paris, *Audrey Hepburn* (New York: G. P. Putnam's Sons, 1996), 270–271.
66. Rebecca Ascher-Walsh, Kristen Baldwin, Anita M. Busch, Steve Daly, Andrew Essex, Daniel Fierman, Jeff Gardinier, David Hochman, Dave Karger, Tricia Laine, Chris Nashawaty, Joe Neumaier, Degen Pener, Megan Quitkin, Jessica Shaw, Tom Sinclair, Benjamin Svetkey, "The Following Summer Movie Preview Has Been Approved for All Audiences by the Editors of Entertainment Weekly" *Entertainment Weekly*, 15 May 1998, 36.
67. William Donati, *Ida Lupino: A Biography* (Lexington: The University Press of Kentucky, 1996), 23–77.
68. Frank Miller, *Movies We Love* (Atlanta: Turner, 1996), 232.
69. David Shipman, *The Great Movie Stars: The Golden Years* (New York: Crown, 1970), 58.
70. Todd McCarthy, *Howard Hawks: The Grey Fox of Hollywood* (New York: Grove Press, 1997), 294.
71. Lawrence J. Quirk, *Paul Newman* (Dallas: Taylor, 1996), 130.
72. Larissa MacFarquhar, "Stranger in Paradise" *Premiere*, June 1997, 72.
73. James Spada, *Streisand: Her Life* (New York: Ivy Books, 1995), 273.
74. Randall Riese, *Her Name Is Barbra* (New York: St. Martin's Paperbacks, 1993), 343.
75. James Spada, *Streisand: Her Life* (New York: Ivy Books, 1995), 273.
76. James Spada, *Streisand: Her Life* (New York: Ivy Books, 1995), 273.
77. James Spada, *Streisand: Her Life* (New York: Ivy Books, 1995), 273.

P

1. Peter Fonda, *Don't Tell Dad: A Memoir* (New York: Hyperion, 1998), 160–162.
2. Ellis Amburn, *The Sexiest Man Alive: A Biography of Warren Beatty* (New York: HarperCollins, 2002), 46.
3. David Shipman, *The Great Movie Stars: The Golden Years* (New York: Crown, 1970), 127.
4. David Shipman, *The Great Movie Stars: The Golden Years* (New York: Crown, 1970), 137.
5. Stephen M. Silverman, *Dancing on the Ceiling: Stanley Donen and His Movies* (New York: Alfred A. Knopf, 1996), 247–249.
6. Alvin Yudkoff, *Gene Kelly: A Life of Dance and Dreams* (New York: Back Stage Books, 1999), 136–139.
7. Axel Madsen, *Stanwyck* (New York: HarperCollins, 1994), 314–315.
8. Axel Madsen, *Stanwyck* (New York: HarperCollins, 1994), 314–315.
9. Barbara Leaming, *If This Was Happiness: A Biography of Rita Hayworth* (New York: Viking, 1989), 324.
10. James L. Dickerson, *Nicole Kidman* (New York: Citadel Press, 2003), 145.
11. John Eastman, *Retakes: Behind the Scenes of 500 Classic Movies* (New York: Ballantine Books, 1989), 251.
12. Peter Biskind, *Easy Riders, Raging Bulls* (New York: Simon & Schuster, 1998), 211.
13. Marshall Terrill, *Steve McQueen: Portrait of an American Rebel* (New York: Donald I. Fine, 1993), 258.
14. Ronald Haver, *David O. Selznick's Hollywood* (New York: Alfred A. Knopf, 1980), 374, 377, 378.
15. David Thomson, *Showman: The Life of David O. Selznick* (New York: Alfred A. Knopf, 1992), 483.
16. Ronald Haver, *David O. Selznick's Hollywood* (New York: Alfred A. Knopf, 1980), 374, 377, 378.
17. R. Dixon Smith, *Ronald Colman, Gentleman of the Cinema* (Jefferson: McFarland, 1991), 143.
18. James Kotsilibas-Davis and Myrna Loy, *Myrna Loy: Being and Becoming* (New York: Alfred A. Knopf, 1987), 145.
19. David Shipman, *The Great Movie Stars: The International Years* (New York: St. Martin's Press, 1972), 41.
20. Marshall Fine, *Bloody Sam: The Life and Films of Sam Peckinpah* (New York: Donald I. Fine, 1991), 244–245.
21. Garry Jenkins, *Harrison Ford: Imperfect Hero* (Secaucus: Birch Lane Press, 1998), 261.
22. Susan Sackett, *The Hollywood Reporter Book of Box Office Hits* (New York: Billboard Books, 1990), 214.
23. Tom Hutchinson, *Rod Steiger* (New York: Fromm International, 2000), 125.

24. Seth Cagin, *Hollywood Films of the 70s: Sex, Drugs, Violence, Rock 'N' Roll & Politics* (New York: Harper & Row, 1984), 150.
25. Jeff Burkhart and Bruce Stuart, *Hollywood's First Choices* (New York: Crown Trade Paperbacks, 1994), 218.
26. Randall Riese, *Her Name Is Barbra* (New York: St. Martin's Paperbacks, 1993), 262.
27. Joe Rhodes, "Back in Action" *TV Guide*, 23 October 1999, 43–44.
28. Daniel Fierman, "The Actor: Ben Affleck" *Entertainment Weekly*, 14 November 2003, 53.
29. Jeffrey Lantos, "He Got Game" *Movieline*, June 2000, 70–71.
30. *New York Daily News* (New York), 2 March 2000.
31. *New York Daily News* (New York), 2 March 2000.
32. David Hochman, "Pearl Bucks" *Entertainment Weekly*, February 11 2000, 8.
33. Michael Schumacher, *Francis Ford Coppola* (New York: Crown, 1999), 371.
34. Michael Goodwin and Naomi Wise, *On the Edge: The Life & Times of Francis Coppola* (New York: William Morrow, 1989), 420.
35. Benjamin Svetkey, "Porn on the 4th of July" *Entertainment Weekly*, 31 January 1997, 20.
36. Michael Fleming, "Casting Glances" *Movieline*, June 1997, 65.
37. Benjamin Svetkey, "Porn on the 4th of July" *Entertainment Weekly*, 31 January 1997, 20.
38. David Shipman, *The Great Movie Stars: The International Years* (New York: St. Martin's Press, 1972), 39–40.
39. Tom O'Neill, "Hollywood's Cast System" *Us*, June 1995, 80, 83, 92.
40. Michael Fleming, "The Perfect Guy for the Perfect Storm" *Movieline*, July 2000, 62, 63.
41. Christine Spines, "Leader of the Pack" *Premiere*, January 2002, 56.
42. Michael Fleming, "The Perfect Guy for the Perfect Storm" *Movieline*, July 2000, 62, 63.
43. Frank Spotnitz, "News & Notes" *Entertainment Weekly*, 30 July 1993, 10.
44. John Eastman, *Retakes: Behind the Scenes of 500 Classic Movies* (New York: Ballantine Books, 1989), 256.
45. Stephen Rebello, "The Next McCarty Era" *Movieline*, August 1998, 56.
46. Laurent Bouzereau, *The DePalma Cut: The Films of America's Most Controversial Director* (New York: Dembner Books, 1988), 37.
47. David Shipman, *The Great Movie Stars: The International Years* (New York: St. Martin's Press, 1972), 397.
48. Lee Pfeiffer and Michael Lewis, *The Films of Tom Hanks* (Secaucus: Citadel Press, 1996), 158.
49. Tom Roston, "The Man Who Knew Too Much" *Premiere*, September 2002, 86.
50. Frank Miller, *Movies We Love* (Atlanta: Turner, 1996), 235, 237.
51. Steve Daly, "The New Recruit" *Entertainment Weekly*, 3 November 2000, 23.
52. Fred Schruers, "Class President" *Premiere*, November 2003, 72.
53. Samuel Fuller, *A Third Face: My Tale of Writing, Fighting, and Filmmaking* (New York: Alfred A. Knopf, 2002), 300.
54. Nellie Bly, *Marlon Brando: Larger Than Life* (New York: Pinnacle Books, 1994), 62.
55. Carroll Baker, *Baby Doll: An Autobiography* (New York: Arbor House, 1983), 91.
56. John Eastman, *Retakes: Behind the Scenes of 500 Classic Movies* (New York: Ballantine Books, 1989), 257.
57. Carroll Baker, *Baby Doll: An Autobiography* (New York: Arbor House, 1983), 91.
58. John Eastman, *Retakes: Behind the Scenes of 500 Classic Movies* (New York: Ballantine Books, 1989), 257.
59. John Eastman, *Retakes: Behind the Scenes of 500 Classic Movies* (New York: Ballantine Books, 1989), 258.
60. Gene Brown, *Movie Time: A Chronology of Hollywood and the Movie Industry from Its Beginnings to the Present* (New York: Macmillan, 1995), 286.
61. Hedy Lamarr, *Ecstasy and Me: My Life as a Woman* (U.S.A.: Bartholomew House, 1966), 293, 300–302.
62. Robert Edelman and Audrey Kupferberg, *Angela Lansbury: A Life on Stage and Screen* (Thorndike: G.K. Hall, and Bath: Chivers Press, 1996), 63.
63. John Eastman, *Retakes: Behind the Scenes of 500 Classic Movies* (New York: Ballantine Books, 1989), 260.
64. Jeff Burkhart and Bruce Stuart, *Hollywood's First Choices* (New York: Crown Trade Paperbacks, 1994), 218.
65. Donald Bogle, *Dorothy Dandridge: A Biography* (New York: Amistad Press, 1997), 162–164.
66. Patrick McGilligan, *Jack's Life: A Biography of Jack Nicholson* (New York, London: W. W. Norton, 1994), 293–294.
67. Joe Russo and Larry Landsman with Edward Gross, *Planet of the Apes Revisited: The Behind-The Scenes Story of the Classic Science Fiction Saga* (New York: Thomas Dunne Books, 2001), 48–49.
68. Charlton Heston, *The Actor's Life: Journals 1956–1976* (New York: E. P. Dutton, 1976, 1978), 271.
69. James Riordan, *Stone: The Controversies, Excesses, and Exploits of a Radical Filmmaker* (New York: Hyperion, 1995), 185.
70. Ron Base, *"If the Other Guy Isn't Jack Nicholson, I've Got the Part"* (Chicago: Contemporary Books, 1994), 243.
71. James Riordan, *Stone: The Controversies, Excesses, and Exploits of a Radical Filmmaker* (New York: Hyperion, 1995), 185.
72. David Shipman, *The Great Movie Stars: The International Years* (New York: St. Martin's Press, 1972), 204.
73. John Baxter, *Woody Allen: A Biography* (New York: Carroll & Graf, 1998), 193.
74. Marshall Terrill, *Steve McQueen: Portrait of an American Rebel* (New York: Donald I. Fine, 1993), 423.
75. Nigel Andrews, *Travolta: The Life* (New York: Bloomsbury, 1998), 215.
76. Christina Kelly, "You Made Gillian Cry" *Jane*, January/February 1999, 108.
77. Frank Castelluccio and Alvin Walker, *The Other Side of Ethel Mertz: The Life Story of Vivian Vance* (Manchester: Knowledge, Ideas & Trends, 1998), 286.
78. Frank Capra, *The Name Above the Title: An Autobiography* (New York: Macmillan, 1971), 471–475.
79. Lawrence Grobel, *The Hustons* (New York: Scribner's, 1989), 638.
80. Joseph McBride, *Frank Capra: The Catastrophe of Success* (New York: Simon & Schuster, 1992), 638.
81. Frank Capra, *The Name Above the Title: An Autobiography* (New York: Macmillan, 1971), 471–475.
82. William F. Nolan, *McQueen* (New York: Congdon & Weed, 1984), 42.

83. Frank Capra, *The Name Above the Title: An Autobiography* (New York: Macmillan, 1971), 471–475.
84. Leslie Van Buskirk, "Johnny Depp" *Us*, February 1994, 41.
85. James Robert Parish, *Whoopi Goldberg: Her Journey from Poverty to Megastardom* (Secaucus: Birch Lane Press, 1996), 277–278.
86. Robert Evans, *Francis The Kid Stays in the Picture* (New York: Hyperion, 1994), 294–295.
87. David Saltman, *Gilda: An Intimate Portrait* (Chicago: Contemporary Books, 1992), 194–195.
88. A. Scott Berg, *Goldwyn: A Biography* (New York: Alfred A. Knopf, 1989), 479, 482.
89. Ronald Haver, *David O. Selznick's Hollywood* (New York: Alfred A. Knopf, 1980), 380.
90. Esther Williams with Digby Diehl, *The Million Dollar Mermaid* (New York: Simon & Schuster, 1999), 363.
91. Christine Spines, "Neil LaBute" *Premiere*, September 2002, 32.
92. Frank Miller, *Movies We Love* (Atlanta: Turner, 1996), 240.
93. Douglas Brode, *The Films of Jack Nicholson* (Secaucus: Citadel Press, 1987), 212–213.
94. Eugene E. Pfaff and Mark Emerson, *Meryl Streep: A Critical Biography* (Jefferson: McFarland, 1987), 7.
95. Jay Boyer, *Bob Rafelson* (New York: Twayne, 1996), 78.
96. David Hochman, "Next of Kim" *Entertainment Weekly*, 3 October 1997, 35.
97. David Shipman, *Judy Garland: The Secret Life of an American Legend* (New York: Hyperion, 1992), 133–134.
98. Ron Base, *"If the Other Guy Isn't Jack Nicholson, I've Got the Part"* (Chicago: Contemporary Books, 1994), 244.
99. Garry Jenkins, *Harrison Ford: Imperfect Hero* (Secaucus: Birch Lane Press, 1998), 247.
100. *New York Daily News* (New York), 21 March 1999.
101. Jeffrey Lantos, "Runaway Funny" *Movieline*, July 1999, 68–69.
102. Benjamin Svetkey, "Clown Jewel" *Entertainment Weekly*, 30 May 2003, 67.
103. James Spada, *Julia: Her Life* (New York: St. Martin's Press, 2004), 116.
104. Michael Fleming, "Fearless Leigh" *Movieline*, April 1999, 63.
105. Michael Fleming, "Casting Glances" *Movieline*, June 1997, 64–65.
106. Tom Russo, "What If…?" *Premiere*, February 2004, 87.
107. Michael Fleming, "Fearless Leigh" *Movieline*, April 1999, 63.
108. Garry Marshall with Lori Marshall, *Wake Me When It's Funny* (Holbrook: Adams, 1995), 206.
109. Frank Miller, *Movies We Love* (Atlanta: Turner, 1996), 241.
110. Donald Spoto, *Laurence Olivier: A Biography* (New York: HarperCollins, 1992), 143.
111. David Shipman, *The Great Movie Stars: The International Years* (New York: St. Martin's Press, 1972), 296.
112. Degen Pener, "Playing the No-Name Game" *Entertainment Weekly*, 12 April 1996, 18.
113. Martha Frankel, "He Puts the X in Sexy" *Movieline's Hollywood Life*, May/June 2003, 96.
114. Michael Atkinson, "The Sober Sensation" *Movieline*, February 1999, 77.
115. Hollywood Kids, "Q&A: Danny Masterson" *Movieline*, May 1998, 38.
116. Chris Nickson, *Matt Damon: An Unauthorized Biography* (Los Angeles: Renaissance Books, 1999), 91.
117. Benjamin Svetkey, "The Faking of the President 1998" *Entertainment Weekly*, 27 March 1998, 28.
118. Martin Gottfried, *Balancing Act: The Authorized Biography of Angela Lansbury* (Boston, New York, London: Little, Brown, 1999), 250.
119. Robert Windeler, *Julie Andrews: A Life on Stage and Screen* (Secaucus: Birch Lane Press, 1997), 174.
120. David Shipman, *The Great Movie Stars: The International Years* (New York: St. Martin's Press, 1972), 245.
121. Andrew Yule, *Life on the Wire: The Life and Art of Al Pacino* (New York: Donald I. Fine, 1991), 200.
122. Laurent Bouzereau, *The DePalma Cut: The Films of America's Most Controversial Director* (New York: Dembner Books, 1988), 63.
123. James Spada, *Streisand: Her Life* (New York: Ivy Books, 1992), 486–487, 490–491, 496.
124. Randall Riese, *Her Name Is Barbra* (New York: St. Martin's Paperbacks, 1993), 489, 498, 500–501, 523.
125. James Spada, *Streisand: Her Life* (New York: Ivy Books, 1992), 486–487, 490–491, 496.
126. Randall Riese, *Her Name Is Barbra* (New York: St. Martin's Paperbacks, 1993), 489, 498, 500–501, 523.
127. James Spada, *Streisand: Her Life* (New York: Ivy Books, 1992), 486–487, 490–491, 496.
128. James Spada, *Streisand: Her Life* (New York: Ivy Books, 1992), 486–487, 490–491, 496.
129. Randall Riese, *Her Name Is Barbra* (New York: St. Martin's Paperbacks, 1993), 489, 498, 500–501, 523.
130. James Spada, *Streisand: Her Life* (New York: Ivy Books, 1992), 486–487, 490–491, 496.
131. Randall Riese, *Her Name Is Barbra* (New York: St. Martin's Paperbacks, 1993), 489, 498, 500–501, 523.
132. Michael A. Lipton and Bonnie Bell, "How Sweet It Is" *People*, 8 February 1993, 46.
133. William Goldman, *Hype and Glory* (New York: Villard Books, 1990), 115–116, 136.
134. David Shipman, *The Great Movie Stars: The Golden Years* (New York: Crown, 1970), 448.
135. James Spada, *More Than a Woman: An Intimate Biography of Bette Davis* (New York: Bantam Books, 1993), 160.
136. James Kotsilibas-Davis and Myrna Loy, *Myrna Loy: Being and Becoming* (New York: Alfred A. Knopf, 1987), 83.
137. John Eastman, *Retakes: Behind the Scenes of 500 Classic Movies* (New York: Ballantine Books, 1989), 270.
138. Ed Sikov, *Mr. Strangelove: A Biography of Peter Sellers* (New York: Hyperion, 2002), 266.
139. John Eastman, *Retakes: Behind the Scenes of 500 Classic Movies* (New York: Ballantine Books, 1989), 271.
140. Stephen Rebello, "Taylor Made" *Movieline*, November 2000, 71–72.
141. Stephen Rebello, *Alfred Hitchcock and the Making of Psycho* (New York: Dembner Books, 1976, 1990), 60, 62, 65.
142. Stephen Rebello, *Alfred Hitchcock and the Making of Psycho* (New York: Dembner Books, 1976, 1990), 60, 62, 65.
143. Janet Leigh with Christopher Nickens, *Psycho: Behind the Scenes of the Classic Thriller* (New York: Harmony Books, 1995), 15.

144. Stephen Rebello, *Alfred Hitchcock and the Making of Psycho* (New York: Dembner Books, 1976, 1990), 60, 62, 65.
145. Stephen Rebello, "Return to Bates Motel" *Movieline*, December/January 1999, 71–72.
146. David Stenn, *Bombshell: The Life and Death of Jean Harlow* (New York: Doubleday, 1993), 56.
147. John Eastman, *Retakes: Behind the Scenes of 500 Classic Movies* (New York: Ballantine Books, 1989), 273.
148. David Shipman, *The Great Movie Stars: The Golden Years* (New York: Crown, 1970), 83.
149. Jami Bernard, *Quentin Tarantino: The Man and His Movies* (New York: HarperPerennial, 1995), 190–191, 196–197, 201–202.
150. Jami Bernard, *Quentin Tarantino: The Man and His Movies* (New York: HarperPerennial, 1995), 190–191, 196–197, 201–202.
151. Claudia Dreifus, "Sam I Am" *Premiere*, June 1995, 94.
152. Jeff Dawson, *Quentin Tarantino: The Cinema of Cool* (New York: Applause Books, 1995), 155, 189.
153. Jami Bernard, *Quentin Tarantino: The Man and His Movies* (New York: HarperPerennial, 1995), 190–191, 196–197, 201–202.
154. Jami Bernard, *Quentin Tarantino: The Man and His Movies* (New York: HarperPerennial, 1995), 190–191, 196–197, 201–202.
155. Lyall Bush, "Waiting for Hitchcock" *Movie Maker*, May/June/July 1997, 36.
156. John Parker, *Bruce Willis: The Unauthorized Biography* (London: Virgin Books, 1997), 8.
157. Jeff Dawson, *Quentin Tarantino: The Cinema of Cool* (New York: Applause Books, 1995), 155, 189.
158. Rebecca Ascher-Walsh, Steve Daly, Jeff Gardinier, David Hochman, Dave Karger, Dana Kennedy, Gregg Kilday, Tricia Laine, Chris Nashawaty, Degen Pener, Erin Richter, Jessica Shaw, Benjamin Svetkey, Caren Weiner, Chris Willman, "Fall Movie Guide" *Entertainment Weekly*, 22/29 August 1997, 94.
159. Jami Bernard, *Quentin Tarantino: The Man and His Movies* (New York: HarperPerennial, 1995), 190–191, 196–197, 201–202.
160. Eric Lax, *Woody Allen: A Biography* (New York: Alfred A. Knopf, 1991), 303.
161. John Baxter, *Woody Allen: A Biography* (New York: Carroll & Graf, 1998), 327–328.

Q

1. Jeff Burkhart and Bruce Stuart, *Hollywood's First Choices* (New York: Crown Trade Paperbacks, 1994), 32.
2. Anthony Holden, *Laurence Olivier: A Biography* (New York: Atheneum, 1988), 75.
3. Steven Bach, *Marlene Dietrich: Life and Legend* (New York: William Morrow, 1992), 203.
4. R. Dixon Smith, *Ronald Colman, Gentleman of the Cinema* (Jefferson: McFarland, 1991), 140.
5. David Shipman, *The Great Movie Stars: The Golden Years* (New York: Crown, 1970), 291.
6. *New York Daily News* (New York), 2 March 2000.
7. David Shipman, *The Great Movie Stars: The Golden Years* (New York: Crown, 1970), 359.
8. Chris Nickson, *Matt Damon: An Unauthorized Biography* (Los Angeles: Renaissance Books, 1999), 71, 76.
9. Marshall Terrill, *Steve McQueen: Portrait of an American Rebel* (New York: Donald I. Fine, 1993), 429.
10. Warren G. Harris, *Clark Gable: A Biography* (New York: Harmony Books, 2002), 302.
11. Frank Miller, *Movies We Love* (Atlanta: Turner, 1996), 247, 249.

R

1. Lawrence J. Quirk, *Paul Newman* (Dallas: Taylor, 1996), 65.
2. Clive Hirschhorn, *The Columbia Story* (London: Hamlyn, 1999), 359.
3. Daniel Bubbeo, *The Women of Warner Brothers: The Lives and Careers of 15 Leading Ladies* (Jefferson: McFarland, 2002), 33.
4. A. Scott Berg, *Goldwyn: A Biography* (New York: Alfred A. Knopf, 1989), 334–336
5. Rachel Abramowitz, *Is That a Gun in Your Pocket?: Women's Experience of Power in Hollywood* (New York: Random House, 2000), 118.
6. John Eastman, *Retakes: Behind the Scenes of 500 Classic Movies* (New York: Ballantine Books, 1989), 278.
7. Jason Bonderoff, *Tom Selleck: An Unauthorized Biography* (New York: Signet, 1983), 127–128.
8. John Baxter, *Steven Spielberg: The Unauthorized Biography* (London: HarperCollins, 1996), 208, 209, 336.
9. Ron Base, *"If the Other Guy Isn't Jack Nicholson, I've Got the Part"* (Chicago: Contemporary Books, 1994), 146.
10. Janice Dickinson, *No Lifeguard on Duty: The Accidental Life of the World's First Supermodel* (New York: ReganBooks, 2002), 165.
11. Garry Jenkins, *Harrison Ford: Imperfect Hero* (Secaucus: Birch Lane Press, 1998), 160.
12. Jason Matloff, "Serial Thrillers" *Premiere*, October 2003, 75.
13. Jason Matloff, "Serial Thrillers" *Premiere*, October 2003, 75.
14. John Baxter, *Steven Spielberg: The Unauthorized Biography* (London: HarperCollins, 1996), 208, 209, 336.
15. Jason Matloff, "Serial Thrillers" *Premiere*, October 2003, 75.
16. John Baxter, *Steven Spielberg: The Unauthorized Biography* (London: HarperCollins, 1996), 208, 209, 336.
17. Tom Russo, "What If...?" *Premiere*, February 2004, 87.
18. Ty Burr, "Good at What Ails Them" *Entertainment Weekly*, Special Oscar Guide March 1997, 37.
19. Peter Bart, *Fade Out: The Calamitous Final Days of MGM* (New York: William Morrow, 1990), 263–264.
20. Yvonne De Carlo with Doug Warren, *Yvonne: An Autobiography* (New York: St. Martin's Press, 1987), 82.
21. *New York Daily News* (New York), 15 November 1999.
22. Kate Buford, *Burt Lancaster: An American Life* (New York: Alfred A. Knopf, 2000), 162.
23. Michael Schumacher, *Francis Ford Coppola* (New York: Crown, 1999), 473.
24. James Kotsilibas and Myrna Loy, *Myrna Loy: Being and Becoming* (New York: Alfred A. Knopf, 1987), 157.
25. Marshall Terrill, *Steve McQueen: Portrait of an American Rebel* (New York: Donald I. Fine, 1993), 426.
26. Joan Collins, *Past Imperfect: An Autobiography* (New York: Berkley Books, 1985), 123.

27. Barbara Leaming, *If This Was Happiness: A Biography of Rita Hayworth* (New York: Viking, 1989), 32–33.
28. David Shipman, *Judy Garland: The Secret Life of an American Legend* (New York: Hyperion, 1992), 183.
29. Tom McGee, *Betty Grable: The Girl with the Million Dollar Legs* (Vestal: The Vestal Press, 1995), 134.
30. Jeff Burkhart and Bruce Stuart, *Hollywood's First Choices* (New York: Crown Trade Paperbacks, 1994), 210.
31. David Shipman, *The Great Movie Stars: The Golden Years* (New York: Crown, 1970), 248.
32. John Russell Taylor, *Hitch: The Life and Times of Alfred Hitchcock* (New York: Pantheon Books, 1978), 156.
33. Donald Spoto, *The Dark Side of Genius: The Life of Alfred Hitchcock* (Boston, Toronto: Little, Brown, 1983), 216.
34. Ronald Haver, *David O. Selznick's Hollywood* (New York: Alfred A. Knopf, 1980), 312–317.
35. Anne Edwards, *Vivien Leigh* (New York: Pocket Books, 1977), 121–125.
36. Gregory Speck, *Hollywood Royalty: Hepburn, Davis, Stewart & Friends At the Dinner Party of the Century* (New York: Birch Lane Press, 1992), 18, 129.
37. Dan Auiler, *Hitchcock's Notebooks: An Authorized and Illustrated Look Inside the Creative Mind of Alfred Hitchcock* (New York: Avon Books, 1999), 308–310.
38. Donald Spoto, *The Dark Side of Genius: The Life of Alfred Hitchcock* (Boston, Toronto: Little, Brown, 1983), 216.
39. Dan Auiler, *Hitchcock's Notebooks: An Authorized and Illustrated Look Inside the Creative Mind of Alfred Hitchcock* (New York: Avon Books, 1999), 308–310.
40. Gregory Speck, *Hollywood Royalty: Hepburn, Davis, Stewart & Friends At the Dinner Party of the Century* (New York: Birch Lane Press, 1992), 18, 129.
41. Donald Spoto, *The Dark Side of Genius: The Life of Alfred Hitchcock* (Boston, Toronto: Little, Brown, 1983), 216.
42. David Shipman, *The Great Movie Stars: The Golden Years* (New York: Crown, 1970), 238.
43. Aljean Harmetz, "Dangerous Rebel" *Premiere*, February 2002, 37, 38.
44. John Eastman, *Retakes: Behind the Scenes of 500 Classic Movies* (New York: Ballantine Books, 1989), 284.
45. Suzanne Finstad, *Natasha: The Biography of Natalie Wood* (New York: Harmony Books, 2001), 138–141, 144, 147–148, 152–153.
46. Aljean Harmetz, "Dangerous Rebel" *Premiere*, February 2002, 37, 38.
47. Suzanne Finstad, *Natasha: The Biography of Natalie Wood* (New York: Harmony Books, 2001), 138–141, 144, 147–148, 152–153.
48. Suzanne Finstad, *Natasha: The Biography of Natalie Wood* (New York: Harmony Books, 2001), 138–141, 144, 147–148, 152–153.
49. David Stenn, *Bombshell: The Life and Death of Jean Harlow* (New York: Doubleday, 1993), 179.
50. Ron Base, *"If the Other Guy Isn't Jack Nicholson, I've Got the Part"* (Chicago: Contemporary Books, 1994), 37.
51. Eric Braun, *Deborah Kerr* (New York: St. Martin's Press, 1977), 121–122.
52. Gillian Flynn, "First Blood" *Entertainment Weekly*, 11 October 2002, 34.
53. Warren G. Harris, *Clark Gable: A Biography* (New York: Harmony Books, 2002), 90.
54. Frank Miller, *Movies We Love* (Atlanta: Turner, 1996), 254.
55. David Shipman, *The Great Movie Stars: The International Years* (New York: St. Martin's Press, 1972), 81
56. Todd McCarthy, *Howard Hawks: The Grey Fox of Hollywood* (New York: Grove Press, 1997), 611.
57. Todd McCarthy, *Howard Hawks: The Grey Fox of Hollywood* (New York: Grove Press, 1997), 412–413.
58. Jeff Burkhart and Bruce Stuart, *Hollywood's First Choices* (New York: Crown Trade Paperbacks, 1994), 212.
59. Todd McCarthy, *Howard Hawks: The Grey Fox of Hollywood* (New York: Grove Press, 1997), 412–413.
60. John L. Flynn, *The Films of Arnold Schwarzenegger* (New York: Citadel Press, 1993), 79.
61. David Shipman, *The Great Movie Stars: The Golden Years* (New York: Crown, 1970), 266.
62. David Stenn, *Clara Bow: Runnin' Wild* (New York: Cooper Square Press, 1988), 240.
63. Ryan Murphy, "Cybill Shepherd: The Us Interview" *Us,* June 1995, 54.
64. Jane Ellen Wayne, *The Golden Girls of MGM* (New York: Carroll & Graf, 2002), 342.
65. David Shipman, *The Great Movie Stars: The Golden Years* (New York: Crown, 1970), 344.
66. David Shipman, *The Great Movie Stars: The Golden Years* (New York: Crown, 1970), 482.
67. Jeff Dawson, *Quentin Tarantino: The Cinema of Cool* (New York: Applause Books, 1995), 55.
68. Jami Bernard, *Quentin Tarantino: The Man and His Movies* (New York: HarperPerennial, 1995), 135–139, 206.
69. Marshall Fine, *Harvey Keitel: The Art of Darkness* (New York: Fromm International, 1998), 185.
70. Michael Fleming, "The Mind Behind the Eyes" *Movieline*, October 2000, 52.
71. Jami Bernard, *Quentin Tarantino: The Man and His Movies* (New York: HarperPerennial, 1995), 135–139, 206.
72. Marshall Terrill, *Steve McQueen: Portrait of an American Rebel* (New York: Donald I. Fine, 1993), 421.
73. David Shipman, *The Great Movie Stars: The International Years* (New York: St. Martin's Press, 1972), 216.
74. Michael Viner and Terrie Maxine Frankel, *Tales from Casting Couch: An Unprecedented Candid Collection of Stories, Essays, and Anecdotes by and About Legendary Hollywood Stars, Starlets, and Wanna-bees...* (Beverly Hills: Dove Books, 1995), 169.
75. Garry Jenkins, *Harrison Ford: Imperfect Hero* (Secaucus: Birch Lane Press, 1998), 251.
76. Andrew Yule, *Life on the Wire: The Life and Art of Al Pacino* (New York: Donald I. Fine, 1991), 236.
77. Jason Bonderoff, *Tom Selleck: An Unauthorized Biography* (New York: Signet, 1983), 129.
78. John Eastman, *Retakes: Behind the Scenes of 500 Classic Movies* (New York: Ballantine Books, 1989), 290.
79. Barry Paris, *Audrey Hepburn* (New York: G. P. Putnam's Sons, 1996), 270.
80. Frank Miller, *Movies We Love* (Atlanta: Turner, 1996), 257.
81. Marshall Fine, *Bloody Sam: The Life and Films of Sam Peckinpah* (New York: Donald I. Fine, 1991), 71.
82. Rebecca Ascher-Walsh, "Reel World" *Entertainment Weekly*, 30 November 2001, 56.
83. 2Rebecca Ascher-Walsh, "Vicious Circle" *Entertainment Weekly*, 1 November 2002, 44.
84. Rebecca Ascher-Walsh, "Reel World" *Entertainment Weekly*, 30 November 2001, 56.

85. Todd McCarthy, *Howard Hawks: The Grey Fox of Hollywood* (New York: Grove Press, 1997), 554–555.
86. Todd McCarthy, *Howard Hawks: The Grey Fox of Hollywood* (New York: Grove Press, 1997), 633.
87. *New York Daily News* (New York), 13 September 1998.
88. George F. Custen, *Twentieth Century's Fox* (New York: BasicBooks, 1997), 325.
89. Andrew Yule, *Sean Connery: From 007 to Hollywood Icon* (New York: Donald I. Fine, 1992), 158.
90. Todd Keith, *Kevin Costner: The Unauthorized Biography* (London: ikonprint, 1991), 173.
91. Jess Cagle, "The Touch of Evil" *Entertainment Weekly*, August 6 1993, 19.
92. Rebecca Ascher-Walsh, "Precious Metal" *Entertainment Weekly*, 14 September 2001, 44.
93. Chris Nashawaty, "The Right Hook" *Entertainment Weekly*, Special Oscar Guide 2002, 82, 84–85.
94. Ron Base, *"If the Other Guy Isn't Jack Nicholson, I've Got the Part"* (Chicago: Contemporary Books, 1994), 216.
95. Susan Sackett, *The Hollywood Reporter Book of Box Office Hits* (New York: Billboard Books, 1990), 246.
96. Susan Sackett, *The Hollywood Reporter Book of Box Office Hits* (New York: Billboard Books, 1990), 246.
97. Chris Nashawaty, "The Right Hook" *Entertainment Weekly*, Special Oscar Guide 2002, 82, 84–85.
98. Ron Base, *"If the Other Guy Isn't Jack Nicholson, I've Got the Part"* (Chicago: Contemporary Books, 1994), 216.
99. Frank Sanello, *Stallone: A Rocky Life* (Edinburgh: Mainstream, 1998), 65.
100. Ron Base, *"If the Other Guy Isn't Jack Nicholson, I've Got the Part"* (Chicago: Contemporary Books, 1994), 216.
101. Chris Nashawaty, "The Right Hook" *Entertainment Weekly*, Special Oscar Guide 2002, 82, 84–85.
102. Frank Sanello, *Stallone: A Rocky Life* (Edinburgh: Mainstream, 1998), 117.
103. Barry Paris, *Audrey Hepburn* (New York: G. P. Putnam's Sons, 1996), 62.
104. Janet Leigh with Christopher Nickens, *Psycho: Behind the Scenes of the Classic Thriller* (New York: Harmony Books, 1995), 19–20.
105. Lauren Bacall, *By Myself* (New York: Ballantine Books, 1978), 220.
106. Suzanne Finstad, *Natasha: The Biography of Natalie Wood* (New York: Harmony Books, 2001), 234–238.
107. Emanuel Levy, *George Cukor, Master of Elegance: Hollywood's Legendary Director and His Stars* (New York: William Morrow, 1994), 90.
108. Warren G. Harris, *Clark Gable: A Biography* (New York: Harmony Books, 2002), 165.
109. Gary Carey, *All the Stars in Heaven: Louis B. Mayer's M-G-M* (New York: E. P. Dutton, 1981), 197–198.
110. Joan Collins, *Past Imperfect: An Autobiography* (New York: Berkley Books, 1985), 164–166.
111. Charlton Heston, *The Actor's Life: Journals 1956–1976* (New York: E. P. Dutton, 1976, 1978), 27.
112. Susan Sackett, *The Hollywood Reporter Book of Box Office Hits* (New York: Billboard Books, 1990), 201.
113. Stuart Kaminsky, *John Huston: Maker of Magic* (Boston: Houghton Mifflin, 1978), 120.
114. Arthur Laurents, *Original Story By: A Memoir of Broadway and Hollywood* (New York: Alfred A. Knopf, 2000), 131.
115. Frank Miller, *Movies We Love* (Atlanta: Turner, 1996), 261.
116. Maureen Stapleton and Jane Scovell, *A Hell of a Life* (New York: Simon & Schuster, 1995), 40.
117. David Shipman, *The Great Movie Stars: The International Years* (New York: St. Martin's Press, 1972), 12.
118. Theodore Gershuny, *Soon to Be a Major Motion Picture: The Anatomy of an All-Star Big-Budget Multimillion-Dollar Disaster* (New York: Holt, Rinehart and Winston, 1980), 29–30, 98–99, 120, 266–273
119. Jeff Burkhart and Bruce Stuart, *Hollywood's First Choices* (New York: Crown Trade Paperbacks, 1994), 213.
120. Christopher Andersen, *Citizen Jane: The Turbulent Life of Jane Fonda* (New York: Henry Holt, 1990), 156.
121. Jeff Burkhart and Bruce Stuart, *Hollywood's First Choices* (New York: Crown Trade Paperbacks, 1994), 213.
122. John Eastman, *Retakes: Behind the Scenes of 500 Classic Movies* (New York: Ballantine Books, 1989), 297–298.
123. Edward Z. Epstein and Joe Morella, *Mia: The Life of Mia Farrow* (New York: Dell, 1991), 136.
124. John Parker, *Warren Beatty: The Last Great Lover of Hollywood* (New York: Carroll & Graf, 1993), 145.
125. Robert Evans, *Francis the Kid Stays in the Picture* (New York: Hyperion, 1994), 137.
126. Jeff Burkhart and Bruce Stuart, *Hollywood's First Choices* (New York: Crown Trade Paperbacks, 1994), 213.
127. Vincent Curcio, *Suicide Blonde: The Life of Gloria Grahame* (New York: William Morrow, 1989), 161.
128. Rebecca Ascher-Walsh, "5 Cars Stud" *Entertainment Weekly*, 18 September 1998, 36–38.
129. David Shipman, *Judy Garland: The Secret Life of an American Legend* (New York: Hyperion, 1992), 250–252.
130. Stephen M. Silverman, *Dancing on the Ceiling: Stanley Donen and His Movies* (New York: Alfred A. Knopf, 1996), 128.
131. Ruth Gordon, *My Side: The Autobiography of Ruth Gordon* (New York: Donald I. Fine, 1976), 308.
132. Jennifer Graham, "Far from Heaven" *TV Guide*, 12 October 2002, 48.
133. John L. Flynn, *The Films of Arnold Schwarzenegger* (New York: Citadel Press, 1993), 124.
134. Leslie Van Buskirk, "Tom Cruise and His Movie Machine" *Us*, 6 August 1990, 25.
135. Christopher Andersen, *Madonna Unauthorized* (New York: Simon & Schuster, 1991), 118, 183.

S

1. Robert A. Harris and Michael S. Lasky, *The Films of Alfred Hitchcock* (Secaucus: The Citadel Press, 1976), 60
2. John Eastman, *Retakes: Behind the Scenes of 500 Classic Movies* (New York: Ballantine Books, 1989), 299.
3. David Shipman, *The Great Movie Stars: The Golden Years* (New York: Crown, 1970), 74.
4. Michael Fleming, "Casting Glances" *Movieline*, June 1997, 66.
5. Garry Jenkins, *Harrison Ford: Imperfect Hero* (Secaucus: Birch Lane Press, 1998), 298–299.
6. Valerie Milano, *Gwyneth Paltrow* (Toronto: ECW Press, 2000), 42–43.
7. Eliza Bergman Krause, Kristen O'Neill, Maximillian Potter, Christine Spines, "The Ultimate Fall Preview: God Bless American Movies" *Premiere*, October 1995, 114.

8. Garry Jenkins, *Harrison Ford: Imperfect Hero* (Secaucus: Birch Lane Press, 1998), 298–299.
9. Mitchell Fink, "The Insider" *People*, 17 July 1995, 33.
10. Ryan Murphy, "No Comment: You Didn't Hear This From Me" *Us*, August 1994, 28.
11. David Shipman, *The Great Movie Stars: The International Years* (New York: St. Martin's Press, 1972), 73, 468.
12. Barry Paris, *Audrey Hepburn* (New York: G. P. Putnam's Sons, 1996), 115.
13. James Spada, *Streisand: Her Life* (New York: Ivy Books, 1995), 36–37.
14. James Riordan, *Stone: The Controversies, Excesses, and Exploits of a Radical Filmmaker* (New York: Hyperion, 1995), 154, 155, 185.
15. Hedy Lamarr, *Ecstasy and Me: My Life as a Woman* (U.S.A.: Bartholomew House, 1966), 168–172.
16. Marshall Terrill, *Steve McQueen: Portrait of an American Rebel* (New York: Donald I. Fine, 1993), 129–131.
17. David Stenn, *Bombshell: The Life and Death of Jean Harlow* (New York: Doubleday, 1993), 214.
18. Charles Higham, *Sisters: The Story of Olivia De Havilland & Joan Fontaine* (New York: Coward-McCann, 1984), 134.
19. Dave Thompson, *Travolta* (Dallas: Taylor, 1996), 80.
20. Jessica Shaw, "The Unusual Suspect" *Entertainment Weekly*, 6 June 1997, 46.
21. Dave Karger, "Love Notes" *Entertainment Weekly*, 8 February 2002, 34.
22. Raymond Strait, *James Garner: A Biography* (New York: St. Martin's Press, 1985), 199–205.
23. 2Ron Base, *"If the Other Guy Isn't Jack Nicholson, I've Got the Part"* (Chicago: Contemporary Books, 1994), 116.
24. John Eastman, *Retakes: Behind the Scenes of 500 Classic Movies* (New York: Ballantine Books, 1989), 302–303.
25. Raymond Strait, *James Garner: A Biography* (New York: St. Martin's Press, 1985), 199–205.
26. John Eastman, *Retakes: Behind the Scenes of 500 Classic Movies* (New York: Ballantine Books, 1989), 302–303.
27. Todd McCarthy, *Howard Hawks: The Grey Fox of Hollywood* (New York: Grove Press, 1997), 133–134.
28. Wensley Clarkson, *John Travolta: Back in Character* (Woodstock: The Overlook Press, 1996), 193.
29. *New York Daily News* (New York), 15 July 2000.
30. *Newsday* (New York), 12 April 2001.
31. Stephen Rebello, "The Corruption of Chris O'Donnell" *Movieline*, May 1995, 88.
32. John Baxter, *Steven Spielberg: The Unauthorized Biography* (London: HarperCollins, 1996), 375–376.
33. John H. Richardson, "Steven's Choice" *Premiere*, January 1994, 70.
34. Spike Lee with Lisa Jones, *Uplift the Race: The Construction of School Daze* (New York: Fireside, 1988), 26–28, 73, 75.
35. Peter Bart and Peter Guber, *Shoot Out: Surviving Fame and (Mis)Fortune in Hollywood* (New York: G. P. Putnam's Sons, 2002), 110.
36. *New York Daily News* (New York), 16 December 1999.
37. Rob Edelman and Audrey Kupferberg, *Matthau: A Life* (Lanham: Taylor Trade, 2002), 236.
38. Michael Fleming, "Daisies and Butterflies" *Movieline*, April 1998, 46–55, 90–91.
39. David Shipman, *The Great Movie Stars: The International Years* (New York: St. Martin's Press, 1972), 159.
40. Suzanne Finstad, *Natasha: The Biography of Natalie Wood* (New York: Harmony Books, 2001), 52–153.
41. James Kotsilibas and Myrna Loy, *Myrna Loy: Being and Becoming* (New York: Alfred A. Knopf, 1987), 192.
42. James C. Robertson, *The Casablanca Man: The Cinema of Michael Curtiz* (London, New York: Routledge, 1993), 57.
43. David Shipman, *The Great Movie Stars: The International Years* (New York: St. Martin's Press, 1972), 237.
44. David Stenn, *Clara Bow: Runnin' Wild* (New York: Cooper Square Press, 1988), 228, 231–232.
45. Stephen Rebello, "The Wow" *Movieline*, February 1998, 53.
46. Kate Buford, *Burt Lancaster: An American Life* (New York: Alfred A. Knopf, 2000), 186.
47. Stig Bjorkman and Alfabeta Bokforlag, *Woody Allen on Woody Allen* (New York: Grove Press, 1993), 171–172, 190
48. David Shipman, *The Great Movie Stars: The Golden Years* (New York: Crown, 1970), 208.
49. Todd McCarthy, *Howard Hawks: The Grey Fox of Hollywood* (New York: Grove Press, 1997), 303.
50. Anne Thompson, "Star Turner" *Entertainment Weekly*, 19 February 1993, 10.
51. Ryan Murphy, "Cybill Shepherd: The Us Interview" *Us*, June 1995, 54.
52. Anne Thompson, "Star Turner" *Entertainment Weekly*, 19 February 1993, 10.
53. David Shipman, *The Great Movie Stars: The International Years* (New York: St. Martin's Press, 1972), 513.
54. Rebecca Ascher-Walsh, "Stealing Booty" *Entertainment Weekly*, 15 November 1996, 42.
55. David Shipman, *The Great Movie Stars: The International Years* (New York: St. Martin's Press, 1972), 528.
56. Patricia Neal, *As I Am* (New York: Simon and Schuster, 1988), 252–253, 260.
57. Rob Edelman and Audrey Kupferberg, *Matthau: A Life* (Lanham: Taylor Trade, 2002), 82–83.
58. Michael Fleming, "Mountains, Mantras and a Movie Star" *Movieline*, October 1997, 60.
59. David Shipman, *The Great Movie Stars: The Golden Years* (New York: Crown, 1970), 239.
60. Steven Soderbergh, *sex, lies, and videotape* (New York: Harper & Row, 1990), 48–49, 55, 56.
61. John Baxter, *Woody Allen: A Biography* (New York: Carroll & Graf, 1998), 389.
62. Steve Daly, "Who's the Man?" *Entertainment Weekly*, 16 June 2000, 26, 28, 33.
63. Jeffrey Zaslow, "Hugh Grant: "You're Getting Me Slightly Wrong." *USA Weekend*, 21–23 May 1999, 6.
64. Ira Nadel, *Tom Stoppard: A Life* (New York: Palgrave Macmillan, 2002), 419.
65. *New York Daily News* (New York), 28 February 1999.
66. Ira Nadel, *Tom Stoppard: A Life* (New York: Palgrave Macmillan, 2002), 419.
67. *New York Daily News* (New York), 28 February 1999.
68. David Shipman, *The Great Movie Stars: The International Years* (New York: St. Martin's Press, 1972), 53.

69. Billy Adams, *Ewan McGregor: The Unauthorized Biography* (Woodstock: The Overlook Press, 1999), 102.
70. Rebecca Ascher-Walsh, "Reel World" *Entertainment Weekly*, 24 March 2000, 64.
71. Stephen Rebello, "A Man of Convictions" *Movieline*, November 1999, 74–75.
72. Stephen Jones, *Creepshows: The Illustrated Stephen King Movie Guide* (New York: Billboard Books, 2002), 93.
73. Stephen Rebello, "A Man of Convictions" *Movieline*, November 1999, 74–75.
74. Lawrence J. Quirk, *Totally Uninhibited: The Life and Wild Times of Cher* (New York: William Morrow, 1991), 227–228.
75. Donna Hoke, "The Quiet Man" *Soap Opera Digest*, 30 May 1989, 38.
76. Roger Friedman, "Sex & Sensibility" *Entertainment Weekly*, 3 May 1991, 23.
77. Stephen Rebello, "The Unsinkable Melanie Griffith" *Movieline*, April 1999, 56.
78. Spike Lee, *Spike Lee's Gotta Have It: Inside Guerrilla Filmmaking* (New York: Simon & Schuster, 1987), 188, 190, 195–197.
79. John Eastman, *Retakes: Behind the Scenes of 500 Classic Movies* (New York: Ballantine Books, 1989), 310–311.
80. Johanna Schneller, "All 'The Shipping News' That's Fit to Print" *Premiere*, December 2001, 79.
81. Marc Shapiro, *Susan Sarandon: Actress-Activist* (Amherst: Prometheus Books, 1983, 2001), 89.
82. Clive Hirschhorn, *The Columbia Story* (London: Hamlyn, 1999), 40.
83. Rebecca Ascher-Walsh, "The Player" *Entertainment Weekly*, 16 April 1999, 24.
84. David Shipman, *The Great Movie Stars: The International Years* (New York: St. Martin's Press, 1972), 173.
85. Michael Fleming, "Daisies and Butterflies" *Movieline*, April 1998, 90.
86. Chris Nashawaty, "Devil's Candy" *Entertainment Weekly*, 24 October 1997, 30.
87. Stephen Rebello, "Drop Dead Delectable" *Movieline*, July 1999, 53.
88. Jenny McCarthy with Neal Karlen, *Jen-X: Jenny McCarthy's Open Book* (New York: ReganBooks 1997), 195–197.
89. Michael Fleming, "Casting Glances" *Movieline*, June 1997, 65.
90. *New York Daily News* (New York), 22 June 2000.
91. Lawrence Grobel, "Dylan Unplugged" *Movieline*, September 2000, 51.
92. Chris Nashawaty, "The Last Temptation of Chris" *Entertainment Weekly*, 9 January 1998, 27.
93. Gregory Kirschling, "Almost Famous" *Entertainment Weekly*, September 1998, 51.
94. Daniel Fierman, "Night of the Living Dread" *Entertainment Weekly*, 9 August 2002, 35.
95. Quentin Falk, *Anthony Hopkins: The Authorized Biography* (New York: Interlink Books, 1989, 1994), 173.
96. James Kaplan, "Dark Victory" *Entertainment Weekly*, 1 March 1991, 26.(Ryan)
97. Michael Fleming, "Casting Glances" *Movieline*, June 1997, 65. (MacDowell).
98. Quentin Falk, *Anthony Hopkins: The Authorized Biography* (New York: Interlink Books, 1989, 1994), 173.
99. Cindy Pearlman, "Flashes" *Entertainment Weekly*, 3 October 1997, 12.
100. Rudy Behlmer, *Memo from David O. Selznick* (New York: The Viking Press, 1972), 337–338.
101. David Shipman, *The Great Movie Stars: The International Years* (New York: St. Martin's Press, 1972), 369.
102. Frank Miller, *Movies We Love* (Atlanta: Turner, 1996), 272, 274.
103. Stephen M. Silverman, *Dancing on the Ceiling: Stanley Donen and His Movies* (New York: Alfred A. Knopf, 1996), 155.
104. James Robert Parish, *Whoopi Goldberg: Her Journey from Poverty to Megastardom* (Secaucus: Birch Lane Press, 1996), 152.
105. James Robert Parish, *Whoopi Goldberg: Her Journey from Poverty to Megastardom* (Secaucus: Birch Lane Press, 1996), 240–241.
106. David Shipman, *The Great Movie Stars: The Golden Years* (New York: Crown, 1970), 213.
107. *The New York Times* (New York), 3 May 1998.
108. Stephen Rebello, "Elizabeth's Reign" *Movieline*, September 1998, 56.
109. Stephen Rebello, "The Unsinkable Melanie Griffith" *Movieline*, April 1999, 56.
110. Veronica Chambers, "Willing" *Premiere*, January 1994, 76.
111. Charles Oakley, "Joshing Around" *Movieline*, November 2000, 77.
112. Erica K. Cardozo, "Casting the Crew" *Entertainment Weekly*, 14 July 1995, 47.
113. Ron Base, *"If the Other Guy Isn't Jack Nicholson, I've Got the Part"* (Chicago: Contemporary Books, 1994), 296.
114. Ron Base, *"If the Other Guy Isn't Jack Nicholson, I've Got the Part"* (Chicago: Contemporary Books, 1994), 290.
115. Ron Base, *"If the Other Guy Isn't Jack Nicholson, I've Got the Part"* (Chicago: Contemporary Books, 1994), 290.
116. Michael Fleming, "Casting Glances" *Movieline*, June 1997, 67.
117. Nigel Goodall, *Demi Moore: The Most Powerful Woman in Hollywood* (Edinburgh: Mainstream, 2000), 171.
118. James Robert Parish, *Rosie: Rosie O'Donnell's Biography* (New York: Carroll & Graf, 1997), 146, 123.
119. Elaine Gallagher, *Candidly Caine* (London: Robson Books, 1990), 138.
120. Stephen Rebello, "The Malibu File" *Movieline*, December/January 1998, 59.
121. *New York Daily News* (New York), 30 June 1999.
122. John Eastman, *Retakes: Behind the Scenes of 500 Classic Movies* (New York: Ballantine Books, 1989), 313–314.
123. David Shipman, *The Great Movie Stars: The Golden Years* (New York: Crown, 1970), 59.
124. Ginger Rogers, *Ginger: My Story* (New York: HarperCollins, 1991), 246.
125. Ingrid Bergman and Alan Burgess, *Ingrid Bergman: My Story* (New York: Dell, 1980), 398.
126. Michael Munn, *The Sharon Stone Story* (London: Robson Books, 1997), 95.
127. Burt Reynolds, *My Life* (New York: Hyperion, 1994), 316.
128. Andrew Essex, "Making It Through the Night" *Entertainment Weekly*, 25 September 1998, 70.
129. Gary Carey, *Judy Holliday: An Intimate Life Story* (New York: Seaview Books, 1982), 175.
130. Tom Hutchinson, *Rod Steiger* (New York: Fromm International, 2000), 103.

131. Peter Bart and Peter Guber, *Shoot Out: Surviving Fame and (Mis)Fortune in Hollywood* (New York: G. P. Putnam's Sons, 2002), 201.
132. David Shipman, *The Great Movie Stars: The International Years* (New York: St. Martin's Press, 1972), 303.
133. Tony Curtis and Barry Paris, *Tony Curtis: The Autobiography* (New York: William Morrow, 1993), 154.
134. Ed Sikov, *On Sunset Boulevard: The Life and Times of Billy Wilder* (New York: Hyperion, 1998), 409–410.
135. Benjamin Svetkey, "The Dress Makes the Man" *Entertainment Weekly*, 25 May 2001, 57.
136. Ed Sikov, *On Sunset Boulevard: The Life and Times of Billy Wilder* (New York: Hyperion, 1998), 409–410.
137. Ed Sikov, *On Sunset Boulevard: The Life and Times of Billy Wilder* (New York: Hyperion, 1998), 409–410.
138. William Goldman, *Adventures in the Screen Trade* (New York: Warner Books, 1983), 14.
139. Elena Oumano, *Paul Newman* (New York: St. Martin's Press, 1994), 52.
140. James L. Dickerson, *Ashley Judd: Crying on the Inside* (New York: Schirmer Trade Books, 2002), 173–174.
142. Warren G. Harris, *Clark Gable: A Biography* (New York: Harmony Books, 2002), 253–254.
143. Esther Williams with Digby Diehl, *The Million Dollar Mermaid* (New York: Simon & Schuster, 1999), 81–91, 94.
144. David Thomson, *Showman: The Life of David O. Selznick* (New York: Alfred A. Knopf, 1992), 391.
145. Lawrence Grobel, "Keeping It Real" *Movieline*, September 2002, 67.
146. John Parker, *Warren Beatty: The Last Great Lover of Hollywood* (New York: Carroll & Graf, 1993), 50.
147. Joan Collins, *Past Imperfect: An Autobiography* (New York: Berkley Books, 1985), 156.
148. John Eastman, *Retakes: Behind the Scenes of 500 Classic Movies* (New York: Ballantine Books, 1989), 315–316.
149. Marshall Terrill, *Steve McQueen: Portrait of an American Rebel* (New York: Donald I. Fine, 1993), 311. (McQueen)
150. Thomas D. Clagett, *William Friedkin: Films of Aberration, Obsession and Reality* (Jefferson: McFarland, 1990), 141–142.
151. Julia Antopol Hirsch, *The Sound of Music: The Making of America's Favorite Movie* (Chicago: Contemporary Books, 1993), 50–56, 59, 62–64.
152. Julia Antopol Hirsch, *The Sound of Music: The Making of America's Favorite Movie* (Chicago: Contemporary Books, 1993), 50–56, 59, 62–64.
153. Edward Baron Turk, *Hollywood Diva: A Biography of Jeanette MacDonald* (Berkeley and Los Angeles: University of California Press, 1998), 318.
154. Julia Antopol Hirsch, *The Sound of Music: The Making of America's Favorite Movie* (Chicago: Contemporary Books, 1993), 50–56, 59, 62–64.
155. Julia Antopol Hirsch, *The Sound of Music: The Making of America's Favorite Movie* (Chicago: Contemporary Books, 1993), 50–56, 59, 62–64.
156. Jeff Burkhart and Bruce Stuart, *Hollywood's First Choices* (New York: Crown Trade Paperbacks, 1994), 48, 220.
157. Jeff Burkhart and Bruce Stuart, *Hollywood's First Choices* (New York: Crown Trade Paperbacks, 1994), 48, 220.
158. David Shipman, *The Great Movie Stars: The International Years* (New York: St. Martin's Press, 1972), 183.
159. *New York Daily News* (New York), 1 April 1999.
160. Holly Millea, "Ghost in the Machine" *Premiere*, February 1995, 54.
161. Lawrence Grobel, "There's Something About Sandy" *Movieline*, April 1999, 51.
162. *New York Daily News* (New York), 4 March 1999.
163. Gillian Flynn, "Web Casting" *Entertainment Weekly*, 11 February 2000, 9.
164. *New York Post* (New York), 2 August 2000.
165. *New York Daily News* (New York), 4 March 1999.
166. Gillian Flynn, "Web Casting" *Entertainment Weekly*, 11 February 2000, 9.
167. Stephen Rebello, "Along Came a Spidey" *Movieline*, April 2002, 65.
168. *New York Daily News* (New York), 27 August 2000.
169. Tom Russo, "Swing Time" *Entertainment Weekly*, 26 April 2002, 42.
170. Nigel Andrews, *Travolta: The Life* (New York: Bloomsbury, 1998), 166.
171. Larry Grobel, "Dr. Michael & Mr. Keaton" *Movieline*, August 1997, 52.
172. David Gardner, *Tom Hanks: The Unauthorized Biography* (London: Blake, 1999), 70.
173. David Gardner, *Tom Hanks: The Unauthorized Biography* (London: Blake, 1999), 70.
174. David Gardner, *Tom Hanks: The Unauthorized Biography* (London: Blake, 1999), 70.
175. Beverly Gray, *Ron Howard: From Mayberry to the Moon ... and Beyond* (Nashville: Rutledge Hill Press, 2003), 102.
176. David Gardner, *Tom Hanks: The Unauthorized Biography* (London: Blake, 1999), 70.
177. John Parker, *Warren Beatty: The Last Great Lover of Hollywood* (New York: Carroll & Graf, 1993), 55.
178. Warren G. Harris, *Natalie & R.J.: Hollywood's Star-Crossed Lovers* (New York: A Dolphin Book, 1988), 73.
179. Suzanne Finstad, *Natasha: The Biography of Natalie Wood* (New York: Harmony Books, 2001), 215.
180. Steven Jay Rubin, *The James Bond Films* (Westport: Arlington House, 1981), 140.
181. David Shipman, *The Great Movie Stars: The Golden Years* (New York: Crown, 1970), 448.
182. Douglas Brode, *The Films of Jack Nicholson* (Secaucus: Citadel Press, 1987), 83–84.
183. Tag Gallagher, *John Ford: The Man and His Films* (Berkeley and Los Angeles: University of California Press, 1986), 146.
184. Frank Capra, *Frank Capra: The Name Above the Title* (New York: Macmillan, 1971), 302.
185. Bob Thomas, *Golden Boy: The Untold Story of William Holden* (New York: St. Martin's Press, 1983), 79.
186. Charlotte Chandler, *Nobody's Perfect: Billy Wilder: A Personal Biography* (New York: Simon & Schuster, 2002), 167.
187. Bob Thomas, *Golden Boy: The Untold Story of William Holden* (New York: St. Martin's Press, 1983), 79.
188. Lauren Bacall, *By Myself* (New York: Ballantine Books, 1978), 220.
189. Raymond Strait, *Alan Alda: A Biography* (New York: St. Martin's Press, 1983), 127–128.
190. James Spada, *Julia: Her Life* (New York: St. Martin's Press, 2004), 62

191. David Shipman, *Judy Garland: The Secret Life of an American Legend* (New York: Hyperion, 1992), 310–311, 313.
192. Randall Riese, *Her Name Is Barbra* (New York: St. Martin's Paperbacks, 1993), 401.
193. Susan Sackett, *The Hollywood Reporter Book of Box Office Hits* (New York: Billboard Books, 1990), 248.
194. Susan Sackett, *The Hollywood Reporter Book of Box Office Hits* (New York: Billboard Books, 1990), 248.
195. James Spada, *Streisand: Her Life* (New York: Ivy Books, 1995), 375–376, 378, 381–382.
196. James Spada, *Streisand: Her Life* (New York: Ivy Books, 1995), 375–376, 378, 381–382.
197. Ellis Amburn, *The Sexiest Man Alive: A Biography of Warren Beatty* (New York: HarperCollins, 2002), 97.
198. James Spada, *Streisand: Her Life* (New York: Ivy Books, 1995), 375–376, 378, 381–382.
199. Leonard Nimoy, *I Am Spock* (New York: Hyperion, 1995), 343–344.
200. Dale Pollock, *Skywalking: The Life and Films of George Lucas* (New York: Harmony Books, 1983), 151–153, 156.
201. Lawrence Grobel, "Off the Beaten Path" *Movieline*, July 1997, 43.
202. John Baxter, *Mythmaker: The Life and Work of George Lucas* (New York: Spike, 1999), 185–188.
203. Dale Pollock, *Skywalking: The Life and Films of George Lucas* (New York: Harmony Books, 1983), 151–153, 156.
204. Dale Pollock, *Skywalking: The Life and Films of George Lucas* (New York: Harmony Books, 1983), 151–153, 156.
205. Dale Pollock, *Skywalking: The Life and Films of George Lucas* (New York: Harmony Books, 1983), 151–153, 156.
206. Michael Logan, "Sense-Ible Beyond His Years" *TV Guide*, 9–15 October 1999, 3.
207. Cheo Hodari Coker, "Return of the Jedi" *Premiere*, June 2002, 51.
208. Tricia Johnson, "Star Search" *Entertainment Weekly*, 25 February 2000, 9.
209. Cheo Hodari Coker, "Return of the Jedi" *Premiere*, June 2002, 51.
210. Tricia Johnson, "Star Search" *Entertainment Weekly*, 25 February 2000, 9.
211. Tricia Johnson, "Star Search" *Entertainment Weekly*, 25 February 2000, 9.
212. Leonard Klady, "The $7 Million Man" *Entertainment Weekly*, 5 March 1993, 9.
213. Chris Nashawaty, "Stomp the World" *Entertainment Weekly*, 22 May 1998, 25–26.
214. Wolf Schneider, "Hype: All the Right Parts" *Movieline*, March 1997, 14.
215. Rebecca Ascher-Walsh, "Reel World" *Entertainment Weekly*, 12 October 2001, 61.
216. Charles Grodin, Jr., *It Would Be So Nice If You Weren't Here...* (New York: Vintage Books, 1989), 157.
217. Candice Bergen, *Knock Wood* (New York: Linden Press/Simon & Schuster, 1984), 324–326.
218. Ann-Margret with Todd Gold, *Ann-Margret* (New York: G. P. Putnam's Sons, 1994), 91.
219. James Spada, *Julia: Her Life* (New York: St. Martin's Press, 2004), 94–95.
220. Julia Phillips, *You'll Never Eat Lunch in This Town Again* (New York: Signet, 1992), 107–108.
221. Axel Madsen, *Stanwyck* (New York: HarperCollins, 1994), 142.
222. Sondra Locke, *The Good, the Bad & the Very Ugly: A Hollywood Journey* (New York: William Morrow, 1997), 95–96.
223. Julia Phillips, *You'll Never Eat Lunch in This Town Again* (New York: Signet, 1992), 139–140.
224. John Parker, *Warren Beatty: The Last Great Lover of Hollywood* (New York: Carroll & Graf, 1993), 195.
225. John Eastman, *Retakes: Behind the Scenes of 500 Classic Movies* (New York: Ballantine Books, 1989), 327.
226. Julia Phillips, *You'll Never Eat Lunch in This Town Again* (New York: Signet, 1992), 139–140.
227. Gary Carey, *Doug & Mary: A Biography of Douglas Fairbanks & Mary Pickford* (New York: E. P. Dutton, 1977), 227.
228. Stephen Lowenstein, *My First Movie: Twenty Celebrated Directors Talk About Their First Film* (New York: Pantheon Books, 2000), 283.
229. Yvonne De Carlo with Doug Warren, *Yvonne: An Autobiography* (New York: St. Martin's Press, 1987), 76–77.
230. David Shipman, *The Great Movie Stars: The International Years* (New York: St. Martin's Press, 1972), 12.
231. Charles Higham, *Orson Welles: The Rise and Fall of an American Genius* (New York: St. Martin's Press, 1985), 225.
232. John Eastman, *Retakes: Behind the Scenes of 500 Classic Movies* (New York: Ballantine Books, 1989), 328.
233. Jay Fultz, *In Search of Donna Reed* (Iowa City: University of Iowa Press, 1998), 75.
234. David Weddle, *If They Move... Kill 'Em!: The Life and Times of Sam Peckinpah* (New York: Grove Press, 1994), 403.
235. Marshall Fine, *Bloody Sam: The Life and Films of Sam Peckinpah* (New York: Donald I. Fine, 1991), 194.
236. Marshall Fine, *Bloody Sam: The Life and Films of Sam Peckinpah* (New York: Donald I. Fine, 1991), 194.
237. Daniel Bubbeo, *The Women of Warner Brothers: The Lives and Careers of 15 Leading Ladies* (Jefferson: McFarland, 2002), 197.
238. A. Scott Berg, *Goldwyn: A Biography* (New York: Alfred A. Knopf, 1989), 210.
239. John Eastman, *Retakes: Behind the Scenes of 500 Classic Movies* (New York: Ballantine Books, 1989), 329.
240. John Baxter, *Woody Allen: A Biography* (New York: Carroll & Graf, 1998), 258.
241. Hugo Vickers, *Vivien Leigh* (Boston: Little, Brown, 1988), 198.
242. Daniel Bubbeo, *The Women of Warner Brothers: The Lives and Careers of 15 Leading Ladies* (Jefferson: McFarland, 2002), 67.
243. James Spada, *More Than a Woman: An Intimate Biography of Bette Davis* (New York: Bantam Books, 1993), 70, 79–80, 82.
244. Ron Base, *"If the Other Guy Isn't Jack Nicholson, I've Got the Part"* (Chicago: Contemporary Books, 1994), 146.
245. Rebecca Ascher-Walsh, "Burt Starts Over" *Entertainment Weekly*, 4 August, 1995, 7.
246. David Shipman, *The Great Movie Stars: The International Years* (New York: St. Martin's Press, 1972), 283.
247. James Robert Parish and Ronald L. Bowers, *The MGM Stock Company: The Golden Era* (New Rochelle: Arlington House, 1973), 424.

248. Ellis Amburn, *The Sexiest Man Alive: A Biography of Warren Beatty* (New York: HarperCollins, 2002), 29.
249. Patricia Neal, *As I Am* (New York: Simon and Schuster, 1988), 206.
250. Peter Harry Brown and Patte B. Barham, *Marilyn: The Last Take* (New York: Signet, 1993), 99.
251. Jeff Burkhart and Bruce Stuart, *Hollywood's First Choices* (New York: Crown Trade Paperbacks, 1994), 37.
252. James Curtis, *Between Flops: A Biography of Preston Sturges* (New York: Harcourt Brace Jovanovich, 1982), 153.
253. Gregg Kilday, "They Don't Know Jack … Ryan" *Premiere*, July 2001, 32.
254. Barry Paris, *Audrey Hepburn* (New York: G. P. Putnam's Sons, 1996), 123.
255. Joshua Rich, Steve Daly, Andrew Essex, Benjamin Svetkey, Jessica Shaw, Kristen Baldwin, Chris Nashawaty, Jeff Jensen, Tricia Johnson, Dave Karger, Josh Wolk, "Summer Movie Preview" *Entertainment Weekly*, 30 April 1999, 50.
256. *New York Daily News* (New York), 27 June 1999.
257. Todd McCarthy, *Howard Hawks: The Grey Fox of Hollywood* (New York: Grove Press, 1997), 512, 539.
258. Robert Evans, *Francis The Kid Stays in the Picture* (New York: Hyperion, 1994), 56.
259. John Eastman, *Retakes: Behind the Scenes of 500 Classic Movies* (New York: Ballantine Books, 1989), 330.
260. John Eastman, *Retakes: Behind the Scenes of 500 Classic Movies* (New York: Ballantine Books, 1989), 330.
261. Andrew Yule, *Sean Connery: From 007 to Hollywood Icon* (New York: Donald I. Fine, 1992), 114.
262. Marilu Henner with Jim Jerome, *By All Means Keep on Moving* (New York: Pocket Books, 1994), 246.
263. Kent Jones, *Memorable Movie Roles: And the Actors Who Played Them* (Avenel: Crescent Books, 1992), 53.
264. John Eastman, *Retakes: Behind the Scenes of 500 Classic Movies* (New York: Ballantine Books, 1989), 331.
265. Bob Thomas, *Golden Boy: The Untold Story of William Holden* (New York: St. Martin's Press, 1983), 59.
266. Maurice Zolotow, *Billy Wilder in Hollywood* (New York: G.P. Putnam's Sons, 1977), 163.
267. Bob Thomas, *Golden Boy: The Untold Story of William Holden* (New York: St. Martin's Press, 1983), 59.
268. Ron Base, *"If the Other Guy Isn't Jack Nicholson, I've Got the Part"* (Chicago: Contemporary Books, 1994), 202.
269. Ellis Amburn, *The Sexiest Man Alive: A Biography of Warren Beatty* (New York: HarperCollins, 2002), 217.
270. Jeffrey Lantos, "Nolte Now" *Movieline*, December/January 1999, 61.
271. Ron Base, *"If the Other Guy Isn't Jack Nicholson, I've Got the Part"* (Chicago: Contemporary Books, 1994), 202.
272. Ellis Amburn, *The Sexiest Man Alive: A Biography of Warren Beatty* (New York: HarperCollins, 2002), 217.
273. Ron Base, *"If the Other Guy Isn't Jack Nicholson, I've Got the Part"* (Chicago: Contemporary Books, 1994), 202.
274. Susan Sackett, *The Hollywood Reporter Book of Box Office Hits* (New York: Billboard Books, 1990), 260.
275. Marshall Terrill, *Steve McQueen: Portrait of an American Rebel* (New York: Donald I. Fine, 1993), 429.
276. Chris Nickson, *Superhero: An Unauthorized Biography of Christopher Reeve* (New York: St. Martin's Paperbacks, 1998), 41–42.
277. John Eastman, *Retakes: Behind the Scenes of 500 Classic Movies* (New York: Ballantine Books, 1989), 333.
278. David Shipman, *The Great Movie Stars: The Golden Years* (New York: Crown, 1970), 215.
279. Jeff Burkhart and Bruce Stuart, *Hollywood's First Choices* (New York: Crown Trade Paperbacks, 1994), 193.
280. Troy Patterson, "For Your Holm-Viewing Pleasure" *Entertainment Weekly*, 29 May 1998, 80.
281. Kate Meyers, "The Neverending Story" *Entertainment Weekly*, 7 November 1997, 40–41.
282. Jim Jerome, "Kathleen Turner Romances the Tube" *TV Guide*, 1 April 1995, 19.
283. Emanuel Levy, *George Cukor, Master of Elegance: Hollywood's Legendary Director and His Stars* (New York: William Morrow, 1994), 87.

T

1. Marshall Terrill, *Steve McQueen: Portrait of an American Rebel* (New York: Donald I. Fine, 1993), 428.
2. David Shipman, *The Great Movie Stars: The Golden Years* (New York: Crown, 1970), 483.
3. Esther Williams with Digby Diehl, *The Million Dollar Mermaid* (New York: Simon & Schuster, 1999), 162–163, 167.
4. R. Dixon Smith, *Ronald Colman, Gentleman of the Cinema* (Jefferson: McFarland, 1991), 165.
5. Barbara Leaming, *If This Was Happiness: A Biography of Rita Hayworth* (New York: Viking, 1989), 345.
6. Michael Atkinson, "The Mystery of Christian Bale" *Movieline*, March 1997, 105.
7. Stephen Rebello, "The Talented Mr. Minghella" *Movieline*, January 2000, 62.
8. Ron Base, *"If the Other Guy Isn't Jack Nicholson, I've Got the Part"* (Chicago: Contemporary Books, 1994), 145.
9. Joshua Rich, Steve Daly, Andrew Essex, Benjamin Svetkey, Jessica Shaw, Kristen Baldwin, Chris Nashawaty, Jeff Jensen, Tricia Johnson, Dave Karger, Josh Wolk, "Summer Movie Preview" *Entertainment Weekly*, 30 April 1999, 30.
10. Kristen Baldwin, "The Hot Rock" *Entertainment Weekly*, 19 September 1997, 6.
11. Frank Miller, *Movies We Love* (Atlanta: Turner, 1996), 276.
12. Warren G. Harris, *Clark Gable: A Biography* (New York: Harmony Books, 2002), 82.
13. David Lewin and Penina Spiegel, "Tarzan Swings" *Us*, 29 September 1981, 29.
14. Ian Woodward, *Audrey Hepburn* (New York: St. Martin's Press, 1984), 192.
15. Robert Lacey, *Grace* (New York: G.P. Putnam's Sons, 1994), 123–124.
16. Mary Pat Kelly, *Martin Scorsese: A Journey* (New York: Thunder's Mouth Press, 1991), 90.
17. Ryan Murphy, "Cybill Shepherd: The Us Interview" *Us*, June 1995, 54.
18. Andy Dougan, *Untouchable: A Biography of Robert De Niro* (New York: Thunder's Mouth Press, 1996), 76, 77.
19. Andy Dougan, *Untouchable: A Biography of Robert De Niro* (New York: Thunder's Mouth Press, 1996), 76, 77.
20. Benjamin Svetkey, "Hip to be Cher" *Entertainment Weekly*, 23 April 1999, 20–21.
21. Alvin Yudkoff, *Gene Kelly: A Life of Dance and Dreams* (New York: Back Stage Books, 1999), 233.
22. Paul Mazursky, *Show Me the Magic* (New York: Simon & Schuster, 1999), 111, 118–120.

23. Ron Base, *"If the Other Guy Isn't Jack Nicholson, I've Got the Part"* (Chicago: Contemporary Books, 1994), 201.
24. Ellis Amburn, *The Sexiest Man Alive: A Biography of Warren Beatty* (New York: HarperCollins, 2002), 217.
25. David Thomson, *Showman: The Life of David O. Selznick* (New York: Alfred A. Knopf, 1992), 638, 648, 656, 657.
26. Lynn Hirschberg, "Mel Gibson" *Rolling Stone*, 12 January 1989, 43, 76.
27. John L. Flynn, *The Films of Arnold Schwarzenegger* (New York: Citadel Press, 1993), 72.
28. John L. Flynn, *The Films of Arnold Schwarzenegger* (New York: Citadel Press, 1993), 193.
29. Jeff Jensen, The Running Man" *Entertainment Weekly*, 11 July 2003, 45–46.
30. Tom Russo, "What If...?" *Premiere*, February 2004, 87.
31. Jeff Jensen, The Running Man" *Entertainment Weekly*, 11 July 2003, 45–46.
32. Mary Kaye Schilling, "Lone Star" *Entertainment Weekly*, 28 November 2003, 87.
33. Shirley MacLaine, *My Lucky Stars: A Hollywood Memoir* (New York: Bantam Books, 1995), 129, 132.
34. Burt Reynolds, *My Life* (New York: Hyperion, 1994), 258.
35. Douglas Brode, *The Films of Jack Nicholson* (Secaucus: Citadel Press, 1987), 236.
36. Minty Clinch, *Harrison Ford* (London: New English Library, 1987), 191.
37. Shirley MacLaine, *My Lucky Stars: A Hollywood Memoir* (New York: Bantam Books, 1995), 129, 132.
38. *New York Daily News* (New York), 3 June 1999.
39. David Shipman, *The Great Movie Stars: The International Years* (New York: St. Martin's Press, 1972), 462.
40. Warren G. Harris, *Sophia Loren: A Biography* (New York: Simon & Schuster, 1998), 122.
41. Mitchell Fink, "The Insider" *People*, 14 August 1995, 33.
42. Stephen Rebello, "The Unsinkable Melanie Griffith" *Movieline*, April 1999, 56.
43. Nancy Griffin, "Cher" *Us*, October 1991, 47.
44. 1995 People Entertainment Almanac (Boston, New York, Toronto, London: Cader Books, 1994), 412.
45. Michael Fleming, "The Mind Behind the Eyes" *Movieline*, October 2000, 52.
46. Rebecca Ascher-Walsh, Kristen Baldwin, Anita M. Busch, Steve Daly, Andrew Essex, Daniel Fierman, Jeff Gordinier, David Hochman, Dave Karger, Tricia Laine, Chris Nashawaty, Joe Neumaier, Degen Pener, Megan Quitkin, Jessica Shaw, Tom Sinclair, Benjamin Svetkey, "The Following Summer Movie Preview Has Been Approved for All Audiences by the Editors of Entertainment Weekly" *Entertainment Weekly*, 15 May 1998, 33.
47. Jane Ellen Wayne, *The Golden Girls of MGM* (New York: Carroll & Graf, 2002), 149.
48. Andrew Yule, *Picture Shows: The Life and Films of Peter Bogdanovich* (New York: Limelight Editions, 1992), 140.
49. Charles Higham, *Sisters: The Story of Olivia De Havilland & Joan Fontaine* (New York: Coward-McCann, 1984), 124.
50. Charles Grodin, Jr., *It Would Be So Nice If You Weren't Here...* (New York: Vintage Books, 1989), 234.
51. Patrick McGilligan, *Robert Altman: Jumping Off the Cliff* (New York: St. Martin's Press, 1989), 368.
52. John Eastman, *Retakes: Behind the Scenes of 500 Classic Movies* (New York: Ballantine Books, 1989), 342.
53. David Thomson, *Rosebud: The Story of Orson Welles* (New York: Alfred A. Knopf, 1996), 293–294.
54. Stephen Rebello, "Born to be Bad" *Movieline*, May 1992, 32.
55. David Shipman, *The Great Movie Stars: The International Years* (New York: St. Martin's Press, 1972), 137.
56. David Shipman, *The Great Movie Stars: The International Years* (New York: St. Martin's Press, 1972), 334.
57. John Eastman, *Retakes: Behind the Scenes of 500 Classic Movies* (New York: Ballantine Books, 1989), 347.
58. Rudy Behlmer, *Memo from Darryl F. Zanuck: The Golden Years at Twentieth Century-Fox* (New York: Grove Press, 1993), 6.
59. Tom McGee, *Betty Grable: The Girl with the Million Dollar Legs* (Vestal: The Vestal Press, 1995), 55.
60. David Shipman, *The Great Movie Stars: The International Years* (New York: St. Martin's Press, 1972), 45.
61. Jill Bernstein, Amy Brill, John Brodie, Alex Lewin, Jason Matloff, Kindra Peach, Maximillian Potter, Sean Smith, Anne Thompson, "Premiere's Ultimate Fall Preview" *Premiere*, September 1997, 49.
62. David Shipman, *The Great Movie Stars: The Golden Years* (New York: Crown, 1970), 189.
63. Christine Spines, "Leader of the Pack" *Premiere*, January 2002, 56.
64. Christine Spines, "Leader of the Pack" *Premiere*, January 2002, 56.
65. Chris Nashawaty, "Three the Hard Way" *Entertainment Weekly*, 8 October 1999, 27.
66. Robert Edelman and Audrey Kupferberg, *Angela Lansbury: A Life on Stage and Screen* (Thorndike: G.K. Hall, and Bath: Chivers Press, 1996), 107.
67. Charlton Heston, *The Actor's Life: Journals 1956–1976* (New York: E. P. Dutton, 1976, 1978), 402–403.
68. Charlton Heston, *In the Arena: An Autobiography* (New York: Simon & Schuster, 1995), 517.
69. Charlton Heston, *The Actor's Life: Journals 1956–1976* (New York: E. P. Dutton, 1976, 1978), 402–403.
70. Charlton Heston, *In the Arena: An Autobiography* (New York: Simon & Schuster, 1995), 517.
71. Murgatroyd, "This and That" *Movieline*, May 1992, 9.
72. Rob Edelman and Audrey Kupferberg, *Matthau: A Life* (Lanham: Taylor Trade, 2002), 127.
73. Andrew Yule, *Sean Connery: From 007 to Hollywood Icon* (New York: Donald I. Fine, 1992), 85–86.
74. Steven Jay Rubin, *The Complete James Bond Movie Encyclopedia* (Chicago: Contemporary Books, 1990), 60, 78, 122.
75. Sondra Locke, *The Good, the Bad & the Very Ugly: A Hollywood Journey* (New York: William Morrow, 1997), 190.
76. David Shipman, *The Great Movie Stars: The Golden Years* (New York: Crown, 1970), 417.
77. Ian Christie, *Gilliam on Gilliam* (London: Faber and Faber, 1999), 88, 90.
78. Jess Cagle, "A View to a Kill" *Entertainment Weekly*, 26 July 1996, 20–21.
79. Mitchell Fink, "The Insider" *People*, 22 July 1996, 35.
80. Paula Parisi, *Titanic and the Making of James Cameron: The Inside Story of the Three-Year Adventure That Rewrote Motion Picture History* (New York: Newmarket Press, 1998), 96–104.

81. Paula Parisi, *Titanic and the Making of James Cameron: The Inside Story of the Three-Year Adventure That Rewrote Motion Picture History* (New York: Newmarket Press, 1998), 96–104.
82. Mike Flaherty, "Secret Agent Man" *Entertainment Weekly*, 15 May 1998, 83.
83. Paula Parisi, *Titanic and the Making of James Cameron: The Inside Story of the Three-Year Adventure That Rewrote Motion Picture History* (New York: Newmarket Press, 1998), 96–104.
84. John Eastman, *Retakes: Behind the Scenes of 500 Classic Movies* (New York: Ballantine Books, 1989), 348.
85. James Robert Parish, *Gus Van Sant: An Unauthorized Biography* (New York: Thunder's Mouth Press, 2001), 197–200.
86. Lyall Bush, "Waiting for Hitchcock" *MovieMaker*, May/June/July 1997, 35.
87. James Robert Parish, *Gus Van Sant: An Unauthorized Biography* (New York: Thunder's Mouth Press, 2001), 197–200.
88. James Robert Parish, *Gus Van Sant: An Unauthorized Biography* (New York: Thunder's Mouth Press, 2001), 197–200.
89. Ginger Rogers, *Ginger: My Story* (New York: HarperCollins, 1991), 246.
90. Dennis Hensley, "The Hot New 39-Year-Old" *Movieline*, August 1998, 72–73.
91. Marshall Terrill, *Steve McQueen: Portrait of an American Rebel* (New York: Donald I. Fine, 1993), 319–320.
92. Ray Carney, *Cassavetes on Cassavetes* (London: Faber and Faber, 2001), 111.
93. Susan Dworkin, *Making Tootsie: A Film Study with Dustin Hoffman and Sydney Pollack* (New York: Newmarket Press, 1983), 7–9, 14–15.
94. Jeff Burkhart and Bruce Stuart, *Hollywood's First Choices* (New York: Crown Trade Paperbacks, 1994), 203.
95. Lawrence J. Quirk, *Totally Uninhibited: The Life and Wild Times of Cher* (New York: William Morrow, 1991), 227.
96. Andrew Yule, *Picture Shows: The Life and Films of Peter Bogdanovich* (New York: Limelight Editions, 1992), 180.
97. Susan Dworkin, *Making Tootsie: A Film Study with Dustin Hoffman and Sydney Pollack* (New York: Newmarket Press, 1983), 7–9, 14–15.
98. Susan Dworkin, *Making Tootsie: A Film Study with Dustin Hoffman and Sydney Pollack* (New York: Newmarket Press, 1983), 7–9, 14–15.
99. Rachel Abramowitz, "Studios Ignoring You? Quick, Make an Indie!" *The New York Times Magazine*, 16 November 1997, 100.
100. *1996 People Entertainment Almanac* (Boston, New York, Toronto, London: Cader Books, 1995), 404.
101. John Russell Taylor, *Hitch: The Life and Times of Alfred Hitchcock* (New York: Pantheon Books, 1978), 280–281.
102. Ed Sikov, *Mr. Strangelove: A Biography of Peter Sellers* (New York: Hyperion, 2002), 202.
103. John Eastman, *Retakes: Behind the Scenes of 500 Classic Movies* (New York: Ballantine Books, 1989), 354.
104. John Eastman, *Retakes: Behind the Scenes of 500 Classic Movies* (New York: Ballantine Books, 1989), 354.
105. Warren G. Harris, *Cary Grant: A Touch of Elegance* (New York: Doubleday, 1987), 80.
106. Barry Paris, *Garbo* (New York: Alfred A. Knopf, 1995), 96.
107. Tom O'Neill, "Hollywood's Cast System" *Us*, June 1995, 83.
108. John L. Flynn, *The Films of Arnold Schwarzenegger* (New York: Citadel Press, 1993), 159, 161.
109. David Shipman, *The Great Movie Stars: The Golden Years* (New York: Crown, 1970), 212.
110. Marshall Terrill, *Steve McQueen: Portrait of an American Rebel* (New York: Donald I. Fine, 1993), 276.
111. Patrick McGilligan, *Jack's Life: A Biography of Jack Nicholson* (New York, London: W. W. Norton, 1994), 206.
112. Anne Thompson, "Steven Soderbergh" *Premiere*, December 2000, 62.
113. Holly Millea, "The Second Coming of Mickey Rourke" *Premiere*, February 2003, 75.
114. Robert Edelman and Audrey Kupferberg, *Angela Lansbury: A Life on Stage and Screen* (Thorndike: G.K. Hall, and Bath: Chivers Press, 1996), 240.
115. Cybill Shepherd, *Cybill Disobedience* (New York: HarperCollins, 2000), 133–134.
116. A.M. Sperber and Eric Lax, *Bogart* (New York: William Morrow, 1997), 336, 343–344.
117. A.M. Sperber and Eric Lax, *Bogart* (New York: William Morrow, 1997), 336, 343–344.
118. John Eastman, *Retakes: Behind the Scenes of 500 Classic Movies* (New York: Ballantine Books, 1989), 357.
119. A.M. Sperber and Eric Lax, *Bogart* (New York: William Morrow, 1997), 336, 343–344.
120. John Eastman, *Retakes: Behind the Scenes of 500 Classic Movies* (New York: Ballantine Books, 1989), 357.
121. A.M. Sperber and Eric Lax, *Bogart* (New York: William Morrow, 1997), 336, 343–344.
122. Jane Lenz Elder, *Alice Faye* (Jackson: University Press of Mississippi, 2002), 170.
123. David Shipman, *The Great Movie Stars: The Golden Years* (New York: Crown, 1970), 365.
124. James Robert Parish and Ronald L. Bowers, *The MGM Stock Company: The Golden Era* (New Rochelle: Arlington House, 1973), 739.
125. Jane Ellen Wayne, *The Golden Girls of MGM* (New York: Carroll & Graf, 2002), 374.
126. David Shipman, *The Great Movie Stars: The International Years* (New York: St. Martin's Press, 1972), 45.
127. Dale Sherman, *Black Diamond: The Unauthorized Biography of Kiss* (London: CG, 1997), 199.
128. Peter Thompson, *Jack Nicholson: The Life and Times of an Actor on the Edge* (Secaucus: Birch Lane Press, 1997), 86.
129. *1995 People Entertainment Almanac* (Boston, New York, Toronto, London: Cader Books, 1994), 392.
130. Sondra Locke, *The Good, the Bad & the Very Ugly: A Hollywood Journey* (New York: William Morrow, 1997), 91–92.
131. John Eastman, *Retakes: Behind the Scenes of 500 Classic Movies* (New York: Ballantine Books, 1989), 359.
132. Jeff Dawson, *Quentin Tarantino: The Cinema of Cool* (New York: Applause Books, 1995), 55.
133. Benjamin Svetkey, "The Pro" *Entertainment Weekly*, 5 June 1998, 28.
134. Michael Schumacher, *Francis Ford Coppola* (New York: Crown, 1999), 398.
135. J. Randy Taraborrelli, *Once Upon a Time: Behind the Fairy Tale of Princess Grace and Prince Rainier* (New York: Warner Books, 2003), 351–352.

136. Barry Paris, *Audrey Hepburn* (New York: G. P. Putnam's Sons, 1996), 270.
137. *New York Daily News* (New York), 24 January 1999.
138. Jennifer Armstrong, Rebecca Ascher-Walsh, Sumeet Bal, Karyn L. Barr, Mandi Bierly, Scott Brown, Bob Cannon, Clarissa Cruz, Steve Daly, Amy Feitelberg, Daniel Fierman, Raymond Fiore, Nicholas Fonseca, Bruce Fretts, Gillian Flynn, Jeff Jensen, Dave Karger, Gregory Kirschling, Alice M. Lee, Nancy Miller, Chris Nashawaty, Joshua Rich, Missy Schwartz, Karen Valby, Josh Young, "Fall Movie Preview" *Entertainment Weekly*, 22–29 August 2003, 75.
139. David Shipman, *The Great Movie Stars: The Golden Years* (New York: Crown, 1970), 527.
140. Marshall Terrill, *Steve McQueen: Portrait of an American Rebel* (New York: Donald I. Fine, 1993), 422.
141. Patrick McGilligan, *Jack's Life: A Biography of Jack Nicholson* (New York, London: W. W. Norton, 1994), 344–346, 368–369.
142. Robert Evans, *Francis The Kid Stays in the Picture* (New York: Hyperion, 1994), 353–358.
143. Peter Biskind, *Easy Riders, Raging Bulls* (New York: Simon & Schuster, 1998), 430–432.
144. Patrick McGilligan, *Jack's Life: A Biography of Jack Nicholson* (New York, London: W. W. Norton, 1994), 344–346, 368–369.
145. Vincent Lo Brutto, *Stanley Kubrick: A Biography* (New York: Donald I. Fine, Books, 1997), 278–279.
146. David Shipman, *The Great Movie Stars: The International Years* (New York: St. Martin's Press, 1972), 423.

U

1. Benjamin Svetkey, "Making Waves" *Entertainment Weekly*, 21 April 2000, 44.
2. Rebecca Ascher-Walsh, Steve Daly, Jeff Gardinier, David Hochman, Dave Karger, Dana Kennedy, Gregg Kilday, Tricia Laine, Chris Nashawaty, Degen Pener, Erin Richter, Jessica Shaw, Benjamin Svetkey, Caren Weiner, Chris Willman, "Fall Movie Guide" *Entertainment Weekly*, 22/29 August 1997, 47.
3. *The New York Times* (New York), 8 June 1997.
4. Ed Sikov, *Mr. Strangelove: A Biography of Peter Sellers* (New York: Hyperion, 2002), 181.
5. Daniel Fierman, "Killer Instinct" *Entertainment Weekly*, 17 March 2000, 28–29.
6. David Shipman, *The Great Movie Stars: The International Years* (New York: St. Martin's Press, 1972), 424.
7. Stephen Rebello, "The Next McCarthy Era" *Movieline*, August 1998, 56–57.
8. *Daily News* (New York), 1 June 2000.
9. Alexander Walker, *Vivien: The Life of Vivien Leigh* (New York: Weidenfeld & Nicolson, 1987), 106–107.
10. *Daily News* (New York), 13 June 1999.
11. Michael Viner and Terrie Maxine Frankel, *Tales from Casting Couch: An Unprecedented Candid Collection of Stories, Essays, and Anecdotes by and About Legendary Hollywood Stars, Starlets, and Wanna-bees...* (Beverly Hills: Dove Books, 1995), 112.
12. Mark Harris, "The $9 Million Maybe" *Entertainment Weekly*, 9 April 1993, 29.

13. Ron Base, *"If the Other Guy Isn't Jack Nicholson, I've Got the Part"* (Chicago: Contemporary Books, 1994), 285.
14. Ron Base, *"If the Other Guy Isn't Jack Nicholson, I've Got the Part"* (Chicago: Contemporary Books, 1994), 241–242.
15. Laurent Bouzereau, *The DePalma Cut: The Films of America's Most Controversial Director* (New York: Dembner Books, 1988), 76.
16. Andy Dougan, *Untouchable: A Biography of Robert De Niro* (New York: Thunder's Mouth Press, 1996), 189–190.
17. Stephen Rebello, "Out of the Line of Fire" *Movieline*, July 1998, 70.
18. Ron Base, *"If the Other Guy Isn't Jack Nicholson, I've Got the Part"* (Chicago: Contemporary Books, 1994), 280.
19. Robert Evans, *Francis The Kid Stays in the Picture* (New York: Hyperion, 1994), 293.

V

1. Warren G. Harris, *Sophia Loren: A Biography* (New York: Simon & Schuster, 1998), 279.
2. James Robert Parish and Ronald L. Bowers, *The MGM Stock Company: The Golden Era* (New Rochelle: Arlington House, 1973), 154.
3. Jeff Burkhart and Bruce Stuart, *Hollywood's First Choices* (New York: Crown Trade Paperbacks, 1994), 202.
4. Dalton Ross, "What to Watch" *Entertainment Weekly*, 27 April 2001, 104.
5. David Shipman, *The Great Movie Stars: The International Years* (New York: St. Martin's Press, 1972), 89.
6. David Shipman, *The Great Movie Stars: The International Years* (New York: St. Martin's Press, 1972), 179.
7. Milos Forman and Jan Novak, *Turnaround: A Memoir* (New York: Villard Books, 1994), 284.
8. Ron Base, *"If the Other Guy Isn't Jack Nicholson, I've Got the Part"* (Chicago: Contemporary Books, 1994), 171.
9. Jeff Burkhart and Bruce Stuart, *Hollywood's First Choices* (New York: Crown Trade Paperbacks, 1994), 192.
10. Jason Bonderoff, *Tom Selleck: An Unauthorized Biography* (New York: Signet, 1983), 129–131.
11. Stephen Rebello, "Nowhere to Hide" *Movieline*, May 1995, 85.
12. Peter Manso, *Brando: The Biography* (New York: Hyperion, 1994), 306.
13. Jeff Young, *Kazan: The Master Director Discusses His Films* (New York: Newmarket Press, 1999), 93.
14. Benjamin Svetkey, "Lava Is a Many-Splendored Thing" *Entertainment Weekly*, 25 April 1997, 33.

W

1. Tom McGee, *Betty Grable: The Girl with the Million Dollar Legs* (Vestal: The Vestal Press, 1995), 166–168.
2. Mark Schwed, "Hollywood Grapevine" *TV Guide*, 3 January 1998, 10.
3. Sean M. Smith, "Is Penelope Cruz Too Beautiful for Words" *Premiere*, March 2001, 72.
4. Tom O'Neill, "Hollywood's Cast System" *Us*, June 1995, 83.
5. James Riordan, *Stone: The Controversies, Excesses, and Exploits of a Radical Filmmaker* (New York: Hyperion, 1995), 218, 231, 233–234.

6. Warren G. Harris, *Audrey Hepburn: A Biography* (New York: Simon & Schuster, 1994), 127.
7. Barry Paris, *Audrey Hepburn* (New York: G. P. Putnam's Sons, 1996), 118.
8. John Parker, *Warren Beatty: The Last Great Lover of Hollywood* (New York: Carroll & Graf, 1993), 88.
9. Ron Base, *"If the Other Guy Isn't Jack Nicholson, I've Got the Part"* (Chicago: Contemporary Books, 1994), 239–240.
10. Lawrence J. Quirk, *Totally Uninhibited: The Life and Wild Times of Cher* (New York: William Morrow, 1991), 230.
11. Randall Riese, *Her Name Is Barbra* (New York: St. Martin's Paperbacks, 1993), 487.
12. John Eastman, *Retakes: Behind the Scenes of 500 Classic Movies* (New York: Ballantine Books, 1989), 366–367.
13. Michael Freedland, *The Warner Brothers* (New York: St. Martin's Press, 1983), 145.
14. David Shipman, *The Great Movie Stars: The Golden Years* (New York: Crown, 1970), 202.
15. Gene Brown, *Movie Time: A Chronology of Hollywood and the Movie Industry from Its Beginnings to the Present* (New York: Macmillan, 1995), 113.
16. David Shipman, *The Great Movie Stars: The Golden Years* (New York: Crown, 1970), 496.
17. Arthur Laurents, *Original Story By: A Memoir of Broadway and Hollywood* (New York: Alfred A. Knopf, 2000), 266.
18. Steve Wulf, "25 Years Ago" *Entertainment Weekly*, 1 March 1999, 82.
19. James Spada, *Streisand: Her Life* (New York: Ivy Books, 1995), 326–328.
20. Randall Riese, *Her Name Is Barbra* (New York: St. Martin's Paperbacks, 1993), 369.
21. Arthur Laurents, *Original Story By: A Memoir of Broadway and Hollywood* (New York: Alfred A. Knopf, 2000), 266.
22. *Daily News* (New York), 30 November 1999.
23. Jeff Lipsky, "Mr. Romano's Neighborhood" *Premiere*, February 2004, 106.
24. Dave Karger, "War Story" *Entertainment Weekly*, 28 November 1997, 43.
25. Ron Base, *"If the Other Guy Isn't Jack Nicholson, I've Got the Part"* (Chicago: Contemporary Books, 1994), 145–146.
26. Suzanne Finstad, *Natasha: The Biography of Natalie Wood* (New York: Harmony Books, 2001), 227–228.
27. Ann-Margret with Todd Gold, *Ann-Margret: My Story* (New York: G. P. Putnam's Sons, 1994), 60.
28. Barry Paris, *Audrey Hepburn* (New York: G. P. Putnam's Sons, 1996), 168–169.
29. John Parker, *Warren Beatty: The Last Great Lover of Hollywood* (New York: Carroll & Graf, 1993), 71.
30. Ron Base, *"If the Other Guy Isn't Jack Nicholson, I've Got the Part"* (Chicago: Contemporary Books, 1994), 145–146.
31. John Eastman, *Retakes: Behind the Scenes of 500 Classic Movies* (New York: Ballantine Books, 1989), 368.
32. David Gardner, *Tom Hanks: The Unauthorized Biography* (London: Blake, 1999), 118.
33. William Goldman, *Which Lie Did I Tell?* (New York: Pantheon Books, 2000), 43.
34. Benjamin Svetkey, "Clown Jewel" *Entertainment Weekly*, 30 May 2003, 67.
35. Andrew Yule, *Sean Connery: From 007 to Hollywood Icon* (New York: Donald I. Fine, 1992), 258.
36. John Eastman, *Retakes: Behind the Scenes of 500 Classic Movies* (New York: Ballantine Books, 1989), 370.
37. Jeffrey Meyers, *Bogart: A Life in Hollywood* (New York: Houghton Mifflin, 1997), 38.
38. David Shipman, *The Great Movie Stars: The International Years* (New York: St. Martin's Press, 1972), 40.
39. Jeff Burkhart and Bruce Stuart, *Hollywood's First Choices* (New York: Crown Trade Paperbacks, 1994), 73–75, 81.
40. Jeff Burkhart and Bruce Stuart, *Hollywood's First Choices* (New York: Crown Trade Paperbacks, 1994), 73–75, 81.
41. John Eastman, *Retakes: Behind the Scenes of 500 Classic Movies* (New York: Ballantine Books, 1989), 271.
42. Jeff Burkhart and Bruce Stuart, *Hollywood's First Choices* (New York: Crown Trade Paperbacks, 1994), 73–75, 81.
43. Jeff Burkhart and Bruce Stuart, *Hollywood's First Choices* (New York: Crown Trade Paperbacks, 1994), 73–75, 81.
44. Peter Fonda, *Don't Tell Dad: A Memoir* (New York: Hyperion, 1998), 215–216.
45. John Eastman, *Retakes: Behind the Scenes of 500 Classic Movies* (New York: Ballantine Books, 1989), 372.
46. David Weddle, *If They Move ... Kill 'Em!: The Life and Times of Sam Peckinpah* (New York: Grove Press, 1994), 319–321.
47. David Weddle, *If They Move ... Kill 'Em!: The Life and Times of Sam Peckinpah* (New York: Grove Press, 1994), 319–321.
48. Marshall Fine, *Bloody Sam: The Life and Films of Sam Peckinpah* (New York: Donald I. Fine, 1991), 124.
49. David Weddle, *If They Move ... Kill 'Em!: The Life and Times of Sam Peckinpah* (New York: Grove Press, 1994), 319–321.
50. Holly Millea, "The Second Coming of Mickey Rourke" *Premiere*, February 2003, 95.
51. Andrew Yule, *Picture Shows: The Life and Films of Peter Bogdanovich* (New York: Limelight Editions, 1992), 115.
52. David Shipman, *The Great Movie Stars: The International Years* (New York: St. Martin's Press, 1972), 450.
53. Chris Nashawaty, "Star Spelled Backward" *Entertainment Weekly*, March 28 2003, 32.
54. Stephen Rebello, "Girl We Love" *Movieline*, April 1998, 94.
55. Stephen Rebello, "Kiss Us, Kate" *Movieline*, March 1998, 118.
56. Stephen Rebello, "One Hundred Percent from the Heart" *Movieline*, November 1998, 81.
57. Michael Atkinson, "The Mystery of Christian Bale" *Movieline*, March 1997, 105.
58. Beverly Gray, *Ron Howard: From Mayberry to the Moon ... and Beyond* (Nashville: Rutledge Hill Press, 2003), 131.
59. Michael Logan, "Hot 'Date'" *TV Guide*, 17 May 2003, 40.
60. A. Scott Berg, *Goldwyn: A Biography* (New York: Alfred A. Knopf, 1989), 158–159.
61. Patrick McGilligan, *Jack's Life: A Biography of Jack Nicholson* (New York, London: W. W. Norton, 1994), 350.
62. Nancy Griffin and Kim Masters, *Hit and Run: How*

Jon Peters and Peter Guber Took Sony for a Ride in Hollywood (New York: Simon & Schuster, 1996), 137.
63. Rebecca Ascher-Walsh, "Testing 'Limits'" *Entertainment Weekly*, 18 September 1998 22, 24.
64. Anne Edwards, *Shirley Temple: American Princess* (New York: Berkley Books, 1988), 109–110.
65. Doug McClelland, *Down the Yellow Brick Road: The Making of The Wizard of Oz* (New York: Pyramid Books, 1976), 55, 63, 66.
66. Anne Edwards, *Shirley Temple: American Princess* (New York: Berkley Books, 1988), 109–110.
67. David Shipman, *Judy Garland: The Secret Life of an American Legend* (New York: Hyperion, 1992), 82–84.
68. Jeff Burkhart and Bruce Stuart, *Hollywood's First Choices* (New York: Crown Trade Paperbacks, 1994), 162–164.
69. Aljean Harmetz, *The Making of The Wizard of Oz* (New York: Alfred A. Knopf, 1977), 119, 122–123.
70. Doug McClelland, *Down the Yellow Brick Road: The Making of The Wizard of Oz* (New York: Pyramid Books, 1976), 55, 63, 66.
71. Jeff Burkhart and Bruce Stuart, *Hollywood's First Choices* (New York: Crown Trade Paperbacks, 1994), 162–164.
72. David Shipman, *Judy Garland: The Secret Life of an American Legend* (New York: Hyperion, 1992), 82–84.
73. Doug McClelland, *Down the Yellow Brick Road: The Making of The Wizard of Oz* (New York: Pyramid Books, 1976), 55, 63, 66.
74. Jeff Burkhart and Bruce Stuart, *Hollywood's First Choices* (New York: Crown Trade Paperbacks, 1994), 162–164.
75. Gerald Clarke, "Beyond the Yellow Brick Road" *TV Guide*, 1 July 2000, 18.
76. David Shipman, *Judy Garland: The Secret Life of an American Legend* (New York: Hyperion, 1992), 82–84.
77. Jeff Burkhart and Bruce Stuart, *Hollywood's First Choices* (New York: Crown Trade Paperbacks, 1994), 162–164.
78. Jeff Burkhart and Bruce Stuart, *Hollywood's First Choices* (New York: Crown Trade Paperbacks, 1994), 162–164.
79. Jeff Burkhart and Bruce Stuart, *Hollywood's First Choices* (New York: Crown Trade Paperbacks, 1994), 162–164.
80. Aljean Harmetz, *The Making of The Wizard of Oz* (New York: Alfred A. Knopf, 1977), 119, 122–123.
81. Jeff Burkhart and Bruce Stuart, *Hollywood's First Choices* (New York: Crown Trade Paperbacks, 1994), 162–164.
82. Doug McClelland, *Down the Yellow Brick Road: The Making of The Wizard of Oz* (New York: Pyramid Books, 1976), 55, 63, 66.
83. David Shipman, *The Great Movie Stars: The Golden Years* (New York: Crown, 1970), 278.
84. Garry Jenkins, *Harrison Ford: Imperfect Hero* (Secaucus: Birch Lane Press, 1998), 229.
85. Nellie Bly, *Marlon Brando: Larger Than Life* (New York: Pinnacle Books, 1994), 82.
86. Kirk Douglas, *Climbing the Mountain: My Search for Meaning* (New York: Simon & Schuster, 1997), 79–83.
87. A. Scott Berg, *Goldwyn: A Biography* (New York: Alfred A. Knopf, 1989), 32–323.

X

1. Nigel Andrews, *Travolta: The Life* (New York: Bloomsbury, 1998), 152.
2. *Daily News* (New York), 1 June 2000.

Y

1. David Shipman, *The Great Movie Stars: The Golden Years* (New York: Crown, 1970), 337.
2. William Goldman, *Which Lie Did I Tell?* (New York: Pantheon Books, 2000), 7.
3. Frank Miller, *Movies We Love* (Atlanta: Turner, 1996), 306, 308.
4. James Spada, *Streisand: Her Life* (New York: Ivy Books, 1995), 445–446.
5. Randall Riese, *Her Name Is Barbra* (New York: St. Martin's Paperbacks, 1993), 459–460, 462.
6. Randall Riese, *Her Name Is Barbra* (New York: St. Martin's Paperbacks, 1993), 459–460, 462.
7. Randall Riese, *Her Name Is Barbra* (New York: St. Martin's Paperbacks, 1993), 459–460, 462.
8. James Spada, *Streisand: Her Life* (New York: Ivy Books, 1995), 445–446.
9. Randall Riese, *Her Name Is Barbra* (New York: St. Martin's Paperbacks, 1993), 459–460, 462.
10. Gregory Kirschling, "Almost Famous" *Entertainment Weekly*, September 1998, 51.
11. John Oller, *Jean Arthur: The Actress Nobody Knew* (New York: Limelight Editions, 1997), 100–102.
12. Frank Capra, *The Name Above the Title: An Autobiography* (New York: Macmillan, 1971), 243.
13. Steven Jay Rubin, *The Complete James Bond Movie Encyclopedia* (Chicago: Contemporary Books, 1990), 451.
14. Eric Braun, *Deborah Kerr* (New York: St. Martin's Press, 1977), 116.
15. Andrew Yule, *Sean Connery: From 007 to Hollywood Icon* (New York: Donald I. Fine, 1992), 75, 80.
16. Rudy Behlmer, *Memo from David O. Selznick* (New York: The Viking Press, 1972), 159.
17. David Shipman, *The Great Movie Stars: The Golden Years* (New York: Crown, 1970), 343.
18. David Shipman, *The Great Movie Stars: The International Years* (New York: St. Martin's Press, 1972), 42.

Z

1. Garry Jenkins, *Harrison Ford: Imperfect Hero* (Secaucus: Birch Lane Press, 1998), 95–96.
2. John Parker, *Sean Connery* (Chicago: Contemporary Books, 1993), 174–175.
3. Elaine Gallagher, *Candidly Caine* (London: Robson Books, 1990), 130.
4. David Shipman, *The Great Movie Stars: The Golden Years* (New York: Crown, 1970), 236.
5. Anthony Quinn with Daniel Paisner, *One Man Tango* (New York: HarperCollins, 1995), 319–321.
6. Michael Caine, *What's It All About?: An Autobiography* (New York: Turtle Bay Books, 1992), 153–155.

INDEX

Numbers in *italics* are pages with photographs.

Aaliyah 159
Abbott, George 182
ABC 205
Abdul, Paula 81
Abdul-Jabbar, Kareem 7
Abel, Walter 131
About Last Night 3
Above Suspicion 3
Abraham, F. Murray 12, 91
Abraham Lincoln 3, 4
Abrahams, Mort 30, 188
Absence of Malice 3
Absolute Power 3
Academy Awards 1, 4, 8, 11, 12, 17, 19, 22, 23, 25, 29, 31, 32, 33, 40, 42, 43, 44, 47, 48, 51, 52, 54, 56, 59, 62, 65, 66, 67, 69, 75, 79, 82, 83, 84, 86, 92, 93, 94, 95, 99, 102, 104, 108, 109, 110, 111, 114, 116, 119, 125, 128, 133, 134, 139, 142, 153, 157, 158, 161, 162, 164, 166, 168, 169, 172, 174, 175, 177, 179, 181, 183, 184, 185, 187, 190, 192, 195, 197, 204, 208, 209, 211, 216, 218, 220, 222, 227, 228, 229, 237–238, 242, 243, 245, 251
The Accidental Tourist 3–4
The Accused 4–5
Ace Ventura: Pet Detective 5
Across 110th Street, 5
Act One 5
Action 184
The Actress 5
Adams, Brooke 66
Adams, Cindy 21
Adams, Dawn 222
Adams, Joey Lauren 154
Adams, Maud 177
Adams, Nick 187
Adam's Rib 41
The Addams Family 5
Addams Family Values 5
Adjani, Isabelle 27, 64, 128

Adler, Stella 261
Adlon, Percy 24–25
The Adventures of Baron Munchausen 6
The Adventures of Marco Polo 6
The Adventures of Pluto Nash 6
The Adventures of Robin Hood 6
The Affairs of Cellini 170
Affectionately Yours 6
Affleck, Ben 65, 168, 177, 184, 212, 231, 232, 256
Affleck, Casey 165
The African Queen 6–7, 200
After the Fall 140
Agnes Browne 7
Aherne, Brian 95, 96, 123, 140, 234
A.I.: Artificial Intelligence 163
Aiello, Danny 45, 72
Aimee, Anouk 36–37, 73, 165, 222, 261
Air Force One 7
Airplane! 7
The Alamo 7
An Alan Smithee Film: Burn Hollywood Burn 7
Albee, Edward 254
Alberghetti, Anna Maria 200, 253
Alberni, Louis 132
Albert, Eddie 138, 233
Albertson, Frank 131, 194
Albright, Lola 21
Alda, Alan 10, 38, 182, 226
Alderman, John 253
Aldrich, Kathryn 198, 199
Aldrich, Robert 125
Aldridge, Katharine 105, 107
Alexander, Denise 253
Alexander, Jane 56, 129, 139, 140
Alexander, Jason 151
Alexander, John 131
Alexander, Melanie 223, 224
Alexander, Ross 162
Alfie 7–8

Algiers 8, 258
Ali (sheik) 144
Ali, Muhammed 118
Alice Doesn't Live Here Anymore 8
Alice in Wonderland 8
Alice's Restaurant 8
Alien 8
All About Eve 8–9
All Fall Down 156
All My Children 5, 119, 256
All Night Long 9
All Quiet on the Western Front 10
All That Jazz 10–11
All the King's Men 11
All the Pretty Horses 11
All Through the Night 1, 11
Allen, Elizabeth 222
Allen, Jay Presson 250
Allen, Joan 63, 174
Allen, Karen 197
Allen, Nancy 50, 141
Allen, Ray 117
Allen, Steve 31
Allen, Tim 72
Allen, Woody 17–18, 29, 45, 52, 62, 114, 125, 129, 157, 189, 195, 202, 213–214, 215, 220
Allgood, Sara 132
Allman, Gregg 226, 227
Ally McBeal 53
Allyson, June 8, 17, 28, 43, 128, 168, 207, 230, 234, 238
Almereyda, Michael 114
Almost Famous 11–12
Almost Grown 215
Along Came a Spider 139
Alonso, Maria Conchita *185*
The Alphabet Murders 12
Alt, Carol 193
Altman, Robert 60, 149, 151, 171, 189, 217
Alvarado, Trini 102, 103
Always 12
Amadeus 12

311

Ameche, Don 110, 149
American Beauty 12
American Gigolo 12–13
American Graffiti 13, 227
American Hot Wax 13
An American in Paris 13
American Psycho 13
The Americanization of Emily 13–14
America's Sweethearts 14
Ames, Leon 131
Amis, Suzy 36
Amistad 14, 241
Anaconda 88
Analyze This 14
Anatomy of a Murder 14–15
Anchors Aweigh 183
Anders, Allison 96
Andersen, Hans Christian 115
Anderson, Eddie 105, 108
Anderson, Elga 93
Anderson, Gillian 114, 189, 220
Anderson, Gordon 45–46, 118
Anderson, Jeff 58
Anderson, Jo 133
Anderson, Judith 198, 199
Anderson, Kevin 102, 103
Anderson, Loni 9, 220
Anderson, Mary 105, 106
Anderson, Paul Thomas 40
Andersson, Bibi 220
Andre the Giant 193
Andress, Ursula 157, 180
Andrews, Dana 143
Andrews, Dean 132, 133
Andrews, Edward 240
Andrews, Julie 29, 48, 56, 117, 169, 192, 214, 222, 223
Andrews, Lois 8
Andy Hardy Comes Home 15
Angel, Heather 31, 198, 199
Angel Eyes 15
Angel Heart 15
Angela's Ashes 15
Angeli, Pier 112, 147, 206, 230, 253
Angels Over Broadway 15
Angie 15–16
Animal House 16
The Animal Kingdom 16
Aniston, Jennifer 45, 118, 176, 204
Ankerson, Ardis 105, 107
Ann-Margret 49, 81, 111, 181, 228, 253
Anna and the King 176
Anna and the King of Siam 16–17
Anna Karenina 17
Annabella 154, 155
Anna-Lisa 222
Annaud, Jean-Jacques 215
Anne of the Thousand Days 17
Annie 17
Annie (TV) 54
Annie Get Your Gun 17
Annie Hall 17–18, 214
Annie Oakley 18
Another Woman 18

Anson, A.E. 150
Anspach, Susan 38, 171
Antoinette, Marie 157
Antonioni, Michelangelo 37, 260
Antony, Mark 57, 58, 68
Antony and Cleopatra 68
Antwone Fisher 18
The Anvil 48
Anwar, Gabrielle 241
Any Given Sunday 18
The Apartment 18, 19
Apocalypse Now 18–19
Apollo 13 19
Apollodorus 47
The Apostle 19–20
Applegate, Christina 96
Aprea, John 19
Apt Pupil 20
Apted, Michael 60
Arabesque 20
Arau, Alfonso 251
Arbuckle, Fatty 180
Archer, Anne 29, 100, 101, 233
Arenas, Reinaldo 29
Arizona 20
Arkin, Alan 36, 39, 40, 129, 176
Arlen, Richard 119
Armani, Giorgio 12
Armstrong, Gillian 168
Arnaz, Lucie 111
Arnold, Edward 59, 131
Arnold, Tom 151, 185
Arnstein, Nicky 94
Around the World in 80 Days 20–21
Arquette, Patricia 134, 185, 242
Arquette, Rosanna 4, 42, 43, 68, 195, 196
The Arrangement 21
Arsenic and Old Lace 21
Arthur 21
Arthur, Beatrice 155
Arthur, Jean 15, 16, 18, 20, 25, 92, 104, 105, 106, 121, 131, 132, 136, 150, 160, 189, 259
As Good as it Gets 21, 208
As the World Turns 42
As Young as You Feel 21
Ashby, Hal 115–116, 141
Ashcroft, Peggy 115, 122, 223
Asherson, Renee 120
Ashford & Simpson 48
Ashley, Elizabeth 26, 253
Ashley, Ted 155
Asner, Edward 133
The Asphalt Jungle 21
Assante, Armand 42
The Associate 21
Astaire, Fred 13, 38, 64, 78, 162, 167, 223, 254
Astor, Mary 73, 74, 125, 154, 155
At First Sight 5
At Long Last Love 173
Athena 21–22
Atherton, William 154
Atlanta, GA 107

Attanasio, Paul 232
Attenborough, Richard 55, 95, 122, 153
Aubrey, Jim 95
Audley, Eleanor 223
Audran, Stephane 35
Auerbach, Norbert 259
Auger, Claudine 240, 241
Aumont, Jean-Pierre 50
Auntie Mame 22, 155
Aurthur, Robert Alan 10
Avalon, Frankie 100, 101, 111, 151
The Avengers 22
Avenue Pictures Productions 76
Averill, James 119
Avery, Margaret 59
Avildsen, John 136, 171–172, 205
Awakenings 22
The Awful Truth 22
Axelrod, George 43
Aykroyd, Dan 3, 16, 98, 171, 172
Aylward, Gladys 129
Ayres, Gerry 165
Ayres, Lew 75, 76, 105, 107, 135
Azaria, Hank 14, 155, 156

The Babe Ruth Story 22
Babenco, Hector 139
Babes on Broadway 22–23
Baby Boom 23
Baby Boy 23
Baby Doll 23
Baby, It's You 23
Bacall, Lauren 37, 47, 62, 68, 127, 186, 205, 226
Bachelor Party 23
Back to the Future 23–24
Back to the Future Part II 24
Back to the Future Part III 24
Backdraft 238
Baclanova, Olga 91, 92
Bacon, Elizabeth 238
Bacon, Irving 131
Bacon, Kevin 85, 88, 128, 132, 133
Bacon, Lloyd 130
Bad Men of Missouri 24
Baddeley, Hermione 223
Badham, John 209
Badham, Mary 118
Baer, Max 193
Bagdad 24
Bagdad Café 24–25
Bainter, Fay 54, 223, 259
Baio, Scott 91
Baja Oklahoma 228
Baker, Carroll 23, 163, 187, 199
Baker, Diane 253
Baker, Lenny 172
Baker, Stanley 222, 223, 261
Balaban, Bob 115, 215
Baldwin, Alec 52, 82, 93, 97, 102, 103, 125, 128, 132, 133, 184, 219, 241, 258
Baldwin, Roger S. 14
Baldwin, Stephen 180

Index 313

Baldwin, William 238, 240
Bale, Christian 13, 126, 235, 256
Balk, Fairuza 96
Ball, Jane 137
Ball, Lucille 25, 31, 41, 47, 99, 105, 106, 111, 112, 117, 119, 120, 155, 156, 231
Ball of Fire 25
The Ballad of Cable Hogue 25
Ballantyne, E.J. 131
Balsam, Martin 51, 248
Bana, Eric 124
Bananas 189
Bancroft, Anne 34, 35, 81, 85, 100, 102, 109, 110, 163, 166, 170, 179, 194, 214, 222, 223, 246
Bancroft, George 131
Band of Angels 119
The Band Wagon 25
Banderas, Antonio 29, 42, 81, 159
Banjo on My Knee 25
Bankhead, Tallulah 105, 106, 108, 134, 135, 147, 152, 197–198, 214, 261
Banks, Leslie 120
Bannen, Ian 232
Bannister, Guy 133
Barabbas 25
Baral, Eileen 223, 224
Barbarella 26
Barclay, Don 131
Bard, Katharine 198, 199
Bardem, Javier 29, 30
Bardot, Brigitte 26, 57, 58, 130, 178, 179
The Barefoot Contessa 26
Barefoot in the Park 26
Barefoot in the Park (play) 26
Baretta 41
Barker, Lex 143–144
Barkin, Ellen 3–4, 27, 28, 42, 43, 68, 109, 156, 216, 239
The Barkleys of Broadway 26
Barnes, Binnie 155
Barr, Roseanne 216
Barrett (Browning), Elizabeth 26, 27
The Barretts of Wimpole Street (1934) 26
The Barretts of Wimpole Street (1957) 26–27
Barrier, Edgar 131
Barris, Chuck 60
Barrow, Clyde 40
Barrymore, Diana 105, 107
Barrymore, Drew 28, 52, 53, 96, 169, 194, 212, 218
Barrymore, Ethel 175, 200
Barrymore, John 48, 61, 74, 110, 156, 162, 195, 205
Barrymore, Lionel 48, 105, 108, 110, 131
Bartholomew, Freddie 66
Bartlett, Martine 222
Barton, James 110

Barton Fink 91
Basehart, Richard 176, 194
Basic Instinct 27
Basinger, Kim 27, 28, 36, 41, 42, 56, 70, 82, 91, 173, 191, 219, 220, 237
The Basketball Diaries 27
Bass, Ronald 197
Bassett, Angela 81, 166, 258
Bassey, Shirley 178
Bates, Alan 10, 220
Bates, Barbara 8, 9
Bates, Florence 198, 199
Bates, Kathy 54, 164, 241
Batman 27
Batman & Robin 27–28
Batman Forever 28
Batman Returns 27, 28
Battle Circus 28
Battle for the Planet of the Apes 28
Baxter, Amy Lynn 14
Baxter, Anne 8, 9, 64, 65, 66, 125, 153, 172, 175, 179, 185, 198, 199, 222, 230, 254
Baxter, Len 125
Baxter, Warner 105, 107, 154, 155
The Beach 29
Beaches 29
Beakel, Walter 109
Beals, Jennifer 87
Bean, Sean 229
The Beatles 17, 206
Beatty, Warren 5, 10, 28, 33, 34, 38, 40, 47, 52, 62, 70, 75, 82, 95, 100, 101, 109, 111, 112, 115, 118, 119, 120, 137, 142, 145, 147, 159, 164, 174, 180, 182, 183, 184, 192, 206, 207, 222, 225, 229, 231, 233, 235, 236, 251, 252, 253, 254, 260
Beau Geste 29
A Beautiful Mind 7, 29
Beavers, Louise 105, 108
Beck, John 197
Beck, Michael 258
Becket 29
Beckinsale, Kate 45, 184, 203
Becky Sharpe 106
The Bedford Incident 29
Bedknobs and Broomsticks 29
Beecher, Janet 105, 108, 257, 258
Beery, Wallace 110, 162, 168
Before Night Falls 29–30
Begelman, David 173
The Beggar's Opera 79
The Beguiled 43
Being There 30
Belack, Doris 243
Belafonte, Harry 5, 190
Bel Geddes, Barbara 8
Bellamy, Ralph 22, 162–163
La Belle Meuniere 30
The Belle of New York 30
Belli, Melvin 100
Bello, Jean 115

Bellows, Gil 216
Belmondo, Jean-Paul 57, 183, 246
Belolo, Henri 48
Beloved 30
Belushi, James 3, 87, 88, 144, 145, 209
Belushi, John 3, 16, 60, 98, 171, 172
Ben-Hur (1925) 31
Ben-Hur (1959) 31
Benard, Maurice 216, *217*
Bender, Lawrence 195, 202
Bendix, William 22
Beneath the Planet of the Apes 30
Benet, Eric 6
Bening, Annette 28, 71, 72, 250
Benjamin, Paul 5, 72
Benjamin, Richard 38, 189
Bennett, Bruce 162, 245
Bennett, Constance 131, 148, 170, 177, 181, 244
Bennett, Joan 105, 106, 107, 154, 155, 167, 170, 220
Benny, Jack 33–34, 85
Benny and Joon 31
The Benny Goodman Story 31
Benson, Robby 102, 116
Bentley, Wes 195–196
Berenger, Tom 32, 46, 62, 132, 188, 192
Beresford, Bruce 62
Berg, Peter 210
Bergen, Candice 37, 109, 110, 111, 112, 113, 228
Bergen, Edgar 223
Bergman, Andrew 36, 122, 212
Bergman, Ingrid 8, 9, 47, 50, 54, 72, 83, 88, 92, 93, 96, 126, 129, 154, 155, 163, 168, 183, 209, 220, 254
Bergman, Sandahl *201*
Bergner, Elisabeth 51, *90,* 115
Berkeley, Busby 17, 88
Berkeley Square 31
Berkley, Elizabeth 87, 218
Berlin 227
Berman, Pandro S. 158, 234
Bernardi, Herschel 223
Bernstein, Armyan 7
Berridge, Elizabeth 12
Berry, Eric 223
Berry, Halle 6, 53, 88, 128, 136, 166, 258
Bertinelli, Valerie 88
Bertolucci, Bernardo 216
Best, Travis 117
Best Foot Forward 31
The Best of Everything 247
Best in Show 31
The Best Little Whorehouse in Texas 31
The Best Things in Life Are Free 32
The Best Years of Our Lives 32
Betrayed 32
The Betsy 32

314 Index

Bettany, Paul 200
The Beverly Hillbillies 224
Beverly Hills Cop 32
Beverly Hills Cop II 32
Beverly Hills Cop III 32
Beverly Hills 90210 154
Beymer, Richard 120, 231, 253
Beyond Borders 32–33
Beyond Rangoon 242
Bianchi, Daniela 93
Biano, Solly 210
The Bible 33
Bicentennial Man 33
Bick, Jerry 171
Bickford, Charles 131, 226, 235
The Bicycle Thief 33
Biehn, Michael 237
Biel, Jessica *207*
Big 33
The Big Broadcast of 1937 33
The Big Broadcast of 1938 33–34
The Big Chill 34, 251
The Big Sky 34
Bikel, Theodore 117
"Bill" 9
Bill, Tony 109
A Bill of Divorcement 34
Billy Budd 34
Billy Liar 34, 73
Binoche, Juliette 64, 208
Bio-Dome 154
Biograph 157
Birch, Thora 12
The Birdcage 34
The Birds 34–35, 158
Birkenhead, Lord 53
Birmingham, AL 118
Birney, David 151
Bishop, Joey 138
Bishop, Kelly *71*
The Bishop's Wife 132
Bisset, Jacqueline 37, 47, 69, 226
Bitter Sweet 35
Bjork, Anita 125, *126*
Black, Jack 216
Black, Karen 60, 66, 82, 83, 100, 101
The Black Bird 35
Black Hand 35
Black Knight 35
The Black Orchid 35
Black Rain 35
Black Widow 35
Blackman, Honor 216
Blade Runner 35
Blaine, Vivian 113, 114
Blair, Betsy 78, 122, 123
Blair, Linda 81, 82
Blake, Robert 10, 40, 41, 94, 95, 127, 255
Blakely, Susan 100, 101, 233
Blakley, Ronee 171
Blame It on Rio 36
Blanchard, Mari 203
Blanchett, Cate 79, 114

Blandick, Clara 257, 258
Blandioi, Clara 132
Blaze 36
Blazing Saddles 36, 155
Blessed Event 36
Bligh, William 168
Blind Date 36
The Bliss of Mrs. Blossom 36–37
Blithe Spirit 37
Blithe Spirit (play) 37
Blixen, Karen 181
Blondell, Joan 90, 105, 108, 112, 245, 256
Blood Alley 37
Blood and Sand 37
Blood Simple 37
Bloodline 37
Bloom, Claire 53, 202, 216
Bloom, Verna 16, 121
Blow Out 37
Blowing Wild 37
Blowup 37
Blue 37, 207
The Blue Angel 37
Blue City 243
The Blue Lagoon 37–38
Blue Skies 38
Blue Velvet 38
Blues Brothers 2000 38
Blues in the Night 38, 236
Bluestein Davis, Susan 62
Blumberg, Nate 75
Blume in Love 38
Blyth, Ann 8, 119, 162, 180, 231
Boardman, Eleanor 83
Bob & Carol & Ted & Alice 38
Bobby Deerfield 3, 38
Body Double 38–39
Body Heat 39
The Bodyguard 39
Boetticher, Budd 247
Bogarde, Dirk 65, 95, 99, 236
Bogart, Humphrey 1, 6, 7, 11, 24, 37, 38, 43, 49, 50, 62, 66, 90, 100, 121, 127, 154, 156, 178, 181, 186, 208, 226, 245, 254
Bogart, Leslie 186
Bogdanovich, Peter 43, 55, 97, 141, 142, 159, 173, 175, 183, 238, 243
Boland, Mary 198, 199
Bolero 131
Boleyn, Anne 17, 155
Bolger, Ray 257
Bologna, Joe 133
Bolt, Robert 73
Bon Jovi, Jon 63
Bond, Ward 131
Bondi, Beulah 110, 131
The Bonfire of the Vanities 1, 39–40
Bonifant, J. Evan 38
Bonney, William H. "Billy the Kid" 184
Bonnie and Clyde 40
Bono, Jerry 223
Bono, Sonny 226, 227

Bononova, Fotunio 132
Boogie Nights 40
Booke, Sorrell, 223
Boone, Richard 147, 173, 229, 255
Boorman, John 242
Booth, James 7, 8, 261
Booth, Karin 8
Booth, Shirley 8, 59, 189, 221
Boothe, Powers 86
Bopha! 40
The Border 40–41
Borge, Victor 223
Borgnine, Ernest 100, 158, 244, 255
Born on the Fourth of July 41
Born to Be Bad 41
Born Yesterday 41
Borsten, Orin 137
Bosom Buddies 33
Boston, MA 182
The Bostonians 41
Bostwick, Barry 160
Bottoms, Sam 45, 46
Bottoms, Timothy 133, 141
Boulting, Ingrid 143
Bound for Glory 41
The Bounty 41
The Bourne Identity 41, 184
Bow, Clara 57, 201, 213
Bowerman, Bill 256, 257
Bowie, David 142, 143, 149
Bowles Locker, Em 105, 107
Bowman, Lee 127
Boxing Helena 41–42
The Boy Who Could Fly 42
Boyd, Stephen 31, 57, 58, 222, 223, 229
Boyer, Charles 16, 17, 49, 50, 95, 96, 175, 206, 252, 258
Boyle, Danny 29, 146
Boyle, Joseph C. 45
Boyle, Lara Flynn 160
Boyle, Peter 92, 229
Boyle, Richard 209
Bracco, Lorraine 80, 109, 196
Bradford, Jesse 108
Bradley, Leslie 223
Bradley, Omar N. 184
Brady, Alice 198, 199
Bram Stoker's Dracula 42
Branagh, Kenneth 52, 116, 159
Brandauer, Klaus Maria 125
Brandenburg, Larry 83
Brando, Marlon 18, 19, 21, 31, 47, 53, 55, 60, 61, 68, 73, 77, 78, 79, 81, 82, 84, 94, 96, 100, 101, 102, 111, 112, 113, 119, 120, 124, 132, 133, 135, 137, 142, 144, 145, 164, 165, 167, 173, 176, 179, 181, 182, 183, 187, 201, 210, 211, 225–226, 227, 232, 233, 236, 250, 251, 258, 260
Braselton, GA 42
The Brave 96
Brazil 42–43

Breakfast at Tiffany's 43
Breaking the Waves 43
Breezy 43
Brennan, Eileen 141
Brennan, Walter 110, 131, 132, 203, 204, 255
Brent, George 49, 65, 95, 96, 123, 175, 178
Breslin, Jimmy 92
Brest, Martin 161–162, 211
Brewster, Diane 203
Brewster's Millions 43
Brice, Fanny 94, 257
The Bride Goes Wild 43
The Bride of Frankenstein 43
The Bridge on the River Kwai 43
A Bridge Too Far 44
Bridges, Beau 151, 230
Bridges, Jeff 84, 87, 119, 133, 137, 138, 141, 151, 176, 182, 235, 246
Bridges, Lloyd 192, 203
The Bridges of Madison County 44
Bridget Jones's Diary 44
Brief Moment 44
Bright Lights, Big City 44
Brightman, Sarah 81
Bring Me the Head of Alfredo Garcia 44
Bringing Out the Dead 240
Bringing Up Baby 44–45, 152
Briskin, Sam 132
Britt, May 91
Britton, Barbara 8
Brix, Herman 235
Broadcast News 21, 45
Broadway 7, 10, 12, 21, 26, 34, 41, 45, 46, 47, 48, 52, 54, 59, 61, 64, 73, 80, 81, 83, 85, 87, 94, 95, 103, 104, 113, 114, 115, 119, 122, 130, 132, 134, 137, 143, 148, 151, 155, 163, 164, 168, 169, 173, 179, 182, 183, 184, 187, 189, 202, 206, 215, 224, 230, 234, 245, 253, 258, 259
Broadway Danny Rose 45
Broadway Melody of 1936 45
Broadway Nights 45
Broccoli, Albert "Cubby" 105, 177, 178, 225, 241
Brock, Alice 8
Broderick, Helen 132
Broderick, Matthew 87, 103, 104, 128, 141, 174, 228, 251
Brodie, Steve 131
Brody, Adrien 232
Brokedown Palace 45
Broken Arrow 45
Broken Lance 45
The Broken Land 45
Brolin, James 95, 177
Bromhead, Gonville 261
Bronco Billy 45–46
Bronson, Betty 31
Bronson, Charles 67, 100, 101, 164, 233, 255

Bronston, Samuel 79, 85
Bronx, NY 46
A Bronx Tale 46
The Brood 66–67
Brooks, Albert 33, 167, 181, 191, 212, 254
Brooks, Avery 154
Brooks, Garth 241
Brooks, James L. 21, 33, 237
Brooks, Leslie 8
Brooks, Louise 43, 194
Brooks, Mel 36, 194
Brooks, Randy 202
Brooks, Richard 100, 127
Brophy, Edward 131
Brosnan, Pierce 27, 104, 105, 148
Brown, Blair 60
Brown, Bryan 234
Brown, Charles 245
Brown, David 139
Brown, Horace 143
Brown, James 255
Brown, Joe E. 162
Brown, Johnny Mack *144*, 235
Brown, Molly 241, 249
Brown, Wally 131
The Brown Derby 108
Browne, Coral 22
Browne, Jackson 184
The Browning Version 46
Bruce, Lenny 145
Bruckheimer, Jerry 13, 62, 185
Bryant, Kobe 117
Bryna Production Company 69
Brynner, Yul 25, 137, 145, 221, 222, 223
The Buccaneer 46
Buccella, Maria Grazia 240, 241
Buchanan, Edgar 131, 132
Buchanan, Jack 25
Buck, Jules 169
Buckner, Susan 111
Buetel, Jack 181, 201
Bujold, Genevieve 17, 66, 100, 101, 115, 241
Bull Durham 46
Bullock, Sandra 28, 68, 127, 141, 153, 191, 208, 219, 224
Bunuel, Luis 17, 18
Burghoff, Gary 151
Burglar 46
Burke, Billie 105, 108, 257
Burke, James 131
Burnett, Carol 17, 81, 175
Burns, Michael 171
Burr, Cheryl 211, 212
Burr, Raymond 121
Burstyn, Ellen 8, 81, 86, 87, 141, 142, 179
Burton, Peter 93
Burton, Richard 17, 20, 29, 48, 57, 58, 60, 72, 109, 144, 148, 169, 173, 182, 204, 208–209, 222, 223, 226, 236, 240, 254
Burton, Tim 27, 28, 78

Bus Stop 46
Buscemi, Steve 91, 148, 202, 246
Busch, Niven 77
Busey, Gary 171
Busey, Jake 126
Bush, Sophia 237
Bushell, Anthony *134*
Bussell, Darcey 208
Butch and Sundance: The Early Days 46
Butch Cassidy and the Sundance Kid 12, 47
Butterfield 8 47
Buttons, Red 117
Byington, Spring 259
Byrne, Gabriel 14, 42
Byrne, Martha 42
Byrne, Michael 128, 129
Byrnes, Edd 64, 65

Caan, James 19, 38, 58, 80, 94, 95, 100, 101, 108, 109, 139, 153, 164, 179, 200, 204, 233
Cabaret 47
Cacoyannis, Michael 261
Cactus Flower 47
Caesar, Julius 57, 58
Caesar, Sid 175
Caesar and Cleopatra 47
Caesar's Palace 180
Cage, Nicolas 41, 83, 84, 102, 103, 122, 155, 156, 181, 185, 200, 222, 224, 225, 240
Cagney, James 36, 50, 66, 90, 93, 104, 116, 121, 135, 139, 140, 162, 167, 169, 194, 203, 239, 246, 247
Caine, Michael 7, 8, 55, 56, 71, 76, 114, 130, 156, 220, 231, 234, 261
Caine, Shakira 156
Cairo 47–48
Calhern, Louis 17, 131
Calhoun, Rory 155, 160
California Angels 46
California Split 48
Callas, Maria 33
Calleia, Joseph 132
Calloway, Cab 190
Calvert, Phyllis 260
Camelot 48
Cameron, James 241
Camille 48
Camino Real 93
Camp, Colleen 3
Camp McCall, NC 32
Campbell, Betty 198, 199
Campbell, Catherine 105, 107
Campbell, Louise 198, 199
Campbell, Martin 33
Campbell, Naomi 46
Campbell, Neve 207, 212
Campbell, Nicholas 66–67
Campbell, Robert 178
Campbell, Tisha 211
Campion, Cris 188
Campion, Jane 128

Canalito, Lee 235
Candy, John 76, 132, 133, 255
Cannery Row 48
Cannon, Dyan 38, 97, 118, 119
Cannonball Run 48
Can't Stop the Music 48
Cantinflas 20
Cantor, Eddie 134
Cape Fear (1962) 48
Cape Fear (1991) 48
Capone, Al 225, 249
Capote, Truman 43
Capra, Frank 21, 92, 104, 132, 140, 150, 160, 165, 189, 205, 259
Capshaw, Kate 3, 35, 50, 51, 129
Captain Blood 49
Captain Corelli's Mandolin 49
Captain Horatio Hornblower 49
The Captain's Paradise 49
Capucine 188, 222
Caravan Pictures 16
The Cardinal 49, 161
Cardinale, Claudia 117
Cardona, Annette 111
Carey, Harry 165, 208
Carey, Macdonald 160
Carey, Mariah 81
Caridi, Carmine 100, 101
Carlisle, Phyllis 229
Carlyle, Robert 15, 126, 216
Carmel, CA 259
Carmor, Roger C. 223
Carnal Knowledge 49
Carne, Marcel 246
Carney, Alan 131
Carney, Art 116, 117
Carnovsky, Morris 259
Caron, Leslie 40, 83, 94, 99, 147, 151, 222, 223
Carousel 49
Carpenter, Cathy 109, 110
Carpenter, David 62
Carpenter, John 86
Carr, Allan 48, 111
Carr, Charmian 223, 224
Carradine, David 41, 137, 142
Carradine, John 91
Carradine, Keith 19, 151, 171, 229
Carrey, Jim 5, 29, 123, 155, 156, 160, 185, 187, 224, 225
Carrie (1952) 49–50
Carrie (1976) 37, 50, 227
Carroll, Diahann 57, 178
Carroll, Jim 27
Carroll, Madeleine 140, 148, 149
Carroll, Nancy 57, 69, 230
Carson, Jack 22, 136, 138, 200
Carson, Johnny 83, 84, 138
Carter, Helena Bonham 43, 85, 159
Carter, Nell 97
Cartlidge, Katrin 247
Cartwright, Angela 192, 223, 224
Casablanca 1, 11, 50, 66
Case, Alan 253
The Case of the Howling Dog 50

Cash, Rosalind 178
Casino 50–51, 58
Cass Timberlane 51
The Cassandra Crossing 51
Cassavetes, John 203, 206, 207, 236, 243
Cassidy, Butch (Robert Leroy Parker) 46, 47
Casta, Laetitia 238
Castellani, Renato 206
Castellano, Richard 100, 101–102
Castillo, Gloria 199
Cat on a Hot Tin Roof 51
Cataldi, Anna 181
Catch-22 51, 110
Cates, Georgina 185
Catherine the Great 51
Catlett, Walter 131
Caulfield, Maxwell 23
Caveman 77
Caviezel, James 15, 121, 184–185
Cecil B. Demented 51
Ceiling Zero 51–52
Celebrity 52
Ceylon 43
Chain Reaction 52
Chakiris, George 253, 255
Chamberlain, Richard 253
The Champ 52
Champion, Nathan D. 119
Chan, Jackie 7
Chancellor, John 172
Chandler, Helen 123
Chandler, Jeff 180
Chaney, Lon 75
Channing, Carol 119, 120
Channing, Stockard 89, 111, 233
Chapin, Doug 223, 224
Chaplin 122
Chaplin, Charlie 33, 56, 57, 104, 105, 162, 166, 224
Chaplin, Geraldine 73, 223, 224
Chaplin, Saul 223
Chaplin, Sydney 141
Chapter Two 175
Charade 20, 52–53, 157
Chariots of Fire 52
Charisse, Cyd 78, 94, 175, 222
Charlie Brown 224
Charlie's Angels 53
Charlie's Angels (TV) 139
Charly 53, 216
Charrier, Jacques 246
Charriere, Henri "Papillon" 183
The Chase 53
Chase, Chevy 16, 214, 225, 243
Chase, Duane 223, 224
Chasin, George 180
Chatterton, Ruth 229
Cheadle, Don 215
Chechik, Jeremiah 22
Cher 5, 23, 28, 35, 44, 60, 68, 81, 84, 89, 110, 129, 137, 138, 142, 143, 159, 161, 162, 166, 216, 226, 227, 236, 238, 243, 251, 256

Cherkassov, Nicolai 145
Cherrill, Virginia 56–57
Cheshire, Happy 131
Chevalier, Maurice 13, 74
Cheyenne Autumn 53
Chicago 54
Chicago, IL 210
Chicken Every Sunday 54
Chicken Run 54
A Child Is Waiting 54
The Children's Hour 54–55
Child's Play 55
Chiles, Lois 67, 111, 112
The China Syndrome 55, 175
Chinatown 55, 247
Chong, Rae Dawn 42–43
A Chorus Line 55
The Chosen 55
Chou, Collin 159
Christensen, Hayden 228
Christian, Fletcher 41
Christie, Agatha 12
Christie, Julie 34, 38, 60, 65, 73, 118, 119, 240, 241
A Christmas Carol (Charles Dickens) 212
A Christmas Story 55
Christopher Strong 55
Christy, Dorothy 222
Churchill, Sarah 207
Chwat, Sam 46
CIA 232
The Cider House Rules 55–56, 225
The Cider House Rules (John Irving) 55
Cilento, Diane 23, 222
The Cincinnati Kid 56
Cincinnati Reds 7
Cinemascope 49
Cinque, Joseph 14
Cisco Pike 184
Citizen Kane 239
City for Conquest 56, 236
City Heat 56
City Lights 56–57
City of Angels 150
City Streets 57
Claire, Ina 99, 112, 158, 197, 198
Clark, Fred 8
Clark, Petula 109, 250
Clarke, Mae 91, 194
Class Action 57
Classe Tous Risques 57
Claudia 57
Claudine 57
Clavel, Aurora 44
Clayburgh, Jill 8, 60, 86, 87, 95, 100, 101, 153, 175, 228, 249
Clayton, Dick 30
Clayton, Jan 222
Clayton, Marion 198, 199
Clear and Present Danger 232
Cleese, John 39, 40
Cleopatra 1, 57, 58
Cleopatra 57–58

Index

Clerks 58, 154
Clift, Montgomery 8, 69, 77, 93, 120, 124, 144, 177, 179, 201, 203, 206, 210, 221, 226, 231, 232, 233, 236, 243, 256, 260
Clinton, Bill 192
Clive, Colin 91
The Clock 58
Clockers 58
Clooney, George 27, 28, 60, 133, 146, 185–186, 202, 238, 240, 249
Close, Glenn 44, 81, 84, 236
Close Encounters of the Third Kind 58
Clyde, Andy 255
Coad, Joyce 198, 199
Cobb, Bill 72
Cobb, Lee J. 81, 82, 145, 203, 204, 205, 255
Cobbs, Renata 217
Cobra (1925) 59
Cobra (1986) 32
Coburn, Charles 131, 132
Coburn, James 13, 14, 44, 154, 184
The Cobweb 59
Coca-Cola 136
Cody, Buffalo Bill 17
Coe, Barry 210
Coen, Ethan 83, 124, 163
Coen, Joel 37, 83, 124, 163
Cohen, Rob 76, 219
Cohn, Harry 11, 20, 22, 41, 93, 104, 112, 115, 121, 131, 140, 183, 187, 259
Cohn, Sam 10
Colbert, Claudette 8, 9, 83, 98, 105, 107, 121, 131, 140, 180, 218, 244, 249
Cold Mountain 59
Cole, Dennis 252
Coleman, Dabney 243, 254
Coleman, Nancy 105, 106
Collaredo, Archbishop 12
Collier, Buster, Jr. 134
Collier, Constance 257
Collins, Cora Sue 172, *173*
Collins, Joan 57, 58, 99, 140, 141, 198, 206, 222
Collins, Ray 131
Colman, Ronald 17, 44, 49, 50, 75, 104, 107, 129, 133, 147, 160, 170, 183, 195, 198, 234, 254
Colmans, Edward 223
The Color of Money 116
The Color Purple 59
Colouris, George 131
Columbia Pictures 6, 11, 20, 25, 35, 41, 42, 47, 52, 78, 93, 94, 96, 97, 99, 109, 112, 121, 127, 136, 160, 165, 173, 178, 183, 186, 221, 259
Columbo 44
Columbus, Chris 33, 116–117
Combs, Sean 18

Come and Get It 59
Come Back Little Sheba 59
Come Back to the Five and Dime, Jimmy Dean, Jimmy Dean 60
The Comedians 60
Comet Over Broadway 60
Coming Home 10, 60
Comingore, Dorothy 180
Confessions of a Dangerous Mind 60
Conlin, Jimmy 131
A Connecticut Yankee in King Arthur's Court (Mark Twain) 35
Connell, Jane 155
Connelly, Chris 109
Connelly, Jennifer 203, 210
Connery, Sean 6, 12, 17, 53, 69, 70, 72, 76, 92, 94, 98, 125, 128, 129, 141, 152–153, 156, 159, 166, 178, 191, 204, 222, 223, 228, 232–233, 240, 254, 260
Connick, Harry, Jr. 128
Connolly, Walter 150
Connors, Chuck 203
The Conqueror 60
Conquest of the Planet of the Apes 28
Conroy, Pat 193
The Constant Nymph 60
Conte, Richard 100, 135
Continental Divide 60
Contreras, Roberto 243
The Conversation 61
Conversation Piece 61
Convoy 61
A Cool Dry Place 61
Coolidge, Jennifer 31
Cooper, Gary 6, 20, 83, 88, 89, 90, 92, 98, 105, 107, 115, 120, 122, 150, 152, 160, 162, 165, 201, 208, 214, 215, 226, 256
Cooper, Gladys 115
Cooper, Jackie 66, 226, 233
Cooper, Merian 88
Cooper, Rocky 226
Coote, Robert 98, 223
Coppola, Francis Ford 19, 34, 42, 61, 85, 86, 100–102, 103, 181, 185, 197, 246
Coppola, Sofia 102, 103
Cord, Alex 255
Corey, Jeff 63
Corey, Wendell *146*
Corman, Roger 148, 225–226, 246, 255
The Corn Is Green 61
Cornell, Katharine 218
Cornfield, Hubert 173
Cort, Bud 115, 116
Cosby, Bill 90
Cosmatos, George Pan 207
Costa, Mary 87
Costa-Gavras 100
Costello, Dolores 73, *74*
Costner, Kevin 3, 4, 7, 32, 33, 39, 46, 81, 85, 98, 125, 132, 133, 164,

168, 171, 177, 188, 191, 192, 211, 241, 249, 251
Cotten, Joseph 50, 121–122, 239
The Cotton Club 61
Counsellor at Law 61
Counsellor at Law (play) 61
The Count of Monte Cristo 61
The Country Girl 61–62
Court, Hazel 140, 222
Courtenay, Tom 73, 95
Courtland, Jerome 222, 223
Courtneidge, Cicely 223
The Courtship of Andy Hardy 62
Cover Girl 62
Coward, Noel 37, 43, 72, 95, 96, 149, 223, 239
Cox, Brian 157
Cox, Wally 29
Cox, Courteney 5, 238
Crabbe, Buster 235
Craig, Michael 222, 223
Craig, Yvonne 253
Crain, Jeanne 8, 9, 54, 126, 153, 169, 179, 185, 188
Crawford, Broderick 11, 41
Crawford, Cindy 255
Crawford, Joan 8, 64, 93, 99, 105, 106, 125, 141, 144, 145, 151, 161, 162, 166, 182, 183–184, 200, 201, 209, 233, 238
Crawford, Johnny 184
Crawford, Michael 119, 120
Cregar, Laird 143
Cremer, Bruno 222
Crenna, Richard 86
Crews, Laura Hope 105, 108, 198, 199
Crimes and Misdemeanors 62
Crimes of Passion 62
Crimes of the Heart 62
Crimson Tide 62
Crisp, Donald 123, 171
Criss Cross 62
Critical Condition 62
Crittenden, Dianne 119, 227
Cronenberg, David 66–67
Cronin, A.J. 137
Cronkite, Walter 172
Cronyn, Hume 58, 249
Crosby, Bing 92, 104, 182, 222, 223
Crosse, Rupert 141
Crouse, Lindsay 191
Crouse, Russell 29, 147
The Crow 62–63
The Crow: City of Angels 63
Crowe, Cameron 11, 12, 84, 134, 210
Crowe, Russell 7, 30, 194, 258
Crowley, Patricia 89, 199, 200
The Crucible 63
Crudup, Billy 11, 121, 124, 241, 257
Cruise, Tom 29, 39, 41, 42, 44, 59, 71, 78, 79, 80, 82, 86, 87, 88, 98, 116, 128, 129–130, 132, 133,

318 Index

134, 163, 168, 197, 204, 208, 216, 241, 243, 251, 257
Cruising 63
Cruz, Penelope 49, 53, 251
The Cry Baby Killer 63
Cryer, Jon 174
Crystal, Billy 14, 122, 254
Cukor, George 34, 41, 66, 105, 106, 107, 121, 140, 146, 169, 205, 234, 236, 245
Cul-de-Sac 64
Culkin, Kit 108
Culkin, Macaulay 38, 108
Culp, Robert 38, 202, 203, 255
Cummings, Constance 69
Cummings, Robert 8, 138, 208
Cummins, Peggy 89
Cuny, Alain 73
Currie, Finlay 196
Curtis, Jamie Lee 38, 39, 42, 76, 77, 110, 114
Curtis, Tony 31, 94, 140, 180, 203, 221
Curtiz, Michael 100, 119, 162–163
Cusack, John 14, 96, 155, 156, 210, 256
Cushing, Peter 114
Cynara 64

Dabney, Augusta 198, 199
Daddy and Them 96
Dafoe, Willem 80, 81, 132, 133, 142, 143, 164, 188, 189, 209, 224
Dahl, Arlene 8, 111, 143
Dahl, Tessa 156
Dailey, Dan 36, 88, 167, 250
Daily Variety 182
Dakota Incident 64
Daldry, Stephen 122–123
Dale, Jim 148
Dall, John 206
Dalton, Timothy 148
Daly, Tim 215, 259
Damage 64, 169
D'Ambrosio, Franc 102, 103
Damn Yankees 64
Damn Yankees (play) 182
Damon, Matt 11, 41, 59, 163, 176, 184, 192, 194, 196, 197, 235, 242
Damone, Vic 100, 101
A Damsel in Distress 64
Dancing Lady 64
Dancing with the Hits 211
Dandridge, Dorothy 46, 37, 188
Danes, Claire 45, 108, 117, 194, 237, 241, 256
D'Angelo, Beverly 120
Daniell, Henry 48
Daniels, Bebe 64, 90
Daniels, Jeff 77, 122, 195
Daniels, William 109, 110
Danner, Blythe 100, 101, 192
Danova, Cesare 31
Danson, Ted 190
Danton, Ray 97

Darabont, Frank 216
D'Arbanville, Patti 76, 77
Darby, Kim 246
Darby's Rangers 64–65
Daredevil 65
Darin, Bobby 243
Dark City 65
Dark Victory 65
Darling 65
Darling, How Could You 65
Darnell, Linda 64, 89, 175
Darvas, Lillie 223
Darvi, Andrea 223, 224
Darwell, Jane 105, 108, 110, 131
Dash, Stacey 190
Da Silva, Howard 248
Dassin, Jules 172, 244
Dauphin, Claude 206, 223
Davalos, Richard 77
Davenport, Doris 105, 106, 253, 254
Davenport, Harry 105, 108, 131
Davenport, Nigel 53, 189, 248
David and Bathsheba 65–66
David Copperfield 66
Davidovich, Lolita 36, 39, 128, 129
Davies, Marion 26, 143, 157
Davis, Bette 6–7, 8, 49, 50, 59, 60, 65, 91, 96, 105, 107, 123, 131, 134, 135, 136, 137, 138, 140, 141, 147, 156, 158, 162, 173, 175, 177, 189, 193, 196, 219, 229, 231, 241, 250, 252, 254, 258
Davis, Brad 8, 62, 86, 161
Davis, Geena 3, 15, 16, 27, 28, 87, 88, 144, 145, 169, 238, 249
Davis, Judy 52, 125, 169, 201
Davis, Sammy, Jr. 5, 48, 138, 172, 190, 255
Dawson, Rosario 6, 135
Dawson's Creek 219
Day, Clarence 147
Day, Clarence, Jr. 147
Day, Doris 109, 110, 119, 120, 134, 150, 167, 182, 205, 222, 223, 224
Day, Laraine 89, 154, 155
Day, Vinnie 147
The Day of the Locust 66
The Day the Earth Stood Still 66
Day-Lewis, Daniel 27, 42, 59, 80, 81, 92, 95, 129, 186, 195, 211, 215, 216
Daylight 66
Days of Heaven 66
Days of Thunder 87, 98
Dead End 1, 11, 66
Dead Poets Society 66
The Dead Zone 66–67
Deakins, Lucy 42
Dean, James 51, 59, 77, 92, 98, 177, 199, 221
Death Becomes Her 67
Death on the Nile 67
Death to Smoochy 117
Death Wish 67

DeBussy, Fleurette 105, 107
De Carlo, Yvonne 24, 49, 62, 74, 75, 93, 119, 166, 197, 229
The Decision of Christopher Blake 67
Dee, Frances 105, 106, 154, 155, 198, 199
Dee, Sandra 99, 127
Deep in My Heart 67
The Deer Hunter 119, 227
DeGeneres, Ellen 195
De Grunwald, Dimitri 163
De Havilland, Olivia 6, 8, 16, 32, 49, 60, 79, 98, 105, 108, 124, 125, 131, 132, 138, 154, 155, 156, 160, 162, 198, 199, 209, 220, 230–231, 238, 242, 259
Dekker, Albert 131
de la Prada, Don Antonio 195
De Laurentiis, Dino 25, 26, 33, 38, 67, 86, 114, 138, 251
The Delicate Delinquent 67
Deliverance 68
Dell, Myrna 8, 131, 132
Delon, Alain 100, 101, 144, 145
Delpy, Julie 208
del Rio, Dolores, 8, 45
Del Ruth, Roy 22
Del Toro, Benicio 29
Demarest, William 131, 203, 204, 255
DeMille, Cecil B. 46, 112, 209, 229
DeMille, Katherine 46
Demme, Jonathan 156, 186, 218
Demolition Man 68
De Mornay, Rebecca 42, 68, 204
Demy, Jacques 165
Deneuve, Catherine 44, 142, 178, 179
De Niro, Robert 14, 15, 22, 33, 41, 42, 45, 46, 48, 58, 60, 72, 83, 86, 94, 95, 99–100, 101, 102, 103, 108, 109, 132, 142–143, 152, 153, 156, 159–160, 162, 164, 167, 176, 180, 212, 235, 249
Dennehy, Brian 86, 133, 157
Dennis, Rusty 159
Dennis, Sandy 254
Dennis the Menace 224
Denny, Simon Baker 126
Denver, John 177
De Palma, Brian 1, 37, 38, 39–40, 50, 76, 186, 211, 227, 249
De Palma, Cameron 76
Depardieu, Gerard 98, 159, 161
Depp, Johnny 31, 42, 51, 60, 74, 78, 92, 96, 128, 129, 172, 190, 224
Derek, John 93
Dern, Bruce 60, 78, 112, 138, 246, 255
Dern, Laura 3, 31, 38, 96, 136, 191, 228
Dershowitz, Alan 202

Deschanel, Zooey 11
De Sica, Vittorio 33
Design for Living 68
Designing Woman 68
Desire Me 68
Desiree 78
Desperately Seeking Susan 68–69
Destry Rides Again 69
DeSylva, Buddy 150, 231
The Detective 69
Detective Story 69
Detmers, Marushka 124
Devane, William 82, 83
Devereaux, Robert (Earl of Essex) 193
The Devil to Pay! 69
The Devils 69, 232
The Devil's Disciple 69
The Devil's Holiday 69, 70
The Devil's Own 69–70
Devine, Loretta 251
De Vito, Danny 87, 88, 132, 133, 181, 195, 251
Devlin, Dean 128
de Vries, Hans 178
Dewhurst, Colleen 179
Dey, Susan 111
Diamond Head 70
Diamonds Are Forever 70
Diary of a Sergeant 32
The Diary of Anne Frank 70
The Diary of Anne Frank (play) 122
Diaz, Cameron 44, 53, 54, 146, 159, 169, 238
DiCaprio, Leonardo 11, 13, 27, 28, 29, 40, 129, 130, 159, 192, 194, 196, 224, 225, 228, 232, 235, 241–242, 257
DiCillo, Tom 148
Dick Tracy 70, 164
Dickens, Charles 212
Dickinson, Angie 76, 80, 97, 151, 203, 222, 223, 253
Dickinson, Janice 197
Die Hard 70
Diener, Joan 143
Diesel, Vin 65
Dieterle, William 79
Dietl, Bo 180
Dietrich, Marlene 8, 9, 37, 69, 95, 96, 168, 183, 197, 226
A Different World 169
Diffring, Anton 222, 223
Dillane, Stephen 253
Dillon, Matt 27, 72, 76, 87, 102, 103, 126–127, 132, 133, 180, 181, 195
Dingle, Charles 131
Dinner at Eight 71
Dirty Dancing 71
The Dirty Dozen 71
Dirty Harry 71
Dirty Rotten Scoundrels 71
Dirty Work 71
Disclosure 71–72

Disney 7, 174
Do the Right Thing 72
Do You Love Me 72
Dr. Jekyll and Mr. Hyde 72
Dr. No 72, 93
Dr. Seuss' The Cat in the Hat 72
Dr. Strangelove or: How I Learned to Stop Worrying and Love the Bomb 73
Doctor Zhivago 73
Dodson, Mary Kay 198, 199
Dodsworth 73
Dodsworth (play) 73, 74
Dogma 73
Doherty, Shannen 154
La Dolce Vita, 73–74
Don Juan 74
Donahue, Elinor 253
Donahue, Troy 184, 225
Donat, Peter 100, 101
Donat, Robert 49, 61, 72, 95, 96, 109, 113, 120, 121, 139, 191, 192, 208
Donen, Stanley 52, 53, 54, 85, 148, 182
Donlevy, Brian 154, 155
The Donna Reed Show 224
Donnelly, Donal 85, *86*, 102, 103
Donnelly, Ruth 132
Donner, Richard 141
Donnie Brasco 74
D'Onofrio, Vincent 94
Dooley, Paul 55
Dorff, Stephen 51, 197, 211
Dorfman, Robert 183
Dorleac, Francoise 64, *200*
Dorn, Philip 50
Double Indemnity 18, 74
Double Jeopardy 74–75
A Double Life 75
Dougherty, Marion 118
Douglas, Kirk 21, 31, 69, 86, 124, 176, 179, 189, 203, 210, 226, 230, 258
Douglas, Melvyn 30, 105, 106, 107, 154, 173, 174, 191, 192
Douglas, Michael 27, 55, 86, 98, 132, 133, 151, 164, 179, 212, 245, 248, 250, 251, 259
Douglas, Paul 18, *19*, 22, 41, 221, 239
Douglas, Sarah 233
Douglass, Stephen 182
Dowell, Raye 217
Down, Lesley-Anne 115
Down and Out in Beverly Hills 75, 79
Down Argentine Way 75
Down to You 75
Downey, Robert, Jr. 14, 127, 171, 176, 210, 240
Downs, Cathy 169
Doyle-Murray, Brian 16
Dracula 75–76
Dragnet 76

Dragon: The Bruce Lee Story 76
Dragonheart 76
Drake, Betsy *123*
Drake, Larry 132, 133
Drake, Tom 160
Draper, Paul 38
A Dream Come True 6
DreamWorks 203, 218
Drescher, Fran 13
Dressed to Kill 76
Dressler, Marie 105, 107, 140
Drew, Ellen 198, 199
Dreyfuss, Richard 10, 12, 13, 55, 58, 60, 75, 76, 79, 94–95, 108, 109, 122, 133, 136, 164, 166, 167, 172, 176, 227, 238, 244, 254
Drive, He Said 76
The Driver 76
Driver, Minnie 108, 219
Driving Miss Daisy 76
Dru, Joanne 201
Drugstore Cowboy 76–77, 170, 242
Drums Along the Mohawk 258
Drury, James 202, 203
The Duchess and the Dirtwater Fox 77
Duchovny, David 18
Dudley, Renee 223, 224
Duel in the Sun 77
Duel in the Sun (Niven Busch) 77
Duets 77
Duhamel, Josh 256
Duke, Patty 250
Dumb and Dumber 5, 77
Dunaway, Faye 40, 53, 55, 80, 82, 111, 112, 113, 135, 166, 172, 175, 240–241, 261
Duncan, Sandy 119, 120
Dune 77
Dunn, James 245, 246
Dunn, Kathy 223, 224
Dunne, Irene 16–17, 88, 96, 105, 107, 121, 126, 147, 175, 177, 180, 223, 252
Dunne, Philip 66
Dunnock, Mildred 115
Dunst, Kirsten 12, 129, 130, 224, 225
Dupuis, Roy 11
Durang, Christopher 18
Durbin, Deanna 257
Durning, Charles 31, 56, 79, 86, 213
Duryea, Dan 131
Duse, Vittorio 103
Dutronc, Jacques 197
Dutton, Charles S. 154
Duvall, Robert 19, 20, 32, 100, 101, 103, 128, 133, 171, 176, 202, 211, 217
Duvall, Shelley 80, 190
Dvorak, Ann 52, 105, 108, 131, 132, 252
Dybas, James 119, 120

Dylan, Bob 40, 184
Dyne, Michael 187

E.T. the Extra-Terrestrial 77
Each Dawn I Die 130
Eagels, Jeanne 69, *70*, 134
Eagle, Emira 258
East of Eden 77–78
East Side, West Side 78
Easter Parade 78
Eastman, Carole 156
Eastwood, Clint 3, 19, 33, 43, 44, 45, 46, 56, 70, 71, 78, 86, 96, 119, 128, 136, 160, 164, 189, 222, 233, 240
Eastwood, Kyle 136
Easy Rider 78
Ebsen, Buddy 203, 204, 257
Eccleston, Christopher 127
Eckhart, Aaron 15, 18
Eckman, Gene 259
Ed 78
Eddy, Nelson 99
Eden, Eleanor 260
Edmunds, William 132
Educating Rita 78
Edward Scissorhands 78
Edwards, Anthony 83, 84
Edwards, Blake 14, 36, 56, 233, 236
Edwards, Vince 100
Egan, Eddie 92
Egoyan, Atom 234
The Egyptian 78
Ehle, Jennifer 190
Eichhorn, Lisa *9*
The Eiger Sanction 78
Eight Men Out 79
Eilers, Sally 135
Eisner, Michael 13
Ekland, Britt 113
El Cid 79
Eldard, Ron 187
Eldridge, Florence 158
Electra, Carmen 211
The Electric Horseman 79
The Elephant Man 77
Elephant Walk 79
Elfand, Martin 177
Elizabeth 79
Elizabeth I 79, 158, 193, 260
Elkins, Hilly 172
Ellenstein, Robert 223
Elliott, Denholm 129, 213
Elliott, Sam 84
Ellis, Edward 165
Ellis, Gloria 253
Elsom, Isobel 166, 223
Emile l'African 30
Empty Nest 86, 186
Enchanted April 169
Endfield, Cy 261
Endless Love 79
Enemies: A Love Story 79
An Enemy of the People 79–80

Enemy of the State 80
England 90, 113, 222, 223
English, Ellia 251
Enigma 80
Entertainment Weekly 4
Ephron, Nora 161, 220
Epps, Omar 154
ER 240
Eraser 80
Ermey, R. Lee 234
Erwin, Stuart 51, 52
Escapade 80
Escape from the Planet of the Apes 80
Esmond, Jill *34,* 107
Esposito, Giancarlo 72
Esposito, Jennifer *232*
Estevez, Emilio 188
Eszterhas, Joe 7
Etting, Ruth 150
Europe 13, 89, 178
Evans, Charles 243
Evans, Edith 115, 223
Evans, Josh 61
Evans, Maurice 95, 96, 188
Evans, Robert 55, 61, 69, 95, 97, 100, 101, 112, 115, 144, 168, 183, 190, 232, 243, 247
Even Cowgirls Get the Blues 80–81
Even Cowgirls Get the Blues (Tom Robbins) 80
Ever After 52, 81
Everett, Rupert 42, 54
Every Which Way But Loose 241
Everybody's All-American 81
Eve's Bayou 81
Evita 80, 81
Ewell, Tom 214, 215
Executive Suite 81
eXistenZ 82
The Exorcist 81–82
Exorcist II: The Heretic 82
Eye of the Devil 82
The Eyes of Laura Mars 82
Eyes Wide Shut 82, 163

Fabares, Shelley 223, 224
Fabian 111
The Fabulous Baker Boys 82
Fahrenheit 451 82
Fairbanks, Douglas 6
Fairbanks, Douglas, Jr. 51, 68, 113, 147, 258
Fairbanks, Lucille 198, 199
Fairchild, Morgan 141, 142
Falana, Lola 59
Falk, Peter 44, 48, 60, 168, 176, 238
Fame 212
Family Affair 82
Family Plot 82–83
Family Ties 23, 24
The Fan 83
Fancher, Hampton 35, 119, 120
Fanny 83

Fantastic Voyage 241
The Far Horizons 20
A Farewell to Arms (1932) 83
A Farewell to Arms (1957) 83, 210
Fargas, Antonio 5
Fargo 83
Farina, Dennis 238
Farley, Chris 218
Farmer, Frances 29, 59, 91, 231
The Farmer Takes a Wife 83
The Farmer's Daughter 83
Farnsworth, Richard 247
Farr, Felicia 139
Farrell, Colin 65, 117, 163, 187
Farrelly, Bobby 216, 238
Farrelly, Peter 216, 238
Farrow, John 224
Farrow, Mia 18, 69, 111, 112, 113, 114, 156–157, 206, 207, 214, 223, 224, 226
Fast Times at Ridgemont High 83–84
Fat City 84
Fatal Attraction 84
Fatal Beauty 84
Father of the Bride 85
Fawcett, Farrah 19–20, 53, 97, 235
Faye, Alice 41, 75, 97, 170, 198, 239, 240, 245
Faylen, Frank 131
Fearless Fagan 85
Feiffer, Jules 190
Feldman, Phil 25
Felicity 77
Fellini, Federico 17, 74
Fenn, Sherilyn 41, 42
Feodorovna, Alexandra 172
Fernandel *20,* 30
Ferrara, Abel 94
Ferrell, Tyra 211
Ferrer, Jose 8, 9, 67, 135, 150, 176
Ferrer, Mel 169, 170, 232
Ferrie, David 132, 133
Feuillere, Edwige 115
A Few Good Men 85
Fiddler on the Roof 85
Fiddler on the Roof (play) 12
Field, Betty 25, 88, 138, 154, 155, 177, 231
Field, Sally 3, 109, 110, 120, 166, 174, 175, 214, 220, 228, 229, 246
Field, Todd 210
Field of Dreams 32, 85
Fielding, Helen 44
Fields, Gracie 155, 165, 166
Fields, Tony 55, 246
Fields, W.C. 66, 131, 132, 162, 244, 257
Fiennes, Joseph 216
Fiennes, Ralph 27, 28, 32, 33, 104, 105, 176, 200, 208, 215, 216, 241
55 Days at Peking 85
Figgis, Mike 229
Fight Club 85

Finch, Peter 57, 58, 72, 79, 95, 172, 222, 223, 232, 233, 236
Fine Kaye, Sylvia 116
Fini Zanuck, Lili 76
Finian's Rainbow 85, 86, 103
Finley, William 186
Finn, Mali 241
Finney, Albert 12, 17, 95, 102, 103, 144, 163, 212, 220, 247
Fiorentino, Linda 27, 73, 160, 161, 243
Firestarter 86
The Firm 86
First Blood 86
First Monday in October 86–87
The First Wives Club 87
Firstborn 62
Firth, Colin 216
Fishburne, Laurence 72, 159, 211
Fisher, Antwone 18
Fisher, Carrie 50, 111, 126, 227
Fisher, Eddie 47, 100, 101
The Fisher King 87
Fisk, Jack 186
Fitzcarraldo 87
Fitzgerald, Barry 131, 132
Fitzgerald, Ella 50
Fitzgerald, F. Scott 112
Fitzgerald, Geraldine 123, 152, 154, 155, 193, 198, 199
5 Against the House 87
Fix, Paul 255
Flame and the Flesh 165
The Flamingo Kid 87
Flanery, Sean Patrick 150
Flap 87
Flashdance 87
Flatliners 87
Fleischer, Richard 25
Fleming, Ian 72
Fleming, Rhonda 147, 203
Fletcher, Louise 171, 179, 239
The Flintstones 87–88
Flora Plum 114
Florey, Robert 100
Flying Down to Rio 88
The Flying Nun 246
Flynn, Errol 6, 49, 105, 107, 124, 165, 193, 234
Flynt, Larry 185
Foch, Nina 219
Foley, James 36, 100
Follow the Fleet 88
Fonda, Bridget 102, 103, 131, 134, 191, 218, 219, 242
Fonda, Henry 25, 68, 73, 74, 80, 81, 83, 86, 87, 110, 134, 138, 140, 145, 154, 164, 165, 172, 175, 182, 184, 203, 214, 251, 254, 255
Fonda, Jane 26, 40, 49, 53, 55, 73, 79, 81, 83, 104, 119, 121, 125, 127, 135, 139, 159, 172, 175, 179, 206, 207, 225, 249, 250, 253
Fonda, Peter 78, 121, 147, 151, 182, 184, 248, 255

Fontaine, Joan 8, 60, 64, 65, 89, 105, 108, 127, 132, 198, 199, 214, 238
Food Giant 142
Fools Rush In 88
Footloose 88
For Me and My Gal 88
For Whom the Bell Tolls 88, 89
Ford, David 210
Ford, Faith 87, 88
Ford, Gerald 111
Ford, Glenn 8, 124, 133, 172, 189–190, 196, 203, 210, 226, 236, 255
Ford, Harrison 7, 33, 35, 37, 46, 61, 66, 69, 70, 76, 93, 97, 109, 115, 125, 126, 129, 132, 133, 136, 164, 165, 167, 184, 185, 191, 197, 202, 208, 211, 219, 227, 231–232, 237, 245, 247, 249, 257, 258, 260
Ford, John 73, 123, 158, 165, 235
Ford, Steven 111
Ford, Wally 131
Foreign Correspondent 89
Forever Amber 89
Forever Female 89
Forman, Milos 12, 54, 156, 179, 196, 250
Forrest, Diana 105, 107
Forrest, Frederic 19, 61
Fort Apache: The Bronx 89
Forte, Nick Apollo 45
The Fortune 89
Forty Carats 89
40 Days and 40 Nights 90
48 Hrs. 32, 90
Forty Guns 90
49th Parallel 90
42nd Street 64, 90
Fosse, Bob 10, 11, 54, 226
Fosse, Nicole 55
Foster, Brandy 196
Foster, Buddy 91
Foster, David 97
Foster, Jodie 4, 37, 38, 64, 74–75, 91, 114, 122, 159, 176, 183, 196, 216, 218, 227, 242
Foster, Preston 154, 155
Foul Play 16
The Fountainhead 90–91
Four Rooms 91
Four Weddings and a Funeral 91
Fowler, Will 181
Fowles, John 92
Fox, James 214
Fox, Michael J. 23, 24, 44
Fox, Rick 117
Fox, Sidney 198, 199, 231
Fox, Susan 105, 107
Fox, Vivica A. 214, 258
Fox Film Corporation 198
Foxes 91
Foxx, Jamie 18
Foy, Bryan 182
Frances 91

Francis 91
Francis, Kay 60, 64, 65, 90, 135, 196, 197, 198, 219, 244
Franciscus, James 30, 260
Franco, James 222
Frank, Anne 70
Frank, Mel 77
Franken, Rose 57
Frankenheimer, John 156, 213, 236
Frankenstein 91
Frankie and Johnny 91
Franklin, Bonnie 253
Frankovich, Mike 47, 226
Franz, Dennis 76
Franz, Eduard 223
Fraser, Agnes 198, 199
Fraser, Brendan 168, 235, 252
Frasier 210
Fraulein 91
Frazier, Joe 205
Freaks 91–92
Frears, Stephen 121
Frechette, Mark 260
A Free Soul 92
Freed, Arthur, 13, 88, 219, 234
Freeman, Mona 8
Freeman, Morgan 39, 40, 139
Freeman, Paul 197
The French Connection 92
The French Lieutenant's Woman 92
Friday 35
Friday the 13th: A New Beginning 92
Friday the 13th: The Final Chapter 92
Friedkin, William 63, 81, 82, 92, 222
Friendly Persuasion 92
Friends 78, 150, 221
Frings, Kurt 181
From Hell 92
From Here to Eternity 93
From Russia with Love 93
The Front Page 93
Frontier Gal 93, 94
Frost, Sadie 42
The Fugitive 93
The Full Monty 15
Fuller, Robert 202
Fuller, Samuel 90, 187
The Funeral 94
Funny Face 94
Funny Girl 94
Funny Lady 94–95
A Funny Thing Happened on the Way to the Forum 12
Fuqua, Antoine 245
Furneaux, Yvonne 222
Fuzz 48
The Fuzzy Pink Nightgown 95

Gabin, Jean 95, 96, 206
Gable, Clark 3, 17, 46, 49, 64, 70, 71, 79, 92, 93, 95, 98, 105, 106, 107, 110, 119, 124, 131, 144, 145,

147, 151, 156, 162, 164, 174, 187, 191, 192, 193, 196, 200, 205, 210, 211, 221, 234, 235, 257
Gable & Lombard 95
Gabor, Eva 222
Gabor, Zsa Zsa 8, 9, 187
Gaines, Richard 131
Gainsborough/Rank 155
Gainsbourg, Charlotte 247
Gaipa, Corrado 103
Gallagher, Peter 215
Gam, Rita 222
The Gambler 95
Gandhi 95, 164
Gandhi, Mahatma 95
The Gang That Couldn't Shoot Straight 95, 101, 102
Gangs of New York 95
Garbo, Greta 17, 61, 65, 90, 95, 96, 126, 162, 167, 174, 183, 195, 200, 234, 244
Garcia, Andy 42, 62, 102, 103, 159, 176, 180, 254
The Garden of Allah 95–96
Garden of the Moon 96
Gardner, Ava 26, 33, 49, 50, 62, 78, 85, 109, 110, 126, 143, 150, 151, 163, 165, 166, 169, 170, 173, 187, 188, 192, 217, 232, 234
Garfield, John 8, 9, 38, 104, 121, 181, 190, 213, 244, 245
Garland, Alex 29
Garland, Beverly 203
Garland, Judy 17, 23, 26, 30, 54, 78, 88, 105, 108, 115, 117, 118, 128, 191, 198, 207, 217, 224, 226, 234, 250, 257, 261
Garner, James 13, 14, 64, 65, 94, 164, 203, 210, 228, 250
Garner, Jeff 228
Garnett, Tay 249
Garr, Teri 58, 223, 224
Garrett, Betty 17
Garrett, Patrick J. 184
Garrison, Jim 132, 133
Garrison, Liz 132, 133
Garrison, Miranda 71
Garson, Greer 8, 78, 123, 167, 178, 191, 192, 261
Gary, Lorraine 133
Gas Food Lodging 96
Gaslight 96
Gassman, Vittorio 102, 103, 222, 223, 250
Gattaca 96
The Gauntlet 96
Gavin, John 70, 194, 232
The Gay Sisters 96
Gaye, Nona M. 159
Gaynor, Janet 25, 65, 105, 108, 147, 154, 155, 177, 199, 215, 252
Gaynor, Mitzi 32, 221, 224
Gazzara, Ben 176, 256
Gazzo, Michael V. 102
Geeson, Judy 230

General Hospital 216, 217
The General's Daughter 96
Genghis Khan 200
Gentleman's Agreement 97
Gentlemen Prefer Blondes 97
George III, King 152–153
George, Chief Dan 147
George, Gladys 105, 108, 229
George, Susan 230
The George Raft Story 97
George White's Scandals 97, 240
Georgia 106
Gere, Richard 12, 13, 37, 54, 61, 66, 70, 129, 161, 176, 177, 191, 202, 226, 249, 251, 259
Geronimo 97
Geronimo: An American Legend 97
Gershe, Leonard 95
Gershon, Gina 218
The Getaway 97
Ghost 97
The Ghost and Mrs. Muir 98
The Ghost & the Darkness 98
Ghostbusters 98
Giannini, Giancarlo 197
Giant 98–99
Gibson, Henry 171
Gibson, Mel 27, 41, 54, 76, 97, 98, 104, 129, 132, 133, 168, 171, 185, 192, 194, 208, 211, 237, 240, 249
Gibson, Tyrese 23
Gidget 110
Gidget Goes Hawaiian 99
Gielgud, John 95, 96, 206, 208, 209
Gifford, Frank 203
Gigi 99
Gigi (play) 99
Gigli 65
Gilbert, Helen 257
Gilbert, John 92, 110, 195, 200, 234
Gilbert, Lewis 7, 8, 78
Gilchrist, Connie 132
Gillespie, Dana 233
Gilliam, Terry 42, 43, 87
Gilmore, Virginia 98, 199
Gimpel, Erica 211, *212*
Gingold, Hermione 99
Girardon, Michele 117
A Girl, a Guy, and a Gob 99
The Girl in the Red Velvet Swing 99
Girl, Interrupted 99
The Girl Next Door 99
The Girl of the Golden West 99
Gish, Lillian 82, 83, 105, 108
Gist, Robert 223
Givenchy 232
Givney, Kathryn 223
Gladiator 30
Glamour 142
Glaser, Paul Michael 208
Gleason, Jackie 92, 175, 189
Glengarry Glen Ross 99–100
Glengarry Glen Ross (play) 99–100

Glenn, Scott 177, 218, 245
Glory 199
Glover, Crispin 24, 256
Glover, Danny 30, 40, 234
Glover, Julian 128, 129
"God Bless the Child" 211
God Is My Co-Pilot 100
Godard, Jean-Luc 161
Goddard, Mark 253
Goddard, Paulette 8, 69, 105, 112, 140, 154, 155, 198, 260
The Godfather 1, 95, 100–102
The Godfather (Mario Puzo) 100
The Godfather Part II 102, 103
The Godfather Part III 85, 102–103
Godzilla 103–104
Goetz, William 210
Goin' South 104
Going My Way 104
The Gold Rush 104
Goldberg, Leonard 74, 75
Goldberg, Whoopi 5, 7, 24, 25, 46, 59, 84, 97, 136, 153, 190, 193, 219
Goldblum, Jeff 128, 132, 133, 193
Golden Boy 104, 130, 259
Golden Boy (play) 104
GoldenEye 104–105, 148
Golden Globe Awards 167, 215, 237
Goldfinger 105
Goldman, William 1, 3, 47, 259
Goldsman, Akiva 232
Goldsmith-Thomas, Elaine 153
Goldthwait, Bobcat 46
Goldwyn, Samuel 6, 25, 59, 73, 107, 112, 113, 147, 196, 258
Goldwyn, Tony 18, 235
Golino, Valeria 191
Gomez Carriles, Lazaro 29
Gone with the Wind 105–108, 199, 231, 249, 260
The Good Mother 108
The Good Son 108
Good Will Hunting 11, 40, 108, 197, 208
Goodbye, Columbus 108
The Goodbye Girl 108–109
Goodbye, Mr. Chips (1939) 109
Goodbye, Mr. Chips (1969) 109
Goodfellas 109
Gooding, Cuba, Jr. 18, 134
Goodman, Benny 31
Goodman, John 87, 132, 133
Goodwin, Bill 131
Goodwin, Harold 256
Gordon, Bert I. 187
Gordon, Gavin 223
Gordon, Keith 76
Gordon, Larry 90
Gordon, Ruth 5, 41, 115, 207, 218, 241
Gorney, Karen Lynn 209, *210*
Gossett, Louis, Jr. 177
Gould, Elliott 10, 38, 48, 60, 91, 149, 159, 176, 230, 243

Gould, Jason 178, 192, 193
Goulding, Edmund 60, 177
Goulet, Robert 148
Gouranis, Anthony 102
Gouranis, James 102
Grable, Betty 17, 72, 75, 97, 99, 113, 114, 121, 145, 149, 155, 160, 170, 187, 198, 239, 250
Grace Quigley 109
The Graduate 109–110, 194, 254
Grady, Bill 106
Graff, Todd 15
Graham, Elaine 217
Graham, Heather 40, 76, 77, 160
Grahame, Gloria 41, 93, 112, 124, 127, 131, 132, 151, 177, 207
Grand Hotel 110
Grandview U.S.A. 110
Granger, Farley 32, 78, 206, 230
Granger, Stewart 47, 153, 226
Grant, Cary 20, 21, 22, 33, 34, 35, 43, 44, 45, 52–53, 64, 72, 113, 116, 118, 119, 122, 131, 132, 145, 149, 150, 152, 157, 160, 164, 168, 169, 173, 174, 175, 180, 187, 196, 201, 203, 205, 206, 208, 226, 236, 239, 244, 250, 254
Grant, Hugh 96, 104, 105, 116, 208, 216, 256
Grant, Kathryn 199
Grant, Lee 121
Granville, Bonita 198
The Grapes of Wrath 110
Grapewin, Charles 131
Grauman's Chinese Theatre 59
Gray, F. Gary 35, 214
Gray, Linda 105, 108
Gray, Spalding 29
Grayson, Diane 192
Grayson, Kathryn 136–137, 191, 234
Grazer, Brian 7
Graziano, Rocky 221
Grease 110–111, 258
Grease (play) 111
Grease 2 23
The Great Escape 209
Great Expectations 111
The Great Gatsby 111–112
The Greatest Show on Earth 112
The Greatest Story Ever Told 112
Greco, Buddy 100, 101
The Greeks Had a Word for Them 112
Green, Gillian 225
Green, Seth 154
The Green Berets 71
Green Fire 61
Green Mansions 112, 221
The Green Mile 113
Greene, Angela 8
Greenquist, Brad 215
Greenwich Village, NY 48
Greenwood, Bruce 74, 75
Greer, Dabbs 113

Greer, Jane 151, 203, 222
Gregg, Julie 100, 101
Gregory, James 30
Greist, Kim 42, 43
Grey, Jennifer 71
Grey, Joel 133
Grey, Lita *104*
Greystoke: The Legend of Tarzan, Lord of the Apes 113
Grier, Pam 195
Griffith, D.W. 3, 157
Griffith, Melanie 1, 3, 21, 27, 32, 36, 38, 39, 40, 50, 68, 70, 216, 219, 229, 238
Griffiths, Rachel 185
Grimaldi, Prince Rainier 51, 68, 158, 246
Grisham, John 241
Grodin, Charles 51, 109–110, 137, 138, 161–162, 191, 228, 238
Grosbard, Ulu 99
Grosso, Sonny 92
Groundhog Day 113
The Group 113
Grover, Cynthia 223, 224
Guetary, Georges 13
Guevara, Che 81
Guinness, Alec 33, 43, 49, 95, 144, 151, 227
The Gunfighter 120
Gung Ho 113
Gunga Din 113
Guns at Batasi 113
Gunton, Bob 216
Gurie, Sigrid 6
Guthrie, Woody 41
Guy, Jasmine 115, 211
Guys and Dolls 113–114
Gwynne, Fred 83, 84

Hackett, Buddy 184, 243
Hackford, Taylor 177
Hackman, Gene 10, 36, 58, 61, 62, 69, 86, 92, 109, 110, 116, 132, 133, 148, 151, 164, 174, 179, 184, 185, 204, 218, 231, 238, 252, 253
Hagen, Jean 41, 219
Haigh, Kenneth 208, 209
Haines, Randa 258
Hair 171
Hale, Barbara 41
Hale, Dorothy 64
Hale, Georgia 56, 57, *104*
Haley, Jack 257
Hall, Anthony Michael 27
Hall, Jon 248
Hall, Thurston 132
Halloween 114
Hallstrom, Lasse 56, 217
Halton, Charles 131
Halton, George 131
Ham, Harry 107
Hamel, Veronica 100, 101
Hamill, Mark 227
Hamilton, George 5, 243

Hamilton, Guy 70
Hamilton, Linda 85, 237, 241
Hamilton, Margaret 257
Hamilton, Murray 109, 110
Hamlet (1948) 114
Hamlet (2000) 114
Hammerstein, Oscar, II 9, 49
Hammond, Kay 3, 37
Hammond, Nicholas 223, 224
Hancock, John Lee 7
The Hand 114
Handler, Evan 80
Haney, Carol 94
Hanks, Colin 228
Hanks, Tom 1, 23, 33, 39, 40, 59, 66, 76, 85, 113, 134, 144, 145, 161, 174, 185, 186, 192, 211, 219, 220, 225, 254
Hannah, Daryl 144, 145, 191, 251
Hannah and Her Sisters 114
Hannibal 114, 157, 232, 248
Hanover Street 115
Hans Christian Andersen 115
The Happening 240–241
Happy Days 111, 225
The Happy Time 115
The Happy Time (play) 115
A Hard Day's Night 206
Hardcore 115
Harden, Marcia Gay 12
Harding, Ann 55, 167, 177, 258
Hardison, Kadeem 72
Harland, Robert 253
Harlem, NY 5
Harlem Nights 115
Harlow 115
Harlow, Jean 41, 64, 91–92, 105, 107, 112, 120, 151, 153, 194, 200, 201, 209, 244, 257
Harlow, Shalom 127
Harold and Maude 115–116
Harper 116
Harper, Jessica 186, 217
Harper's Bazaar 62
Harrelson, Woody 31, 121, 128, 171, 185, 241
Harrer, Heinrich 215
Harris, Barbara 82, 83, 171, 250
Harris, Ed 3, 19, 41, 42, 246
Harris, Jo Ann 43
Harris, Jonathan 223
Harris, Julie 93, 188, 250
Harris, Richard 48, 51, 87, 148, 154, 173, 178, 189, 212, 255, 258
Harrison, Linda 133
Harrison, Rex 16, 17, 57, 58, 98, 159, 169, 212
Harrold (Ladd), Midge *104*
Harron, Mary 13
Harry and Son 116
Harry and Tonto 116
Harry Potter and the Chamber of Secrets 116–117
Harry Potter and the Sorcerer's Stone 117

Hart, Linda 186
Hart, Melissa Joan 211
Hart, Moss 5
Hart, Richard 68
Hart Carroll, Lisa 237
Hartford, Dee 141
Hartley, Mariette 97
Hartnett, Josh 90, 184, 185
Hart's War 117
Harvey, Laurence 7, 8, 144, 206, 207, 232
Harvey, Lilian 97, 240
Harvey, Rodney 76, 77, *170*
The Harvey Girls 117
Hatari! 117
Hatfield, Hurd 187
Hatter's Castle 117
Hauer, Rutger 141
Haven, Annette 38, 39
Haver, June 99, 149, 250
Hawaii 117
Hawke, Ethan 7, 257
Hawkins, Jack 141
Hawks, Howard 14, 34, 44–45, 59, 62, 113, 117, 126, 141, 157, 166, 180, 200, 201, 203, 204, 210–211, 214, 232
Hawn, Goldie 54, 67, 68, 77, 133, 214, 243
Hawthorne, Nigel 152, 153
Hayden, Sterling 133, 203, 255
Haydn, Richard 98, 223
Haydon, Julie 105, 108, 198, 199
Hayek, Salma 88, 213
Hayes, Billy 161
Hayes, Gabby 203, 204
Hayes, Helen 83, 189
Haynes, Roberta 93
Haysbert, Dennis 150
Hayward, David 171
Hayward, Leland 158
Hayward, Susan 8, 9, 29, 57, 65, 66, 105, 106, 126, 198, 199, 202, 250, 254
Hayworth, Rita 15, 37, 41, 121, 124, 140, 154, 155, 170, 180, 183, 198, 213, 230, 235
Haze, Jonathan 148
He Got Game 117
Head Over Heels 117, 164
Headly, Glenne 70
Hearst, William Randolph 26
The Heart Is a Lonely Hunter 118, 142, 246
Heartbreakers 118
Heartburn 118
Heather, Jean 74
Heatherton, Joey 253
Heaven Can Wait 118–119
Heaven Knows, Mr. Allison 119
Heaven's Gate 119
Heche, Anne 194, 218, 219
Heckerling, Amy 84
Hedren, Tippi 34, 35, 158, 224
Heflin, Van 131, 255

Heims, Jo 43
The Helen Morgan Story 119
Helldorado 119
Hellman, Lillian 135
Hello, Dolly! 119–120
Hell's Angels 120
Helm, Ann 253
Helm, Brigitte 37, 43
Helm, Fay 198, 199
Helmond, Katherine 41, 241
Help! 206
Hemingway, Ernest 88
Hemingway, Mariel 27
Hemingway's Adventures of a Young Man 120
Hemmings, David 37
Henie, Sonia 83
Henner, Marilu 13, 21, 35, 56, 130, 161, 209, 233
Henreid, Paul 50, 165, 175, 252
Henry, Charlotte 8
Henry II 29
Henry V 120
Hepburn, Audrey 12, 20, 37, 43, 49, 52, 53, 57, 61, 70, 73, 81, 83, 89, 94, 99, 109, 112, 117, 127, 129, 150, 151, 169, 172, 175, 178, 181, 196, 202, 205, 208, 210, 222, 223, 232, 235, 246, 247, 253
Hepburn, Katharine 6, 7, 8, 16, 32, 41, 44, 55, 65, 72, 79, 92, 98, 105, 106, 109, 121, 123, 127, 148, 152, 158, 167, 177, 178, 187, 189, 198, 213, 217, 234, 245, 258
Herbert, F. Hugh 212
Herbert, Hugh 131, 257
Here Comes Mr. Jordan 118
Heroes 120
Hershey, Barbara 29, 35, 44, 84, 114, 141, 142
Hersholt, Jean 110, 131
Herzfeld, Jim 160
Hesterberg, Trude 37
Heston, Charlton 25, 30, 31, 64, 65, 68, 69, 70, 85, 120, 133, 145, 149, 167, 178, 184, 211, 226, 240, 255
Hewitt, Jennifer Love 45, 63, 118, 141, 256
Hewitt, Martin 79
Heywood, Anne *53*, 216
Hickey, William 193, 194
Hickman, Dwayne 187
Hickock, Dick 127
Hicks, Catherine *39*
Hicks, Russell 132
Hicks, Taral 46
Higgins, Colin 31, 115
Higgins, Diane 223, 224
Higgins, Susie 223, 224
High Noon 120
High Road to China 120
High Sierra 1, 11, 50, 66, 121
Hill, George Roy 47
Hill, Karen 109

Hill, Lauryn 53
Hill, Marianna 200
Hill, Walter 43
Hiller, Arthur 14
Hiller, Wendy 146, 168, 192
Hilliard, Harriet 88
The Hi-Lo Country 121
Hilton-Jacobs, Lawrence 224
Hinds, Samuel 131, 132
Hines, Gregory 61, 90
The Hired Hand 121
Hirsch, Judd 181
His Girl Friday 121
His Kind of Woman 121
Hit the Deck 121
Hitchcock, Alfred 34–35, 83, 89, 125, 158, 175, 183, 194, 198, 199, 206, 208, 224, 230, 243, 250
Hitchcock, Jane 173
Hitler, Adolph 90
Hobart, Rose 147
Hoblit, Gregory 117
Hobson, Valerie 111
Hobson's Choice 121
Hocus Pocus 121
Hodge, John 146
Hodiak, John 143
Hoffa 156
Hoffman, Dustin 35, 60, 66, 94, 100, 101, 108, 109, 110, 114, 128, 139, 141, 143, 145, 152–153, 164, 174, 176, 188, 189, 190, 194, 197, 230, 243, 247, 250, 251, 252–253
Hoffman, Philip Seymour 126, 200
Holbrook, Hal 66, 67, 223
Hold 'Em Jail 121
Holden, Beverly 180, 181
Holden, William 8, 13, 14, 20, 43, 81, 86, 87, 98, 104, 130, 149, 164, 165, 172, 173, 182, 187, 197, 203, 206, 210, 214, 215, 226, 230, 233, 255
A Hole in the Head 121
Holiday 121
Holland, Tom 84
Holliday, Judy 41, 97, 221
Holliday, Polly 243
Holloway, Stanley 169
Holly, Lauren 5
Hollywood, CA 5, 16, 47, 48, 63, 68, 104, 106, 107, 155, 182
Hollywood Reporter 69, 182
Holm, Celeste 8, 54
Holm, Ian 234
Holman, Herbert Leigh 107
Holmes, Katie 49, 126
Holt, Tim 245
Home Alone 108
Home Alone 2 108
Honeymoon 121–122
The Honeymoon Express 256
Honeymoon in Vegas 122
The Honeymoon Machine 122
The Honeymooners 116

Honkytonk Man 136
Hook 122
Hook, Henry 261
Hope, Bob 21, 33, 34, 113, 221
Hopkins, Anthony 41, 92, 95, 98, 114, 130, 152–153, 157, 159, 164, 174, 218
Hopkins, Bo 184
Hopkins, Miriam 59, 105, 106, 131, 134, 147, 174, 177, 242
Hopper, Dennis 64, 65, 78, 244, 246
Horman, Ed 164
Horne, Lena 47, 48, 50, 217
The Horse Whisperer 122
Horton, Edward Everett 131
Hoskins, Bob 122, 166, 176, 249
Hot Millions 122
Hot Saturday 122
The Hotel New Hampshire 122
Hounsou, Djimon 14
The Hours 122–123
A House Divided 123
Houseboat 123
Houseman, John 81
Houston, Sam 7
Houston, Whitney 39
How Green Was My Valley 123
How the Grinch Stole Christmas 123
How to Be Very, Very Popular 124
How to Lose a Guy in 10 Days 124
How to Steal a Million 124
Howard, John 131
Howard, Ken 151, *252*
Howard, Leslie 31, 44, 49, 91, 105, 107, 129, 186, 195, 198, 205
Howard, Mary 198, 199
Howard, Ron 7, 29, 173, 225
Howard, Trevor 72, 151, 169, 206
Howards End 169
Howell, C. Thomas 23
The Hucksters 124
Hudson, John 64, 65
Hudson, Kate 11–12, 124
Hudson, Rochelle 252
Hudson, Rock 31, 46, 83, 98, 145, 157, 169, 188, 210, 213
Hudson, Ruben 217
Hudson Hawk 124
The Hudsucker Proxy 124
Hughes, Albert 92
Hughes, Allen 92
Hughes, Howard 93, 170, 201, 205, 257
Hughes, John 153
The Hulk 124
Hull, Henry 131
Hull, Warren 110
Hulswitt, Mart 223
Human Desire 124
The Hunchback of Notre Dame 124–125
Hunnicutt, Arthur 203, 204
Hunt, Helen 21, 38, 45, 103–104
Hunt, Peter 179

The Hunt for Red October 125, 231
Hunter, Holly 21, 37, 45, 73, 86, 195, 242
Hunter, Ian 49, 162
Hunter, Kim 188
Hunter, Ross 127, 240
Hunter, Tab 64, 65, 199, 210
Huppert, Isabelle 119
Hurley, Elizabeth 22, 127, 141, 219
The Hurricane 125
Hurt, John 8, 77, 80, 81, 119, 126, 218
Hurt, Mary Beth 120, 129
Hurt, William 3–4, 39, 132, 136, 139, 164
Husbands and Wives 125, 169
Hush...Hush, Sweet Charlotte 125
Hussey, Ruth 154, 155
Huston, Angelica 5, 7, 44
Huston, John 7, 33, 84, 154, 156, 165, 183, 193–194, 196, 201, 245
Huston, Walter 162, 165, 196, 245
Hutton, Betty 17, 97, 112, 209
Hutton, Jim 254
Hutton, Timothy 79, 181, 204
Hyatt, Bobby 199
Hyer, Martha 194, 203
Hyman, Bernie 117
Hyson, Dorothy 198, 199
Hytner, Nicholas 54, 63

I Confess 125–126
I Hate Hamlet 80
I Love Lucy 155
I Love Trouble 126
I Remember Mama 126
I Thank a Fool 126
I Wanna Hold Your Hand 126
I Was a Male War Bride 126
Ice Age 126
The Ice Storm 126
I'd Climb the Highest Mountain 126
Idle, Eric 7
Idol, Billy 237
If...Dog...Rabbit 126–127
Iglesias, Julio 81
I'll Be Seeing You 127
I'll Cry Tomorrow 150
Imitation of Life 127
The Impatient Years 127
In a Lonely Place 127
In & Out 127
In Cold Blood 127
In Living Color 5
In Love and War 127
In My Life 17
"In My Life" 17
In Name Only 127
In Search of Gregory 161
In the Arena (Charlton Heston) 69
In the Bedroom 169
In the Cool of the Day 127
In the Cut 128
In the Good Old Summertime 128
In the Line of Fire 128

"In the Navy" 48
Incognito 128
Indecent Proposal 31, 128
Independence Day 128
Indiana Jones and the Last Crusade 128–129
Indiana Jones and the Temple of Doom 35, 129
The Inn of the Sixth Happiness 129
Insomnia 153
Inspector Clouseau 129
Interiors 129
Intermezzo 107, 129
Intersection 129
Interview with the Vampire 129–130
Interview with the Vampire (Anne Rice) 129
Invisible Stripes 130
The Ipcress File 130
Ireland, John 131, 201, 203
The Irish in Us 6
Irma La Douce 130
Irons, Jeremy 42, 129, 253
Irreconcilable Differences 130
Irvine, William C. 119
Irving, Amy 58, 161, 197, 209, 227
Irving, Colin 55–56
Irving, John 55
The Island 130
The Island of Dr. Moreau 130–131
Islands in the Stream 131
Israel, Neal 23
It All Came True 1, 11
It Could Happen to You 131
It Happened One Night 131, 218
It's a Wonderful Life 131–132, 230
Ivanek, Zeljko 122
Ivanhoe 132
Iverson, Allen 117
Ives, Burl 14, 203, 204
Ivy 132

J. Arthur Rank 99, 179
J.F.K. 132–133
Jack Frost 133
Jackie Brown 133
Jackman, Hugh, 54, 258
Jackson, Glenda 35, 69, 77, 232
Jackson, Jonathan 228
Jackson, Joshua 219
Jackson, Kate 53, 60, 139
Jackson, Michael 1
Jackson, Peter 149
Jackson, Samuel L. 72, 133, 139, 154, 195, 202, 215, 216
Jacobi, Lou 130
Jacobs, Arthur 30, 80, 189
Jacobs, Tracey 60
Jacobsson, Ulla 220
Jaeckel, Richard 255
Jaffe, Sam 150, 193–194
Jaffe, Stanley 4
Jager, Lisa 223, 224
Jagger, Bianca 226, 227
Jagger, Dean 50, 131

Jagger, Mick 7, 80, 226, 227
Jaglom, Henry 244
Jane, Topsy 34
Jane Eyre 133
Janssen, David 47, 94, 100, 210
Janssen, Famke 160
Jarman, Claude, Jr. 259
Jaws 133
The Jazz Singer (1927) 134
The Jazz Singer (1952) 134
Jealousy 134
Jean-Baptiste, Marianne 247
Jeanmaire, Zizi (Renee) 115
Jeans, Isabel 99, 223
Jeffreys, Anne 207
Jeni, Richard 7
Jenks, Frank 131
Jenner, Bruce 233
Jergens, Adele 8
Jerry Maguire 134, 146
Jessel, George 8, 134
Jewison, Norman 85
Jezebel 105, 134–135
Jimmy and Sally 135
Joan of Arc 208, 209
The Joey Bishop Show 21
Johansson, Scarlett 122
Johnny Belinda 135
Johnny Guitar 135
Johnny Mnemonic 135
Johnny Suede 135
Johns, Glynis 90
Johnson, Ben 141, 142, 255
Johnson, Celia 192
Johnson, Don 184, 192, 249
Johnson, Mark Steven 65
Johnson, Michelle 36
Johnson, Monica 212
Johnson, Richard 72
Johnson, Van 58, 160, 172, 203, 230
Jolie, Angelina 32, 33, 96, 99, 114, 141, 189
Jolson, Al 134, 135
The Jolson Story 135
Jones, Allan 99
Jones, Anissa 81, 82
Jones, Annie 5
Jones, Carolyn 203
Jones, Christine 17
Jones, Dudley 12
Jones, Jack 223, 224
Jones, James Earl 36, 72
Jones, Jennifer 26, 27, 49, 50, 57, 61, 77, 137, 144, 152, 190, 222, 230, 236, 237
Jones, Quincy 59
Jones, Shirley 49, 177, 189–190, 194, 222, 223
Jones, Steven A. 152
Jones, Tommy Lee 19, 35, 75, 132, 133, 160, 171, 174, 250, 257
Jordan, Dorothy 88, 105, 108
Jordan, Neil 166
Jory, Victor 131, 162

Joseph II, Emperor 12
Josie and the Pussycats 135
Joslyn, Allyn 131
Jourdan, Louis 99, 206, 222, 223
Jovovich, Milla 140
Juarez 135
Judd, Ashley 74, 75, 114, 140, 141, 152, 185, 221
Judgment at Nuremberg 135
Juke Girl 135
Julia 135
Julia, Raul 108, 109, 139
Jumpin' Jack Flash, 136
June Bride 136
Junger, Gil 35
Jungle Fever 136
Junior Bonner 136
Jurado, Katy 45
Jurassic Park 122, 136
Jurgens, Curt 129
Jussim, Jared 134
Just for You 136
Just Tell Me What You Want 136
Justin, John 222, 223

Kahn, Madeline 56, 155
Kane, Carol 141
Kanew, Jeff 66
Kanin, Garson 41, 158
Kaplan, Jonathan 4
Kapur, Shekhur 79
The Karate Kid 136
Karath, Kym 223, 224
Karloff, Boris 21, 91
Kasdan, Lawrence 4, 34, 39, 156, 252
Kasznar, Kurt 67, 115, 223
Katcher, Aram 243
Katharine of France, Princess 120
Kathleen 136–137
Katt, William 227
Katz, Sam 45
Katzenberg, Jeffrey 218
Kaufman, Andy 155, 156
Kaufman, Bob 243
Kaye, Danny 115, 116, 221, 254
Kaye, Nora 252
Kazan, Elia 23, 77, 93, 100, 102, 143, 179, 225, 236, 250, 256
Kazan, Lainie 21
Kazantzakis, Nikos 125
Keach, Stacy 81, 82, 84, 230
Keaton, Buster 110
Keaton, Diane 3, 23, 37, 68, 79, 100, 101, 108, 119, 129, 153, 156, 157, 168, 189, 236, 237
Keaton, Michael 27, 28, 113, 132, 133, 173, 195, 225
Kedrova, Lila 261
Keel, Howard 138, 182, 219
Keeler, Ruby 64, 90, 231
Keitel, Harvey 19, 58, 82, 126, 159, 160, 202, 216, 247
Keith, Brian 161, 173, 194, 222, 223, 255

Kellerman, Sally 95, 151, 226
Kelley, David E. 160
Kelley, DeForest 227
Kelly, Gene 13, 35, 62, 78, 88, 113, 137, 157, 183, 219, 233, 236
Kelly, Grace 26, 27, 34, 35, 51, 61–62, 68, 94, 98, 99, 113, 158, 165, 172, 179, 222, 223, 235, 246
Kelly, Patsy 222
Kelly's 5
Kennedy, Arthur 144, 255
Kennedy, John F. 133, 182
Kennedy, Madge 158
Kent, Jean 46, 153, 201, 202
Kepros, Nicholas 12
Kern, Jerome 9
Kerr, Deborah 6, 82, 85, 93, 113, 117, 119, 137, 146, 165, 196, 200, 213, 260
Kerr, John 59, 199
Key West, FL 5
Keyes, Evelyn 41, 177, 180, 198, 99
The Keys of the Kingdom 137
The Keys of the Kingdom (A.J. Cronin) 137
Khan, Genghis 60
Khan, Princess Kukachin 6
Kibbee, Guy 131, 162
Kidder, Margot 233
Kidman, Nicole 22, 28, 50–51, 54, 79, 82, 87, 97, 128, 167, 183, 191, 194, 219, 242
Kiel, Richard 225
Kilbride, Percy 131
Kiley, Richard 148
Kill Bill: Vol. 1 137
The Killers 137
The Killing of Sister George 137
Kilmer, Val 5, 27–28, 62, 98, 102, 103, 130–131, 135, 159, 208, 241, 256
Kimmins, Anthony 49
Kind, Diana 209
King, Henry 49, 222, 232, 236
King, Martin Luther, Jr. 21
King, Morgana 100, 102
King, Stephen 67
The King and I 137, 223
King Kong 137–138
The King of Comedy 138
The King of Marvin Gardens 138
King Rat 138
Kings Row 138
Kingsley, Ben 95, 164
Kinnear, Greg 74, 75, 208
Kinskey, Leonid 75
Kinski, Klaus 87
Kirkland, Patricia 138
Kirkland, Sally 102
Kirshner, Mia 152
Kiss and Tell 138
Kiss Me Kate 137, 138
Kiss Me Stupid 138
Kiss of the Spider Woman 139
Kiss the Girls 139

Kissinger, Henry 174
Kitaen, Tawny 23
Klein, Chris 228
Kline, Kevin 34, 54, 67, 87, 127, 164, 176, 195, 220, 259
Klinger, Michael 64
Klitschko, Vladimir 176
Klugman, Jack 233
Klute 139
Knaiz, Judy 119
Knepper, Robert 96
Knife in the Water 139
Knight, Christopher 231, 253
Knight, Pat 8
Knight Without Armour 139
Knute Rockne, All American 139
Koch, Howard W. 178
Kohner, Susan 253
Konstantin, Leopoldine 175
Kopelson, Arnold 93
Korda, Alexander 6, 51, 107, 139
Korshack, Sidney 95
Korsmo, Charlie 122
Kotch 139
Kotto, Yaphet 5
Kovic, Ron 41
Kozlowski, Linda 215
Kramarsky, David 63
Kramer vs. Kramer 139–140
Kranz, Gene 19
Kristofferson, Kris 61, 115, 119, 184, 220
Kruger, Hardy 117, 208
Kruger, Otto 131
Kubrick, Stanley 73, 82, 248
Kudrow, Lisa 1
Kuffs 140
Kurney, Caroline 194
Kutcher, Ashton 90, 184
Kwan, Nancy 258
Kyme 211

L.A. Confidential 42
The L-Shaped Room 151
Laage, Barbara 140
La Belle, Patti 59, 97
LaBute, Neil 190
LaCava, Gregory 170
Ladd, Alan 69, 74, 98, 104, 239
Ladvenu, Martin 208, 209
The Lady Eve 140
Lady for a Day 140, 189
The Lady from Shanghai 140
Lady Godiva Rides Again 140
Lady L 140
The Lady Vanishes 140–141
Ladyhawke 141
Laemmle, Carl, Jr. 231
Lafitte, Jean 46
Lake, Ricki 214
Lake, Veronica 77, 231
Lamarr, Hedy 8, 50, 69, 77, 96, 112, 144, 187, 209
Lamas, Fernando 143, 144, 190
Lamas, Lorenzo 111

Lambert, Christopher 113
La Motta, Vickie 196
Lamour, Dorothy 154, 155, 197
Lancaster, Burt 31, 51, 65, 67, 69, 71, 86, 93, 100, 112, 113, 124, 135, 137, 139, 145, 165, 176, 178, 184, 197, 203, 204, 206, 213, 255
Lanchester, Elsa 6, 43
Land of the Pharaohs 141
Landau, Martin 62, 132, 133
Landers, Audrey 55
Landis, Carole 180
Landis, John 16, 245
Landon, Michael 203, 253
Lane, Diane 37, 38, 102, 103, 122, 134, 191
Lane, Nathan 34, 151
Lane, Priscilla 105, 108, 208
Lang, Margaret 198, 199
Lang, Walter 137
Lange, Hope 189, 190, 194, 253
Lange, Jessica 44, 91, 104, 137, 138, 153, 156, 174, 191, 209, 214, 243
Langham, Rhea 107
Lansbury, Angela 8, 29, 61, 89, 117, 140, 150, 155, 156, 179, 187, 192, 240, 245
Lansing, Joi 8
Lansing, Sherry 232
Lanza, Mario 231
La Plante, Laura 239
Lara Croft: Tomb Raider 141
Lardner, Ring 79
Las Vegas, NV 23, 180, 203, 227
La Salle, Eriq 217
Lass, Barbara 64
The Last Detail 141
The Last of Mrs. Cheyney 141, 184
The Last of the Dogmen 141, 142
Last of the Mohicans 42
The Last Picture Show 141–142
The Last Samurai 59
Last Summer 142
Last Tango in Paris 142
The Last Temptation of Christ 142–143
The Last Tycoon 143
Late Night with David Letterman 24
Latin Lovers 143–144
Laughing Sinners 144
Laughlin, John 62
Laughlin, Tom 194
Laughter in the Dark 144
Laughton, Charles 6, 8, 66, 109, 130, 155, 168, 207
Laura 144
Laurents, Arthur 78, 252
Laurer, Joanie 237
Laurie, Piper 194, 203
Laven, Arnold 196
Laverne & Shirley 55
Law, Jude 59, 81, 92, 96, 224, 225
Lawrence, Carol 222, 223, 253
Lawrence, Gertrude 8, 9
Lawrence, Marc 91

Lawrence, Martin 35
Lawrence, T.E. 144
Lawrence of Arabia 144
Layton, Joe 17
Lazenby, George 178–179
Lea, Nicholas 241
Leachman, Cloris 141
A League of Their Own 16, 144–145
Leak, Jennifer 109, 110
Lean, David 14, 73, 144
Leary, Denis 126
Leasure, Althea 185
LeBlanc, Matt 78, 150
Ledger, Heath 167
Lee, Ang 124, 126
Lee, Anna 123
Lee, Brandon 62, 63, 76
Lee, Bruce 76
Lee, Christopher 114
Lee, Dorothy 121
Lee, Jason Scott 76
Lee, Lila 217
Lee, Linda 105, 107
Lee, Pamie 223, 224
Lee, Peggy 134
Lee, Spike 58, 72, 136, 154, 211–212, 217, 232
Leeds, Andrea 59, 105, 108, 198, 199
Legends of the Fall 145
Leguizamo, John 215, 216
Lehman, Ernest 120
Leibman, Ron 176
Leigh, Janet 85, 194, 205, 212
Leigh, Jennifer Jason 68, 82, 83, 84, 124, 191, 215, 242
Leigh, Vivien 65, 66, 79, 89, 92, 105, 107, 114, 120, 123, 125, 183, 191, 192, 198, 199, 202, 213, 217, 230, 231, 249, 259, 260
Leisen, Mitchell 200
Le Mat, Paul 84
Lemmon, Jack 10, 47, 99, 100, 119, 130, 132, 133, 139, 164, 165, 172, 203, 221, 254
Lenny 145
Leno, Jay 98
Lenz, Kay 43
Leonard, Robert Z. 99
Leonowens, Anna 137
The Leopard 145
Lerner, Alan Jay 169
Lerner, Irving 231
LeRoy, Mervyn 90, 196
Lester, Mark L. 86
Lester, Richard 204, 240
Lethal Weapon 237, 249
Let's Make Love 145
Letterman, David 24
Lettieri, Al 97
Letty Lynton 145
Levant, Oscar 219
Levene, Sam 113, 131
Levine, Joseph E. 44, 259
Levine, Peter 166

Levinson, Barry 72, 197
Lewis, Jerry 67, 138
Lewis, Juliette 42, 48, 125
Lewis, Lennox 176
Li, Jet 159
The Liberation of L.B. Jones 145
Liberty Films 132
"Liebestraum" 9
The Lieutenant Wore Skirts 145
The Life and Death of Colonel Blimp 145–146
A Life Less Ordinary 146
The Life of David Gale 146
A Life of Her Own 146
Life of Riley 22
Life with Father 147
Life with Father (play) 147
Lili 147
Liliom 147
Lilith 147
Lilith (J.R. Salamanca) 147
Lillie, Beatrice 257
Lincoln, Abbey 182
Lincoln, Abraham 3
Lincoln, Mary Todd 3
Linder, Cec 105
Lindfors, Viveca 222
Lindo, Delroy 154
Lindsay, Howard 147
Lindsay, Margaret 96
Lindstrom, Pia 93
Lion's Gate Films 13, 166
Liotta, Ray 171
Lipton, Robert 109
Lithgow, John 157
Little, Cleavon 36
Little, Natasha 80
Little Big Man 147
Little Caesar 147
Little Egypt 147
The Little Foxes 147
The Little Foxes (play) 147
The Little Prince 148
The Little Shop of Horrors 148
Little Women 148
Liu, Lucy 53, 54
Live from New York (James A. Miller, Tom Shales) 1
Lively, DeLee 55
Livesey, Roger 113, 145, 146
The Living Daylights 105, 148
Living in Oblivion 148
Livingston, Ron 177
Livingstone, Mary 239
Llewellyn, Desmond 93
Lloyd, Emily 125, *161*
Lloyd, Harold 45
Lloyd, Jake 227, 228
Lloyd's of London 148–149
Loaf, Meat 16
Lo Bianco, Tony 100, 101, 108, 109
Locke, Sondra 43, 45, 56, 96, 118, 142, 229, 246
Lockhart, Anne 114
Lockhart, Gene 131

Lockhart, June 114
Lockhart, Kathleen 131
Lockin, Danny 119, 120, 223
Lockwood, Gary 165, 226
Lockwood, Margaret 46, 89, 117, 153, 179, 201, 202, *260*
Loder, John 208
Logan, Joshua 48, 83, 187, 210, 224, 235
Logan, Shirley 105, 107, 198, 199
Loggia, Robert 132, 133, 194
Loken, Kristanna 237
Lolita 149
Lollobrigida, Gina 57, 58, 73, 74, 124–125, 140, 141
Lom, Herbert 79
Lombard, Carole 25, 44, 95, 104, 105, 106, 107, 112, 121, 127, 131, 164, 170, 174, 193, 221, 238, 242
London, England 27, 80, 231, 258, 261
London, Julie 203
Lone, John 151
Long, Beverly 199
Long, Earl 36
Long, Shelley 77, 130, 136
The Long Goodbye 149
The Long Hot Summer 158
The Longest Day 149
Longmire, Adele 105, 107
Look for the Silver Lining 149
Looking for Mr. Goodbar 149
Lopes, Lisa "Left Eye" 135
Lopez, Jennifer 81, 88, 153, 213, 248
Lord, Jack 194
Lord of the Rings: The Fellowship of the Ring 149
Lords, Traci 76, 77
Loren, Sophia 20, 26, 35, 60, 73, 123, 140, 163, 175, 192, 238, 249
Lorenzo's Oil 149
Lorimar 63
Lorring, Joan 61
Los Angeles Film Critics Awards 237
Los Angeles Lakers 237
Loser 149
Lost Horizon 150
Lost in Space 150
Lost in Translation 103
Lost Souls 150
The Lost Weekend 150
Louise, Anita 6, 34, 49, 105, 106, 162, 198, 199
Love, Courtney 85, 99, 167, 185
Love, Edmund 71
Love and Pain (and the Whole Damn Thing) 150
The Love Boat 224
Love Field 150
Love in the Afternoon 150
Love Me or Leave Me 150–151
Love on the Run 151
Love Story 101, 151, 183

Love! Valour! Compassion! 151
Love with the Proper Stranger 151
Lowe, Edmund 157, *158*
Lowe, Rob 3, 77
Loy, Myrna 16, 31, 32, 37, 59, 80, 85, 131, 141, 151, 162, 168, 183–184, 197, 200, 202, 213, 239
Lualdi, Antonella 117
Lucas, George 13, 50, 128, 166, 197, 227, 228
Lucasfilm 228
Lucchesi, Gary 177
Lucci, Susan 44, 118, 119
Lucky Lady 151
Ludwig 151
Luft, Lorna 118
Luft, Sid 226
Lugosi, Bela 75, 91
Luhrmann, Baz 54, 167, 256
Lukas, Paul 252
Luke, Derek 18
Lumet, Sidney 10, 136, 168, 172, 250
Lumiere 151
Luna, Barbara 253, 258
Lundigan, William 8, 9
Lupino, Ida 8, 90, 123, 136, 138, 140, 222, 231
LuPone, Patti 81
Lurie, Rod 252, 253
Das Lusitania Songspiel 18
Lynch, David 29, 38, 42, 77, 203
Lynch, Jennifer 41–42
Lynch, Kelly 27, 76, 77, 195, 242
Lyne, Adrian 84, 128
Lynley, Carol 40, 49
Lynn, Jeffrey 105, 107, 134
Lyon, Sue 40, 149
Lyonne, Natasha 176
Lyons, Carole 223, 224

M. Butterfly 151
M. Butterfly (play) 151, 152
Macao 151
Macbeth 152
Macchio, Ralph 136
Macdonald, Andrew 29, 146
MacDonald, Jeanette 35, 99, 161, 196, 206, 223
MacDonald, Marie 41
MacDowell, Andie 91, 113, 124, 215, 218
MacEwen, Linda 238
MacGowran, Jack 81
MacGraw, Ali 19, 32, 55, 61, 95, 97, 100, 101, 108, 111–112, 119, 136, 183, 222
MacLachlan, Kyle 114, 132, 215, 218
MacLaine, Shirley 10, 11, 20, 30, 36, 37, 40, 47, 65, 76, 81, 94, 119, 120, 130, 221, 237, 238, 246, 249
MacLane, Barton 131
MacLeod, Gavin 223

MacMahon, Aline 179
MacMurray, Fred 3, 18, 19, 32, 74, 154, 193, 233, 245–246
MacRae, Gordon 49, 177, 182
Macy, William H. 83
Mad City 152
Mad Dog and Glory 152
The Mad Miss Manton 152
Madame Bovary 152
Madame Butterfly 152
Made in America 153
Madigan, Amy 3
The Madness of King George 152–153
Madonna 15–16, 36, 41, 42, 43, 54, 68, 70, 81, 82, 88, 102, 103, 145, 168, 191, 208, 218, 220, 249
Madrid, Spain 251
Madsen, Michael 171, 195, 202
Madsen, Virginia 102, 103
Maggiorani, Lamberto 33
Magic 153
The Magic Bow 153
Magnani, Anna 35, 206
The Magnificent Ambersons 153
The Magnificent Seven 202
Magnum, P.I. 48, 197, 202
Maguire, Tobey 224, 225
Mahoney, John 210
Maid in Manhattan 153
The Main Event 153
Main Line Films 42
Maisie 153
Major Dundee 154
Major League 154
Major League 2 154
Make Room for Daddy 224
Malanowicz, Zygmunt 139
Malcolm X 154
Malden, Karl 176, 184
Malet, Arthur 122
Malice 242
Malick, Terrence 66
Malikyan, Kevork 197
Malkovich, John 128, 132, 174, 176, 204
Mallrats 154
The Maltese Falcon 1, 11, 50, 66, 154–155
Mame 155
Mamet, David 3, 100
The Mammy (Brendan O'Carroll) 7
Mamoulian, Rouben 58, 104
Man About Town 155
A Man for All Seasons 8, 155
The Man from Down Under 155
The Man in Grey 155
Man on the Moon 155–156
Man Trouble 156
The Man Who Came to Dinner 156
The Man Who Loved Women 237, 238
The Man Who Would Be King 156
The Manchurian Candidate 156
Mancuso, Nick 197
Mangano, Silvana 25, 61, 73, 74

Manhattan Melodrama 156
Manhattan Murder Mystery 156–157
Manheim, Camryn 144, 145, 219, 220
Manhunter 157
Mankiewicz, Joseph L. 9, 14, 58, 113
Mannequin 157
Mannequin 2: On the Move 157
Manners, David 75, 76
Mannheim, Lucie 37
Manoff, Dinah 111
Man's Favorite Sport? 52–53, 157
Man's Genesis 157
Mansfield, Jayne 198, 199
Mantegna, Joe 72, 102, 103
Manterola, Patricia 238
The Many Loves of Dobie Gillis 231
Marathon Man 109
March, Fredric 17, 32, 44, 46, 49, 50, 61, 65, 68, 83, 95, 96, 105, 107, 131, 134, 139, 147, 154–155, 165, 175, 205
Marchand, Nancy 158
Marcias, Enrico 259
Marcovicci, Andrea 120
Margotta, Michael 19, 76
Marie 157
Marie Antoinette 157
Marie Galante 157, 158
Marin, Cheech 151, 241
Marjorie Morningstar 157–158
Marley, John 100
Marlowe, Hugh 8
Marlowe, Scott 253
Marnie 158, 224
The Marrying Kind 158
The Marrying Man 219
Mars, Kenneth 194
Marsden, James 192
Marsh, Jean 140
Marsh, Mae 157
Marshal, Alan 95, 96
Marshall, Brenda 154, 155
Marshall, Connie 212, *213*
Marshall, E.G. 129
Marshall, Ellie 8
Marshall, Frank 122
Marshall, Garry 29, 87, 91, 175, 191
Marshall, George 200
Marshall, Herbert 50
Marshall, Marian 8
Marshall, Penny 22, 33, 91, 100, 101, 144, 145, 171, 172
Marshall, Red (Charles) 131
Marshall, Rob 54
Martin, Dean 67, 95, 138, 182, 189, 203, 260
Martin, Dewey 34
Martin, George 17
Martin, Jack 132, 133
Martin, Marcella 105, 106
Martin, Mary 92, 224
Martin, Steve 39, 71, 127
Martinelli, Elsa 117

Martinez, A 216
Martinez, Olivier 29
Martino, Al 100, 101
Martino, John 100, 102
Marty 158
Marty (TV) 179
Marvin, Lee 71, 86, 133, 149, 154, 182, 184, 203, 204, 255
Marx, Groucho 105, 107
Mary Hartman, Mary Hartman 111
Mary of Scotland 158
Mary Reilly 158
Mary Shelley's Frankenstein 159
MASH 151
Mask 159
Mask of Zorro 159
Mason, James 20, 47, 72, 73, 118, 119, 149, 153, 155, 226, 254
Mason, Marsha 56, 108–109, 175
Mason, Tom 19
Masquerade 159
Massee, Michael 63
Massey, Raymond 21, 125, 131
Masterson, Danny 192
Masterson, Mary Stuart 31, 191
Mastrantonio, Mary Elizabeth 57, 204
Mastroianni, Marcello 102, 103
Matheson, Tim 16
Mathews, Dorothy 105, 107
Mathis, Samantha 45
The Matrix 159
The Matrix Reloaded 159
The Matrix Revolutions 159
Matthau, Carol 139
Matthau, Walter 12, 39, 40, 47, 71, 86, 87, 93, 139, 188, 212, 214–215, 222, 223, 240
Mattingly, Hedley 223
Mature, Victor 169, 204, 250
Maverick 159
Maxwell, Marilyn 8–9
Mayer, Louis B. 17, 59, 64, 66, 71, 99, 107, 140, 145, 183, 200, 209, 239, 240, 257, 259
Mayer Selznick, Irene 106, 107
Mayhew, Peter 227
Mayo, Archie 6
Mazar, Debi 218
Mazursky, Paul 38, 75, 76, 79, 116, 167, 172, 236
Mazzello, Joseph 122
Mazzocone, Carl 42
MCA 260
McAndrew, Marianne 119, 120
McCabe & Mrs. Miller 159
McCallum, Rick 228
McCambridge, Mercedes 135
McCann, Chuck 118
McCarey, Leo 22, 198
McCarthy, Andrew 157
McCarthy, Eugene 118, 119
McCarthy, Jenny 28, 87, 154, 186, 211, 218, 248–249
McCarthy, Joseph 15

McCartney, Paul 206
McCarty, Walter 117
McConaughey, Matthew 14, 168, 241, 252
McCourt, Frank 15
McCourt, Malachy 15
McCoy, Tim 20
McCrea, Joel 83, 89, 127, 202, 203, 235
McCullogh, Rohan 233
McDaniel, Hattie 105, 108, 132
McDermott, Dylan 218
McDonald, Marie 9
McDonnel, Austine 105, 107
McDonnell, Mary 44, 141, *142*
McDormand, Frances 37
McDowall, Roddy 30, 123, 188
McDowell, Malcolm 184
McDuffie, Lizzie 105, 108
McEntire, Reba 241
McGann, Paul 216
McGavin, Darren 55, 67, 210
McGill, Bruce 16
McGillis, Kelly *4*, 23, 27, 42, 43, 68, 243
McGiver, John 223
McGoohan, Patrick 72, 117
McGovern, Elizabeth 132, 133, 215
McGregor, Ewan 29, 127, 146, 167, 216
McGuire, Dorothy 16, 57, 92, 112, 239
McHale's Navy 159
McHugh, Frank 131
McKee, Lonette 136, 173, *174*
McKellen, Ian 20
McKenna, Frances 223, 224
McLaglen, Victor 113
McLuhan, Marshall 17, 18
McNaughton, John 152
McQuarrie, Christopher 29
McQueen, Chad 19
McQueen, Steve 18, 19, 32, 39, 43, 44, 47, 55, 56, 58, 61, 71, 76, 80, 86, 89, 92, 95, 96, 109, 111, 112, 119, 122, 127, 131, 138, 149, 151, 154, 172, 183, 189, 196, 198, 202, 209, 222, 233, 234, 242, 243, 244, 247, 251, 255
McQueeney, Patricia 167
Meade, Mary 9
Meadows, Audrey 88
Mean Streets 159–160
Medavoy, Mike 114
Meek, Donald 131
Meeker, Ralph 95, 225, 226
Meet Joe Black 22
Meet John Doe 160
Meet Me After the Show 160
Meet Me in St. Louis 160
Meet the Parents 160, 228
Megaforce 160
Megna, Ave Maria 223, 224
Mekka, Eddie 55
Melcher, Martin 223

Melnick, Daniel 10–11, 230
Memmoli, George 235
Men Don't Leave 160
Men in Black 160
Men in Black II 160–161
Mendes, Sam 12
Menjou, Adolphe 8, 93, 131, 132
Menzies, Heather 223, 224
Le Mepris 161
Mercer, Beryl 10
Mercer, Julia Ann 133
Merchant, Vivien 187
Meredith, Burgess 204, 205, 223
Merivale, Phillip 131
Merkel, Una 3, *4*, 45, 257
Mermaids 103, 161
Merrick, David 55
Merrill, Gary 8, 9, 210
Merrill, Lynn 105, 107
The Merry Widow (1934) 161
The Merry Widow (1952) 143
Messing, Debra 159
Metcalf, Mark 16
Meteor 161
Mewes, Jason 58, 154
Meyers, Nancy 130
MGM 12, 13, 17, 26, 31, 37, 41, 45, 48, 49, 50, 58, 59, 61, 62, 64, 68, 72, 73, 78, 80, 84, 95, 96, 107, 110, 113, 124, 136, 137, 138, 143, 146, 152, 156, 165, 166, 175, 183, 183, 191–192, 195, 196, 198, 200, 205, 217, 220, 221–222, 231, 233, 234, 235, 239, 249, 257
Michael 161
Michaels, Lorne 80, 190
Michele, Michael 115
Michell, Keith 222, 223
Micki & Maude 161
Midler, Bette 17, 81, 89, 137, 138, 164, 171, 176, 208, 219, 238
Midnight Cowboy 161, 162
Midnight Express 161
Midnight Run 161–162
A Midsummer Night's Dream 6
Mifune, Toshiro 227
Mighty Aphrodite 52, 134
Milan, Italy 12
Milani, Chef 132
Mildred Pierce 162–163
Miles, Sarah 73
Miles, Sylvia 121
Miles, Vera 194, 222, 250
Milestone, Lewis 93
Milland, Ray 44, 49, 95, 96, 105, 107, 123, 146, 150, 203, 226
Miller, Allan 153
Miller, Ann 78
Miller, Arthur 140, 205
Miller, Jason 81, 82
Miller, Jonny Lee 81
Miller, Marilyn 149
Miller, Penelope Ann 85
Miller, Robert Ellis 118

Miller, Troy 133
Miller's Crossing 163
The Million Dollar Mermaid (Esther Williams) 143
The Millionairess 163
Mills, Hayley 149
Mills, John 121
Mimieux, Yvette 73
Mindel, Allan 77
Mineo, Sal 199
Minghella, Anthony 59, 235
Ministry of War 146
Minnelli, Liza 21, 47, 81, 82, 83, 226, 227, 229
Minnelli, Vincente 99
Minority Report 163
The Miracle 163
Miracle on 34th Street 163
The Miracle Worker 163
The Miracle Worker (play) 163
Miramax 54, 59, 75, 90, 216, 253
Mirisch, Walter 253
The Mirror Crack'd 163
The Mirror Has Two Faces 163
Les Miserables 164
Misery 164
The Misfits 164
Missing 164
Mission: Impossible II 163, 258
Mission to Mars 117, 164
Mississippi Burning 164
Mr. and Mrs. Smith 164
Mister Buddwing 164
Mr. Majestyk 164
Mister Roberts 164–165
Mr. Skeffington 165
Mr. Smith Goes to Washington 104, 132, 165
Mitchell, Cameron 190
Mitchell, Margaret 107
Mitchell, Thomas 131, 132, 137
Mitchum, Robert 35, 37, 48, 71, 86, 92, 93, 119, 124, 131, 149, 164, 169, 170, 172, 176, 181, 184, 203, 206, 255
Moby Dick 165
The Mod Squad 165
The Model Shop 165
Modine, Matthew 18, 23, 24, 127, 132, 176, 243
Mogambo 165, 235
Mohr, Jay 184
Mol, Gretchen 207
Molina, Alfred 185
Molly and Me 165–166
Mommie Dearest 166
Mona Lisa 166
Monaco 35, 68, 94, 158, 246
Money for Speed 8
Mongkut, King 137
Monkey Business 166
Monroe, Marilyn 1, 8, 9, 21, 23, 43, 46, 51, 57–58, 78, 90, 97, 99, 113, 114, 124, 130, 140, 172, 187, 221, 231

Monsieur Verdoux 166
Monster's Ball 166
Montalban, Ricardo 143, 230, 244
Montana, Lenny 100, 102
Montand, Yves 13, 58, 102, 103, 145, 178
Montez, Maria 37, 93, *94*
Montgomery, Elizabeth 88
Montgomery, George 64, 155
Montgomery, Robert 44, 68, 110, 113, 131, 136, 145, 151, 154, 155, 156, 164, 168
Moody, Ron 178
The Moon and Sixpence 166, 229
Moon Over Parador 79
Moonlighting 70
Moonstruck 162, 166
Moore, Cleo 9
Moore, Demi 4, 27, 28, 71, 85, 87, 97, 128, 144, 145, 174, 180, 208, 219, 220
Moore, Dudley 21, 163, 225, 236
Moore, Grace 161, 206
Moore, Joanna 157
Moore, Julianne 114, 122, 123, 194, 217, 248
Moore, Mandy 54
Moore, Mary Tyler 181, 214
Moore, Pauline 198, 199
Moore, Roger 72, 120, 177
Moore, Terry 99, 199
Moore, Victor 131, 257
Moorehead, Agnes 125, 218, 230
Morali, Jacques 48
Moran, Bugs 225, 226
Moran, Dolores 9
Moranis, Rick 5, 87
More, Margaret 155
More American Graffiti 166, 227
Moreau, Jeanne 25, 73, 85, 109, 110, 124, 151, 156
Moreno, Dario 57
Moreno, Rita 137
Morgan, Debbi 81
Morgan, Dennis 24, 100, 136
Morgan, Frances 211, 212
Morgan, Frank 17, 257
Morgan, Glen 256
Morgan, Helen 119
Morgan, Michele 50
Moriarty, Cathy 35, 196
Morison, Patricia 198, 199
Morituri 167
Mork & Mindy 167
Morley, Karen 16
Morley, Robert 223
Morris, Wayne 130, 137
Morrow, Barry 197
Morrow, Rob 130, 131
Mortensen, Viggo 42, 113, 149, 242
Moscow on the Hudson 167
The Mosquito Coast 167
Mostel, Zero 8, 12, 85, 115
Mostow, Jonathan 237
Mother 167

Mother Carey's Chickens 167
Mother Wore Tights 167
Moulin Rouge 54, 167, 183, 216
Mourning Becomes Electra 167
Movieline 11, 12
Mozart, Constanze 12
Mozart, Wolfgang Amadeus 12
Mrs. Miniver 167
Mrs. Soffel 167
Mrs. Winterbourne 167
MTV 193
Muir, Jean 49, 162, 198, 199
Muldoon, Wendy 223, 224
Mulholland Drive 203
Mullally, Megan 204
Mulligan, Robert 151
Mulroney, Dermot *148*, 169
The Mummy 167
The Mummy Returns 167
Munchausen, Baron Karl Friedrich Hieronymous von 6
Muni, Paul 61, 121, 154, 155, 210, 211, 213
Munson, Ona 105, 108
Murder by Death 167
Murder, Inc. 167
Murder on the Orient Express 167
Murphy, Eddie 32, 46, 62, 90, 98, 113, 115
Murphy, George 88
Murray, Bill 16, 27, 66, 67, 98, 113, 152, 185, 197, 225, 256
Murray, Don 46, 210
Murray, Peggy 119, 120
Muse, Clarence 50
Music for the Millions 167
The Music Man 167
Music of the Heart 167
Mutiny on the Bounty 144, 167
My Best Friend's Wedding 169, 238
My Cousin Vinny 169
My Darling Clementine 169
My Fair Lady 109, 169, 178
My Favorite Martian 138
My Forbidden Past 169–179
My Gal Sal 170
My Man Godfrey 170
My Own Private Idaho 170
My Three Sons 18
Myers, Mike 72, 218, 220
Myra Breckinridge 170

NAACP 128
Nahan, Stu 83, 84
Nair, Mira 185
Najimy, Kathy 121
Nan, Lin 129
The Nanny 13
Nash, John Forbes, Jr. 29
Nashville 171
Nathanson, Michael 165
National Board of Review Awards 237
National Society of Film Critics Awards 237

National Velvet 171
Natural Born Killers 171
Natwick, Mildred 115
Nazimova 198, 199
NBC 169, 210
Neagle, Anna 35, 196, 223
Neal, Patricia 8, 90, 109, 110, 214, 231, 254
Neame, Ronald 190
Neeson, Liam 15, 28, 66, 104–105, 192, 211
Negri, Pola 233
Neighbors 171–172
Neill, Sam 136
Nelligan, Kate 91, 192, 193
Nelson, Judd 5
Nelson, Lori 199
Nelson, Ozzie 88
Nelson, Ricky 203
Nelson, Ruth 22
Nesbit, Evelyn 99
Nesbitt, Cathleen 82, 83, 223
Ness, Eliot 249
Network 172
Neufeld, Mace 125, 232
Never on Sunday 172
Never So Few 172
Neville, John 6
New Girl in Town 256
New Line Cinema 130, 131, 149, 256
New York, NY 104, 118
New York Daily News 195–196
New York Film Critics Circle Awards 237
New York Giants 22
New York Yankees 22
Newley, Anthony 7, 8
Newman, Nell Potts 183
Newman, Paul 3, 10, 12, 36, 38, 46, 47, 51, 55, 56, 71, 73, 77–78, 86, 89, 92, 116, 119, 126, 127, 132, 133, 138, 140, 151, 156, 157, 158, 164, 176, 177, 178, 181, 183, 184, 187, 196, 198, 204, 209, 210, 221, 229, 236, 237, 240, 241, 244, 250
Newman, Susan Kendall 126
Newsweek 228
Newton, Robert 258
Newton, Thandie 53
Newton-John, Olivia 81, 110, 111, 258
Next Stop, Greenwich Village 172
Next Time I'll Sing to You 261
Niagara 172
Niagara Falls 172, 173
Nicholas, Ron 253
Nicholas and Alexandra 172
Nicholls, Allan 171
Nichols, Barbara 238
Nichols, Mike 34, 49, 51, 89, 108, 109, 110, 118, 143, 192, 254
Nicholson, Ivy 141
Nicholson, Jack 10, 18, 19, 21, 27,

39, 40, 41, 45, 55, 58, 60, 63, 75, 76, 78, 81, 82, 91, 100, 101, 104, 108, 109, 111, 112, 118, 123, 128, 132, 138, 143, 148, 153, 156, 174, 177, 179, 183, 188, 191, 204, 206, 207, 222, 230, 231, 237, 244, 246, 247, 256
Nick of Time 172
Nickelodeon 173
Nielsen, Brigitte 201
Nielsen, Connie 164
Nielsen, Leslie 194
The Night of the Following Day 173
The Night of the Iguana 173
Night Shift 173
Nimoy, Leonard 227
Ninchi, Annibale 74
9½ Weeks 173, 174
1941 173
Ninotchka 173–174
Nirvana 167
Nissen, Greta *120*
Niven, David 20, 72, 95, 96, 149, 196, 198, 213, 222, 223
Nixon 174
Nixon, Marian 199
Nixon, Marni 169
Nixon, Pat 174
Nixon, Richard 174
No Man of Her Own 174
No Small Affair 174
No Time for Comedy 108
No Way Out 175
Noble, Tricia 119, 120
Noel, Hattie 105, 108
Noiret, Phillippe 58, 102, 103
Noises Off 175
Nolan, Doris 121
Nolan, Jeanette 152, 194
Nolan, Lloyd 154, 155, 225
Nolte, Nick 19, 48, 75, 86, 89, 90, 109, 114, 126, 128, 132, 192–193, 220, 227, 233, 248
Norma Rae 175
Norman, Marc 216
Norris, Christopher 223, 224
North, Jay 223, 224
North, Sheree 32, 124, 145, 186, 203
North by Northwest 175
The North Star 175
Northwest Passage 175
Norton, Edward 65, 117, 127, 155, 156, 192, 197, 212
Norton, Ken 204, 205
Nothing in Common 175
Notorious 175
Nouri, Michael 87
Novak, Kim 16, 82, 87, 183, 186, 187, 235, 250
Novello, Ivor 95, 96
The Novice 80
Now, Voyager 175
Nugent, Elliott 136
Nugent, Sharon 253
Nunn, Bill 72

Nunn, Terri 227
Nurse Betty 176
Nuts 176
Nuyen, France 258
Nye, Louis 223

O 176
Oakes, Susan 253
Oakie, Jack 113
Oakley, Annie 17, 18
Oates, Warren 44
Ober, Philip 93
Oberon, Merle 6, 54, 55, 60, 65, 95, 96, 123, 241, 258
The Object of My Affection 176
Obradors, Jacqueline 219
O'Brien, Edmond 8, 93, 144, 203, 255
O'Brien, Margaret 136, 199
O'Brien, Pat 93, 139
O'Carroll, Brendan 7
Ocean's 11 176
O'Connor, Donald 91, 219, 254
O'Connor, Kevin J. 126
O'Connor, Una 132
Octopussy 177
Odone, Michaela 149
O'Donnell, Chris 28, 61, 127, 160, 192, 193, 211, 224, 225, 241
O'Donnell, Rosie 7, 88, 121, 144, 145, 219, 220, 235
Of Human Bondage 50, 177
Of Mice and Men 177
Office Space 177
An Officer and a Gentleman 177
O'Hara, Catherine 31, 87, 88
O'Hara, Maureen 24, 72, 92, 99, 123, 198
O'Keeffe, Miles 235
Oklahoma! 49, 177
Old Acquaintance 177
Old Gringo 178
The Old Maid 178
Oldman, Gary 42, 132, 133
Olin, Lena 27, 39
Oliver! 178
Oliver! (play) 178
Oliver, Edna May 258
Oliver, Gordon 131–132
Olivier, Laurence 30, 34, 43, 49, 50, 65, 66, 75, 79, 95, 96, 100, 101, 107, 114, 116, 120, 123, 135, 138, 139, 145, 146, 147, 149, 169, 183, 191, 192, 193, 195, 198, 199, 202, 206, 213, 226, 229, 258
Olmstead, Gertrude 59
Olsen, Moroni 132
Olson, James 196
The Omega Man 178
The Omen 178
On a Clear Day You Can See Forever 178
On Golden Pond 174, 178
On Her Majesty's Secret Service 178–179

On the Waterfront 179
Onassis, Jacqueline (Kennedy) 182
Once in a Lifetime 179
Once Upon a Dream 179
Once Upon a Time in America 142
One Desire 179
One Flew Over the Cuckoo's Nest 179, 218, 225
One Flew Over the Cuckoo's Nest (play) 179
One Glorious Day 180
100 Rifles 48
One Million B.C. 180
One Million Years B.C. 180
One Minute to Zero 180
One Tough Cop 180
O'Neal, Griffin 52
O'Neal, Patrick 222, 223
O'Neal, Ryan 7, 39, 52, 76, 100, 101, 130, 151, 153, 183, 204, 252
O'Neal, Tatum 183
O'Neil, Barbara 105, 108
O'Neill, Jennifer 100, 101, 204
Only Angels Have Wings 180
The Only Game in Town 180
Only Yesterday 180
Only You 180
Operation Petticoat 180
Orbach, Jerry 62
Ordesky, Mark 149
Ordinary People 181
Orion Pictures 68
Ormond, Julia 145, 208
Oscars *see* Academy Awards
O'Shea, Katie 141, 183–184
O'Shea, Milo 248
Osment, Haley Joel 227, 228
Osmond, Marie 81, 111
O'Sullivan, Maureen 105, 108, 213, 214, 224, 259
Oswald, Lee Harvey 132, 133
Otis, Carre 255–256
O'Toole, Peter 29, 73, 80, 81, 109, 132, 133, 144, 169, 206, 231, 261
Out of Africa 181
Out of Sight 181
Out of the Fog 181
Out of the Past 181
Outcast Lady 181
The Outlaw 181
The Outlaw Josey Wales 136
The Outrage 181
The Outsiders 181
The Outsiders (TV) 170
Overall, Park 86, *186*
Owen, Clive 32, 33
Owen, Patricia 222
Owen, Reginald 131
Owen, Tony 119
The Owl and the Pussycat 182
The Owl and the Pussycat (play) 182
Ozzie and Harriet 88

PT 109 182
Pacino, Al 1, 3, 18, 19, 37, 38, 58,

60, 61, 62, 63, 66, 81, 82, 86, 91, 95, 99–100, 101, 139, 143, 145, 156, 164, 176, 180, 185, 191, 192, 202, 204, 211, 227, 249, 251
Pacula, Joanna 42, 43
Page, Geraldine 179, 232, 234
Paget, Debra 99
Pagnol, Marcel 30
Paid 182
Paige, Janis 135, 203
Paint Your Wagon 182, 255
Paiva, Nestor 132
The Pajama Game 182
The Pajama Game (play) 94, 182
Pakula, Alan J. 228, 229
Pal Joey 183
Pal Joey (play) 137
Palance, Jack 71, 97, 169, 171, 203
Palin, Michael 42
Palmer, Leland 10
Palmer, Lillie 222
Paltrow, Bruce 77
Paltrow, Gwyneth 22, 32, 33, 40, 53, 54, 77, 79, 114, 124, 145, 190, 203, 208, 216, 220, 241
The Panic Room 183
Papas, Irene 246
Pape, Lionel 123
Paper Moon 183
Papillon 183
The Paradine Case 183
Paramount Pictures 3, 4, 8, 13, 28, 31, 32, 34, 35, 37, 49, 65, 69, 79, 88, 89, 97, 98, 100, 100, 102, 103, 112, 113, 115, 129, 157, 161, 183, 188, 207, 221, 230, 232, 238, 243, 247
Pare, Michael 188
Parker, Alan 15, 81, 161
Parker, Bonnie 40
Parker, Eleanor 92, 115, 222, 223
Parker, Mary-Louise 242
Parker, Michael 170
Parker, Sarah Jessica 91, 103, 104, 176
Parkes, Walter 203
Parkins, Barbara 249, 250
Parks, Larry 62, 135
Parks, Michael 19
Parnell 141, 183–184
Parr, Catherine 260
Parrish 184
Parsons, Louella 69, 158
Parton, Dolly 78
The Partridge Family 111
Pasadena Playhouse 199
Paseornek, Michael 166
Pasternak, Joseph 69, 191
Pat Garrett and Billy the Kid 184
Patinkin, Mandy 81, *118*, 157, 177, 259
Patric, Jason 86, 97, 128, 208
Patrick, Robert 237
Patriot Games 184, 231
Patterson, John Henry 98

Patton 184
Patton, George S., Jr. 184
Patty, Miriam 198, 199
Paul, Adrian 104, 105
Paulie 184
Pavan, Marisa 206
Paxton, Bill 103–104, 241, 248
Paycheck 184
Paymer, David 7
Payne, Eric 217
Payne, John 163, 167
Peaker, E.J. 119
Pearce, Guy 65
Pearl Harbor 184–185
Peck, Gregory 20, 37, 49, 65, 66, 68, 77, 94, 97, 120, 128, 129, 132, 133, 137, 145, 165, 176, 178, 183, 196, 203, 205, 226, 249, 251, 255, 259
Peckinpah, Sam 25, 44, 56, 97, 184, 203, 230, 255
Peggy Sue Got Married 185
Penn, Arthur 100
Penn, Chris 94, 202, 246
Penn, Sean 36, 41, 83, 84, 85, 96, 121, 176, 197, 200, 248
Penthouse 14
The People vs. Larry Flynt 185
People Will Talk 185
Peppard, George 43, 253, 255
Perez, Rosie 185, 214, 247
Perez, Vincent 63
The Perez Family 185
The Perfect Storm 185–186
A Perfect World 186
Perkins, Anthony 34, 77, 92, 144, 221, 235
Perkins, Elizabeth 85, 87
Perkins, Millie 70, 253
Perlich, Max 76, 77
Peron, Eva 81
Peron, Juan 80, 81
Perrine, Valerie 95, 137, 138
Perrineau, Harold, Jr. 256
Perry, Frank 142
Perry, Luke 193
Perry, Matthew 78, 128, 150, 169, 221
Perschy, Maria 157
Persoff, Nehemiah 259
Pesci, Joe 72, 132, 133
Peter III, Czar 51
Peters, Bernadette 171
Peters, Jean 187, 250
Peters, Jon 27, 153, 208, 226, 227
Petersen, Wolfgang 33, 186
Petrie, Donald 253
The Petrified Forest 186
The Petrified Forest (play) 186
Petty, Lori *68*, 144, 145
Pfeiffer, Michelle 27, 28, 32, 36, 39, 42, 43, 46, 70, 74, 75, 81, 82, 85, 91, 149, 150, 180, 191, 218, 249, 250, 254
The Phantom 186

Phantom of the Paradise 186
Phffft! 186
Phifer, Mekhi 18
Philadelphia 186–187, 211
The Philadelphia Story 187
Phillippe, Ryan 228
Phillips, Don 84
Phillips, Julia 229
Phillips, Lee 210
Phillips, Michelle 100, 101, 191
Phoenix, Joaquin 194, 218, 242, 256
Phoenix, River 62, 129, 130, 170
Phone Booth 187
Piazza, Ben 106
Piccoli, Michel 103, 161
Pickens, Slim 73
Pickford, Mary 147, 157, 229, 233
Pickup on South Street 187
Picnic 187
Picnic at Hanging Rock 187
Picture Mommy Dead 187
The Picture of Dorian Gray 168, 187
Pidgeon, Walter 123
Pilbeam, Nova 198, 199
Pillow Talk 187
Pillsbury, Sarah 68
Pinchot, Bronson 246
The Pink Panther 188, 244
Pinkett Smith, Jada 53, 214
Pinky 188
The Pirate 78
Pirates 188
Pistone, Joe 74
Pitillo, Maria 103, 104
Pitt, Brad 22, 41, 59, 62, 69, 77, 83, 85, 135, 145, 146, 159, 204, 208, 212, 215, 216, 238, 241
Pittman, Tom 63
Pitts, ZaSu *10,* 207
Place, Etta 47
Planet of the Apes (1968) 30, 188
Planet of the Apes (2001) 117, 176
Plato, Dana 81, 82, 191
Plato, Kay 82
Platoon 188–189
Platt, Louise 105, 106–107
Play Dirty 189
Play It Again, Sam 189
Play Misty for Me 189
Playboy 87, 224, 248
The Player 189
Players Directory 165
Playing by Heart 189
Plaza Suite 189
Pleasence, Donald 64, 114, 161, 215, 260
Pleshette, Suzanne 34, 35, 205, 253
Plowright, Hilda 223
Plowright, Joan 169
Plummer, Amanda 195, 220
Plummer, Christopher 130, 222, 223, 236
Pocketful of Miracles 189–190

Index

Pogostin, Leo 21–22
Pogue, John 219
Point Break 190
Poitier, Sidney 5, 182, 190, 230
Polanski, Roman 55, 64, 139, 188, 207
Polk, Oscar 105
Pollack, Sydney 3, 59, 82, 86, 191, 208, 243, 252
Polley, Sarah *11*
Pollock 12
Polo, Marco 6
Polo, Teri 160
Pons, Lily 161
Ponti, Carlo 35, 73, 100, 238
Pontiac Moon 190
"Poor Jud Is Dead," 177
The Pope of Greenwich Village 32
Popeye 190
Porgy and Bess 190
Porter, Eric 222, 223
Porter, Jean 131, 132
Portman, Eric 155
Portman, Natalie 122, 126
Portrait of Jennie 190
The Poseidon Adventure 190
Posey, Parker 185
Posse 190
Possession 190
Post, Ted 30
Postcards from the Edge 81
Poster, Meryl 54
Postlethwaite, Pete 209
The Postman Always Rings Twice (1946) 190
The Postman Always Rings Twice (1981) 191
Potter, Monica 117, 164
Pounder, CCH 24, 25
Powell, Anthony 122
Powell, Dick 162, 181
Powell, Eleanor 45, 88
Powell, Jane 21, 22, 121, 207, 214, 231
Powell, William 16, 49, 50, 61, 129, 147, 156, 170, 173, 174, 198, 199, 205, 226
Power, Tyrone 97, 104, 110, 123, 138, 149, 204, 221, 226, 232, 250
Practical Magic 191
The Practice 160
The Preacher's Wife 39
Prefontaine, Steve 256, 257
Premiere 18
Preminger, Otto 14, 15, 50, 89, 137, 144, 206, 209
Prentiss, Paula 38, 157, 189
Presenting Lily Mars 191
Presley, Elvis 110, 111, 197, 226, 227, 253
Pressman, Edward R. 63
Preston, Kelly 134, 217
Preston, Robert 55, 138, 155, 168, 239, 248
Presumed Innocent 191

Pretty Baby 191
Pretty Woman 191
Price, Alan 226, 227
Price, Vincent 8, 89, 95, 96, 131, 132
Price, Will 106
Pride and Prejudice 191–192
The Pride and the Passion 192
Primal Fear 192
Primary Colors 192
The Prime of Miss Jean Brodie 17, 192
The Prime of Miss Jean Brodie (play) 155
The Prince and the Showgirl 43
Prince of the City 192
The Prince of Tides 192–193
The Princess Bride 193
The Princess Comes Across 193
Printemps, Yvonne 99
Prinze, Freddie, Jr. 224–225
The Private Lives of Elizabeth and Essex 193
Private Parts 193
The Prizefighter and the Lady 193
Prizzi's Honor 193–194
Proctor, Elizabeth 63
The Producers 194
Proof of Life 194
Prowse, David 227
Pryce, Jonathan 42, 80, 81, 241
Pryor, Richard 43, 61, 62, 90, 154
Psycho (1960) 194, 212
Psycho (1998) 194
The Public Enemy 194
Puglie, Frank 132
Pullman, Bill 250
Pulp Fiction 1, 195
Purdom, Edmund 78, 231
The Purple Rose of Cairo 45, 195
Purviance, Edna *166*
Pushing Tin 96
Puzo, Mario 100, 101

Quaid, Dennis 7, 18, 33, 76, 81, 132, 133, 161, 177, 192, 197, 219, 220, 234, 249
Quaid, Randy 141, 197
Qualen, John 131
Queen Christina 195
Queen Latifah 54, 214
Queen of the Damned 195–196
The Queen's Affair 196
Queensland, Australia 130
The Quick and the Dead 196
Quigley Down Under 196
Quilley, Denis 222, 223
Quine, Richard 14
Quinlan, Kathleen 233
Quinn, Aidan 14, 31, 68, 69, 142, *143*, 215, 241
Quinn, Anthony 5, 25, 38, 46, 87, 100, 124, 125, 145, 154, 155, 261
Quinn, Francesco 188
Quinn, Patricia 8

Quintanilla Perez, Selena 213
Quo Vadis? 196

Rabwin, Marcella 106
The Rack 196
Racklin, Marty 243
Radio Flyer 196
Radner, Gilda 190
Raeburn, Mavis 198, 199
Rafelson, Bob 138, 156, 244
Raffin, Deborah 233
Raffles (1930) 196
Raffles (1940) 196
Raft, George 1, 11, 38, 50, 66, 74, 97, 121, 130, 135, 154, 174, 193, 213, 225
Ragghianti, Marie 157
Raging Bull 196
Ragtime 196
Raiders of the Lost Ark 129, 197
Railsback, Steve 86
Raimi, Sam 133, 225
Rain, Douglas 248
Rain Man 197
Rainbow Island 197
Rainer, Luise 80
The Rainmaker (1956) 197
The Rainmaker (1997) 197
Rains, Claude 8, 43, 66, 79, 131, 132, 165, 175
The Rains Came 197–198
Raise the Titanic 198
Raising Arizona 163
Raitt, John 182
Rally Round the Flag, Boys 198
Rambova, Natacha 59
Ramis, Harold 16, 98
Ramona 198
Randall, Tony 12, 260
Randolph, Lillian 132
Random Harvest 50
Ransohoff, Martin 56
Rappe, Virginia 180
Rathbone, Basil 8, 95, 96, 105, 107, 125
Ratner, Brett 200
Ratoff, Gregory 8
Ray, Aldo 93
Ray, Billy 117
Ray, Mary 105, 107
Ray, Nicholas 127, 199
Ray, Rene 198, 199
Ray, Terry 105, 107
Raymond, Gene 104, 132
The Razor's Edge 97, 198
Reagan, Nancy (Davis) 8, 9, 167
Reagan, Ronald 8, 50, 109, 110, 135, 138, 210, 214, 245
Reap the Wild Wind 198
Rear Window 179
Rebecca 198–199
Rebecca of Sunnybrook Farm 199
Rebel Without a Cause 199
Recco, Donna-Marie 14
Reckless 200

Red Cross 238
The Red Danube 200
Red Dragon 157, 200
Red Dust 145, 200
Red Garters 200
The Red-Headed Woman 201
Red Line 7000 200
Red River 201
Red Sonja 201
Redford, Robert 1, 12, 18, 19, 29, 37, 41, 44, 47, 53, 60, 100, 101, 109, 111, 112, 119, 132, 151, 156, 164, 181, 191, 192, 204, 206, 207, 229, 233, 242, 243, 250, 252, 253, 254, 259
Redgrave, Lynn 122
Redgrave, Michael 72
Redgrave, Vanessa 48, 69, 92, 135, 155, 169, 232
Redman, Joyce 222–223
Reed, Alan 194
Reed, Carol 178, 239
Reed, Donna 8, 20, 43, 62, 93, 119, 131, 132, 168, 203, 230
Reed, Oliver 240
Reed, Robi 211
Reeve, Christopher 12, 13, 39, 41, 114, 207, 208, 233
Reeves, Keanu 28, 42, 135, 159, 170, 176, 185, 221, 224
The Ref 201
Reflections in a Golden Eye 201
Reid, Beryl 137
Reid, Frances 198, 199
Reid, Wallace, Jr. 181
Reiner, Rob 85, 164, 193, 210, 254
Reinhardt, Gottfried 162
Reinhardt, Max 162
Reinhold, Judge 83, 84, 185
Reiser, Paul 23
Reisz, Karel 95
The Reluctant Widow 201–202
Remick, Lee 14, 181, 199, 255, 261
Remington Steele 105, 148
Rendezvous 202
Renfro, Brad 20
Rennie, Michael 66
Reservoir Dogs 195, 202
Return of the Seven 202
The Revengers 202
Revere, Anne 131, 132, 259
Reversal of Fortune 202
Revolution 202
Reynolds, Audrey 198, 199
Reynolds, Burt 30, 31, 40, 45, 48, 56, 68, 70, 90, 95, 100, 101, 179, 220, 225, 231, 233, 234, 237, 246, 253, 260
Reynolds, Debbie 5, 94, 167, 177, 199, 249
Reynolds, Joyce 9
Reynolds, Marjorie 9, 198, 199
Rhames, Ving 202
Rhett, Alicia 105, 106, 198, 199

Rhodes, Hari 28
Rhys-Davies, John 197
Ribisi, Giovanni 165
Ricci, Christina 126, 136, 149, 256
Rice, Anne 129–130
Rice, Joan 140
Rich, Allan 71, 72
Rich and Famous 202
Richard III 202
Richards, Ariana 136
Richards, Denise 141, 218
Richards, Marty 54
Richard's Things 202
Richardson, John 178
Richardson, Marie 82
Richardson, Miranda 19, 20, 169
Richardson, Ralph 79
Richardson, Salli 190
Richardson, Tony 144
Rickman, Alan 5, 117, 204
Ride the High Country 202–203
Ridges, Stanley 131
Riegert, Peter 16
Rifkin, Ron 119, 120
Rigg, Diana 178, 179
Riley, Pat 237
The Ring 203
Ringwald, Molly 191
Rio Bravo 203–204
Rio Lobo 204
Riskin, Robert 150
Risky Business 204
Ritchie, Michael 130
Ritt, Martin 174, 175, 176
Ritter, John 43
Ritter, Tex 141, 142
Ritter, Thelma 256
Rivera, Geraldo 171
Rivers, Joan 28
RKO 77, 106, 127, 132, 148, 170, 205
Roach, Hal 244
Robards, Jason 25, 87, 198, 225, 226, 236, 240, 255
Robbins, Gale 9
Robbins, Jerome 253
Robbins, Tim 124, 189, 216
Robbins, Tom 80
The Robe 204, 226
Roberts, Burton Bennett 39, 40
Roberts, Eric 42, 177, 180, 226
Roberts, Julia 14, 27, 32, 33, 57, 86, 87, 102, 103, 126, 127, 128, 131, 146, 153, 158, 159, 191, 208, 216, 219, 220, 221, 228, 229
Roberts, Leona 105, 108
Roberts, Lynn 198, 199
Roberts, Rachel 187
Robertson, Cliff 159, 182, 194
Robertson, Dale 160
Robin and Marian 204
Robin Hood: Prince of Thieves 204
Robinson, Dewey 162
Robinson, Eartha 211, 212
Robinson, Edward G. 53, 54, 56,
61, 121, 147, 154, 155, 186, 188, 213, 230, 245
Robson, Flora 85, 198, 199
Robson, May 140, 189, 258
Roc 154
Rochon, Lela 258
The Rock 98
Rock, Chris 235
Rock, Dr. 209
Rock Star 204
Rockne, Knute 139
Rockwell, Sam 60, 135
Rocky 204–205
The Rocky Horror Picture Show 217
Rocky III 205
Rodgers, Raby 223
Rodgers, Richard 49
Rogers, Anthony 178
Rogers, Charles R. 170
Rogers, Ginger 8, 17, 25, 26, 56, 88, 90, 115, 121, 127, 158, 166, 167, 175, 220, 242
Rogers, Wayne 202, 203
Rogers, Will 180
Roland, Gilbert 95, 96
Rollins, Howard E. 196
Rollins, Rowena 9
Roman Holiday 205
The Romance of Rosy Ridge 205
Romance on the High Seas 205
Romano, Ray 252–253
Romanus, Robert 83
Romberg, Sigmund 67
Rome, Italy 25
Rome Adventure 205
Romeo and Juliet (1936) 205–206
Romeo and Juliet (1954) 206
Romeo and Juliet (1968) 206
Romeo Must Die 159
Romero, Cesar 75, 95, 96, 223
Ronet, Maurice 144
Rooker, Michael 154
The Rookie 7
Rooney, Mickey 23, 31, 62, 91, 162
Roos, Fred 100–101, 102, 227, 260
Roosevelt, Franklin Delano 108, 184, 185
The Roots of Heaven 206
Rope 206
Rose, Billy 94
Rose, Felipe 48
Rose, George 223
Rose, Pete 7
Rose Marie 206
The Rose Tattoo 206
The Rose Tattoo (play) 206
Rosebud 206
Rosemary's Baby 69, 206–207
Rosenman, Howard 153
Ross, Diana 39, 59, 153, 226, 227
Ross, Frank 259
Ross, Herbert 54, 88, 109, 228–229, 246, 252
Ross, Katharine 32, 47, 109, 110, 112

Ross, Shirley 239
Rossellini, Isabella 44
Rossen, Robert 11, 147
Rossi, Tino 30
Roth, Joe 15–16, 57, 153
Roth, Tim 91, 117, 202, 229
Roughshod 207
Rounders 207
Rourke, Mickey 7, 15, 32, 34, 76, 102, 103, 128, 245, 256
Rouvenol, Jean 198, 199
Rowlands, Gena 18, 213, 214, 243
The Royal Tenenbaums 228
Royal Wedding 207
Royle, Selena 131
Rubinstein, John 47, 115, *116*
Rudd, Paul 55, 56, 176
Ruddy, Albert S. 97, 101
Rudin, Scott 122, 168, 215, 218
Ruffalo, Mark 128, 218, 222, 256, 259
Ruggles, Wesley 20
Ruggles of Red Gap 207
Ruhmann, Heinz 223
Rule, Ja 18
Rule, Janice 187
The Rules of Attraction 207
Rumble Fish 34
The Running Man 207–208
Rush 208
Rush, Geoffrey 164
Russell, David O. 240
Russell, Harold 32
Russell, Jane 97, 113–114, 150–151, 181
Russell, Kurt 28, 46, 136, 228, 237
Russell, Rosalind 8, 73, 121, 147, 162, 167, 197, 198, 200, 202, 234
Russell, Theresa 35
Russo, Gianni 100, 101
Russo, James 72
Russo, Rene 28, 128
Ruth, George Herman "Babe" 22
Rutherford, Ann *15,* 105, 108, 198, 199
Ruthless People 208
Rutledge, Ann 3
Ryan, Irene 132
Ryan, John 30, 100, 101
Ryan, Meg 4, 32, 33, 74, 75, 97, 128, 150, 159, 195, 108, 216, 218, 219, 220, 228, 229, 242, 254
Ryan, Robert 255
Rydell, Mark 129, 174, 176
Ryder, Alfred 223, 224
Ryder, Winona 52, 63, 79, 102, 103, 124, 134, 150, 161, 176, 194, 208, 216, 228, 229, 251

Sabotage 208
Saboteur 208
Sabrina (1954) 208
Sabrina (1995) 208
Sacajawea 20
Sagal, Boris 178

Sahl, Mort 44
The Saint 28, 208
Saint, Eva Marie 175, 177, 179, 194, 223, 238, 240
Saint Joan 208–209
St. John, Jill 70, 253
St. Johns, Adela Rogers 92
St. Louis Blues 225
The St. Valentine's Day Massacre 225–226
Saks, Gene 26, 47, 155
Salieri, Antonio 12
Salinger, Pierre 182
Salt, Jennifer 100, 101
Saltzman, Harry 178, 179
Salvador 209
Sampson, Will 225
Samson and Delilah 112, 209
San Fernando Valley, CA 142
San Giacomo, Laura 102, 103, 215
Sanchez, Jaime 255
Sanchez-Gijon, Aitana 251
Sand, Paul 153
The Sand Pebbles 209
Sanda, Dominique 142
Sande, Walter 131
Sanders, George 8, 9, 89
Sandler, Adam 71
Sands, Diana *57,* 182
Sands, Julian 41
Sands, Tommy 253
Sanford, Erskine 131
Sanford, Midge 68
Santa Barbara 193
The Santa Clause 2 72
Sarandon, Susan 44, 46, 139, 149, 180, 204–205, 214, 217, 236, 238, 241, 242, 256
Saratoga 209
Saratoga Trunk 209
Sarelle, Leilani 27
Sarrazin, Michael 151, 161, *162*
Sarsgaard, Peter 218, 259
Saturday Night Fever 209, 210
Saturday Night Live 3, 16, 32, 190
Sautet, Claude 57
Savage, John 161, 209, 229
Savalas, Telly 71
Saving Private Ryan 209
The Saviors of God (Nikos Kazantzakis) 125
Savoca, Nancy 247
Saxon, John 100, 101
Say Anything 210
Sayles, John 23, 79
Sayonara 210
Sayres, Jo Ann 198, 199
Scacchi, Greta 27
Scarface (1932) 210–211
Scarface (1983) 211
Scary Movie 211
Scary Movie 2 211
Scent of a Woman 211
Schaake, Katrine 204
Schaech, Jonathon 228

Schaefer, George 79–80
Schaffner, Franklin 131, 188
Schary, Dore 6, 22, 146, 165, 200
Schatzberg, Jerry 174
Scheider, Roy 10, 11, 81, 82, 92, 132, 133, 222, 247, 250
Scheinman, Andy 164
Schell, Maximilian 55, 222, 223, 244
Schepisi, Fred 217
Schildkraut, Joseph *51,* 61
Schindler, Oskar 211
Schindler's List 211
Schlesinger, John 34, 65, 66, 161
Schnabel, Julian 29
Schneider, Bert 76
Schneider, Maria 142
Schneider, Romy 261
School Daze 72, 211–212
Schreiber, Live 251
Schroder, Rick 20, 27, 52
Schroeder, Barbet 219
Schubert, Franz 30
Schumacher, Joel 28, 87
Schurz, Carl 53–54
Schwartz, Leonard 45
Schwarzenegger, Arnold 7, 207, 208, 237, 244
Sciorra, Annabella 102, 103, 128
Scofield, Paul 8, 147, 208, 209, 222, 223
The Score 212
Scorsese, Martin 48, 50–51, 58, 95, 116, 138, 142, 143, 152, 160, 173, 196, 235, 240
Scott, Debralee *111*
Scott, Dougray 81, 258
Scott, George C. 48, 73, 86, 100, 101, 115, 124, 131, 172, 176, 184, 196
Scott, Hazel 50
Scott, Larry B. 211
Scott, Martha 92, 123, 131
Scott, Randolph 202, 203
Scott, Ridley 35, 114, 238, 248
Scott, Robert L. 100
Scott, Tony 83
Scott, Zachary 8, 245
Scott Thomas, Kristin 122
The Scout 212
Scream 212
Scream 3 211
Screen Actors Guild 24
Scrooge 212
Scudda-Hoo! Scudda Hay! 212, 213
Sea of Grass 213
The Sea Wolf 213
Seagal, Steven 234, 248, 249
Seaton, George 14
Seberg, Jean 208, 209
Seconds 213
The Secret Call 213
Sedgwick, Kyra 176
Segal, George 10, 35, 38, 60, 138, 151, 163, 182, 236, 243, 254

Segal, Vivienne 161
Seidelman, Susan 68
Selby, David 202
Selena 213
Sellars, Elizabeth 223
Selleck, Tom 27, 48, 120, 160, 196, 197, 202, 250
Sellers, Peter 73, 113, 129, 138, 163, 178, 188, 194, 244, 248
Seltzer, Will 227
Selznick, David O. 16, 17, 49, 50, 64, 65, 66, 77, 83, 96, 105, 106, 107, 108, 120, 137, 138, 156, 183, 190, 198, 199, 218, 236, 239, 260
Selznick, Myron 105, 106, 107
Selznick International Pictures 57, 106
Seneca, Joe 72
Separate Tables 213
September 213–214
Serato, Massimo 222, 223
Serenade 214
Sergeant Pepper's Lonely Hearts Club Band 161
Sergeant York 214
Serial Mom 214
The Servant 214
Set It Off 214
Seven 77, 145
Seven Brides for Seven Brothers 214
7 Women 214
The Seven Year Itch 214–215
Seven Years in Tibet 215
Seventh Heaven 215
sex, lies, and videotape 215
Sexton, Charlie 62
Sexual Perversity in Chicago 1
Seyler, Atheny 223
Shadows and Fog 215
Shaft 215–216
Shakespeare, William 158, 206, 216
Shakespeare in Love 216
Shakur, Tupac 23
Shalako 53, 179, 216
Shallow Grave 216
Shallow Hal 216
Shandling, Garry 181
Shane 136
Shannon, Peggy 213
Sharif, Omar 73, 94, 144
Shatford, Bobby 185, 186
Shavers, Ernie 205
Shaw, Artie 221
Shaw, Clay 132, 133
Shaw, Robert 133, 229
Shaw, Victoria 223
The Shawshank Redemption 216
She-Devil 216, 217
Shea, John 259
Shearer, Moira 115, 207
Shearer, Norma 8, 26, 67, 98, 105, 106, 143, 157, 167, 175, 177, 181, 182, 191, 192, 200, 201, 220, 244
Sheedy, Ally 83, 84, 243
Sheehan, Winfield 198

Sheen, Charlie 27, 41, 76, 102, 103, 132, 133, 188, 251
Sheen, Martin 19, 86, 100, 101, 209
Sheinberg, Sid 133
Shelley, Mary Wollstonecraft 43
The Sheltering Sky, 216
Shelton, Ron 36, 46, 241
Shentall, Susan 206
Shepard, Sam 213, 214
Shepherd, Cybill 55, 66, 67, 82, 83, 97, 100, 101, 112, 132, 133, 136, 141, 142, 143, 149, 173, 201, 214, 226, 227, 235, 245
Sheridan, Ann 50, 56, 105, 106, 126, 160, 162, 169, 170, 230
Sheridan, Margaret 201
She's Gotta Have It 217
Shields, Brooke 37, 38, 79, 191
Shiffrin, Bill 64, 65
Ship of Fools 217
The Shipping News 217
Shire, Talia 100, 101, 204, 205
Shirley, Anne 105, 108, 167, 198, 199
Shock Treatment 217
Shopworn 217
Shore, Dinah 137
Short, Martin 185
Short Circuit 243
Short Cuts 217
Show Boat 137, 217
Showgirls 218
Shrek 218
Shrek 2 218
Shue, Elisabeth 210
Shyamalan, M. Night 248
Shyer, Charles 130
Sidney, George 138
Sidney, Sylvia 8, 56, 57, 230, 252, 258
Signoret, Simone 261
Signs 218
The Silence of the Lambs 4, 114, 157, 218
Silliphant, Sterling 244
Silva, Cindy 7
Silver, Joel 70–71, 124
Silver, Ron 79, 87, 202
Silverado 251
Simmons, Bob 72
Simmons, Gene 87, 246
Simmons, Jean 5, 79, 113, 114, 151, 205, 260
Simon, Carly 226–227
Simon, Neil 108, 109, 175, 189
Simon, Simone 215, 229
A Simple Plan 218
Simpson, Don 29, 62, 71, 72
Simpson, O.J. 196, 237
Simpson, Ray 48
Simpson, Russell 110
Simpson, Valerie 48
Sinatra, Frank 49, 69, 71, 93, 94, 101, 102, 103, 113, 116, 121, 138,
148, 156, 165, 172, 178, 179, 180, 182, 183, 189, 203, 221, 226, 250
Sinatra, Frank, Jr. 100, 101
Since You Went Away 218
Singer, Bryan 20, 60
Singer, Lori 88
Singin' in the Rain 219
Single White Female 219
Singled Out 154
Singleton, John 23, 215, 216
Sister Act 219
The Sisters 219
Six Days, Seven Nights 7, 219
Six Degrees of Separation 219
Six Degrees of Separation (play) 219
The Sixth Sense 228
Sizemore, Tom 132, 133, 171, 209
Skala, Lilia 223
Skerritt, Tom 66, 67
Skinner, Cornelia Otis 105, 108
The Skulls 219
Skye, Ione 42, 96, 210
Slater, Christian 62, 129, 130, 210
Slater, Helen 215
Sleepers 219
Sleeping with the Enemy 219
Sleepless in Seattle 219–220
Sleuth 220
Slezak, Walter 8, 223
Sliding Doors 22, 220
Sloane, Everett 8
Small Time Crooks 220
"Smells Like Teen Spirit" 167
Smiles of a Summer Night 220
Smilin' Through 220
Smith, Alexis 8, 67, 226
Smith, Anna Nicole 88
Smith, Bubba 193
Smith, Charles Martin 13
Smith, Constance 235
Smith, Dick 102
Smith, G. Albert 51, 52
Smith, Jaclyn 53
Smith, John 210
Smith, Kent 132
Smith, Kevin 58, 65, 154
Smith, Maggie 17, 122, 150, 168, 192, 245
Smith, Perry 127
Smith, Will 18, 54, 80, 159, 160, 219
Smokey and the Bandit III 175
The Snake Pit 220
Snider, Paul 226
Snipes, Wesley 83, 136, 154, 215–216, 228
Snodgress, Carrie 204
Snyder, Tom 83, 84
So I Married an Axe Murderer 220
Soap 241
Soapdish 220
Sobieski, Leelee 12, 129, 130
Soderbergh, Steven 176, 215
A Soldier's Daughter Never Cries 220

The Solid Gold Cadillac 221
Solomon and Sheba 221
Some Came Running 221
Some Like it Hot 221
Somebody Up There Likes Me 221
Someone Like You 221
Somers, Suzanne 13
Something's Gotta Give 221
Somewhere I'll Find You 221–222
Sondergaard, Gale 257, 258
The Song of Bernadette 222
Sonnenfeld, Barry 160
Sonny 222
Sons and Lovers 222
Sons of the Desert 222
Sorcerer 61, 222
Sorvino, Mira 52, 134, 152, 185, 232
Sorvino, Paul 174
Sossamon, Shannyn 207
Sothern, Ann 8, 117, 131, 132, 153, 261
Soul, David 86
The Sound of Music 130, 222–224
The Sound of Music (play) 130
South Pacific 224
Spacek, Sissy 50, 132, 133, 141, 142, 157, 186, 237, 249
Spacey, Kevin 12, 19, 54, 146, 155, 156, 217
Spader, James 132, 133, 215, 228
Spano, Vincent 23, 102, 103
Sparkle 224
Spears, Britney 54
Speed 224
Speed the Plow 79
Speed 2: Cruise Control 224
Speedman, Scott 77
Spider-Man 224–225
Spiegel, Sam 43, 143, 179, 230, 231
Spielberg, Anne 33
Spielberg, Steven 12, 14, 23, 24, 33, 44, 58, 59, 77, 122, 128–129, 133, 136, 153, 163, 197, 211, 241
Splash 225
Splendor in the Grass 182, 225, 253
Spy Game 29, 41
The Spy Who Loved Me 225
Stack, Robert 64, 65, 173
Stagecoach 226
Stahl, Nick 11
Stalag 17 226
Stallion Road 226
Stallone, Sylvester 32, 45, 60, 61, 66, 68, 86, 180, 204, 205, 233
Stalmaster, Lynn 40, 141, 233
Stamos, John 193
Stamp, Terence 7, 8, 34, 37
Stand Up and Be Counted 226
Stanley, Kim 46
Stanley, Richard 130
Stansfield, Lisa 128
Stanton, Harry Dean 132, 133
Stanwyck, Barbara 8, 9, 18, 25, 37, 41, 44, 45, 65, 90–91, 96, 104,

124, 125, 134, 135, 140, 146, 150, 152, 160, 162, 178, 179, 183, 208, 217, 229, 233, 239, 249, 261
Stapleton, Jean 25
Stapleton, Maureen 189, 206
Star 80 226
A Star Is Born (1954) 226
A Star Is Born (1976) 226–227
Star Trek: Generations 227
Star Wars 50, 227
Star Wars: Episode I—The Phantom Menace 227–228
Star Wars Episode II—Attack of the Clones 228
Stargate 228
Starger, Martin 159
Stark, Joy 223, 224
Stark, Ray 94, 182, 228, 252
Starr, Blaze 36
Starr, Ron 202, 203
Starship Troopers 228
Starsky & Hutch 228
Starsky & Hutch (TV) 208
Start the Revolution without Me 228
Starting Over 175, 228
State Fair 228
Steel, Dawn 88
Steel Magnolias 228–229
Steele, Tommy 85
Steelyard Blues 229
Steenburgen, Mary 3, 104, 190, 237
Steiger, Rod 55, 73, 83, 100, 101, 158, 177, 179, 184, 203, 221
Stella Dallas, 229
The Sterile Cuckoo, 229
Sterling, Jan 41, 135
Sterling, Robert 210
Sterling, Tish 223, 224
Stern, Howard 14, 71, 193
Stevens, Connie 254
Stevens, Dodie 253
Stevens, George 98, 112, 132
Stevens, Mark 163
Stevens, Stella 25, 97, 243
Stewart, James 25, 68, 72, 108, 110, 116, 131, 132, 160, 165, 169, 175, 184, 187, 206, 214, 215, 226, 230, 255
Stewart, Paul 236
Stickney, Dorothy 115
Stickney, Phyllis Yvonne 211
Stigwood, Robert 81
Stiles, Julia 176
Stiller, Ben 160, 216, 228
Sting 142, 143, 191
The Sting 12, 156, 229
Stockwell, Dean 34, 77, 100, 101
Stoddard, Haila 105, 107
Stoker, Austin 28
Stoltz, Eric 23, 24, 27, 83, 84
Stone, George E. 147
Stone, Lewis 245
Stone, Oliver 18, 33, 41, 81, 114,

133, 171, 174, 185, 188, 189, 209, 248, 251
Stone, Sharon 27, 28, 50, 51, 70, 79, 84, 88, 104, 105, 128, 129, 220, 248
Storm Center 229
Stormy Monday 229
The Story of Dr. Wassell 229
The Story of Three Loves 230
Stovall, Count 245
Stowe, Madeleine 96, 191, 217
The Stranger 230
Strangers on a Train 230
Strasberg, Lee 102, 204, 205
Stratford, Tracy 223, 224
Stratten, Dorothy 238
Stratton, Ethel 230
Stratton, Monty 230
The Stratton Story 230
Straw Dogs 230
The Strawberry Blonde 230
Streep, Meryl 44, 58, 67, 81, 86, 92, 118, 120, 135, 139, 156, 168, 181, 191, 220, 235
Street Scene 230
A Streetcar Named Desire 230–231
A Streetcar Named Desire (play) 184
Streisand, Barbra, 8, 9, 47, 60, 81, 82, 91, 94, 96, 119, 120, 137, 138, 139, 153, 163, 176, 178, 182, 192, 193, 208, 209, 220, 226, 227, 251, 252, 259
Strick, Joseph 118, 248
Strickland, Gail 139–140
Stritch, Elaine 151, 213, 214
Strictly Dishonorable 231
The Stripper 231
Striptease 231
Stroker Ace 237
Stroud, Pauline 140
Strudwick, Shepperd 105, 107, 223
Stuart, Gilchrist 223
Stuart, Randy 9
The Student Prince 231
Studs Lonigan 231
Sturges, John 14
Sturges, Preston 140, 231
Styne, Jules 94
Suddenly, Last Summer 231
Suddenly, Last Summer (play) 231
Sullavan, Margaret 8, 105, 121, 131, 177, 180, 198, 199
Sullivan, Annie 163
Sullivan, Brad 192
Sullivan's Travels 231
The Sum of All Fears 231–232
Summer and Smoke 232
Summer of Sam 232
The Sun Also Rises 232
The Sundance Kid (Harry Longbaugh) 47
Sunday, Bloody Sunday 232–233
Sunderland, Nan 73, 74
Sunset 233
Sunset Boulevard 233

Sunshine, Ken 225
Super Soap Weekend 256
Superman 233
Superman II 233
The Superstars 205
Susan Lennox (Her Fall and Rise) 234
Sutherland, Donald 132, 133, 181, 206, 228, 229, 230, 234, 241, 257
Sutherland, Kiefer 85, 187, 241
Suvari, Mena 12, 149, 176
Suzman, Janet 172
Swank, Hilary 114, 153
Swann, Lyn 105, 107
Swanson, Gloria 8, 65, 161, 233
Swardstrom, Brian 117
Swayze, Patrick 76, 97, 190, 242, 244
Sweeney, D.B. 132, 133
Sweeney Todd 103
Sweet Bird of Youth 234
The Sweet Hereafter 234
Sweet November 185
Switch Back 234
Switching Channels 234
Sylbert, Richard 70
Sylvia Scarlett 234

T, Mr. 205
Tai-Pan 234
Taka, Miiko 210
Take a Letter, Darling 234
Take Me Out to the Ball Game 234
A Tale of Two Cities 234
The Talented Mr. Ripley 59, 235
Tales That Witness Madness 235
Tall Story 83, 235
Tallichet, Margaret 105, 106, 253, 254
Tam Lin 30
Tamblyn, Russ 253
Tammy Tell Me True 99
Tandy, Jessica 8, 76, 230
Taps 204
Tarantino, Quentin 133, 137, 195, 202
Tarzan 235
Tarzan, the Ape Man (1932) 235
Tarzan, the Ape Man (1981) 235
A Taste of Honey 235
Tatagliore, Paul 195
Tate, Sharon 56, 206, 207, 223, 224, 250
Taurog, Norman 95
Taxi 235
Taxi (TV) 13
Taxi Driver 4, 173, 235
Taylor, Don 80, 200
Taylor, Elizabeth 8, 17, 26, 29, 47, 49, 50, 51, 57, 58, 60, 79, 88, 98, 119, 120, 130, 132, 147, 151, 157, 163, 170, 180, 182, 196, 205, 224, 231, 236, 249, 254, 260
Taylor, James 226–227

Taylor, Juliet 236
Taylor, Mary 198, 199
Taylor, Robert 35, 95, 96, 151, 175, 180, 194, 196, 221, 226, 250
Taylor, Rod 34, 35, 92, 182, 203, 260
Taylor, Sandra 193, 248
Taylor, Zola 258
Tea with Mussolini 236
The Teahouse of the August Moon 236
Tempest 236
Temple, Gertrude 23, 162
Temple, Shirley 22, 23, 121, 122, 136, 137, 138, 147, 162, 172, 190, 257
Temujn (Genghis Khan) 60
10 236
The Ten Commandments 59
Tender is the Night 236
Tennant, Victoria 3
Tequila Sunrise 237
Terkel, Studs 81, 82
The Terminator 237
Terminator 2: Judgment Day 237
Terminator 3: Rise of the Machines 237
Terms of Endearment 237–238
Terrell, John Canada 217
Terry, Helen 198, 199
Tetzel, Joan 198, 199, 223
Tewkesbury, Joan 239
Texas Rangers 219, 238
The Texas Wheelers 171
Thalberg, Irving 92, 110, 144, 157, 191, 205
That Certain Feeling 238
That Kind of Woman 238
That Old Feeling 238
Thau, Benny 143
Thaxter, Phyllis 57, 233
Thelma & Louise 238
There's Something About Mary 238
Theron, Charlize 54, 184, 185, 218
Thesiger, Ernest 43
Thewlis, David 130, 131
They All Kissed the Bride 238
They All Laughed 238
They Died with Their Boots On 238
Thibeau, Jack 19
Thieves 238
Thieves Like Us 239
The Thin Man 16, 168, 239
The Thin Red Line 220
Thinnes, Roy 82, 83
The Third Man 239
This Boy's Life 239
This Could Be the Night 239
This Earth Is Mine 239
This Gun for Hire 239
This Is My Affair 239
This Property Is Condemned 254
This Way Please 239
Thomas, Danny 1, 135
Thomas, Henry 145

Thomas, Leonard 211
Thomas, Melody 223, 224
Thomas, Phillip Michael 224
The Thomas Crown Affair 240
Thompson, Carlos 222, 223
Thompson, Emma 27, 63, 73, 91, 122
Thompson, J. Lee 81, 82
Thompson, Jack 211
Thompson, Lea 191
Thompson, Marshall 58, 249
Thomson, Scott 83, 84
Thornton, Billy Bob 96
Thoroughly Modern Millie 119
Thorpe, Dick 22
A Thousand Acres 240
365 Nights in Hollywood 240
Three Kings 240
The Three Musketeers (1948) 240
The Three Musketeers (1973) 240
Three of Hearts 240
The Thrill of It All 240
Thulin, Ingrid 117
Thunderball 240–241
Thurman, Uma 1, 22, 27, 39–40, 80, 158, 176, 195
Thurston, Carol 229
Tibbetts, Martha 52
Tibbs, Casey 201
A Ticket to Tomahawk 250
Tierney, Gene 54, 78, 98, 123, 144, 187, 232
Tierney, Lawrence 91, 179
Tiffin, Pamela 228, 254
Tightrope 241
'Til We Meet Again 241
Tillman, Fred 5
Tilly, Meg 4, 12, 83, 84, 195
Time Bandits 241
A Time to Kill 241
Tin Cup 241
Titanic 11, 29, 108, 241–242
TLC 135
To Be or Not to Be 242
To Die For 242
To Each His Own 242
To Have and Have Not 62
To Kill a Mockingbird 118
To Live and Die in L.A. 189
To Wong Foo Thanks for Everything, Julie Newmar 242
Tobey, Ken 34
The Today Show 84
Todd, Mike 20
Todd Lincoln, Mary
Tokovsky, Jerry 165
Toland, Virginia 9
Tom Horn 242–243
Tomei, Marisa 15, 16, 134, 152, 169, 180, 185, 249
Tomlin, Lily 80, 171, 179
Tone, Franchot 121, 122, 154, 155, 168
The Tonight Show with Johnny Carson 84, 138

340 Index

Tony Awards 64, 206
Too Late Blues 243
Tootsie 243
Top Gun 5, 29, 243
Topaz 243
Topkapi 244
Topol 85
Topper 244
Toren, Mike 223
Torn, Rip 78
Torrent 244
Tortilla Flat 244
Total Recall 244
A Touch of Class 35
Toulouse-Lautrec 216
Toumanova, Tamara 50
Tovarich 244
The Towering Inferno 244
Towne, Robert 237, 247, 257
Townsend, Stuart 149, 195, 196
Tracks 244
Tracy, Lee 36, 131
Tracy, Spencer 11, 14, 41, 49, 53, 54, 56, 59, 65, 66, 72, 85, 98, 104, 113, 119, 145, 157, 158, 171, 184, 187, 203, 213, 217, 246, 247, 259
Trading Places 32, 245
Traffic 29, 245
Training Day 245
Tramont, Jean-Claude 9
Trapper John, M.D. 224
Travels with My Aunt 245
Traven, B. 245
Travers, Henry 131, 132
Travis, Nancy 85, 220
Travis, William Barrett 7
Travolta, John 12–13, 19, 21, 37, 54, 55, 56, 66, 74, 86, 89, 96, 102, 103, 110, 111, 129, 130, 133, 141, 152, 161, 172, 173, 177, 189, 192, 195, 209, 211, 217, 225, 227, 249, 258
The Treasure of the Sierra Madre 245
A Tree Grows in Brooklyn 245–246
Trenholme, Helen 50
Trevor, Claire 135, 226, 231
Tribute to a Bad Man 246
Les Tricheurs 246
Trick or Treat 246
Trikonis, Gina 253
Trikonis, Gus 253
Trintignant, Jean-Louis 58, 214
The Trip 246
Tripplehorn, Jeanne 27, 86, 113
TriStar Pictures 220
Trouble in Paradise 90
True Crime 240
True Grit 246
True Romance 246
Truffaut, Francois 58, 82
Truhitte, Daniel 223
The Truman Show 156, 246
Tryon, Tom 194

Tucci, Maria 100, 101
Tucker, Chris 35
Tucker, Preston 246
Tucker, Sophie 165, 166
Tucker: The Man and His Dream 246
Tufts, Sonny 137
Tully, Tom 132
Tulo, Marilu 233
The Tumbler, 145
Tune, Tommy 119, 120
Turman, Glynn 227
Turner, Debbie 223, 224
Turner, Janine 88
Turner, Kathleen 39, 42, 43, 44, 45, 70, 185, 214, 251
Turner, Lana 14, 31, 41, 51, 72, 75, 89, 105, 106, 117, 143–144, 146, 152, 165, 191, 194, 221, 222, 240
Turner, Tina 59, 84, 97
The Turning Point 246–247
Turturro, John 72, 102, 103, 174
Tushingham, Rita 235
Twain, Mark 35
20th Century 198
20th Century-Fox 7, 9, 16, 32, 33, 43, 47, 52, 54, 57, 65, 78, 83, 97, 104, 108, 136, 137, 145, 147, 149, 163, 166, 169, 192, 198, 221, 232, 236, 239, 241, 257, 261
24-Hour Woman 247
21 Grams 247
20,000 Years in Sing Sing 247
Twin Peaks 114
Twister 45, 104
Two for the Road 247
The Two Jakes 75, 247
Two of a Kind 258
2001: A Space Odyssey 248
Tyler, Beverly 205
Tyler, Liv 53
Tyler, Tom 235
Tyne, Billy 185
Typhoon 248
Tyson, Mike 176
Tzavaras, Roberta 168

U-571 248
U-Turn 248
Ufland, Harry 19
Ulee's Gold 248
Ullman, Liv 76, 89, 202
Ullman, Tracey 88, 214, 220
Ulysses 248
Unbreakable 248
Unconquered 201, 248
Under Siege 2: Dark Territory 248–249
Unfaithful 249
Union Pacific 249
United Artists 51, 91, 188, 189, 204, 220, 221, 259, 261
United States 90, 222
United Talent Agency 60
Universal 9, 31, 51, 61, 65, 69, 76, 83, 91, 99, 111, 133, 136, 138, 154, 157, 162, 168, 180, 204, 208, 216, 231, 257
An Unmarried Woman 249
The Unsinkable Molly Brown 249
Untamed Heart 249
The Untouchables 249
Urban Cowboy 13, 249
Ure, Mary 202, 222, 223
Urich, Robert 224
Ustinov, Peter 12, 140, 188, 244, 251
The Usual Suspects 19, 29

Vaccaro, Brenda 100, 101
Vadim, Roger 26, 73
Valentino, Rudolph 59
Vallee, Rudy 100, 101
Valley Girl 84
The Valley of Decision 58, 249
Valley of the Dolls 249–250
Valley of the Kings 250
Valli, Alida 100, 102, 183
Vallone, Raf 100, 103, 161
Valmont 250
Vance, Courtney B. 219
Vance, Vivian 22, 155, 189
Van Der Beek, James 192, 219, 228
Vandervoort, Benjamin 149
Van Devere, Trish 100, 101
Van Dien, Casper 228
Van Dyke, Dick 175, 210
Van Dyke, W.S. 239
Vanguard Pictures 77
Van Sant, Gus 76–77, 80–81, 108, 170, 194, 242
Varden, Norma 194, 223
Varela, Leonor 238
Variety 109
Vaughn, Vince 61, 194, 228
Vawter, Ron 215
Vega, Isela 44
Veidt, Conrad 50
Ventura, Lino 58, 222
Vera-Ellen 21, 22, 30, 121, 214
The Verdict 250
Verdon, Gwen 11
Verdugo, Elena 166, 229
Verhoeven, Paul 27
Vermont, Monique 223, 224
Vernon, Jackie 118
Vernon, John 16
Vertigo 250
Victor/Victoria 250
Vidor, King 90, 91, 259
Vienna, Austria 51
View from the Top 124
Vignola, Bob 132
Viharo, Robert 19
The Village People 48
Vincent, Jan-Michael 133
Vint, Alan 19
Vinton, Bobby 100, 101
The VIPs 60, 249
Virtuosity 250

Index 341

Visconti, Luchino 145
Viva Zapata! 250
Voight, Jon 10, 52, 60, 68, 114, 126, 133, 151, 159, 161, 184
Volcano 250
Volonte, Gian Maria 102, 103
von Detten, Erik 228
von Habsburg, Empress Carlotta 135
Von Hessert, Cornelia R. 62
von Kurowsky, Agnes 127
von Sternberg, Josef 37
Von Sydow, Max 114
Von Trapp, Captain Georg
Von Trapp, Maria 222, 223
Voscover, George 223
Vuille, Georges-Alain 234

Wabash Avenue 250
Wachowski, Andy 159
Wachowski, Larry 159
Wagner, Richard 151
Wagner, Robert 199, 205, 251
Wahl, Ken 89
Wahlberg, Mark 28, 40, 176, 180, 185, 186, 204, 228, 240
Waiting to Exhale 39, 251
Wake Island 22
Wald, Jerry 162–163
A Walk in the Clouds 251
A Walk on the Moon 251
Walken, Christopher 35, 66, 67, 114, 119, 126, 143, 151, 213, 214, 227
Walken, Glenn 19
Walker, Kathryn 171, 172
Walker, Robert 58
Wall Street 251
Wallace, Dee 77
Wallach, Eli 93, 102, 103, 124, 177
Walley, Deborah 99
Wallis, Hal B. 17, 59, 65, 162, 197, 232, 246
Wallis, Shani 178
Walston, Ray 64, 83, 138
Walters, Charles 17, 21–22
Walters, Julie 78
Walthall, Henry B. 150
Wanger, Walter 8
Wanted: Dead or Alive 43
War and Peace 251
The War Lover 251
The War of the Roses 251
Ward, Sela 27
Ward, Simon 240
Warden, Jack 213
Wargames 251
Warner, David 25, 241
Warner, H.B. 131
Warner, Jack 38, 50, 65, 67, 100, 104, 108, 131, 134, 135, 147, 169, 181, 182, 203, 226, 230, 254
Warner, Julie 85
Warner Brothers 6, 7, 24, 28, 36, 46, 50, 63, 64, 65, 68, 74, 80, 81, 90, 91, 93, 104, 107, 108, 112, 124, 126, 127, 134, 135, 136, 138, 139, 149, 155, 160, 162, 167, 169, 171, 176, 178, 181, 182, 186, 199, 205, 209, 214, 219, 230, 244, 245, 253, 259, 260
Warren, Lesley Ann 108, 223, 224, 233
Warren, Phil 132
Warrick, Ruth 8
Washbourne, Mona 223
Washington 35
Washington, Denzel 14, 18, 30, 62, 83, 150, 154, 186, 250
Wasson, Craig 38, 39
Watch on the Rhine 252
Waters, Elizabeth 258
Waters, Ethel 47, 48
Waters, John 51, 214
Waterston, Sam 79, 129, 129, 213, 214
Waterworld 7
Watkins, Linda 105, 107
Watson, David 30
Watson, Ella 119
Watson, Emily 43, 44, 79
Watson, Lucile 198, 199
Watts, Naomi 203
Waxman, Henry 59
Way Down East 252
The Way of the Gun 29
The Way to Love 252
The Way We Were 252
Wayans, Damon 134
Wayans, Keenen Ivory 211
Wayne, John 37, 49, 50, 60, 71, 77, 119, 120, 149, 165, 173, 184, 201, 203, 226, 246
Weathers, Carl 204, 205
Weaver, Fritz 223, 224
Weaver, Sigourney 8, 17, 18
Weaving, Hugo 149
Webb, Clifton 8, 21, 25, 64, 144, 175
Webb, Jack 16
Webber, Andrew Lloyd 81
The Wedding Planner 252
Weidler, Virginia 22, 23, 162
Weinstein, Bob 195
Weinstein, Harvey 54, 59, 195, 253
Weinstein, Henry 236
Weintraub, Jerry 177
Weir, Peter 66, 187, 246
Weissman, Jeffrey 24
Weissmueller, Johnny 235
Weisz, Rachel 44, 52
Weitman, Robert 73
Welch, Joseph N. 14, 15
Welch, Raquel 48, 119, 170, 180, 191, 240, 241, 250
Welcome Back Kotter 66, 111, 224
Welcome Home Roxy Carmichael 103
Welcome to Mooseport 252–253
Welcome to Sarajevo 253
Weld, Sylvia 198, 199

Weld, Tuesday 40, 56, 149, 175, 206, 207, 214
Welles, Orson 22, 30, 33, 79, 133, 138, 140, 152, 165, 173, 225, 230, 239
Wellman, William 65, 194
Wells, Frank 155
Werich, Jan 260
Werner, Oskar 82
West, Adam 27
West, Carinthia 233
West, Mae 105, 108, 233
West Side Story 253
The Westerner 253–254
Whale, James 43, 91
What Price Beauty? 59
Whatever Happened to Baby Jane 125
What's Up Doc? 252
Whelan, Arleen 9
When a Man Loves a Woman 254
When Harry Met Sally 218, 229, 254
Where the Heart Is 254
Whitaker, Forest 84
White, Carol 230
White, Christine 223
White, George 97
White, Sanett 217
White, Ted 92
White Christmas 254
White House 108
The White Sister 254
White Witch Doctor 254
Whitehead, O.Z. 110
Whitesell, Patrick 232
Whiting, Leonard 206
Whitman, Stuart 194, 203
Whitney, Liz 105, 107
Whittingham, Carolyn 198, 199
Whorf, Richard 38, 154, 155
Who's Afraid of Virginia Woolf 254
Why Do Fools Fall in Love 258
Wickwire, Nancy 223
Widdoes, James 16
Widdoes, Kathleen 100, 101
Widmark, Richard 176, 203
Wieand, Dick 92
Wiest, Dianne 18, 114, 125
The Wild Angels 255
The Wild Bunch 255
Wild Orchid 255–256
Wild River 256
Wilde, Cornel 112, 210
Wilder, Billy 18, 74, 130, 134, 150, 214–215, 221, 226, 233
Wilder, Gene 36, 75, 194, 228
Wilding, Michael 49
Wilke, Robert J. 121
Will Success Spoil Rock Hunter? 256
Willard 256
William, Warren 140
William Shakespeare's Romeo + Juliet 256
Williams, Abigail 63
Williams, Billy Dee 84
Williams, Cara 41

Williams, Cindy 227, 245
Williams, Dick Anthony 154
Williams, Emlyn 223
Williams, Esther 21–22, 51, 143, 144, 167, 190, 221, 222, 234
Williams, JoBeth 3, 139
Williams, Paul 186
Williams, Robin 6, 22, 27, 33, 34, 40, 66, 132, 161, 162, 167, 174, 190, 208
Williams, Tennessee 51, 93, 232
Williams, Treat 63, 126, 192
Williams, Vanessa L. 166, 211
Williamson, Mykelti 134
Williamson, Nicol 20, 79–80, 144, 148, 204
Willis, Austin 105
Willis, Bruce 7, 36, 39, 40, 46, 67, 68, 69, 70–71, 117, 195
Willis, Victor 48
Willow 256
Wilson, Carey 62
Wilson, Dooley 50
Wilson, Lois 45
Wilson, Marie 41
Wilson, Owen 228
Wilson, Patrick 7
Wilson, Rita 219, 220
Wilson, Scott 127
Wilson, Trey 163
Win a Date with Tad Hamilton! 256
Winchell, Walter 106, 209
Wincott, Michael 132, 133
Windom, William 80
Windtalkers 225
Winfrey, Oprah 59
Wing, Leslie 87
Winger, Debra 21, 27, 32, 45, 46, 48, 84, 108, 144, 145, 157, 176, 185, 197, 216, 237, 239, 249, 254
Wings 259
Winkler, Henry 75, 110, 111, 173
Winner, Michael 67
The Winning of Barbara Worth 256
Winningham, Mare 76, 77
Winslet, Kate 44, 52, 63, 80, 108, 159, 241, 256
Winters, Shelley 22, 28, 62, 75, 93, 105, 106, 147, 187, 190, 221
Wise, Robert 66, 209, 223–224, 246, 253
Wiseman, Joseph 72
Wish You Were Here 125
The Witches of Eastwick 256–257
Withers, Googie 179
Witherspoon, Cora 198, 199, 257
Witherspoon, Reese 48
Without Limits 257

Witt, Alicia 224, 225
The Wizard of Oz 108, 257–258
Wolfe, Tom 40
Wolff, Caroline 239
Wolheim, Louis 93
A Woman Rebels 258
Wong, B.D. 151, *152*
Wood, Elijah 149
Wood, Evan Rachel 129, 130
Wood, Lana 70
Wood, Natalie 26, 38, 40, 52, 108, 112, 127, 136, 157, 163, 181, 199, 205, 206, 207, 212, 225, 249, 250, 253
Wood, Peggy 223
Woodard, Alfre 81, 97, 195
Woods, Edward 194
Woods, James 132, 133, 209, 211
Woods, Maurice 245
Woodward, Joanne 25, 57, 58, 177, 198
Woolley, Monty 21, 144, 156
Working Girl 1, 258
The World of Suzie Wong 258
World War II 32
Worley, Joanne119 120
Worth, Irene 192, 193, 223
Wrestling Ernest Hemingway 258
Wright, Ben 223–224
Wright, Jeffrey 215, 216
Wright, Teresa 77, 92, 147, 175, 222
Wright Penn, Robin 28, 86, 136, 193, 204, 208, 248
Writers Guild Awards 236
Wunsch, Robert 80
Wuthering Heights 258
Wyatt, Jane 111
Wyatt Earp 195
Wyle, Noah 145
Wyler, William 13–14, 31, 32, 49, 50, 69, 73, 89, 92, 94, 123, 132, 145, 147, 205, 254
Wyman, Jane 92, 150, 259
Wynn, Ed 257
Wynn, Keenan 58, 233
Wynter, Dana 91, 223

X, Malcolm 154
The X-Files 189
X-Men 258
Xanadu 258

"Y.M.C.A." 48
Yablans, Frank 102
A Yank at Oxford 259
Year of the Comet 259
The Yearling 259
Yentl 161, 259

Yeoh, Michelle 159
Yordan, Philip 231
York, Alvin C. 214
York, Michael 7, 47, 151
York, Susannah 155, 261
You Can Count On Me 259
You Can't Take It with You 132, 259
You Only Live Twice 260
You'll Never Eat Lunch in This Town Again (Julia Phillips) 229
Young, Gig 44, 210
Young, Loretta 31, 41, 69, 83, 90, 105, 107, 108, 125, 131, 148, 149, 154, 155, 198, 199
Young, Mary 131
Young, Otis 141
Young, Robert, 8, 175
Young, Roland 131, 244
Young, Sean 27, 28, 35, 70, 197, 251
Young, Terence 37, 93, 241
The Young and the Restless 224
Young Bess 260
Young Cassidy 73, 260
The Young in Heart 260
The Young Lions 260
The Young Mr. Pitt 260
Youngblood Hawke 260
Yulin, Harris 129

Zabriskie Point 260
Zaillian, Steven 232
Zane, Billy 102, 241
Zanuck, Darryl F. 9, 16–17, 25, 37, 46, 66, 75, 78, 89, 97, 98, 110, 123, 137, 138, 140, 149, 160, 163, 167, 169, 188, 198, 215, 239, 250, 257, 261
Zanuck, Richard D. 76, 133, 250
Zardoz 260
Zee and Co. 261
Zeffirelli, Franco 52, 236
Zellweger, Renee 44, 54, 63, 134, 146, 167, 176
Zemeckis, Robert 23, 24, 67
Zeta-Jones, Catherine 14, 32, 33, 54, 141, 167, 186, 245
Zieff, Howard 153
Ziegfeld Follies 261
Zimbalist, Efrem, Jr. 210
Zimbalist, Stephanie 118, 119
Zinnemann, Fred 93, 155, 177, 181
Zoolander 228
Zorba the Greek 261
Zorba the Greek (Nikos Kazantzakis) 125
Zorina, Vera 88, *89*
Zulu 261
Zuniga, Daphne 88

J. Dean -
Somebody up there likes me.
Cat on a hot Tin Roof
Friendly Persuasion
Fear Strikes out
Oklahoma